A History of the Old South

THE MACMILLAN COMPANY
NEW YORK • CHICAGO
DALLAS • ATLANTA • SAN FRANCISCO
LONDON • MANILA

IN CANADA
BRETT-MACMILLAN LTD.
GALT, ONTARIO

A History of
the Old South

CLEMENT EATON
Professor of History
University of Kentucky

NEW  YORK

The Macmillan Company

To
Mary Elizabeth Allis

Preface

———◆———

D URING the ante-bellum period strong similarities existed between the North and the South, similarities which have not properly been recognized. Nevertheless, despite an underlying homogeneity, there were differences between the two sections so sharp as to constitute a Southern Way of Life and a Northern Way of Life. In presenting this regional history of the South the purpose has been to keep the attention of the reader focused on the way of life of the people. It has been necessary to consider those differences which made the South a unique region and the interrelations between "the South" and the nation of which it was a part. Therefore a vast amount of general American history has been omitted or placed in the background while emphasis has been given to those characteristics which are peculiarly "Southern" and the historic processes which produced them.

The students of the Old South have constantly sought to find a unifying principle in the history of a complex area, spacious enough to include several European nations. The eminent Southern historian, Ulrich B. Phillips, could not find it in the political realm, for although the Southern states at times acted as a *bloc* in Congress to defend slavery or their economic interests, they did not attain political unity except during the four years of the existence of the Confederacy. Phillips began by thinking that the factor differentiating the people of the North and the South was climate and geography, but he ended by concluding that "the central theme of Southern history" was the presence of the Negro in large numbers, leading to a continuous struggle to keep the South "a white man's country." Other historians have advanced different theses of integration, such as the rise of Southern nationalism after 1820, the ruralness of Southern society, the struggle of the planter class to dominate, the South as a conscious political minority within the nation, the native American composition of the population due to the dwindling of immigration after 1800, and the protracted colonial status of the section. Certainly, also, there has been a long continuity

in the history of the South of violent resistance to any outside interference with or criticism of its way of life. The integrating theme
in this study of the Old South is the emergence of a regional culture,
created by all classes of Southern society rather than by an elite,
aristocratic group.

A generous characteristic of the profession of American scholars
has been a willingness to give frank criticism to a colleague who is
writing a book. Availing myself of this spirit of cooperation, I have
asked a number of my colleagues and friends to read chapters dealing with fields in which they are specialists. Among those who have
thus contributed to the accuracy of this volume are Professors
Wendell H. Stephenson of Tulane University, James W. Patton of
North Carolina State College, Lawrence H. Gipson of Lehigh University, Fletcher M. Green, J. Carlyle Sitterson, Edgar W. Knight,
and Milton Heath of the University of North Carolina, Dr. Christopher C. Crittenden, of the North Carolina Department of Archives
and History, Thomas D. Clark, J. Merton England, Bennett H. Wall,
and James F. Hopkins of the University of Kentucky, J. Winston
Coleman, Esq., of Lexington, John Hope Franklin of Howard University, Joseph C. Robert of Duke University, Benjamin Eaton, Jr.,
of Raleigh, North Carolina, and Charles Edward Eaton of the University of North Carolina. To my alma mater, the University of
North Carolina, to those who instructed me as a graduate student
at Harvard, particularly Professors Frederick Merk and Arthur M.
Schlesinger, to Lafayette College, to the University of Wisconsin,
and to the University of Kentucky, I owe a debt of gratitude.

I have tried to confine the citations in this volume principally to
direct quotations, manuscript sources, and articles in historical journals. I am indebted to many authors whose works are listed in the
bibliography.

CLEMENT EATON

Lexington, Kentucky

Contents

Illustrations

———◆———

Maps

———◆———

Maps

CHAPTER I

Southern Land and Southern Blood

ON February 18, 1861, Jefferson Davis stood on the portico of the Capitol in Montgomery, Alabama, and delivered his inaugural address as president of the Southern Confederacy. On that occasion a new song, "Dixie," was played by a band before an audience of enthusiastic Southerners. Like the cradles, coffins, patent medicines, crinoline skirts, tall silk hats, indeed, most of the manufactured articles which the South used, "Dixie" was imported from the Yankees. It was on a stage in New York City in 1859 that Dan Emmett of Mount Vernon, Ohio, a blackface minstrel, sang for the first time, "I wish I was in the land of cotton—Dixie land." Its stirring tune and pervading nostalgia were so appealing that it became the unofficial anthem of the Confederacy.

As to the derivation of the term, the land of Dixie, there are several explanations and conjectures. The most reasonable account of its origin is that it came from French-speaking Louisiana, where ten dollar bills circulated with the numeral *Dix* printed upon them. Louisiana, accordingly, was colloquially called "Dix's Land," or "Dixie," a nickname which was gradually applied to the Southern states as a region. Another theory, which seems both dubious and ironic, is that the term was derived from the name of a Northern slave-owner, Dixie, whose farm was located in the state of New York. He treated his slaves so kindly that when he sold them down South, they longed for their old home, "Dixie's Land," and sang of it as an earthly paradise. Still another hypothesis is that Dixie was a corruption of the name of Jeremiah Dixon, who surveyed the Mason and Dixon line.

The boundaries of the land of Dixie will always be a subject of debate, for sentiment had a part in determining them. The sentiment of Southernism, the feeling of a kinship with the South, was an important criterion in drawing the frontier of the South. More soldiers from Kentucky fought for the Union than for the Confederacy, yet Kentucky was economically and psychologically a part of the Old South. It is a significant and surprising fact that in 1860 Kentucky had a larger number of slaveholders than any other Southern state except Virginia and Georgia, although states like South Carolina, Mississippi, and Alabama owned far more slaves than did the Bluegrass state. The curving frontier line of the Old South included eastern Maryland, a land of tobacco plantations and of slaves, as well as the western part of Virginia (with the exception of the Panhandle) which in the course of the Civil War separated from the mother state. Although Delaware remained a slave state until 1865, her connections, going back to colonial days, were with Pennsylvania and the Middle States, which made her loyal in sentiment to the Union during the Civil War. Missouri, a border slave state, was more definitely Southern, tempered, however, by the influence of the West and of a large German population in the St. Louis area. In 1850 the persons of Southern nativity in Missouri outnumbered those of Northern birth considerably more than three to one. Kentucky far surpassed any other state in contributing population to Missouri with Tennessee and Virginia ranking second and third.

Prior to the outbreak of the Civil War the best sociological test of whether a state was "Southern" or "Northern" rested upon the question of whether it gave legal recognition to slavery or not. The dividing line between free and slave states east of the Allegheny Mountains was the Mason and Dixon line, which had been surveyed in 1767 by two English surveyors as the final settlement of a boundary dispute between Pennsylvania and Maryland. After John Randolph of Roanoke had popularized the phrase "Mason and Dixon line" during the Missouri Compromise debates, this surveyor's line became the symbolic boundary between the North and the South. Beyond the Allegheny Mountains the Southern frontier ran along the Ohio River and, crossing the Mississippi, embraced that part of Missouri below the Missouri River, the state of Arkansas, and eastern Texas.

Within this area there were in 1860 fifteen states which recognized slavery as a legal institution. Only eleven of them, however, joined the Southern Confederacy.

The South has a rich diversity of terrain. The largest region is the Coastal Plain, a low, sandy surface which was formed both by the elevation of the sea-bed through geologic changes and by the ceaseless action of rivers depositing sediment. The Coastal Plain was also called the Tidewater because the rivers traversing it were affected by the ebb and flow of the tide. The width of the Coastal Plain varies greatly, extending as much as two hundred and fifty miles inland in North Carolina, and constituting almost the whole of the peninsula of Florida. The belt of land nearest to the ocean is swampy, producing cypress trees and live oaks, the latter often festooned with gray Spanish moss, "like a Dunker's beard." Much of the Coastal Plain also was covered by immense pine forests—the varieties of the longleaf, the slash, the short-leaf, and the loblolly, or "old field pine."

Beyond the Coastal Plain is the Piedmont region, a zone of rolling hills extending westward to the mountains. The Piedmont is separated from the Coastal Plain by the fall line, which was once the ancient shore line. Here a break in the terrain causes the rivers coming down from the hilly hinterland to develop waterfalls and rapids, providing a source of power for mills and factories. Furthermore, the falls of the rivers, being the heads of navigation to the sea, were the natural location for inland cities, such as Richmond, Raleigh, Columbia, Augusta, and Montgomery. The climate of the Piedmont is cooler and more salubrious than that of the Coastal Plain and the soil, frequently red clay, nourishes hardwood trees—oaks, chestnut, hickory, and walnut. In the colonial period the Tidewater was the seat of culture and political power, but in modern times the Piedmont has become the most prosperous region of the South.

The first mountain barrier to the westward advance of settlement was the Blue Ridge, a low, forest-covered range that extends from Pennsylvania into Georgia. The Blue Ridge broadens in its southwesterly course into the Blue Ridge Province, containing the Great Smokies of North Carolina and such peaks as Clingman's Dome and Mount Mitchell, well over six thousand feet in height, the tallest mountains east of the Mississippi. On the other side of the Blue Ridge

Province is a long depression or trough in the mountains, running in a southwesterly direction, called the Great Valley, which is traversed by several rivers, particularly the Shenandoah in Virginia and the Holston in Tennessee. Down this corridor from Pennsylvania came the German and Scotch-Irish settlers through the back door of the South, looking for good limestone soils. To the west of the Great Valley is an extensive highland known as the Appalachian

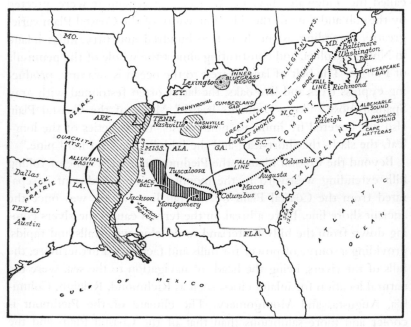

THE PHYSICAL SOUTH

Based partly on map, "Physical Divisions of the United States," by N. M. Fenneman at end of article by him in *Annals of the Association of American Geographers*, XVIII (December, 1928), 261–353.

Plateaus. Where the states of Virginia, Kentucky, and Tennessee meet, there is a narrow pass through the mountains called Cumberland Gap, through which the pioneers crossed over to the lush lands of "Kaintuck." Near the center of the state of Kentucky is located the Lexington Bluegrass basin, whose soluble limestone soil nourishes the famed blue-grass which produces fine horses. The Nashville, Tennessee, basin is another region of limestone soil, very fertile and adapted to raising cattle and horses. Between these two centers of fertility and culture lies an area where the pennyroyal, an aromatic herb, which the natives call "pennyrile," grows luxuriantly.

The Appalachian Plateaus slope gradually to the rich alluvial lowlands of the Mississippi Valley. Below Montgomery, Alabama, there is another zone of dark, highly productive soil, called the "Black Belt," which extends into northeastern Mississippi in the shape of a crescent. Across the Mississippi in Texas there is an opulent belt of "black waxy" soil which in the ante-bellum days was white with fields of cotton. Eastern Texas, indeed, was a part of the Old South, but after passing the 98° of longitude one steps into the West, for the lack of sufficient rainfall makes this country a range for cattle rather than an agricultural region.

To the north, in Arkansas and extending into Missouri, is a group of low mountains, the Ouachita and the Ozarks, inhabited by the mountain whites, who long retained the pioneer pattern of living. Thomas Hart Benton has painted pictures of their drab existence, relieved by violent outbursts of passion, of religious emotion, of drunkenness, and of break-down dancing to the fiddle. Since the mountains practically prohibited the transportation of crops to market, the men tended to develop a semi-Indian philosophy as reflected in the folksong:

> Chickens a-crowin' on Sourwood Mountain
> Call up yore dogs and let's go a-huntin'.
>
> Say, old man, I want your daughter
> To wash my clothes an' carry my water.
>
> Ducks in the pond, geese in the ocean,
> Devil's in the women if they take a notion.

In addition to the physical terrain, climate and rainfall must be considered as important elements of the Southern environment. Captain John Smith wrote concerning the Virginia climate: "The Sommer is hot as in Spaine; the Winter colde as in France or England." [1] A later writer has described the summer of the lower South as "90° in the shade." There are three belts of climate below the Mason and Dixon line, based on the length of the growing season— the upper South, where the growing season is six months, the middle

South, eight months, and the deep South, nine months. Killing frosts occur as far south as St. Augustine and New Orleans, and at times cold "northers" suddenly chill the weather of balmy Texas. Also a wide variation of rainfall occurs within the Southern states. Although droughts occur at intervals the upper South has an annual precipitation of forty to fifty inches, while much of the lower South has a downfall of rain of fifty to sixty inches. In the strip of territory along the Gulf coast and in the mountainous area of the Carolinas and Georgia the rainfall is so copious that sixty to a hundred inches of precipitation is prevalent. Running like a sad rhythm through Southern history is the constant erosion of the soil, which in the colonial and ante-bellum periods caused many Southern people to be always "on the move" and today Southern farmers pay a heavy bill for fertilizer.

In various subtle ways the Southern people have been affected by a warm climate, but contrary to popular belief, the climate does not seem to have been of decisive importance in producing a difference of Southern speech from other varieties spoken in the United States. Modern students believe that the most important cause for the peculiarities of Southern speech was the survival in the South of the English language as spoken in the seventeenth and eighteenth centuries, which was brought over by the colonists.[2] The pronunciations of *get* as "git," *ask* as "ax," *boil* as "bile," *oblige* as "obleege," and *master* as "marster" or "marse," were common usages in the southern part of England during the seventeenth century. Even the dropping of final *g*, as in "darlin" for *darling*, or elision of *r*—supposedly common Southern failings—were practices of old English speech during the period of emigration. Likewise, the pronunciation of *e* as *i* in such words as *tennis* ("tinnis"), *men* ("min"), and *pen* ("pin") is an archaic form of old English pronunciation. Furthermore, the Southern colonists brought over with them pronunciations peculiar to the numerous dialects of the mother country, especially those of southern and southwestern England. Expressions such as "gwine" for *going* and "ain't" for *isn't* antedate the coming of the Negroes to the South. Many of the pronunciations and even the drawl which are regarded today as peculiarly "Southern" were also current in New England in the seventeenth and eighteenth centuries.

The variation of Southern speech from the New England and also the General American or Western type should not be attributed primarily to the linguistic laziness of the people, induced by a languorous climate, but to the greater conservatism of the South in not changing its speech. In the late eighteenth century there was a change of speech in the London district when the broad *a* became fashionable and standard British pronunciation. In general, Southern speech continued to retain the older pronunciation of *a*. There were exceptions, however, in Tidewater Virginia and in the Charleston district, which had close connections with England and which tended to imitate more readily the fashions current in the mother country. New England was also similarly affected and, moreover, the influence of New England "schoolmarms" and the printed page tended to eradicate some of the elisions of *r's* and final *g's* which continued in Southern speech.

The influence of the Negroes may have tended to make Southern speech more conservative and archaic. The Negroes imitated the phonetics of the master class, and they were unaffected by the influence of spelling and the printed page. Consequently, they tended to perpetuate the older type of speech of the English colonists. The slaves imported a few words from Africa into Southern speech, such as "goober" for *peanuts*, "yam" for *sweet potato*, "cooter" for *terrapin*, and "voodoo" for *magic*, and probably some African inflections and grammar survived in Negro speech, but in general the Negro imitated the white man's speech and forgot his old African tongue. The word "boss," which the Negroes often used in addressing white men, was of Dutch origin, probably introduced through the slave trade.

The places where the old English speech survived most tenaciously were the eastern sand banks and the mountains. Here the inhabitants were insulated from progressive currents and also only to a slight degree were affected by the controls of the printed page. They seldom saw a Negro, and consequently could not have been influenced by Negro corruptions of speech. Yet many of their pronunciations and expressions were similar to those used by the Negroes, such as "hit" for *it* and "tote" for *carry* and "pore" for *poor*. Old pronunciations and archaic words were also preserved by the continuance of folksongs and ballads brought from the British Isles by the colonists.

The American environment wrought a revolution in the habits of the European colonists. The Englishman was a heavy beef and mutton eater. In America his descendants became primarily pork eaters but supplemented their "hog and hominy" fare with venison, bear meat, and turkey. In the rank, virgin soil of the South, wheat tended to grow up in tall stalks without much grain, while corn flourished. Consequently, the Southerner was nourished on corn bread and hominy or "grits" in contrast to wheat bread, which was universally consumed both in England and in the North. Why the colonists did not continue the English practice of drinking huge quantities of ale and beer is a mystery. Ultimately they developed into rum drinkers on account of the West India trade and in the South distilled a potent alcoholic beverage from Indian corn. In England the half-timbered cottage with thatch roof was the home of the laboring man; in the Southern colonies, the abundance of wood led to the construction of the log cabin, with a roof of shingles instead of thatch. In the mother country the high, stiff-backed chair was the seat of repose; in America, where the restless frontier spirit prevailed, the rocking-chair became the emblem of the dynamic energy of the people, who even in their leisure, must always be "on the move." As many of these restless Americans rocked, they exercised their jaws chewing tobacco and spitting, a habit which gave way in the twentieth century to gum chewing.

From the aboriginal inhabitants in America the colonists learned many ways of adapting themselves to the environment of the New World. Contrary to a prevalent stereotype, most of the Southern Indians were engaged extensively in a primitive agriculture, raising maize, sweet potatoes, squash, melons, pumpkins, gourds, and tobacco, to which they introduced their white conquerors. The white man learned from this primitive people how to make canoes, how to girdle trees, how to hunt game, how to make moccasins, how to cultivate tobacco and smoke it, and how to adapt himself to forest warfare. Perhaps the Indian eloquence, heard at councils and on treaty-making occasions, affected Southern oratory, giving to it a more florid tone. Certainly college boys are indebted to the Cherokee Indians for the game of lacrosse, which they played with a deerskin ball and racquets about two feet in length, accompanied by furious betting on the part of the spectators. Today the main physical survivals of Indian culture in the South are the mounds which they built, especially the remarkable group at Moundville, Alabama, containing one mound fifty-eight feet high, and those at Etowah and Macon, Georgia. These strange relics of a vanished people were principally truncated pyramids of earth forming platforms for the council and ceremonial houses rather than mounds for burial purposes.

Although environment has been a potent factor in the evolution of Southern society, the civilization of the Old South did not arise entirely as the result of a passive people yielding to the all-powerful determination of physical geography. After all allowance is made for the modifying effect of the environment—the fact remains that American culture was largely a continuation of European civilization in a new land. Furthermore, the facts of nature alone—a warm climate and the diversity of Southern topography—would not have created the virulent sectionalism which led to the Civil War. Regionalism is partly man-made, a human or artificial creation. Indeed, so different are some of the regions within the land of Dixie that until the slavery issue became emotionalized it was difficult to get the Southern states to act as a unit.

The basic stock of the settlers of the South was English. Census officials have estimated from a study of the personal names in the first census that 82.1 per cent of the American people in 1790 were of English ancestry, but these estimates undoubtedly exaggerated the importance of the English element, for many foreign immigrants anglicized their names. Indeed, more recent studies indicate that the English element in the American colonies in 1775 constituted only 60 per cent of the white population. In the Southern colonies, the soundest estimates indicate that nearly two-thirds of the white population was of English blood, the next largest national group being the Scotch and Scotch-Irish, approximately 20 per cent, and the third being the Germans, over 5 per cent. The Celtic Irish in the colonial South were approximately 5 per cent and the French between 2 and 3 per cent of the white population.[3] The colonial period was pre-eminently the time of the mixing bowl or of the melting pot in the

South. After 1800 foreign immigration flowed into the North but, with the exception of large seaports and a few river towns, avoided the land of Dixie, so that this region has remained the most "American" part of the United States. Its population has been derived predominantly from colonial lineage.

The first wave of immigration from England to the American colonies took place between 1607, the date of the founding of Jamestown, and 1642, the date of the Puritan Rebellion in England. This Great Migration, as it has been called, carried approximately 40,000 people to Bermuda and the West Indies, 18,000 to New England, and only 9,500 to Virginia and Maryland. Later in the century the West India island of Barbados, where the development of large slave-tilled sugar plantations drove out poor men, became a secondary source of immigration to the southern mainland colonies, particularly to South Carolina.

The settlement of the Virginia colony was initiated and financed by a commercial company, the London Company (later called the Virginia Company). The company's administration was a failure and it made no profits out of its huge investment of £200,000. In 1624 its charter was annulled and Virginia became a royal colony. It was disclosed at the trial of the company which resulted in its dissolution that it had sent out a total of six thousand colonists since the granting of its charter in 1606, but that in February, 1624, only twelve hundred and seventy-five persons were left in Virginia. Lack of proper food, disease, the hardships of the wilderness, and the Indian massacre of 1622 had taken a frightful toll of human life. In the process of becoming acclimated many settlers died from an intermittent fever, "the Virginia sickness," which was described by Ebenezer Cook in the satirical poem, *The Sot-Weed Factor: or, a Voyage to Maryland* (1708):

> With Cockerouse [a man of quality] as I was sitting,
> I felt a Feaver Intermitting;
> A fiery pulse beat in my Veins, From Cold I felt resembling Pains:
> This cursed seasoning I remember
> Lasted from *March* to cold *December*.

Immigration into the Southern colonies was also promoted by several noble proprietors and by a humanitarian board of trustees. The first settlement of Maryland, at St. Mary's on the Chesapeake Bay in 1634, was directed by Lord Baltimore, a Catholic nobleman to whom the land between the Potomac River and the fortieth degree of latitude had been granted as a proprietary province. Lord Baltimore not only wished to make his colony an asylum for persecuted Catholics but also to gain profits from its settlement. Actually, relatively few Catholics emigrated to Maryland, and it became necessary for Lord Baltimore to protect the Catholic minority from persecution by the Maryland Toleration Act of 1649. The colonization of the Carolinas was promoted by the eight Lord Proprietors to whom in 1663 the imperial domain between Virginia and Spanish Florida had been granted by Charles II. Georgia was founded seventy years later by a group of twenty-one trustees, headed by the Irish Earl of Egmont and General James Oglethorpe, who hoped to provide a land of opportunity for imprisoned debtors and at the same time to develop a buffer colony against the Spanish in Florida. Recent studies have disclosed, however, that "only a handful of debtors ever came to Georgia—a dozen would be a fair estimate." [4]

Immigrants left the British Isles for the Southern colonies on account of a variety of motivations. The political troubles in England, particularly the struggle between the king and Parliament, sent immigrants across the Atlantic. The inclosure movement, by which agricultural lands were converted into sheep pastures, the high land rents resulting from monetary inflation, exhaustion and erosion of soils, the class structure of English society, which made it difficult to improve one's station in life and drove sons of the gentry to seek larger economic opportunities in the colonies, were some of the stronger reasons for emigration. Although the population of England was hardly larger than three million people in the early part of the seventeenth century, those sections of England, the central and southeastern portions, from which many of the immigrants came were regarded as overpopulated. Love of adventure, the missionary impulse, and flight from religious persecutions played a minor role in immigration as compared with economic motives. Perhaps the greatest immigration agents were the suppliers of indentured servants who persuaded naive country lads to emigrate by painting rosy pictures of America.

Indeed, the promotional literature of the seventeenth century affected the literate members of society who were maladjusted in England and seeped down into the lower strata of ignorant country folk. One of the first boosters of Virginia was Captain John Smith, who in 1624 published his *Generall Historie of Virginia, New England, and the Summer Isles,* which portrayed the richness and opportunity of this virgin land. Possibly he had his eye on a big sale of his volume when he wrote such passages as the one below describing a Virginia mask which he witnessed:

Then presently they were presented with this anticke; thirtie young women came naked out of the woods, onely covered behind and before with a few greene leaves, their bodies all painted . . . singing and dauncing with most excellent ill varietie, oft falling into their infernall passions, and solemnly againe to sing and daunce . . . they solemnly invited him to their lodgings, where he was no sooner within the house, but all these Nymphes more tormented him than ever, with crowding, pressing, and hanging about him, most tediously crying, Love you not me? love you not me? [5]

Immigrants were attracted to the Southern colonies not only by economic opportunities but by that elusive quest of men for political freedom. The first charter of the London Company contained the seed of democracy in the provision that the colonists who emigrated to Virginia should retain the liberties and the rights of Englishmen "as if they had been abiding and born, within this our Realm of *England.*" In 1619 a new treasurer of the company, Sir Edwin Sandys, ordered the summoning of a representative assembly at Jamestown, the prototype of later American legislatures. Efforts to establish feudal institutions in the Southern colonies failed in the presence of frontier conditions. John Locke's fantastic frame of government for Carolina, based on a feudal land-holding nobility, was not even put into operation. Although Lord Baltimore granted over sixty patents for the establishment of manors, relatively few Americans were willing to become tenants when ownership of land could be easily acquired, and consequently in the course of years the manors were subdivided into tobacco plantations.

The attempt to establish a paternalistic government in Georgia also was of short duration. In the early years of the colony the settlers had no legislature, being ruled by a trusteeship, of which Oglethorpe was the chief administrator. The colonists were required to plant mulberry trees for the raising of silk worms and were prohibited from holding slaves, importing rum, or owning more than 500 acres of land. This regime caused many settlers to abandon Georgia for colonies with a freer government and larger economic opportunities. The Trustees accordingly were forced gradually to relax their restrictions and in 1751 gave up their charter. Georgians thus attained the freedom of other colonists, the freedom to get drunk, to rest in the shade while their black slaves were working, to hold as much land as they could win by honesty or unscrupulousness, and to wrangle with the royal governor in their legislature.

A valuable admixture to the English blood in the Southern colonies was brought by the coming of French immigrants. The original impulse which drove these Gallic colonists across the Atlantic Ocean to Southern shores was religious intolerance. During the last half of the seventeenth century the French government severely persecuted its Protestant inhabitants, called Huguenots, who were located chiefly in western and northern France. The Huguenot emigration scattered Frenchmen throughout the American colonies, but the largest concentration of Huguenots in America was located in South Carolina. They began to enter this colony in 1680, but after the Revocation of the Edict of Nantes (1685), which had granted toleration to Protestants, they came in increasing numbers. Although a few of these immigrants were from aristocratic lineage, the majority of them belonged to the middle class of France, being skilled workers, petty tradesmen, and farmers. The French settlers became plantation owners and merchants in Charleston, intermarried with the English, and most of them eventually joined the Church of England. At the close of the colonial period the French element constituted about 3 per cent of the population of South Carolina. Despite their small numbers, the French element has made a notable contribution to the leadership of the Southern region, producing Marion, Moultrie, Legaré, Poinsett, the Le Conte brothers, Matthew Fontaine Maury, and John Sevier.

At the beginning of the French and Indian War the British gov-

ernment deported approximately seven thousand of the French inhabitants of its Canadian province of Acadia for security reasons.
These simple peasant farmers were uprooted from their homes and
scattered among the thirteen colonies. Some of the Acadians settled
in Baltimore, where they established a French church. A group of
eleven hundred and forty of these unfortunate people were transported to Virginia, but so unwelcome were they that the legislature appropriated £5,000 to ship them to England. When nine
hundred and forty-two Acadians arrived on the shores of South
Carolina without warning Governor Glen strongly protested, because they were Catholics and because this alien group constituted
a danger to the colony. The legislature ordered their dispersal
throughout the parishes and sold those who refused to work as indentured servants. A heavy rate of mortality, partly owing to smallpox, reduced their number, so that in 1760 only two hundred and ten
Acadians remained in South Carolina. Following the Treaty of Paris
(1763) most of the dispersed Acadians left the English colonies,
some of them emigrating to Louisiana and others managing to get
back to their homeland. They have been aptly described as "Acadian
transients." [6]

Advancing from the seacoast along the river valleys, the English
settlers had reached the fall line in Virginia by 1676, the time of
Bacon's Rebellion. Beyond this line of demarcation lay a region of
hills and forests, which had been explored as early as 1671 by Thomas
Batts and Robert Fallam, sent out by Captain Abraham Wood who
had a trading post at modern Petersburg on the falls of the Appomattox. Their explorations extended as far as the New River, one of the
branches of the Kanawha, and they were perhaps the first English
to reach the headwaters of streams flowing into the Mississippi River.
This western hinterland attracted the eye of Lieutenant-Governor
Alexander Spotswood, who developed ambitious plans of expanding the Virginia colony and of preventing the French from hemming
the English into the narrow region of the coastal plain. At the same
time he was eager to increase his personal fortune by land speculations and Indian trade. Since he found that expansion along the
James River, the best avenue into the Piedmont, was blocked by the
Byrd family, who had obtained the land about the falls of the river

on which Richmond is located, he began to advance up the Rappahannock River. In 1714, he imported some Germans whom he located in the back country on the Rapidan River at a colony which he named Germanna. These immigrants, brought over to work the iron deposits which had been discovered near the falls of the Rappahannock, were given no lands but were tenants on the governor's land. In the same year Spotswood established Fort Christiana on the Meherrin River, a tributary of the Roanoke, for the purpose of Indian trade.

In 1716 the governor led a party of gentlemen, provided with a liberal supply of wine and liquor, to the top of the Blue Ridge, where they drank copious toasts in Champagne, Claret, and Burgundy. In preparation for the journey the horses of the company had been equipped with horseshoes, a practice that was not usually followed in the Tidewater, where the soils were sandy and free from stones. To commemorate this trip of exploration and assertion of England's claims Spotswood created the order of the Knights of the Golden Horseshoe and gave to each of the adventurers a gold pin in the shape of a horseshoe.

The leaders of the movement into the Virginia Piedmont were the wealthy planters of the Tidewater. Since tobacco-growing as practiced in the colonial period quickly exhausted the soil, large reserves of virgin soil were needed. Consequently, when lands in the Tidewater began to wear out, the far-sighted planters began to plan for the future by acquiring lands in the Piedmont. Furthermore, money was to be made by speculating in western lands. The advance into the Piedmont along the James was led by the aristocratic Randolph family, their friends, and relatives. Frequently the Tidewater planter would send his overseer and a gang of slaves into the western wilderness to clear the ground, build a house, and prepare for the later removal of the planter's household. The Beverley family, for example, obtained a district of more than 100,000 acres in the Valley of Virginia at the site of the present town of Staunton. William Byrd II patented an enormous number of acres along the Roanoke River, including the famous Indian trading island of Occaneechee, where the Dan and the Staunton rivers unite to form the Roanoke, and here he built a hunting lodge, "Bluestone Castle." Many of these large grants of land were held by speculators who had secured them on the condition of settling one family on the land for every thousand acres patented. To facilitate the settlement of the back country of Virginia two huge empty counties were created in 1720, Spotsylvania in northern Virginia, and Brunswick in the southern Piedmont.

The advance of the frontier in the colonial period was not always the simple process described by some historians, in which the vanguard of settlement was led by small pioneer farmers followed after a time interval by substantial farmers and planters. Frequently, the movement of acquiring western lands in the South was initiated by wealthy planters seeking reserves for tobacco lands.[7] However, many small tobacco farmers left the Tidewater and moved into the Piedmont in quest of virgin soils. Here they continued the culture of tobacco, which they transported to market by floating the hogsheads in canoes and double-canoes (the latter originated in 1749 by the Reverend Robert Rose of Virginia) down the rivers, or by rolling them along the ground. In this picturesque method of transportation the hogshead was drawn by a horse hitched by means of a pair of shafts to a pole which pierced the cylinder heads. Numerous yeomen who settled in the Valley of Virginia became wheat farmers, engaged in subsistence farming, for the problem of transportation to the seacoast was so difficult as to discourage the extensive cultivation of tobacco. Still other small farmers occupied the wild lands of southwest Virginia, including the Roanoke Valley region.

In the back country of North Carolina ex-indentured servants and yeomen farmers from Virginia settled on the land as squatters without a legal title. William Byrd II maligned the inhabitants of this region by insinuating that the chief colonizing agents of the rude Carolina frontier were the sheriffs of Virginia who stimulated the emigration of undesirable citizens into the wilderness to the south. The best lands of the Carolina back country were monopolized by rich speculators. Furthermore, the oldest and most populous part of the colony, the Granville Tract, was controlled by the noble Granville family of England. Their agent, located at Edenton, granted land patents and collected quit-rents, but he found his job of collecting quit-rents from squatters a perilous enterprise. A huge tract of land, "a principality," in western North Carolina was granted in 1736 by the Crown to Henry McCulloh and associates on condition of settling on the land six hundred European Protestants within ten years. When the son of the proprietor, Henry Eustace, attempted to survey this domain, on which squatters had located, his agents were beaten by mobs and eventually he was frustrated in his dream of obtaining a princely revenue from his wild lands in Carolina. Despite the undemocratic system of granting large areas of land to individuals, the North Carolina back country was populated by poor people. Between 1733 and 1754 the population of the colony more than doubled, chiefly by the settlement of the back country, and by the middle of the eighteenth century it contained a white population twice the size of South Carolina's white inhabitants.

The occupation of the back country of South Carolina was artificially stimulated by the provincial government. In 1730 the royal governor, Robert Johnson, secured the adoption of a scheme for the settlement of poor Protestant immigrants in eleven townships on the frontier. The motives for this colonization scheme were to guard the colony from the peril of Indian and Spanish attacks and by increasing the white population to diminish the danger from servile insurrection. So many slaves had been imported into the colony that they formed two-thirds of the population and were a constant danger to security, which was demonstrated by the Stono insurrection of 1739. Under Governor Johnson's scheme each white immigrant who settled in one of these outlying townships was given fifty acres of land for each member of his household, agricultural tools, a cow and calf for each five persons, provisions for a year, and freedom from payment of quit-rents for ten years. Also either the Crown or the colony paid the passage of many of these settlers who located on the exposed frontier. The colony set aside the customs receipts from the duty on slaves as a fund to pay these charges. Attracted by these terms a group of Swiss, largely French-speaking, in 1735 founded Purrysburg on the Savannah River, where they produced silk. Other settlements of Swiss and Germans were made during the decade of the 1730's at Amelia, Saxe Gotha, and Orangeburg. Also

Scotch-Irish came directly from Belfast to found Williamburg township and Welsh Baptists arrived from Delaware to settle at Queens-
boro in the Pee Dee Valley. All of these settlements were in the
Coastal Plain below the fall line, where the colonists cultivated
wheat, corn, hemp, flax, and indigo. The settlers of this period came
through the port of Charleston or from the older settlements of the
colony. No other English colony gave such liberal inducements to
stimulate immigration.[8]

The hilly region between the fall line and the Blue Ridge was the
cradle of the typical American pioneer and has felicitously been
called "the Old West." It was settled largely by German and Scotch-
Irish immigrants, who entered the South from Pennsylvania through
the corridor of the Great Valley. The first settler to locate in the
northern end of the Shenandoah Valley was Adam Miller or Müller
from Lancaster, Pennsylvania, who brought a group of German
families in 1726 or 1727 to this rich agricultural region. In 1732 Jost
Hite led a migration of sixteen families from Pennsylvania to the
Valley of Virginia. Most of these Pennsylvania "Dutchmen" had
come to the great immigrant port of Philadelphia from the Rhine
Valley and from southern Germany. In the old country they had
been peasants, badly exploited by their landlords, the remains of
whose romantic castles one sees today on a trip down the Rhine.
The Germans were driven from their homeland partly on account of
religious persecution (after the Elector of the Palatinate, John
William, had tried to force his people early in the eighteenth century
to accept Catholicism) but predominantly by a desire to escape
from the low standard of living in the Rhine Valley caused by
avaricious landlords and the devastation of invading armies.

When the desirable lands of the Pennsylvania back country had
been absorbed, they pushed southward into the Great Valley and
spilled over the Blue Ridge into the Piedmont of Virginia and the
Carolinas. Entering Maryland, they settled around Hagerstown
and Frederick. In the Shenandoah Valley, the towns of Winchester,
Stephensburg, Strasburg, and Woodstock became distinctly Germanic in atmosphere. In North Carolina the Germans settled especially in the Piedmont counties of Rowan, Guilford, Forsyth,
and Davidson, with Salisbury as the principal town. Thus a "new

Germany of the South" was created, based on a Pennsylvania-German culture rather than the unmodified civilization of the old country.

Only recently have scholars recognized the many valuable contributions to the society of the Southern back country made by non-English stocks.[9] The Germans, for example, brought with them the art of building superior log cabins, constructed of squared rather than round logs, and mortised at the ends by a peculiar notch. The German craftsmen of Pennsylvania had developed an effective rifle with a long barrel, later known as the "Kentucky long rifle." In the Conestoga Valley of Pennsylvania they had invented the Conestoga wagon, a durable, covered wagon, which, with some adaptations, became the "prairie schooner" of the Far West. The skill of the German craftsmen did much to make the back country economically independent of the Tidewater and of the shipment of manufactured goods from Europe. The German immigrants into America brought with them the art of making glazed pottery, and they produced superior tinsmiths, cabinet makers, wagon makers, tanners, coopers, and iron workers.

Into the back country of the Southern colonies they imported their churches and German pietism. Many an old father gave his young son emigrating to America a large Gothic Bible inscribed with his blessing. Such an inscription was written on the flyleaf of the Bible of John Conrad Clement who left Hesse-Darmstadt in 1765 for Pennsylvania and whose children trekked down the Great Valley to the neighborhood of the village of Mocksville in Piedmont, North Carolina, carrying the sacred book with them. The old German father wrote in the Bible given to his son about to depart for America, "if I am no more with thee in body, yet am I with thee in spirit and with my prayers, for prayer is a strong tower against crafty attacks of Satan and of the world and of our corrupt flesh and blood . . . Be this the end and good night forever. . . . The Spirit of God lead and direct thee and me and us all in his time out of this wearisome and troubled life into the eternal blessed life through Jesus Christ our Lord to whom be praise and honor from eternity to eternity, Amen." [10]

The most interesting group of Germans in the back country were the Moravians, a religious sect officially known as the *Unitas Fratrum*, founded early in the eighteenth century by religious refugees living on the estate of Count Zinzendorf in Moravia. In 1753 they purchased a large tract of land in the Piedmont region of North Carolina which had been selected by the Moravian Bishop Spangenberg. From their center in America at Bethlehem, Pennsylvania, they sent a group of brothers ahead to build houses and prepare for the migration of families to their new home in the wilderness. Three little German villages, Bethabara, Bethania, and Salem were founded (the last in 1776), destined to become a part of the modern city of Winston-Salem. They erected communal houses, such as the Brothers' House, in which the single men lived, and the virginal Sisters' House, still surviving at Salem, as well as dignified brick churches. Their architecture was sober and Germanic in style, with red tile roofs, arched hoods over the doors, and vaulted cellars. The religion of the Moravians was based on brotherly love and peace, and their graveyards were characterized by uniform, horizontal grave stones, a symbol of the democracy of the dead. Among their unique ceremonies were a beautiful Easter service at dawn and the Love Feast, in which lighted candles were held by the congregation and Moravian sugar bread was served. Furthermore, they established missions among the Indians and the Negro slaves.[11]

These Pennsylvania-Dutchmen brought with them a deep love for music. The Moravians had trombone choirs that played the fervent, emotional, religious music of the German folk. Also they had a talented organ maker, Joseph Bullitschek who in 1773 made the organ for the Bethania church, an instrument which is still capable of producing exquisite tones. In the vicinity of the Blue Ridge Mountains of Virginia lived the Germans, Joseph Funk and his sons, who for nearly fifty years made their home, called "Singer's Glen," a center not only for teaching music but for publishing music books.

The German settlers were regarded as "odd-looking" people by their English neighbors. They wore wide-brimmed hats with low crowns and peculiarly cut coats without lapels. The Amish and Mennonites among them abstained from the sinful device of buttons, while both the young and the old men grew patriarchal beards. From Pennsylvania they hauled their iron stove plates, decorated with

Bible scenes, their dower chests on which were painted birds and tulips (the Persian flower of love), and their quaint Bibles. They continued to eat sauerkraut and doughnuts, to drink clabber milk, and to sleep under feather mattresses. Their weddings were picturesque affairs, somewhat reminiscent of Peter Brueghel's paintings, in which a prodigous dinner was served and the groomsmen wore white embroidered aprons. Much hilarity was evoked on these occasions by the attempts of the guests to steal the bride's slipper.

Gradually the German inhabitants gave up their folk art and their peculiar customs. At the end of the eighteenth century they began to abandon speaking their original tongue. The churches, Lutheran, German Reformed, Mennonite, Dunker, and Moravian, were the last strongholds of the German tongues. In 1855 the Moravian Church at Salem abandoned keeping the church records in the language of their forefathers. In a number of cases, even the trace of German origin was eradicated by the anglicizing of surnames— Müller becoming Miller; Schmidt, Smith; Klein, Short, Small, or Little; and Hoenes, Hanes.

Although the Germans of the South surrendered in many respects to their environment, they continued their type of agriculture, perhaps their greatest contribution to their adopted land. The English settlers of the Tidewater had pursued a type of agriculture that stripped the soil of its fertility, sacrificing the soil in order to conserve labor and produce a money crop for export. The Germans, on the other hand, practiced a careful and far-sighted agriculture. They were skilled in choosing good soils for their farms, especially the rich limestone soils. Their lands were conserved by crop rotation, by developing meadows, by preserving their woodlands, and by a careful husbandry of deep ploughing and of the use of animal manures. Instead of concentrating on a single exhaustive crop, such as tobacco, they engaged in a diversified subsistence agriculture. It is true that the location of their settlements, distant from markets, contributed to saving them from the absorption in tobacco culture, but their Germanic traditions were also important in their continuance of a thrifty agriculture.[12] While the English farmer exhausted the fertility of his soil and abandoned his farm, the Germans saved the soil and transmitted their farms, undepleted, to their children. Wherever the

Germans tilled the land, there stood the large Swiss-type barns, more commodious than their houses. In contrast to these thrifty farmers the English of the Tidewater, according to a French traveler of 1788, "know not the use of barns," providing neither shelter nor hay for their cattle during the winter and thus depriving their families of milk.[13]

Through the Great Valley from Pennsylvania the Scotch-Irish followed the Germans into the back country of the South. The home of these hardy immigrants had been northern Ireland, the Ulster district, to which their forefathers had been transported from lowland Scotland by James I to hold the wild Irish down and make Ireland Protestant. The immigrants who left Belfast for Philadelphia were principally Presbyterian Scotsmen, but they also included an admixture of Celtic Irish and of English who had originally crossed over into the Scottish lowlands, from whence they had gone to northern Ireland. In Ireland these transplanted Scotsmen tilled small farms, which they leased from landlords for a hundred years, and developed a thriving industry of weaving linen and woolen cloth. In the first half of the eighteenth century their leases began to expire and their absentee landlords demanded higher rents— "rack rent." Furthermore, the British mercantilists secured the passage of legislation excluding the export of Irish woolens to England, although the linen industry was encouraged. Added to these economic grievances was a religious injustice, the establishment of the Anglican church in this Presbyterian district, which forced the Scotch-Irish to pay taxes to support Anglican clergymen whom they did not desire. Consequently, the Scotch-Irish began to leave Ireland in droves to find new homes in America.

They came in such numbers to the United States during the eighteenth century that they far exceeded the great Puritan immigration into New England of the preceding century. Finding the good lands near the Atlantic seaboard occupied or preempted, they were forced to push on to the frontier. In Pennsylvania they founded towns in the hinterland such as Carlisle and Pittsburgh. Then they began to settle in great numbers in the Southern Piedmont during the three decades preceding the Revolution. The migration of John C. Calhoun's ancestors illustrates this movement of the Scotch-Irish into the South. The Calhoun family first settled in western Pennsylvania in 1733, then moved to the New River Valley in Wythe County, Virginia, and made a final remove to the frontier region near Abbeville, South Carolina, during the French and Indian War. Calhoun's grandmother was killed by the Cherokee in the course of that war.

The Scotch-Irish had strongly marked characteristics which made them admirably suited to become the cutting edge of the frontier. Tall, angular, with jutting chins and forceful countenances, they were noted for their fighting qualities, their tenacity of will, and their practicality. They were self-reliant and devoted to principle—these serious Presbyterian folk, who often lacked humor, demonstrativeness, and an appreciation for esthetic qualities. Accustomed to turbulent border fighting in Ireland, they made excellent frontiersmen and Indian fighters. They were distinguished from their German neighbors by their zest and capacity in politics. Many Southern statesmen, including several Presidents, were descended from this virile stock—Andrew Jackson, John C. Calhoun, George McDuffie, James K. Polk, the Breckinridges, Andrew Johnson, and Woodrow Wilson.

The Scotch-Irish settlers brought an element of vigorous industry into the South. Although they readily accepted slavery, they were nevertheless industrious and thrifty farmers, intent on improving their condition in life. They had a tradition of opposition to landlordism which caused them to become a thorn in the flesh of proprietors and quit-rent collectors, often squatting on the unoccupied lands, and proclaiming that the soil should be free to actual settlers. The Scotch-Irish women brought their spinning wheels and looms from the old country, and one of the important tasks of the Scotch-Irish maidens in the Piedmont was spinning flax and making linen and woolen cloth for the household. The men frequently were distillers of corn liquor and of apple and peach brandy, occupations that did not conflict with their stern Presbyterianism.

Closely related to the Scotch-Irish were the Highland Scot and Welsh settlers. The latter have been ignored by social historians, but two of the South's eminent men, Thomas Jefferson and General George H. Thomas, were descendants of Welshmen. In 1735 the

Prince of Wales sailed from the port of Inverness to Georgia, bringing one hundred and thirty Highland men and fifty women and children. Their lands in Scotland had been confiscated as a result of participating in Jacobite uprisings. Consequently they were glad to accept land in America even if it was located on the exposed frontier of the Altamaha River in Georgia. Here they founded the town of New Inverness (later called Darien) near the mouth of the river. They are noted for their opposition to the introduction of slavery in the colony, which was especially urged by the inhabitants around Savannah. The Highland Scots of New Inverness, under the leadership of John Mohr McIntosh, joined with the German settlers at Ebenezer in 1738 to petition the trustees to continue the prohibition of slavery. They produced many valuable citizens of Georgia, such as the great planter, Thomas Spalding of Sapelo Island.

The North Carolina contingent of the Highland Scottish immigration came at a later date, following the defeat of "Bonnie Prince Charlie" at the battle of Culloden Moor in 1746 and the cruel suppression of the Scottish rebellion by the Duke of Cumberland. The Highland emigration was also stimulated by the expansion of sheep grazing which deprived many small farmers of their livelihood and by the break-up of the clan system in the eighteenth century, which produced crime and disorder. Then the tacksmen system, by which the tacksman, or chief tenant, would sublet to lesser tenants, resulted in oppression and "rack rents," thus increasing unrest in Scotland and emigration to America. The Highland Scots who came to North Carolina settled at Fayetteville (called Cross Creek before the Revolution) on the Cape Fear River. They retained their Gaelic speech and their Presbyterian faith, as well as a fierce loyalty to an oath. At the beginning of the American Revolution, having sworn loyalty to the king, they became Tories who fought valiantly for the royal cause in the battle of Moore's Creek Bridge near Wilmington (February 27, 1776).

This immigrant stock—both Highland Scots and Scotch-Irish—made two extremely valuable contributions to the spiritual life of the South, by the introduction of the Presbyterian Church, and by the impulse they gave to the education of the youth. They remained staunch followers of John Knox with his fatalistic and gloomy interpretation of the Christian faith. Wherever they went, they established their Presbyterian church, which emphasized the importance of honesty and truthfulness, the sacredness of a contract, or the convenant. Since their church required educated ministers and a laity well-read in the Bible, they were also a great force in establishing academies, and later such colleges as Hampden-Sydney, Washington and Lee, Davidson, and Oglethorpe University in the South and Princeton in New Jersey.

The type of immigrants who settled in the South was fully as important a determinant of its civilization as the molding force of the terrain and climate. If Virginia or the Carolinas had been populated by Asiatics, instead of by Englishmen, Germans, Scots, and French, there is every reason to believe that a type of society would have arisen different from that which did develop. In other words, culture importation, the mental baggage which the immigrants brought with them, had a profound and continuing influence on the rise of Southern civilization. The old question of which is stronger, heredity or environment, applies to societies as well as to individuals.[14] The Southern heritage was predominantly English, but it was enriched by the cultural contributions of other Western European peoples. This heritage was powerfully modified by the Southern environment which produced the plantation way of life described in succeeding chapters.

Citations

1. JOHN SMITH, The Generall Historie of Virginia, New-England and the Summer Isles (London, 1624), 21.
2. CLEANTH BROOKS, JR., "The English Language in the South," R. C. Beatty and W. R. Fidler (eds.), Contemporary Southern Prose (Boston, 1940), and G. P. Krapp, The English Language in America (New York, 1925), I, 39–40; 64–65; II, 56, 199, 225.
3. "Report of the Committee on Linguistic and National Stocks in the United States," Annual Report of American Historical Association, 1931 (Washington, 1932), I, 307, 124.
4. A. B. SAYE, New Viewpoints in Georgia History (Athens, Ga., 1943), preface, v; also p. 31.

5. Smith, *Generall Historie*, 67.
6. R. A. Hudnut, and H. Baker-Crothers, "Acadian Transients in South Carolina," *American Historical Review*, XLIII (April, 1938), 500–513.
7. T. P. Abernethy, *Three Virginia Frontiers* (University, La., 1940), has made a significant modification of Frederick Jackson Turner's theories.
8. R. L. Meriwether, *The Expansion of South Carolina, 1729–1765* (Kingsport, Tenn., 1940).
9. Notably, T. J. Wertenbaker, *The Old South; the Founding of American Civilization* (New York, 1942), Chap. V.
10. MS. in possession of Miss Mary Jane Heitman, Mocksville, North Carolina, translated by Adelaide L. Fries.
11. Adelaide L. Fries (ed.), *Records of the Moravians in North Carolina* (Raleigh, 1922–1947), 7 vols.; *The Road to Salem* (Chapel Hill, 1944).
12. R. H. Shryock, "Cultural Factors in the History of the South," *Journal of Southern History*, V (August, 1939), 341–342.
13. J. P. Brissot de Warville, *New Travels in the United States of America Performed in 1788* (New York, 1792), 234.
14. Wesley F. Craven has shown that the evolution of local government, the county system and the sheriff, as well as the development of the Anglican church in Virginia represented a compromise between old English institutions and the molding effect of American environment. *The Southern Colonies in the Seventeenth Century, 1607–1689* (Baton Rouge, 1949), 168–172; 178–182; 269–309. R. S. Cotterill has described how English settlers discarded their old ways of life and developed new habits of diet, new methods of building houses, new crops, and new ideas in America. *The Old South* (Glendale, Calif., 1939), Chap. II.

CHAPTER II

Origin of the Plantations and Towns

THE plantation system of the South had its roots in the economic and social conditions of the colonial period. The two basic elements in this system were the acquisition of large estates and the use of a considerable labor force, consisting at first of white indentured servants and later of black slaves. The main incentive for the rise of such large units of agricultural production was the profits to be obtained from the cultivation of tobacco and rice on a large scale for the European market. In the seventeenth and eighteenth centuries the large planter had the advantage over the small farmer in marketing the staple crops, in obtaining credit from the London factors, in purchasing supplies in bulk, and in having his own wharf.

The method of cultivating tobacco on relatively virgin soils also led to the development of large plantations. Tobacco was planted for four or five years in succession in the same field, a practice which exhausted the fertility of the soil, but brought quick returns.[1] Such rapid exploitation of the land, as well as the operation of erosion, led to the constant abandonment of old fields and the clearing of new fields. This wasteful frontier method of agriculture was followed primarily because of the high cost of labor and the illimitable reserves of land in America rather than because of ignorance or carelessness. Nevertheless, it had bad results. Every planter realized the necessity of acquiring extensive reserves of land, and this need led to the growth of lonely plantations and the dispersion of population. Consequently, the tobacco planters marched slowly to the West, leaving behind them abandoned tobacco fields which in the course of years became covered with pine trees and broomsedge.

By the time of the Revolution much of Tidewater Virginia and Maryland had been left in a state of desolation.

The accumulation of large estates in the South was facilitated by the "headright" system, by which a person who imported a slave or an indentured servant received a grant of fifty acres of land. This practice led to great frauds. Some unscrupulous planters magnified the number of servants whom they had imported or the number of acres patented by adding zero's to the documents. A collusion between landgrabbing squires and colonial officials often made possible the accumulation of broad estates. Also, aspiring planters consolidated their landholdings by marrying widows possessed of goodly acres. The break-up or subdivision of these semi-feudal landholdings was prevented to a considerable extent by the laws of primogeniture and entail. According to the rule of primogeniture, the lands of an estate were inherited intact by the oldest son if the father died without a will, but as a matter of fact, many planters divided their plantations among their children by their wills. The aristocratic law of entail permitted the descent of estates and of slaves to be fixed, so that they could not be sold, but must be inherited by the family from generation to generation. By the time of the Revolution, however, many estates were not entailed, and the law had become so burdensome that the legislature frequently docked entails on plantations.

Measures could have been taken to give free land to poor farmers and to prevent or retard the growth of huge estates. The strict enforcement of the payment of quit-rents would have discouraged the holding of vast tracts of unused lands, but the payment of this tax on the land, usually two shillings per hundred acres, was often evaded. When some of the royal governors, like Francis Nicholson and Alexander Spotswood of Virginia, tried to prevent the rise of land monopoly, to expose frauds, and to sue the great planters for arrears in quit-rents, they were defeated by the influential men who profited from landgrabbing and who dominated the colonial government. Spotswood, finding that it was fruitless to "buck" the powerful planters and champion the cause of a more democratic distribution of the land, reversed his policy and joined the scramble to obtain huge land grants. Although the quit-rent system was a relic

of feudalism, the efficient collection of these taxes on large preserves
of unused land would have forced a fairer distribution of the land.
These dues were thoroughly hated in the South and the Middle
colonies where they were with difficulty collected. New England
was free from this burden. In Pennsylvania on the eve of the Revolution, only one-third of the amount due was collected, in Virginia less
than one-half, in South Carolina between £2,000 and £3,000, but
in Maryland nearly the entire rent roll of £8,000 was exacted.

The growth of extensive estates in the South formed the economic
substratum for a dominant aristocracy. "King" Robert Carter, noted
for his haughty demeanor, died in 1732, possessing 333,000 acres of
land and seven hundred slaves. Other examples of regal estates were
Beverley's Manor at Staunton, the immense landholdings of the
Byrd family of "Westover," the estates of the Carroll and Dulany
families in Maryland, the Granville tract and the McCulloh "principality" in North Carolina, and the plantations of Sir James Wright
in Georgia. A huge domain between the Potomac and Rappahannock
rivers was granted in 1673 by Charles II to the Earl of Arlington
and Lord Culpeper.* This area, known as the "Northern Neck of
Virginia," contained approximately one million acres of land from
which the family collected the hated quit-rents. This immense grant
was eventually inherited by Thomas Lord Fairfax, who in 1747
settled at "Greenway Court," near Winchester, the only British
peer who made his permanent residence in the colonies. These great
estates of the eighteenth century were made possible by the introduction of the institution of Negro slavery. The only landholdings
comparable to them in the northern colonies were those of the
Narragansett (Rhode Island) planters and the spacious estates of
the Hudson Valley which had been initiated by the patroon system.

The prime requisite for success in founding a permanent English
colony in Virginia was the discovery of a profitable export commodity. In 1612 John Rolfe pointed the way to prosperity by discovering a method of curing the Virginia tobacco which removed

---

* It is a complicated story which Douglas S. Freeman has skillfully told in
George Washington, a Biography (New York, 1948), I, 4–14, and Appendix,
447–513. In 1649 Charles I granted the Northern Neck to seven favorites. In
1688 Lord Culpeper, who had previously become proprietor, secured a re-
newal of the grant in perpetuity with greatly expanded boundaries.

its bitter taste and enabled it to supplant Spanish tobacco in the English market. Sir Walter Raleigh had popularized the smoking of the American weed among the gentry of England, but conservatives strongly condemned the use of tobacco for hedonistic purposes. In 1604 King James wrote a violent pamphlet against the use of tobacco entitled "Counter-Blaste to Tobacco," in which he declared that smokers were "guilty of sinful and shameful lust." But his condemnation could not prevent a steady demand for the delightful plant, and soon the Jamestown planters were growing tobacco in the streets. Charles I, who succeeded James in 1625, was also hostile to the growth of a crop which produced only unsubstantial smoke. He tried to establish a royal monopoly by a contract to buy and sell the entire Virginia output, but his action was vigorously resisted by the planters. Nevertheless, he aided the colonists by prohibiting the cultivation of tobacco in England and by excluding the more desirable Spanish tobacco from the English market or admitting only a very small quantity.

The Virginia Company and the British government made strenuous efforts to divert the colonists from growing tobacco and turn their energies into more productive channels. They encouraged silk culture, wine making, the cultivation of olives, almonds, ginger, citrus fruits, indigo, cotton; the establishment of iron works; and the manufacture of glass beads. The colonial legislature by means of bounties and the British government by the Trade Acts sought to encourage a diversification of agriculture in the southern colonies. The crucial battle for a more wholesome economy was fought in the early years when the necessary capital and skill for experimentation was lacking. Furthermore, tobacco throve, while the desirable plants for a self-sufficing empire withered or were killed by nipping frosts.

Tobacco was an ideal crop to ship across the Atlantic, for it had small bulk and high value, so that it could bear the expense of the high freight rates. Consequently it became the dominant economic interest, the money crop, of the Chesapeake Bay country. It was also grown in the Albemarle Sound region of North Carolina. The competition of this tobacco, however, caused the Virginia Assembly in 1679 to pass an act forbidding the importation of Carolina tobacco into Virginia or its shipment through Virginia ports. This selfish policy of the Old Dominion struck a serious blow at North Carolina, for the province lacked good harbors and was dependent upon Norfolk for the shipment of its tobacco. For fifty years the province was held back in its economic development by Virginia's embargo. Finally, in 1731, shortly after North Carolina became a royal colony, the Albemarle planters secured the disallowance of the Virginia discriminatory law.

The tobacco plant was cultivated on rich virgin soil beneath the tall trees of the forest, which had been killed by the process of girdling. The Indians had taught the colonists this easy way of clearing the land by cutting a band of bark from the tree, causing it to die. The wind tore the branches from these dead monarchs of the forests and later the colonists built fires around the trunks and burned them. During the colonial period plows were not practical in cultivating the plants beneath the girdled trees; hoes had to be used.

Tobacco at first brought a high price, five shillings a pound, but overproduction caused the price to fall rapidly so that as early as 1630 it had declined to two pence a pound. To remedy the situation the Virginia government turned to the expedient of crop control (a forerunner of the Roosevelt policies of the AAA), and in 1629 limited each planter by law to the cultivation of only three thousand plants and in the following year, to two thousand. Such restrictions, however, proved to be ineffective, for the neighboring colony of Maryland refused to cooperate and expanded its crop when Virginia limited its production. In 1682, after prices fell to a disastrous level, some of the small planters staged a tobacco riot, during which they went through the fields, cutting down the plants in order to curtail overproduction.

Tobacco became a legal medium of exchange in Virginia, Maryland, and North Carolina. Very few gold and silver coins circulated in the colonies, partly as a result of the mercantilistic policy of England, and therefore tobacco filled a dominant position in the currency. Salaries of ministers were paid in tobacco, usually 16,000 pounds. Since there were two important varieties of the plant grown in Virginia, the Sweet-Scented, which was the more valuable, and the Oronoko, which was the common variety, the clerical salaries were unequal. Fortunate was the parson whose lot fell in a Sweet-Scented parish. In order to keep up the quality of Virginia tobacco, the colony provided for a rigid system of inspection by officials. The Inspection Law of 1730 required that bonded inspectors should be appointed at public warehouses to examine all tobacco for export and burn all inferior tobacco. For good tobacco stored in warehouses the inspectors gave receipts which were legal tender for debts and taxes.

The tobacco trade had a profound influence on the development of society in the Chesapeake Bay country. It was a life-saver in providing the colonists with a valuable money crop to pay for imports from England and the continent. The tobacco ships arrived from England late in the fall or the early winter, bringing with them luxuries and necessities from the mother country. Sailing up the rivers, they stopped leisurely at the individual wharves of the planters, unloading their goods, and engaging tobacco for the return trip. They did not return to England with their freight of tobacco until the spring. Throughout the colonial period there was a dearth of ships to carry staple exports to Europe, a condition which placed the planter in an unfavorable position in bargaining for cheap freight rates. Indeed, the cost of transporting tobacco to England was excessive, partly on this account, but also because of the uneconomical method of loading the ships. Instead of loading and unloading at central towns, the sea captains spent many days going from plantation to plantation, thus piling up the expense of sailors' wages, storage, loss of interest on the capital invested in ships, etc. The prevalent freight rates of £7 a ton was equal to approximately 18 per cent of the gross sale price of tobacco. Efforts were made by the Virginia assembly to force the trade into ports of entry through the creation of towns by legislation, but since the large planters found the old system more convenient and profitable to them such laws were repealed.

The tobacco trade was carried on through London factors. These businessmen were commission merchants who received the assignment of tobacco and sold it on commission. They credited the planter with the balance after various charges, commissions, tariff duties, and freight rates had been paid. The total of these charges was so great that the planters usually received only about 35 per cent of the gross sale price. The captains of the tobacco ships brought orders from the planters for English goods. The factors obtained these goods from various shops and warehouses in London and dispatched them to the planter in the fall and winter trips. The planters bitterly complained at times that shop-worn and unfashionable goods were sent to them—the refuse of the London shops. Also often the amount of articles ordered was greater than the profits from the sale of the tobacco assignment and thus many planters were thrown into chronic debt.[2]

During the period of the Commonwealth in England, the decade 1650–60, the Southern planters enjoyed practically free trade with the world. They exported a large amount of their tobacco to the continent, especially to Holland, and secured cheap freight rates in the Dutch ships. But after the restoration of the Stuarts in 1660, the tobacco trade was severely regulated to secure a revenue for the king. Tobacco from the American colonies was thus channeled into English ports, where it paid a tariff duty ranging from 200 per cent of the value in 1660 to 600 per cent in 1705. Although the incidence of this excessive tax fell chiefly on the British consumer, the high retail price of tobacco which resulted must have restricted the market for Southern tobacco and thus adversely affected the interests of the tobacco planters.

While the Chesapeake Bay colonies were exploiting tobacco, the younger colonies to the south were developing rice, indigo, and naval stores as valuable commodities of export. The fur trade and the sale of Indian slaves to the West Indies had formed an unsubstantial and transitory foundation upon which to build a Carolina aristocracy. The introduction of rice culture, however, provided an economic substratum for plantation life. Rice had been unsuccessfully tried in Virginia before the middle of the seventeenth century, but the swampy lands of coastal South Carolina with its warmer climate proved a favorable location for rice plantations. There is a tradition, which may be true, that the cultivation of rice in South Carolina resulted from the introduction in 1694 of seed from Madagascar. At first this cereal was cultivated on small streams and swampy land by impounding rain and swamp water to be used in the periodic flowings of the rice fields. In 1758 a planter of the Georgetown district, McKewn Johnstone, developed the tidal flow method. By this means the rice fields adjacent to the rivers and streams flowing into the ocean were flooded with fresh water by the flow of the tide pushing the river water upstream. Dikes, sluices, "trunks," or water gates, and canals made it possible to flood the rice fields with fresh water at the proper intervals. If salt water got into the fields, however, they were ruined for several years.

Rice culture was extended to include the sea islands and the coastal region of South Carolina, the southeastern corner of North Carolina, and the coast of Georgia. Negro slavery was admirably suited to rice growing. The slaves were given fixed tasks in the fields and when their tasks had been completed they were allowed to enjoy any leisure time they had earned. The cultivation of rice was subject to many hazards, such as hurricanes which might drive salt water into the fields and thus temporarily ruin them, floods that would break levees and dikes, the activity of alligators and muskrats that might start disastrous breaks in the embankments, or the depredation of the yellow and black "rice birds" (bobolinks). After the cereal had ripened in September, it was cut with a sickle, threshed with flails, or by the treading of animals, and then taken to a mill which removed the husks by the pounding of pestles in mortars and finally polished the grains.

A superior type of rice known as Carolina Gold Seed rice was developed prior to the Revolution.[3] A slave could tend about four acres of this cereal, as well as raise provisions for himself. A good hand usually raised at least four barrels of rice, weighing five hundred pounds each, which brought fifty shillings per hundred weight in a favorable market. The English trade acts required rice to be shipped to English ports for distribution, despite the fact that Great Britain and the British West Indies together consumed less than one-fifteenth of the colonial exports of rice. In 1730, however, the British government permitted the export of Carolina rice directly to ports on the continent of Europe south of Cape Finisterre (the northwestern tip of Spain). Although the Southern colonies monopolized the rice trade with Portugal, only about 22.6 per cent of their total exports of rice was absorbed by countries south of

Cape Finisterre. More than 74 per cent of the Carolina rice was sold to Holland, Germany, Denmark, and Sweden, and thus had to detour by England.

The dry land crop of colonial South Carolina and Georgia was indigo. The successful growing of this crop was begun in 1742 by a remarkable woman, Eliza Lucas, on her plantation of "Wappoo" near Charleston from seed sent by her father, the governor of the West Indian island of Antigua. In 1748 the British government offered a bounty of six pence a pound, which greatly stimulated production. Eight years later Moses Lindo, a West Indian Jew, came to Charleston and taught the planters his skill in grading indigo. There were three kinds of indigo produced: (1) the copper-colored variety, used in dyeing woolens, which brought the highest price, (2) the purple, used in the dyeing of linens, and (3) the blue variety, used by the silk industry. Besides its use in the dyeing industry, indigo was employed by domestic householders in the laundering of clothes. The South Carolina planters could raise only two crops of indigo annually as contrasted with three or four crops in the French West Indies, and also their indigo tended to be hard on the surface without being fully cured in the center.

Indigo was obtained from the leaves of a plant that looked somewhat like asparagus. After it was cut during full bloom, the plant was placed in a vat of water and beaten while it was fermenting. At a certain stage limewater was added, which precipitated the indigo material and caused it to sink to the bottom of the vat. The water was then drained and the indigo pressed into cubes. A slave could tend about four acres, which usually yielded less than one hundred pounds an acre. With the addition of the British bounty, the indigo grower made large profits in the colonial period, so that some planters doubled their capital every three or four years. The American Revolution, resulting in the discontinuance of the bounty and the loss of a favorable market, struck a serious blow to the Carolina indigo industry. Then a plague of caterpillars and the competition of East India indigo and of cotton completed the ruin of indigo growing in the South. In modern times a coal-tar product has been substituted for vegetable indigo.

In North Carolina the chief export became naval stores, consisting of turpentine, tar, and pitch. The vast forests of long-leaf pine in the coastal region were ideally suited for supplying the British navy and shipping industry with these indispensable products. So distinctive of North Carolina was this forest industry that the inhabitants were nicknamed "Tar Heels." Turpentine was obtained by cutting gashes in the pine trees, from which the sap flowed into small boxes attached beneath the gashes. Tar was made by burning pine logs in kilns covered with sand and clay. The supremacy of North Carolina in the production of naval stores did not decline until after the Civil War.

The principal source of labor in the Southern colonies during the seventeenth century was the importation of white indentured servants. In England the farm hands and laboring class received miserably low wages. For example, a ploughman in the first half of this century received fifty shillings a year. The Inclosure Movement had produced a number of unemployed agricultural laborers, while the Elizabethan poor law prevented the free migration of laborers from one parish to another by making each parish responsible for its poor. Such poor people found it almost impossible to save £6, the average cost of passage to America. The only method by which they could transfer their labor from a cheap market in England to a dear market in America was the indenture system, really a credit, or installment system to pay the passage money of crossing the Atlantic. The servant signed a contract by which he sold his labor to a master for a period usually of four or five years.

Immigration into the colonies was vastly stimulated by the profitable business of securing servants for the American market. Some sea captains made a business of transporting redemptioners, those servants who were given the privilege of selecting their masters within a period of two weeks. John Harrower, an indentured servant in Virginia, describes in his diary, 1773–1776, a class of merchants called "Soul drivers" who met immigrant and convict ships at the docks to buy servants, whom they drove through the colonies "like a parcell of Sheep" to sell to the highest bidder.[4] Such servants were sold for prices ranging from £20 for the highest type, Scottish soldiers captured after the Jacobite revolt, to £4 for Irish vagrants.

Most of the indentured servants were young men and women

under twenty-five years of age. They could look upon their four years of service in the new world as an apprenticeship in the art of growing tobacco. According to the testimony of George Alsop, an indentured servant, who wrote a description of Maryland in 1666, their lot was not hard in comparison with working conditions in England. They worked only five and one-half days in the week; in the winter they did very little work; and during the hot summer days they were allowed a three-hour rest period in the middle of the day. They were fed much better food than was available to the English laboring class, enjoying turkey, huge oysters, and venison so often that it became a "tiresome meat." [5] After a servant had fulfilled his contract he was given "freedom dues." These rewards varied in the different colonies, but usually consisted of an outfit of clothing, a certain number of barrels of corn, and agricultural tools or a musket, or a money payment. In Maryland he was given fifty acres of land until 1683, in North Carolina a similar amount of land during the proprietary period, in South Carolina fifty acres of land in the eighteenth century, but in Virginia he was not given land.

Under some masters indentured servitude approximated the conditions of slavery. The master had the right to punish his white servant by whipping, and the servant could not leave the plantation without permission. If a servant married without consent or if a maid servant had an illegitimate baby, the term of service was extended for one year. If a servant ran away and was arrested, he or she was punished by extending the term of service two days extra in Virginia and ten days in Maryland for every day of absence. Cruel treatment led to strikes and revolts on the part of white servants, particularly caused by the failure of masters to observe the custom of the country in providing their white servants with meat at least three times a week. The servants were protected from abuse to a considerable extent by custom and by their right to appeal to the courts.

The labor shortage in America was so great that it led to the dark crime of kidnapping. There were professional agents in England known as "spirits" who kidnapped "drunks" in taverns and young persons on the streets to ship them to America for sale as servants. The illegal abduction of servants became so serious that in 1664 the

British government created a Registry, which recorded the name, age, birthplace, and the terms of contract of each servant going to America, as well as an acknowledgment that the servant left the shores of England without coercion. Perhaps more cruel than kidnapping in its total effect was the deception of thousands of naive country lads and girls by agents called "crimps" in England and "newlanders" in Germany who portrayed America in a rosy and fallacious light.

The British government used the Southern colonies as well as the islands of Jamaica and Barbados as a dumping ground for convicts. Besides genuine criminals there was a class of political prisoners (much smaller in number than the jailbirds) who were transported to America to be sold as bond servants. In seventeenth century England there were over two hundred crimes listed as felonies punishable by death, but many petty criminals, especially thieves, were pardoned on condition of being transported to America. These jailbirds from the great prisons of Newgate and Old Bailey were undesirable citizens, and both Virginia and Maryland passed laws prohibiting their entrance into the colony. Such laws protecting the colonies from the immigration of convicts, however, were disallowed by the English government.

A careful student of this subject has found that during the last half of the seventeenth century a total of 4,431 persons were pardoned in England for transportation to America, but most of these were sent to Jamaica and other islands in the West Indies.[6] The merchant or captain who transported these criminals had to give bond to land them in America and had to pay various fees, equal to £3, but the services of the criminal could be sold in the colony and the importer received a headright of fifty acres for each convict. In 1717 the British Parliament passed a law facilitating the transportation of felons to America and setting the terms of exile at seven years for minor offenders and fourteen years for the more serious criminals. Furthermore, the government paid merchant contractors to transport these undesirable citizens to America. Most of the convicts sent to the mainland colonies were taken to Virginia and Maryland, where their sale to the tobacco planters was very profitable. The latest student of white bondage in the American colonies has estimated from reliable data that during the eighteenth century over 20,000 convicts were received by Virginia and Maryland, the principal colonies to which criminals were sent.[7]

Although the convict was exiled for seven years from England, his period of service as an indentured servant in the colonies was usually less than that term. Defoe in his novel of the famous whore and thief, *Moll Flanders*, who was transported to Virginia, has given a graphic account of the hardened criminals sent to the Southern colonies. "Many a Newgate-bird became a great man," one of his characters in Virginia says, "and we have several justices of the peace, officers of the trained bands, and magistrates of the towns they live in that have been burnt in the hand." Yet he shows how in this young society they could rehabilitate their lives, and acquire tobacco land, tools, and supplies from the merchants "upon the credit of their crop before it is grown." (A forerunner of the crop lien after the Civil War.) [8]

Throughout the seventeenth century white servants, rather than slaves, performed most of the labor of clearing the land and cultivating the tobacco fields. Between fifteen hundred and two thousand indentured servants came into Virginia annually and considerable numbers into Maryland. In 1671 Governor Berkeley estimated that in Virginia there were six thousand white indentured servants and two thousand slaves in a total population of forty-five thousand people. The by-product of this form of labor was the development of a large class of yeoman farmers. Until 1660 it was easy for ex-indentured servants to acquire land and rise in the world, since tobacco brought good prices.[9] A number of former indentured servants became members of the House of Burgesses. In 1632 six of the forty-four burgesses had been servants, and the legislature of 1663 contained thirteen ex-servants. Chief Justice Roger B. Taney of Maryland and General Thomas Sumter of South Carolina, "the Game Cock of the Revolution," were descended from indentured servants.

The golden age for the indentured servant in the Southern colonies ended with the restoration of the Stuarts, when Charles II ascended the throne. In Pennsylvania, on the other hand, the height of the importation of servants was reached in the eighteenth century.

The passage of the Navigation Acts of 1660 and 1663 deprived Virginia and Maryland of a free world market for their tobacco and of cheap freight rates in Dutch ships. This adverse blow caused the profits from the cultivation of tobacco to fall and made it difficult for the freedman to acquire land. The raising of tobacco for a small profit was more efficiently conducted on large estates tilled by slave labor, and the planters often supplemented their income by the fur trade and by selling merchandise to the farmers. The stream of white indentured servants which had invigorated the middle class of Virginia for a century dwindled by 1718 to a trickle of only 101 servants, and after that time until 1768 chiefly skilled artisans were imported as indentured servants.

Accordingly, the yeoman class in Virginia and Maryland declined, and the society of the tobacco colonies became decidedly more aristocratic. Contemporaneous with this great social revolution, the character of immigrants into the Southern colonies also changed from English settlers of the seventeenth century to Germans and the Scotch-Irish of the eighteenth century. During the five years preceding the Revolution, however, immigration from England, which had fallen off so greatly since 1689, was strongly revived; the port of Annapolis, Maryland, for example, showed a striking rise in the arrivals of indentured servants and convicts from England.

Maryland and Virginia represented the Promised Land to many poor and landless men in England. Undoubtedly emigration to these Southern colonies marked a step upward for the majority of the emigrants. Nevertheless, the hardships and disillusionments of the early years of planting the colonies left a bad tradition concerning the New World for some time. In order to refute such reputation John Hammond wrote in 1656 his glowing promotional pamphlet entitled *Leah and Rachel, or, the Two Fruitfull Sisters Virginia and Mary-land*. "The Country is reported to be an unhealthy place," he wrote, "a nest of Rogues, whores, desolate [sic] and rooking persons; a place of intolerable labour, bad usage and hard Diet, etc.," but Hammond proclaimed Virginia and Maryland to be superior to England as homes for poor people.[10] He was undoubtedly right, for labor was much more valuable in the Southern colonies, perhaps four or five times more so, than in England. The indentured servants had to go through a seasoning process in which many of them died from malaria, "the Virginia sickness," but after 1671 the planters learned the use of Peruvian bark, or quinine, as a remedy, which greatly decreased the mortality from the disease.

What happened to the servant after his indenture had been completed? In some cases he went to the frontier and became a yeoman farmer. But the pleasant generalization that the majority of the freed servants became sturdy yeoman farmers has been questioned by a recent student. He takes the view that many of these servants were riffraff, poor human material for colonists, who lacked the ambition to become independent farmers. He concludes that only 7 per cent of the 5,000 indentured servants who came to Maryland in the decade 1670–80 seized the opportunity to acquire the free grant of fifty acres of land and settle as farmers. Some sold their rights immediately, only a small fraction even went to the trouble of proving their rights to the fifty-acre grant, while the majority became either artisans, laborers, overseers, or "poor whites," or returned to England.[11]

In the last quarter of the seventeenth century the black tide of Negro slavery overwhelmed the white workers in the Virginia and Maryland tobacco fields. Africa contained great reservoirs of black slaves which could be used as a cheaper and more stable labor force than white indentured servants to cultivate the staple crops of the Southern colonies. Mungo Park, who made his famous exploration of Africa in 1795, estimated that three-fourths of the native Africans (probably an exaggeration) were held in slavery, in most cases in a brutal and relentless type of bondage. The kind-hearted Bishop Las Casas is credited with introducing African slavery into the West Indies to save the Indians who were dying rapidly under Spanish exploitation. Captain John Hawkins, a devout man, was the pioneer Englishman in the slave-trading business to the New World (1562), and it is an ironic commentary on the divorce of religion from humanitarianism that his slave ship was named *Jesus*.

Negro servants were introduced into the American colonies in 1619 when a Dutch ship brought twenty Negroes to Jamestown and sold them to the planters, technically as long-term indentured servants. Slavery was gradually established by custom and by the middle of the seventeenth century was legally recognized in Virginia, the status of a person being determined by whether the mother was a slave or free person. For a long time there was considerable doubt whether Christian baptism freed a slave, but in 1667 the Virginia legislature settled the question by enacting a law which declared that baptism did not affect the legal status of a slave. When slavery supplanted white servitude in the Southern colonies, the laws governing the slaves greatly resembled the laws regulating the white indentured servants.

The English did not participate extensively in slave trading until the reorganization of the Royal African Company in 1672 (founded in 1662, with the king's brother, the Duke of York, as president). This company was given a monopoly of the African slave trade until 1697 when private traders were admitted for a period of fourteen years to this traffic in human flesh upon the payment of 10 per cent duty. The slave trade was carried on through means of "factories," or trading establishments, defended by forts on the west coast of Africa. In 1750 the Royal African company had nine factories, the chief of which was Cape Coast Castle, with a strong fort built on a huge rock that projected into the sea. It was an expensive enterprise to maintain these forts and trading posts. In fact, the company was prevented from going into bankruptcy by an annual grant from Parliament of £10,000. The competition of French slave traders, who paid more for their human merchandise than the English company, was especially formidable since the French African Company was heavily subsidized by its government. In 1750 the African slave trade was again thrown open to private traders, who were incorporated as "The Company of Merchants Trading to Africa." Two years later the old corporation came to an end, the British government paying to the company £112,142 for its assets.

During the first half of the eighteenth century Bristol and Liverpool were the great slave-trading ports of the British Empire. In 1750 a total of one hundred and fifty-five British and colonial ships were engaged in the slave trade, of which twenty came from the American colonies, principally from Rhode Island. Toward the close of the colonial period, however, there were one hundred and fifty Rhode Island ships employed in this traffic in human flesh as compared with one hundred and ninety-two English ships, a record to which Southerners pointed during the antislavery controversy.

These ships were engaged in a triangular trade with England or the American colonies, the west coast of Africa, and the West Indies. To Africa the slave ships carried trading goods, bars of iron, rum— "well-watered," firearms, lead, beads, and cloth, which they exchanged for slaves. The latter were transported to the sugar islands of the West Indies and exchanged for molasses, rum, and gold coins. In New England the molasses was manufactured into rum to exchange for more slaves. The "middle passage" was the leg of the journey between Africa and the West Indies. During the passage across the Atlantic the slaves were confined in close quarters, the space between some decks being only three feet high, and they were manacled except when taken upon the top deck in small numbers for exercise and while their quarters were being cleaned with vinegar. The middle passage was at times a journey of horror, with slaves dying from dysentery, smallpox, and the yaws. Some slaves committed suicide by the strange African device of swallowing the the tongue. There was a strong human stench that was wafted from a slave ship. The average mortality of the slaves on the middle passage has been estimated by the best authorities at from 8 to 13 per cent.[12] Indeed, the captains of slave ships tried to preserve the health of their valuable cargo. Nevertheless, this trade was a brutal process of eliminating the weak and sickly, for a large number of slaves died on the trek from the interior to the "factories" on the seacoast.

The slaves of the Southern colonies came from many different tribes of Africa with various characteristics. Some of them were Mohammedans, such as the Foulah Negroes, who could read and write and who performed ablutions and rites of prayer and refrained from the drinking of liquor. The slaves that brought the best prices were the Gold Coast, or Whydah Negroes, and the Coromantees (Koromantyns). These people were strong, coal-black, and warlike, but dangerous because they were not as docile as other Negroes and more liable to insurrection. There were also Paw Paws, or Popows, noted for their thieving propensities, Senegalese, unusually intelligent, and Angolas, who were more submissive. The Eboes, prognathous in facial angle, were particularly emotional and prone to commit suicide. Mandingoes were a more delicate type of Negro with thinner lips, less kinky hair, and a less offensive odor than the other Negroes. The Gaboons were noted for garrulity, while the natives of the Congo were regarded as exceptionally stupid. All these immigrants from Africa had to go through a seasoning process, often fatal, in America and the West Indies, where they grew accustomed to the strange food and the climate and were trained to work by distribution among the older slaves. A far greater number of slaves were imported into the British West Indies, where the mortality was very high and the natural increase very low, than into the Southern colonies. The Southern colonies received their slaves largely from the West Indies instead of directly from Africa.

Negro workers were well suited to the hot climate of the South. They perspired freely, and were less subject to malaria and hookworm than the whites; they were less expensive than white servants also because they required hardly any clothes. The gang system was evolved to direct their reluctant labor. Usually a plantation employed about thirty slaves and an overseer; the work was routinized; and the staple crops of rice and tobacco did not permit the slave to hide from the observation of the overseer. Slaves increased in the Southern colonies until at the end of the colonial period they constituted two-thirds of the population of South Carolina, approximately one-half of the population of Virginia, and one-third of the population of North Carolina, Maryland, and Georgia. In South Carolina were the largest slaveholdings, an average of thirty-three slaves to a master, but in the other Southern colonies the ratio was much lower. There were some colonial "millionaires," such as Ralph Izard of South Carolina, who owned 594 slaves, Charles Carroll of Maryland, 316, George Mason of "Gunston Hall," 300, and George Washington, 188, but these men were rare exceptions to the generality of planters.

The Negroes lived in whitewashed log or frame huts which were usually congregated in a "quarter" that satisfied their gregarious instincts. Each week they were given an allowance of cornmeal, bacon, and molasses, or rice. The women worked in the fields as well as the men, but were given leisure during the child-bearing period. In America the Negroes were probably healthier than in Africa, lived in superior houses, had medical attention, and came into contact with the Christian religion. Although the South Carolina slave code, affected by the code of Barbados, was harsh, it was tempered in practice. The slaves of Virginia and Maryland seem to have been more humanely treated. Nevertheless, the diary of William Byrd II indicates that even the most educated Virginia planters lost their tempers at times and inflicted severe punishment on their slaves. Mrs. Byrd would fly into a rage and beat the maid with tongs or brand her servants. Byrd himself tortured his slaves occasionally by putting a bit with a screw on the tongue of the offending slave. Philip Fithian, a tutor in the household of Robert Carter of Virginia, saw a Negro coachman chained to the coach and was told by a Virginian that his peculiar method of punishing a Negro was to curry him with a curry comb and then after salting him to rub him with dry chaff.

It has been assumed by many students of American history that slavery was a serious handicap to Southern development. But in the colonial period slavery was probably an economic benefit to the Southern colonies and it was not regarded as a moral stigma. Slavery gave the planters a stable labor supply that had many advantages over white indentured servitude. Its establishment in the South was the natural outgrowth of economic "laws," especially Wakefield's law, which laid down the premise that the presence of plentiful and cheap land suitable for agriculture and the lack of labor bred slavery, for free men seldom will work for wages when they can become independent farmers.

On the basis of black slavery the golden age of colonial aristocracy and culture in the South arose. Slaves were necessary to the large-scale production of tobacco and rice, the export of which had the effect on the Southern colonies of strengthening the social and cultural ties with England. Slavery also was an important element in the development of leadership, in producing such qualities as the habit of command, poise in the presence of dependents, a feeling of responsibility for a large family of blacks and whites, and the military virtues. This economic institution gave the privileged classes the concentration of wealth and the leisure which enabled them to build beautiful Georgian homes, cultivate the social graces, and import luxuries and books from Europe. If Virginia, Maryland, and the Carolinas had remained free labor colonies, it is doubtful if the South would have produced the culture of a William Byrd II, the plantation life of "Mount Vernon" or "Monticello," or the galaxy of able leaders who led in the Revolutionary movement. Like feudalism or serfdom, Southern colonial slavery was a mixture of good and bad. The evils implicit in slavery, especially its pernicious effects on the whites and its economic drawbacks, became more apparent in the nineteenth century.

Although the slave-tilled plantations were dominant in the economy of the colonial South, the rise of seaports also played a vital role in its development. A web of commerce connected the Southern colonies with England, based on a reciprocal exchange of goods in contrast to the one-way commerce of the ante-bellum period. In 1769 the exports from the Southern colonies to Great Britain were four times more valuable than the products sent thither from the colonies above Maryland. At the same time Southerners imported goods from the Mother country twice as valuable as those imported by the Northern colonists. The Northern colonies, on the other hand, had a much larger commerce with southern Europe and the West Indies than the Southern colonies enjoyed.

The port of Baltimore, which had attained a population of 6,000 by the eve of the Revolution, was not only a tobacco port but a center for grist mills and an outlet for the grain of the German and Scotch-Irish of Pennsylvania, who used the Susquehanna River as a means of transportation. From Norfolk, the principal harbor of Virginia, were shipped thousands of hogsheads of tobacco to England as well as large quantities of pork, beef, flour, and lumber to the West Indies. Norfolk profited greatly from the fact that the North Carolina coast was landlocked, so that much of the tobacco and corn of that colony was carried to the Virginia port. In the Albemarle Sound area Edenton was visited by small New England vessels and in the Cape Fear region Brunswick and Wilmington competed with each other to become the main seaport of North Carolina. Shortly before the Revolution Wilmington surpassed its rival, and today Brunswick is a dead town in a forest with only the ruins of St. Philip's church remaining to remind the curious visitor of its colonial glory.

Charles Town (Charleston) was the most thriving port of the colonial South, having an important export trade in deerskins, rice, indigo, beef, pork, corn, lumber, and naval stores. It is interesting to observe also among its exports in 1748, 296,000 oranges. In that year two hundred vessels carried the exports of the city to distant markets—68 to Europe, 87 to the West Indies, and 37 to northern ports. In return, extensive invoices of luxuries were imported for the rich merchants and the grandees of the rice plantations. In the middle of the eighteenth century Governor James Glen lamented the fact that the South Carolinians imported so many luxuries, which he listed as Flanders laces, Dutch linens, French cambrics and chintzes, silks, gold and silver lace, Hyson tea and other East Indian goods, and great quantities of Madeira wine.

In the Southern colonies many of the outstanding merchants were Scots. Frequently as agents of large merchandising firms in England and Scotland, they rose in the New World by buying plantations and marrying daughters of prominent planters. The career of John Norton is a success story of a young merchant who was sent out in 1743 by the firm of Flowerdew and Norton, merchants of London. Locating his store at Yorktown in Virginia, he bought land, imported Negroes, and eventually was elected to the House of Burgesses. Moreover, he executed numerous commissions for planters, such as buying special orders of merchandise for them and even placing their children in English schools. The charge of these colonial merchants was usually a commission of 5 per cent for purchasing goods and 5 per cent for selling tobacco and other exports.

The records of the firm of John Norton and Sons give a vivid insight into colonial commerce, especially the type of goods imported by the Virginia planters and the exports of this colony. Typical cargoes leaving the York River, for example, were: January 13, 1767, the ship *Sally*, Thomas Lilly, captain, cleared for London with 394 hogsheads of tobacco, 14 casks and one box of ginseng, 4 hogsheads and 8 casks of snake root, 3 hogsheads of deerskins, 5 casks of copper ore, 20 tons of pig iron, and 19 tons of bar iron, 15,000 staves, and 3,000 feet of plank; February 3, 1767, the ship *Murdock*, John McCunn, master, cleared for Glasgow with 434 hogsheads of tobacco, 36 tons of pig iron, 14,000 staves, and 10 bags of cotton; February 4, 1767, the ship *Rebecca*, John Anthony, master, cleared for Barbados with 4,300 bushels of corn, 176 bushels of peas, and 4,000 shingles.

The ledgers of John Norton and Sons also reveal the fashionable and luxurious tastes of the tobacco planters, their love of gay clothes, their medicine, their taste for books. This Virginia store imported such items as a red silk bonnet for a child three years old, a pair of "turned stays for a girl about 8 years old," fashionable silver shoes, quilted petticoats, cambric, satin, silver buckles, chinaware, damask table cloths, a silver laced hat for a boy four years old, a green silk tippet, mourning rings, red morocco shoes for a child, and other luxurious articles of apparel which had to conform to the latest fashions of London.[13] They also imported many delicacies for Virginia epicures—Hyson tea, lemons, almonds, raisins, chocolate, cheese, anchovies, capers, and snuff. To counteract ill effects of wine and rich foods which produced gout and other distempers they imported medicines, such as powdered jalop, gentian, laudanum, myrrh, Jesuit's Bark, and the Poor Knight of Windsor's Red Fit Drops. Nor were the soul and mind of the gentry neglected in the consignment of goods from England, which contained religious books, medical books, Latin grammars, law books, and even popular novels, like *Tristram Shandy*.

The trade of North Carolina was more complex, but less valuable than the commerce of either Maryland, Virginia, or South Carolina. In general, the trade currents of the North Carolina ports followed a triangular pattern. Ships from the Northern colonies brought manufactured goods to the Carolina ports, exchanged them for exports of naval stores, tobacco, and other raw materials, and cleared for West India ports or England, returning to New England or the middle colonies with British goods. It is indicative of the rudimentary economy of the colony that the ships entering the colony carried freight amounting to only 60 per cent of their capacity, and some of those direct from Europe came in ballast. North Carolina exported a variety of commodities, naval stores and tobacco predominating, but also deerskins, corn, blackeyed peas, lumber, cypress shingles, staves, snake root, tallow, butter, flax, hemp, myrtle wax, salt fish, beef, pork, furs, potash, and pearlash. Scottish firms, such as John Hamilton and Co., established branch stores in the interior, where the merchants assembled products from many small farmers for exportation. In the latter part of the colonial period this firm sold goods imported from England at an advance of 50 per cent wholesale and 100 per cent retail on the invoices. Much of the retail business was based on credit to many small purchasers as well as to the large planters. The risks of the merchants were great, and their profits in the latter colonial period do not seem to have been unreasonable. By furnishing long-term credits the British and Scottish firms which exported goods to the merchants rendered a valuable service to the Southern colonies.

After population spread into the Piedmont, direct contacts of the tobacco planters with their factors in England began to diminish. Country stores arose in the interior which furnished the yeoman farmers with merchandise brought up the rivers in boats or overland by wagoners. These stores accumulated tobacco, flour, and salt meat which they sent in turn to the large merchants on the seacoast, such as Niel Jameison at Norfolk, who owned ships trading in West India and British ports. At the falls of the rivers interior towns arose where gristmills were located and where goods had to be transshipped around the obstructions in the rivers. Such towns were Alexandria, Fredericksburg, and Richmond in Virginia, Cross Creek or Fayetteville in North Carolina, Orangeburg in South Carolina, and Augusta in Georgia.

The commerce of the Southern colonies was harassed at times by pirates, especially from 1650 to 1720, a period which has been called "the golden age of piracy." The haunts of these gangsters of the ocean were the Bahama Islands, particularly Nassau, then called New Providence, and the hide-outs behind the sand bars of the Carolina coast. Indeed, Ocracoke Inlet, south of Cape Hatteras, became the capital of the Southern pirates. The pirates made a practice of providing themselves with food supplies by landing on some of the West Indian islands and smoking meat, which was called by the Indians, "boucanning," from which the term buccaneer was probably derived. The Caribbean sea was infested with pirates led by

Henry Morgan, a redemptioner of Barbados, whose followers in 1671 sacked the city of Panama. Along the sea lanes of the Northern colonies and in the Indian Ocean operated another celebrated pirate, Captain Kidd, who was hanged in 1701.

The most notorious pirates who operated along the Carolina coast were Edward Teach, known as "Blackbeard," and Captain Stede Bonnet. Teach was a melodramatic villain who curled his long black beard and mustachios, burned brimstone on his ship to overawe his men, and was reputed to have had fourteen wives. His boldest deed was to intercept a ship sailing from Charleston in 1718 with some prominent Charlestonians on board. He held these citizens as hostages until the town authorities sent the medical and other supplies that he demanded. Teach openly appeared at Bath and Edenton, North Carolina, where Governor Charles Eden and Tobias Knight, Secretary of the colony, were suspected of sharing his booty. Stede Bonnet also frequented the Carolina coasts. A former major in the British army, he had become a wealthy and respected citizen of Barbados until 1717 when he turned to the trade of a buccaneer. Although he knew nothing of navigation, nevertheless, by the sheer force of his personality, he was able to command the crew of his ship, the *Royal James*, in a brief but amazing career of piracy.

In 1718 a campaign was undertaken to eliminate the nuisance of these gangsters of the ocean. In that year a British fleet under Woodes Rogers drove the pirates from their great base at New Providence Island. At the same time Governor Alexander Spotswood of Virginia sent out an expedition to capture "Blackbeard," who was killed in battle near Ocracoke Inlet. Finally, the governor of South Carolina dispatched Colonel William Rhett to the Cape Fear region. His ship pursued the *Royal James* until both the pirate vessel and Rhett's ship were stranded within pistol shot of each other. Victory depended on which ship was first freed by the tide. Colonel Rhett's ship was the lucky one, and he captured Stede Bonnet and his crew, whom he took to Charleston for trial. The pirate leader, so brave in battle, was terrified as he faced the gibbet and begged piteously for his life. But stern justice was administered by the hanging of Bonnet and twenty-two of his crew. The significance of these early buccaneers is that they brought into the colonies much needed gold and silver, sold goods cheaply, and paid high prices for provisions. When they began, however, to interfere with the rice and tobacco trade, the Southern colonies were stirred to action to eliminate these criminals.

Citations

1. WILLIAM TATHAM, *An Historical and Practical Essay on the Culture and Commerce of Tobacco* (London, 1800), 5–27; 107–129.
2. J. S. BASSETT, "The Relation between the Virginia Planter and the London Factor," *Annual Report of the American Historical Society for the Year 1901* (Washington, 1902), I, 551–575.
3. D. C. HEYWARD, *Seed from Madagascar* (Chapel Hill, 1937).
4. "Diary of John Harrower, 1773–1776," *American Historical Review*, VI (Oct., 1900), 77.
5. C. C. HALL (ed.), *Narratives of Early Maryland, 1633–1684* (New York, 1910), 354–360.
6. A. E. SMITH, "The Transportation of Convicts to the American Colonies in the Seventeenth Century," *American Historical Review*, XXXIX (October, 1933), 238.
7. A. E. SMITH, *Colonists in Bondage* (Chapel Hill, 1947), 119.
8. DANIEL DEFOE, *The Fortunes and Misfortunes of the Famous Moll Flanders* (The Bibliophilist Society, 1931), 71.
9. PROFESSOR T. J. WERTENBAKER has made a basic study of indentured servants in *Planters of Colonial Virginia* (Princeton, 1922); see also R. B. MORRIS, *Government and Labor in Colonial America* (New York, 1941).
10. HALL, *Narratives of Early Maryland, 1633–1684*, 284.
11. SMITH, *Colonists in Bondage*, 299.
12. U. B. PHILLIPS, *American Negro Slavery* (New York, 1940), 38; ELIZABETH DONNAN (ed.), *Documents Illustrative of the History of the Slave Trade to America* (Washington, 1935), IV, 35, 97, 175–8; GUNNAR MYRDAL, *An American Dilemma* (New York, 1944), I, 121; II, 1202.
13. F. N. MASON (ed.), *John Norton and Sons, Merchants of London and Virginia* (Richmond, 1937).

CHAPTER III

The Rise of a Native Aristocracy

A CCORDING to the romantic tradition, the Southern colonies were settled by Cavaliers or aristocrats. New England, in contrast, was so unfortunate as to be populated by humble folk, particularly the plebeian Round Heads who fought for Parliament during the civil war which rent England. In 1649 after King Charles I had been beheaded, Governor Berkeley invited the royalists to seek asylum in Virginia. The historian, John Fiske, has popularized the idea of an exodus of Cavaliers from England to Virginia, pointing out that the population of Virginia increased from fifteen thousand in 1649, the date of the regicide of Charles I, to thirty-eight thousand in 1660, when the Stuarts were restored to the throne.[1] It seems reasonable to conclude that a larger number of royalists came to Virginia than to Puritan New England, for in Virginia the Anglican Church was established and country estates could be acquired. Some of these immigrants were of gentle blood, but the term "Cavalier" was a political designation, including common foot soldiers and tradesmen who supported the king in the Puritan Revolution.

Modern research has discredited the old idea that Southerners were descended principally from Cavalier, or aristocratic origins, while New Englanders came from Round Head, or plebeian immigrants. Actually, the great majority of immigrants to both areas during the colonial period belonged to the middle or lower classes of Englishmen. Titled persons who made their permanent residence in America were extremely rare. Those who were in a fortunate position in the mother country were unlikely to emigrate to a raw country, which was the haven for the poor, the discontented, and the socially maladjusted. It has been estimated that at least one-half of all the white immigrants to the colonies south of New England arrived as indentured servants. An eminent authority on the colonial South, Thomas Jefferson Wertenbaker, has dispelled many illusions concerning the aristocratic origins of the great majority of Virginians, who above all Southerners have prided themselves on descent from gentle blood. The continuous immigration of white indentured servants, who became freemen at the expiration of their terms of indenture, was constantly refreshing the class of yeoman. A study of the quit-rent roll of Governor Francis Nicholson of 1704 indicates that 90 per cent of the people of Virginia at that time were small farmers and that 65 per cent of them owned neither slaves nor indentured servants. Indeed, a realistic picture of Virginia in the seventeenth century shows it to be a land of small yeoman farmers, with a sprinkling of large planters.

The Wertenbaker thesis maintains that most of the prominent families of Virginia, the "F. F. V.'s," or First Families of Virginia, who attained wealth and prestige in the colonial period were derived from middle class or bourgeois origins, particularly the merchant class, in England and Scotland.[2] The Byrd family who developed an elegant style of life at "Westover" were descended from a London goldsmith, the Blands from a skinner, and the founder of the great Carter family was an immigrant of nameless background. The Lees, the Washingtons, and the Randolphs, however, came from the English squirearchy. The tone of society in Virginia of the seventeenth century was bourgeois rather than cavalier. In the Southern colonies, as well as in New England, this century has been described as the age of pewter and of small cottages rather than of silver and of Georgian mansions. The aristocratic code of honor and the practice of dueling were absent from the mores of Southerners of the seventeenth century, attaining a vogue only late in the colonial period.

It is probable that modern scholarship has swung to the extreme left in discarding the older Cavalier tradition. Philip Alexander Bruce in *Social Life of Virginia in the Seventeenth Century* has brought forward an impressive amount of evidence to show the gentle birth of many Virginia families. Although very few titled persons came to the colony to reside, some younger sons of the gentry and of the nobility emigrated to the tobacco colonies. The laws of primogeniture and entail, which reserved the ancestral estate for the eldest son, necessitated the younger sons entering trade or the professions or emigrating to the colonies. Consequently, many of the merchants and members of the guilds had the same blood and rearing as the country gentry. Some of the Virginia families were descended from ship captains and from officers of the royalist troops during the Puritan Revolution. Bruce observed that the Rent Roll of Governor Nicholson did not apply to the Northern Neck of Virginia, between the Rappahannock and Potomac rivers, where many of the powerful aristocracy were settled. Even in the narrow limits of the settled part of Virginia in the seventeenth century there were at least four hundred and fifty families who owned from one thousand to ten thousand or more acres. Indeed, he concluded, in conflict with the Wertenbaker thesis, that "one in every four families in Virginia at the end of the seventeenth century owned from five hundred acres to twenty thousand acres," a proportion of large landed proprietors comparable to the distribution of the gentry in aristocratic England.[3]

It is much more to the credit of the Southern aristocracy of the eighteenth century, however, that most of its members arose by their own efforts from virile middle class stock than that they were transplanted from a decadent aristocracy of the Old World. The development of a native aristocracy in the Southern colonies was aided by the continuous operation of certain powerful forces, the most important of which was the acquisition of large plantations tilled by slaves and protected from disintegration by the laws of primogeniture and entail. In addition, the immigrants from England brought with them a traditional conception of social stratification. Consequently, it was natural for them to continue in the New World social distinctions, expressed in the titles of address, the yeoman being called "goodman," the gentleman, "Mister," a member of the governor's council, "Esquire," and high civil officials, "Honorable." Military titles also flourished in this truncated society which was devoid of a nobility. Around the royal governor clustered a group known as "the governor's set," composed of the great planters, the Anglican clergy, and the lawyers, who formed the nucleus of the colonial aristocracy. Also merchants who had acquired wealth frequently purchased plantations, married planters' daughters, and thus entered this upper group of colonial society. Indeed, the social position of merchants in the colonial South was very honorable, but in the ante-bellum period trade and mercantile pursuits were disparaged.

During the decade before the Revolution a new class of lawyers arose in the colonies who became leaders in public affairs. In Maryland, particularly, legal skill was in constant demand by the large planters to protect their vested interests, and accordingly the lawyers in that province became a powerful and affluent group. The lawyers of colonial days learned their law by apprenticeship to an established lawyer, using as a textbook the *Institutes of the Laws of England* by "Old Coke," whom Jefferson praised highly as preserving traditions of liberty, while Blackstone's text, published 1765–69, on the other hand, made Tories of later generations of lawyers. The law profession in the colonial South is admirably mirrored in the manuscript diary of Waightstill Avery, a Connecticut Yankee educated at Princeton, who settled in Mecklenburg County, North Carolina, in 1769. In the practice of his profession he rode from one courthouse to another, often spending the night in "nasty" log cabins, at times losing his way among the woods, the few people he saw too ignorant to direct him, nearly drowning in crossing fords, and suffering from ague and fever. Indeed, his diary pictures a society of strong contrasts, on the one side, containing "Gentlemen Merchants," "Gentlemen Attorneys," some of whom were deists, and cultivated planters, and on the other side, rude farmers, who entertained themselves on court days by getting drunk and by fights of "bruising, Goughing, Biting, and balloching." [4]

When Avery arrived in North Carolina, at the time of the Regulator troubles, lawyers were bitterly hated because they were accused of charging excessive fees, despite the law regulating fees. However, the fee book of Avery, which is preserved in the Draper Collection at the University of Wisconsin, indicates that his profits were not exorbitant according to relative standards today—fifteen shillings for small cases and one Pound, five shillings, for larger cases. During six months in 1775 he recorded fees totaling £164 from 146 cases, which compares favorably with the earnings of Jefferson as a lawyer during this period—£147 cash and £223 uncollected, from 198 cases in the year 1769.

Aristocratic distinctions were reflected by the marked difference between the dress of the upper class and of the common people. The aristocrats dressed in a lavish and colorful fashion, wearing scarlet, pearl, or yellow vests, waistcoats, knee breeches, and long coats of various colors, silk stockings, ruffles on their shirts, shoes with silver buckles. Toward the close of the seventeenth century the long locks of the Cavaliers were cut off and periwigs, which were very expensive, were donned. They were oiled or greased, and powder was dusted upon them. In the wig-wearing days the gentleman put on a linen or worsted nightcap when he laid aside his heavy wig, for otherwise a shorn head would have been a comical sight in my lady's boudoir. By the time of the American Revolution wigs had been abandoned, and aristocrats wore their hair in a queue, powdered, beneath three-cornered cocked hats. "Ladies" wore large hoop skirts, made of rich silks and satins, stays or corsets, high-heeled shoes, and elaborate coiffeurs. Children were dressed very much like grown-ups.

Members of the poorer class were clad in homespun, or "Osnibrick," a coarse cloth made in Osnabrück, Germany. The men often wore buckskin breeches or leggins, while the women spun and wove out of flax and wool linsey-woolsey cloth, from which they made shapeless dresses. If a common man or woman dared to dress above his class, he was fined, as in New England, for such impudence and extravagance. A tradesman was even fined for participating in the aristocratic sport of horse racing. Democracy in clothes did not arrive until the early part of the nineteenth century, after the French Revolution had popularized the pantaloons of the peasants, the *sans culottes*, and stigmatized the breeches of the aristocrats. James Monroe was the last President to wear the knee breeches of the colonial aristocrats.

One of the strong props of the Southern aristocracy was their control over local government. The basic unit of local government was the county, modeled after the English shire. In South Carolina the normal functions of the counties were performed by the parishes, of which there were twenty-five during the colonial period. The county governments which operated in the colonial and ante-bellum periods were remarkable instances of the union of executive, legislative, and judicial functions in the hands of one political body. Later the idea of the separation of governmental powers became a cardinal principle of American political theory, but actually the organization of the county governments continued to ignore this theory. In each county there were usually eight or more justices of the peace, appointed by the governor for an indefinite period. They were chosen as a rule from the aristocratic families and served without pay. These amateur judges tried petty cases individually, but once a month they met at the county seat and constituted a court to try the more serious cases. The law which they recognized was the common law of England as modified and expanded by the colonial statutes. Not only did this group form a judicial body, but they also exercised administrative functions, such as apportioning local taxes, supervising the roads, and issuing certificates for land grants. The sheriff of the county, appointed annually by the governor, collected the taxes, for which he received a fee of 10 per cent, arrested criminals, had charge of the jail, executed orders of the county court, and summoned jurors.

The county of the Tidewater was subdivided into two or three parishes, which were both religious and governmental divisions. In the thinly settled western districts, however, there was frequently only one parish to a county. The executive body of the parish was the vestry, consisting of twelve of the leading members of the Episcopal Church. Originally elected by the people, the vestry was converted into a closed corporation that filled vacancies in its membership by co-option. The vestrymen selected the clergyman, administered the parish glebe, or church land, looked after the poor, decided various church matters, apportioned the parish taxes, and presented lawbreakers to the county court.

The most democratic feature in the provincial government was the lower house of the legislature, called the House of Burgesses in Virginia and the House of Commons in South Carolina. It was composed in Virginia of two representatives from each county and from each of the towns of Jamestown, Williamsburg, and Norfolk, as well as a representative from the College of William and Mary. These representatives were the only officers elected by the people. Until 1670 the right to manhood suffrage was allowed in Virginia but after the Bacon Rebellion property and religious qualifications of voting confined this privilege to the upper classes. Furthermore, the *viva voce* method of voting and plural voting, or the right of a property owner to vote in each county where he had a plantation, strengthened the control of the aristocracy. A Virginia election has been vividly described by Robert Beverley in *The Candidates; or the Humors of a Virginia Election* (1770), the first American comedy.[5] Instead of voting for demagogues who tried to lure them with liquor and barbecues, the voters elected aristocrats, possessing learning and character. Throughout the eighteenth century the representatives in the legislature were chosen from the leading families of the counties.

The colonial assemblies regarded themselves as similar to Parliament in England and entitled to Parliamentary privileges. A noteworthy difference between the two bodies, however, was that the members of the colonial legislatures, except in South Carolina, were paid for attendance. They elected a Speaker to preside over their meetings and to act as spokesman. Their independence was curtailed by the fact that the governor had the authority to summon, to prorogue, and to dissolve the assembly. Many memorable conflicts occurred between the legislature, representing the interests of the colonists, and the royal governor, representing the prerogative of the king. The greatest power of the assembly was its control over the purse, through which it could bring pressure to bear on the governor to accede to its will by refusing to appropriate money for his salary. The Virginia, Maryland, and Georgia assemblies, however, lost this valuable power of protecting their interests before the colonial period had ended. In Virginia the imperial government was granted as early as 1680 a permanent tax of two shillings on the export of each hogshead of tobacco, the receipts of which were set aside to pay the governor's salary.

The colonial legislatures were given liberal discretion in making laws, for seldom did the British government after 1713 exercise its right of disallowing the laws of the Southern assemblies. Less than 3 per cent of the laws passed by the North Carolina legislature were disallowed in England, and nearly nine-tenths of the Virginia colonial laws were confirmed. Nevertheless, the British government possessed a double check over colonial legislation, in the first instance, by the veto of the royal governor, and then by the disallowance of the privy council. This practice of annulling colonial laws was exercised to protect the royal prerogative and the interests of British merchants as well as to prevent the passage of colonial laws that conflicted with the common law or the statutes of Parliament. Colonial laws went into force after their passage by the assembly. Laws objectionable to the British government might operate for months or years in the colonies, owing to the delay of disallowing them, caused by the difficulty of communication across three thousand miles of ocean and by the procrastination of officials in England.

In all the Southern colonies the Council was an aristocratic feature of government. As a rule, it was composed of twelve or more men, recommended by the governor, but appointed by the king. Usually chosen from the leading planters, the members exercised great control over the administration by virtue of their wealth, prestige, and knowledge of local conditions. The Council formed the upper house of the legislature, served as the advisory body for the governor, and sat as the supreme court of the colony. The only appeal from its decisions in civil cases was to the king, in cases involving over £300. This clique of wealthy colonials usually sided with the governor in the struggle with the lower house of the legislature, but occasionally they supported the popular cause, as when in 1635 the Virginia Council deposed Governor Sir John Harvey and sent him back to England.

At the apex of the colonial administration was the royal governor. He arrived in the colony with a set of instructions drawn up in England, and his function was to represent the royal authority. His powers were very extensive, including the appointing power, the authority to summon and dissolve the assembly, to veto laws, and to pardon, the control over the military forces of the colony, the power to grant land patents with the consent of the council, and the authority to issue proclamations. His salary was frequently lucrative, for example, in Virginia he was paid £2,000, which was perhaps equivalent to $50,000 in present currency. Many of the royal governors were unfit appointees, favorites of the king, placemen, or bankrupt nobles who came to America to recoup their fortunes.

Nevertheless, the Southern colonies had a few excellent royal governors, such as the Scotsmen, Spotswood and Dinwiddie in Virginia, Glen in South Carolina, and Wright in Georgia, who identified themselves with colonial interests and made excellent administrators. The royal type of government gradually superseded the corporate and proprietary types, so that at the outbreak of the Revolution all the Southern colonies were royal colonies with the exception of Maryland.

The life of the aristocracy of the colonial South is much better known than the mute, inglorious history of the common people, who have left few written records. In the Tidewater small farmers lived as humble neighbors to the great planters. Indentured servants were brought over from England and the continent to serve not only as laborers but also as teachers and skilled artisans. The diary of John Harrower, an indentured servant who taught the children of Colonel William Daingerfield of "Belvidera" near Fredericksburg, Virginia, indicates that an indentured servant of intelligence could be well respected by the planters. Harrower made extra money by teaching the children of neighboring planters for a fee and by writing love letters for illiterates. Besides the skilled artisans in the Southern colonies, who received good wages, there were some free agricultural laborers. During the wheat harvest Colonel Daingerfield, for example, supplemented his own labor supply by hiring free laborers. Modern studies have shown that there also existed a number of white farm tenants and leaseholders in the colonial South, particularly in Maryland, where the great landholders advertised for tenants.

The settlement of the back country introduced a vigorous and independent group of yeoman farmers into Southern society, who became the main force in fighting the battles of the common man. The struggle that arose between the back country inhabitants and the Tidewater squirearchy was really a conflict between two different ways of life, produced in part by geographic differences. The Tidewater was a maturer region than the hinterland, possessing more wealth, more education, closer contacts with Europe, and a greater refinement of life. The back country, on the other hand, was handicapped by difficulties of transportation and consequently was forced to rely upon a subsistence type of agriculture. Except in certain favored river valleys, it was the home of the yeoman and the small farmer.

The most palpable difference between the two sections was the dominance of slave labor in the Tidewater and the prevalence of free labor in the interior. The Germans of the back country, especially, were opposed to the introduction of slavery into their communities. Exceedingly thrifty, these immigrants from Pennsylvania had a contempt for the shiftless slave labor which they had observed in the South. Slavery was not adapted to their type of self-sufficient farming, based on wheat, potatoes, barley, oats, hay, and orchard products. Their large families of sturdy sons and buxom, hustling girls afforded an abundance of intelligent and careful labor. Moreover, they were unaccustomed to slave labor when they entered the South and their churches were opposed to slaveholding on moral grounds. Consequently, in areas with a large German population, such as Shenandoah County, Virginia, and the Salisbury district in North Carolina, only a small percentage of the families held slaves.

Social differences between the back country and the Tidewater were very pronounced. The people of the Tidewater were overwhelmingly English in stock; the inhabitants of the back country, in contrast, had a strong infusion of German and Scotch-Irish blood. The Tidewater gentry tried to imitate the manner of living of the English squirearchy; the inhabitants of the back country, on the other hand, hated snobbery and the pretensions to aristocracy. In the Tidewater the Anglican Church was dominant; in the back country, dissenting sects, such as Presbyterians, Lutherans, and Baptists prevailed. The people of the back country felt a sort of inferiority complex in the presence of the more polished Tidewater aristocrats. In Virginia the inhabitants of the Great Valley and the more primitive regions of the Piedmont were called "Cohees," probably from the uncouth phrase used by them, "Quo(th) he," while the eastern planters were called "Tuckahoes" from an edible swamp root grown in eastern Virginia. The "Tuckahoes" were hedonistic, loving good wine and companionship; the "Cohees," having a different set of values, were too busy tilling their fields to waste time on social pursuits.

Poor people lived both in the Tidewater and the back country,

but our knowledge of them in comparison with the favored aristocrats is very inadequate. Travelers in the colonial period hardly
deigned to notice them. Thomas Anburey, a lieutenant in Burgoyne's army, who after the surrender at Saratoga was quartered
near Charlottesville, declared that the lower class in Virginia was
smaller in proportion to the whole population than perhaps in any
country in the world. They dwelt in log cabins which had oiled
paper or wooden shutters instead of glass in the windows, wooden or
leather hinges on the doors, and chimneys made frequently of
wooden sticks held together by clay. Although the journal of
Benjamin H. Latrobe, later to become architect of the national
Capitol, was written thirteen years after the colonial period had
ended, his description of the poor whites of Virginia is probably an
accurate picture of the lower class throughout the eighteenth century. He described "the hundreds of half-starved, miserably lodged,
idle, besotted and fever-smitten families that inhabit the country on
the Potomac, and indeed all the back country of the slave States—." [6]
They fished and hunted, owned a few pigs and a cow, which were
kept at hardly any expense in the woods, cultivated a few acres of
land, chiefly raising corn and cabbage. The women were prolific
breeders of children and, like Indian squaws, were beasts of burden.
The bare-footed men did very little labor, but their great source of
bliss was whiskey. Some of these poor whites were tenants to
great land-owners or possessed small farms or hired themselves
occasionally as agricultural laborers.

Social stratification was very discernible in the amusements of
gentlemen and the ruder diversions of the common people. The
aristocrats of the Tidewater were passionately fond of stately dances
such as the minuet and the Virginia reel, of following the latest styles
of dress in England, and of traveling in their coaches, decorated with
coats-of-arms. They were heavy drinkers and gamblers. One of these
aristocrats, George Washington, kept a careful record over a period
of four years of his losses and gains at cards, computing a gain of
£72 and a loss of £78. They attended cock fights, played billiards,
bowled on the green, and were enthusiasts over racing and breeding fine horses. Fox hunting was *par excellence* the sport of the
aristocrats. The red fox, it is believed, was imported about 1680

from England, so that the country gentlemen of Virginia could imitate a distinctive diversion of the English squires.

The lower classes, particularly in the backwoods, found amusement in shooting matches to test their marksmanship and in wrestling and boxing contests in which there were no rules of fair play. Biting, scratching, "Abelarding," and especially gouging out the eye of an opponent were practiced. Anburey described some ruffians as keeping the nails of their thumbs and second fingers long and pointed, hardening them over a candle flame, in order to be ready to "gouge" more effectively.[7] According to William Tatham, however, the farmers kept their nails long in order more easily to "sucker" tobacco or pinch off the superfluous sprouts. The common people delighted in betting on quarter races, which were different from the longer races over oval tracks patronized by the aristocrats. The quarter races were held on straight courses of one-fourth of a mile, usually near "ordinaries," the colonial name for taverns. The common people also enjoyed corn-shuckings and log-rollings, at which liquor was served, group singing occurred, and practical jokes were played.

One of the most riotous holidays of the plebeians, as well as of the aristocrats, was muster day. Several times a year the militia was drilled and reviewed by its officers at the various county seats. Every able-bodied freeman between the ages of eighteen and forty-five was enrolled in the militia and required to attend muster or be fined. It was his duty to keep a rifle or a musket and a supply of powder and lead. The colonial militia system encouraged the growth of an aristocratic spirit, for the officers were appointed by the governor from the prominent families. Travelers in the South were impressed by the many captains, majors, colonels, and generals whom they met—a substitute for European titles of nobility. After the Revolution, however, the militia system tended to the growth of a democratic spirit, for the officers, including even major-generals, were elected. Consequently, there arose a feeling of equality between the privates and the officers and a lack of proper discipline. On muster day the American freeman appeared on the parade grounds in various quaint and ridiculous uniforms, and the musters were accompanied by much drinking, fighting, and electioneering.

The inhabitants of the back country developed a bitter grievance against the people of the Tidewater, because the latter did not give them a fair share in the control of the government. It was natural that Tidewater planters were not disposed to allow the reins of government to pass into the hands of the newcomers, who arrived in waves of immigration from Pennsylvania. Consequently, the colonial legislatures apportioned representation so that the yeomen of the back country, who owned few slaves, were either not represented at all in the legislature or under-represented. In Virginia the counties, regardless of size or population, sent two representatives each to the House of Burgesses. The back country counties were much larger than the Tidewater ones and when they filled up with population, a great inequality of representation resulted. In South Carolina the up-country was practically unrepresented in the legislature and the twenty-five lowland parishes sent delegates of varying numbers without much correlation to population. Furthermore the influence of the back country in the making of laws was greatly curtailed in the Southern colonies by the high property qualifications for office-holding and voting. In South Carolina on the eve of the Revolution the members of the General Assembly were required to own five hundred acres in a "settled" plantation and *ten slaves*. The colonial legislatures, thus constituted, ignored pretty much the needs and petitions of the back country. The Tidewater region was not very responsive to voting taxes for frontier defense, building roads, and improving internal navigation, or to freeing the dissenters of the back country from the necessity of paying taxes to support the Anglican Church.

On two notable occasions the back country engaged in armed conflict with the lowland aristocracy in an attempt to obtain justice. In 1676 the small farmers and frontiersmen of Virginia arose against the misrule of Governor William Berkeley. Berkeley had been sent to the colony as governor in 1642 when he was a young man of fashion in London, the author of a play called "The Lost Lady." For ten years his rule was popular except for his persecution of the dissenters from the Church of England. In 1644 he defeated the Indians under the leadership of the aged Opechancanough after they had killed many settlers. Thus a vast area of western land was opened for settlement. Also he had advanced the economic interests of the colony, particularly by his liberal policy in regard to foreign trade. With a munificent salary and a fine estate at "Greenspring," four miles from Jamestown, this bachelor governor entertained lavishly. A staunch royalist, he succeeded in having the Virginia Assembly recognize Charles II as king after the regicide of Charles I. For such loyalty to the crown Virginia was later given the title of a dominion within the British realm and was called the Old Dominion. In 1652 Berkeley was deposed from his governorship by the Puritan Commonwealth, but after the overthrow of the Puritan regime in England he resumed his old position in 1660.

In this second period of administration he became exceedingly reactionary and autocratic. By giving special favors to members of the Council and of the House of Burgesses and by allowing them to acquire land unlawfully, he reduced these branches of the colonial government to pliant tools of his will. He refused to hold any elections for new members of the legislature but continued to adjourn the old assembly from year to year since its personnel, elected in the first flush of enthusiasm for the royal cause after the restoration of Charles II, was favorable to him. Moreover, he had grown avaricious and arbitrary with the passing of the years, especially after his marriage to an heiress.

The immediate cause for the uprising against the tyrannical governor was an unauthorized expedition against the Indians led by Nathaniel Bacon. Bacon was a well-educated member of the English country gentry who had recently arrived in the colony and had acquired a plantation near the falls of the James. When his overseer was murdered by the Indians, he led an expedition against them without waiting to secure the consent of the governor. For this offense he was proclaimed an outlaw by Berkeley, whose Indian policy was based on the protection of the frontier by a series of forts or garrisons. Upon his return from chastising Indians he was pardoned, but he became dissatisfied with the arbitrary rule of the governor and his clique and led a revolt of the yeomen and small planters to obtain democratic reforms. At first Bacon defeated the troops of Berkeley and his aristocratic followers and captured the capital of Jamestown, which he burned. Led step by step into more radical courses, he appealed to the people of Maryland to unite with his forces to resist misrule of the king's officers. But this early American revolt collapsed in the autumn of 1676 when the leader suddenly and mysteriously died.

Almost a century later the back country again arose to fight the ruling oligarchy in the Regulator movement of North Carolina.[8] The inhabitants of the Piedmont in this colony had many grievances, their under-representation in the legislature, the excessive legal fees charged by corrupt officials, the collection of quit-rents, the absorption of the best lands by speculators in the huge Granville tract, the requirement that dissenters pay taxes to support the Anglican church, and the erection of a magnificent palace at New Bern by Governor William Tryon with the taxes taken from the people. Incited by two popular agitators, Hermon Husband and Rednap Howell, writer of doggerel satires, the outraged farmers of the back country formed mobs, called "Regulators," who interfered with the operation of the courts and attacked hated county officials. Waightstill Avery recorded in his diary, April 12, 1769: "A Set of Banditti who stiled themselves Regulators had on the evening before brought a large quantity of hickory Switches to menace the Clerk of the court (or Col. Spencer) whom they threatened and flogged his writer."

In May, 1771, Governor Tryon marched westward with an army of a thousand and sixty-eight men, commanded by an enormous number of commissioned officers, and attacked the Regulators in the battle of Alamance Court House. The Regulator army, an unwieldy mob of about two thousand men, was defeated and the ringleaders were executed. Some of the defeated Regulators, embittered by the failure of the popular cause, emigrated to the pioneer settlements of east Tennessee. A somewhat similar movement of "regulators" in the up-country of South Carolina was more successful, for they secured their main contention, the establishment of circuit courts in the interior districts, which made it unnecessary for the inhabitants of the back country to travel long distances to attend court at Charleston.

Thus a sectionalism arose within the Southern colonies that has left enduring traces. An interesting hangover of the pervasive force of such sectionalism was displayed well into the twentieth century at the University of North Carolina, where boys from the western part of the state joined the Dialectic Literary Society and those from the eastern section, the Philanthropic Society. Political alignments were often determined by the bitter resentments generated by sectionalism. Patrick Henry led the back country patriots in Virginia in the Revolutionary movement against the conservatism of the Tidewater aristocrats. In some communities, the Tories were motivated in siding with the British government by their hatred of the lowland gentry who joined the patriot cause. Hostile feelings between the East and the West were allayed somewhat by the expansion of slavery and of tobacco and cotton plantations into the Piedmont. But intra-state sectionalism was kept alive until the very end of the ante-bellum period by quarrels over internal improvements, slave taxation, public education, and apportionment of representation. Even in the Civil War one of the most important reasons for the existence of Unionism in the Appalachian Highlands was the influence of the deep scars of sectionalism rather than any devotion to the cause of preserving the Union.

While the Tidewater planters were evolving an aristocratic type of society and government, they were also adapting English architecture to the American environment. The first settlers built cabins of vertical logs, instead of the familiar cabins of the American frontier having horizontal logs daubed with clay, or they constructed half-timbered cottages with thatched roofs reminiscent of the English country-side. Later they built unpainted frame houses with roofs of clapboard shingles and chimneys at the ends instead of the middle of the house, such as were common in the colder climate of New England. These comparatively small houses represented a survival of mediaeval or Gothic architecture, which lingered for a surprisingly long period in the Tidewater South, even beyond the eighteenth century. Characteristic of this style were thick walls, the cross design of the homes of the squires, the overhang, casement windows with diamond-shaped panes, and gable roofs. The churches, such as St. Luke's at Smithfield, Virginia, probably the oldest Protestant church building in the New World, were also Gothic in architecture, adorned with massive square towers and Gothic arches. Relatively few buildings in the seventeenth century

Southern colonies were constructed of brick, partly because of the difficulty of procuring lime for mortar. Two of the rare brick edifices of this century which have survived are the Adam Thoroughgood cottage in Princess Anne Country and the so-called Bacon's Castle, south of the James River near Williamsburg, a mediaeval-looking manor house with steep roof, chimneys containing three stacks, and Flemish curved gable ends.

In the eighteenth century a new style of architecture arose in the colonies that expressed the wealth and stately elegance of the aristocracy. This new style was imported from England and was called Georgian after the name of the three Georges who ruled England from 1714 to 1820. The planters selected their designs from the English architectural books, such as those written by James Gibbs and Batty Langley. The work of the great English architects, Inigo Jones and Sir Christopher Wren, profoundly influenced American colonial architecture. Indeed, the first important Georgian building in the South was Brafferton Hall at William and Mary College, designed by Sir Christopher Wren or a disciple, and completed in 1723.

In contrast to the Gothic houses of the seventeenth century, the Georgian houses were symmetrical, usually rectangular in shape, and more commodious. On the exterior the Georgian house was adorned with classic details, beautiful classic doorways, large symmetrical sash instead of casement windows, dormer windows, cornices, balustrades on the roofs, pilasters, etc. Some of these mansions, such as the Brewton House in Charleston and "Shirley" in the James River Valley, had exquisite double-decker porticoes supported by white classic pillars. The Southern mansions were built for coolness, containing a large central hallway, high ceilings, chimneys on the end walls, and detached kitchens. The interiors of these Georgian homes were characterized by elegant simplicity, expressed in the white paneling, classic mantels, and beautiful stairways. Although this architecture of the Georgian period was an imitation of the current English style and had little originality, nevertheless it produced beautiful and dignified homes, an ideal setting for the well-poised aristocrats of the eighteenth century.

The lover of colonial architecture can find two notable shrines of

Georgian architecture at Williamsburg and at Annapolis, Maryland. Williamsburg has been restored, not to say glorified, as a colonial village by the wealth of John D. Rockefeller, Jr. One of the most appealing buildings of Old Williamsburg was the Governor's Palace, so similar to Eaton Hall in England, of seventeenth century Renaissance style. Other notable edifices were the Capitol, which was designed in 1699, the so-called Christopher Wren building on the campus of William and Mary College, and the Raleigh Tavern, built in 1735, where young Tom Jefferson danced with the entrancing Rebecca Burwell, who rejected his suit, and where many of the Revolutionary meetings took place. In Annapolis the Georgian style flowered in such homes as the Hammond House, one of the most exquisite houses in America, designed and built by an indentured artisan, William Buckland, the Chase House, and the Paca House. No account of Georgian architecture in America should neglect "Gunston Hall" on the Potomac, the home of George Mason, with its Chinese Chippendale interior, or the lovely "Westover," residence of the Byrds on the James River. Outside of these homes were notable gardens of the formal English type, with boxwood borders, neatly clipped and pruned, growing herbs for the medicine chest, and sweet-smelling flowers, such as the gardenia, the honeysuckle, and the cape jessamine.

The furniture of these Georgian homes was often imported from England, or made by native cabinet makers who followed dominant English styles. The earliest of the grand styles of colonial furniture was the Chippendale (named after Thomas Chippendale, a London cabinet maker), which flourished from 1740 to 1780. The Chippendale chair was characterized by the cabriole, or bowed leg, with claw and ball foot, and the back was carved into graceful designs, such as the tracery of Gothic rose windows, the Chinese Chippendale design, and the "ladder back." The Hepplewhite style, which flourished from 1775 to 1795, was distinguished by lightness and delicacy. The chair, the card table, the highboy, all had straight, tapering legs, fragile in appearance, precarious furniture for a lusty "beef-eater" or a gouty old gentleman. Hepplewhite carved the backs of his chairs into the shapes of a heart, or an oval, or a shield, and he was fond of using satinwood inlay and of painting festoons and decorations on his handiwork. The Sheraton style, which flourished at the close of the eighteenth century, resembled the Hepplewhite in its delicacy and use of inlays of exotic woods, but it was more strongly built. The chairs, having square or rectangular backs with a cross rail a little above the seat, were supported by fluted legs. In all these styles mahogany wood was the principal material, and the chairs, sofas, and love seats were covered with sumptuous damask and brocades.

The elegant aristocrats who lived in these Georgian homes on the eve of the Revolution had achieved a happy adaptation of English culture to the American environment. In the Southern colonies they had begun to evolve a way of life different from the pattern of the English squires or from the communal life of New England. During the seventeenth century there had been a much higher degree of similarity between the cultures of the northern and southern colonies than was apparent in the eighteenth century. In this last century the Southern colonies became differentiated from New England by the shaping forces of environment, by the substitution of Negro slavery for white indentured servitude, by the development of staple crops, the dominance of the Anglican Church, and the emergence of a powerful plantation aristocracy. In the middle of the eighteenth century the South was more cosmopolitan in its mental outlook than ever in its history. Not only had immigration added variety to the pattern of the Southern population, but the tobacco and rice aristocrats were kept in continuous contact with European culture through the intercourse of a flourishing trade. Furthermore, the intellectual horizon of the colonists was broadened by the connection with the British Empire and its officials and by the practice of wealthy planters of sending their sons to Europe to be educated.

But the culture of the colonial South was narrowly confined to an upper class. Governor William Berkeley in 1671 thanked God that there were no free schools or newspapers in Virginia, for the former bred disobedience and heresy, and the latter spread libels against the government. Actually, there were at least two free schools in Virginia at that time, the Syms school and the Eaton school, endowed by the wills of two enlightened and benevolent men. Also in the eighteenth century there were free schools in Charleston, New Bern, and other Southern towns, founded by the Society for the Propagation of the Gospel in Foreign Parts, and the Winyah Indigo Society's school at Georgetown. In Annapolis, was King William's School which developed after the Revolution into St. John's College. Nevertheless, the education of the youth was regarded in the colonial South as a private responsibility, which was assumed by the planter, who either taught his children himself or employed a tutor, or sent them to schools in England.

The delightful journal of Philip Fithian, tutor in the home of "Councillor" Robert Carter of "Nomini Hall" in the years 1773–74, gives an insight into the method of educating children by a tutor on the plantation. Fithian, a graduate of Princeton, who was preparing to become a Presbyterian minister, accepted the job of a tutor in Virginia with some trepidation, for he had heard that Virginia was a worldly place, where he might be corrupted. He was paid a salary of £40 a year to teach the seven Carter children and a nephew, English, Latin, Greek, mathematics, and the history of England. In addition to this education in books, the Carter children were instructed in music and formal dancing by masters who traveled on regular routes from plantation to plantation. The Southern gentry were genuinely concerned in giving their children a Renaissance type of education. Besides a knowledge of the classics, they were taught to ride, to dance, to play on some musical instrument, to speak English correctly, to acquire an amateur knowledge of English law, to keep accounts, and to manage a plantation. Yet the realization of this ideal of versatility was often defeated by the laziness of Southern youth, as Fithian found, by their passionate love of horses and out-of-doors life and by their delight in dancing, fine clothes, and gay parties.

To supply educated ministers for the colony and to provide an Indian school, William and Mary College was founded at Williamsburg in 1693, the second oldest college in the country. The founder of this notable institution was Reverend James Blair, Commissary of the Church of England in Virginia, a masterful figure who sat on the governor's council. The student at this pioneer college first entered the grammar school where he was taught Latin and Greek, and then he put on the cap and gown of a student in the college proper, where he studied rhetoric, logic, ethics, and mathematics as well as the classic authors. William Byrd II noted in his diary in 1712 that there were only twenty-two students at the college and that the head master was dismissed for being a sot. Fithian observed on the eve of the Revolution that some of the professors were seen drunk in the streets and that they gambled with cards all night in the public tavern. Nevertheless, there were other eminent professors at the college, such as George Wythe who became the first professor of law in America, and Professor William Small, who inspired Thomas Jefferson when he was a student at Williamsburg. Also the Phi Beta Kappa Society was founded at William and Mary in 1776 to encourage scholarship and debating. Some of the most eminent statesmen produced by the South, such as Jefferson, Marshall, Monroe, Edmund Randolph, and John Tyler, were educated at William and Mary College. Many Southerners, however, especially from South Carolina, went to England to be educated as gentlemen; despite the culture of the upper class in South Carolina there was no college in the colony. A study of Americans who were admitted as students to the Inns of Court in England prior to 1860 reveals that two-thirds of them came from the Southern colonies and states.[9]

The culture of the Southern planters was indicated to some extent by their libraries. The library of Ralph Wormeley of "Rosegill" in Virginia was one of the best seventeenth century colonial collections of books, 385 volumes, of which twenty-six were medical books and eighty were religious works. Over one-third of the library of "King" Carter at "Corotoman," or approximately one hundred titles, were law books. George Washington, although he was not a voracious reader, had a library of 903 volumes at "Mount Vernon." The finest library in the American colonies was at "Westover" on the James River, where William Byrd II had gathered nearly 4,000 volumes. Another superb library was the collection of "Councillor" Carter at "Nomini Hall," which contained a wide variety of books by such authors as Locke, Grotius, Puffendorf, Sidney, Blackstone, Palladio, Voltaire, Molière, Donne, Chaucer, Dryden, and Congreve. At the close of the eighteenth century the greatest book connoisseur in the South was Thomas Jefferson who gathered a library which he estimated at between nine and ten thousand volumes. A large proportion of these libraries of the colonial planters consisted of Greek and Roman classics, but there were many works on their shelves dealing with such practical subjects as agriculture, law, medicine, architecture, gardening, and military science. Recent studies have shown that the planters did much "purposeful reading," and that religious books occupied a large space in their libraries.[10] In addition to these private collections, Dr. Thomas Bray, Commissary of the Church of England to Maryland, established libraries in each of the thirty parishes of that colony, with the stipulation that any inhabitant could borrow books by promising to return them within one to four months. The Society for the Propagation of the Gospel in Foreign Parts, which he also founded in 1701, started libraries for public use in other Southern colonies.

The outstanding literary figure in the Southern colonies was William Byrd II, whose major works were not published until long after his death in 1744. Byrd was trained as a man of fashion in London, where he enjoyed the life of the coffee houses, the companionship of wanton women and of pleasure-loving nobles, and the drama of the English stage. In fact, he never cured himself of his nostalgia for England, which he regarded as "home." On his James River estate of "Westover" he arose at five o'clock in the morning and regularly read before breakfast a portion of Homer, Terence, Petronius, or the Greek version of Josephus, or a passage from the Hebrew. He also read Italian, Dutch, and French works in the original, as well as kept up with current English literature. In 1728 he wrote his most important work, *History of the Dividing Line*, which described his experiences as one of the commissioners who surveyed the boundary line between Virginia and North Carolina. Although it was written partly to gain adequate remuneration for his arduous labor in surveying the boundary, it gives a vivacious, if prejudiced, picture of social conditions in North Carolina at the time. It has also real literary merit because it is permeated with the comic spirit, an aristocratic type of wit, that contrasts pleasurably with the dull religious literature produced in contemporary New England, the land of "the saints."

The most colorful historian of the colonial South was the sarcastic and forthright Robert Beverley. A member of the Virginia aristocracy, Beverley suffered various misfortunes which caused him to retire to his huge estate of "Beverley Park" where he lived a solitary and Spartan life until his death in 1722. His *History and Present State of Virginia*, published in London in 1705, describes the early settlement of the colony, its natural history, its laws and government, as well as the customs and manners of the Indians. Possessing an ardent love of his native land, he tried to encourage his fellow Virginians to become economically independent of England. Accordingly, he set them an example by using native manufactures and by making wine from his own vineyards. The first edition of his history is filled with ironic references to the colonial officials, but in a second edition (1722) he deleted most of his pungent criticism of his contemporaries.

The most cultivated community and the only "city" of the Southern colonies was Charleston. Its population of approximately 12,000 inhabitants was far below that of Philadelphia, the largest city of the American colonies in 1776, which boasted 35,000 people. Moreover, at least half of the population of Charleston was composed of Negroes. In the early part of its history it did not have local autonomy but was ruled by the provincial legislature which the planters controlled. The inhabitants of this semi-West Indian city were threatened by dangers of slave insurrections, disastrous fires and by epidemics, such as yellow fever and smallpox. The great fire of 1740, which destroyed a large part of the city, caused the enactment of a law that all houses within the limits must be built of stone or brick. Charleston was the second city in America to have a fire engine. Despite its delightful location, it was one of the most unhealthful spots on the continent, although it was much freer from malarial mosquitoes than the surrounding rice plantations. This fortunate exemption partly explains why the rice grandees lived in the city during the hot seasons. Thus Charleston virtually became a city state, the focus of plantation culture.

Travelers who visited Charleston and the homes of the rice planters were surprised at the high state of culture of the upper class of society. Wrote Johann David Schoepf, a physician to German troops during the Revolution, "Throughout, there prevails here a finer manner of life, and on the whole there are more evidences of courtesy than in the northern cities." [11] The architecture of colonial Charleston was influenced partly by the West Indies—many of the brick houses were stuccoed and colored with soft pink, green, yellow, and blue tints. Iron balconies and tile roofs also suggested French Huguenot ancestry. In addition to these styles of architecture there were numerous symmetrical Georgian houses ornamented with classical details. The classical influence was also expressed in St. Philip's church and the aristocratic St. Michael's, built in 1752, patterned after the London church, St. Martins-in-the-Fields. Although South Carolina failed to establish a colonial college, it had a remarkable Charleston Library Society, founded in 1748, which accumulated a large circulating library. In 1732 an apprentice of Benjamin Franklin founded the *South Carolina Gazette* at Charleston, four years before the *Virginia Gazette* was started at Williamsburg.

Charleston had a remarkably rich cultural life for a remote colonial town. This city had the first scientific museum in America, and scientific studies were carried on by Doctor John Lining and Doctor Alexander Garden, the last an amateur botanist after whom the gardenia is named. Charleston was the home of the first colonial to hold a genuine degree of Doctor of Medicine, William Bull, who in 1734 received a medical degree from the University of Leyden. In 1762 one of the earliest musical societies in the colonies was organized, the St. Cecilia Society, at which distinguished concerts were given. In the Charleston theater, founded in 1735, traveling troupes of English actors, particularly the Hallams, performed the plays of Shakespeare and the latest London successes. At the same time social life was stimulated by twenty different clubs in the city, such as the Hell-Fire Club. Indeed, the club movement was widespread throughout the colonies, producing such various organizations as political clubs, Masonic lodges, smoking societies, the Maryland Jockey Club, and even golf clubs, introduced by Scotsmen at Savannah and Augusta.

The colonial planters were appreciative of the fine arts, especially portrait painting, but were not creative in this field. Between 1700 and 1728, Henrietta Johnson, an English woman who had settled in

Charleston, was doing charming portraits of the rice planters in pastel. She had been called the first woman painter in America as well as the first Southern artist. A little later Jeremiah Theus, a Swiss, was painting coats-of-arms and crests for coaches and chaises, as well as portraits of the Charleston grandees. The Boston painter, John Singleton Copley, also painted the portraits of some of the colonial dignitaries of the South in their colorful costumes of silks and satins, such as the portraits of Mr. and Mrs. Izard of South Carolina, and of the North Carolina merchant, John Burgwin. In Maryland the Swedish-born painter, Gustavus Heselius (d. 1775), and his son, John, worked at their profession. Gustavus painted a "Last Supper" for St. Barnabas Church, Queen Anne's County, which is the earliest religious painting produced in the United States that has survived. John Heselius is noted chiefly for being the first teacher of Charles Willson Peale.

Charles Willson Peale, a native of Queen Anne's County, Maryland (d. 1827), will occupy a permanent place in the history of American art as the painter of portraits of George Washington in his prime. He was an amazingly versatile and dynamic person. His youth was spent as an apprentice to a saddler, but during his long life he worked as a silver smith, made coaches and clocks, and lectured as a popular scientist. His most curious skill was the making of false teeth, notably a set for President Washington that were held in place by creaking springs. After he had acquired the skeleton of a mastodon, he learned taxidermy and started a famous museum of natural history and a portrait gallery in Philadelphia. Peale studied art under Benjamin West in England and returned to America to become a portrait painter. He fought as a soldier in the Revolution, and he has preserved to posterity the appearance of Washington as a colonel of Virginia militia (1772) and as commander of the Revolutionary army. His portraits of the national hero lack the subtlety and penetration of character that Gilbert Stuart's portraits of the aged Washington have, but Peale's likenesses are realistic and show Washington's countenance before its expression was altered by his false teeth. Peale was a prolific father, who named his sons Raphael, Rubens, Titian, and Rembrandt, the latter attaining fame as a portrait painter.

Culture is much deeper than a taste for the fine arts or the accretion of knowledge; it is also concerned with the spirit, the province of religion. In all of the Southern colonies the Church of England became the established, or the official, church. The clergyman, chosen by the parish vestry, was given a glebe (a house and several acres of land) and was paid a salary from the taxation of the freemen regardless of their creed. Supervision over the American churches was exercised by the Bishop of London, who sent over commissaries to represent him. On account of the scattered population, it was often necessary for the colonial parishes to depart from the practices of the church in England. The dead were buried in family graveyards instead of the consecrated churchyards. Various violations of the liturgy occurred, such as the failure of the ministers to wear the proper vestments and the performing of marriages in private houses. The clergymen were unable to perform the sacraments or conduct religious services at the right intervals since they had to travel by horseback to distant churches in their parishes. Consequently "chapels of ease" were established in remote places, where prayers and printed sermons were read by laymen. A further difficulty which hampered the growth of the Anglican church in America was that ministers had to cross the Atlantic to be ordained.

In the seventeenth century the Southern colonies were far more Puritanical in laws and mores than the Cavalier tradition represents them. Compulsory attendance at church on Sundays was a rigidly enforced law, and profane swearing or Sabbath-breaking were severely punished by the magistrates. In the eighteenth century, however, a more worldly atmosphere prevailed and greater laxity in religious performances occurred. The clergy had slight supervision over them, and some ministers were a disgrace to their profession. The Reverend Andrew Burnaby who traveled in Virginia, 1759–60, described the clergy, about sixty-five in number, as in general men of "sober and exemplary lives." On the other hand, Fithian's journal portrays a certain Parson Giberne, one of the most popular and admired preachers in Virginia, who stayed up late three nights in succession drinking and playing cards, a bout which sent him reeling to bed. Fithian also noted that the minister in his parish preached only fifteen minutes, contrasting with the long two-hour sermons of New England. His description of a Sunday in Virginia just before the Revolution suggests that the people were far less Puritanical than their predecessors of the seventeenth century. The men assembled at the church early in order to talk over business and politics. The lower classes used Sunday for rude diversions, while the Negroes spent the holy day fishing, working in their gardens, or patching their quarters. Indeed, Virginia had a reputation for having no "heart religion" but for being a land of tippling, gambling with cards or dice, dancing, and swearing. The young tutor in the Carter family wrote in praise of Priscilla, a girl in her teens, "she never swears, which is here a distinguished virtue." [12]

The religion of the planters seems to have been predominantly formal, practical, and decorous. William Byrd II, for example, went to church regularly and took the sacrament, but it was difficult for this worldly gentleman to stay awake during the sermons. At night he invariably said his prayers, recording in his secret diary, written in a shorthand which has recently been decoded, "I said my prayers and had good health, good thoughts, and good humor, thank God Almighty." He also read many sermons and other religious works along with his daily stint of reading in the classics. Nevertheless, his religion did not prevent him from quarreling with his wife, cheating her at cards in order to establish male ascendancy, avariciously trying to monopolize land, or violating the sexual moral code. At sixty-five years of age he confessed in his secret diary, "played the fool with Sally, God forgive me." [13] Nor did his religion place a taboo on his enjoyment of the hedonistic pleasures of the fashionable set, gay parties, drinking heavily, dancing, gambling with dice, and attending horse races and cock fights. He had the comfortable belief that his sins would be forgiven.

The Anglican Church was the church of the colonial aristocracy and did not meet the emotional needs and the democratic striving of the common people. These needs were satisfied by the rise of dissenting sects such as the Quakers, the Baptists, and the Presbyterians. The Quakers were the first dissenters to invade the South. When they began to arrive in the colonies during the decade of the 1650's, they were severely persecuted in New England where some of them were hanged, but in Virginia they were merely fined or expelled. The Quakers found a refuge in the back country of North Carolina, which George Fox, the founder of the sect, visited in the decade of the 1670's. The violent persecution of this devoted group of Christians, who refused to take oaths, or show respect for authority, or fight in the militia, was stopped after the passage of the Toleration Act by Parliament in 1689. The Baptists spread from Rhode Island and Philadelphia into the Southern colonies by means of itinerant preachers, who were often arrested as vagrants or disturbers of the peace. The Methodist Church was introduced into the Southern colonies by John Wesley, the founder, and George Whitefield, the great evangelist, in the decade of the 1730's. During the colonial period the Methodists did not organize a separate church but remained affiliated with the Anglican Church. The immigration of the Scotch-Irish into the back country of the South spread the Presbyterian faith, based on Calvinism.

Around 1740 the Southern colonies were deeply agitated by the Great Awakening, a religious movement that was a reaction from the formalism of the Episcopal Church. The Great Awakening was accomplished by a series of revivals which swept through the thirteen colonies, perhaps the first social movement in which all the colonies shared prior to the political movement of opposition to British mercantilism. The ministers of the Great Awakening preached the necessity of a religious experience—first, a conviction of sinfulness, and then the great emotional catharsis of being pardoned. They discounted education and wealth, and preached in barns and open-air gatherings as well as in churches. There were economic reasons also for the Great Awakening in the South, since the dissenting sects were bitterly resentful against the compulsion of paying taxes to support the Anglican clergy and against the monopoly which the latter enjoyed of performing marriages, thus reserving to themselves the profits of the marriage fees. The two leaders of this far-reaching religious movement in the South were the traveling evangelist, George Whitefield, and Samuel Davies, who engaged in a heroic crusade to spread the Presbyterian faith in the Virginia back country. The Great Awakening appealed to the common people and stimulated the growth of the Baptist, Methodist, and Presbyterian churches. The Presbyterians split into two factions over the question of accepting the new methods of evangelism, the "New Lights," and the "Old Side." The conservative and aristocratic Church of England frowned upon the unconventional and emotional methods of saving souls adopted by the apostles of the Great Awakening.

This emotional and more primitive type of religion was suited to the mores of a semi-frontier people. Likewise, rural conditions in the South hastened marriages and encouraged large families. John Lawson, who wrote a natural history of North Carolina before he was burned at the stake by the Tuscarora Indians in 1711, observed concerning the Carolina girls: "They marry very young; some at Thirteen or Fourteen; and She that stays till Twenty is reckoned a Stale maid. . . ." [14] Widows with property were snapped up quickly by ambitious suitors in this day of the "belleship of widows." Divorces were not sanctioned by the Anglican Church and were therefore rare in the colonial South. A large family of children was an asset in a huge, empty country. The upper class as well as the common people were very prolific, but there was an appalling amount of infant mortality among both the whites and the blacks. Mrs. Robert Carter, the gracious mistress of "Nomini Hall," had seventeen children; Patrick Henry was a member of a family of nineteen; Henry Clay's mother had sixteen children, and John Marshall was one of fifteen children.

Women in the American colonies either willingly or perforce accepted male dominance. Nevertheless, there was many a spirited lady, such as William Byrd's first wife, who put up a stiff fight to live her own life. Byrd quarreled furiously with her when, in a fit of temper, she beat one of her slaves with a pair of tongs, and again when she extravagantly ordered a long list of luxurious goods from England, and on another occasion when she differed with him in regard to the new method of singing Psalms. He reveals his childish desire to be the cock of the walk in his account of an altercation with Mrs. Byrd because she wished to pluck her eyebrows before going to the governor's ball. "My wife and I quarreled about her pulling her brows. She threatened she would not go to Williamsburg if she might not pull them; I refused, however, and got the better of her, and maintained my authority." [15] Occasionally a Southern woman, like Eliza Lucas in South Carolina or Margaret Brent in Maryland, overcame great obstacles and participated in the world of affairs which was dominated by the lordly males.

The legal position of women in the colonial South, as in New England, reflected attitudes that went back through the Middle Ages to Biblical times. The English common law, which prevailed in the colonies, recognized male supremacy, so that a husband could legally administer reasonable chastisement to his wife by whipping her. The married woman could not make a will or a contract or sue in court, and in case of divorce the husband was entitled to the custody of all the children. The husband acquired all the property that his wife owned or inherited and also any wages she might earn. The single woman, however, had the right to sue, make contracts and wills, and control her property. A widow was entitled to a dower in her husband's estate of one-third of his personal property and the use for life of one-third of his lands and slaves. The independence of women today would have shocked our ancestors, who held with *The Spectator* that "separate purses between man and wife" were "as unnatural as separate beds." [16]

The household routine of our colonial forefathers seems remote from modern habits. Cooking was done in the large open-hearth fireplace of the kitchen, which on the Southern plantations was detached from the house. Dinner was served at three o'clock in the afternoon. The numerous flies were brushed away by little Negro boys with peacock-tail fans. In the evening after supper the planter might "prattle with the ladies and drink whipped syllabub." At nine o'clock he usually retired to his high canopied bed, but his rest was likely to be disturbed by bedbugs, for the slovenly servants, even in the homes of the most elegant aristocrats, did not keep the houses very clean. Baths were not taken often, although William Byrd II (and later Thomas Jefferson) made it a rule to wash his feet daily.

The folkways of the American people were illustrated in the medical practice of colonial days. Great faith was placed in concoctions, brews, and elixirs, consisting of such revolting ingredients as toads, snails, snakes, urine, cow and hen dung, mixed with various herbs like rosemary and lavender. The sovereign herb was ginseng,

whose root was dug in the wilds of the Southern colonies. William
Byrd II, an amateur scientist and a member of the Royal Society,
praised it extravagantly, as a panacea for practically all ailments except declining virility. It was exported in large quantities from
Southern ports and was much desired by Chinese physicians. Actually, the ginseng root had little medical value except for its psychic
effects on believers in its efficacy. Obstetrics was practiced largely by
midwives, contributing to a very high mortality rate among infants
and mothers. Physicians in the colonial South had to learn their
craft as a rule by an apprenticeship to an established physician. The
German physician, Johann David Schoepf, in 1783 described a typical country doctor who lived in Edenton, North Carolina, a town
of a hundred frame houses. The doctor had an apothecary shop in
which he sold little besides tartar-emetic, flowers of antimony, salt-
petre, and Peruvian bark.

Practitioners of the eighteenth century resorted to heroic measures of empiricism, relying mainly on bleeding, purging, and blisters. George Washington had a strong and hearty constitution, but
in his last illness in 1799 he could not survive the ignorant medical
practice of his age. On a snowy December day he came from a tour
of his plantation and sat down to dinner without changing his wet
clothes. As a consequence, he developed a sore throat and a bad
cold. To combat his sickness he was bled four times, losing at the
first bleeding a half-pint of blood. His power of resistance was
further weakened by doses of calomel and by blisters. It is not
strange that the great man died under such treatment. Remarkable
is the contrast between the age when people were bled during illness and our own time when patients are strengthened by blood
plasma and extra blood from blood banks.

The two most useful medical discoveries made during the colonial
period (by accident) were the introduction of cinchona, or Peruvian bark, as a specific for malaria, and the adoption of the practice
of inoculation to prevent or lessen the ravages of smallpox. The
Peruvian Indians had discovered a remedy for malaria by using a
native bark, which was named cinchona after the wife of the viceroy
of Peru, who brought this medicine in 1640 to Spain, whence fourteen years later it was carried to England. The method of inoculating

persons to prevent smallpox was imported by Lady Mary Wortley Montagu from Constantinople into England from whence it was introduced into Boston about 1720 by Cotton Mather and Doctor Zabdiel Boylston. This innovation provoked bitter opposition from the conservative clergy who regarded this Turkish practice as an interference with the inscrutable ways of Providence.

The Southern colonies had the crudeness and shortcomings, as well as the virtues, of a new country. The observations of Durand of Dauphiné, a Huguenot gentleman who landed in Tidewater, Virginia in 1686, point out this condition. He crossed the ocean with a group of immigrants who were to be sold as indentured servants, including "twelve prostitutes & fifteen of the boldest & most insolent young scoundrels in England." He found a distinct difference between the lower class and the gentry, as did Janet Schaw almost a century later when she visited North Carolina and wrote her delightful *Journal of a Lady of Quality*. The former were rude and uncivil, disposed to fleece the foreigner, while the latter were very hospitable. All classes were heavy drinkers of rum, brandy, punch, and wine, and "every body smokes, men, women, girls, and boys from the age of seven years." Durand was impressed by the laziness of the people and the vast amount of time they consumed in visiting each other. He observed the harshness of the legal code: "Robbery is punished so severely that if a man is convicted of having stolen a chicken, he is hanged." [17] This new land had execrable roads, zigzag rail fences, the signs of a thriftless agriculture, swarms of mosquitoes and prevalent malaria, and lack of towns, in contrast to Europe. At the same time the French traveler was impressed by the beauty and fertility of the country, its cheap or free land, its freedom from beggars, and its religious toleration.

The most striking social fact about the Southern colonies was that from the plantations was emerging a remarkable class of gentlemen. Durand has drawn charming vignettes of some of the planters of the late seventeenth century, such as Ralph Wormeley of "Rosegill" and Colonel William Fitzhugh of "Ravensworth." Wormeley had studied at Oxford and was a hospitable and cultivated gentleman. When Durand approached "Rosegill" he thought he was entering a large village, for the house of the planter was surrounded by so many out-buildings. Wormeley owned a vast amount of land in scattered plantations, but his labor force was only twenty-six slaves and twenty indentured servants. Colonel Fitzhugh illustrated the lavish hospitality of the planters when he entertained a group of twenty unexpected guests, furnishing them with beds, as well as quantities of alcoholic beverages, and sending for three fiddlers, a jester, a tight-rope dancer, and an acrobat who tumbled around.

Doctor Alexander Hamilton's *Itinerarium*, perhaps the best travel account of the colonial period, makes some comparisons between the societies of the Southern and Northern colonies which give a valuable perspective. Hamilton was a well-educated Scotch physician who practiced medicine at Annapolis. In 1744 he made a leisurely trip for the sake of his health from Annapolis to Boston, which he described with humor and with a penetrating insight into the character and manners of the American colonists. He discovered that medical science in the Northern colonies was as primitive as in the Southern colonies. "The doctors here [at Albany] are all barbers" he wrote in disdain of their empiric trade of dosing and of shaving. He noted wretchedly poor people on his route, families who ate out of a dish without fork, spoon, or knife, ignorant and relentlessly inquisitive rustics of New England, comparable to the poor farmers below the Potomac, and the prevalence of hard drinking, tobacco chewing, and immoderate swearing. The most significant intellectual difference between the Southern and Northern colonies was reflected in their attitudes toward religion. Doctor Hamilton observed that disputation about religion was more in vogue in New England, and the Sabbath day was kept more fanatically in this land of white steeples than in the tobacco plantation region. Indeed, he declared that to talk in the dialect of New England about theology—original sin, reprobation, regeneration, justification, etc.—would in "our part of the world" be like speaking in Greek or Arabic.[18] At the conclusion of his *Itinerarium*, he summarized his observations by noting that he had found little difference between the various provinces in the manners and character of the people, especially as to politeness and humanity, but that the Northern colonies were better settled than Maryland, healthier, and more civilized in the large towns.

STEPHEN FOSTER OF PENNSYLVANIA WHO WAS ONE OF
THE CREATORS OF THE LEGENDARY SOUTH

A portrait by John Vanderlyn, 1775–1852. (Courtesy of the Kirby Hall
of Civil Rights, Lafayette College.)

THE TOBACCO PLANT IN TIDEWATER NORTH CAROLINA

The eighteenth century tobacco plant in America was smaller than its modern descendant, approximately two or three feet high. (Courtesy of North Carolina Department of Conservation and Development.)

HARVESTING HEMP IN KENTUCKY

Hemp was an ante-bellum money crop of Kentucky and Missouri, which was temporarily revived during World War II. (Courtesy of J. Winston Coleman, Jr.)

If culture is interpreted to include the development of a class of refined "gentlemen" and "ladies," the Southern colonies in the eighteenth century were richly provided with that asset. At the time of the Revolution, Anburey described the plantation of "Tuckahoe" on the upper James and its owner, Colonel Randolph, who exhibited the qualities of leadership which distinguished the colonial aristocracy. The house at "Tuckahoe" was built for hospitality and pleasure as well as for a living place, containing many guest rooms and a commodious ballroom equipped with four "sophas" for lounging. A lover of fine horses, the colonel had imported from England the magnificent dappled-gray "Shakespeare" to head his stud. When a popular clamor arose against the hospitality shown to the paroled officers of Burgoyne's troops at Charlottesville, Colonel Randolph and other planters of breeding resisted such illiberality, for being gentlemen of affluence and authority, they disdained the popular clamor. Nevertheless, the Revolution introduced a spirit of equality, the "levelling principle," into the caste system of colonial days. Anburey saw three countrymen enter the mansion of "Tuckahoe" and sit down with the colonel, pulling off their muddy boots and spitting on the floor, as they discussed the terms for grinding their grain at the colonel's mill.

Although "the first gentlemen of Virginia" have been elaborately delineated by historians, the first gentlemen of Carolina have been neglected. A typical gentleman of this class has been described by John Davis, a tutor on "Ocean Plantation" near Coosahatchie, South Carolina, at the close of the eighteenth century. The master, a member of the powerful Drayton family, treated the young tutor with the utmost consideration, providing him with a horse, a library, and an abundant supply of "segars." When the family moved in May to another estate on the Ashley River, near magnificent Drayton Hall, the home of an elder brother, Davis wrote, "I was now breathing the politest atmosphere in America." [19] Indeed, a society which produced the Pinckneys, the Rutledges, the Middletons, the Manigaults, the Izards, and the Draytons contained much culture. Some of the homes and gardens of Tidewater South Carolina, such as "Drayton Hall," "Middleton Place," "Magnolia," "Mulberry," and "The Elms," vied in elegance with the famous Virginia mansions of

"Mt. Airy," "Blenheim," "Marmion," and "Carter's Grove." The proprietors of these ancestral estates were not as a rule play-boys, enervated by slavery and luxury, but industrious, masterful leaders.

Yet a truthful picture of Southern society in the eighteenth century cannot omit the prevalence of idleness and laziness among many of the people. Harry Toulmin, a traveling English minister, observed in Tidewater Virginia in 1793 the ennui of little villages abounding with "indolent young men, who have no religion and no business, and who kill their time no more than perhaps six days in the week at a public billiard table." [20] He explained this phenomenon as produced by slavery and a warm climate. But this curse of the South continued long after the end of slavery until the spread of education, the improvement of transportation, better health, and wider industrial opportunities lessened the stagnation of ruralness.

Citations

1. JOHN FISKE, *Old Virginia and Her Neighbors* (Boston, 1900), II, 16; T. J. Wertenbaker notes that population in Virginia expanded from 15,000 in 1649 to 40,000 in 1662, but attributes this immigration, not to a "Cavalier exodus" from England, but to "the prosperity which attended the economic freedom of the Commonwealth period." *The First Americans* (New York, 1929), 313.
2. T. J. WERTENBAKER, *Patrician and Plebeian in Virginia* (Charlottesville, 1910).
3. P. A. BRUCE, *Social Life of Virginia in the Seventeenth Century* (Richmond, 1927), 99.
4. Diary of Col. Waightstill Avery, 1769, Draper Collection, North Carolina MSS. (Wisconsin Historical Society Library).
5. Edited by J. B. Hubbell and D. Adair, *William and Mary Quarterly*, Third Series, V (April, 1948), 217–257.
6. B. H. LATROBE, *The Journal of Latrobe* (New York, 1905), 34.
7. THOMAS ANBUREY, *Travels through the Interior Parts of America* (London, 1789), II, 349, 375; see also William Tatham, *op. cit.*
8. J. S. BASSETT, "The Regulators of North Carolina (1765-1771)," *Annual Report of American Historical Association for the Year, 1894* (Washington, 1895), 140–212.
9. J. G. DER. HAMILTON, "Southern Members of the Inns of Court," *North Carolina Historical Review*, X (October, 1933), 274.

10. L. B. WRIGHT, *The First Gentlemen of Virginia: Intellectual Qualities of the Early Ruling Class* (San Marino, 1940), Chap. V.
11. J. D. SCHOEPF, *Travels in the Confederation [1783–1784]* (Philadelphia, 1911), II, 167.
12. H. D. FARISH (ed.), *Journal and Letters of Philip Vickers Fithian, 1773–1774* (Williamsburg, 1943), 65.
13. M. H. WOODFIN (ed.), *Another Secret Diary of William Byrd of Westover for the Years, 1739–1741* (Richmond, 1942), 70.
14. JOHN LAWSON, *The History of Carolina, Containing Exact Description and Natural History of that Country* (Raleigh, 1860), 143.
15. L. B. WRIGHT (ed.), *The Secret Diary of William Byrd of Westover, 1709–1712* (Richmond, 1941), 296.
16. J. C. SPRUILL, *Women's Life and Work in the Southern Colonies* (Chapel Hill, 1938), 366.
17. DURAND OF DAUPHINÉ, *A Frenchman in Virginia* (Privately Printed, 1923), 114.
18. ALEXANDER HAMILTON, *Hamilton's Itinerarium* (St. Louis, 1907), 199–200.
19. JOHN DAVIS, *Travels of John Davis in the United States of America, 1798 to 1802* (Boston, 1910), II, 130.
20. HARRY TOULMIN, *The Western Country in 1793* (San Marino, 1948), 30.

CHAPTER IV

Breaking the Bonds of Empire

T'HE British government attempted to force trade between the American colonies and the mother country to conform to a theory known as mercantilism. Although businessmen as a group scorn "theory" as impracticable, often they are slaves unconsciously to theories or to ideas which have been outmoded by the dynamics of society. Such a theory was mercantilism, which enthralled the business man and the politicians of the seventeenth and eighteenth centuries. Mercantilism was a European, rather than a peculiarly British, system of "state" economics which matured in the seventeenth century. In a revived form today it is called economic nationalism.

The goal of the mercantilists was a self-sufficing state or empire. Mercantilism of the seventeenth and eighteenth centuries was based on the fallacy that wealth consists of the quantity of gold and silver money accumulated by a country, which was to be obtained by a favorable balance of trade. The mercantilists believed that the main function of colonies was to supply raw materials and furnish markets for the manufactured goods of the mother country and that colonies should be prevented from diversifying their economy and passing out of the colonial stage through the development of their own manufactures. The mercantilists also maintained that the carrying trade should be confined to the ships of the mother country and its dependent colonies, which would contribute to the development of a powerful navy. The faults of this rigid theory of empire were that its narrow economic nationalism often got out of alignment with natural economic laws, that it stimulated trade wars, and that in practice the interests of colonies were at times sacrificed for the benefit of special economic groups within the mother country.

In the case of Great Britain the adoption of mercantilism as a policy came gradually and tentatively. After the fact of mercantilism had emerged, a theory justifying it developed. The British government and commercial companies had taken steps toward the realization of a self-sufficing empire by the encouragement of new crops in the American colonies. They had attempted, for example, to develop a silk industry that would free England from dependence on the Mediterranean countries. Also the production of wine and olive oil had been artificially encouraged. The early regulation of the tobacco trade by the Crown adumbrated the policy of "enumerated commodities" which was to become a cardinal part of the trade acts. The British government was driven to apply mercantilism to the American colonies as a result of the desire to monopolize vital raw materials, to secure a revenue from the colonies, to build a merchant marine and navy, and to favor such pressure groups as the British shopkeepers and the lobby of the West Indies planters.

The first important act of Parliament to carry out the principles of mercantilism was the Navigation Act of 1651. This law was really a measure to strike a blow against the Dutch who were rapidly absorbing much of the carrying trade of the world, including the freightage of tobacco from the Southern colonies. The Navigation Act required that all goods shipped from the colonies to England, or in the coastal trade, must be transported in English or colonial ships, the captain and the majority of the crew of which must be English or colonials. Furthermore, all commodities imported into England or the colonies must be carried in English or colonial bottoms or by vessels belonging to the European countries in which the goods were produced. After 1654, the year in which the war between England and Holland ended, this law was disregarded by the colonies.

With the restoration of Charles II to the throne, however, there was an intensification of the regulation of colonial trade in accordance with mercantilistic ideas. The dominance of the British merchants and ship-owners over Parliament was demonstrated by the passage of trade acts designed to benefit their interests. In 1660 a more stringent Navigation Act was passed at the urgent solicitation of George Downing, Harvard College graduate and ardent imperialist. This law required that the crews of English and colonial ships should be three-fourths Englishmen or colonials, and British monopoly was extended by the stipulation that these ships engaged in the carrying trade must be built in British or colonial shipyards. The effect of these laws was to protect the New England ship-building industry and merchant marine, but at the same time to injure the tobacco planters of Maryland and Virginia who had to pay higher freight rates after the exclusion of the Dutch competition. The navigation acts, nevertheless, contributed to the creation of a powerful British navy.

The Restoration policy of strict regulation of colonial trade was carried a step farther by the act of 1660 establishing a list of "enumerated goods" which must be shipped to English ports, even if such goods were destined for continental ports. This list included sugar, tobacco, cotton, indigo, ginger, and dye woods, none of which was produced in the Southern colonies in any appreciable quantity, except tobacco. From time to time, however, additions were made to this list: rice in 1704, naval stores in 1705, copper and furs in 1722, and lumber in 1764. Colonial commerce was further restricted by the Staple Act of 1663, which required that all commodities, except salt for the New England fisheries and wine from the Azores and Madeira Islands, imported from Europe to America had to go through British ports. The Southern colonies throughout the colonial period did not have the privilege that New England and the Middle Colonies enjoyed of importing their salt directly from the Cape Verde Islands, Portugal, or Spain. Although they could obtain a strong, corrosive salt from Turk's Island or Tortuga in the West Indies, they were forced to import most of their salt for beef and pork from the Northern colonies at an increased price and higher freight charges. Another instance of discrimination between different parts of the empire was that Ireland, and Scotland until the Act of Union of 1707, were considered foreign countries as far as the trade laws were concerned.

There were strong inducements for Southern planters to evade the trade laws since the main markets for rice and tobacco were in continental Europe. In order to suppress evasions of these acts, Parliament passed a law in 1673 which required a bond that enumerated goods would be shipped only to England, or, as an alternative, that the exporter must pay a high "plantation duty" at the shipping port if he carried his cargo to another colonial harbor. In 1696 a drastic law was enacted by the Parliament requiring colonial governors to take an oath to enforce the trade laws and establishing vice-admiralty courts in the colonies to try smugglers. These courts dispensed with local juries who were prone to be lenient with evaders of the trade acts. In 1733 a lobby of absentee West India planters put pressure on Parliament to pass an obnoxious bill, known as the Molasses Act, which favored their special interest. This law placed a prohibitive duty of sixpence a gallon on all molasses shipped from the French and Spanish West Indies into British possessions. The enforcement of this act would have affected adversely the West India trade of the Southern colonies, but fortunately for the American colonies as a whole it became a dead letter law until it was revived in 1764 by George Grenville. The New Englanders were the chief offenders in the smuggling business. On the other hand, according to Governor Glen of South Carolina (1750), "No Country in this Part of the World hath less illegal Trade than *South Carolina;* at least, so far as I can learn." [1]

As to the effect of the trade laws on the Southern colonies, there is a considerable divergence of opinion among American scholars. The imperial school of historians have discarded the view held by Bancroft and older historians that the trade laws were acts of tyranny which produced the American Revolution. They maintain that the Trade Acts did not seriously affect the economic prosperity of the colonies, for it was to the advantage of the colonies to buy and sell in England. They point out that these laws, especially those affecting the Northern colonies and the West India trade, were not enforced until 1764 and that there were no great protests against them until the decade preceding the Revolution.

They observe that the colonists did not appreciate the value of a self-sufficing empire or the economic benefits which they received from the imperial connection. The tobacco planters, for example, were given a monopoly of the British market by tariffs that practically excluded the superior Spanish tobacco. English farmers were forbidden to grow tobacco, and royal dragoons were sent to trample the fields of violators of this law. Moreover, the Southern colonies received a high bounty for the export of indigo, naval stores, and pig iron. Also the colonists did not appreciate the protection of the British navy and army. The lightness of imperial taxation was another example of the liberality of the British empire before 1763. Indeed, the chief taxes which the colonists had to pay were a poll tax to the local government and a tithe for the support of the Anglican church. In the Southern colonies, they were required to pay a quit-rent of two shillings per hundred acres, but this charge on the land was frequently uncollected. Governor Arthur Dobbs reminded the assembly of North Carolina in 1754 that although the British government was loaded with debts it "hath not only protected these colonies but indulged them in . . . the easiest taxes (spent for their support) of any Civilized nation of the Globe." [2]

Unlike New England, the Southern colonies fitted well into the scheme of a self-sufficing empire. New England and the Middle Colonies had a climate much like that of the British Isles, producing raw materials and products which were not greatly needed in the mother country. Consequently, they had to obtain money to pay for the unfavorable balance of trade with England by trade with the West Indies and Africa. The Southern colonies, on the other hand, produced semi-tropical products such as rice, tobacco, indigo, and naval stores, the staples that England needed. Furthermore, the British laws which prohibited the colonies from manufacturing for inter-colonial export, the Hat Act, the Woolens Act, and the Iron Act, scarcely affected the Southern colonies, except possibly impeding the growth of an incipient iron industry in Virginia and Maryland.

The British trade laws, however, bore unequally upon different economic interests in the colonies. They favored the West India sugar planters, who were given a monopoly of the British market. The rice planters also persuaded Parliament to take rice off of the enumerated list in 1730, allowing them to export rice directly to markets south of Cape Finisterre (located on the northwest corner of Spain). From 1767 to the Revolution, moreover, rice, which had paid a duty of approximately six shillings, four pence a hundredweight, was admitted free of customs into England, but an export duty of eight pence per hundredweight was imposed. A large portion of the rice sent to England on the eve of the Revolution, amounting to 79 per cent, was re-exported and also 40 per cent of the indigo was re-exported. The production of indigo was aided by a bounty of six pence a pound and, furthermore, indigo paid no duty in England.

So profitable was the bounty on naval stores that North Carolina had little complaint to make of the working of the mercantilist system. This bounty was inaugurated in 1705 as a result of the difficulty in England of obtaining tar and pitch from Sweden. After the Stockholm Tar Company had been granted a monopoly on these forest products by the Swedish government the price to English customers had been doubled. Furthermore, the Great Northern War between Sweden and Russia, 1699–1721, seriously threatened England's supply from the Baltic countries. To encourage colonial production Parliament granted bounties of £4 a ton on tar and pitch and £3 a ton on turpentine imported from the colonies, thus equalizing the costs of production in America with the costs in the Baltic countries. As a result of these subsidies practically a new industry was created in the Carolinas to produce tar after the Swedish model from green trees rather than from fallen trees and pine knots. But the Carolinians resisted changing to this technique, and accordingly the bounty was discontinued for four years, 1725–1729. As a consequence, the importation of tar and pitch from the colonies into England dropped from 81,033 barrels to 34,277 barrels and the importation of naval stores from the Baltic countries was resumed. In 1729 the bounties were restored owing to the clamor of the colonial naval stores producers, the merchant marine interests, which had suffered from the decline of this trade, and the advocates of mercantilistic policies. Thus Carolina tar, although often mixed with chips and sand and less desirable than Swedish tar, captured the English market and cost the British taxpayers an annual sum of approximately £34,000 for bounties during the decade prior to the American Revolution.[3]

The yoke of the trade and navigation laws was most galling to the tobacco planters of the Chesapeake Bay country. In respect to freight rates, the tobacco planters of the seventeenth century found that the use of Dutch vessels was the cheapest method of getting their crops to market. A realistic student of the effect of the Navigation Acts on the thirteen colonies has observed that the Dutch paid most for American goods, carried freight most economically, and granted the most liberal terms of credit, so that in a free market the American colonies would have been drawn irresistibly into the economic orbit of the Netherlands.[4] Such an extreme view, however, discounts the tastes of the colonists who were habituated to English goods and who were affected by strong emotional bonds with the motherland. All this Dutch trade, except smuggling, was stopped by the Navigation Acts of the Stuarts.

An ironic fact about the tobacco trade was that a very large proportion of the American tobacco was re-exported from England to the continent of Europe. In 1773 Great Britain used less than four million pounds of the golden leaf, while 100,482,007 pounds were re-exported, mostly to Holland and Germany. The shippers of re-exported tobacco received a refund, or drawback, of nearly the whole of the tariff duty, but the tobacco planter was forced to pay additional freight, insurance, commissions, and handling charges that went into the pockets of British businessmen. Such indirect routing of tobacco was clearly unjust and a violation of the natural laws of economics.

The tobacco planters suffered heavy burdens, indeed, from the application of mercantilism. England was not the natural entry port for Southern tobacco, and the customs duty on this luxury was exceedingly great. In 1732 the tobacco planters presented a petition to the British government, *The Case of the Planters of Tobacco in Virginia*, in which they asked that the tariff duty be reduced from six and a half pence to four pence, that the government provide warehouses to store the tobacco until the duty was paid, and that no duty be charged on re-exported tobacco. There is good reason to believe that the indirect routing of tobacco and rice through England cost the planters a considerable share of the profits of their crops. After the American Revolution had broken the restraints of the Trade Acts, the tobacco planters, who had sent 99.8 per cent of their exports for the foreign market to England in 1773, sent only 62.2 per cent in 1790 and 31.7 per cent in 1821. The shipment of rice to England in 1790 also dropped to less than one-half the amount sent during the later colonial period.

The tobacco trade led the planters into chronic debt to the British merchants. This condition was produced primarily by the low prices for tobacco received by the planters in comparison with the increased costs of production. In 1697 planters received one and a half pence a pound for their tobacco, but after the outbreak of Queen Anne's War the price dropped to one-fourth of a penny a pound in 1704 and for a period of ten years there was a depression; from 1724 to 1734 occurred still another period of severe depression; and still another decade of prevailing low prices coincided with the French and Indian War. At times the planters consigned their annual crop to an agent in England and received not a cent for the labor and expenditure of a year. The planters usually overestimated the prices that their crops would bring in England and ordered a larger supply of luxuries and necessities than the returns from their tobacco justified. The debts of the planters thus accumulated and were passed from father to son, for their estates were often protected from foreclosure by the law of entail.

The tobacco planters of the eighteenth century were caught in an economic squeeze. While the price of their staple remained low during the eighteenth century, the cost of production increased greatly. The planter paid a commission to his factor in England of 2½ per cent for selling his tobacco, based not on the colonial price of tobacco, but the English wholesale price, and 2½ per cent for purchasing manufactured goods. He had to pay heavy freight, insurance, and handling charges. The price of his labor force increased from £25 for a slave hand in 1700 to between £50 and £80 for a slave in the 1770's. Furthermore, the erosion of the light soil of the Tidewater and the exhaustion of the tobacco lands as the result of the lack of the proper rotation of crops reduced the yield for the same amount of labor. None the less, the Tidewater tobacco plantations were able to continue to compete with the fresher soils of the Piedmont because of their accessibility to market. The tobacco planters were never able to control production in order to adjust the supply to the demand, and nature itself upset any orderly plan of production by its variations of weather, floods, and plant disease.

Nor did the individualistic planters develop a successful marketing system which would eliminate the over-charges of middlemen.

The money policy of the British government in regard to the American colonies, some historians believe, was far more injurious to the economic development of the colonies than were the Trade Acts. Not only did England prohibit the export of English coins to the American colonies but also even forbade them to mint a supply of money from foreign bullion. A slight concession was granted in 1722 when the colonies were allowed to issue copper currency in values of farthings, half pennies, and pennies. This illiberal policy was based partly on a mistaken notion of mercantilism that the amount of gold and silver a nation retained was the measure of its wealth.

Throughout the colonial period the American colonies were constantly being drained of specie. This condition was caused by the unfavorable balance of trade with England, the interest charges on debts, especially those of the Southern planters, and the paper money issues which depreciated and drove coins from circulation. The colonists were therefore forced to devise expedients like tobacco warehouse certificates in Virginia, Maryland, and North Carolina and buck skins in less developed regions to serve for money. They also obtained the specie needed to compensate for the unfavorable balance of trade with the mother country by importing foreign coin, especially through the trade with the West Indies and with pirates. Consequently, the colonists were accustomed to use such foreign coins as gold Portuguese "Joes," French livres, Dutch guilders, and Spanish gold pistoles, doubloons, and silver pieces of eight. Although foreign coins circulated almost exclusively in the colonies, the nomenclature of English currency as a rule was employed in business transactions.

The most universal coin used in the colonies was the Spanish piece of eight, or peso, containing eight reals, first issued by Spain in 1497. It had different values in different colonies, being worth five shillings in Virginia at the close of the seventeenth century. It was overvalued in terms of English sterling in order to prevent the shipment to England of the scanty supply of foreign cash in the colonies. In 1704 a royal proclamation prescribed that the piece of eight should not be valued in any colony at more than six shillings "proclamation money." Called the Spanish dollar after 1728, it had the advantage of being milled on the outer edge to prevent "clipping" or shaving off a portion of the silver content. In 1786 this unit of currency was adopted by the Congress of the Confederation as the model for the American dollar.

Since the colonies lacked specie they resorted to paper money. Bills of exchange, or drafts of a planter or colonial merchant on a London factor, were also used to supply in part the deficiency of coin, particularly to pay for imports. During Queen Anne's War the Southern colonies began to issue paper money, at first public promissory notes authorized by the colonial legislatures. Such paper money was frowned upon by the British government, which was very solicitous of the interests of British merchants. Royal governors were instructed to veto paper money acts or they were disallowed in England. Some colonies, like South Carolina, tried to aid the debtor interest by creating a Land Bank which issued paper money to land-owners with land as a security. The demand for paper money was especially strong in the back country. The lack of an adequate circulating medium intensified the antagonism between the debtor and the creditor interests in the colonies and prevented the accumulation of capital for new industries. In 1764 Parliament passed an act forbidding the colonial legislatures to issue paper money as legal tender, although they could issue it for local purposes with provision for redemption. Accordingly, a severe money shortage existed in the colonies during the decade preceding the Revolution. This policy of drastically regulating the money supply of the colonies was only a part of the larger system of mercantilism which bred a deep sense of grievance in the minds of the colonists and was the prelude to the American Revolution.

Until 1763, nevertheless, the Southern colonies were reasonably content with their position within the British Empire. But this amicable relationship was disturbed as a result of the French and Indian War which led to a reorganization of the British Empire unfavorably to American liberty. This great struggle for empire between France and England, called in Europe the Seven Years' War, was caused by clashes over colonial expansion and by power politics.

It was precipitated by the advance of the Indian traders of Pennsylvania and the land speculators of Virginia into the Ohio Valley during the middle of the eighteenth century.

Speculation in western lands offered a lucrative opportunity at this time to Southern planters, for immigration and the great growth of population had put pressure on the acquisition of lands. Accordingly, the Loyal Land Company, the Greenbriar Company, and the Ohio Company were formed to exploit the Western country. Among their stockholders were such persons as George Mason, the Washington brothers, Dr. Thomas Walker, Peter Jefferson, father of the future President, and Lieutenant-Governor Robert Dinwiddie of Virginia. The most important of these enterprises was the Ohio Company, which in 1749 received a grant of 200,000 acres in the Ohio Valley on condition of settling two hundred families in that region within seven years. During the next year the company sent out Christopher Gist, a famous frontiersman of Maryland, to explore the Ohio River and report on the location of good lands. As a base for the fur trade, the company established a trading post at Will's Creek (now Cumberland, Maryland) near the great bend of the Potomac River. In 1752 the treaty of Logstown, an Indian village eighteen miles below the forks of the Ohio, was concluded with the Indians, giving permission for the Ohio Company to erect two fortified trading houses on the Ohio River and to plant settlements south of the river.

It was unfortunate for the welfare of the British Empire in America that colonial rivalries hampered this penetration of the Ohio Valley. The Ohio Company planned to build a fort below the forks of the Ohio River at McKee's Rocks, but they were opposed by the Pennsylvania fur traders with the backing of their provincial government. The Pennsylvania authorities believed that the forks of the Ohio lay within the limits of their colony, whose western boundary had been fixed at five degrees west of the Delaware River. This line had not been surveyed at that time. They attempted to thwart the expansion of the Virginia company toward the northwest, especially by turning the Indians of the region against the Virginia traders. Furthermore, the Ohio Company itself was hindered from a vigorous prosecution of its designs by powerful rivals within the Virginia colony, particularly the Blair and the Greenbriar companies, which dominated the colonial council.

In the meanwhile, the French governor of Canada, Marquis Duquesne, began to build a chain of forts from Lake Erie down the Allegheny River to the forks of the Ohio. Alarmed by the French advance, Governor Dinwiddie of Virginia sent George Washington, then twenty-one years old, to warn the French that they were trespassing on English territory (1753). Washington was guided through the wilderness by Christopher Gist, who on one occasion during the journey saved the life of the young Virginian. The French at Fort Le Boeuf laughed at Washington's demand that they retire from their forts along the Allegheny River. The Ohio Company had failed to realize the significance of the forks of the Ohio River, but Washington's report pointed out its strategic value, and the company now hastened to send an expedition which began to build a rude fort at this point. The French also sent a detachment of soldiers to the forks of the Ohio, who drove away the Virginians before they had completed their fort, and erected Fort Duquesne on the coveted location. Shortly afterwards, in April, 1754, Washington precipitated the French and Indian War by a petty clash with a French scouting party which he met at Great Meadows in southwestern Pennsylvania. Since the war was fought largely by British regulars, and on the Canadian border, the Southern colonies were affected only slightly by its military activities—principally by Indian attacks on their frontiers which followed the defeat of Braddock near Fort Duquesne in 1755.

The expense of a long war, however, resulted in the accumulation of an enormous imperial debt which did affect the Southern colonies. The British government after the conclusion of peace in 1763 determined to raise more revenue in the colonies in order to lighten the burdens of taxpayers at home. Thus a new policy was adopted, which in effect reorganized the loose colonial system. The British ministry under the lead of George Grenville began vigorously to enforce the trade acts, which had in some cases become dead letter laws. In 1764 the enactment of the Sugar Act seriously threatened the illegal trade of the colonies with the West Indies. One aspect of this new policy was the passage of a Stamp Act, March 22, 1765, which placed a graduated stamp duty on all legal documents, play-ing cards, newspapers, pamphlets, and even college diplomas. This tax was an innovation. Previously Parliament had enacted trade and customs laws, taxing the colonists indirectly at the seaports, but the Stamp Act levied a direct, internal tax.

The promulgation of the Stamp Act produced a tremendous repercussion in the American colonies. The first great protest against this revenue act was made in the Virginia legislature by Patrick Henry. At this time Henry was twenty-nine years old and had already acquired a reputation as a radical. Born on the Virginia frontier in Hanover County, he had developed a love of freedom and "an itch for popularity." He had not made a success in private life, for he was too lazy to study or work at a business. Failing as a country storekeeper, he acquired a smattering of law and became a lawyer, a member of "a talking profession," and a representative in the House of Burgesses. He delighted in playing the fiddle, in joking with his neighbors, and in hunting and fishing. According to Thomas Jefferson, he would hunt for weeks without changing his shirt or taking a bath, and it bored him to read a book. Nevertheless, this tall, red-headed, young man was a natural orator, who seemed to young Jefferson "to speak as Homer wrote." [5] Patrick Henry be-came a powerful figure in the Revolutionary movement because he devoted his talents as an agitator to arousing the fears of Americans that their political liberty was endangered by Parliamentary taxation of the colonies. Not an intellectual himself, he reached with his emotional oratory and slogans the great mass of Americans who did not read the newspapers or pamphlets containing the constitutional arguments of the intellectuals.

Henry was a volcanic radical in his youth and a conservative in his old age. He had gained fame as a radical in the Parson's Case of 1763, in which he maintained that the king and his Privy Council had no constitutional right to veto a law of the colonial legislature. In the Virginia legislature of 1765 he made one of the most effective speeches in the history of American oratory. Carried away by his own extemporaneous oratory he declaimed against the usurpations of the British monarch, comparing him to Caesar, Charles I, and Cromwell, although the real culprit in the attempt to tax the colonies was Parliament, which had passed the Stamp Act. A French spy who witnessed the occasion recorded that after the Speaker had called Henry to order for treasonable utterance, he made an apology for his flaming words and declared his loyalty to the Crown.[6] Later in the evening this backwoods radical was seen walking down the streets of Williamsburg clad in buckskin breeches leading a lame horse.

In addition to his bold speech, Henry introduced seven resolutions in regard to the Stamp Act. They maintained that the colonists possessed all the rights of Englishmen, that taxation without representation was a violation of the British constitution, and that the Virginia assembly alone had the right to tax the colony. His sixth and seventh resolutions declared that the colony was not bound to obey an act of Parliament taxing the colonies, and that anyone who should assert the contrary was an enemy of the colony. When these resolutions were presented to the Virginia assembly most of the members had gone home, leaving only thirty-nine of the one hundred and sixteen members present. Five of Henry's resolves were passed by narrow majorities in the rump legislature, but the radical sixth and seventh resolutions were rejected. The vote was along sectional lines, the Piedmont representatives favoring, while the aristocratic Tidewater representatives voted in the negative.

Opposition to the Stamp Act was expressed by mobs and by a Stamp Act Congress which met in October, 1765, in New York and asserted the doctrine of no taxation without representation. The colonies of North Carolina, Georgia, and Virginia, however, were unrepresented in this Congress. Petitions were sent to the king, the House of Lords, and the House of Commons asking for the repeal of the Stamp Act. The colonists found a more efficacious means of bringing about the repeal of the obnoxious measure than petition, namely, a boycott against the importation of British goods. The English merchants then forced Parliament to repeal the act, but at the same time it passed the Declaratory Act asserting the right of Parliament to legislate for the colonies "in all cases whatsoever."

In the complex influences that contributed to the growth of revolutionary feeling after 1765 economic interests played a significant but not an exclusive role. One imponderable economic motive, the desire of planters to free themselves from the incubus of debts owed to British merchants, may have had some influence in their participation in the Revolutionary movement. The planters had the usual psychology of debtors to creditors, which was intensified by their belief that the British merchants habitually fleeced them. By the time of the American Revolution the indebtedness of the colonists to their English creditors amounted to £4,000,000, of which approximately one-half was owed by Southern planters.[7]

Another important economic grievance which exacerbated the relations between England and the Southern colonies was the imperial policy in regard to western lands. The Proclamation Line of 1763 had been intended as a temporary expedient to prevent Indian warfare, but this measure was retained as a part of British policy and enforced by the Earl of Hillsborough and Lord Dartmouth, Secretaries of State for the colonies, who were hostile to westward expansion. In 1768 the British government adopted the policy of a boundary line between the settled area and the Indian country which would be changed periodically as a result of negotiation with the Indians.

The Virginia expansionists feared that the British government would yield to the pressure of groups of speculators in England and in the Northern colonies and grant huge areas of land in the West to their rivals. A group of Pennsylvania merchants and fur traders, headed by Samuel Wharton and William Trent, was urging the British authorities to make a large grant for a colony in the present state of West Virginia to be called Vandalia when the Revolution stopped their designs. In 1774 the Crown issued stringent new regulations for the sale of western land, doubling quit-rents, requiring the sale of all tracts at auction to the highest bidder, and forbidding the practice of an irregular survey to include only choice fertile lands within a tract. Also in this year the Quebec Act attached all the territory north of the Ohio River and west of Pennsylvania to the Catholic province of Quebec, reserving it as an Indian country and fur trading preserve. Thus the British government on the eve of the Revolution frustrated one of the strongest urges in American history, westward expansion.

Despite the importance of these economic factors, the main

grievance of the American colonists seems to have been political. Contrary to the economic deterministic view of twentieth century historians, the fear of the loss of political rights seems to have been uppermost in the thinking of eighteenth century Americans. Although the revived mercantilistic system of regulating trade was a source of irritation, the issue of taxation by Parliament seems to have been of more vital concern to the American colonists as a whole. In the final analysis the colonists were resolved not to submit to the new imperial policy of Great Britain after the French and Indian War which threatened their political liberty.

As early as 1760 the inhabitants of the tobacco colonies had evolved a bold and independent spirit which was the forerunner of the American Revolution. This fact was noted by the Reverend Andrew Burnaby who was traveling in Virginia and Maryland at that time. "The public or political character of the Virginians," this Englishman wrote, "corresponds with their private one: they are haughty and jealous of their liberties, impatient of restraint, and can scarcely bear the thought of being controlled by any superior power. Many of them consider the colonies as independent states, not connected with Great Britain, otherwise than by having the same common king, and being bound to her by natural affection." [8] Thus the inhabitants of the English colonies in America had imperceptibly become Americans. During the next ten years the American colonies developed more vigorously this rudimentary idea of a federal empire, in which each component should pass laws and levy taxes for itself through its own legislature. Their concept of the federal, rather than the unitary, empire was belatedly adopted by the British government in 1931 by the Statute of Westminster.

The American Revolution cannot be adequately explained without considering the growth of the colonial mind. Two profound influences had changed the mental outlook of the colonists of 1775 from the temper and point of view of their seventeenth century forefathers. They had been affected by the American environment, particularly the plantation and the American frontier, and by the European Enlightenment. The principal effect both of the frontier and of the plantation life was to intensify the natural tendency of men to resist the imposition of outside authority or intermeddling

with their affairs. Southern planters were little kings on their plantations, and they resented the intrusion of distant British authority,
which had become more efficient and meddlesome, upon the liberties
that they had previously enjoyed. The European Enlightenment
liberated their minds from excessive reverence for authority of all
kinds, particularly religious and governmental. The old patterns of
thought which had upheld authority were breaking down under the
impact of the growing scientific spirit, following the epochal discoveries of Isaac Newton. This spirit was manifest in the growth of
rationalism in religion, in the emergence of new economic doctrines
of laissez-faire, which found classic expression in Adam Smith's
The Wealth of Nations, and in the spread of the natural rights
philosophy elaborated by John Locke and Rousseau. The natural
rights philosophy taught the dignity of man, that he has certain
natural rights which must be respected by government.

The masses would probably have remained inert if they had not
been stirred to action by a well-organized and determined minority
of radicals. In Charleston, South Carolina, the most effective agitator
was Christopher Gadsden, who led the mechanic and lower classes
in the "Liberty Tree Party," although he himself belonged to the
aristocracy. Public opinion was inflamed by such dramatic episodes
as the burning of the tea ship, *Peggy Stewart,* at Annapolis, Maryland, and the Edenton (North Carolina) Tea Party, in which a group
of ladies burned their household supplies of tea to protest against
Parliamentary taxation. A powerful weapon in arousing the colonists
was the boycott of British goods, which was enforced in the local
communities by committees of safety, dominated in the Southern
colonies by planters and lawyers. Also cooperation with the
Northern radicals was advanced by committees of correspondence.

The drastic punishment of Boston after the Tea Party of December 16, 1773, crystallized the spirit of resistance in the colonies.
Virginia generously sent food to the New England city, whose
harbor had been closed until the destroyed tea had been paid for.
The indentured servant, John Harrower, noted in his diary that his
master, owner of a plantation near Fredericksburg, had donated
one hundred bushels of wheat and fifty bushels of corn to the inhabitants of Boston on this occasion. The Virginia assembly set

aside June 1, 1774, as a solemn day of fasting and prayer to protest against the punishment of Boston by the "Intolerable Acts"—a dramatic piece of propaganda to arouse the people. Lord Dunmore, the governor, dissolved the legislature for this disloyal act, but the burgesses assembled in the Apollo Room of the Raleigh Tavern at Williamsburg and summoned the first Continental Congress to meet in Philadelphia.

A clash at arms between the colonial patriots and royal troops occurred at Lexington, Massachusetts, on April 19, 1775. Two months later the Second Continental Congress appointed George Washington commander-in-chief of the Continental army. He was, in reality, an amateur, but less so than his subordinate generals, his chief of artillery, Henry Knox, for example, being a Boston bookseller, and his greatest general, Nathanael Greene, being a Rhode Island blacksmith. For over a year after the battle of Lexington the colonists fought for redress of grievances rather than for independence. On June 7, 1776, Richard Henry Lee of Virginia introduced a resolution proposing a declaration of independence. This resolution was adopted July 2, and two days later a formal Declaration of Independence written by Thomas Jefferson was accepted by a unanimous vote.

Public opinion in the Southern as well as the Northern colonies, however, was seriously divided in regard to the support of the Revolution. In Virginia there were perhaps fewer Loyalists or Tories than in any other colony and in Maryland they were also very weak. In North Carolina the Tories and the Patriots (often called Whigs) were about evenly matched, while in South Carolina and Georgia perhaps a majority of the population were hostile to the independence movement.[9] It is a significant fact that Massachusetts contributed more soldiers to the Continental army than did the five combined Southern states.[10]

Various motives explain the loyalty of Southern Tories to the British Empire. The Scottish merchants as a rule were opposed to the Revolution since it would destroy their trade connections with England. The Anglican clergy was disposed to remain loyal, because of the establishment of the Church of England in the Southern colonies and its close connection with the mother country. The "governer's set" was naturally loyal to the royal government. The *Letters from America*, written by William Eddis, secretary of Governor Robert Eden of Maryland, reflect the point of view of this group who were hostile to the revolutionary movement. Although the great planters and lawyers of the Southern colonies as a whole supported the patriotic cause, there were some who became Tories or pursued a non-committal or inactive course during the Revolution. In Maryland the most prominent Loyalist was Daniel Dulany, a brilliant lawyer, who wrote an influential pamphlet in 1765 against the Stamp Act, in which he maintained that taxation without representation was a violation of the English common law. After hostilities began, however, he became a Loyalist, and most of his property was confiscated by the Maryland Assembly. In Virginia William Byrd III, Lord Fairfax, and John Randolph, the Attorney General, were Loyalists, while Robert Carter of "Nomini Hall" took no part in the Revolution. In South Carolina some of the large planters and lawyers, such as Rawlins Lowndes, were opposed to radical measures that would lead to independence, yet they favored resistance to Parliamentary taxation. Ultimately they joined the revolutionary movement, hoping that England would make concessions and that a reconciliation would take place.

In each of the colonies there were local and special influences that operated to turn men to the Tory or the Patriot cause. Many of the inhabitants of the back country, particularly former Regulators, were disposed to remain loyal because of their hatred of the Tidewater aristocracy who had denied them equality in the colonial assemblies. The Scotch Highlanders of North Carolina remained true to their oath of allegiance to the king and fought for the British. The German Moravians of North Carolina adopted a neutral attitude in the contest. In Virginia the odious conduct of the last royal governor, Lord Dunmore, who tried to foment a servile insurrection in 1775 and who ordered the seaport of Norfolk to be burned, tended to consolidate wavering opinion behind the Patriot cause. Also, the Virginia government allowed the numerous debtors of British merchants to settle their debts by paying sums due into the state treasury in depreciated paper money. In Maryland the Catholics were led by Father John Carroll, who aided the Continental Congress in trying to enlist the support of the French Canadians, while the very wealthy planter, Charles Carroll, espoused the Whig cause and set an example to other Catholic land-owners. On the other hand, in Georgia there were several factors favoring the Loyalist side, the generosity of Parliament in giving the colony an annual subsidy of £8,000, the presence of hostile Indian tribes on the frontier, the popularity of the royal governor, Sir James Wright, and the proximity of the British province of East Florida, which could be used as a base for attack on the Georgia frontier.

The South was relatively free from the devastation of British armies until near the end of the war. Failing in the North, the British military command undertook a campaign in the South which at first was successful, resulting in the capture of the seaports of Savannah (December 29, 1778) and of Charleston (May 12, 1780). An attempt by General Horatio Gates to retrieve the American cause in the South ended in ignominious disgrace when his green troops fled from the battlefield of Camden, South Carolina. The fighting in the South often assumed the character of a civil war, Tories against Patriots. In the battle of King's Mountain on the border between North and South Carolina (October 7, 1780), a band of backwoodsmen led by Isaac Shelby, John Sevier, and William Campbell administered a decisive defeat to the Tories commanded by Colonel Patrick Ferguson and checked the British use of the Tories. After an indecisive battle at Guilford Court House, North Carolina, the British commander, Lord Cornwallis, retired to the Yorktown peninsula in Virginia. Here he was surrounded by American forces under Washington and LaFayette, as well as by a French fleet and a French army under Rochambeau. Thus trapped, the British army was forced to surrender, October 19, 1781, but the war did not end formally until the signing of the Treaty of Paris two years later.

The impact of the Revolution on the economic, social, and political life of the South was profound. In the first place, it resulted in significant changes in the distribution of land and in the dislocation of Southern agricultural staples. Certain tremendous concentrations of land, such as the Lord Baltimore estate, the Lord Fairfax estate, the Granville Tract, and the extensive holdings of Sir James Wright

in Georgia, were broken into small farms and plantations by the
confiscation of Tory property. Southern agriculture was affected
by the withdrawal of the British bounty on indigo, by the loss of the
monopoly of the British tobacco market, and by the stoppage of

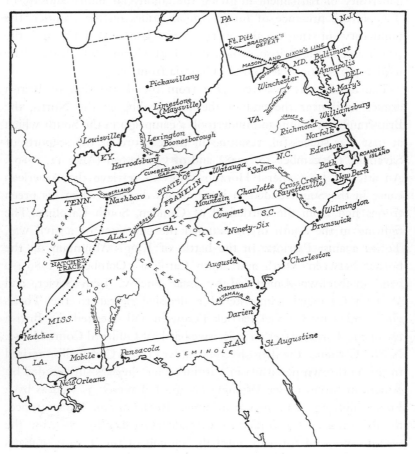

THE SOUTH IN THE EIGHTEENTH CENTURY

the trade with the British West Indies, lasting until President Jackson
secured the reopening of it in 1830. Advantages were gained by the
removal of the burden of quit-rents and by the abolition of primogeniture and entail. Primogeniture, however, did not disappear in
South Carolina until 1791.

The Southern states shared in the post-war economic depression that affected the whole nation. In order to relieve the debtor class, the states issued large quantities of paper money, especially in 1785 and 1786. In South Carolina the paper money issues were conservatively managed and they did not depreciate badly, owing partly to the Hint Club, which sent ropes as reminders to persons who would not accept the paper currency of the state. In North Carolina and Georgia the radicals triumphed over the conservatives and secured the passage of inflationary paper money bills. In North Carolina the paper currency declined to one-half the value of specie. Virginia, however, escaped the evil consequences of the paper money rage. She had paid her Revolutionary soldiers with land warrants for wild land in Kentucky, and the conservatives controlled the state.

The American Revolution stimulated a movement to eradicate slavery from the South. Not only did the natural rights philosophy of the Revolutionary period predispose men's minds to unshackling the fetters of the slaves, but the unprofitableness of slavery in the tobacco region following the Revolution created economic conditions favorable to an emancipation movement. The Southern states abolished the African slave trade during this period, Virginia in 1778, Georgia being the last, in 1798. Jefferson was the leader in his native state in urging the adoption of a plan for the gradual emancipation of the slaves. Although his advice was not followed, Virginia did pass a law in 1782 making the process of emancipating slaves by individual masters much easier. In 1784 Jefferson drew up an ordinance for the government of the unsettled Federal territory, which he presented to the Congress of the Confederation. It contained a provision abolishing slavery after the year 1800 in all the vast region of the Mississippi Valley then owned by the United States. When this measure was defeated by one vote, Jefferson lamented: "Thus we see the fate of millions unborn hanging on the tongue of one man, and Heaven was silent in that awful moment!" [11] The Negro historian W. E. B. DuBois has pointed out that the most favorable opportunity to effect the emancipation of the slaves came in the period following the Revolution before the invention of the cotton gin (1793). Nevertheless, the great opportunity of peaceful emancipation was allowed to slip by, and it never came again, for the expansion of cotton culture resuscitated the languishing institution and men's economic interests became more deeply involved in perpetuating slavery.

Social life in the Southern states was affected indirectly by the Revolution in many ways. The officers of the American army established the Society of the Cincinnati to perpetuate patriotic memories, but it was regarded by stern republicans as an aristocratic organization that should not be countenanced. Anglophobia, generated by the Revolution, continued for many years to affect American politics, and the precedent of elevating military heroes into political positions was established. The Revolutionary struggle also contributed to the spread of dueling, especially in the Southern colonies. The example of the French officers who aided the American cause was contagious in the adoption of this artificial code of honor which required men to fight duels when they thought themselves insulted or their honor impugned. After Alexander Hamilton was killed by Aaron Burr in a duel in 1804, the pernicious practice was strongly condemned by public opinion in the North and fell into disuse in that region, but in the Southern states dueling flourished until the Civil War. A humanitarian movement arose during and after the American Revolution which led to the revision of the harsh criminal codes of the colonial period. In Virginia, Jefferson, who was a student of the Italian legal reformer, Beccaria, succeeded in revising the criminal code in 1779 so that only two crimes, treason and murder, were made punishable by death.

The American Revolution had a liberating influence on the religious life of the South. The Church of England was disestablished in the Southern states, and the principle of the separation of the church and state was gradually accepted. In Virginia, Jefferson drafted a noble Statute for Religious Freedom, which was introduced into the legislature in 1779. This bill declared that "all men shall be free to profess, and by argument to maintain, their opinions in matters of religion, and that the same shall in no wise diminish, enlarge, or affect their civil capacities." It was not adopted at that time, but while Jefferson was absent as minister in France, the question was revived in 1784, when a bill was introduced to pay the teachers of the Christian religion by a general assessment on tax-

payers. This proposal was supported by a combination of Episcopalians and Presbyterians as well as by the Revolutionary leaders,
George Washington, Patrick Henry, and Richard Henry Lee. The
fight in the legislature for the principle of religious toleration and
the complete separation of church and state was led by James
Madison, who in 1786 secured the passage by the legislature of
Jefferson's famous statute. In contrast to the liberal action of the
Southern states in disestablishing the Anglican Church, the Congregational Church in Connecticut was not disestablished until 1818 and
in Massachusetts not until 1833.

The Revolution contributed to the nationalizing of the American
churches. John Wesley, the English founder of Methodism, had
opposed the American Revolution, but at the conclusion of the war
he advised a separate organization of the American church. This step
was taken at the Baltimore Conference, Christmas, 1784, when a set
of doctrines and a constitution were adopted for the new church,
which was named the Methodist Episcopal Church. Francis Asbury,
the first American bishop of the church, spread its influence over the
back country and among the poorer classes by the establishment of
the typical American institution of the Methodist circuit rider.
Despite a frail body and frequent sickness he traveled incessantly on
horseback to preach to touchingly ignorant and naive people in the
South and West, who gathered to hear him in barns, in the forests,
and in humble log cabins, as well as in the more formal church buildings. His journal shows that he was imbued with the booster spirit.
When he died in 1816 he had traveled approximately three hundred thousand miles during his religious crusade, had preached more
than sixteen thousand sermons, and had ordained at least four
thousand ministers.

In contrast to English practice, but following the precedent of the
colonial charters, all the colonies adopted written constitutions during the Revolution. South Carolina was the first Southern state to
draw up a constitution, in March, 1776, while Georgia was the last,
in February, 1777. In framing these fundamental laws, Maryland,
Virginia, and South Carolina were firmly controlled by the conservatives. The new constitutions were hastily drawn up by a few
dominant personalities such as George Mason in Virginia, Samuel

Chase, Charles Carroll, and William Paca in Maryland, Willie Jones and Richard Caswell in North Carolina, and John Rutledge in South Carolina. Furthermore, they were not submitted to the people for ratification.

The Revolution did not disturb seriously the power of the colonial aristocracy. In no case was free manhood suffrage granted by the new constitutions of the Southern states. In Maryland and South Carolina a property qualification of fifty acres of land, in Virginia twenty-five acres of settled land or fifty acres of unsettled, was required of all voters; in North Carolina and Georgia all taxpayers were permitted to vote. Relatively high property qualifications were imposed on members of the legislature and state officials. Even in one of the most radical of the Southern states, North Carolina, a state senator had to own three hundred acres of land, while the conservative constitution of Maryland prescribed a property qualification for senators of £1,000, and South Carolina, the most aristocratic of the states, required a senator to own an estate worth £2,000. Members of the lower house of the legislature had to be substantial citizens, owning £500 of property in Maryland, £250 in Georgia, and one hundred acres in North Carolina. The governor of South Carolina had to be a patrician worth £10,000 or more, but in North Carolina the qualification was only £1,000. In addition to these property qualifications on voting and office-holding, the colonial aristocracy perpetuated its power by arranging representation in the legislature so that the wealthy slave-owning Tidewater outvoted the Piedmont with its larger population of poorer freemen.[12]

The Revolutionary constitutions reflected the experience of the colonists in their struggle with the royal governors. The powers of the governors were severely curbed by depriving them of the veto power, the authority to summon or dissolve the legislature, and most of the appointive power. In South Carolina the chief executive was called President until 1779 when the title governor was substituted. Although the principle of separation of the executive, legislative, and judicial powers was universally held in the states, the legislature was given excessive authority over the government. Not only did it exercise many of the executive functions, such as the appointive power, but it also elected the governor and the judges. The lower house of the legislature was chosen by a minority of the people in annual elections, while the upper house was elected by popular vote only in Virginia and North Carolina. In Maryland the senators were chosen by an electoral college, in South Carolina by the lower house, and in Georgia there was no upper house. Georgia and South Carolina represented the extremes of government in the Southern states, South Carolina having the most aristocratic frame of government, and Georgia the most democratic form. Only in Georgia were the judges selected by popular vote, and its radical unicameral legislature had no parallel in the United States, save the eccentric constitution of Pennsylvania. The early state constitutions revealed a distrust of democracy and of executive authority, a tender regard for the rights of property, and were in many respects at variance with the philosophy of the Declaration of Independence.

Nevertheless, the Revolutionary constitutions made a long step toward the ideal of human liberty in the incorporation of bills of rights. The first and most important of these statements of personal liberties was the Declaration of Rights drafted by George Mason of "Gunston Hall" and adopted June 12, 1776, as a part of the Virginia constitution. It served as a model for other states, and some of its doctrines were incorporated three weeks later in Jefferson's Declaration of Independence. These bills of rights were based on the concept of the limited state, derived from a social compact. The Virginia Declaration of Rights declared that men are "by nature equally free and independent" and that they have certain natural and inalienable rights which governments should respect. These bills of rights preserved both the ancient and recently acquired liberties of Englishmen, such as the rights of jury trial, indictment by a grand jury, freedom from excessive bail or from cruel and unusual punishments or arbitrary arrests, the right of petition, freedom of speech and of the press, and religious toleration. Included in these documents were the principles of the separation of church and state and the subordination of the military to the civil government. The preservation of civil liberties by a written constitution is one of the most enduring achievements of the Revolutionary period. Although the natural rights theory which underlay the bills of rights has been discredited, the doctrine of the free individual, the assertion of the dignity of American citizens, found in these documents, remains as a precious heritage of our Revolutionary past.

Citations

1. JAMES GLEN, *A Description of South Carolina* (London, 1761), 48.
2. L. H. GIPSON, *The British Empire before the American Revolution* (Caldwell, Idaho, and New York, 1936–1946), VI, 9.
3. J. WILLIAMS, "English Mercantilism and Carolina Naval Stores, 1705–1776," *Journal of Southern History*, I (May, 1935), 169–185.
4. L. A. HARPER, "The Effect of the Navigation Acts on the Thirteen Colonies," *The Era of the American Revolution*, edited by R. B. Morris (New York, 1939), 5.
5. A. A. LIPSCOMB and A. A. BERGH, *The Writings of Thomas Jefferson* (Washington, 1903), I, 5, 12; XIV, 341.
6. "Journal of a French Traveller in the Colonies, 1765," *American Historical Review*, XXVI (July, 1921), 745.
7. J. C. MILLER, *Origins of the American Revolution* (Boston, 1943), 15.
8. ANDREW BURNABY, *Travels through the Middle Settlements in North-America in the Years 1759 and 1760* (London, 1775), 24.
9. R. O. DeMOND, *The Loyalists in North Carolina during the Revolution* (Durham, 1940), 60–61.
10. LORENZO SABINE, *The American Loyalists* (Boston, 1847), 31.
11. BERNARD MAYO (ed.), *Jefferson Himself* (Boston, 1942), 109.
12. FLETCHER M. GREEN, *Constitutional Development in the South Atlantic States, 1776–1860* (Chapel Hill, 1930) is a pioneer work in the realistic study of southern constitutional history.

CHAPTER V

Through the Cumberland Gap

Lay down, boys, an' take a little nap,
Fourteen miles to the Cum-ber-land Gap.

The first white man in Cumberland Gap
Was Doctor Walker, an English chap.

Daniel Boone on Pinnacle Rock,
He killed Indians with an old flintlock.

I've got a woman in Cumberland Gap
She's got a boy that calls me "pap."

Lay down, boys, an' take a little nap,
They're all raisin' Hell in Cumberland Gap.

CUMBERLAND GAP has the romantic interest in the history of the American frontier that the pass of Thermopylae had in ancient Greece. It was the scene of conflicts between Indians and frontiersmen and it was the funnel through which the westward movement passed. Located at the point where the three states of Virginia, Kentucky, and Tennessee meet, it was discovered in 1674 by an illiterate frontiersman, Gabriel Arther, who had been sent to the Cherokee country by Abraham Wood, the Indian trader located at the falls of the Appomattox (present day Petersburg). In 1750 the pass was rediscovered and named by Dr. Thomas Walker of Virginia, agent of the Loyal Land Company, who built a cabin near Barbourville, Kentucky. Through this famous rift in the mountains ran the Great Warrior Path which was used by the Shawnee and Iroquois Indians to attack the southern tribes. "Stand at Cumberland Gap," wrote Frederick Jackson Turner in his epochal essay on the significance of the frontier in American history, "and watch the procession of civilization, marching single file—the buffalo following the trail to the salt springs, the Indian, the fur-trader and hunter, the cattle-raiser, the pioneer farmer—and the frontier has passed by." [1]

Thus, Turner stated his great generalization that has had such a fruitful influence on the interpretation of American history. He conceived of the frontier not only as a region of thin population, the edge of settlement, a line moving westward, but also as a sociological process whereby society in America was continually evolving from more primitive stages into higher and more complex forms. The first frontier of the explorer and hunter was followed by the second stage of evolution, the frontier of the fur trader; then came the frontier of the cattle pens, at times supplemented by the mining frontier; agricultural advance into the lonely wilderness was led by the pioneer farmer with his axe on his shoulder; and finally the substantial farmer firmly established civilization with his school and church. Turner believed that the frontier left a strong imprint on American society as it moved westward, like the terminal moraines of a retreating glacier. The American frontier converted the European settler into an American and developed distinctive American qualities, such as individualism, a love of democracy, resourcefulness and versatility, optimism, a feeling of nationalism, and a curious blend of materialism and idealism. The frontier, he believed, offered an escape for disappointed or underprivileged persons in the East, a safety valve for labor in the older part of the country.

The Turner frontier thesis has been recently attacked as presenting too great a simplification of American history. [2] The revisionists have pointed out that Turner's theory was primarily geographic determinism, leaving very little freedom to the individual personality, and that it failed to take account sufficiently of cultural ideas and institutions brought from Europe. Turner's safety valve thesis particularly has been severely attacked, since few laborers in the eastern cities had either the skill needed to cope with the wilderness or the money to escape from bad laboring conditions to the frontier. Furthermore, the fact that emigration to the West was greatest during boom periods and declined during periods of depression throws serious doubts on the validity of the safety valve theory. In his

SLAVE DECK OF THE BARK, "WILDFIRE"

Note the filed teeth of the Africans. This ship, engaged in smuggling slaves, was captured by the U. S. Navy and brought to Key West, Florida, April 30, 1860. (From a daguerreotype, published in *Harpers' Weekly*, June 2, 1860.)

PICKING COTTON IN SOUTH CAROLINA
(Courtesy of U. S. Forest Service.)

CUTTING SUGAR CANE IN LOUISIANA
(Courtesy of U. S. Department of Agriculture.)

analysis of the various stages of the frontier he failed to appreciate the significant role of the land speculator and the overlapping of frontiers. Even Turner's originality has been denied recently by scholars who observe that his basic ideas were derived from census officials, especially Francis A. Walker, Superintendent of the Census of 1870, and Henry Gannett, and from his teachers at the University of Wisconsin. Despite these criticisms, Turner's frontier thesis has great value in explaining social evolution in the South, where the frontier process was modified and colored by the presence of Negro slavery. Turner's ideas are especially fruitful in pointing the way to the study of regionalism, or sectionalism, in American history, which underlies so much of American politics. He believed that the history of the nation could be understood only by studying the emergence of sections and the way they acted, illustrating their behavior by various maps. Thus he has furnished an invaluable tool for the historian of the South.

The frontiersman encountered a cordon of Indian tribes on the western frontier whose land he coveted and with whom traffic in furs and deerskins brought risky profits. The domain of the Algonkin family, containing many tribes who were linguistically related, extended from Canada far into the Carolinas. In eastern North Carolina, surrounded by Algonkins, was a mysterious island of Iroquois stock, the Tuscarora. This tribe was defeated in a war with the whites in 1713 and shortly thereafter emigrated to New York to join the League of Five Nations. The Cherokee, who inhabited the hill country and mountains of the Carolinas, Georgia, and Tennessee, also spoke an Iroquoian language. They were perhaps the finest of eastern Indians, splendid physical specimens, much taller than the neighboring Creeks, brave, dignified, and honest. This intelligent and warlike Indian nation, numbering approximately fifteen thousand people in colonial times, dwelt in circular cabins of peeled logs, grouped in about sixty towns, of which Echota and Great Tellico in eastern Tennessee were the leading tribal centers.

Below the Cherokee and to the westward were a group of tribes that belonged to the Muskhogean family, the Creeks in Georgia and Alabama, the Seminole in Florida, the Choctaw in Mississippi, and the Chickasaw in northern Mississippi. The Creeks were the most numerous of the Southern tribes, numbering at the height of their power twenty-five thousand people. The Choctaw and Chickasaw pursued a fierce warfare against each other, encouraged by their white allies, the French and the English. There were remnants also in the colonial South of its oldest Indian inhabitants, the Siouan family, the main body of which had retreated across the Mississippi River to the Great Plains: the Catawba tribe, who dwelt along the river of that name in North and South Carolina, the Santee, Congaree, and Wateree tribes in South Carolina, and the Biloxi in southern Mississippi. In 1670 the Catawba were estimated to include seven thousand people, but so hated were they by the other tribes, who waged ceaseless war on them, that by the time of the Revolution, they had dwindled to five hundred people.

The trade with the Southern Indians in the colonial period was based first at Charleston, South Carolina, and later at Augusta, Georgia. Two or three hundred traders, many of them Scotsmen, were engaged in this lucrative, but risky commerce. They lived in the Indian villages and frequently married Indian women. The Indian maids, as William Byrd II discovered, during a trip into the hinterland of North Carolina, anointed their heads with bear grease which became rancid and smelled to high heaven. The white traders, dwelling remote from the restraints of civilized life, were noted for their immoral characters. Although they often provoked wars, they also at times acted as a tranquillizing influence. Their most difficult problem was the judicious use of credit, for if their customers were allowed to accumulate a large burden of debt, they would be tempted to liquidate the debts by murdering the traders.

Very few beaver skins were obtained in the trade with the Southern Indians, but vast quantities of deerskins were secured by barter. Bundles of the latter formed the main export of Charleston until the rise of the rice plantations in the eighteenth century. At the peak of the trade, in 1748, approximately 160,000 deerskins were sent from South Carolina to England. The profits of this Indian commerce were absorbed largely by the Charleston merchants, who outfitted the traders and handled the export of the skins. This traffic has left its imprint on American colloquial language. The slang word used today, "a buck" for a dollar, dates from frontier days when a buckskin, the hide of a male deer, was recognized as a standard unit of exchange or of current money.

Trade with the whites revolutionized the habits of the Indians and deprived them of their old independence. Giving up the use of the bow and arrow, they came to depend on the white man for guns, powder, and lead. They needed the assistance of blacksmiths and gunsmiths, and they required such articles as cloth, needles, brass kettles, axes, hoes, mirrors, and even tobacco and rum. These goods were carried by pack horses along paths through the woods to the Indian villages. The English traders could procure manufactured goods more cheaply than their French and Spanish rivals, and deerskins fortunately brought a better price in England than in either France or Spain. Consequently the English traders could pay better prices for skins and furs than could their Latin rivals. Toward the middle of the eighteenth century the South Carolina traders organized the Sphynx Company, in which Governor Glen was a partner, in order to break into the monopoly of the French over the Choctaw trade. Despite their ability to offer higher prices for deerskins, this attempt was a failure because the French suppressed the faction of the Choctaw, led by Red Shoe, who were disposed to trade with the English. The constant demand of the traders for hides led to an enormous slaughter of deer in the Southern forests comparable to the destruction of the buffalo herds on the great plains of the West.

A dark phase of the Carolina Indian trade was the traffic in Indian slaves. In 1708 there were in South Carolina fourteen hundred Indian slaves and only twenty-nine hundred Negro slaves. The Indians, however, made poor servants and were worth only one-half the price of black slaves. Accordingly, it became a policy of Carolinians to sell Indian captives to New Englanders, including Puritan preachers, or to dispose of them in the West Indies. After Indian wars the captives constituted a valuable booty, frequently sold as slaves in these remote markets.

To control Indian relations with the whites, the British government created a Superintendent of Indian Affairs for the southern frontier. From 1762 to 1779 John Stuart served in this position, seeking to preserve peace, regulating the fur trade, and negotiating treaties for the cession of land. Stuart pushed the western limit of settlement far beyond the mountains by obtaining land cessions from the Indians by the Treaty of Hard Labor in 1768 and two years later by the Treaty of Lochaber.

The task of preserving stable relations with the Indians was rendered difficult by the encroachment of white settlers on their hunting grounds and by the presence of white renegades or diplomatic agents of foreign powers residing among them. Some of these adventurers, such as Christian Priber and Alexander Arbuthnot of a later period, were apparently sincere friends of the Indians who tried to protect their interests from unscrupulous whites. Priber, a German who had a naive conception of "the noble red man," lived among the Cherokee, studied their language, adopted their dress and customs, and sought to establish a Utopian socialist republic among them which embraced not merely common ownership of land, but also common ownership of wives and children. His activities as "prime minister" caused his arrest by the Georgians, and he died in 1743 a prisoner of James Oglethorpe. Unlike the altruistic motives of Priber, the impulses that sent William Augustus Bowles, a native of Maryland, an actor, a painter, and a British army officer, to intrigue among the Creek Indians, were the love of adventure and the lust for profits. Elected a Creek chief, he launched an ambitious project of establishing free ports on the Gulf of Mexico, flying the Creek flag. His leadership in plundering raids of the Creeks resulted in his arrest in Florida by the Spaniards, who imprisoned him in Morro Castle at Havana, where he died in 1805.

The most significant of these adventurers was the quarter-breed, Alexander McGillivray. Son of a Scotch trader, he was educated in Charleston by his uncle, a Presbyterian minister. Returning to live among the Creeks, he became their most influential chief. By playing the English, the Spanish, and the American governments against each other, he increased his own fortunes and those of the Creek tribes. On his plantation by the Coosa River, he employed gangs of Negro slaves and maintained separate houses for his many wives. His wealth was derived in part from his connection as "sleeping partner" with the Scottish firm of Panton, Leslie, and Co., who had obtained a monopoly of the Creek trade. So astute a diplomat was he, that at the time he was drawing a pension from Spain, he was also wearing the gaudy uniform of an officer of the American army and collecting a salary from the United States government. Nevertheless, until his death in 1793, he was a valuable agent in keeping the Creeks at peace with their white neighbors.

Control over the Indians on the border between Florida and the United States was exerted by Spain through the powerful Scottish trading firm of Panton, Leslie, and Co., which had been organized during the American Revolution by loyalists from Georgia. William Augustus Bowles tried to break its monopoly of trade with those Indians within the Spanish sphere of influence. In two plundering expeditions (1795 and 1802), he led bands of Creeks who robbed the company of goods worth $30,000. The Indians of the Southern border became dependent on the company for vital supplies of manufactured goods, ammunition, and weapons, for which they were held deeply in debt. During the decades of the 1790's and the early 1800's the company tried to collect these debts by securing the cession of large tracts of land. While Jefferson was President the Federal government entered into collusion with the firm, now headed by John Forbes, who agreed to put pressure on the Indians to sell valuable lands on the Mississippi River in return for the aid of the government in collecting the company's bad debts. This partnership was too powerful for the Indians to resist, but it revealed an unscrupulous lust on the part of Jefferson for acquiring land for his country.[3]

At the time of the Revolution, Kentucky, though teeming with wild game, was unoccupied by any Indian tribe. The Shawnee, an Algonkin tribe, had a famous trading village, Eskippakithiki, in central Kentucky near Winchester, but they had abandoned it in 1754. The Iroquois, with the aid of the white man's guns, prevented this beautiful country from being appropriated by any tribe. When the Long Hunters and Daniel Boone entered Kentucky it was indeed a debatable land between the northern and southern tribes, "the dark and bloody ground."

Around the name of Daniel Boone has grown a mighty legend, which has magnified the exploits and the importance of this worthy pioneer. The myth-making process began with the publication in 1784 of John Filson's *Discovery, Settlement, and Present State of*

Kentucke. Filson was a schoolmaster and Kentucky's first historian, who claimed to have preserved in this volume's Boone's autobiography, but who used such stilted language and embroidered the plain narrative of the old frontiersman to such an extent that his work is unreliable. John James Audubon also contributed to the Boone myth by his anecdotes and his description of the hero as gigantic in size. Actually, Boone was of medium height, although extraordinarily agile and muscular. The only authentic picture of him was painted by Chester Harding in 1819, the year before Boone died, when he was a hale old man of eighty-five years. He had mild blue eyes, and in young manhood light hair and yellow eyebrows, a fine forehead, and a Roman nose. He had a passion for the untrammeled life of the wilderness, and in association with "civilized" men, he was unworldly. Pleasant, quiet-spoken, and free from the frontier vices, he was distinguished by a remarkable serenity of mind.

The great frontiersman Daniel Boone was born in 1734 near Reading, Pennsylvania, into a Quaker family who engaged in weaving, the trade of blacksmith, and farming. In 1751 they emigrated to the Yadkin Valley in the back country of North Carolina, where at Joppa graveyard in Davie County is the grave of Squire Boone, Daniel's father. The young "Nimrod of the Yadkin" took part in the Braddock expedition during the French and Indian War, not as a fighter, but as a teamster and blacksmith. In 1765 he visited Pensacola, Florida, and thought of settling there, but his wife refused to move. Although his spelling and grammar were semi-literate, he became highly skilled in the ways of the woods and in the use of his flintlock rifle. He acquired such an accurate knowledge of Indian character and warfare that he could "think Indian."

The Boone myth represents its hero as the first explorer of Kentucky, and also as the first white man to plant a settlement in Kentucky. Neither of these claims is true. Boone was only one of a considerable number of explorers and hunters who visited Kentucky and Tennessee before the region was settled. In the decade of the 1760's the Long Hunters, or groups of men who hunted for considerable periods of time in the western wilderness, had traversed a large part of Kentucky and Tennessee and had named many of the natural features of the country. Indeed, Boone was told of "Kaintuck," a paradise for hunters, by John Finley, a Pennsylvania fur trader who had hunted in that region. He first met Finley in the Braddock campaign, but in the winter of 1768–69 Finley wandered into the Yadkin Valley as a peddler and fired Boone's imagination by his narrative of Kentucky. Boone was desperately poor at this time, and he welcomed an opportunity to recruit his fortunes by a trip into this fabulous hunting ground for peltry and deerskins, which sold for a dollar a skin. Piloted by Finley, he and several associates in the spring of 1769 passed through the Cumberland Gap into Kentucky, where they collected many deerskins and beaver furs. In the winter of 1770 Boone spent three months living alone in the wilderness of Kentucky, but he found this dangerous life exhilarating. Although he and his brother Squire, who had joined him, gathered a valuable supply of furs, they were robbed by a band of Cherokee as they were returning home.

In September, 1773, Boone led a party of frontiersmen and their families to plant a settlement in this fabulous land. The expedition was attacked by Indians in Powell's Valley near Cumberland Gap, during which Boone's eldest son was killed, and the group became so discouraged that they returned home. As a result of this disaster, the first white man to accomplish a settlement in Kentucky was not Boone but James Harrod of Pennsylvania, who in 1774 founded Harrodsburg in central Kentucky. The outbreak of Lord Dunmore's War caused the temporary abandonment of the little settlement, but it was reoccupied the next year.

The Boone myth also neglects the important role of Judge Richard Henderson in the settlement of Kentucky. Henderson was a wealthy aristocrat, member of a law firm of Salisbury, North Carolina, who was an insatiable land speculator. In 1774 he formed the Transylvania Company to buy the Indian claims to the rich lands of Kentucky between the Cumberland and Kentucky rivers. In the following year he assembled more than a thousand Cherokee at Sycamore Shoals on the Watauga River (in northeastern Tennessee) and purchased from them by treaty their shadowy claim to Kentucky as well as a path from Long Island in the Holston River to the Cumberland Gap. Although they were given £10,000 worth of trading goods, the sale was vehemently opposed by a faction led by

Dragging Canoe and Groundhog-Sausage. Finally, the white men won over the fickle savages with the aid of the friendly chief Little Carpenter. It is doubtful whether the Cherokee could have given a valid title to this area of wild land, which they did not occupy. Furthermore, the right of the Transylvania Company to purchase this huge tract of land between the Kentucky and Cumberland rivers from the Indians without a Crown grant was highly dubious.

In the spring of 1775 Boone, as an employee of the Transylvania Company, with thirty axemen blazed Boone's Trace which became a part of the Wilderness Road through the Cumberland Gap to the Bluegrass region of Kentucky. On the Kentucky River he founded the pioneer settlement of Boonesborough. A few weeks later Judge Richard Henderson led another contingent of settlers to this capital of Transylvania. In May, 1775, Henderson summoned a legislature to meet under a gigantic elm at Boonesborough, which drew up a bill of rights guaranteeing religious liberty and a democratic form of government. Henderson and his associates conceived of the Transylvania colony as a proprietary colony like Maryland. They hoped to make lucrative profits from the sale of land and from charging an annual quit-rent of two shillings for each hundred acres.

The grandiose plans of the Transylvania proprietors were thwarted by the independent spirit of the frontiersmen who had settled at various stations in Kentucky. The resistance movement to the proprietorship was initiated by the men of Harrodsburg, who were urged to bold action by George Rogers Clark. This tall red-headed adventurer, who was born near Charlottesville, Virginia, the son of a planter, was engaged in surveying in Kentucky at the time. In 1776 he and another delegate were selected by the people of Harrodsburg to carry a petition to the Virginia government protesting against the claims of Henderson and his partners and asking to be incorporated into Virginia. After a journey of incredible hardships and peril along the Wilderness Road he arrived at Williamsburg. His mission was eminently successful, for the Virginia authorities sent a large supply of powder to Kentucky and in December, 1776, created the county of Kentucky, embracing all the scattered settlements in this vast area. Thus the ambitious project of the state of Transylvania collapsed, but Henderson was compensated by a grant of 200,000 acres of land at the mouth of the Green River, where the town of Henderson stands today.

Daniel Boone's later career in Kentucky demonstrated that shrewdness in woodcraft and Indian warfare did not fit a man for coping with the complexities of a more civilized society. Shortly after his founding of Boonesborough he graduated from hunter and explorer to frontier surveyor. The Kentucky land system became a mass of conflicting and overlapping claims, because of the loose and unsystematic surveys which were often based on the location of trees or other temporary landmarks. Boone took out patents for numerous tracts of land ranging from four hundred acres to ten thousand. Unfortunately he failed to follow the proper legal procedure in recording his titles, so that his land was taken away from him by a series of ejection suits. For a while he became a tavern keeper and merchant at Limestone (Maysville), the chief gateway to Kentucky from the north. He was also appointed a justice of the peace and represented Fayette County in the Virginia legislature. This master of woodcraft was robbed of $20,000 as he slept in a tavern during a journey to Richmond in 1780 to purchase land warrants for himself and neighbors. Disgusted with his failures, the loss of land, and the disappearance of the old freedom of the frontier as a result of the growth of population, he abandoned Kentucky in 1788 and lived in the valley of the Great Kanawha River. Ten years later he removed to the Femme Osage Creek in eastern Missouri. Here he was granted a thousand arpents of land by the Spanish authorities, became a syndic, or official, and went on long hunts for bear and deer. He enjoyed a serene old age, dying in 1820, but not before he had made a last visit to Kentucky to pay his old debts. His body was later brought back to the scene of his early exploits and interred at Frankfort on the banks of the Kentucky River.

During the course of the American Revolution the Kentucky settlements were forced to defend themselves from formidable Indian attacks. In addition to Boonesborough, there had developed a number of isolated little settlements such as Harrodsburg, Logan's Fort, Bryan's Station, Limestone on the Ohio River, and Lexington, which was named by the frontiersmen after they had received news of the battle of Lexington in far-off Massachusetts. These settlements were protected from Indian attacks by palisades built around the clusters of cabins, with block houses at the four corners of the enclosure. Brave Indian fighters and land seekers, such as George Rogers Clark, Simon Kenton, the Todds, and the Calloways, kept Kentucky from being abandoned as a result of the Indian menace.

Indian attacks on the Kentucky frontier during the Revolution were instigated by the commandant at Detroit, Governor Henry Hamilton, called the "Hair Buyer" by his savage allies. In January, 1778, Boone and a party of frontiersmen were engaged in boiling salt water from the springs of the Lower Blue Licks in huge kettles when they were surprised by a band of Indians and Boone was captured. The captives were taken to the Shawnee village of Little Chillicothe in Ohio, where Boone was adopted as a member of the family of the chief, Black Fish. However, the skilled frontiersman managed to escape from his captivity and to reach Boonesborough in time to warn settlers to strengthen the fortifications and prepare for an attack. Early in September, 1778, Black Fish appeared before Boonesborough with four hundred warriors including some forty French-Canadians. Finding the inhabitants alert, they laid siege unsuccessfully to the palisaded village for nine days, a record for Indian constancy in continuing a siege.

In August, 1782, occurred the darkest hour in Kentucky's struggle to survive Indian warfare. A band of braves, led by British officers and including the famous renegade Simon Girty, attacked Bryan's Station, five miles from Lexington, but were repulsed. The frontiersmen were so elated over this success that a force of one hundred and eighty-two men under Colonel John Todd set out in pursuit of the retiring enemy. When they reached the Licking River, in northern Kentucky, Boone and other experienced frontiersmen advised caution and waiting for reinforcements, but a dare-devil spirit led to an impetuous charge across the river. Here near the Blue Lick Springs the main body of the Indians were lying in ambush. The Kentuckians fought bravely but were badly defeated and left seventy of their number dead on the field of battle.

The most effective method of protecting the Kentucky frontier was to capture the Illinois country and its chief military post, Detroit, the source of instigation and of supply to hostile Indians. Such a plan was carried out by George Rogers Clark in a bold campaign during 1778–79. Commissioned by Governor Patrick Henry and given £1,200 of depreciated paper money, he gathered a little army of 175 men at his rendezvous and base of operations on Corn Island near the site of Louisville. He was accompanied from Fort Pitt down the Ohio River by thirteen families in flatboats who founded at the falls of the river the future city of Louisville. In a thrilling campaign of surprise and bold initiative he captured the Creole towns of Kaskaskia, Cahokia, and Vincennes. He took as prisoner the British lieutenant governor of the Northwest, Lord Henry Hamilton, who has left a fascinating journal of his experiences as he he was conducted by an armed guard, in imminent peril of being mobbed, along the Wilderness Road to the jail at Williamsburg, Virginia.⁴ This conquest of the Northwest country strengthened the claim of the United States during the negotiation of the Treaty of Paris to this region and to the Mississippi River as our western boundary. The apogee of Clark's life was attained in the Revolutionary War, when he was less than thirty years old, but his later career was a sad anti-climax. Virginia voted him two swords but failed to pay him for his services and expenditures in the conquest of the Northwest. Finally settling at Louisville, he drank to excess and died in 1818, a morose and frustrated hero of the frontier.

Throughout the Revolution population continued to flow into Kentucky along the Wilderness Road from Cumberland Gap to Louisville on the Ohio River, passing through the little frontier settlements of Logan's Station (Stanford), Danville, and Harrodsburg. The Wilderness Road was fed by the Great Valley Road which followed the Indian warpath down the Shenandoah and Holston valleys to Cumberland Gap. Hundreds of pioneers entering Kentucky were scalped by the Indians and this pathway through the Cumberland Gap was bloody and dangerous indeed until Colonel William Whitley of "Sportsman Hill" in 1794 led a punitive expedition against the Chickamauga Indians. Two years before this smashing blow against the Indians the old pack trail had been widened into a wagon road as a result of the effort of Kentucky's first governor, Isaac Shelby.

Along the Wilderness Road in 1796 came Moses Austin, famous in connection with the colonization of Texas, who described the poverty-stricken procession of humanity he passed, some of them barefoot and ragged, seeking the Promised Land:

Ask these Pilgrims what they expect when they git to Kentuckey the Answer is Land. have you any. No, but I expect I can git it. have you any thing to pay for land, No. did you Ever see the Country. No but Every Body says its good land. can any thing be more Absurd than the Conduct of man, here is hundreds Travelling hundreds of Miles, they Know not for what Nor Whither, except its to Kentuckey, passing land almost as good and easy obtain, the Proprietors of which would gladly give on any terms, but it will not do its not Kentuckey its not the Promis.d land its not the goodly inheratence the Land of Milk and Honey. and when arriv.d at this Heaven in Idea what do they find? a goodly land I will allow but to them forbiden Land. exhausted and worn down with distress and disappointment they are at last Oblig.d to become hewers of wood and Drawers of water.[5]

This seeking of the Promised Land was the essence of the restless spirit of the American pioneer. Elizabeth Madox Roberts in one of the finest of American historical novels, *The Great Meadow,* has portrayed this magnification in the minds of the home-seekers of "Caintuck," the lush land, with "soil as rich as cream," the wild plum in bloom, the game at the salt licks, and the green, velvety meadows.

The frontiersmen who settled the trans-Appalachian region were not a homogeneous group. The majority came from the Piedmont and Great Valley region and were humble farmers, "cabin and corn patch men." There were some pioneers, like Daniel Boone who left the old settlements in imminent danger of being imprisoned for debt, or like Simon Kenton, the famous scout, who fled from Virginia to escape the law after he had brutally beaten a rival suitor. Others were speculators, or foreign immigrants, or aristocrats like Colonel David Meade who sent his slaves ahead from Old Virginia to prepare a plantation for the removal of his family. Near Lexington in the Bluegrass he developed one of the most famous plantations in Kentucky, "Chaumiere du Prairie." In Kentucky and Tennessee the frontiersmen encountered tremendous canebrakes, particularly in the river bottoms, whose leaves prevented their cattle from starving and nourished the bears that furnished meat for the family. Contrary to the common misconception, the frontiersmen frequently suffered from ill health, particularly from diseases which have practically

disappeared or have greatly diminished in our era, such as malaria
or ague, the milk sickness, smallpox, scalded feet, and rheumatism.
The milk sickness, caused by drinking the milk of cows that had
eaten of the white snakeroot, killed Nancy Hanks, the mother of
Lincoln. The speech of the frontiersmen was picturesque and earthy,
redolent of their life in the wilderness, containing such phrases as
"playing possum," "I'm stumped," "the latchstring hangs out," "log-
rolling," and "he won't do to tie to," which have survived in the
American idiom.[6]

In the conquest of the Southern frontier, the American axe played
a decisive role which has hardly been noticed by historians. The
settlers of the Tidewater had brought with them an axe of ancient
Roman design, weighing about three pounds, with wide flaring
blade, lacking a pounding head, and held by a long straight handle.
By 1740, however, the "American axe" had been evolved, having a
blunt head, weighing up to seven pounds, and perfectly balanced.
The "Kentucky Long Eye" with a blade 4¾ inches wide was popular
in the Coastal Plain in the 1830's while in the Piedmont the "Kentucky Small Eye" was the "very pattern wanted." Country blacksmiths in the interior and Negro artisans on the plantations fash-
ioned rough axes, but after the frontier had passed, many small
farmers purchased their axes from merchants in the towns at the fall
line, who secured them during a yearly trip to New York or from
seaport towns like Charleston. An enterprising agent of a Yankee
axe company wrote to his employer that in the back country, where
the population was chiefly white, superior axes were appreciated, but
in the slaveholding districts "the Slave holders accustom themselves
to considering any tool good enough for a Negro to use and spoil." [7]

In 1769 the spearhead of the westward movement had penetrated
the rugged mountains in the extreme northeastern corner of Tennessee, where land seekers from Virginia had founded a settlement in
the Watauga Valley. The pioneers of this new frontier had come
largely from the Piedmont, an area called by Professor Turner, "the
Old West," where they had learned much of frontier skill. To this
remote corner of the Southern frontier also had emigrated some of
the Regulators after their defeat at the battle of Alamance. When
North Carolina ignored the petition of the settlers of the Watauga

Valley to establish a local government for them, they formed the Watauga Association (in 1772 or 1773) creating a frontier democracy. This frame of government established a legislature of thirteen members, one from each little fort or palisaded settlement. Belatedly, in 1776, North Carolina incorporated the Watauga settlement, including the whole future state of Tennessee, into Washington County.

The two most forceful leaders in the rude settlements of Tennessee were James Robertson and John Sevier. Robertson, a closemouthed, uneducated, but fearless frontiersman of Scotch-Irish descent, arrived in 1770 from Wake County, North Carolina. Sevier was born and reared in the Shenandoah Valley of Virginia, where he matured rapidly and married at the age of seventeen. Tall, handsome, debonair, he was the cavalier type in this rough wilderness environment. Indeed, he was one of the few cultivated men on the frontier. He combined a gift for making friends and for diplomacy with the virile fighting qualities which made "Nolichucky Jack" a terror to the Cherokee on the warpath.

After Sevier had superseded the quiet Robertson as the leader of the Watauga settlement, Robertson moved to a new frontier, the Nashville limestone basin. In the winter of 1779–80 he led a group of pioneers overland to the French Lick in the Cumberland valley where he founded Nashborough (Nashville). In this undertaking he was the agent of Richard Henderson, the ambitious land speculator. Another party, led by Colonel John Donelson, including his daughter, Rachel, the future wife of Andrew Jackson, went down the Tennessee River by flatboats, up the Ohio, and then up the Cumberland River to Nashville. They arrived at this frontier settlement in the winter of 1780, after an Odyssey of nearly a thousand miles of peril from Indian ambuscades and water hazards.

The early history of Tennessee was strongly colored by the activity of powerful land speculators. A group of land grabbers, headed by William Blount, persuaded North Carolina's legislature in 1784 to cede her western lands to the Congress of the Confederation in order to secure protection from the Indians for prospective settlers on their vast holdings. Later in the same year, this act of cession was repealed by a new legislature. In the interval, the people of east Tennessee met in a convention at Jonesborough and set up the precocious state of Franklin. The Blount group of speculators was opposed to this independence movement, but finally joined it to control it and protect their land titles. Indeed, one of their men, John Sevier, was elected the first governor. The formation of the state of Franklin was not purely the spontaneous assertion of frontier democracy which the older historians portrayed, but was at least partly motivated by land speculation.

The government of North Carolina proclaimed the formation of the state of Franklin null and void. Also Congress refused to act favorably on a petition of the inhabitants of Tennessee to recognize the new state. None the less, despite Indian warfare and the efforts of North Carolina to restore control over the rebellious inhabitants, this little frontier republic precariously survived for four years. A faction opposed to Sevier, led by John Tipton, tried to subvert the *de facto* state and to reduce it to subordination to North Carolina. At times two governments were functioning in the region; rival sheriffs and competing courts clashed; and blood was shed in internal strife. Finally Sevier was captured and taken to prison at Morganton, North Carolina, but melodramatically escaped. Not until the Federal Constitution was adopted did this opera bouffe war come to an end and the state of Franklin succumb. Then Sevier was pardoned from the charge of being a traitor, and in 1790 North Carolina retroceded her western lands to the national government.

The Tennessee and Kentucky communities needed outlets to the ocean for the marketing of their crops. Unfortunately, Spain controlled the two best outlets, the mouth of the Mississippi and the route by the Tombigbee River to Mobile. Spain used her strategic position as a lever to try to detach the western settlements from the United States and to persuade them to join her empire. Thus arose the so-called Spanish Conspiracy, most active in 1786–87, when the West was incensed by the proposed Jay-Gardoqui Treaty, which would have surrendered the right of Americans to navigate the Mississippi River for a period of twenty-five years. In Tennessee a group of land speculators, John Sevier, William Blount, and others, flirted with Spain in the hope of securing an outlet along the Tombigbee River for a colony which they planned at Muscle Shoals.

In Kentucky the leader of the Spanish Party was the adventurer, James Wilkinson, who later intrigued with Aaron Burr. In 1787 Wilkinson, who had established himself as a merchant and speculator at Frankfort which he founded, made a trip to New Orleans to confer with Spanish authorities. He advised Spain that the best method of protecting Louisiana from an attack by the Westerners, aided by a fleet of Great Britain, was to foment an independence movement in Kentucky. He accepted the role of Spanish agent in return for a pension and the right to ship Kentucky produce to New Orleans. Wilkinson's motive seems to have been purely mercenary, to extract money from Spain. The great majority of Kentuckians, however, remained loyal to the Confederation of states, and only a few prominent leaders, such as Judge Benjamin Sebastian, negotiated with Spain to secure bribes. Any chance for the success of a separatist movement was destroyed by the Pinckney Treaty of 1795, which granted the right of deposit in New Orleans, and by the purchase of Louisiana in 1803. Consequently, when Aaron Burr initiated his conspiracy in 1806, he found the western states loyal to the United States, but willing perhaps to countenance a filibustering expedition against Spain.

During its formative years Kentucky was a battleground between the radical and the conservative forces for the control of the government. The settlement of Kentucky was accelerated by the practice of Virginia of paying its Revolutionary soldiers in land warrants entitling the holder to locate his grant in western lands. Many of these warrants were purchased cheaply by speculators. The advance of the frontier into the Bluegrass region was financed by speculators, and most of the good land was acquired by masterful men with money. "The Bluegrass country," a recent scholar has observed, "was never a poor man's frontier." [8] The poor people settled principally below the Green River, where they followed the leadership of the demagogue Felix Grundy. They demanded manhood suffrage, election of all local and state officials by the people, the ballot instead of the *viva voce* method of voting practiced in Virginia, a legislature of one chamber, and, strangely, the abolition of a bill of rights. The reason for this last demand was the fear of the radical party that a bill of rights would protect vested interests, including

slavery, which they wished to abolish. In the constitutional convention of 1792, the leader of the antislavery group was the Presbyterian minister David Rice, but he was defeated in the attempt to
make Kentucky free soil. The conservatives, led by George Nicholas,
wished to make the new state a replica of Virginia with the institution of slavery as the basis of aristocratic control.

The constitution which emerged from this conflict was a compromise. Although it contained provisions for manhood suffrage,
the second in the nation to do so, the ballot, and the apportionment
of representation in the legislature according to population, slavery
was preserved, ministers were disqualified from serving in the
legislature, and both the governor and the Senate were to be chosen
by an electoral college. With such a frame of government, influenced both by Virginia and by the democratic constitution of
Pennsylvania, Kentucky was admitted into the Union in 1792 as
the first state beyond the Appalachians. Seven years later a new
constitutional convention was convened, in which the radicals succeeded in abolishing the electoral college. However, the Virginia
practices of the *viva voce* method of voting and of the appointment
of sheriffs and justices of the peace by the governor were adopted.
An attempt by reformers and idealists like the Lexington editor,
John Bradford, and the youthful Henry Clay to incorporate in the
constitution a provision for the gradual abolition of slavery was
defeated by the conservatives.

Tennessee was the second state in the West to be admitted into
the Union (in 1796). Although its constitution granted manhood
suffrage, it contained a number of aristocratic features. Land speculators had a powerful influence in its politics. One of the most
aggressive of these men was Andrew Jackson, who joined in a
partnership with John Overton to found the city of Memphis in
1819. Overton became perhaps the richest citizen of Tennessee and
a member of the "Nashville Junto" that promoted the Presidential
candidacy of Jackson. Political democracy, however, was not
achieved in Tennessee until the reforms of the constitutional convention of 1834.[9]

In the economic development of Kentucky and Tennessee, the
introduction of the steamboat played a major role. The first steam-

boat to make the voyage upstream from New Orleans to Louisville, Kentucky, was the *Enterprise* in the year 1815. The epochal nature of this event was registered in the decline of Lexington as the metropolis of the West, following the introduction of the new mode of transportation. Lexington was an inland town fifteen miles from the Kentucky River, but it was on the main road from the Ohio River at Limestone to the interior of Kentucky and it was the capital of the Bluegrass. In 1810 it was a thriving center of trade, with a population of 4,326, and was rapidly developing manufactures— ropewalks, bagging and cordage factories, textile mills, powder mills, etc., which made its citizens ardent for protective tariffs. The coming of the steamboat caused a sharp decline in its economic supremacy, for in the decade of the 1820's Louisville at the falls of the Ohio surpassed it. But Lexington remained the cultural and political center of Kentucky. It boasted the pioneer newspaper of the West, the *Kentucke Gazette*, founded by the surveyor John Bradford in 1787 during the agitation for statehood. Moreover, it contained Transylvania University, the home of Henry Clay and many cultivated and aristocratic citizens, that entitled it to be called the "Athens of the West."

From Nashville, Tennessee, a famous frontier path, nearly six hundred miles long, ran through Indian territory to Natchez on the Mississippi River. In 1801 treaties with the Indians permitted the Natchez Trace to be widened into a wagon road, and two years later a mail service was established. Along this road came pioneers from Kentucky and Tennessee to settle the Southwest, for it was a short-cut to the longer route down the Mississippi River. Flatboatmen and the crews of arks which had drifted down the Mississippi often returned by the Natchez Trace, especially before the days of steamboats. Unfortunately, this lonely road was infested with robbers and murderers, such as the homicidal maniac "Little Harpe," Samuel Mason, a Revolutionary soldier and justice of the peace in Kentucky who turned to the trade of highwayman, Joseph Hare, the dandy, and John A. Murrell and his gang.

Natchez at the end of the journey was the extreme western point of the frontier in 1800. Originally a French town, which was destroyed by the Natchez Indians in 1729, Natchez became once more a center of settlement when the English acquired this territory in 1763 and built Fort Panmure. After the conquest of the town by Galvez during the American Revolution it remained under Spanish rule until 1798. In that year Natchez was surrendered to the United States in fulfillment of the Pinckney treaty (also called San Lorenzo) of 1795, which had fixed the boundary between Florida and the United States at the thirty-first degree of latitude. The chief relic of Spanish rule was the palace of the Governor Gayoso, "Concord," which survived well into the nineteenth century. At first the main crops were tobacco and indigo, especially the "pigeon neck" variety, so called because of its prismatic colors. After the introduction in 1795 of the Whitney gin, cotton became the great money crop.

Following the Louisiana Purchase in 1803, the Natchez region rapidly advanced in prosperity and culture. A considerable number of educated men settled there, so that probably the earlier generation of settlers was more cultivated than their sons. The surprising luxury enjoyed by this remote frontier town is indicated by a manifest of goods imported into Natchez in 1801 by the merchant John McDonogh in the ship "Carlisle" from Baltimore, Maryland. From the cargo there were landed 720 casks of claret, 2,400 bottles of Medoc wine, 15 pipes of brandy, 70 dozen of men's white stockings, 312 dozen kid gloves, 18 gross white playing cards, 96 reams of "faint blue" paper, wall paper of various kinds, including "9 muses dark grounded," as well as such articles of luxuries as sweet oil, almonds, soap, cambrics, and linen. As early as 1790, Andrew Marschalk, an army officer, had introduced a printing press, and nine years later a newspaper was started. Many rich planters and professional people built beautiful homes in and around Natchez-on-the-Bluff, but below, on the river bank, flourished wicked and rowdy Natchez-under-the-Hill, where hundreds of flatboats and steamboats floated at the docks.

Contrary to a common misconception, this rapidly maturing town on the frontier did not favor *laissez-faire* methods of government, but strictly regulated many business activities.[10] The surrounding region of farmers and planters revolted from the dominance of the town after Jefferson appointed the young Republican W. C. C. Claiborne as governor of Mississippi Territory. The farmers and

planters obtained control of the legislature and deprived the aristocrats of Natchez of the advantage of having the capital located in
their city. They transferred the seat of government to the brand-new
village of Washington, six miles to the east, and here also they located
the pioneer Jefferson College, chartered in 1802, but not opened
until 1811. In 1808 Christian Schultz in his *Travels on an Inland
Voyage* described the worldly, hedonistic atmosphere of this river
town of three thousand inhabitants as follows: "all make love; most
of them play [gamble]; and a few make money. With Religion they
have nothing to do." [11] In truth, Natchez at this time was a prismatic
blend of the frontier, evidenced by skins of the "spotted tiger"
killed in the surrounding wilderness hanging in the stores, the river
trade with its boastful half-horse, half-alligator boatmen and their
copper-colored prostitutes, and of the slave-tilled cotton economy,
which was destined to make Natchez one of the wealthiest and most
cultured communities in the United States.

Citations

1. F. J. TURNER, *The Frontier in American History* (New York, 1921),
   12.
2. G. W. PIERSON, "The Frontier and American Institutions: a Criticism
   of the Turner Theory," *New England Quarterly*, XV (June, 1942),
   224–255; M. Kane, "Some Considerations of the Frontier Concept
   of Frederick Jackson Turner," *Mississippi Valley Historical Review*,
   XXVII (December, 1940), 379–400; and F. A. Shannon, "A Post-
   Mortem on the Labor-Safety-Valve Theory," *Agricultural History*,
   (January, 1945), 31–37.
3. R. S. COTTERILL, "A Chapter of Panton, Leslie and Company," *Journal of Southern History*, X (August, 1944), 275–292.
4. This manuscript is in the Harvard University library, extracts from
   which are found in R. L. Kincaid, *The Wilderness Road* (Indianapolis, 1947), 139–145.
5. *American Historical Review*, V (April, 1900), 525–526.
6. EVERETT DICK, *The Dixie Frontier, A Social History* (New York,
   1948), chap. XXX.
7. A. R. MOEN, Petersburg, Virginia, August 22, 1831, to Mess. Collins
   & Co., Hartford, Connecticut, MS. owned by Professor T. D. Clark,
   University of Kentucky.

8. ABERNETHY, *Three Virginia Frontiers*, 65.

9. T. P. ABERNETHY, *From Frontier to Plantation in Tennessee* (Chapel Hill, 1932).

10. C. S. SYDNOR, *A Gentleman of the Old Natchez Region: Benjamin L. C. Wailes* (Durham, 1938), Chap. I.

11. CHRISTIAN SCHULTZ, *Travels on an Inland Voyage* (New York, 1810). II, 134.

CHAPTER VI

Ascendancy of the Southern Federalists

WHILE the Revolution was in progress the thirteen colonies formed a loose central government under the Continental Congress. In November, 1777, the Continental Congress adopted a constitution entitled "The Articles of Confederation," but it was not ratified by all the states until four years later. The reason for this delay was that Maryland refused to sign the document until the states had agreed to surrender their claims of western land to the central government. The claims of Virginia, under a sea to sea charter and by Clark's conquest of the Ohio region, were especially obnoxious to a small state like Maryland which had a narrowly limited western boundary. After Virginia surrendered her claims and it became evident that the various titles of the states to western territory would be given to the central government, Maryland ratified the Articles of Confederation. Not until 1802, however, did Georgia surrender her claim to western lands, the last of the states to do so.

The adoption of Articles of Confederation represented a victory of the radicals over the conservatives in the struggle between conflicting interests, or "parties," of the Revolutionary period. The Articles of Confederation were permeated by the spirit of the Declaration of Independence, based on the idea that liberty could best be preserved by decentralization. But the conservatives were hostile to a constitution which permitted the thirteen sovereign states to give a free rein to the radicals within the states. In contrast to the big business leaders of the New Deal period, who advocated state rights, the property interests of the 1770's and 1780's sought a more centralized government to curb rampant democracy.[1]

The older historians, influenced by Federalist propaganda, have exaggerated the weaknesses and centrifugal tendencies of the government during the Confederation, which was called by John Fiske "the critical period" of American history. They have, for example, continued the myth that the states erected tariff barriers against each other, when, in reality, the discriminations were directed against Great Britain. The new central government, like the Weimar Republic, was discredited by an economic depression, which has been exaggerated by historians. After the crisis of the Revolution had passed, the radicals lost their organization and the conservatives finally won the upper hand by calling the Constitutional Convention of 1787. The property interests were aided in this victory by the alarm produced by Shays' Rebellion of the veterans and small farmers of Massachusetts in 1786 and by the menace of paper money inflation.

The immediate steps that led to the calling of a Constitutional Convention in Philadelphia in 1787 were taken by Southern men. In 1785 a conference was held at "Mount Vernon," Washington's estate on the Potomac, to secure cooperation between Maryland and Virginia over the navigation of the Potomac River. At this meeting a decision was made to invite all the thirteen states to a convention at Annapolis, Maryland, the following year for the purpose of adopting uniform trade regulations. Only five states attended, but one of the delegates, Alexander Hamilton from New York, proposed the summoning of another convention with a much larger scope than the consideration of commercial measures, namely to revise the old Articles of Confederation. The Congress of the Confederation finally called such a convention to meet at Philadelphia on May 14, 1787, to which all the states, except Rhode Island, sent delegates.

The ace in this counter-revolution movement was securing the attendance at the convention of Washington, who was finally persuaded to go. The Virginia delegation, by far the most brilliant and useful of the various state groups, included James Madison, George Mason, the author of the Virginia Declaration of Rights, George Wythe, one of the great liberals of America, and the youthful Governor Edmund Randolph, a polished orator, the spokesman for the delegation. Patrick Henry, although chosen a delegate, refused to attend because he was hostile to a strong central government and "smelt a rat." Thomas Jefferson was also absent, for he was serving as minister to France. All the Virginia delegates, except Madison, lived in the Tidewater area.

James Madison was the most valuable member of the Constitutional Convention. He was better prepared than any other delegate by his study of the history of the various leagues and confederations of the past. Although he was only thirty-six years old at the time, he had a profound grasp of the problems of government, especially in relation to economic interests. He prepared "the Virginia plan" which represented the views of the larger states as to the basis of representation. The sessions of the convention were secret, and the newspapers did not report its proceedings. However, Madison took a front seat in the Convention and kept an accurate set of notes on the debates, which constitute our only complete account of the great debates on the framing of the Constitution. Strangely, these notes were not published until 1840. He has rightly been singled out as "the father of the Constitution," although the completed document was the work of many minds and a number of compromises.

The other Southern states sent, in general, their conservative leaders. From South Carolina came John Rutledge, called "Dictator," Charles Cotesworth Pinckney, Revolutionary leader, the brilliant Charles Pinckney, only twenty-nine years old, next to the youngest member of the convention, who claimed erroneously in his old age to have presented the blueprint upon which the Constitution was based, and Pierce Butler, proud of descent from the Duke of Ormond, a great planter strongly devoted to the preservation of slavery. Of Maryland's five delegates three were conservatives, but Luther Martin, a Princeton graduate, was an able and strenuous advocate of the point of view of the small farmers and the debtors. The delegation from North Carolina contained the land speculator, William Blount, William R. Davie, later instrumental in founding the University of North Carolina, Richard Dobbs Spaight, an owner of seventy-one slaves, and Hugh Williamson, the intellectual leader of the group. Williamson was born in Pennsylvania and was graduated from the University of Edinburgh, and afterwards located in

Edenton, North Carolina, as a merchant and physician. From Georgia came Abraham Baldwin, a Yankee educated at Yale, one of the founders of the University of Georgia, and William Few, who has been described as "almost unique among the members of the Convention in being a representative, in origin and education, of the small farming class." [2] The delegates of Delaware included Richard Bassett, owner of the six-thousand-acre estate of Bohemia Manor, and John Dickinson, famed as a pre-Revolutionary pamphleteer.

The Southern delegates were chosen, as in the Northern states, not by popular vote, but by the legislatures, which in turn were elected by property holders. These delegates were particularly concerned with the establishment of a government that would benefit their economic interests by preventing the states from issuing a flood of paper money, by paying the bondholders of the public debt, by establishing tariff laws, by protecting speculators in western land, and by safeguarding Southern slaveholders from the dangers of servile insurrection and from the loss of fugitive slaves. A number of the Southern delegates were speculators in western lands, and fifteen of the members of the convention were slaveholders. To conclude that these delegates were dominated solely by their economic interests would be unjust. The legislatures chose their best and most intelligent men to send to the Constitutional Convention, and it was highly probable that such forceful personalities would have accumulated considerable property. Most of the delegates seem to have been motivated by a desire to give their country a government strong enough to preserve the republican experiment of government in America which was in danger of disintegrating. Conservative men had been frightened by the menace of debtors securing the passage of laws favorable to their interest, such as paper money and stay laws. Consequently, they believed that one of the most fundamental functions of government was to protect property.

The Constitutional Convention had been called for the purpose of revising the old Articles of Confederation. Nevertheless, the delegates resolved to create a new government instead of trying to revamp the old decentralized government of the Confederation. In so doing, they accomplished a peaceful revolution. The revolutionary nature of their proceedings is clearly seen in their decision that when nine of the thirteen states accepted the new Constitution, it should go into effect in those states. The old Articles of Confederation had prescribed a unanimous consent of the states for any alteration of the frame of government. In drawing up the Constitution, the delegates were guided primarily by English models of government and by their practical experience with the colonial governments and with the weakness and inefficiency of the Confederation.

On May 29, four days after the Convention opened, Edmund Randolph presented the Virginia Plan in a series of resolutions for a new frame of government for the thirteen states. This blueprint became the basis of discussion and the matrix of the completed document. The essential point to note about the Virginia plan was that it proposed a legislature of two houses, in which representation should be proportional to population, rather than the equal votes of states, big and little, which was the rule in the unicameral legislature of the Congress of the Confederation. The upper house, according to this plan, was to be chosen by the lower house from candidates nominated by the state legislatures. The Madison draft of a constitution encountered violent opposition from the small states, whose counter-proposal for equal representation of the states was presented by William Paterson and is known as the New Jersey Plan.

A compromise offered by Oliver Ellsworth of Connecticut, called the Grand Compromise, was finally adopted. According to this decision the states were given equal representation in the upper house, or Senate, selected by the state legislatures, but representation in the lower house was apportioned according to population. Two qualifications to this solution were added, namely, that all money bills must originate in the lower house and that no amendment should ever be made which would deprive any state without its consent of its equal vote in the Senate.

Apart from the struggle between the large and small states over the basis of representation, the real cleavage in the Convention was between the Northern and Southern states, which had conflicting economic interests. One of the questions in which Northern and Southern interests were opposed was the status of the slaves in apportioning representation in Congress. The Southern delegates wished slaves to be counted as population in determining the numbers of representatives each state should have in the House of Representatives. The Northern delegates opposed this formula, pointing out that slaves were considered as property in the South. They argued that slaves should not be counted at all as persons in apportioning representation, but should be taxed as persons in assessing direct taxes on the states, a proposition highly repugnant to the Southerners. The latter demanded slave representation in Congress to protect slavery from any attempt to abolish it that might later be made by the Northern states. They threatened to leave the convention unless such security was given them. Finally, a compromise was adopted by which slaves were to be counted as three-fifths their actual number in apportioning both representation and direct taxes. This three-fifths compromise (called the Federal ratio) was suggested by the fact that under the Articles of Confederation such a ratio had been proposed in assessing requisitions for taxes on the states. It was a genuine victory for the South since direct taxes were levied by the Federal government only three times during the existence of slavery, while the Federal ratio gave to a Southerner residing in a state with a large preponderance of slaves, such as South Carolina, or Mississippi, political power in the House of Representatives almost equal to the vote of two Northerners.

The adoption of the three-fifths ratio made the South more willing to accept the Constitution and especially to agree to another compromise favorable to the North. This adjustment was in regard to the power of enacting tariff laws. The Southern delegates demanded that all tariff laws should require the vote of a two-thirds majority, for they feared that the power of levying duties on imports or exports would be used to exploit the staple-producing states. Ultimately a compromise was worked out which granted to Congress the authority to pass tariff bills by a simple majority vote, but prohibited that body from levying an export duty, which would have fallen heavily on the agricultural class of the South.

Another compromise that primarily affected the Southern states related to the prohibition of the slave trade. The upper South, which had a superfluity of Negro field hands, wished to close the African slave trade, but Georgia and South Carolina demanded that it remain open. These two states of the lower South secured allies in the

New England shipping states, which were gaining profits from importing slaves into the South. This pressure group was able to force the adoption of a compromise leaving the African slave trade open for a period of twenty years, during which Congress was prohibited from laying an import duty on slaves greater than ten dollars a head.

A great majority of the members of the Convention seem to have been ashamed of the existence of slavery in this country, and when a committee under the leadership of Gouverneur Morris phrased the Constitution in final form, it carefully avoided including the words slave or slavery in the famous document. The fugitive slave clause of the Constitution, for example, used a euphemism in referring to slaves as follows: "No person held to service or labor in one state, under the laws thereof, escaping into another, shall in consequence of any law or regulation therein be discharged from such service or labor, but shall be delivered up on claim of the party to whom such service or labor may be due."

The Southern delegates shared the aversion to democracy that dominated the Convention. A reaction of the pendulum from the enthusiasm for human rights of the Revolutionary period had swung in the direction of protecting property rights from the depredations of a numerical majority. In 1787 democracy, as has been wittily observed, was in disgrace. Shays' Rebellion, the stay laws, and the paper money panaceas had frightened the property classes, evoking the specter of social revolution. Consequently, most of the fifty-five members of the Convention wished to curb rabid democracy by a system of checks and balances and indirect elections in order to make property safe. The Virginia Plan presented by Randolph had provided for representation in Congress to be based both on population and on the wealth of the citizens of a state measured by the amount of taxes paid. Baldwin of Georgia declared in the Convention that the Senate "ought to be the representation of property." The wealthy Pierce Butler of South Carolina, "contended strenuously" according to Madison's Notes, "that property was the only just measure of representation," [3] a theory of government which was supported by William R. Davie of North Carolina, and John Rutledge and Charles Cotesworth Pinckney of South Carolina.

The Constitution was completed by September 17, 1787, and was then signed by twenty of the thirty Southern delegates. Four of the Virginia delegates, George Mason, James McClurg, George Wythe, and Edmund Randolph failed to sign the document. William R. Davie and Alexander Martin of North Carolina, Luther Martin and John Francis Mercer of Maryland, William Pierce and William Houston of Georgia were the other Southern delegates who did not sign, either because of opposition to the document, or because they had left the Convention. The objections of Mason to the Constitution are an important critique on that frame of government by one of the ablest and wealthiest of Southern planters. He deplored the absence of a bill of rights protecting civil liberties, the compromise on the slave trade, which he believed should be closed entirely, and the absence of a cabinet for the President. His objections also reflected the fear which the agricultural class held that the North would control the government and exploit the South. Consequently, he demanded that commercial and navigation acts should be passed only by a two-thirds vote of Congress. He declared that the Constitution gave excessive power to the Senate and that the judiciary would become so powerful that it would destroy the state courts, and finally he saw great danger in the elastic clause of the Constitution.[4]

The Constitution was not submitted to popular vote but to specially summoned conventions. The delegates to these conventions, however, seem to have followed, with few exceptions, instructions from the electorate. In all the Southern states, and in most of the Northern states, there were property qualifications for voting for the members of these conventions. It is surprising to find that only a small fraction, certainly less than one-fourth, of the white adult males voted in this election which was to determine under what type of government they and their descendants should live. Non-voting of the qualified voters in truth has had a long continuity in the United States. Although many of the non-voters in 1788 were kept away from the polls by lack of property, a large majority of those qualified failed to exercise their sovereign privilege of voting in this critical election on account of indifference, travel difficulties, etc.

An instructive parallel exists between the debate over the adoption of the Federal Constitution and the debate today over the strengthening of the United Nations government. In 1787–88 it was difficult to get Americans to think nationally: in 1948 it is equally difficult to persuade people to think internationally. As a recent writer has suggested, the debate over the ratification of the Constitution was "the Great Rehearsal" for the acceptance of a world federation. Most of the arguments pro and con in the debate of 1787–88 are applicable today in regard to entrusting stronger powers to a world government. There was the fear of small states that they would be dominated by the large states; there was the fear of provincial people of oppression by a distant centralized government; and there was the belief among many Southerners that the economic interests of their region would be sacrificed in a more closely knit union, where the congress would be controlled by the numerically stronger North. Indeed, the strong consciousness of sectional interests was clearly exhibited in these debates, antedating by many years the famous clash between the Northern and Southern states in 1820 over the admission of Missouri to the Union. There were men both in the South and in New England who agreed with Benjamin Randall of Sharon, Massachusetts, that "Our manners are widely different from the southern states" and that in any close union the two sections would continually be at variance.[5] Thus early, serious differences between the Northern and Southern states, as well as a struggle between the planting and the commercial classes, were foreshadowed.

In general, there was an economic and geographic alignment of classes in the nation over the question of ratifying the Constitution. The back country, as a whole, was opposed while the Tidewater area supported the movement to establish a stronger central government. In Virginia 80 per cent of the Tidewater voted for and 20 per cent against the adoption of the Constitution; the Piedmont, 26 per cent for, and 74 per cent against ratification, the Shenandoah Valley, 97 per cent for, and 3 per cent against ratification.[6] In North Carolina all the six towns represented in the convention of 1788, except Hillsborough in the Piedmont, favored the ratification of the Constitution. The wealthy planters, the merchants, and the business people of the South were usually Federalists, as those who favored the Constitution were called. The Anti-Federalists, or opponents of the adoption of the Constitution, were usually debtors or small farmers and yeomen. The debtor class objected to restrictions placed by the Constitution on the states' issuing paper money or impairing the obligation of a contract. Some of the agitators of the Revolution, such as Patrick Henry and Sam Adams, were hostile to the ratification of the Constitution because they believed that the new semi-federal, semi-national government would crush personal liberty. Fortunately, the Federalists were better organized, more aggressive, and better informed on the nature of the proposed government than the Anti-Federalists. Furthermore, they had the advantage of using the arguments of a very able series of essays, called "The Federalist Papers," written by James Madison, John Jay, and Alexander Hamilton.

Delaware, elated over the victory of the small states in obtaining the Grand Compromise, was the first state to ratify the Constitution, December 7, 1787—by a unanimous vote. Georgia quickly followed, January 2, 1788, also by a unanimous vote, partly motivated by a desire to secure the protection of a strong central government against the Indians and the Spaniards on her frontier. In Maryland Luther Martin and Samuel Chase, later to be a Justice of the Supreme Court whom the Jeffersonians impeached, fought vigorously against ratification, but they were defeated by a vote of sixty-three in favor to eleven against accepting the Constitution. South Carolina likewise overwhelmingly ratified the new document. Rawlins Lowndes, an aristocrat of the low country, was the leader of the up-country opposition. He objected to the Constitution because of its prohibition of the slave trade after twenty years, because of the excessive power of the Senate, and because he believed that it inadequately protected minority rights. He wished his epitaph to contain the words, "Here lies the man that opposed the Constitution because it was ruinous to the liberty of America." [7]

In Virginia occurred the ablest debate in the nation on the merits of the Constitution. The Anti-Federalists had as their spokesmen some of the most prominent men of the state, Patrick Henry, George Mason, Richard Henry Lee, James Monroe, and John Tyler. On the other side were Madison, George Wythe, Edmund Pendleton, "Light Horse Harry" Lee, and John Marshall. Although Washington was not a member of the ratifying convention, his support of the Constitution had great weight in forming public opinion, particularly in influencing the Revolutionary soldiers. Patrick Henry took a leading part in opposing the ratification of the Constitution and was greatly feared by the Federalists. At this time he was fifty-three years of age, but was prematurely old. Having lost his hair early in life, he wore a brown wig, which he would twist awry on his bald head in a comical manner during his excitement in orating on the dangers of establishing a strongly centralized government. He pointed out the expense of the new government, the dangerous power of the Supreme Court, and the failure to safeguard personal liberty by a bill of rights, and he strenuously objected to its national character, based on the people rather than the states. He gained the support of most of the Kentucky delegates in the convention by arousing their fear that the congress of the proposed government, dominated by the North, would surrender the right to navigate the Mississippi.

The Federalists won a great triumph when Governor Edmund Randolph, who had refused to sign the Constitution in Philadelphia, changed his attitude and spoke in favor of Virginia accepting the new instrument of government. He had favored a stronger central government, but had refused to sign the Constitution because he believed that it should be amended by another Convention. Now he had concluded that it was wise for his state to ratify in order to prevent a dissolution of the Union, and later to secure amendments. This method of promising amendments was the strategy of victory. The Virginia Convention, after a violent struggle, ratified the Constitution, June 25, 1788, by a narrow margin of ten votes. Hugh Blair Grigsby, who made a thorough study of Virginia's ratification of the Constitution, reached the conclusion that two-thirds of the people of that state were opposed to this new frame of government.[8] Victory was attained by the Federalists partly because of the under-representation of the back country in the Convention. Shortly before Virginia's decision, Vermont had ratified the Constitution, making the ninth state to do so, thus furnishing enough acceptances to establish the new government.

In North Carolina a convention met at Hillsborough, in the Piedmont section of the state, July 21, 1788, to decide the question of ratifying the Constitution. The convention was dominated by Willie Jones, a wealthy aristocrat who held democratic views. Jones advocated a procedure proposed by his friend, Thomas Jefferson, that North Carolina should refrain from joining the new government until the Constitution had been amended and a bill of rights had been added. This argument as well as the influence of the paper money crowd swayed the convention to adjourn without ratifying the Constitution. The Anti-Federalists in the convention included some of the old Regulators, such as Thomas Person of Granville County, and the Presbyterian leader, Reverend David Caldwell of Guilford County. In the eastern part of the state the Anti-Federalist leader was Timothy Bloodworth of Wilmington, a versatile man whose career combined farming, preaching, and the trade of blacksmith with his political activities as the organizer of the mechanics and small farmers against the merchants and wealthy planters, who were in general Federalists. North Carolina remained outside of the Union until November 22, 1789, when a second convention met at Fayetteville and ratified the Constitution. Thus North Carolina was next to the last state in the Union in joining the Federal government, Rhode Island being the last.[9]

Fortunately for the secure establishment of the central government, the friends of the Constitution were in general elected to Congress, both from the Southern and Northern states. An exception to this rule was Virginia, which sent Richard Henry Lee and William Grayson, staunch Anti-Federalists, to the Senate. After the Constitution went into effect in 1789 and the first ten amendments were added two years later (1791), new issues arose that led to the emergence of our first national parties, the Federalist and Republican parties. The three most important issues that caused this political alignment were the financial proposals of Alexander Hamilton, the interpretation of the Constitution, and sympathies in foreign affairs. The Federalists supported Hamilton's financial measures, advocated a liberal interpretation of the Constitution, and were sympathetic to England. The Southern Federalists represented the old aristocratic families who held a conservative viewpoint. Interested in protecting property from the assaults of radicalism, they looked upon manhood suffrage with strong disapproval. The Republicans, under the lead of Jefferson, opposed the efforts of Hamilton to favor the commercial classes, advocated a strict interpretation of the Constitution, and were ardent supporters of the French Revolution. In contrast to the Federalists they worked for more democracy in government.

The greatest of the Southern Federalists was George Washington. This Virginia planter disclaimed any connection with a political party and, in fact, strongly advised his countrymen in his farewell address (September 17, 1796), which was revised by Hamilton, to avoid the formation of parties on a geographical basis or to give encouragement to the party spirit. More than any other Southern statesman, Washington had a national outlook. In his cabinet Jefferson, Secretary of State, and Hamilton, Secretary of the Treasury, represented opposing points of view and were constantly seeking to determine the policy of the administration. Although the President did not have the brilliant creative intellect of Hamilton nor the culture and philosophic mind of Jefferson, he had finer judgment than either of his subordinates. Gradually he decided more frequently for the Hamiltonian measures against the Jeffersonian point of view, until Jefferson resigned in 1793. Later Edmund Randolph, the Attorney General, and the other Southerner in the cabinet, also resigned, so that the President's advisers became entirely Northern Federalists. Washington leaned to the Federalist side because he saw the wisdom of strengthening the central government. His nationalism was displayed in his will, in which he directed that part of his estate be devoted to the foundation of a national university.

When Washington retired from office in 1797, he had lost his popularity in the South and Federalism was on the wane. He was not the genial type of Southerner who could win friends by cordial and democratic manners. Fond of ceremony and form, he drove in a coach pulled by four or six horses with out-riders and lackeys in livery. He held stately levees or receptions on Tuesdays at which the guests were not invited to sit down and the President formally bowed instead of shaking hands. Indeed, this dignified and reserved man encouraged no familiarity from his visitors or associates. He was a poor speech maker and consequently lacked that resource of appealing to the people. Moreover, there were a number of specific reasons why Washington's second administration was bitterly criticized below the Potomac. After France had established a republic and executed her monarch in 1793, she was attacked by a coalition of monarchies, including England. The French cause was very popular in the South, but Washington was determined to preserve the neutrality of the United States and refused aid to our former ally. He also firmly repressed the Whiskey Rebellion of 1794 by calling out fifteen thousand militia against the poor farmers of Pennsylvania who were distilling corn whiskey and refusing to pay the inequitable excise tax. Finally, Washington was severely condemned for his support of the Jay Treaty of 1795, which ended a threat of war with England by truckling, Southerners thought, to the hated Britishers. Also he was regarded as the tool of Hamilton.

The Federalist party stood for policies and principles which were growing in disfavor in the South. This party was aristocratic in tone and showed a distrust of political democracy, while the South under the lead of Thomas Jefferson was moving toward a more democratic type of government. Hamilton's financial schemes of funding the national debt at par, which benefited speculators, his policy of a tariff that would aid manufactures, his advocacy of a National Bank and of a liberal interpretation of the Constitution were unpopular in the South, a predominantly agricultural region which feared the control of the central government by the Northern business interests. Although Jefferson aided in the passage of the Assumption Bill, by which the debts of the states were assumed by the national government, the legislature of his native state protested vehemently against this measure. In a memorial to Congress the Virginia legislatur declared that the Federal government had no authority delegated to it by the Constitution to assume the state debts. It asserted "the doctrine of sentinelship," that the state legislatures should be the sentinels to prevent the encroachment of the Federal government on the rights and powers of the states.

Bucking this trend of the South away from Federalism was Patrick Henry, who had become a land speculator and who had strangely been converted from Anti-Federalism to a support of the Federalist party. At this time the old Revolutionary leader was living at "Red Hill," his plantation on the Staunton River in the back country, broken in health and fortune. President Washington offered him the post in his Cabinet of Secretary of State (1795) and later Chief Justice of the Supreme Court, which he declined, although he was greatly flattered by these offers. Consequently when Washington asked him to be a candidate for the Virginia House of Delegates to fight in behalf of the Federalist cause, he consented and won the election after a brilliant speech against the youthful John Randolph, a candidate for Congress, at Charlotte Courthouse in 1799. He died in this year, an example of a flaming radical in his youth who had grown conservative in his old age.

The swing of the South to state rights was seen especially in the refusal of Georgia to appear as a defendant before the Supreme Court in the case of Chisholm versus Georgia (1792). Georgia maintained that it could not be sued by a private citizen of another state without its consent, since it was a sovereign state. A resolution introduced into the legislature declared that acquiescence in this suit "would effectually destroy the retained sovereignty of the States, and would actually tend in its operation to annihilate the very shadow of State government, and to render them but tributary corporations to the government of the United States."[10] Accordingly, Georgia refused to appear before the Federal court and a decision by default was given in favor of Chisholm. The protest of Georgia and of other states led to the ratification in 1798 of the Eleventh Amendment, which exempts states from suits by citizens of another state or of a foreign state in the Federal courts.

Federalist principles and the Federalist party were more strongly entrenched in South Carolina than elsewhere in the South. This allegiance may be partially explained by the presence in that state of a powerful aristocracy of rice planters and merchants, to whom the Federalist doctrine of government by the well-born was appealing. The South Carolina Federalists had some very able leaders, Charles Cotesworth Pinckney and Thomas Pinckney, John Rutledge, and Robert Goodloe Harper. The last was a very aggressive and insolent spokesman of the aristocratic point of view, a Princeton graduate, who changed from a zealous Anti-Federalist to an over-zealous Federalist, but in 1801 he married a daughter of the wealthy Carrolls of Maryland and moved to Baltimore. In 1796 Thomas Pinckney was the Federalist candidate for Vice President and in

1804 and 1808 his brother Charles Cotesworth Pinckney was the Federalist nominee for President.

The leader of the Republican party in the state, on the other hand, was an ambitious young lawyer, Charles Pinckney, a cousin of the Federalist Pinckneys, who had made the opposite switch of political principles from Robert Goodloe Harper. He was called "Blackguard Charlie," or apostate, by the aristocratic clique of Charleston, who looked upon him as a demagogue. Under his lead the state was redeemed from Federalism, casting its electoral vote in 1800 for Thomas Jefferson. The Alien and Sedition laws, which will be discussed in the next chapter, contributed greatly to the ruin of the Federalist party in the South. The dissensions in the party, especially the rivalry between Hamilton and Adams, and the unpatriotic conduct of New England Federalists during the War of 1812 also did much to weaken the party. By 1815 the party of Washington and John Marshall was dead. Its traditions and fundamental principles were carried on by the National Republicans and later by the Whig Party, the parties of conservatism.

After the death of Washington in 1799 the outstanding Southern Federalist was John Marshall. Born in a log cabin in the Piedmont region of Virginia, he spent his youth on the frontier without the advantage of much schooling. Nevertheless, the "blue blood" of the Randolphs flowed through his veins, and he was a cousin of Thomas Jefferson. Perhaps the greatest factor in molding his views and making him such a strong nationalist was his four years of experience in the Revolutionary army. Here he conceived a deep admiration for Washington and a realization of the weakness and inefficiency of the state governments. After the victory at Yorktown, Marshall studied law at William and Mary College for six weeks, taking notes on the lectures of the famous George Wythe, but his mind must have been far away from the dry rules of law, for the name of his sweetheart, Mary Ambler, was scribbled over the pages of his notebook. With a guinea in his pocket, he married Mary Ambler, then only seventeen years of age, and began to practice law in Richmond.

He became the leading Federalist of Virginia, whose ability was recognized by John Adams in appointing him an envoy to France during the X.Y.Z. affair, then briefly Secretary of State, and finally

Chief Justice of the Supreme Court. This last appointment was made by Adams in 1801, after the Federalists had been defeated at the polls, but before Thomas Jefferson was inaugurated as President. Thus Jefferson was deprived of the opportunity of appointing his choice, the eminent Virginia jurist, Spencer Roane, a strong believer in state rights, to this position. Although the Federalist Party was retired from power in 1801, its principles survived in the judicial decisions of John Marshall, who served as Chief Justice until his death in 1835.

This remarkable man was very Southern in his personality, manners, and tastes, but his political and economic philosophy belonged to the North, to the moneyed interests and industrial society of that region. Six feet tall, with raven black hair, shaggy eyebrows, and rough-hewn features, he possessed a virile and forceful personality combined with great geniality and kindliness. He dressed in the negligent fashion of the Southern planters and had very democratic manners. Indeed, after he became Chief Justice, he continued to buy the fish and meat for the family and bring them home in a market basket. He enjoyed pitching horse-shoes with the citizens of Richmond, gambling with cards, drinking Madeira wine, attending balls and barbecues, and forgetting his judicial dignity in the companionship of convivial clubs. One of the most attractive of his traits was his devotion to his invalid wife. During her illness he would take off his shoes and enter the house in his stocking feet in order not to disturb her.

As a Supreme Court judge, Marshall was dominated by his Federalist principles. He was never learned in the law, he knew little concerning the principles of economics, and he was very indolent. His five-volume biography of Washington was lifeless and full of plagiarisms. Nevertheless, he was a man of powerful intelligence and of reasoning ability. His judicial decisions were based largely on his splendid common sense and his strong Federalist bias. Many of his opinions ranged far outside of the strict limits of the case and would be regarded as *obiter dicta* from the standpoint of a narrow definition of the judicial function. His Federalist prejudices, however, happened to correspond with the need of the times to strengthen the central government.

These prejudices, or principles if you will, were a decided leaning in favor of property rights and an equally strong feeling of nationalism. During the long period when he was Chief Justice, his decisions were usually at variance with the prevailing views and the economic interests of his native section, the South. Indeed, he bitterly disliked and distrusted his cousin, Thomas Jefferson, and the latter's political principles, which became the faith of the Southern states. Democratic in manners, Marshall showed a deep distrust of the extension of political democracy. In this prejudice, he represented the Hamiltonian view of government.

Marshall wrote 519 of the 1,106 opinions delivered by the court during his long occupancy of the position of Chief Justice. It would be unwise to attempt to give a resumé even of his most famous decisions, such as the Marbury versus Madison Case (1803), in which he established the power of the Supreme Court to declare a law of Congress unconstitutional, or the Dartmouth College Case (1819), in which he ruled that a charter was a contract which a state legislature could not annul so as to impair the obligation of a contract. Nevertheless, it is appropriate to take up several distinctly Southern cases which illustrate Marshall's bias in behalf of property rights and the increase of the powers of the national government.

One of these decisions, Fletcher versus Peck (1810), greatly curtailed the powers of the state governments and also reflected Marshall's concern to protect property rights as against the rights of society. The Fletcher versus Peck case dealt with the Yazoo Land Fraud. The legislature of Georgia had been corrupted by several land companies, to which a huge area of thirty-five million acres of land in the present states of Alabama and Mississippi had been sold in 1795 for approximately a cent and a half an acre. The people of the state were so outraged by this fraudulent transaction, in which every member of the legislature except one had been bribed, that in the next election, 1796, they chose a new group of legislators, who repealed the dishonest grant. Marshall declared this latter law of the Georgia legislature unconstitutional and therefore null and void, because it impaired the obligation of a contract. This decision set a precedent of the Supreme Court declaring a *state* law unconstitutional.

In one of his most notable decisions, McCulloch versus Maryland (1819), Marshall definitely rejected the interpretation of the Constitution which was popular in the South, the strict interpretation of that document. Rather, he put the imprint of judicial authority upon the implied powers doctrine of Hamilton and thus tremendously expanded the Federal power. The case arose as the result of Maryland attempting to tax out of existence a branch of the United States Bank at Baltimore. The cashier, McCulloch, appealed to the Supreme Court for protection. Maryland was represented by the famous Luther Martin, whose drunkenness caused the court obligingly to adjourn until he became sober. Marshall decided in this case that Congress had a constitutional right to charter the United States Bank and that a state could not tax an agency of the Federal government, for the power to tax was the power to destroy.

The decision which aroused most resentment in his native Virginia was Cohens versus Virginia (1821). The Cohen brothers had violated a law of Virginia in selling lottery tickets in that state. These lottery tickets were authorized in the District of Columbia by a law of Congress. The Cohen brothers appealed from an adverse decision of the State Supreme Court to John Marshall's court. Marshall ruled that the Supreme Court could review and reverse decisions of the highest state courts and that, despite the Eleventh Amendment, the Supreme Court could hear cases on appeal from individuals against states if the latter had originally instituted the suit. The decision aroused the wrath of Spencer Roane, the Chief Justice of the Supreme Court of Virginia, and of Thomas Jefferson, in retirement at Monticello. These Virginians expressed Southern opinion in criticizing Marshall's decision as overthrowing the rightful balance between the Federal and the state governments.[11]

Marshall dominated the Supreme Court almost as an autocrat. Not only did he write nearly half of the opinions delivered during his tenure, but only eight times did he dissent from the majority opinion. When Madison appointed a Republican, Joseph Story, as associate justice, Story was converted by Marshall to his nationalist views. Marshall was a judicial lawmaker rather than a learned and objective judge. It has been correctly said that this country has been governed since 1787 by three constitutions, the limited one drawn up at Philadelphia by the framers, the expanded one formulated by the judicial decisions of John Marshall, and the Constitution as modified by the Reconstruction Amendments. Although the views of Marshall and Washington in favor of strengthening the national government, were rejected by the agrarian South, the course of history has vindicated them. Indeed, the Federal government has become far more centralized and powerful than even John Marshall ever dreamed.

Citations

1. MERRILL JENSEN, *The Articles of Confederation* (Second Edition, Madison, 1948), vii-xv, 239–245, and *The New Nation* (1950).
2. C. A. BEARD, *An Economic Interpretation of the Constitution of the United States* (New York, 1914), 90.
3. GAILLARD HUNT and J. B. SCOTT (eds.), *The Debates in the Federal Convention of 1787 . . . Reported by James Madison* (New York, 1920), 190.
4. P. L. FORD (ed.), *Pamphlets on the Constitution of the United States* (Brooklyn, 1888), 327–32.
5. CARL VAN DOREN, *The Great Rehearsal, The Story of the Making and Ratifying of the Constitution of the United States* (New York, 1948), 203–204.
6. O. G. LIBBY, *The Geographic Distribution of the Vote of the Thirteen States on the Federal Constitution, 1787–8* (Madison, 1894), 34–35. The area of West Virginia voted 16 to 1 for ratification.
7. ALLEN JOHNSON and DUMAS MALONE (eds.), *Dictionary of American Biography*, XI, 473.
8. H. B. GRIGSBY, *The History of the Virginia Federal Convention of 1788*, (Richmond, 1891), I, 41.
9. L. I. TRENHOLME, *Ratification of the Federal Constitution in North Carolina* (New York, 1932).
10. H. C. HOCKETT, *The Constitutional History of the United States, 1776–1826* (New York, 1939), I, 284–285.
11. The history of the constitutional development of the United States has been written almost entirely from the Federalist point of view. A brilliant exception, however, is Charles Grove Haines, *The Role of the Supreme Court in American Government and Politics, 1789–1835* (Berkeley, 1944). See especially his discussion of Marshall's opposition to democratic ideals and principles, Chap. XVII.

CHAPTER VII

The Party of Thomas Jefferson

AMERICAN politics has been characterized by an ebb and flow of conservatism and liberalism. A flowing tide of liberalism reached a high point in the adoption of the Declaration of Independence and of such social reforms as the abolition of primogeniture and entail and the disestablishment of the Anglican church. After the Revolution conservative reaction led to the framing and ratification of the Federal Constitution, in which many checks were placed on rabid democracy. For ten years after the new government went into operation the aristocratic and conservative class of society controlled the administration. During this period, however, a new party, the Republican, was gathering strength to overthrow the dominant Federalist faction in the election of 1800. Jefferson shrewdly analyzed the economic alignment of the two parties in a letter to Philip Mazzei in 1796. The Republican party he described as containing "the whole landed interest and a great mass of talents," while the Federalist group was portrayed as "an Anglican monarchical aristocratical party, merchants, speculators, holders of bank stock and government bonds, and timid men." [1] Jefferson's characterization of his own party was not strictly correct for many of the aristocratic planters of the Tidewater were Federalists.

Nevertheless, the Republican party appealed powerfully to Southern farmers and small planters and to dissatisfied groups out of power in the Northern states. In Virginia Jefferson had been a representative of the back country farming interest and of the dissenters against the conservative Tidewater planters. Hamilton's financial measures and his doctrine of the loose construction of the Constitution were regarded by these agricultural groups as hostile to their economic interests and as favoring a "moneyed aristocracy."

Furthermore, Southern farmers had a reasonable distrust of centralizing power in a distant government (the program of the Federalists), which in a day of slow travel and communication could not have an adequate understanding of local conditions and needs, but which might exercise a dangerous power of interference with their lives. Such a limitation of the powers of government which the Jeffersonians advocated could be safely practiced at this time, for the United States was fortunate in having no powerful armed neighbors, whose menace would require a large degree of centralization of the powers of government.

The outstanding leader in the democratic agrarian revolt was Thomas Jefferson, but he was assisted by a number of able secondary leaders. In the South James Madison, James Monroe, John Taylor, John Randolph, and John Breckinridge were active in the cause of the Republican party. Although the Republican party derived its greatest support from the South, it was powerfully aided by some Northern leaders of factions out of power and representatives of the underprivileged classes. Jefferson was not a sectional leader; indeed, he abhorred geographical parties. In his Cabinet he appointed Albert Gallatin from Pennsylvania, and Levi Lincoln, Henry Dearborn, and Gideon Granger from New England. Jefferson had the wonderful power of phrasing the ideals of his youthful party, reminding one in this respect of Woodrow Wilson, but he also knew the practical art of organizing the forces of opposition into a victorious party. In truth, he was much more than the brilliant expounder of Southern economic interests, for he realized the dignity of human nature and the rights of personality of even the humblest individual. Although he has frequently been portrayed as a dreamer and a theoretical person, in the long view of history he has proved to be more practical than Alexander Hamilton, the cynical "realist," for he based his political philosophy on a sounder and more optimistic view of human nature.

The Virginia background of Jefferson gave him an excellent preparation to become the leader of a democratic movement. His boyhood was spent on a plantation in the Piedmont region of Virginia, near Charlottesville, which in the eighteenth century was one of the newer settled areas of the colony, although it was not the crude frontier of Boone and Crockett. Influenced to some extent by this semi-frontier region, he was principally the product of the culture of the colonial aristocracy. Although his father was a self-made man, recent researches show that he came from good stock and was associated with the gentry.[2] Jefferson's mother, Jane Randolph, was a member of one of the first families of Virginia. When he was seventeen, he entered the College of William and Mary, where he displayed a passion for learning comparable to the zest for knowledge manifested by Goethe, the great European exponent of self-culture. Fully as important in educating the young Virginian as his college courses were his friendships with three cultivated men in Williamsburg, Professor William Small, who stimulated his interest in science, George Wythe, his law instructor, who influenced him in the direction of liberalism, and Governor Francis Fauquier, a charming man of the world, a free thinker, who often invited the young student to dinner. Jefferson was a violin player and one of his great pleasures was to join Governor Fauquier and others in a quartette of chamber music.

In his early youth he developed an enduring passion for the study of the antique world. He mastered the Greek and Latin languages so that he could read the classics in the original. In his notebooks (the so-called *Literary Bible*) he copied passages from the wisdom of Euripides, Cicero, Horace, Tacitus, and other classical writers. But his attitude toward the past was far from being uncritical and sentimental. Indeed, his study of the ancient world, as a modern scholar has observed, revealed to him "the dark side of humanity" and liberated him from a reverence for tradition. From his classical studies Jefferson derived many fruitful ideas of architecture, a lifelong interest in the growth of language, particularly through neologisms, and a passionate love of political and intellectual freedom. Jefferson's remarkable serenity, although partly the result of temperament and good health, was undoubtedly strengthened by his unceasing conversation with classical authors who taught the individual to become "impassible and unassailable by the evils of life, and for preserving his mind in a state of constant serenity."[3] Jefferson mingled his knowledge of antiquity with his daily experience in government, agriculture, and observation of people, each illuminating the other. His education in the classics did not stop with his college days at Williamsburg, but was continuously enriched by constant reading of the great literary works of Greece and Rome.

After completing seven years of study at the College of William and Mary and in the law office of Wythe, Jefferson began to practice law at Charlottesville. Although he obtained a good income from his profession, he disliked controversy and the necessity of making public speeches. His aversion to the legal profession was expressed in his statement that the lawyer's trade is "to question everything, yield nothing, and talk by the hour." Fortunately, Jefferson did not have to depend upon his profession for a living. He became a wealthy young man through inheritance from his father and by his marriage to a widow who owned considerable property. One of the large landed proprietors of the South, he owned ten thousand acres of land, divided into nine plantations, which were cultivated by two hundred and four slaves. His income enabled him to satisfy his tastes in buying books, in acquiring musical instruments, and in enjoying the delights of a gentleman farmer without the sweat and toil of physical labor in the sun.

Returning from Philadelphia after he had composed the Declaration of Independence, he entered upon one of the most fruitful periods of his life when, as a member of the Virginia legislature, he worked for "the great reforms." He succeeded almost immediately in having the law of entails abolished, which he regarded as equivalent to cutting the roots of the tree of aristocracy in his native state. The repeal of the law of primogeniture came later as well as his famous statute for religious freedom, which was not adopted until 1786. He made an important contribution in revising the legal code of Virginia with "a single eye to reason" and the public welfare.[4] He proposed abolition of capital punishment for all crimes except murder and treason, but this humanitarian measure was not adopted until nearly twenty years later. The legislature abolished the slave trade in 1778, a reform that he had urged, but the successful bill was introduced by another man. The two most basic reforms that he advocated, which would have revolutionized the state and probably have prevented the Civil War, the gradual emancipation and colonization of the slaves and a liberal system of free public education, were rejected. It is a significant commentary on the evolution of his democratic thought that he proposed to retain the property qualification on voting in Virginia's first constitution but to give gratis to each adult male citizen fifty acres of land, which would enable him to qualify for the suffrage.

From June, 1779, to June, 1781, he was war governor of Virginia. In striving to furnish supplies and soldiers for the Continental army he neglected local defense, and the state was ravaged by invading armies. Accordingly, he was severely criticized for his administration of state affairs. So keenly was he hurt by these attacks that he resolved never again to hold public office. This period of bitterness was accentuated by grief over his wife's death, marking the nadir of his life. Despite his renunciation of public office, we find him serving for six months in the Congress of the Confederation and in 1784 going to Paris as the American minister. Thus, for five years he was absent from the United States at a period when the Federal constitution was being drafted and ratified. Nevertheless, he had a significant influence in securing the addition of the first ten amendments to the Constitution, known as the Bill of Rights. He advised his followers in America that he favored the ratification of the Constitution by nine states, insuring its acceptance, but that four states should withhold ratification until a bill of rights had been added. It is indicative of Jefferson's economic liberalism that he advocated the incorporation in this bill of rights of a provision outlawing monopolies, which was not adopted.

Despite his idealistic theories and philosophic outlook, Jefferson was a practical politician. One of the first important examples of his willingness to engage in the art of practical politics to attain his objectives was his deal with Hamilton in the summer of 1791 over the assumption of the state debts. Hamilton proposed that the national government take over about eighteen million dollars of state debts and pay them at par. The Virginia legislature strongly opposed this proposal in a resolution drafted by Patrick Henry, pointing out the danger to liberty and "the prostration of agriculture at the feet of commerce" by the adoption of such an unconstitutional measure perpetuating an enormous debt upon the nation. Nevertheless, Jefferson agreed to secure enough votes to pass this measure if Hamilton would use his influence to locate the national capital on the banks of the Potomac after a ten-year period in Philadelphia. The deal went through, and the South thus obtained the seat of the nation's capital. The District of Columbia was created out of adjoining parts of Maryland and Virginia, but in 1846 the Virginia portion, containing the town of Alexandria, was retroceded to the Old Dominion.

In this same summer of 1791 Jefferson's skill as an adroit politician was demonstrated by his "botanizing trip" up the Hudson River. At that time he and James Madison went ostensibly on a botanical excursion, but actually for the purpose of forming political alliances in New York, where Governor George Clinton, the Livingston clan, and Aaron Burr, the manipulator of St. Tammany Society of New York City, were opposed to the Federalist administration. In 1792 Virginia, North Carolina, Georgia, and New York voted for George Clinton for Vice President instead of for John Adams. Thus began the Virginia-New York Alliance, which has played such a significant role in the Republican and Democratic parties from the day of Jefferson, through the administrations of Jackson and Van Buren, to the recent period of Franklin Delano Roosevelt.

After Jefferson resigned from Washington's cabinet in 1793, he devoted himself to organizing a political party of opposition. By a variety of means he built up the Republican party. He gathered around him some of the most brilliant of the Southern leaders, particularly James Madison, who was converted from his strong Federalist allegiance. Realizing the need of propaganda and the fact that the newspapers were controlled by the Federalists, he gave Philip Freneau, the poet, a clerkship in the State Department, which enabled the latter partly to support himself while he was editing the *National Gazette*, the journal of the Republican party. Also Benjamin Franklin Bache, a grandson of Benjamin Franklin, edited the *Aurora* in Philadelphia, which violently attacked the Federalist policies. Jefferson hated to make public speeches, but he accomplished much in mobilizing his party by writing letters to key men in the states and by conversation. He and his cohorts continually attacked the Federalist party as having "monarchical" designs. Furthermore, he capitalized on the mistakes which the Federalist party made, especially the Alien and Sedition Acts. In 1796 Jefferson was the candidate of the Republicans for President against John Adams, who won the election by the narrow margin of three electoral votes. Jefferson became Vice President, which made him presiding officer of the Senate and gave him further opportunities quietly to organize his party.

A splendid opportunity to agitate for the advancement of the Republicans occurred in the autumn of 1798, when the Federalists secured the passage by Congress of the Alien and Sedition Acts. The Sedition Act was rightly regarded as a violation of the First Amendment of the Constitution protecting the freedom of speech and of the press. Moreover, these laws were harshly enforced by partisan Federalist judges, and most of the persons prosecuted were Republican editors. Jefferson determined to arouse the people to protest against these arbitrary acts and at the same time to formulate a platform for his party. Since he was Vice President, however, he felt that he should not take an open part in the attack. Consequently, his authorship of a strong protest against the arbitrary acts of the Federalists, called the Kentucky Resolutions, was concealed. These resolutions were introduced into the Kentucky legislature by John Breckinridge and adopted by that body on November 16, 1798. A month later the Virginia Resolutions, drafted by James Madison, but introduced into the legislature by John Taylor of Caroline, were passed. They were less radical than the Jefferson resolutions. The political character of the Virginia and Kentucky Resolutions has been overemphasized so that their significance as a restatement of civil liberties in America has not been properly recognized.[5]

These documents were written at a time when Americans believed in a social compact, or contract among citizens, as forming the true basis of government. According to this view, sovereignty was divided by the Federal Constitution between the states and the central government. The question who should determine the violations of the compact, the Constitution, whenever the Federal government should encroach upon the rights of the states had not yet been decided. Marshall's decision of Marbury versus Madison establishing the right of judicial review by the Supreme Court was not rendered until 1803. Jefferson and Madison maintained in their resolutions that in the absence of an umpire between the states and the Federal government, the states or the people had this power—in the words of the Kentucky resolution, "That the government created by this compact was not made the exclusive or final judge of the extent of powers delegated to itself." [6]

The Virginia and Kentucky Resolutions restated the theory that the Federal government was a government of strictly limited and delegated powers. The Alien and Sedition Acts, they asserted, were unconstitutional and therefore null and void. They called upon the sister states or "co-states" to remonstrate and secure the repeal of the obnoxious laws. These resolutions were a protest against the trend toward centralization, or a "general consolidated government." The Virginia and Kentucky Resolutions were the appeal of a minority against the tyranny of a majority. They reflected the fear of the Southern states that the central government would be controlled by the commercial interests of the North which would use their power to injure the agricultural interests of the South. This fight of Jefferson and Madison to preserve the federal character of the central government was not a disunion movement, for both men were loyal to the Union. Rather, the Republicans had a strong suspicion that the Federalists were trying to change the original character of the central government. The people should be aroused, they believed, to resist the first attempt to convert the Federal government into a highly centralized and powerful institution. Jefferson and Madison were therefore fighting for a limited national government, or constitutionalism.

None of the states responded favorably to the Virginia and Kentucky Resolutions. Several of the Northern states definitely said that the Supreme Court, and not the states, was the proper agency to determine when infractions of the Constitution had been made by Congress. In rebuttal, the Kentucky legislature, on November 22, 1799, passed some additional resolutions, in which for the first time the word "nullification" was used. The core of the second Kentucky Resolutions was the statement, "That the several states who formed that instrument [the Constitution] being sovereign and independent, have the unquestionable right to judge of the infraction; and, *That a nullification of those sovereignties, of all unauthorized acts done un·der the color of that instrument is the rightful remedy."* [7] The Virginia and Kentucky Resolutions are important documents in Southern political theory, for the compact theory of the Constitution which they expounded contained the germs of the South Carolina nullification movement and of the secession doctrines.

In 1800 Jefferson and Aaron Burr became the candidates of the Republican party for President and Vice President. In accordance with the provision of the Constitution at that time, the electors cast two votes without specifying which ballot was for President and which one for Vice President. Since all the Republican electors voted both for Burr and Jefferson, it happened that both men received seventy-three electoral votes while the Federalist candidates, John Adams and Charles C. Pinckney, received sixty-five and sixty-four respectively. Thus Jefferson and Burr were tied for the majority vote for President, and a choice had to be made by the House of the Representatives. This body contained many Federalists who wished to defeat Jefferson by voting for Burr. The New York politician disclaimed any desire to defeat the will of his party and supplant Jefferson. Moreover, he refused to bargain with the Federalists and maintained a neutral attitude. Jefferson also refused to bargain, but his friends gave assurances to the Federalists. On the thirty-sixth ballot he was elected over Burr when several Federalists under the leadership of James A. Bayard of Delaware abstained from voting. The defect of the Constitution which permitted Presidential electors to cast plural votes was remedied by the adoption of the Twelfth Amendment.

The election of 1800 has often been called a peaceful revolution. The Republicans believed that they had overthrown an aristocratic monarchical group in control of the government and restored a republican regime. Jefferson walked to the Capitol from his boarding-house to be inaugurated instead of riding in state in a coach attended by liveried servants. Thus he symbolized his belief in republican simplicity as contrasted with Federalist ceremony and aristocratic attitudes. As President, he discarded the practice of seating guests at the dinner table of the White House in accordance with their rank or importance and instituted the democratic principle of pell mell. Even in his negligence and simplicity of dress he dramatized his belief in republican simplicity. Once he offended the pompous English minister, Anthony Merry, who was dressed in diplomatic uniform, by receiving him clad in slippers without heels. Jefferson's emphasis on the fact that clothes do not make the man was illustrated by a vivid description of his appearance written by a New England Senator, William Plumer:

In a few moments after our arrival a tall, high-boned man came into the room. He was dressed, or rather undressed, in an old brown coat, red waistcoat, old corduroy small-clothes much soiled, woolen hose, and slippers without heels. I thought him a servant, when General Varnum surprised me by announcing that it was the President.[8]

Yet Jefferson was an aristocrat, not of the European model, but a republican aristocrat. He had the tastes of an aristocrat. He gave elegant dinners at the White House, with the aid of his French chef. His generous hospitality is indicated by the fact that his wine bill for the first year in office was $2,800. The critical Senator Plumer has described a delightful dinner with the President in which eight different kinds of wine were served, including Tokay that cost a guinea a bottle. Jefferson on this occasion was well-dressed, with a new black suit, silk hose, clean ruffled linen, and hair highly powdered.[9] Furthermore, the man presiding at the table (he was a widower at this time) was the most brilliant conversationalist in America. Jefferson loved music, architecture, and the collecting of fine books. Although he hated dogs, he loved birds—he brought to live with him in the White House a pet mockingbird which would perch on his shoulder or finger. Like most of the Southern gentry, he delighted in fine horses, frequently riding his beautiful saddle horse, "Wildair," about the streets of Washington.

Jefferson was the product primarily of the Enlightenment of the eighteenth century and of Virginia plantation influences. He was not unique among the plantation gentry, for many of the liberal aristocrats of his period were very much like him, differing from him principally in degree rather than in quality. It was the fashion in the eighteenth century for men to be versatile, and Jefferson became the most versatile of our Presidents. He was an accomplished violinist until in middle life he broke his right wrist, which caused him to give up his violin playing and to learn to write with his left hand. His talents included the art of practical invention, which enabled him to devise an improved type of plow, a polygraph for writing several copies of a letter, the swivel chair, later to become the throne of bureaucrats, and numerous gadgets for his home at "Monticello." He was a collector of American Indian vocabularies and was one of the first paleontologists in the United States, studying the fossils of prehistoric animals. In politics, he was not only a skilled diplomat and a practical statesman, but America's leading political philosopher. He was also one of the finest amateur architects of this country. His literary skill was exhibited in his political pamphlets, his *Notes on Virginia* (1784), his inaugural addresses, his *Anas,* his *Parliamentary Manual,* and his numerous letters.

His versatility, however, may not have been as deeply based as his extravagant admirers have claimed for him. We know that there was little originality in his composition of the Declaration of Independence, which was strongly influenced by the writings of John Locke. Indeed, Jefferson's mind was empiric and practical, which tended to make him an opportunist. His character and personality were so complex that, as a recent biographer has observed, his portrait cannot be painted in broad brush strokes of black and white. Perhaps the best insight into his many-sided nature is afforded by his epitaph, in which he wrote down the achievements for which he wished to be remembered.

> Here was buried Thomas Jefferson,
> Author of the Declaration of American Independence,
> Of the Statute of Virginia for Religious Freedom,
> And Father of the University of Virginia.

The "revolution of 1800" was not so profound a change as has been depicted. Actually it was the transfer of the power of the central government from the control of a commercial aristocracy into the hands of a landed aristocracy. Jefferson formulated the theory of a republican form of government, but the practice of this theory was largely left to the succeeding generation. The psychology of the common man toward the government was not greatly changed until the Jacksonian movement of the 1820's and 1830's. The victory of the Republicans in 1800 arrested only temporarily the growing centralization of the Federal government, and it is significant that much of the Federalist program was retained. Indeed, Jefferson did not indiscriminately discharge Federal officeholders, but steered a middle course between preserving a non-partisan civil service and the later Spoils System.

The theory of politics held by the agricultural South was admirably stated by Jefferson in his first inaugural address, March 4, 1801. In broad outlines he sketched the ideal of a *laissez-faire* government—"a wise and frugal Government, which shall restrain men from injuring one another, shall leave them otherwise free to regulate their own pursuits of industry and improvement, and shall not take from the mouth of labor the bread it has earned." For the defense of the state he proposed to rely on the militia instead of the standing army, and he upheld the supremacy of the civil over the military authority. In foreign affairs the nation should pursue a policy of peace and no "entangling alliances." His first inaugural address was permeated with the spirit of reconciliation with the Federalists, who had so bitterly attacked him. He declared that although the will of the majority must prevail, the rights of minorities must be protected.

The Jeffersonian administration bears many resemblances to the "New Deal" of the decade of the 1930's. Their theories of taxation were strikingly similar, based on placing the incidence of taxation on the rich. To Dupont de Nemours Jefferson wrote in 1811 advocating a system of taxation of imports by which, after the public debt had been discharged, "the farmers will see his government supported, his children educated, and the face of the country made a paradise by the contributions of the rich alone without being called on to spare a cent from his earnings." [10] Although radical in thought at times and surprisingly violent in speech on occasion, Jefferson was opportunistic like Franklin D. Roosevelt, and he was not much of a radical after he came into power. Indeed, he adopted a considerable part of the Hamiltonian program, and, after he became the leader of a political party, he did nothing constructive in attacking the greatest social evil of his age, slavery.

In his conduct of foreign affairs, Jefferson was not isolationist, despite his recommendation of avoiding foreign alliances. He had the modern concept that nations, having a common feeling for democracy and a similar ideology should support each other by moral, political, and economic means short of war. When the French overthrew their absolute monarchy, Jefferson wrote to George Mason: "I look with great anxiety for the firm establishment of the new government in France, being perfectly convinced that if it takes place there it will spread sooner or later all over Europe. On the contrary a check there would retard the revival of liberty in other countries. I consider the establishment and success of their government as necessary to stay up our own and to prevent it from falling back to that kind of a half-way house, the English constitution." [11] Later he anticipated the Good Neighbor policy of Franklin Delano Roosevelt in proposing "a cordial fraternization" between the republics of Latin America and the United States.

On the other hand, Jefferson was an ardent pacifist who neglected the navy, in contrast to Roosevelt, the advocate of building a more powerful navy to meet the dangers of a European war. A Jeffersonian aberration was a scheme of constructing a number of small gunboats and anchoring them in the ports and mouths of the rivers to be manned by the citizens of the surrounding country in case of an invasion. By this "mosquito fleet" he hoped to save money, but it proved totally impractical. When England and France violated our rights on the high seas and immediately after the British warship *Leopard*, fired on our frigate, the *Chesapeake*, in 1807, Jefferson restrained his country from a declaration of war. Instead, the Republican Congress passed the Embargo Act, which prohibited American vessels from leaving the harbors of the United States for foreign ports.

Franklin Delano Roosevelt drew much of the support for his liberal program from the under-privileged classes of the cities. Jefferson, on the other hand, compared the mobs of large cities to sores on the body politic, unsuitable raw material to make good citizens in a republic. Preeminently the leader of the Southern agrarians, he placed great faith in the virtue and judgment of small, independent farmers, who were property owners as contrasted with the proletariat of the cities. He wished to keep America rural as long as possible in order to prevent the duplication of the unhappy conditions of the mature countries of Europe. American yeoman farmers and planters might temporarily be misled by propaganda, he believed, but the returning good sense of the people would correct their mistakes. Strangely, Jefferson seldom used the words "democratic" or "democracy," but referred to the American experiment of government as "republican." The word "Democratic" as applied to the political party which Jefferson founded was first used alone as the party label in 1844.

The Southern planters and farmers, who desired a decentralized government, found a spokesman in Jefferson. If the South had possessed a more balanced economy, undoubtedly there would have been less emphasis on state rights in the history of that section. Over and over again crops up the fear of Southerners that a strong central government would be controlled by the Northern states which would pass adverse legislature against Southern interests, particularly in regard to slavery and the tariff. The South, therefore, advocated a strict interpretation or construction of the Constitution to confine the Federal government to its delegated powers. In addition to this fear Jefferson had another strong reason for favoring localism in government. An ardent admirer of the New England town meeting, he urged the Southern states to divide their counties into wards, or "ward-republics" he called them, which would enable every citizen to participate in direct government. He believed that if political power was kept largely in the hands of the states and of the local communities the people would have an opportunity to watch their officials more closely and thus prevent corruption.

The democratic leader of 1800 and the democratic leader of 1936 found a conservative Supreme Court hostile to their policies and therefore they tried to curb its power. Jefferson's attempt to reform the judiciary by the initiation of impeachment proceedings was motivated particularly by his opposition to the centralizing tendency of the Supreme Court. This attack on the independence of the judiciary failed when the trial of Justice Samuel Chase in 1805 resulted in acquittal despite the fact that the Republicans had the requisite majority in the Senate to convict. Jefferson continued, however, to oppose a Supreme Court that was "independent of the Nation" and therefore he proposed that, instead of the tenure of the judges being for life, their appointments should be renewed every four or six years. Indeed, Jefferson's writings give strong support to a modern questioning of the wisdom of judicial review.

The great Virginian was a firm advocate of majority rule, not merely of the original majority who drafted the Constitution but of the continuing majority. He appealed to young men in all ages by declaring that "the earth belongs in usufruct to the living; that the dead have neither power nor rights over it. . . ." [12] Literally, he held that each generation should make its own laws and not be bound by the dead hand of the past—a generation being twenty to thirty-four years. He was youthful in spirit also in his flexibility, in adapting himself to changed conditions. During the War of 1812 he became convinced that the United States must give up the ideal of a rural Arcadia and develop a more balanced economy by manufacturing enough goods to be independent of Europe. On his plantation of "Monticello" he himself had erected a nail factory. He took great strides away from his former doctrine of the negative, *laissez-faire* state by proposing that after the public debt had been liquidated the surplus Federal revenues should be used to build national roads and canals and to support a national university.

Jefferson's political philosophy was derived partly from his experience during the fermenting period of the American Revolution and partly from the insemination of liberal European thought. The works of the English democratic thinkers of the seventeenth and eighteenth centuries, such as those of John Locke, Algernon Sidney, and Bolingbroke, as well as the writings of the Scotsman, Lord Kames, had a profound influence on the development of his political philosophy. With the exception of Montesquieu's *Spirit of the Laws*, French political writings do not seem to have greatly affected him. After he had matured his philosophy of life, he spent five delightful years as American minister to France, where he acquired such a decided taste for French wines, music, and cookery that homely old Patrick Henry is reported to have said, "Tom Jefferson has abjured his native vittles." Instead of succumbing to French influences, however, his experiences and observations in France served chiefly to strengthen him in his robust Americanism. Later in his career the Physiocrats and Ideologues, especially Destutt de Tracy, appealed to him, since some of their philosophy clarified and confirmed certain ideas he himself had evolved through his experience and observation.

Jefferson was the most effective exponent of intellectual liberty that America has produced. Uniformity of opinion or of religion, he believed, is neither possible nor desirable any more so than is the standardization of face or stature. The masses of the people tend to be intolerant of critics or persons who disagree with their prejudices in vital matters. Dissent gives them a sense of insecurity. Likewise, dictatorships cannot permit an uncensored press or an untrammeled radio. The lovers of liberty, on the other hand, have always been concerned with the protection of minority rights and the preservation of freedom of expression. The preservation of the right of holding heterodox opinions is a perennial problem in a democratic government, for the tyranny of the majority, is more formidable, as the great Catholic historian Lord Acton observed, than the tyranny of the minority. In our own time this fact has been demonstrated by the attempts to suppress the "subversive propaganda" of those opposed to capitalistic society, by the spy hunt of the Congressional Committee on Un-American activities, and by the doctrine of "guilt by association."

The use of the force of civil government to bring about a uniformity of opinion Jefferson regarded as a violation of the rights of personality and as producing hypocrisy. In the preamble to his famous Virginia Statute of Religious Freedom he declared that the civil government should interfere with the expression of opinions only when they "break into overt acts against peace and order." [12a] Let the government practice toleration, he urged, for truth will prevail over lies and propaganda provided free argument and debate are allowed, "errors ceasing to be dangerous when it is permitted freely to contradict them." Only by zealously guarding civil rights, especially the freedom of speech, of religion, and of assembly, he thought, could the right of dissent by individuals and minorities be maintained. Thus the minority would have the opportunity, through debate and persuasion, to become the majority controlling the government.[13]

This leader of the early Republicans was too great a realist to believe that political democracy could flourish in a soil of tremendous inequalities of wealth. He concluded that, although an equal division of property was impracticable, "legislators cannot invent too many devices for subdividing property." [14] Believing that the small landholders were the most precious part of the state, he wished to see the United States a land of modest fortunes, in which the government should assist the weaker members of society to acquire a reasonable share of property, and reduce bloated fortunes by indirect government action. His sympathy for the poor man is revealed in a letter he wrote to Marquis de Lafayette urging the latter to travel incognito through France to observe the living conditions of the people. "You must ferret the people out of their hovels as I have done," he wrote, "look into their kettles, eat their bread, loll on their beds under pretense of resting yourself, but in fact, to find if they are soft. You will feel a sublime pleasure in the course of this investigation, and a sublimer one hereafter, when you shall be able to apply your knowledge to the softening of their beds or the throwing a morsel of meat into their kettles of vegetables." [15] An example of this disinterested love for humanity was his smuggling of some Italian rice in his pockets through the customs in order to introduce a superior variety into the Southern states. His zeal for human welfare caused him to think of practical means of lessening the drudgery of life. He proposed, for example, the installation of small steam engines in the homes, run by the kitchen fire to pump water for household use and fire protection.

Jefferson's reputation has had a curious fluctuation of popular favor and neglect. In the Presidential election of 1804 his popularity was at its height when he carried every state in the Union except Connecticut and Delaware. Jeffersonian ideas underlay the democratic movement of the Jacksonian era. When the proslavery argument reached its full bloom in the decade of the 1850's, however, the ruling class in the South scrapped his natural rights theory and dismissed the Declaration of Independence as glittering generalities. While his native section repudiated much of his liberalism, although holding to his state rights doctrine, Jefferson obtained new followers and popularity in the North among the abolitionists and Republicans. Lincoln's speeches and writings are saturated with Jeffersonian thought. Following the Civil War the Southern people regarded Lee, not Jefferson, as their greatest man after Washington. During the

Populist revolt of the 1880's and 1890's, the shirt-sleeve leaders of the farmers, such as Tom Watson of Georgia, appealed to the magic name of Jefferson as the champion of the common man. Then the fame of the philosopher-statesman declined, to be revived once more by historical biographers in the decade of the 1920's and later by the political needs of the party of Franklin Delano Roosevelt. Ironically, the opponents of the Roosevelt administration, especially the Liberty League, also claimed Jefferson to be on their side, pointing to him as the advocate of state rights and of a *laissez-faire* government and as disapproving of a third term for President. Finally, the rise of Hitler and the Fascist ideology led to the exaltation of Jefferson as the supreme exponent of democracy and Americanism. Very recently the American people have been reminded of this superb liberal leader in many ways, by a Jefferson coin, a Jefferson stamp, by the speeches of the "New Dealers," by the building of a marble memorial to him on the tidal basin at Washington, and by the undertaking of publishing his entire writings.

The party of Thomas Jefferson has been regarded as peculiarly the champion of state rights within the United States. The doctrine of state rights was not a monopoly of the South, however, for it was frequently used as a defense mechanism by different sections of the country to protect their interests against a hostile majority in control of the government. Suspicion is aroused concerning the sincerity of this plea of state rights by the fact that when the exponents of state rights obtained control of the government they lost their enthusiasm for their cherished doctrine. Even Jefferson and Madison, authors of the Virginia and Kentucky Resolutions, when they became Presidents abandoned their extreme state rights position, to which they were so devoted as leaders of a faction out of power. The acquisition of Louisiana in 1803, which is discussed in the following chapter, is an example of Jefferson's flexibility or opportunism in departing from his principles of state rights and strict construction of the Constitution.

The trend of the Republican party after 1801 from its adherence to state rights led to a split in its ranks. The group which became disgruntled at the leadership of Jefferson were called the "Old Republicans" since they were staunchly loyal to the doctrine of state rights and the strict interpretation of the Constitution. The out-standing political leaders in this clique were John Randolph of Roanoke, John Taylor, William Branch Giles, and James Monroe of Virginia. The Speaker of the House, Nathaniel Macon of North Carolina, joined the discontented faction, probably because of his ruralism. He idealized an agrarian society where men did not live close enough to each other to hear their neighbor's dogs barking. This group of Old Republicans were also called "tertium quids," or a third something, neither loyal Jeffersonians nor Federalists.

In addition to their devotion to the original principles of the Republican party, some of the leaders had personal grudges against the President. Monroe had been chagrined by the failure of Jefferson to submit to the Senate a treaty which he had made with England. Randolph had been humiliated by his mismanagement of the impeachment of Justice Chase, for which he illogically blamed Jefferson. The "Quids" bitterly attacked Jefferson and his cabinet for the settlement of the Yazoo fraud question, by which five million acres of land were appropriated to satisfy the claims of *bona fide* purchasers of land from the Yazoo companies. In 1808 the "Quids" supported Monroe as a candidate of the party for President in opposition to Madison, Jefferson's choice.

Of the opponents of the Jefferson administration, John Randolph of Roanoke was the most feared. He was the greatest master of satire and invective that the South has produced. Reared on the plantation of "Bizarre," a scion of the aristocratic Randolph family, he carried the individualism, pride, and arrogance of the Southern planter to the extreme limits of caricature. He was remarkably precocious as a youth but so unstable that he left both William and Mary College and Princeton without completing his studies. In 1799 he was elected to Congress at the age of twenty-six and within two years he had been chosen chairman of the Ways and Means Committee which made him leader of the Republicans in the lower house of Congress. In 1805 he had a quarrel with Jefferson, following the Chase impeachment fiasco, and from this time on, he became the Great Opposer—vehemently attacking the administration in the Yazoo fraud, in the attempt to acquire West Florida, and in the passage of the Embargo Act. He violently condemned the maintenance of a standing army, proposing to rely for the defense of the country upon the militia. Also he was one of the early Southern "watchdogs over the Treasury." Unavailingly he tried to prevent a declaration of war against England in 1812 as well as the adoption of nationalizing measures of the Republicans after the Treaty of Ghent. In 1820 he was one of the most extreme opponents of the Missouri Compromise. During a long career of various inconsistencies, there was one fixed principle from which he never deviated, a fanatical devotion to state rights.

John Randolph was the outstanding eccentric of the Old South. He presented a strange appearance with his slender legs, like pipe stems, his projecting chin, dark, sad eyes, wrinkled face, and high, feminine voice. He did not need to shave, and he seems to have been impotent sexually. Always unhappy, with frail health and jangled nerves, he lashed at his enemies with a mordant tongue and was ready to fight a duel at the least insult. He would appear in Congress booted and spurred, carrying a riding whip, and followed by his dogs. Although he had a scorn for common people and for political democracy, this perverse aristocrat was an enthusiastic supporter of Andrew Jackson for President. Jackson repaid his support shrewdly by sending the trouble-maker as minister to Russia, where the severe climate ruined his delicate health. There was an appealing humane side in the nature of this Virginia planter. Once he was asked who was the most superb orator he had heard. He promptly replied, "A slave. She was a mother and her rostrum was the auction block." [16] In later life he was afflicted with periods of insanity. He died in 1833, leaving a will which emancipated his four hundred slaves.

More important than Randolph as an intellectual expounder of the doctrines of state rights was John Taylor of Caroline County, Virginia. This Southern planter had a passionate love for agriculture and the way of life based on it. Although he was a Senator for a brief period, he avoided office-holding and devoted his strong mind to writing pamphlets and books and fashioning a political philosophy suited to the agrarian interests of the South. Taylor violently opposed the centralization of political power in the Federal government because he believed that such power would be used by the Northern majority to exploit the South. In 1788 he opposed the ratification of the Federal Constitution by his native state, and ten years later he proposed to Jefferson the idea of forming a Southern Confederacy. Jefferson discouraged such a disunion movement, reminding Taylor that the oppressive Federalist rule would be temporary and that free governments always breed dissenting groups, for which secession was not the right remedy.

Taylor ardently supported Jefferson's early policies, even the purchase of Louisiana. But he refused to change his principles when the majority of his party followed a nationalistic course. Joining the "Quids," he supported Monroe for President in opposition to Madison, Jefferson's choice. In his prolix pamphlets and books such as *An Inquiry into the Principles and Policy of the Government of the United States* (1814), *Construction Construed* (1820), and *Tyranny Unmasked* (1822), he attacked the establishment of a national bank, the increase of the public debt, and the enactment of a protective tariff as a surrender of the Federal government to the Northern capitalists. John Marshall's decisions whittling down the powers of the states alarmed and incensed him. He pointed out the economic bases of political parties and warned the South of the danger of a moneyed aristocracy controlling the central government. Taylor's plea for a balanced government, in which the rights of the states were preserved, became more popular in the ante-bellum South as that section realized more clearly its minority position in the Union.

Citations

1. Lipscomb and Bergh, *Writings of Thomas Jefferson*, IX, 335–336.
2. Marie Kimball, *Jefferson the Road to Glory, 1743–1776* (New York, 1943), Chap. I.
3. Karl Lehmann, *Jefferson, American Humanist* (New York, 1947), 138.
4. Dumas Malone, *Jefferson the Virginian* (Boston, 1948), the best biography of Jefferson, chaps. 17–20.
5. A. Koch and H. Ammon, "The Virginia and Kentucky Resolutions:–," (*William and Mary Quarterly, Third Series*) V (April, 1948), 145–176.

6. H. S. COMMAGER (ed.), *Documents of American History* (New York, 1947) I, 155.

7. *Ibid.*, I, 184.

8. HENRY ADAMS, *History of the United States of America During the Administration of Thomas Jefferson* (New York, 1930), Book II, 366.

9. WILLIAM PLUMER, *William Plumer's Memorandum of Proceedings in the United States Senate, 1803–1807* (New York, 1923).

10. GILBERT CHINARD, *Thomas Jefferson, the Apostle of Americanism* (Boston, 1946), 494–495.

11. LIPSCOMB and BERGH, *op. cit.*, VIII, 123–124.

12. Quoted in H. S. Commager, *Majority Rule and Minority Rights* (New York, 1943), 22.

12a. This quotation should read "break out into overt acts against peace and good order." Julian P. Boyd (ed.), *The Paper of Thomas Jefferson* (Princeton, 1950), II, 546. In the 1786 edition of his *Notes on Virginia* Jefferson took liberties with the original texts of the bill and the act, printing a hybrid version. *Ibid.*, 547–553.

13. CLEMENT EATON, "The Jeffersonian Tradition of Liberalism in America," *South Atlantic Quarterly*, XLIII (January, 1944), 2–5.

14. P. L. FORD (ed.), *The Writings of Thomas Jefferson* (New York, 1892–99), VII, 35.

15. LIPSCOMB and BERGH, *op. cit.*, VI, 109.

16. W. C. BRUCE, *John Randolph of Roanoke, 1773–1833* (New York, 1922), II, 251.

CHAPTER VIII

The Creoles Become Southerners

CONTRARY to a prevalent misconception, the Creoles were persons of Latin extraction born in the colonies without any admixture of Negro blood. There were two types of Creoles in the South, the Spanish in Florida and Texas, and the French in Louisiana. The military and governmental center of the Creoles in Florida was St. Augustine, founded in 1565, the oldest town in the United States, from which radiated Catholic missions into the hinterland as far north as Guale ("Wallie") or coastal Georgia and the sea islands. After the Franciscan missions were destroyed by Indian revolts and attacks from South Carolina during Queen Anne's War, Spain showed a remarkable indifference to her remote settlements in Florida. Chiefly soldiers and priests came to the flowery peninsula and no Protestants, heretics, or Jews were allowed to enter the Spanish colonies. The settlement at St. Augustine was maintained primarily to assert Spanish ownership of Florida and to provide a military base for the protection of the Bahama Channel through which the treasure fleet from Mexico sailed to Spain. It is indicative of the inert policy of Spain that the chief motive for establishing the western outpost of Pensacola in 1698 was not any ambition toward expansion, but merely to prevent the French from seizing a strategic location.

Under Spanish control (which was interrupted for twenty years during the English occupation, 1763–83) the Creoles of Florida lived a somnolent and backward existence. They failed to develop a valuable export commodity or to advance beyond a frontier civilization. Nevertheless, it is unhistorical to perpetuate the old stereotype of the Spaniards in the New World, the so-called black legend, which vastly exaggerates the Spaniard's intolerance, laziness, pride, hostility to innovation, lack of local self-government, and cruelty toward the Indians. It must be remembered that Florida was on the periphery of the Spanish empire in America and that at the center a remarkable colonial civilization arose in such cities as Mexico City, Lima, and Havana. Since Florida represented a frontier outpost, it is not surprising that after this region was acquired by the United States in 1821 the remains of Spanish culture were relatively slight.

The attempt of France to establish an empire on the Gulf coast, on the other hand, has left enduring effects upon the deep South. The voyage of La Salle from Canada down the Mississippi River to its mouth in 1682 formed the basis of the French claim to the land which they named Louisiana. La Salle failed in the attempt to plant a colony at the mouth of the great river, but one of his followers, a mendacious priest named Father Louis Hennepin, revived the interest of the French in colonizing this remote region by publishing a volume, *New Discovery* (Utrecht, 1698), which was widely read in Europe. In this book he claimed to have discovered the mouth of the Mississippi two years before the memorable voyage of La Salle. French secret agents erroneously reported that the English were preparing an expedition under the guidance of Father Hennepin to seize the mouth of the Mississippi River to forestall French occupation. The French Minister, Count de Pontchartrain, sent out an expedition in 1699 under the Sieur de Iberville to found a colony at this strategic place. This Canadian soldier located his colony, not at the mouth of the Mississippi, but to the eastward at Old Biloxi (now Ocean Springs) in the present state of Mississippi. In 1702 the settlement was moved to a site on the Mobile River, and eight years later it was transferred to the location of the modern city of Mobile.

The dominant figure in the early history of Louisiana was a younger brother of Iberville, the Sieur de Bienville. Only twenty-one years of age in 1701 when he was placed in charge of the Louisiana colony, he governed it at intervals for over forty years. He became an adept in Indian diplomacy, studied the languages and characteristics of neighboring tribes, and treated them with frankness and bonhomie. His greatest achievement was the founding of New Orleans in 1718, whose site, a hundred miles above the mouth of the

Mississippi River, he had selected the previous year at a place "having one of the finest crescents on the river."

During the early years of Louisiana, King Louis XIV, engaged in war, paid little attention to his far away colony on the Gulf coast. In 1712 he turned over the responsibility of the colony to a rich merchant, Antoine Crozat, who was given a monopoly of its trade with the exception of beaver furs. The appointment of Lamothe Cadillac, the founder of Detroit, as governor, failed to bring prosperity to the province, and Crozat became so disappointed at the lack of financial profits from his investment that in 1717 he surrendered his charter to the king.

After the failure of Crozat's monopoly, a Scotch speculator, John Law, in 1717 organized the Company of the West (popularly known as the Mississippi Company) to exploit Louisiana. This company was given a monopoly of trade and the right to work the supposed gold and silver mines. Its stock was sold to the public through a remarkable campaign of advertising which puffed up this remote region as an earthly paradise. A wild orgy of speculation in its stock followed in France, known as the Mississippi Bubble. Law exercised such a great fascination, even hypnotic power, over the French people that he deluded all classes, from perfumed noblemen to his own coachman.

In return for the privileges of its charter, the company agreed to transport six thousand white colonists and three thousand slaves to Louisiana. Here, however, was the rub. It was difficult to get substantial French peasants to emigrate. Consequently, the Company of the West (later entitled Company of the Indies), in its eagerness to obtain human material for its colony, sent over many worthless and vicious settlers, men and women picked up from the streets of Paris, from prisons, houses of correction, and hospitals. The agents of the police of Old Orleans collected prostitutes and vagrants, in order to send them to swell the population of its namesake in the New World.[1] In 1718 the Company transported over eight hundred colonists without proper provision for feeding them. They were dumped upon the shores of Louisiana and Governor Bienville had a difficult time absorbing them into his weak colony. Few were willing to work as agricultural laborers, and no mines of silver and gold were discovered. Among the worthless rabble that came over was a group of substantial German peasants who settled above New Orleans on the "German coast" of the Mississippi River. The most productive immigrants brought into the colony by the Company were large numbers of black slaves.

In 1720 the Mississippi Bubble burst, one of the most famous swindles in history. The glowing dreams of quick profits which the specious Scotsman had conjured in the minds of French "suckers" were not realized. Indeed, Louisiana remained an unprofitable colony, a financial loss to the French treasury, as long as France held it. When Law's dazzling stock manipulations failed, he fled from France penniless, and a large number of French people suffered bankruptcy as a result of placing confidence in him. In 1731, after a disastrous Indian war, the Company of the Indies surrendered its charter and Louisiana reverted to a royal colony.

One of the potent reasons for the failure of the French to thrive in Louisiana was their inability to win and hold the friendship of neighboring Indian tribes. In order to overawe the hostile Natchez, Cadillac established Fort Rosalie at Natchez. When these savages killed some French travelers, an expedition was sent against them which was called by Gallic wits "La Guerre aux Poules," or "The Chicken War," because the chief spoils were some captured chickens. In 1729 the Natchez massacred the garrison and settlers at Fort Rosalie. The French retaliated the following year by a grim war which liquidated this brave and warlike people. The remnants of the defeated nation fled for refuge to the Chickasaw Indians in the present state of Tennessee. Ten years afterward Bienville began a war against the Chickasaw which ended in failure. He was so chagrined over its result, as well as depressed by ill health, that he resigned his governorship and left for France, never to return to Louisiana.

The last important Indian trouble which the French in Louisiana experienced was with the Choctaw, a powerful tribe inhabiting the present states of Mississippi and Alabama. The French regarded these Indians as their property, and in 1736 they built Fort Tombecbé on the upper waters of the Tombigbee River in Alabama to maintain their ascendancy over them. A faction of the Choctaw, however, under the leadership of Rouge Soulier (Red Shoe) was alienated from the French and sought trade connections with the English. Red Shoe had greatly resented the seduction of his favorite wife by a Frenchman and determined to secure vengeance. In 1746 during King George's War the followers of Red Shoe killed the French traders among them. The English seized this opportunity to send James Adair, an Indian trader who subsequently wrote a *History of the American Indians* (1776), to extend their influence over the disaffected Choctaw. This effort was frustrated, however, by the assassination of Red Shoe the next year by a pro-French warrior. There followed a fratricidal war between the pro-English and pro-French factions of the Choctaw nation. The Louisiana authorities cynically encouraged this civil war, which eventually resulted in the establishment of exclusive French influence over the Choctaw. By the Grandpré treaty of 1750 the French agreed to expel all English traders and to continue to make war against the Chickasaw, inveterate enemies of both the Choctaw and the French.

The ineptitude of the French of Louisiana in handling Indian affairs contrasts with the success of the Canadian French in dominating the Algonkin tribes. Two adverse economic factors, however, contributed to the signal failure of the Louisiana colony to develop a lucrative Indian trade. Beaver furs from the Illinois country which were shipped down the river to New Orleans spoiled on account of the warm climate. Furthermore, the French could not secure manufactured goods to use in the Indian trade as cheaply as their English competitors.

Louisiana suffered from a bad governmental system. The administration of the province was divided between the royal governor, who had charge of military defense and Indian relations, and the *ordonnateur*, or intendant, who had charge of finances and justice, assisted by a superior council in which the people were represented by six of the principal inhabitants. The two executive officers were supposed to serve as a check on each other. They were to act jointly in matters relating to commerce, agriculture, and the increase of population. This duplex system of government led to innumerable quarrels and the hampering of efficient administration. At times the wives of the intendant and of the governor waged bitter social wars, posting lampoons against each other on the street corners. Nor did this system check the spread of corruption among the officials, for most of them came to Louisiana to exploit their jobs in order to return, well-laden, in the words of Gayarré, the Creole historian, "to their cherished native country, to the beautiful France, which they could not forget." [2] Such a governor was the Marquis de Vaudreuil who for ten years, from 1743 to 1753, ruled Louisiana with a splendor, luxury, and pomp that were a faint reflection of the reign of Louis XIV in France. Unfortunately, this gay and magnificent governor was a corruptionist, who made illegal profits out of his office. Like the neighboring colony of Florida, Louisiana did not enjoy political freedom. The inhabitants had no control over their government; everything was decided in France or by the royal officials. The laws were the customs of Paris, which did not provide a jury system. Even prices at the market were regulated by the intendant.

The French in Louisiana, however, did not establish the feudal system of landholding which predominated in Canada. The arable land was divided into little farms, consisting of a frontage of one arpent (182 feet) on the river and forty arpents deep. Also some large estates cultivated by slave labor were established. The fertile alluvial soil of the Mississippi River valley was protected from inundation by the erection of levees which finally attained a height of twenty or thirty feet; New Orleans was protected by a levee as early as 1729. The chief crops of the Creole farmers were tobacco, indigo, and rice. Although sugar cane was introduced into Louisiana from Hayti by the Jesuits in 1751, it did not become an important crop until the close of the century.

In order to control the numerous slaves a black code was promulgated (1724). The *Code Noir* contained some humane provisions, such as laws forbidding masters to work their slaves on Sunday or holidays or sell young children from their mothers or torture their slaves. Furthermore, all slaves were required to be instructed in the Catholic religion, and emancipated slaves were to enjoy the same rights and privileges as free-born persons. On the other hand, this slave code placed numerous harsh restrictions on the servile population to prevent insurrection and ordered runaway slaves to be branded with a fleur-de-lis on one shoulder and to have their ears cut.

The chief cause for the feeble expansive power of France was the lack of an invigorating stream of immigrants. As in Spanish Florida, Jews were prohibited from immigrating into the colony, and, in general, Protestants also were excluded. Thus France failed to utilize some of her best emigrating stock, the French Huguenots, who would have entered French colonies if permitted. Since the Catholic population of France had little desire to emigrate to a wilderness country, the Crown resorted to various expedients to increase the colonial population. Prisoners were set free if they would marry prostitutes and go to Louisiana. Abbé Prevost's novel, *Manon Lescaut*, published in 1732, relates the story of a beautiful but immoral girl who was transported from a French jail along with others of "the frail sisterhood" to be married by the settlers. In 1728 the king sent over a shipload of virtuous maidens, each provided with a casket of clothes, (hence they were called "casket girls") to be married to the French colonists. Early marriages, boys at eighteen, and girls from twelve to fourteen years of age, were encouraged. Soldiers were granted honorable dismissals to become permanent settlers in the country.

The expansion of Louisiana was motivated by military, trade, and imperial considerations, rather than by a drive for agricultural exploitation. During Cadillac's administration, St. Denis was sent in 1713 to establish a French fort on the Red River at Natchitoches. The following year he attempted to open a trade across Texas with the inhabitants of northern Mexico, but he was arrested, his goods confiscated, and he was imprisoned in Mexico City. He managed, however, to secure his release and to resume his position as commandant of Natchitoches. Here he developed a remarkable influence over the western Indians, who admiringly called him "Big Legs," and established a profitable trade between Natchitoches and the Spanish southwest. Indeed, the French avoided any serious conflicts with their Spanish neighbors either on their eastern or western frontiers, because of the lack of ambition of the Spaniards, the vast vacant spaces between the centers of French and Spanish colonization, and the friendliness of the ruling families of those two nations.

The far-flung colony of Louisiana, despite its great potentialities, languished under French rule. Neglected by the royal government, it did not thrive by its own efforts. An inflated currency tended to paralyze commercial activity. In the decade of the 1750's only a half dozen ships a year came from France to the port of New Orleans, as contrasted with the flourishing commerce of the English island of Barbados which employed over two hundred and twenty vessels in 1748. The colony had few exports to send to France in return for manufactured goods. The tobacco was of inferior quality to the Chesapeake Bay staple; lead mining failed, partly on account of the distance of the mines from New Orleans; indigo, the chief staple, was exported in small quantities. The weakness of the Louisiana colony was exhibited during the French and Indian War, when it remained practically passive during that life and death struggle for empire.

At the end of the French and Indian War, France was willing to abandon her unprofitable colony of Louisiana. By the secret treaty of Fontainebleau in 1762 Louisiana west of the Mississippi and the Isle of Orleans were ceded to Spain, her ally in the war, as a consolation prize for the loss of Florida to the English. The Creoles of Louisiana were greatly perturbed at this surrender of their colony, not only because of attachment to France, but because they feared the effect of the exclusive Spanish trade laws. Spain was very slow, however, in taking possession of her new province. Not until the spring of 1766 did a Spanish governor, Don Antonio de Ulloa, arrive with an escort of ninety soldiers. His haughty and aloof manners, his proclamation that the Spanish trade laws must be obeyed, and his disagreement with the Creoles over the redemption of the inflated paper currency finally provoked a rebellion. In 1768 Don Antonio was forced to flee, and the excitable Creoles proclaimed their loyalty to France.

The Spanish officials of Carlos III then debated whether to retain Louisiana or offer to return it to France. The decision was to keep it as a buffer colony for Mexico and to gratify Spanish pride. Furthermore, they resolved to make an example of this rebellious colony by a severe punishment. In 1769 Don Alexander O'Reilly, a limping Irish general, who had fought for Spain in the war of the

Austrian Succession, was sent to Louisiana with a strong force of soldiers to put down the insurrection. The leaders of the revolt were executed or imprisoned and Spanish authority was firmly established. Although the Creole inhabitants called him "Bloody O'Reilly," he sought to reconcile the French population to Spanish rule by conciliatory measures, by appointing Frenchmen to office, and by establishing in New Orleans the Cabildo, a council and court for the colony. Spanish administration was very venal; the local offices were purchased or in some cases inherited.

Nevertheless, the government of Louisiana under Spain was more efficient and unified than the French administration had been. Despite the fact that Spanish law forbade trade with the English, this trade was winked at by the governor. By the Grand Pragmatic of Free Commerce in 1778, Spain liberalized her colonial policy, abolished the system of convoyed fleets, and permitted trade between Louisiana and all the ports of France, Spain, the colonies, and the United States. Thus in "the last cycle" of Spanish rule in the New World, elements of freedom and common sense were permeating the old exclusive Spanish policy.[3]

During the Spanish period of Louisiana history, two new elements of French stock were added to the population. In 1764 the first group of Acadian exiles arrived, ten years after the expulsion from Acadia. The emigration was small, for according to a census taken in 1787 there were only 1,587 Acadians in Louisiana. These people were poor peasants, most of them illiterate, and far different from the sentimental picture of them in Longfellow's "Evangeline." They settled permanently in the bayou region southwest of the Mississippi River, especially along La Fourche and Bayou Teche. Here they were called "Cajuns" by the Americans. Preserving the dialect of Normandy, modified by the incorporation of English and Louisiana Creole words, they formed a backward and unprosperous people, comparable to the "poor whites" of the English colonies.

The last important French element to immigrate to the Southern region were Santo Domingo planters and their families. In 1791 the mulattoes of this Caribbean island began a revolutionary movement which stirred up the black slaves and resulted in the massacre of many of the French-speaking planters. The Santo Domingo master class who survived fled to Louisiana and also to Charleston. It is estimated that over ten thousand of these refugees entered the United States and Louisiana, some of them bringing their slaves. Many of these planters were cultivated and art loving and were responsible for starting the French theater in New Orleans. The Santo Domingans contributed teachers of French, musicians, pastry-makers, fencing masters, and wig-makers to the art of pleasant living in the South.

The Spanish rule of Louisiana was mainly a military occupation; few Spaniards except officials and soldiers emigrated to the new colony. The French Creoles, even opulent sugar planters, were largely illiterate, uniformly Catholic in religion, indolent and un-ambitious. The women were described as vivacious, beautiful as Georgian women, with red lips and white teeth, their complexions lighter than those of the men, but their beauty vanished early. The houses of the Creoles were made of cypress logs with steep roofs and were raised seven or eight feet above the ground. Galleries or porches were built on all sides of the typical one-story houses. In New Orleans drainage of the unpaved streets was in open sewers after the mediaeval fashion. The city suffered at intervals from yellow fever and was generally unhealthy. The citizens enjoyed the privilege of going to a French theater and of hearing operas, but culture was confined to a small class. Indeed, Louisiana did not have a newspaper until 1794 when the *Moniteur de la Louisiane* was established. The population of New Orleans shortly before the United States acquired the province was approximately twelve thousand people, black and white; Lower Louisiana had about sixty thousand people, exclusive of Indians, Upper Louisiana (Missouri) about ten thousand.[4]

In October, 1800, Napoleon Bonaparte forced Spain to cede to him the province of Louisiana by the secret treaty of San Ildefonso. President Jefferson did not learn of the existence of this secret treaty surrendering Louisiana to France until May, 1801. He wrote to the American minister in Paris, Robert R. Livingston, "The day that France takes possession of New Orleans . . . we must marry ourselves to the British fleet and nation." [5] On October 16, 1802, the Spanish intendant at New Orleans, apparently acting under pressure of the French, refused to American vessels the right of deposit which had been previously granted. The West was deeply aroused over the prospect of losing its outlet for the Mississippi River trade. The time for action had come. Jefferson determined first to use diplomacy, to try to buy the island of Orleans, on which the city of New Orleans was located, and West Florida. James Monroe was sent as envoy extraordinary to cooperate with Livingston to effect this object. The American representatives were authorized to offer as high as fifty million francs ($10,000,000) for New Orleans and the Floridas.

Before Monroe arrived (April 13, 1803) Napoleon through his foreign minister, Talleyrand, offered to sell the whole of Louisiana. The reasons for this swift change of policy were that the French dictator planned to renew the war with England, and Louisiana would then be an easy prey for the British navy. Also Napoleon had failed to recover the control of France over the island of Santo Domingo, a vital part of his project of recreating a French colonial empire in the western hemisphere. He had sent his brother-in-law, General Leclerc, with a formidable army to the island, but Leclerc had to contend with dauntless Negro guerrillas led by the "Black Napoleon," Toussaint L'Ouverture. After he had captured the Negro leader and sent him as a prisoner to France, he still could not conquer the people of Santo Domingo, who were aided by the terrible scourge of yellow fever, which decimated the French army and killed Leclerc himself. Against the proposed sale of Louisiana Lucien and Joseph Bonaparte bitterly protested to their brother during an interview while he was taking a perfumed bath. The Little Corsican replied to their patriotic outbursts by a violent splashing in the bathtub that covered them with foam and water and caused their precipitate retreat.

When Talleyrand made the offer to our representatives to sell the whole of Louisiana, Livingston and Monroe jumped at the opportunity, afraid that the fickle emperor would change his mind. The treaty was signed April 30, 1803, surrendering this imperial realm to the United States for eighty million francs, or approximately $14,500,000. The Constitution of the United States did not expressly give the President and Congress the right to purchase foreign territory, an obstacle which caused great concern to Jefferson and the Republicans, believers in strict interpretation of that document. Jef-

ferson proposed a constitutional amendment to make legal the purchase of Louisiana, but Livingston pointed out that Napoleon might
change his mind and that it was highly expedient to conclude the
bargain as soon as possible. Jefferson then suppressed his constitutional scruples and urged the Senate to ratify the treaty and Congress to appropriate the money, disregarding "metaphysical sub-
tleties." [6] Finally the treaty was ratified by the Senate over the opposition of the Federalists, and Louisiana was formally transferred
to the United States, December 20, 1803.

The treaty of cession stated that the boundaries of Louisiana
should be those that the province had when France possessed it prior
to 1763 and when acquired from Spain. These boundaries were
vague. The western limit of the province was the Rocky Mountains
and the French had claimed that Louisiana extended to the Rio
Grande River, thus including Texas. Jefferson and Madison also believed that we had acquired West Florida by the treaty. A remarkable
fact about the treaty was that France technically did not own Louisiana, for its government had failed to carry out the treaty of San
Ildefonso of 1800 by not fulfilling its promise to deliver Tuscany
in Italy to a member of the Spanish royal family. Furthermore, the
French had given a solemn pledge that Louisiana would not be transferred to a third power. Indeed, the French had not even taken
formal possession of the province or sent a governing official to
Louisiana. Only shortly before the transfer to the United States
agents, the Spanish governor formally surrendered the province to
a French prefect, who then promulgated the *Code Napoleon* as the
law of the province.

The treaty provided that the inhabitants of Louisiana should become citizens of the United States and enjoy all the rights and privileges of that status and the protection of their religion. In 1804 Congress created the territory of Orleans, with its capital at New Orleans, and later the upper part of the vast region purchased from
France was organized into Louisiana Territory with its capital at St.
Louis. At first the President was given autocratic authority over the
territory of Orleans, but he appointed a mild and benevolent governor, W. C. C. Claiborne. This denial of the privileges of American citizens to the inhabitants led to a petition of protest to Con-

gress, drafted by Edward Livingston, a younger brother of our French minister, who had emigrated to New Orleans. Congress then amended the law regulating the government of the territory by granting an elective legislature and a delegate to Congress. Not until 1812, however, when Louisiana was admitted as a state in the Union, did the inhabitants enjoy "all the rights, advantages, and immunities of citizens of the United States."

Although the purchase of Louisiana insured the loyalty of the West to the United States, this acquisition did not quench the desire of the frontiersmen to seize further territory from the Spaniards. Wrote the Kentucky leader, John Adair, to James Wilkinson: "Mexico glitters in our Eyes—the word is all we wait for." [7] In 1805 a serious threat of war with Spain arose, during which the inhabitants of Kentucky and Tennessee were eager to attack the Mexican provinces. In that year, Vice President Aaron Burr, defeated for political office and discredited in the East by his fatal duel with Hamilton, went down the Ohio and Mississippi rivers to explore the possibilities of turning western feelings to his advantage. He was cordially received by such prominent leaders as Henry Clay, ex-Senator John Brown, and Senator John Adair of Kentucky, and Andrew Jackson. His chief friend and conspirator in the West, however, was James Wilkinson, governor of Louisiana Territory and commander of the American army in the West.

Opposed to Burr in Kentucky was a small Federalist clique led by ex-Senator Humphrey Marshall and Joseph Hamilton Daveiss, the United States district attorney. Their mouthpiece was the recently founded *Western World* of Frankfort, which published sensational charges of treason against Burr and prominent Kentucky Republicans. These accusations and rumors led to an investigation of Burr by a grand jury at Frankfort. He was defended by Henry Clay and was acquitted. A brilliant opportunist, Burr was apparently ready to resort to any scheme that would bring him money and power. To different persons this plausible intriguer told different stories as to his objective. He approached the English and Spanish ambassadors with proposals to revolutionize the western part of the United States and to incite a secession movement, but this intrigue seems to have been motivated only by the desire to extort money. Rather,

Burr apparently had in mind a plan to lead a filibustering expedition against Spanish territory in the Southwest, predicated on the imminence of a war between Spain and the United States. The elimination of the danger of war in 1806, however, caused the supple adventurer to shift his objectives. Obtaining money from Harman Blennerhassett, a gullible Irishman who lived on an island in the Ohio River, and from Joseph Alston, his South Carolina son-in-law, he purchased a large tract of land on the Ouachita River in Louisiana. Here he planned as one of his enterprises to found a colony which might become a base for an attack against Mexico. Another immediate objective, according to the findings of a recent historian, was to lead a filibuster expedition against Spanish West Florida, seizing Baton Rouge and Mobile.[8]

Whatever Burr's real designs were, he was betrayed by his confederate, James Wilkinson. This unscrupulous adventurer decided in the autumn of 1806, before Burr's expedition had started, to betray his fellow-conspirator. Alarmed by the unfavorable publicity of Burr and doubting his success, he used the occasion to extract money from the Spaniards and also to win Jefferson's favor by posing as a great patriot. Instead of provoking a war with Spain over the hostile demonstrations of that nation against the western frontier, he concluded an agreement, setting up a Neutral Ground between the Sabine River and the Arroyo Hondo. Then he sent a note to President Jefferson from Louisiana warning of a treasonable plot concocted by Burr.

On November 27, Jefferson issued a proclamation announcing that a military expedition against the dominions of Spain was being prepared on the western waters and ordering all American citizens to withdraw immediately from such a criminal enterprise. As a result, the country was aroused against the little band of adventurers, which consisted of less than sixty men, who left Blennerhassett's Island on December 10, 1806, and floated down the Ohio and Mississippi rivers toward Louisiana. Burr did not join the expedition until it had reached the mouth of the Cumberland River. When the flotilla of nine boats entered Mississippi Territory late in January of the following year, Burr was arrested and subsequently tried in Richmond, Virginia, before a Federal Circuit Court presided over by

Chief Justice Marshall. In this famous trial Marshall narrowly interpreted the definition of treason given in the Constitution, ruling out
constructive treason. Jefferson was eager to convict Burr, apparently for political reasons. Nevertheless, Burr was acquitted of the
charge of treason, which seems to be a just verdict, for there was no
reliable evidence that his expedition was engaged in anything worse
than undertaking the founding of an agricultural colony and possibly a filibuster expedition against Mexico or West Florida.

The acquisition of the Louisiana Purchase territory added to our
population the Creoles who have made distinctive contributions to
the pattern of Southern civilization. Although they have been overwhelmed numerically by the immigration of the English since 1803,
they still constitute an important and colorful minority in the cities
of New Orleans and Mobile and in the surrounding country. Their
language has survived in the lower South for over two hundred
years, but in the twentieth century it has been steadily losing
ground, for members of the younger generation prefer to speak
English and are rapidly forgetting their mother tongue. The Creoles
tended socially to keep to themselves and did not mingle freely with
the Protestant "Americans." This fact, as well as the lack of a democratic system of education, partly explains their failure to contribute
many eminent leaders to the nation.

The French Creoles made important contributions to legal institutions in Louisiana. The Black Code was adopted by the Spanish
rulers of the province and later by the Americans when Louisiana
was acquired by the United States. Louisiana was for many years the
only Southern state that prohibited the sale of slave children under
ten years of age from their mothers. The Civil Code of the state,
adopted in 1825, the work of Edward Livingston and two Creole
jurisconsults, continued the Roman law of French and Spanish
regimes as the fundamental law of the state. Eighty per cent of the
provisions of this code were taken verbatim from the Code Napoleon.
Louisiana was the only state in the Union whose law was based on
the Roman law rather than on the English common law. The courts
of ante-bellum Louisiana were conducted in the two languages
spoken by the people. In the twentieth century Louisiana furnished
a chief justice of the United States, Edward White, whose doctrine,

"the rule of reason," may have been affected by his Catholic heritage and his training in Louisiana law.

During the French and Spanish occupation of Louisiana the Catholic Church was firmly rooted. The clergy were under the jurisdiction of the Bishop of Quebec, who placed the Capuchins in charge of lower Louisiana while the Jesuits were made supreme in upper Louisiana and the Illinois country. The Jesuits, however, tried to secure a foothold in New Orleans, which resulted in a resounding war between the two orders. In 1727 some Ursuline nuns sailed to New Orleans, where they took charge of the hospital and founded a girls' school. Their convent on Chartres Street, built in 1731, is one of the oldest buildings in the Mississippi Valley. The Catholic Church was responsible for introducing whatever education was given to the Creole youth. During the Spanish regime an attempt was made (in 1789) by Father Antonio de Sedella to introduce the Inquisition in order to crush all heretics in the colony, but this emissary of the Inquisition was expelled by the governor.[9]

The French have made enduring contributions to Southern agriculture and practical arts. The Creoles introduced sugar cane into the lower South, and in 1795 Etienne de Boré discovered a method of granulating sugar from Louisiana cane syrup which laid the foundations for the great sugar plantations of ante-bellum days. Also the French began the practice of building levees to prevent the Mississippi River from flooding the plantations and the city of New Orleans. They developed the lead mining industry in Missouri and were foremost in exploring the Mississippi Valley.

Many useful loan words have been incorporated in the American language from the speech of the French inhabitants of the Gulf coast. From the French of Louisiana the following words have been borrowed: bayou, levee, crevasse, chute, bureau, depot (which the Negroes in the South still use in preference to the more dignified term railroad station), picayune, and lagniappe, referring to the pleasant custom of tradesmen giving their customers something extra beyond their purchase, an additional yam, or fig, or flower as a sign of good will. The French of the Missouri country were noted fur traders, from whom as well as from the French settlers from the North were derived such words as prairie, batteau, pirogue, rapids, portage, voyageur, cache, gopher, and brave for Indian warrior. The French Creoles developed a patois in which they orally transmitted proverbs, folklore, and songs, such as "Belle Amerikaine," "Un Pauvre Hobo," and "Jolie Blonde."

The Creoles also contributed a hedonistic element to the society of the lower South. The carnival of Mardi Gras which came before Lent was a colorful pageant and a time of merriment which has continued to be observed in New Orleans and Mobile to the present day. The city of New Orleans became the pleasure metropolis of the Mississippi Valley, although its reputation as a city of sin flourished only after Louisiana became a part of the United States. Orange wine, absinthe, the delicacies of frog legs, bouillabaisse, poulet Creole, Creole gumbo, and pralines were distinct French contributions to the art of good food and drink. The Creoles also developed an institution of concubinage with beautiful octoroon and quadroon maidens, and masked balls added gaiety to the worldly life of the Latin quarter. Americans who came down the Mississippi were shocked at the Creole Sundays, when the Sabbath day was devoted to pleasure. Furthermore, these Latins were passionately fond of gambling, lotteries, and dancing. French dancing and fencing masters taught the unsophisticated Americans those continental arts.

The Creoles of Louisiana developed a literature and furnished the picturesque material for an important school of local color that developed after the Civil War. Charles Gayarré, who wrote an admirable history of Louisiana in the decade of the 1850's, was not only the outstanding Creole writer but probably also the greatest historian produced by the ante-bellum South. The Creoles, including Creole Negroes, wrote French poetry and dramas. In the decades of the 1880's and 1890's the Creole civilization was portrayed by George Washington Cable, Kate Chopin, Grace King, and Lafcadio Hearn. These writers described the architecture, customs, and characteristics of Old Louisiana. They presented the tragedy of the mixture of white and Negro blood. Their stories and romances recreated the flavor of a semi-tropic civilization affected by Negro slavery and by the Latin temperament.

The passing of French culture from Upper Louisiana forms a little-known but fascinating chapter in the social history of the Southwest. St. Genevieve was begun in 1735 as the shipping point of the lead mining district of Missouri, and St. Louis was founded in 1764 by Pierre Laclede, the agent of a French fur trading company. This town became the center of the fur trading activities of the West, and French Creole trappers dominated the fur trade of the hinterland and of the Rocky Mountains. When the United States took possession of the Missouri territory in 1804, the Creoles dreaded the American occupation, fearing that their complicated land titles might not be respected and distrusting the democracy of the newcomers. The mass of the *habitants* were unambitious, hedonistic, and illiterate, but the small upper class, including the Chouteau family of St. Louis, for example, were better educated than the Americans, possessing good libraries and reading the writings of the French free thinkers.[10] Some of these aristocrats owned large plantations, tilled by slave labor, while others had gained affluence from the fur trade, the lead mines, and from merchandising.

The coming of the Americans wrought a revolution in this civilization of Old Missouri, for the six thousand Creoles and Negro slaves reported by the Spanish census of 1799 were overwhelmed by the inrush of the Americans which increased the population of the territory to 66,586 by 1820. The horizontal log cabin of the American frontiersman superseded the French log cabin built of vertical logs; French geographical names were corrupted or displaced; the Gallic Sunday with its gayety was frowned upon by the intolerant Protestant settlers; in 1808 the *Missouri Gazette*, the first newspaper of the region, was published in English; by 1821, when Missouri became a state, much of French culture had been erased and the Creoles were rapidly being assimilated by American civilization. Nevertheless, faint traces of by-gone French culture survive in Missouri to this day.

Citations

1. D. M. Quynn (ed.), "Recruiting in Old Orleans for New Orleans," *American Historical Review*, XLVI (October, 1940), 832–836.
2. Charles Gayarré, *History of Louisiana* (New Orleans, 1885), II.

3. H. I. Priestley, *The Coming of the White Man, 1492–1848* (New York, 1929), Chap. VII.

4. J. A. Robertson, *Louisiana under the Rule of Spain, France, and the United States, 1785–1807* (Cleveland, Ohio, 1911), I, 71, 149–150, 170, 172.

5. Lipscomb and Bergh, *Writings of Thomas Jefferson*, X, 313.

6. Ford, *Writings of Thomas Jefferson*, X, 7.

7. T. R. Hay and M. R. Werner, *The Admirable Trumpeter, A Biography of General James Wilkinson* (New York, 1941), 219.

8. T. P. Abernethy, "Aaron Burr in Mississippi," *Journal of Southern History*, XV (February, 1949), 9–21.

9. George Washington Cable, *The Creoles of Louisiana* (New York, 1884).

10. Harvey Wish, "The French of Old Missouri (1804–1821): A Study in Assimilation," *Mid-America*, XXIII (July, 1941), 167–189.

CHAPTER IX

The War Hawks and Expansion

T HE War of 1812, which was largely brought on by the pressure of Southern and Western Congressmen, seems to have been an act of folly from the viewpoint of Southern interests. It was, as a whole, an inglorious war for the United States and did not accomplish the objectives of its Southern proponents. Rather, it increased the power of the central government and contributed largely to the growth of New England manufactures and a high tariff policy, both of which developments were later violently opposed by the South.

It is a moot question how important individual leaders are in provoking or restraining the war fever. The personality of President Madison is particularly significant in studying the drift to war in 1812. A Tidewater Virginian, born at Port Conway in 1751, he was graduated from the College of New Jersey (Princeton), where he studied Hebrew and theology, intending to become a minister. His early career was marked by a high idealism.[1] When he entered politics, he refused to follow the Southern custom of soliciting votes by treating the sovereign voters with liquor. Madison was a brilliant scholar, but he was unsuited to be President during the critical years preceding the War of 1812 or to be a successful war leader. Vacillating—the vice of scholars—timid, and gullible, he was unable to resist the more aggressive personalities of the war party or steer a firm course. Unlike Jefferson who had been a real leader, dictating quietly the party program, he lacked the political art and seems to have had little influence on Congress.

When Madison became President he inherited a problem of maintaining the rights of the United States on the high seas. Great Britain was fighting to survive against the imperialist ambitions of Napoleon. In this fierce struggle American neutral rights were violated by both belligerents. Madison continued Jefferson's policy of attempting to preserve peace by diplomacy and economic coercion. Macon Bill no. 2, passed in May, 1810, provided that if Great Britain would repeal its Orders in Council or France its Berlin and Milan decrees, violating our neutral rights, the United States would enforce an economic boycott against the other nation failing to follow suit within a period of three months. Thereupon, Napoleon duped President Madison by pretending to repeal his offensive measures against our ships, a ruse which caused the President to revive a policy of non-intercourse against Great Britain, whose government refused to repeal the Orders in Council. Accordingly, the net result of the Macon Bill no. 2 and Napoleon's trickery was to arouse a strong feeling in the United States to declare war against England.

Since England and France were almost equally culpable in violating our neutral rights, there was abundant reason to declare war against France as well as England. Indeed, the sympathy of Americans should have been with England in her struggle to preserve her freedom against the ruthless military dictator Napoleon, as John Randolph observed. But anglophobia was strong among the dominant Republicans, and France had not impressed American seamen, while Great Britain had been a serious kidnaper of our citizens, impressing over six thousand American seamen, a number which popular rumor magnified to over ten thousand. Moreover, the Westerners believed that the British in Canada incited the Indians on the frontier to hostilities and furnished them with guns and ammunition, a charge which the British denied. Just at this time Tecumseh organized the Indians of the Ohio valley to resist the advance of the American pioneer and sought the aid of the Southern Indians. The real cause for Indian warfare, however, was not British instigation but a determination of the Indians to save their hunting grounds from the rapacious Westerners.

In the Congressional elections of 1810 and 1811 a number of young representatives were sent to Washington who were eager to declare war against England. A group of these ardent patriots from the South and the West boarded at the same tavern and were called "the war mess." Their leader was Henry Clay of Kentucky, thirty-four years of age, who was elected Speaker of the House of Representa-

tives in a period when the lower house of Congress was more respected and powerful than the Senate.[2] These young men bitterly
criticized the "if policy" of Madison, his failure to assert vigorously
American rights against the British and the French. They came
chiefly from the frontier regions or the back country of the South
and gained the name "War Hawks" because of their advocacy of
war with England. Clay used his power as Speaker to appoint War
Hawks on the important committees of the House of Representatives
and his eloquent voice was exerted to arouse Americans to a declaration of war against England as an obligation of honor and as necessary to preserve our export trade.

From Kentucky came, besides Clay, Richard Mentor Johnson, one
of the most vociferous of the War Hawks. Born at Beargrass, Kentucky, he had three brothers slain by the Indians. He was a colorful
figure, indeed, noted in Congress for disdaining such effeminate apparel as a cravat and for shocking conventional morality by having a
Negro mistress, Julia Chinn, who bore him two daughters. During
the course of the War of 1812 he was reputed to have killed Tecumseh, which led to his nickname "Tecumseh Johnson." From
Tennessee came Felix Grundy, a brilliant criminal lawyer and practical politician, and also John Sevier, the old frontiersman and Indian fighter. Georgia sent two War Hawks to Congress in the persons of the belligerent, red-headed George M. Troup and William
H. Crawford. The ablest delegation of War Hawks was a brilliant
trio from South Carolina, John C. Calhoun, Langdon Cheves, and
William Lowndes. The last was a remarkably tall young man (6 feet
6 inches in height) with golden hair and low voice, gifted in intellect and in winning friends. If the preponderance of war sentiment
was in the West and in the newer parts of the South, the Tidewater
area also had some prominent advocates of war, such as Secretary of
State James Monroe, and the old Jeffersonian leader, Nathaniel
Macon of North Carolina.

The motives that led the War Hawks to demand a war with England were a remarkable mixture of idealism and material considerations. In the first place, these youthful legislators—"Young America"
—believed that the United States should take a bold and manly stand
against insult and oppression. Madison and "the regular troops" of

the Republican party, led by Albert Gallatin, realized that the United States was totally unprepared for war and tried to restrain the rash and headstrong enthusiasm for war of the young leaders. However, the War Hawks were expressing deep social forces of their section, especially for expansion. Kentucky wished the United States to seize Canada, but there was considerable sentiment south of the Blue-grass state also to add Canada to the United States in fulfillment of manifest destiny. Clay held out the prospect of an easy conquest of Canada, which, he boasted, the Kentucky militia alone could accomplish. Furthermore, the Westerners were desirous of eradicating the power of the British in Canada to instigate attacks on the American frontier, or, in Clay's eloquent words, "to extinguish the torch that lights up savage warfare." [3]

In addition to a desire to uphold national honor, the Southern states were affected by two powerful economic motives in their advocacy of war. The lower South was eagerly desirous of seizing Florida which controlled the outlets of several important Southern rivers. Florida was weakly defended by Spain, an ally of England. John Randolph declared that the motive for the War of 1812 was "agrarian cupidity." Not only was there the urge of southward expansion, but also, prior to the war, the Southern farmers were suffering from a decline in the price of their agricultural exports. They believed that British interference with foreign commerce was responsible for this loss. Nathaniel Macon declared, "We must either prepare to maintain the right to carry our produce to what market we please, or to be content without a market." [4]

The War Hawks acted with considerable inconsistency in preparing the country for the approaching war. There were less than seven thousand men in the regular army, and the navy of sixteen ships was ridiculously small in comparison with the naval power of Great Britain. The War Hawks voted for a large increase in the army, which could be used in the conquest of Canada and the Floridas, but some of the most ardent patriots, such as Johnson and Grundy, opposed a large expansion of the navy, which would be useless in fighting Indians or conquering the interior lands of Florida and Canada. Moreover, the War Hawks were very solicitous not to throw cold water on the martial fervor of the South and West by heavy taxation to pay for the prosecution of an expansionist war.

Madison finally yielded to the martial spirit of the South and the West. The old charge that he was forced by the War Hawks to recommend war as a price of renomination for President, however, is untrue, for he was nominated by a Congressional caucus unanimously two weeks before his war message. On June 1, 1812, Madison sent his message to Congress citing the outrages that would justify a war against England—impressment of American seamen, violation of the three-mile limit of our shores, paper blockades, Orders in Council, and the suspicion of British instigation of Indian outrages. He said nothing in the war message about other great driving forces of the war fever in the South and the West, such as expansionist feeling, anglophobia, and resentment over the foreign export situation.

The vote on a declaration of war, June 18, 1812, revealed the fact that the country was seriously divided in opinion. In the Senate the vote for war was 19 to 13, but in the House of Representatives the vote was 79 in favor and 49 opposed. A majority of the Congressmen from New England, New York, and New Jersey—the maritime sections of the country—voted against a declaration of war. It is a strange paradox that the two sections of the country, the West and the South, which had few ships and sailors and therefore had suffered least from the British violation of the freedom of the seas were precisely the regions eager for war, while New England was bitterly opposed to this vindication of the national honor. In Congress Ohio, Kentucky, Tennessee, Georgia, and South Carolina voted unanimously for war, Maryland was divided 6 to 3, while coastal Virginia and North Carolina were pro-war, the Piedmont anti-war. There was one intensely Southern Congressman, John Randolph of Roanoke, who made a violent speech against our entry into a war with England in which he pointed out that by attacking England we were aiding Napoleon, the enslaver of Europe.

The United States seems to have blundered into war. British public opinion demanded the repeal of the obnoxious decrees against American neutral commerce, but delay in revoking the Orders in Council was caused by the assassination in May, 1812, of Prime Minister Perceval. On June 16, however, Lord Castlereagh, the Foreign Minister, announced that the Orders in Council would be suspended. It is possible that if a cable had existed at that time, the American Congress would not have declared war against England. The revocation of the Orders in Council actually took place five days after the declaration of war by the United States.

Three military campaigns were fought in the South during the War of 1812, the British invasion of the District of Columbia and Maryland in 1814, the Creek Campaign of the same year, and the battle of New Orleans, January 8, 1815. Kentucky volunteers played an important part in the victories of the American armies on the northwest frontier. William Henry Harrison, a Virginia aristocrat, who had been governor of Indiana Territory, commanded the American troops at the victory of the Thames River in lower Canada (1813). Another Southern officer, Winfield Scott of Virginia, won the battles of Chippewa and Lundy's Lane (1814), which were across the Canadian border not far from Buffalo, New York.

It was fortunate for the unprepared and disunified American nation that England had her hands full fighting Napoleon during the early years of the war. In April, 1814, Napoleon was forced to abdicate his throne, thus releasing a number of veteran troops of England for use in the American war. In June, 1814, a force of 4,500 British regulars under General Robert Ross was sent from Bordeaux to the Chesapeake Bay country. Ross landed at Benedict, Maryland, forty miles from Washington, and marched unopposed along the Patuxent River until he came to the village of Bladensburg, about five miles from the capital. Here he was opposed by approximately six thousand green militia under the incompetent General W. H. Winder and a naval detachment under Commodore Joshua Barney. The British sent a shower of Congrieve rockets among the untrained militia, terrifying them. Consequently, they fled in the direction of Washington with the British regulars running after them, giving rise to the nickname of "the Bladensburg races" (August 24, 1814). The British officers arrived at the White House in time to eat the dinner prepared for the hastily retreating President and Mrs. Madison. After burning the White House, the Capitol, and the public buildings, the victorious army retired. In an attack on Baltimore, however, they were repulsed, and General Ross was killed. Fort

McHenry, which defended the sea approaches to the city, was too strong to be captured. Its defense inspired the composition of the national anthem, "The Star Spangled Banner," by Francis Scott Key.

The instigation to hostilities by Tecumseh and the disgraceful surrender of Detroit early in the war by General William Hull had the effect of encouraging the Upper Creek Indians, called "Red Sticks," to attack the Southern frontier. On August, 1813, they captured Fort Mims at the junction of the Alabama and Tombigbee rivers, scalping and killing the five hundred men, women, and children in the fort. Andrew Jackson, major general of Tennessee militia, was ordered to lead an army against the "Red Sticks" and administer severe punishment. At this time he was in bed suffering from a pistol wound inflicted in a tavern brawl in Nashville. Nevertheless, he arose from his sick bed, carrying his arm in a sling, and took command of the undisciplined militia. He maintained a stern discipline over this force, suppressing a mutiny by using part of his army to keep another part from returning home. In March, 1814, he attacked the main town of the "Red Sticks" at Horseshoe Bend on the Tallapoosa River, near the present city of Montgomery, and killed all but about fifty of an estimated number of eight hundred warriors as well as making prisoners of five hundred squaws and children. He then built Fort Jackson at the juncture of the Coosa and Tallapoosa rivers, where he dictated a treaty by which the Creeks surrendered over twenty million acres of choice land in southern Georgia and Alabama. The Southern Indians never forgot the merciless vengeance of "Long Knife," as they called Jackson.

Jackson's campaign against the Creeks was followed by the most dramatic event of the war, the battle of New Orleans. The British sent an expeditionary force of seven thousand five hundred veterans of the Napoleonic war, under the command of Sir Edward Pakenham, brother-in-law of the Duke of Wellington, to capture New Orleans. The defenses of this city had been badly neglected, but on December 1, 1814, the masterful Jackson was placed in charge of the forces guarding the city, consisting of between six and seven thousand Kentucky, Tennessee, and Louisiana militia. Two colorful elements among this motley army were four hundred Negro soldiers and the pirates of Barataria, who had infested the Gulf coast. The leaders of the pirates were Jean and Pierre Lafitte, who were offered tempting rewards to aid the British, which they patriotically refused, and Dominique You, who rendered effective service as an artillerist.

Instead of going up the Mississippi, the British took an unexpected route by Lake Borgne across the swamps to New Orleans. On January 8, 1815, the main battle took place, lasting less than half of an hour, at Chalmette's plantation a few miles from New Orleans. Showing his contempt of American soldiers, Pakenham ordered a frontal assault on Jackson's improvised fortifications, made partly of cotton bales. Jackson directed his men to hold their fire until the redcoats were in easy rifle range. The charging British, in close order, were mowed down by the accurate fire of the Southern militia, Pakenham was killed, and the British lost two thousand men, killed and captured. The American loss was only thirteen soldiers killed in this most spectacular victory ever won by an army of the United States. However, this victory had no military significance, for it was fought two weeks after the peace treaty had been signed at Ghent, Belgium. If a cable had existed at that time, the battle would never have been fought, and very likely Andrew Jackson would not later have been elected President.

But this victory over John Bull made an important contribution to American pride in the nation, as exhibited in the song, "The Hunters of Kentucky":

> But Jackson he was wide awake,
>   And was not scar'd at trifles,
> For well he knew what aim we take
>   With our Kentucky rifles.
> So he led us down to Cypress swamp,
>   The ground was low and mucky,
> There stood John Bull in martial pomp
>   And here was old Kentucky.
> Oh Kentucky, the hunters of Kentucky!

The Treaty of Ghent, which was signed on Christmas Eve, 1814, was an inglorious peace treaty, for it was silent about the original American grievances of impressment and interference with our neutral trade. In fact the British representatives came to the conference with the demeanor of a conquering nation, actually demanding a

cession of American territory. The South and West were represented on the United States peace commission by Henry Clay. The
American delegation made the mistake of taking a house together
in the old Belgian town of Ghent. The gambling, swearing, drinking, and late hours of Henry Clay caused dissension, especially shocking the austere Puritan member, John Quincy Adams. Adams was
determined to secure the right of New Englanders to continue to
fish off the grand banks of Newfoundland, but was little concerned
in preventing the British from obtaining the right to navigate the
Mississippi. Clay, on the other hand, had no interest in fish for New
Englanders but was determined to exclude the British from the Mississippi River. He succeeded in "saving the Mississippi River" exclusively for the citizens of the United States. The main result of the
treaty of Ghent was to restore the *status quo*. Yet the War of 1812
had some effect in producing economically and spiritually a Second
Declaration of Independence from England. The only tangible gains
the South derived from this war for expansion were the appropriation of much of the land of the Creeks after their crushing defeat,
the bloodless conquest of Mobile in 1813 by General James Wilkinson, and the making of a Presidential candidate, Andrew Jackson.

During the five years following the Treaty of Ghent the Southern
states reached a peak of national feeling, from which there began a
recession in 1820 that continued until long after the Civil War. Part
of this enthusiasm for the nation was an afterglow of the war feeling. The disloyal example of New England, culminating in the Hartford Convention, impressed Southerners with the virtue of being
patriotic. The executive branch of the Federal government was controlled by Virginia Presidents until 1825, a factor in Southern satisfaction with the central government. Moreover, the westward movement, following the conclusion of the War of 1812, tended to
produce a more nationalistic outlook. The abolitionist movement had
not yet arisen to foment bitter sectional discord.

The nationalistic trend in the South after the war was shown in
the support of a protective tariff by a number of Southern Congressmen. The war had actually benefited the rebellious New England
states more than any other section by the encouragement it gave to
the rise of manufacturing. With the conclusion of peace English

manufacturers tried to destroy the infant American industries by "dumping" cheap goods on the American market. To prevent this catastrophe, Congress passed the protective tariff of 1816. The bill was introduced by William Lowndes of South Carolina and was vigorously supported by John C. Calhoun. The vote of the Southern states in Congress on the tariff of 1816 was twenty-five for the measure and thirty-nine against it. Lowndes, Henry Clay, and Calhoun supported the enactment of a protective tariff because they had visions of the development of Southern manufacturing and furthermore believed that such mills would increase the demand for cotton and raise its price. There were already small textile factories arising in the Carolinas, Kentucky, and Georgia. In 1810 North Carolina had fifty-six small mills and Georgia ninety-one. Also a strong motive for the considerable Southern support of a protective tariff in 1816 was the desire to make the country economically free of foreign nations. By 1820, however, the Southern states realized that a protective tariff was against their interest and therefore they voted overwhelmingly against an effort to raise the tariff in that year. From this time on, the South, in general, voted against protective tariffs with the exception of special groups like the sugar planters, the iron interests, and the hemp growers and manufacturers.

The South also displayed its nationalistic feeling in supporting the chartering of the Second National Bank. In 1816 a committee with Calhoun as the leading member drafted a bill creating a national bank, in which both the government and private investors held the stock. This bank was given the privilege of keeping the government deposits without paying interest, but it was required to transfer government funds without charge. The charter was to run for twenty years and granted the institution the privileges of issuing bank notes, acceptable for government dues, and of establishing branch banks in the states. President Madison signed the bill despite the fact that he had opposed Hamilton's First National Bank as unconstitutional. Two prominent Southerners, John Randolph of Roanoke and John Taylor of Caroline, refused to follow the new trend of the Republican party toward nationalism but fought strenuously against the chartering of this powerful financial institution.

During this period of nationalism, Calhoun introduced his "Bonus

Bill" in December, 1816, to use the bonus of $1,500,000 which the Second National Bank paid for its charter to build national roads and canals. He advocated this bill as a military measure, to provide roads for defense and as a means of binding the rapidly growing country into a strong union. He had no constitutional scruples in regard to his proposal, for he believed that such expenditures were authorized by the "common defense" and "general welfare" clauses of the Constitution. The "Bonus Bill" passed Congress but was vetoed by Madison on his last day of office. In the vote in the House of Representatives the Southern states were nearly evenly divided, with a slight preponderance against the bill.

The South did receive the advantage of obtaining one great national road built with Federal funds, the so-called National Road, which began at Cumberland, Maryland, on the Potomac River in 1811 and by 1818 was completed as far as Wheeling, Virginia. The eastern end of the road was so heavily used that it began to wear out by 1822, when a bill was introduced into Congress to establish toll gates and use the toll receipts for the repair and upkeep of the road. It passed Congress, but was vetoed by President Monroe as unconstitutional. Monroe's veto message marks a return to the strict construction of the Constitution held by the early Republicans, the victory of a rigid theory over the interest of the nation.

In 1820 Monroe was reelected President with only one dissenting vote. There was no opposition party worthy of the name, for the Federalist party had practically disappeared. The Republican party, dominated by Southern leadership, had changed greatly since its victory in 1800. In the course of twenty years it had abandoned much of its devotion to strict construction of the Constitution and had adopted some of the salient policies of the Federalists. The last of the Virginia dynasty, President Monroe, promulgated the "Monroe Doctrine" of 1823, which is one of the greatest documents in the history of American nationalism. It is interesting to note that Monroe proposed to incorporate in this famous message to Congress a strong expression of American support to democratic movements both in Spain and Greece, but was deterred by his Secretary of State, John Quincy Adams, who also contributed to Monroe's message its non-colonization doctrine.

The War of 1812 temporarily checked the westward movement of population, but after the conclusion of peace there developed so extensive a migration of settlers into the region beyond the mountains that the period from 1815 to 1836 is rightly called "The Great Migration." One reason for this expansion was the crushing defeat of the Creeks by Jackson in 1814 and the large land cessions extorted from them. The advance guard of this folk movement to the rich lands of the Southwest was formed by pioneer farmers who built log cabins and cleared the land by the process of girdling. Most of this group were semi-nomadic, restless "movers," who sold their pioneer clearings to more substantial farmers and once more moved westward. Many of these pioneer farmers were cattle and hog raisers who used the public domain for their range. The cattle and hogs did not have to be fed and sheltered during the winter months as in the North. The more substantial farmers and planters who removed to the Southwest frequently sent out sons or neighbors to spy out the land and report on fertile sites for farms. There was a tendency for groups to settle this new country, a group of neighbors, a congregation, or a large family and its relatives. The rapid filling up of the Gulf area and the lower Mississippi Valley is indicated by the dates at which states in this region were admitted into the Union, Louisiana in 1812, Mississippi in 1817, Alabama in 1819, Missouri in 1821, and Arkansas in 1836.

The flow of population from the upper South to the Old Northwest had considerable influence on American political history. In the first quarter of the nineteenth century many Quakers from Virginia and North Carolina migrated across the Ohio River to escape living in a slave country. Thus they removed valuable antislavery elements from the South and weakened the cause of liberalism in that region. Along with the Quakers went many poor farmers of the Southern upland stock. Among this group was the family of Abraham Lincoln who moved from Kentucky first into Indiana, living in a "half-faced" log cabin, and then to Illinois. These Southern settlers had found by experience in their native region that the soil was most fertile where the trees grew tallest. Consequently, they avoided the rich prairie lands north of the terminal moraine line, made by the retreating glaciers of geologic ages, and confined their settlement to the region of the hardwoods in southern Ohio, Indiana, and Illinois. Many of them were quite illiterate; after the Democratic party arose they usually voted the Democratic ticket. Some of them had favored the introduction of slavery into Illinois and Indiana when the latter became states. So formidable was the movement to establish slavery in Illinois in 1822–24 during the agitation for the revision of the constitution that it was defeated only by the strenuous campaign of Edward Coles, a friend of Jefferson, who had emigrated from Virginia to avoid living in a slave state. The southern parts of Ohio, Indiana, and Illinois traded with the lower South via the Mississippi River, and until 1850 they might be regarded as a part of the "Greater South." During the Civil War this region contained numerous Southern sympathizers, called Copperheads.

The migration of Southerners was directed as a rule along isothermal lines, to regions where the climate, soil, and the type of crops grown were similar to those of their old home. Consequently, the westward movement advanced along parallel lines of latitude into contiguous areas. The presence of river systems as means of transportation also affected the westward flow of population. In 1850 over 142,102 natives of Virginia were living in the upper Southern states of Kentucky, Tennessee, and Missouri, 155,978 in the old Northwest, and only 38,311 in the lower South. The slaves of the lower South were far more frequently natives of "Old Virginia" than the free settlers. Maryland sent very few of her native sons to the deep South. In North Carolina the trend of the southward movement of population was about equally divided between the upper and the lower South, 103,315 natives of the state living in 1850 in the former region, and 107,912 in the latter. South Carolina and Georgia were the chief contributors of population to the young states of the Southwest. Missouri at the time of the great debate over its admission was settled largely by people from the upper South, while Arkansas was a child of Tennessee. Texas also received a large contingent of settlers from this state. In Louisiana a remarkable number of New Yorkers settled, largely because of the commercial attraction of New Orleans. In general, the emigrants to the lower South seem to have come predominantly from the Piedmont region rather than the Tidewater area. The westward movement of population into the Mississippi valley was stimulated by boom times such as the periods 1813–19, 1833–37, and 1853–57, and noticeably slackened during times of depression.[5]

One of the best examples of these emigrating planters was Colonel Thomas Dabney of "Elmington" in the Tidewater district of Virginia. Dabney lived in a fine old ancestral house, endeared by many memories, but the worn-out tobacco lands of the estate could no longer support the elegant life of former days. Accordingly, in 1835 he decided to sell "Elmington" and transfer his slaves to richer land. His fast-expanding family—his wife bore him sixteen children—demanded an ampler income than "Elmington" could supply. Before he abandoned his native state he was given an elaborate testimonial dinner at which Governor John Tyler presided. With his two hundred slaves, he set out overland to his new home in Hinds County, Mississippi, forty miles east of Vicksburg. Here he had purchased the lands of several farmers, which he combined into a plantation that ultimately contained four thousand acres. The pioneer farmers invited him to house-raisings and log-rollings, but when he came with a gang of Negroes and directed them from his horse while wearing gloves, they resented his aristocratic manners.

The westward march of the cotton planter was attended by a great rise in land prices. Under the Harrison Land Act of 1800 a settler could buy land from the Federal government on credit. The minimum amount of land sold to a buyer was 320 acres (in 1804 reduced to 160 acres) and the minimum price was $2 an acre. The poor man could thus easily acquire a farm, for he was required to pay only the first installment of fifty cents an acre, after which he could begin to plant a cotton crop, paying the remainder of the purchase price within four years. Public land was sold at auction, and land offices for the sale of the southwestern lands, released by Indian treaties, were located at Milledgeville, Georgia, and Huntsville and Cahaba, Alabama. Wild speculation raised the prices of the virgin lands of the Southwest until the panic of 1819 temporarily held up the westward movement of settlers. During this period of migration, a picturesque settlement of French exiles, some of them former officers in Napoleon's army, founded Demopolis on the Tombigbee River

(1817), where they attempted to cultivate olives and vineyards for wine making.

In 1820 the Federal government changed the land law by abolishing the credit system, but the minimum price of government land was reduced to $1.25 an acre. The auction system was retained, however, and settlers were allowed to surrender the land which they could not pay for and were given full title for the amount which their installments covered. Nevertheless, the substitution of the cash system for the credit system did not seem to restrain speculation successfully. Settlers borrowed paper money from the "wild cat" banks and the "pet banks" of the decade of the 1830's. In July, 1836, President Jackson issued his Specie Circular, which announced that only gold and silver coin would be accepted for land payments. This executive order precipitated the panic of the following year. In 1836 the sale of public lands reached the peak of twenty million acres, but the depression years which followed reduced the sales of the public domain by 1841 to a million acres.

When the United States acquired Missouri by the Louisiana Purchase, there were already several settlements in the region, notably St. Louis, St. Charles, and New Madrid. The latter, located on the west bank of the Mississippi opposite the mouth of the Ohio, had been founded in 1789 by a Pennsylvania land speculator, George Morgan. Following the conclusion of the war of 1812, population flowed into this wild country, so that by 1818 the territory had attained the population of sixty thousand people requisite for admission into the Union. Accordingly, in that year Missouri territory applied for admission as a state, and in February, 1819, the Committee on Territories reported such a bill to the House of Representatives. At this point Representative James Tallmadge, Jr., of New York introduced an amendment to the bill, prohibiting any further immigration of slaves into the proposed state and providing for the emancipation of those born into slavery thereafter. Such children of slave parents, however, could be held to service until they had attained the age of twenty-five years.

The principal motives behind this Northern attempt to restrict the expansion of slavery seem to have been political rather than humanitarian considerations. The North had long resented the three-fifths Federal ratio which gave the South representation in Congress for its slaves.[6] Indeed, the Southern states had twenty more Representatives in the lower house of Congress than they would have had if only white population had been counted. Senator Rufus King of New York, leader of the free soil men in the Senate, pointed out that under the unfair rule of slave representation, the votes of five Southerners were equal to those of seven Northerners in selecting both the President and members of the House of Representatives. Up to this date a balance had been maintained in the Union of an equal number of free and slave states. The admission of Missouri as a slave state would upset this equilibrium in the Senate. It is to be noted, however, that in 1820 the free states had a great preponderance of votes in the House of Representatives, one hundred and five Representatives, as compared with only eighty-one from the slave states.

One of the most acrimonious debates in the history of Congress took place over the Tallmadge amendment. The chief spokesmen of the Southerners were Senators John Tyler of Virginia and William Pinkney of Maryland. Tyler admitted that slavery was an evil to be eradicated, but he argued that the evil would be ameliorated by the distribution of the slaves over a wide area, which would lead to better treatment of them. Pinkney, one of the foremost orators of his age, denied that Congress had the right to place restrictions on the admission of states into the Union, a practice which would reduce the Union to a league between giants and dwarfs rather than between equals. The Tallmadge amendment was passed by the House of Representatives, but rejected in the Senate.

In February, 1820, a compromise, proposed by Senator Jesse B. Thomas of Illinois, was adopted. According to this arrangement, Missouri was admitted as a slave state, but slavery was prohibited in the remainder of the Louisiana Purchase territory north of a line of latitude 36° 30', which was the projection of the southern boundary of Missouri. At the same time the sectional balance in the Senate was maintained by admitting Maine as a free state. Thus the *first* Missouri Compromise bill passed Congress. A factor in securing the passage of this act was a fear on the part of some of the Northern Republicans that the Old Federalist party would be revived on the antislavery issue, and consequently they voted for a compromise. The Southern Representatives were almost equally divided over the acceptance of the compromise, thirty-eight for, and thirty-seven against it, the extreme state rights men opposing the settlement.

A constitution for the new state was drawn up in a convention at St. Louis in the summer of 1820 and submitted to Congress for approval. Unfortunately, it contained a provision authorizing the legislature to exclude free Negroes and mulattoes from entering the state. This provision caused a storm of protest from the Northern members of Congress. At this juncture Henry Clay came froward and was influential in the adoption of the *second* Missouri Compromise. The legislature of Missouri gave a pledge that it would never pass a law which would deprive citizens of other states of the privileges and immunities granted under the Federal Constitution. Such a pledge, however, could not be binding, except morally, upon later legislatures. With this understanding, the President proclaimed the admission of Missouri as a state, August 10, 1821.

The debate on the Missouri Compromise is a landmark in the growth of sectionalism in the United States. It created a sense of unity among the slave states, the embryo of Southern nationalism, for they realized the need of a phalanx to oppose the rising antislavery sentiment of the North. Thomas Jefferson at "Monticello" was so alarmed by the great sectional struggle over the admission of Missouri as a slave state that he wrote: "this momentous question, like a fire bell in the night, awakened and filled me with terror. I considered it at once the knell of the Union." On account of this struggle over slavery, the old statesman feared a cleavage between the North and South along a geographical line "recurring on every occasion and renewing irritations, until it would kindle such mutual and mortal hatred, as to render separation preferable to eternal discord." [7] What Jefferson predicted was realized in the future—the rise of "the irrepressible conflict."

The North won this first round of the sectional battle. The Northwest, which had previously been in alliance with the South, joined the Northeast and voted preponderantly for Tallmadge's Amendment, shifting thus the balance of power. Also the principle of curbing slavery in the West was established. Although the area in the Louisiana Purchase territory above the 36″ 30′ line was much greater than the portion alloted to the expansion of slavery, most Southerners believed that the interdicted territory was barren and unsuited to the expansion of slavery. Moreover, thirty-four years later that part of the famous document, which contained the phrase that slavery should be "forever prohibited" was repealed.

While Congress was debating over the admission of Missouri into the Union, the President negotiated a treaty for the purchase of Florida. Florida had been coveted by Southerners, including the Virginia dynasty of Presidents, for many reasons. It was regarded as included within "the natural boundaries" of the United States and as necessary to give our country control of the Gulf of Mexico. Some of the large Southern rivers had their outlets in the Spanish-controlled coasts of West Florida. This weakly held colony, moreover, had become a decided nuisance to the inhabitants of the southern border of the United States. Runaway slaves found refuge in this territory and it harbored predatory Indians who were a constant menace to peaceful Southern farmers and planters. The cotton planter, eager to find fresh lands for his staple, cast avaricious glances on the valuable agricultural lands in this region preempted by the lackadaisical Spaniards.

Shortly after the Louisiana purchase, our minister, Robert Livingston, asserted that our title included West Florida as far as the Perdido River, which flowed to the east of Mobile Bay. Jefferson and Monroe adopted this pleasant conception of the treaty, but Spain indignantly denied that Louisiana included West Florida. The Louisiana purchase treaty was ambiguous, for it ceded to the United States the province of Louisiana with the same boundaries that it had when France possessed it and when Spain had control of it. In French possession, prior to the transfer to Spain in 1763, the province extended east to the Perdido River. In that year, however, England acquired Florida from Spain and divided the province into East Florida and West Florida with a western boundary of the Mississippi and Iberville rivers. Thus Louisiana in Spanish hands from 1763 to 1783 extended no further eastward than the Mississippi and Iberville rivers. After the Floridas were restored to Spain in 1783, the

Spanish government attached the administration of West Florida to the royal governor at New Orleans.

In 1804 Congress passed the Mobile Act placing the disputed territory, including Mobile, in a customs district, an assumption that led to a violent protest from the Spanish government. The following year James Monroe was sent to Europe on a special mission to obtain West Florida. He tried to put pressure on the weak Spanish government to yield, but Godoy, the Prime Minister and paramour of the Queen, who had acquired the pompous title of Prince of the Peace, refused to surrender. The key to a successful extortion of West Florida from the Spanish was the powerful French emperor and his venal minister, Talleyrand, who understood only the language of military force or of money. Jefferson decided to resort to the latter unscrupulous means of gaining Napoleon's aid in acquiring the coveted land. Accordingly, in December, 1805, he sent a secret message to Congress asking for an appropriation of two million dollars to be used for this purpose. He hoped to persuade the French emperor to put pressure upon the unwilling Spanish government to yield this morsel of territory to the United States. The appropriation was voted in February 1806, but the political situation in Europe changed and frustrated this attempt to win a land which Jefferson claimed already belonged to us by right.

West Florida was annexed to the United States by the medium of force rather than by sinuous diplomacy. After Napoleon began to dominate Spain by placing his brother, Joseph Bonaparte, on the Spanish throne, the American inhabitants of the western part of Florida feared that France would try to extend its rule over this Spanish colony. Accordingly, on September 22, 1810, a group of one hundred and four American settlers under Philemon Thomas started a revolution by seizing the Spanish garrison at Baton Rouge and declaring West Florida free and independent of Spain. They erected the first lone star republic, having a flag of blue woolen cloth with a silver star, and applied for annexation to the United States. A month later President Madison issued a proclamation not only absorbing the little republic between the Mississippi and the Pearl rivers, but also the territory of the Gulf coast to the Perdido River. Mobile, none the less, continued to be held by the Spaniards. It was not until after the War of 1812 had begun that we obtained possession of this Creole town. An expedition led by General James Wilkinson took possession of Mobile in April, 1813, the only piece of territory gained by the war. When Louisiana was admitted to the Union in 1812 that part of Florida between the Mississippi and Pearl rivers was incorporated in the new state.

In 1811 an Indian agent of the United States on the southern border, General George Matthews, attempted to seize East Florida for his government by instigating a revolution against the Spanish in that province. Some gunboats of the United States were ordered to the Atlantic coast of Florida, ostensibly to prevent the smuggling of merchandise and of slaves into the country. Also two hundred soldiers were dispatched to the East Florida border. With such a show of force and with the connivance of the Secretary of State, James Monroe, General Matthews established contacts with the leaders of a revolutionary party, especially John McIntosh, who called themselves the "patriots." Matthews, who had been a Revolutionary soldier and a former governor of Georgia, was a colorful figure, almost illiterate, but full of energy and rashness despite his seventy-two years. He was aided by the imperialistic natives of Georgia who were eager to liquidate the Spanish rule in Florida. On March 18, 1812, the "patriots" captured Amelia Island and then laid siege to St. Augustine, supported by the United States troops. After the hullabaloo raised by the John Henry papers (revelations of a British intriguer who tried to start a secession movement among the New England Federalists), Monroe decided to repudiate Matthews and he was dismissed as agent in April, 1812. The siege of St. Augustine by American troops, however, was not abandoned until the following September, and the captured territory was not given up until Congress had twice refused to approve the occupation.[8]

Spain continued to hold East Florida with a relaxed and nerveless grasp by means of three weak garrisons at Pensacola, St. Marks, and St. Augustine. Runaway slaves had built a fort on the Apalachicola River, called Negro Fort, where they defied capture. On Amelia Island, above St. Augustine, there was a nest of pirates under Gregor MacGregor. British agents, such as Lieutenant Colonel Edward Nicholls, circulated among the Creek and Seminole Indians of the southern border. Criminals frequently escaped across the border. Florida was indeed a nuisance to the United States.

As a consequence of Indian hostilities on the southern border, President Monroe ordered General Andrew Jackson to raise some militia and chastise the offending Indians. In 1818 he crossed the international boundary line in hot pursuit of marauding Indians. When they fled to the Spanish fort of St. Marks for protection, he proceeded to seize the fort and to hang several Seminole chiefs. He was unable, however, to catch one of the principal Seminole leaders, Billy Bowlegs, whose village lay on the Suwannee River. Warned by a Scotch trader and friend of the Indians, Alexander Arbuthnot, Bowlegs escaped to the Everglades. Jackson then arrested Arbuthnot as well as a young soldier of fortune, Robert Ambrister, who was employed by the Scotch trader, as instigators of Indian warfare. Arbuthnot had aroused the anger of Jackson by telling the Indians that Jackson's Creek treaty of 1814 was no longer valid and by offering to furnish hostile Indians with gunpowder. These two British subjects were tried by court martial and executed. Arbuthnot, a white-haired old gentleman, was hanged from the topsail yard of his trading vessel, the *Chance*, while the young adventurer, Ambrister, was accorded the honor of being shot by a firing squad. Then Jackson marched to Pensacola, drove out the Spanish garrison, and raised the American flag above the fort. Thus this American general had violated international law and trampled upon the rights of both Spain and England.

By many Americans of the South and the West Jackson was hailed as a hero for his high-handed conduct. But British public opinion was so inflamed over the affair that Lord Castlereagh had some difficulty in preserving peaceful relations with the United States. Furthermore, Henry Clay made a spirited speech in Congress condemning Jackson's arbitrary and dangerous course. The latter defended himself by declaring that he had received authority from President Monroe for his action through a private correspondence with a Tennessee Congressman, John Rhea. Monroe, on the other hand, denied that he had given Jackson authority to seize Spanish forts and hang British citizens. The Cabinet considered the problem of disciplining Jackson. The Secretary of War, John C. Calhoun, advocated the trial of the unruly general by court martial, but Secretary of State John Quincy Adams stoutly upheld Jackson's conduct, and no action was taken. Furthermore, resolutions introduced into Congress censuring Jackson for his Florida invasion were defeated. Pensacola and St. Mark's, nevertheless, were returned to Spain.

Indirectly, Jackson's invasion of Florida was responsible for Spain's decision to turn over the troublesome province to the United States. Before the irruption of the headstrong general into Florida, Adams had been negotiating without success for the purchase of East Florida. He now had a trump card. He declared that Spain should police her border efficiently and that if the United States were forced to send another expedition into Florida against the Indians, American soldiers would remain. Furthermore, he demanded payment of the claims, amounting to approximately five million dollars, of American citizens against Spain.

The Spanish government was not as solicitous to retain Florida as to prevent the United States from recognizing the independence of the revolted Latin-American republics. The Spanish officials realized that as long as they delayed selling Florida, the government of the United States would be cautious about recognizing these rebellious colonies of the mother country. Henry Clay and others in Congress were vigorously demanding that the United States should recognize these young republics. The invasion of Florida, however, frightened Spain, which now decided to accept the inevitable and cede Florida rather than lose it by force.

The treaty transferring Florida to the United States was signed February 22, 1819, by Adams, representing the United States, and De Onis, the Spanish ambassador at Washington. By its terms Spain agreed to surrender East Florida and recognize the legality of our occupation of West Florida. In return, the United States assumed the claims of its citizens against the Spanish government and surrendered our contention that Texas was a part of the Louisiana Purchase. The Sabine river was agreed upon as part of the western boundary of Louisiana.

Hoping to prevent the United States from recognizing the revolted republics of Latin America, the Spanish government delayed ratifying the treaty. Finally in 1821 the transfer of Florida to the

United States was consummated. Monroe appointed Jackson to be the first military governor of the new province. The general proved to be an unfortunate appointment, for he was surprisingly sensitive over questions of punctilio and became involved in quarrels with the retiring Spanish governor. Disappointed in the lack of jobs for his friends and relatives, he soon resigned from this unpleasant position.

At the time of its acquisition by the United States, the population of East Florida was estimated at 15,000 people and of West Florida at 5,000 people, mostly poor whites and frontiersmen. The territory did not attract many American settlers for a number of years. Land titles were dubious as a result of Spanish claims and during the decades of the 1830's and 1840's the United States army was engaged in a long and costly war against the Seminole Indians. Florida was divided economically and socially into three distinct sections: East Florida, including the area east of the Suwannee River, with St. Augustine as its center, where sugar and oranges were produced; middle Florida, with Tallahassee as its center, settled after 1825 by Southern cotton planters; and West Florida, with Pensacola as its center of population. Florida under the rule of the United States did not prosper much more than it had under the control of Spain. Indeed, Florida did not become a state until 1845, when it was admitted into the Union to balance the free state of Iowa. The movement for statehood was strong among the inhabitants of the Tallahassee district, but the bitter sectional feelings of East Florida caused its leaders to propose the separation of the territory by the Suwannee River and the admission of only the western portion as a state, the eastern part remaining a territory until a later date when it should become the separate state of East Florida.

The civilization of the Spanish Creoles has influenced the pattern of life in the lower South chiefly through the avenues of Texas and New Orleans rather than from the original base of Spanish settlement in Florida. The destruction of the Spanish missions in Florida, Georgia, and South Carolina eradicated the influence of mission architecture on the South Atlantic states.[9] In St. Augustine, however, there remain a few relics of Spanish occupation, a baroque Spanish cathedral, the old Spanish fort of San Marcos (now christened Fort

Marion), built of coquina stone, or a formation of coral and sand quarried from St. Anastasia Island, the picturesque stone gate of the vanished wall about the town, the unpretentious Spanish governor's house, used as a post office by the Americans, the Treasury, and several old houses, such as the Geronimo Alvarez House. In another quarter of the South, the San Antonio valley of Texas, there are five Spanish missions, including the famous Alamo, which preserve the traditions of Spanish architecture.

The most important and numerous monuments of Spanish architecture in the South are to be found at New Orleans. Contrary to a common impression, the architecture of the old quarter of New Orleans is not primarily French but Spanish. The old French city of Bienville and of "the Grand Marquis," Vaudreuil, was destroyed by disastrous fires in 1788 and 1794. The principal public buildings were rebuilt in Spanish style by the generosity of the wealthiest citizen of New Orleans, Don Andres Almonaster. The picturesque Cabildo (City Hall) which stands on Jackson Square, formerly Place d'Armes, the Charity Hospital, and the Capuchin Convent were built by him. Many of the houses of the Vieux Carré are of Spanish architecture, constructed of stucco, painted in many pastel colors, with patios in the rear, balconies of wrought or cast iron, long windows protected from the burning sun by shutters.

To the Spanish settlers in the New World Southern agriculture owes much. The Spaniards introduced many plants, fruits, vegetables, and domestic animals into America. They were responsible for bringing the sweet orange to Florida, which had originally grown in China and had been carried to Spain by the Moors. From Europe they transported to their American colonies wheat, sugar cane, rice, alfalfa, "mission figs," apples, apricots, lemons, cherries, pears, and walnuts. Certain flowers, such as geraniums, red carnations, and lilies came over on Spanish caravels. Domesticated bees, called by the Indians the "white man's flies," were brought over for honey and to pollinate certain European flowers, such as apple blossoms. When the Spaniards arrived, the American native horse, whose bones have been found in the tar pit of the Rancho la Brea near Los Angeles, had become extinct. But some of the Spanish horses escaped and propagated the wild horses of the Western plains. Although the

American continent had millions of buffalo, there were no native cows. Spanish cattle escaped, however, and became the ancestors of the wild long-horned cattle of Texas.

The Spanish settlers of the Southwest have enriched the American language in many ways. The terminology of the cattle country is Spanish because the cowboys were taught much of their skill in handling cattle by the Mexican *vaqueros*. The American cowboy adopted the costume of his Mexican predecessor, the wide-brimmed sombrero, the chaps, the lariat, and even the Mexican saddle. The lingo of the cattle country, the use of the rodeo, the remuda, the practice of branding cattle, the corral were inherited from the Spanish-American cattleman. Many words of common usage in the Southwest, such as canyon, tornado, mesa, plaza, adobe, burro, patio, presidio, peon, poncho, bronco, desperado, calaboose, and vamoose were derived from the Spanish language. Also the American miner profited from Spanish pioneering efforts in the Southwest. The young republic of the United States adopted the Spanish piece of eight, or milled dollar, as the basis of our coinage. Our debt to Spanish mining adventures is reflected in such words of Latin origin as bonanza, placer, eldorado, and vigilante. A study of Spanish words incorporated in the speech of the United States reveals the fact that the Spanish in Texas and the Southwest had a greater significance in American civilization than the Latin element in Florida. The reason for this development was that the Spaniards in Florida were always numerically weak and when the province was acquired by the British and later by the United States most of the Spanish inhabitants moved away.

Citations

1. The personality of Madison is portrayed in IRVING BRANT, *James Madison the Virginia Revolutionist* (Indianapolis, 1941), and *James Madison the Nationalist, 1780–1787* (Indianapolis, 1948).
2. The best modern study of the War of 1812 is A. L. Burt, *The United States, Great Britain and British North America* (New Haven, 1940), Chaps. XI–XV.

3. J. W. Pratt, *Expansionists of 1812* (New York, 1925), 40.
4. W. H. Goodman, "The Origins of the War of 1812: A Survey of Changing Interpretations," *Mississippi Valley Historical Review*, XXVIII (September, 1941), 184.
5. W. O. Lynch, "The Westward Flow of Southern Colonists before 1861," *Journal of Southern History*, IX (August, 1943), and F. L. Owsley, "The Pattern of Migration and Settlement of the Southern Frontier," *ibid.*, XI (May, 1945), 147–176.
6. A. F. Simpson, "The Political Significance of Slave Representation, 1787–1821," *Journal of Southern History*, VII (August, 1941), 314–342.
7. Lipscomb and Bergh, *Writings of Thomas Jefferson*, XIV, 247–249.
8. Isaac J. Cox, *The West Florida Controversy, 1798–1813* (Baltimore, 1918), Chaps. 9–11.
9. See John Bartram, "Diary of a Journey through the Carolinas, Georgia, and Florida," *Transactions of the American Philosophical Society*, New Series, XXXIII, Part I, 51–55.

CHAPTER X

Characteristics of Southern Agriculture

THE traveler in the ante-bellum South was impressed by the wide spaces of woodland between the lonely houses and cleared fields. He observed also the zigzag rail or Virginia worm fences around these fields. The rails for these fences were split from logs by means of wedges and hickory or butternut mauls, such as Abraham Lincoln used. The long-continuing tradition of the frontier made it necessary for every farmer to defend his fields from ranging cattle. Not until after the Civil War did another philosophy of fences prevail, which required the cattle raiser to confine his cattle and prevent them from eating the crops of his neighbor.

Very noticeable were the differences between Northern and Southern agriculture, particularly the fact that the planters were engaged in producing crops for foreign export. A large number of Southern farmers, however, were employed in the same type of agriculture, subsistence farming, as prevailed above the Ohio and the Mason and Dixon line. Southern agriculture was further differentiated from Northern agriculture by the widespread development of the plantation, with its gang system of labor based on black slaves. The plantation was variable in size but frequently consisted of a thousand to fifteen hundred acres of land. Its size was limited by the walking distance of an hour or so from the slave quarters to the most distant fields. The relative proportions of the different types of plantations is indicated roughly by the Census of 1850, which lists 74,031 cotton plantations (producing more than five bales), 2,681 sugar plantations, including the smallest, 15,745 tobacco estates producing

3,000 pounds or more, 8,327 hemp plantations, and 551 rice plantations, each raising 20,000 pounds and over.[1]

The distribution of the different types of plantations was determined by geographic fitness. The locale of the rice district was a narrow strip of coastal South Carolina and Georgia, and a spur in southeastern North Carolina. The sugar-growing region was almost exclusively confined to Louisiana below the Red River and to a few valleys in Texas. The tobacco kingdom covered the upper South, including Missouri. Hemp as a staple crop was grown almost entirely in Kentucky and Missouri. The Cotton Kingdom enjoyed an imperial realm, with a northern boundary including the southern part of North Carolina, the middle area and the Mississippi Valley district of Tennessee, Arkansas, and eastern Texas. Although the large plantation was the rule in the cultivation of rice and sugar, both cotton and tobacco in the nineteenth century could be profitably grown by small farmers. The farms of the yeomen who were engaged in subsistence agriculture were scattered throughout the South, but they were concentrated in the border states and the Piedmont region.

A social revolution occurred in the Southern states as a result of the enormous expansion of the cultivation of cotton. The earliest-known home of cotton seems to have been India, where it was woven into cloth—calico, named after the city of Calicut, madras named after Madras, and muslin named after the Moslems. It was introduced into Spain by the Moors from the Orient, and Columbus brought back cotton from the Bahama Islands. This fiber was also manufactured into cloth by the Aztecs of Mexico and the Incas of Peru. During the colonial period small quantities of the plant were grown, but it did not become a major crop in the South until after the invention of the cotton gin in 1793. There were two main kinds of cotton which were cultivated in the South, the long-staple variety, used in fine fabrics, and the short-staple variety. Long-staple cotton not only had a greater length than the short-staple species, but its glossy black seed could be detached from the lint far more easily than the green seed of the short-staple variety.

Unfortunately, the long-staple type of cotton could be grown only in a restricted area, the sea islands which fringed the coast of South

Carolina and Georgia and the adjacent littoral. This superior strain of cotton, often called sea island cotton, was introduced about 1786 into Georgia from the Bahama Islands by Loyalist refugees. The export of this valuable fiber reached its peak in the decade of the 1820's, when eleven million pounds a year were sent abroad. Sea island cotton had certain disadvantages, the small yield per acre of only one hundred and fifty pounds, the failure of the boll to open fully, thus retarding the picking of it, and the need of skillful handling. The short-staple variety, on the other hand, had the advantage of being a hardy plant which could be grown on the uplands and the interior of the South. It made a fine replacement for the dying indigo industry, as soon as a machine was devised to gin or separate the fiber from the seed.

The need for a cotton gin was supplied by a versatile Yankee inventor, Eli Whitney. Shortly after graduating from Yale College at the age of twenty-seven, Whitney took passage on a ship for the South to secure a position as a tutor. On the ship he met the vivacious widow of General Nathanael Greene, who invited him to visit her at "Mulberry Grove," a plantation near Savannah which had been given to the general by the grateful people of Georgia. Here he was inspired to experiment with making a practical gin by hearing the talk of the planters about the need for a machine to separate the lint from the green cotton seed. In the spring of 1793 he completed the model of a machine which, operated by hand, would do the work of ten men, or by horse power, the work of fifty men. It was a simple mechanism consisting of rollers equipped with wire teeth that rotated against a hopper box constructed of slats. The revolving rollers tore the cotton from the seed, leaving the seed in the hopper. When the rollers became clogged with the lint, Mrs. Greene suggested cleaning them with a broom, a homely device which gave Whitney the idea of adding another cylinder equipped with brushes which revolved in an opposite direction and with greater speed than the wire-teeth roller.

Whitney formed a partnership with Phineas Miller, Mrs. Greene's manager and future husband, to exploit the invention, which was patented March 4, 1794. They hoped to reap a golden harvest by retaining a monopoly of the cotton-ginning business, exacting a toll of one-third of the cotton ginned by their machines. But the simple construction of the machine, which could be made by any competent blacksmith, frustrated this design for a monopoly. Improvements were made by other inventors, such as Hodgin Holmes, a mechanic of Augusta, Georgia, who received a patent May 2, 1796, for a gin which substituted iron disks for the wooden rollers with wire teeth. Planters and business men disregarded the patent rights of Whitney, and Southern jurors would not convict the infringers. Although some of the Southern states contributed considerable sums of money to Whitney and his partner, the latter spent much time and money to protect their patent rights and gained little profit from the invention.

Preceding the invention of the Whitney gin, the Industrial Revolution had begun in England, based on a series of inventions of machines to spin cotton and woolen thread and weave it into cloth in factories. In 1790 an Englishman, Samuel Slater, introduced the cotton mill, operated by water power, into the United States at Pawtucket, Rhode Island. Following the conclusion of the War of 1812, cotton factories, aided by a protective tariff, began to multiply in New England. Consequently, the English and American textile factories were hungry for Southern cotton. This demand was increased later by the invention in 1846 of the sewing machine by Elias Howe, which was perfected by Isaac M. Singer in the decade of the 1850's.

The cotton gin made it practicable to grow short-staple cotton at a profit. Formerly it took one hand a day to gin a pound of this cotton, but the improved gin multiplied the effectiveness of a man so that he could clean 350 pounds of cotton a day. The cultivation of cotton was admirably suited to the gang labor of slaves, since the low height of the cotton plant made it easy for an overseer to supervise the slaves, for they could not hide from his gaze.[2] The chief limitation of the cotton crop was that it required a long growing season, at least two hundred days free from killing frosts. Consequently, the ante-bellum cotton belt did not extend into Virginia, Kentucky, Maryland, or Missouri. As late as 1825 Virginia planters experimented with cultivating cotton, but they abandoned the attempt after a trial. Although the cotton belt had a northern limit, its extension westward was prevented only by barren soil or lack of sufficient rainfall. The production of cotton was also limited by the fact that a gang of slaves could plant and cultivate a much larger acreage of the valuable staple than they could pick, and it was difficult to secure extra laborers during cotton-picking time. If the South could have developed a practicable mechanical picker, such an invention would have enormously lightened the work on a cotton plantation and would have considerably reduced the number of slaves needed. But this invention did not appear, partly because the bolls of the cotton plant ripen at different times.

The varied activity which was pursued on a typical cotton plantation is illustrated by the plantation journals which have survived. One of these manuscripts, the journal of W. S. Hyland who owned a plantation near Warrenton, Mississippi, reveals the amazing amount of work obtained from the slaves during the cotton-picking season.[3] There were from twenty to twenty-five cotton pickers, men, women, and children, on the plantation during the years 1847–1861, working under an overseer. The hands began picking cotton about August 20 and continued until the early part of January, picking over the fields from three to five separate times. The best slaves averaged over 300 pounds a day at the height of the season. In 1852 "Little Mary" led the gang of cotton pickers, picking 2,073 pounds of cotton in a week of six days, while one slave, Bob, picked 540 pounds on October 6, 1856. The plantation produced about 150 bales of cotton, which varied in weight but averaged 450 pounds. The plantation had its own gin, which was operated by slaves. In addition to the money crop, cotton, the plantation produced an ample supply of corn, meat, pumpkins, sweet potatoes, and peas. The labor record shows that very little time was lost by sickness of the slaves although there was an epidemic of diphtheria which took a heavy toll of the lives of the children, and the deaths of several mature slaves from consumption and pneumonia are recorded. The slaves on this plantation worked a full day on Saturday and when rain prevented them from picking cotton they were employed in other work such as gathering and shucking corn, gathering potatoes, sewing, and repairing the worm fences.

The method of cultivating cotton in the ante-bellum South tended to exhaust the soil, especially on account of the failure to practice an intelligent rotation of crops and to check soil erosion. Consequently, the cotton planters began a steady march westward to acquire virgin soil, leaving a wake of desolate and abandoned countryside. These abandoned lands were often called in the later ante-bellum period "Gone to Texas" farms. The advance of the cotton planters toward the setting sun has been compared to the devastating effect of an army invading a peaceful land. The first stage in the westward retreat (or advance) of the cotton planters was the extension of cotton culture into the Piedmont area of the Atlantic seaboard states. This advance brought the plantation system and slavery into the back country, thus tending to unify the back country and the Tidewater. It can be illustrated by the rapid progress of slavery into the Piedmont counties of South Carolina. In 1790 slaves constituted only one-fifth of the population of this region but by 1830 the black population of this region nearly equaled the white.

In the meanwhile cotton and slavery were expanding into the rich bottom lands of the Gulf area. The old, impoverished soils of the Atlantic seaboard could not compete with the fresh, incredibly fertile lands of the Gulf states. The Atlantic seaboard states, however, still produced the major part of the cotton crop up to 1830, but by 1835 the Gulf states had far outstripped the Atlantic states in the production of the fleecy staple. From this date to the Civil War the Gulf states and Arkansas produced three-fourths of the crop grown in the United States. In 1859 the record crop of 4,541,285 bales was grown in the land of Dixie. The weight of the bale in the Southwest, where baling presses and screws prevailed, was approximately 500 pounds, but in the Atlantic seaboard states the weight was around 300 pounds. On the eve of the Civil War considerably over three-fourths of the Southern cotton crop was sent to Europe. Cotton provided approximately 60 per cent in value of the exports of the United States.

The profits from green-seed cotton grown on virgin soil were at first very alluring. In 1801 the price was 44 cents a pound, and on rich soil a bale an acre was grown. In these early years the lucrative returns from growing cotton with slave labor was demonstrated by Wade Hampton who raised six hundred bales of cotton on six hundred acres of his plantation near Columbia, South Carolina. His crop was valued at $90,000. The value of cotton declined rapidly, however, so that in 1811 it brought only 8.9 cents a pound, and in 1812 when news of the declaration of war against England reached the lower South, the price broke disastrously. Thus early was revealed the evils of dependence on a foreign market. Overproduction began to plague the cotton producers, and they never developed a sensible crop control plan that would adjust the supply to the

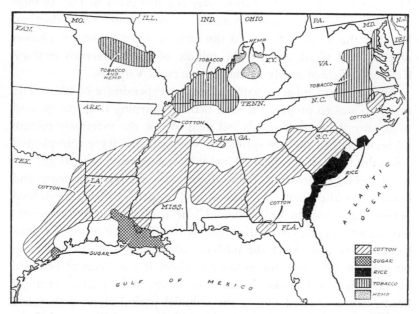

STAPLE CROPS OF THE OLD SOUTH, 1860

Adapted from a map in U. B. Phillips, *Life and Labor in the Old South*
(Boston, 1929)

demand. Prices fluctuated violently, in the decade 1839–49 dropping to prices below the cost of production, but in the decade preceding the Civil War, rising to profitable levels of 11 and 12 cents a pound.

In colonial days tobacco was the money crop of the Tidewater, but in the nineteenth century the center of tobacco growing shifted to the Piedmont. By 1840 little tobacco was raised in the Virginia and Maryland Tidewater, and this region, once dominated by great tobacco plantations, was reoccupied by yeoman farmers. This movement was caused partly by the exhaustion and erosion of the soils in the older region, but also it was accentuated by the fact that tobacco in this later period could be cultivated most profitably on small farms. In the Virginia–North Carolina tobacco district the typical farm contained only five and one-half acres in tobacco, which required the work of two hands. The cultivation of tobacco crossed the mountains and spread into Kentucky, Tennessee, Ohio, and Missouri, casting a dark shadow over the prospects of the Atlantic seaboard, for such dispersion resulted in tremendous overproduction. By 1843 the western surpassed the eastern states in the production of the royal weed, and by the middle of the nineteenth century Kentucky yielded nearly as much tobacco as Virginia.

The raising of tobacco required a great expenditure of labor. The first step was to prepare the seed beds by burning over the ground to destroy the seed of weeds and then to sow the extremely minute tobacco seed. In the late spring the young plants were transplanted from the beds to the fields. Not only was it necessary to kill the weeds and fast-growing Johnson grass by frequent plowing and hoeing, but the plants also had to be "topped" by an experienced person, they had to be "suckered," or the subordinate leaves removed, and a ceaseless warfare against the fat green tobacco worms had to be waged. After the tobacco matured, it was cut and hung on poles in tall, log tobacco houses, where it was "cured" or dried by slow fires and smoke. It was now ready to be packed in hogsheads, that contained during the colonial period about a thousand pounds of tobacco but through most of the ante-bellum period approximately fourteen hundred pounds. Then came the problem of transportation to market, either by boat down the rivers or by rolling the hogsheads along the miserable roads. Before the tobacco could be exported it had to be inspected at warehouses by officials appointed by the governor. In colonial days all condemned tobacco had to be burned, but this requirement was abandoned in 1805 in Virginia and in 1817 in North Carolina.

Up to 1840 most of the tobacco raised in the South was exported. The British purchased 40 per cent of the tobacco exported from Virginia, the French 20 per cent, the Italians 15 per cent, and the North Europeans, 25 per cent. From 1800 to 1860 the British government placed a heavy duty on tobacco, three or four shillings a pound, equivalent to an *ad valorem* duty of 900 per cent. The assumption, which has been current in American economic history, that the exports of tobacco declined following the outbreak of the Revolution until about 1840 has been challenged by a recent scholar.[4] He points out that this error was based on the statistics of the exports of hogsheads, which changed in weight. The record production of tobacco in the Southern colonies was attained in the five years preceding the Revolution, then there was a decline; a spurt of exports, however, in 1790–92 surpassed the colonial record, and in eight separate years before 1840 exports exceeded those of 1792, the banner year of the eighteenth century. It is true that tobacco production in the Virginia district did not exceed colonial production until the decade of the 1830's, but there was a large expansion in the crop of the states across the mountains. So great was the increase in the cultivation of tobacco during the last decade of the antebellum period that production in Virginia and Kentucky was doubled and in North Carolina was tripled. The record year for the export of cured tobacco from the United States was 1859 when twice as much tobacco was exported as the colonial amount.

The growing of tobacco in North Carolina and Virginia was revolutionized by the discovery of a new variety, "Bright Yellow Tobacco." This discovery was accidentally made by Stephen, a young slave employed as blacksmith and overseer on the farm of Abisha Slade in Caswell County, North Carolina. In 1839 this intelligent Negro youth discovered a method of curing a new type of tobacco by using charcoal as fuel. The product, "Bright Yellow Tobacco," it was also found, grew not on rich bottom lands, but on poor, silicious soil. In the decade of the 1850's, the Slade brothers developed and publicized the technique of cultivating and curing this variety, which was sold for four times the price of ordinary dark tobacco. Thus in the last decade of the ante-bellum period a new type of fancy tobacco was developed, which was at first used as the ornamental cover of plug tobacco, but after the Civil War became the basis of the great cigarette industry.

The price which the farmer received for his tobacco fluctuated violently according to the law of supply and demand. It was difficult to control the quantity of tobacco grown, partly because of an eighteen months' interlude between the planting of the crop and the marketing of it. Also the weather played a tremendous and ominous role in the prosperity of the tobacco country. Consequently, most of the planters were distinctly weather conscious, as their diaries show. Freshets, hail, storms, droughts, hostile insects ruined crops and raised prices. On the other hand, a bountiful and gracious Nature produced such bumper crops that prices cascaded downward. Prices ranged from 3½ cents a pound in the early 1800's to a high point of 14½ cents in 1816 after the war with England, to 7.8 cents just prior to the Civil War. Great overproduction in the last few years before secession caused gloomy thoughts concerning the future of their money crops to shadow the minds of the tobacco growers.

A crop that competed with tobacco in Kentucky and Missouri was hemp. In colonial days the British government had tried to encourage the growing of this fiber so essential to the shipping industry by offering bounties of £6 per ton, but little hemp was exported. Hemp and flax were grown widely, however, in the frontier regions of the South, where they were used in making coarse cloth. In Kentucky hemp was grown for commercial purposes principally in the Bluegrass region of Lexington and the districts around Louisville and Maysville (burley tobacco did not become the money crop of the Bluegrass until after the Civil War). A magnificent description of the growing and harvesting of hemp in Kentucky is contained in James Lane Allen's novel, *The Reign of Law*. The hemp seed were sown broadcast over the plowed field, growing up in slender stalks which attained a height of ten feet or more. After the crop was ripe it was reaped by cutting with a hemp knife. The substance of the hemp which held the fibers was then allowed to rot, and the stalks were broken by a crude hand machine. As a result of the protection afforded by the tariff and the high prices of 1826–28, the production of hemp expanded greatly in the Bluegrass region of Kentucky, in middle Tennessee, and in Missouri. Henry Clay, who had married the heiress of a hemp-growing family, became a powerful advocate in Congress of tariff protection which was needed in competition with the superior water-rotted Russian hemp, Manila hemp, and Scottish hemp bagging. Since hemp bagging and bale ropes were used on the Southern cotton bales, the demand of the hemp growers and manufacturers for tariff protection clashed with the interests of the cotton growers.

The failure of the Kentucky hemp growers to supply heavy cordage for the navy is a fascinating story of the bureaucratic mind of the navy and of the independent nature of Southern farmers. The Kentucky growers prepared their fiber for the market by the dew-rotting process, which was satisfactory for cotton bagging and for bale rope but not for the tarred rope used by the navy. The stronger and more flexible water-rotted variety was imported from Russia and was used by the navy throughout the ante-bellum period. Congress tried on numerous occasions to encourage the production of water-rotted hemp for the navy as a patriotic measure, but its efforts were defeated by the inflexible bureaucracy of the navy and by the inertia and conservatism of the American hemp growers. The navy did send agents into the hemp-growing region, but it gave them little authority and usually refused to buy Kentucky water-rotted hemp unless it was sent for inspection to the national rope factory at the Charlestown Navy Yard in Massachusetts. Accordingly, the agents were unable to procure much Kentucky hemp that would meet the specifications of the navy. An ardent propagandist for persuading the Kentucky and Missouri farmers to adopt the water-rotted process in preparing hemp was David Myerle, who exhausted his fortune in this missionary work but was frustrated by a variety of factors.[5] In 1852 a navy yard and rope factory were established by Congress at Memphis, but although the factory had the finest machinery in the world, it received little Southern hemp and was abandoned two years later. Some of the reasons given for the apathy of the Kentuckians toward producing water-rotted hemp were that it smelled badly, and ignorant farmers thought it spread disease, that the Kentucky water pools were needed for their cattle and blooded horses, and that some Kentucky hemp which had been sent to the Charlestown Navy Yard had been unfairly rejected by the Yankees, thus discouraging further shipments.

The depletion of the fertility of the soils of the tobacco region in the eighteenth and early nineteenth centuries stimulated the plant-

ers to study scientific agriculture. George Washington led the way
in trying to rehabilitate his plantation of "Mount Vernon." Not only
did he read the works of the English agricultural reformers, such
as Jethro Tull's *The Horse-Hoeing Husbandry*, but he practiced
a more intelligent rotation of crops, introduced new crops, such as
turnips, lucern (alfalfa), and chicory, and imported an Arabian stal-
lion to improve the breed of horses. The king of Spain sent Washington a pedigreed jack, "Royal Gift," and Lafayette later sent him a
jack from Malta to produce mules. All his reforming efforts, however, availed little, for he had neglected "Mount Vernon" during
such a long period of time while he was in the public service.
Twenty-five years after his death a neighbor described the condition of this former regal estate as, " a more widespread and perfect
agricultural ruin could not be imagined." Jefferson also was ardently interested in improving Southern agriculture, making many
experiments, but "Monticello," with its abandoned old fields, was
sold after his death to Lieutenant Uriah Levy for two thousand, five
hundred dollars. Yet Jefferson's son-in-law, Thomas Mann Randolph,
who assumed the management of "Monticello," pointed the way
to the future by introducing into the Piedmont the new method of
contour plowing, i.e., plowing horizonally along the hills, following their curvatures, which was to become an efficient method of
checking erosion.

Agricultural reform in Virginia and Maryland was preceded by a
great rise in the price of wheat caused by the Napoleonic wars. Also
the price of tobacco reached a nadir during the period of the embargo and the War of 1812. Consequently a shift began from a reliance on the soil-exhausting crop of tobacco to wheat. Furthermore,
intelligent planters were studying methods of increasing the fertility
of soils. In 1784 John A. Binns of Loudon County, Virginia, experimented with gypsum, or plaster of Paris, as a fertilizer, resulting in
the spread of the gospel of gypsum in the years following the War
of 1812. A pioneer work on Southern agriculture was written by
John Taylor of Caroline County, Virginia, *The Arator*, which was
published in book form in 1813. He advocated rotation of crops,
deep plowing, and especially the use of vegetable material for
manures.[6]

The greatest agricultural reformer of the Old South was without doubt Edmund Ruffin of Virginia. After studying the chemistry of soils, he concluded that much of the exhausted arable lands of the upper South had acid conditions which must be neutralized before they could become highly productive. His remedy was to apply marl, a fine shell deposit found in eastern Virginia, to neutralize acid soils. This doctrine he expounded in his *Essay on Calcareous Manures*, published in 1832. In the next year he founded the *Farmers' Register*, to advocate the new cult of the use of marl and scientific methods of farming. He made his plantations at "Coggin's Point" on the James River and "Malbourne" on the Pamunkey River laboratories for agricultural experiment, demonstrating the practical value of his ideas by enormously increasing his production of corn and wheat. His fame spread, and he was invited by North Carolina, Georgia, and South Carolina to conduct agricultural surveys in those states and give his expert advice concerning the renovation of their agriculture.

In the decade of the 1830's the agricultural revolution in the upper South was well on its way. Agricultural societies were founded to exchange information on the best methods of farming, and fairs were held which awarded prizes for superior agricultural products and livestock. Fielding Lewis of Fredericksburg began to use lime instead of marl to neutralize acid soils with excellent results, an example which was followed by the aristocratic planters in the James River Valley, the Harrisons at "Brandon," Hill Carter at "Shirley," and others. John Cocke of "Bremo" urged his fellow Virginians to turn away from the cultivation of tobacco and grow wheat and *clover*, and to abolish the overseer system. Mules were gradually substituted for the slow-moving oxen or the horses of the colonial period. Mules became the ideal draft animal for the Southern plantation since they were strong, fast at the plow, tough and capable of withstanding the abuse of the slaves, and long-lived. The cradle was substituted for the scythe in reaping wheat. Above all, the work of the reformers rescued Southern agriculture from the control of illiterate and routine-ridden overseers and made farming a serious profession, worthy of study for gentlemen. So significant was the agricultural renaissance based on wheat instead of tobacco and on scientific cultivation, that Virginia and Maryland were enjoying a new agricultural prosperity in the last decade of the ante-bellum period.

The agricultural revolution in the lower South occurred later than the Maryland and Virginia renaissance and differed in several respects from its predecessor. Agricultural reform in the cotton belt was led by a group of planters and farmers in middle Georgia, especially in Hancock County. The reform began partly as a result of low prices for cotton in the decade of the 1840's. Georgia had suffered seriously from the emigration of its young men to the West, from the depletion of its soils by erosion, and from the unintelligent cultivation of cotton. Furthermore, the Georgia land lottery, by which thirty million acres of fresh land in the territory from which the Indians had been removed were presented free to Georgia farmers by a lottery system, had encouraged the abandonment of land instead of the practicing of thrifty agriculture. The reformers of Hancock County, organized into a Planter's Club, determined to stay on their farms and increase their value. Accordingly, led by David Dickson, they developed improved strains of cotton seed, checked erosion, bred quality livestock, introduced new crops such as grasses, peaches, and strawberries, and adopted more intelligent methods of utilizing slave labor. In 1844, when the price of cotton sank to the lowest point that it had ever reached, a Georgia planter, Dimos Ponce, proposed a crop control plan of reducing the acreage of cotton which was quite similar to the New Deal plan of the decade of the 1930's. However, he could not secure the cooperation of the individualistic farmers of the South to put his proposal into operation. Southern farmers tried to increase production by the importation of guano (after 1845) from islands off the coast of Peru and by the use of cotton seed, which had formerly been thrown away, as fertilizer. The efforts of the planters and farmers of Georgia to reform agricultural practices of the cotton belt spread to the lower South. Georgia became known as the "Empire State of the South." [7]

The experiments of Southern planters in growing new crops, in improving the breed of livestock, and in developing scientific methods of agriculture have never been properly appreciated. Thomas

Spalding, owner of most of Sapelo Island, Georgia, was an example of a planter who was a constant experimenter, seeking to diversify Southern crops. He tried to revive silk culture in Georgia, to develop olive orchards, and to introduce sugar culture in this state. Other planters experimented with different strains of cotton, sent peaches to the New York market, introduced Angora goats from the Orient, and studied methods of conserving the soil through drainage, deep plowing, rotation of crops, and fertilizers. They read papers before numerous agricultural societies, were active in agricultural fairs at which prices were awarded, and patronized the agricultural periodicals which were founded below the Mason and Dixon line.

Some of the best of these publications were *The American Farmer* of Baltimore, founded by John Skinner in 1819, the *American Turf Register and Sporting Magazine*, also edited by Skinner, which contributed much to improving the breed of American horses, and the *Southern Agriculturist* of Charleston. Joseph Bond, a progressive cotton planter of Georgia, sent the *Soil of the South* (published in Columbus, Georgia) to each of his six overseers. The *American Cotton Planter* of Montgomery, Alabama (1853–1861), was edited by a physician, Dr. N. B. Cloud, who advocated a more diversified economy for the South by growing more grain, raising more stock, and manufacturing textiles from cotton. Another physician, Dr. M. W. Phillips of "Log Hall," Mississippi, edited the *South-Western Farmer* of Raymond, Mississippi, in which he also advocated the diversification of crops as well as the moral culture of the slaves through *oral* instruction in religious truths. Finally a New Yorker, Dr. Daniel Lee, became the editor of a flourishing publication in Augusta, Georgia, *The Southern Cultivator* (founded in 1843), which had attained a circulation of 10,000 subscribers by 1852. It is interesting to observe that he was converted to the opinion that Southern slavery was "upon the whole a good thing." [8] He became the first professor of agriculture at Franklin College (the University of Georgia), holding a chair established in 1854 by a philanthropist.

Some of the largest fortunes from the pursuit of agriculture were accumulated by the rice planters. The richest of the Carolina rice planters was Nathaniel Heyward, who referred to his rice planta-

tions on the Combahee River as "gold mines." In 1805, during the
Napoleonic wars when rice brought a higher price than at any subsequent time before the Civil War, he made a net profit of $120,000
on his rice plantations. When he died in 1851, he had acquired seventeen plantations and 2,087 slaves, making him the largest slaveholder
of the South. His goal in life seemed to have been continuously to
amass slaves and multiply plantations.

Rice planting was not an occupation for the poor man. It required a considerable capital outlay to build the dikes and flood
gates along the rivers, to erect the pounding mills which removed
the husks and polished the rice, and to maintain large gangs of
slaves. The rice plantations lay in the malarial districts of South
Carolina, which forced the planter to abandon residence on his
plantation from early May to November. The Negroes were thus
left largely under the control of the overseer, but the task system
of labor tended to protect them from inhuman treatment. The
planters had to assume grave hazards in the operation of their plantations. Floods and tropical storms at times destroyed crops and the
dikes that kept out the salt water which ruined the rice fields. Alligators and muskrats might start a break in the dikes that would result in great loss. Epidemics such as cholera or yellow fever were a
constant menace to slave property.

The rice plantations of the Carolinas and Georgia led to an economy of concentrated slaveholdings. Governor William Aiken had a
rice plantation on Jehossee Island which had a labor force of seven
hundred slaves. The English actress, Fanny Kemble, who married
one of the rice grandees of Georgia, Pierce Butler, kept a journal of her residence on the rice plantation of "Butler's Island" in
1838–39. She has left a bitterly prejudiced account of slavery and
the life of a rice planter. Later she obtained a divorce from her
husband, and Butler's fortune fell on evil days so that after the
panic of 1857 he was forced to sell his slaves at auction, four hundred and twenty-nine men, women, and children bringing $303,850.
On the other hand, the portrait of an ideal rice planter, James Hamilton Couper of "Hopeton" on the Altamaha River, has been drawn
by the English geologist, Sir Charles Lyell, who has written perhaps
the fairest travel account of the Old South. Couper was educated at

Yale and by travel in Europe, during which he studied the diking system of Holland. Unlike most Southerners, he kept superb plantation records, which are now preserved in the Southern Collection of the University of North Carolina. He arose at six o'clock in the morning and planned his day on the basis of a strict economy of precious hours. The "Hopeton Plantation" employed five hundred slaves of various ages and both sexes. Lyell reported that the Negroes on the plantation lived in neat and comfortable cottages and that they received more food usually than they could eat. Each prime hand produced about four and one-half barrels of rice, each barrel containing five hundred pounds, which sold at prices ranging around three or four cents a pound. The slaves were managed by a white overseer and a Negro driver who had been the son of a Mohammedan prince of the Foulah tribe. The tasks of the slaves were often completed in five hours. The Negroes were allowed to raise and sell chickens, to sell their catch of fish, and to make cypress tubs and canoes, the latter selling for four dollars. Punishments were rare. The "Hopeton Plantation," indeed, was a splendid example of paternalism.[9]

The rice industry in South Carolina did not expand very much after the close of the eighteenth century. A major factor in this lack of growth was the competition of cotton, made possible by the Whitney gin. Rice growing in South Carolina declined in the last decade of the ante-bellum period. Indeed, the rice industry on the Atlantic seaboard reached the high point of its development in the middle of the nineteenth century, which was also the heyday of slavery. In the ante-bellum period, the Carolina planters began to process their rice at mills in Charleston instead of on the plantations. They also developed "Carolina Gold Rice," which was superior both to the oriental and the Mediterranean rice. During the Civil War many of the rice plantations were ruined, their labor force scattered, and the mansions of the planters destroyed by Sherman's army. The rice culture in the Atlantic seaboard never recovered, partly because of the competition of rice lands in Louisiana, Arkansas, and Texas. A series of tropical storms, especially the great one of 1906, destroyed the surviving rice plantations. The abandoned fields relapsed into a state of wild nature, covered with water and reeds, and some of them were converted by wealthy Northern sportsmen into game preserves. *Sic transit gloria mundi.*

Sugar cane was introduced into Louisiana from Santo Domingo by Jesuit priests, but only the cane syrup was at first produced. After the great slave insurrections in Santo Domingo in 1791–95, Louisiana became a refuge for many of the French sugar planters who brought with them their knowledge and skill in the culture of the sugar cane and the manufacture of sugar. In 1795, a French soldier, Etienne de Boré, as previously mentioned, succeeded in granulating sugar from the Louisiana cane juice. His profit of $12,000 on his crop pointed the way to riches in Louisiana. But sugar cane was an exotic in this region, for the growing season did not permit it to attain full maturity, as it did in the West Indies. The cane in the West Indies is normally a twelve months' crop, but Louisiana has killing frosts in winter, which prevented the maturing of the cane. In 1817, however, the Louisiana planters began to plant ribbon cane, obtained from the Philippines, which matured one month earlier than the West India variety. In the West Indies the cane crop did not require replanting for a dozen years, but in Louisiana, for lucrative returns, it had to be planted every three years. Furthermore, the yield from the same acreage was only half as large as in the West Indies, sometimes only one-third. Consequently, Louisiana sugar could compete with the West India product only because of the protection of the American tariff and the remarkably fertile soil of the delta region of Louisiana. Efforts were made to extend the area of sugar-growing into Georgia, Florida, and the Carolinas, but the climate of the more northern region was not favorable to it, and the profits from cotton were greater than from sugar except in years of low prices for cotton. Sugar culture did expand into Texas, where there were forty plantations on the Brazos and other rivers during the last decade of the ante-bellum period.

The cane was planted by laying the stalks in a furrow and covering them with a plow or a hoe. From the joints of these stalks sprouted the new cane. One-fourth to one-fifth of the crop had to be saved for seed—placed in mattresses covered with dirt. The stalks grew higher than a man by the late summer, before the fatal frost fell. Just before the frost was due the cane was cut by Negro slaves with a cane knife, and the leaves were stripped. The grinding season then began, a time when slaves worked eighteen hours a day, on Sunday, as well as on week days. The cane was run through rollers which extracted the juice, but fully a third of the juice was reabsorbed by the *bagasse* (crushed cane) and lost to the planters. The cane juice was boiled, which evaporated the water in the juice, and from this process came brown sugar and the by-product, molasses. White sugar was made in refineries usually located in the city.

The equipment on the sugar plantations after the 1830's was quite expensive, requiring a capital outlay of twelve to fourteen thousand dollars. The sugar machinery on large plantations was run by steam engines. The boiling process in open cauldrons required two or three cords of wood for each ton of sugar, but the invention of the vacuum pans, which were introduced in 1832, greatly reduced the cost of fuel. The sugar was stored in large hogsheads of one thousand pounds, which were frequently made by Negro artisans on the plantation.

The sugar plantation was really a capitalistic enterprise, and the sugar planters were business men as well as planters. For successful operation the industry required big plantations and a much larger proportion of prime field hands, strong sturdy men, rather than women and children, than were employed on the cotton plantations. "Magnolia" plantation in Plaquemines parish, forty-six miles below New Orleans, was a good example of the large sugar plantations, and fortunately its Plantation Journal is preserved in the Southern Collection of the University of North Carolina. This estate consisted of 2,213 acres, of which 950 acres were in cultivation. It had a frontage of two and one-third miles on the Mississippi River, which was prevented from flooding the plantation by a high levee. In 1856 it had a working force of one hundred and eighteen adult slaves, of whom seventy-two were males. In 1861 "Magnolia" produced 1,800 hogsheads of sugar, which placed it fourth in production among the Louisiana plantations. The sugar sold for 7½ cents a pound, and the estate made a gross income from selling sugar and molasses of $148,000.[10]

Although huge profits were attained in certain years by the sugar planters, there were various expenses and vicissitudes that cut down profits. In fact, the production of these plantations varied tremendously from year to year largely because of the wavering prices and the vicissitudes of the weather. The expansion and contraction of sugar-growing were facilitated by the fact that the raising of sugar and cotton could be interchanged in the border sugar parishes. When the price of sugar fell below the margin of profit, some of the planters shifted to cotton growing. An early frost might curtail the crop or a *crevasse* in the levee might ruin the labor of a season or of years. Cholera or yellow fever might decimate the valuable slaves on the plantation.

In 1854 Frederick Law Olmsted, a Northern traveler, made some intelligent observations concerning the sugar plantations in Louisiana. The owner of a large plantation bought on credit declared that success at operating a sugar plantation was like betting on a throw of dice. The year before Olmsted arrived, the planter had been lucky and had made a crop in which the molasses alone paid all his expenses, while the sale of the sugar brought him 25 per cent on his investment. Many planters went heavily into debt in acquiring plantations with the proper equipment and an adequate force of prime slaves. A few bad crops following each other would throw into bankruptcy a sugar planter who had bought his land on credit. Olmsted cites a profit of over 10 per cent in a favorable year on a plantation with an investment of $147,200.[11] Each slave, who cultivated approximately five acres on the average, produced five thousand pounds of sugar and one hundred and twenty-five gallons of molasses. The molasses sold for 18 cents a gallon and the sugar for 5½ cents a pound, making an earning of $297.50 for each hand. The peak of the production of Louisiana sugar was attained in 1853–54 when nearly 450,000 hogsheads were produced, a record yield in the ante-bellum period. Yet this bountiful crop brought considerably less money to the planters than the crop of 1859–60, which was approximately one-half smaller.

The expenses on a sugar plantation were usually higher than those on a cotton plantation. Most sugar plantations produced only a part of the food needed for the slaves. Consequently, they imported considerable quantities of pork, rice, cowpeas, beef, and corn. Also some plantations such as "Magnolia" bought lumber and coal used in the manufacture of sugar from Mississippi flatboatmen. The proprietor had to purchase mules and horses at intervals to replenish his stock. Moreover, large supplies of cheap clothing for the Negroes, agricultural implements, doctor's bills, the cost of freight, the factor's commission of 2½ per cent, the services of a skilled white sugar maker and of an engineer, reduced the net profits derived from the sale of sugar and molasses.

Profits on sugar plantations were possible because of high protection given to the industry by the tariff laws. From 1821 to 1832 there was a specific duty of 3 cents a pound on brown sugar and 4 cents on white sugar—equivalent to an *ad valorem* duty on crude sugar of around 60 per cent. This munificent protection was reduced to 2½ cents in 1833 and during the decade of the 1850's to less than 1 cent per pound on raw sugar. From 1848 to 1861 the *ad valorem* protection of sugar was 30 per cent. The sugar planters maintained that sugar could be produced profitably in the West Indies for 3 cents a pound but in Louisiana for not less than 5½ cents a pound. They justified the tariff by pointing out that internal trade with the rest of the Southern states and the Ohio Valley in the purchase of pork, corn, tobacco, etc., consumed three-fifths of the money derived from sugar.

The sugar planters of Louisiana were frequently wealthy and cultured men. Duncan F. Kenner, for example, was sent to Miami University in Ohio and then spent four years of study and travel in Europe. He was active in politics and was a student of the scientific method of growing sugar. During the Civil War this large slave-owner was an advocate of emancipating the slaves in order to secure European recognition. William J. Minor of Natchez, Mississippi, an example of the absentee sugar grower, owned three large plantations in Louisiana containing 9,300 acres and four hundred slaves, property worth approximately a million dollars. His plantations nearly doubled their value in the last decade before the Civil War, although the annual net return on the valuation of the property was only 5½ per cent.[12] Minor studied at the University of Pennsylvania and displayed a love of books. Like many of the wealthy sugar planters, he was a Whig, in favor of a protective tariff on sugar and opposed to secession. His rules for his overseers were a model of justice and of understanding human nature. The McCollam brothers, who had a plantation called "Ellendale," were examples of self-made sugar planters. When they acquired "Ellendale" in 1851 for $50,000 it was plastered with twenty-six mortgages, but by 1860 they had developed a plantation worth $150,000, largely through shrewd management. They, too, were Whigs who sent their children to college and lived the good life. Nevertheless, there were drawbacks to living on a sugar plantation, such as the unhealthiness of the climate in the lowlands, the mosquitoes that "nearly eat you up," breaks in the levees, loneliness, and the tribulations of slave labor.

In contrast to the planters, the small farmers of the South were engaged principally in growing food crops. This absorption in subsistence agriculture can be attributed to their lack of transportation facilities (for many of the small farms were remote from navigable streams or from highways and railroads), to their location in the uplands or regions unsuitable to the growth of staples, to lack of capital, and other factors. The typical farmer raised corn, rye, barley, oats, and wheat. In the coastal plain he might cultivate a patch of sweet potatoes or of peanuts largely to feed hogs, or raise sorghum for molasses. He supplemented his crops of grain with raising livestock in small numbers. In the cotton and tobacco districts the small farmers frequently raised a bale of cotton or a small quantity of tobacco for the purpose of obtaining money to buy sugar, salt, powder, and lead. In a recent study of farmers in ante-bellum Mississippi, the author found that in a representative sample of counties less than 7 per cent of the cotton produced in 1860 was raised by non-slaveholders.*

The main crop of the farmers was corn, which was easy to cultivate and admirably suited to the Southern climate and soil. This cereal was far more extensively cultivated than cotton below the Mason and Dixon line. Even in Mississippi, the heart of the Cotton Kingdom, only a bale and a half of cotton per person were produced in 1860 whereas thirty-five bushels of corn were raised for each inhabitant of the state. From this grain the farmers made corn pone, hoe cakes, "grits," roasting ears, and fed their stock. The moun-

---

* Herbert Weaver, *Mississippi Farmers 1850–1860* (Nashville, 1945), 100–101.

taineers converted this cereal into corn liquor, called "bald-face whiskey," which was a potent alcoholic beverage. A single farmer could cultivate thirty acres of corn and obtain thirty bushels an acre from fertile soil as well as harvest a crop of cowpeas planted between the rows. Corn sold for 52 cents a bushel in 1840 and 95 cents in 1859. In 1849 the Southern states produced 60 per cent of the corn grown in the United States, but ten years later the proportion had declined to 52 per cent of the national yield, a result of the opening of the vast cornfields of the Middle West. The largest corn-producing states of the South were Kentucky, Tennessee, and Virginia.

Wheat was another important crop of the yeoman farmer. It was grown extensively in the upper South, but it did not thrive in the lower South. Furthermore, cornbread was the staple of Southern diet while bread made from flour was regarded as a luxury. With inadequate scientific knowledge the wheat farmer had to struggle at times against the ravages of the Hessian fly and of such diseases as smut and rust. He learned, however, to increase the production of his crop from six bushels an acre in Tidewater Virginia at the beginning of the nineteenth century to twelve or fifteen bushels on an average in the decade of the 1830's, as a result of the introduction of clover as a cover crop and of plaster to increase fertility. Wheat was grown in Maryland, Virginia, and North Carolina as a staple crop by some large planters, as well as by the yeomen. Virginia was the leading wheat-producing state of the South, and Richmond and Baltimore were two of the largest centers in the United States for milling flour. During the sixty years of the ante-bellum period the average price for wheat was $1.14 a bushel, but in 1860 it sold for $1.40 a bushel.

The Southern states surpassed the Northern states in the raising of livestock during the ante-bellum period. In 1860 the fifteen Southern states had approximately three-eighths of the population of the nation, including the Negroes. Nevertheless, the South could boast of owning 90 per cent of the mules in the country, 60 per cent of the swine, nearly 45 per cent of the horses, 52 per cent of the oxen, and more than one-half of the poultry. Although the South had 40 per cent of the dairy cows of the United States, it produced less than 20 per cent of the butter and only 1 per cent of the cheese made in the United States. The slaves, in general, were not fed on dairy products, and the absence of ice and the lack of near markets discouraged the production of milk and butter in extensive quantity. The Southern farmers also failed to take proper care of their hogs and breed for quality. The typical Southern hog was a plebeian animal, often called "a razor back," who roamed about in the woods and meadows, shifting for himself.

The concept of the Southern states devoting their agricultural energies to a one-sided cultivation of staple crops for export omits the role of the yeoman farmers. Although some areas of large plantations, such as the sugar-producing district, imported a considerable proportion of their food and livestock and even bales of hay, the South as a whole supplied its own food, with a surplus to spare. Most cotton planters raised bountiful crops of corn, and those planters who purchased corn and meat for their slaves justified this practice on the ground that the labor of the slave was more valuable in producing staple crops.[13] Nevertheless, it has been observed by a penetrating student that the South as a whole practiced a less diversified type of agriculture in 1860 than was the case in 1850.[14] During this decade cotton was bringing high prices, and according to the census reports there was a decline within the decade in the per capita production of such basic food materials as corn and hogs although wheat production increased.

A constant criticism that has been made of Southern agriculture was its excessive devotion to one crop such as cotton, and the consequent failure to diversify its agriculture. However, there were strong economic reasons to condone this persistence in the one-crop economy, which became even more dominant after the Civil War. The lack of adequate transportation facilities was a vital factor in the rule of King Cotton. Cotton was easy to transport along the rivers, dirt roads, and railroads of the South; it did not spoil waiting for transportation or for a market, as wheat or corn might. To experiment with perishable crops was a risky business before the days of the refrigerated cars. Furthermore, merchants and factors who furnished credit to farmers frequently insisted on the planting of cotton.

The occupation of the gentleman farmer in the ante-bellum South was in some respects a delectable avocation. But it is a mistake to think of the life of the average Southern farmer as an independent one. If he grew staple crops for export, foreign wars might cut off his markets and overproduction make his bountiful crops bring ruinous prices. American farmers were individualists and never worked out a plan to control production and insure fair prices. The Southern farmer, moreover, was a hostage to Nature, with no insurance against the destruction of his crops by drought, hail, storms, and injurious insects. Epidemics might carry off his valuable slaves or he might lose them by their running away. Although insurance was occasionally taken out on the lives of slaves, this practice was not generally followed. Fortunately, the Mexican boll weevil had not crossed the Rio Grande at this period to devastate the cotton region. If this plague had come before the Civil War instead of a half-century later, one is tempted to speculate whether it would have led to an emancipation of the slaves. The Atlantic seaboard farmer had to meet the competition of the virgin soils recently opened in the Southwest. All Southern farmers, except perhaps the sugar planters, believed themselves to be exploited by the Federal protective tariff. Many of them were in semi-vassalage to their factors who sold the crop for them and advanced credit at high rates of interest. Finally, the planters and farmers had to rely on the reluctant and inefficient labor of black slaves, who were a constant source of exasperation unless the master adopted a philosophy of fatalism or resignation.

Citations

1. J. D. B. De Bow (Supt.), *Compendium of the Seventh Census* (Washington, 1854), 178.
2. A splendid description of the Southern cotton plantation is found in U. B. Phillips, *Life and Labor in the Old South* (Boston, 1929).
3. MS owned by Professor T. D. Clark, University of Kentucky.
4. J. C. Robert, *The Tobacco Kingdom* (Durham, 1938), 128–131.
5. J. F. Hopkins, "A History of Hemp Industry in Kentucky." Unpublished Ph.D. Dissertation, Duke University, 1948.

6. Avery O. Craven, *Soil Exhaustion as a Factor in the Agricultural History of Virginia and Maryland, 1606–1860* (Urbana, 1932) is a basic book in the economic study of the Old South. See also Kathleen Bruce, "Virginian Agricultural Decline to 1860: A Fallacy," *Agricultural History* (January, 1932), VI, 3–13.

7. J. C. Bonner, "Genesis of Agricultural Reform in the Cotton Belt" *Journal of Southern History*, IX (November, 1943), 473–500.

8. A. L. Demaree, *The American Agricultural Press*, 1819–1860 (New York, 1941), 374.

9. Sir Charles Lyell, *A Second Visit to the United States of North America* (London, 1849).

10. J. C. Sitterson, "Magnolia Plantation, 1852–1862: a Decade of a Louisiana Sugar Estate," *Mississippi Valley Historical Review*, XXV (September, 1936), 197–210.

11. F. L. Olmsted, *A Journey in the Seaboard Slave States* (New York, 1856), 656–673; 686–688.

12. J. C. Sitterson, "The William J. Minor Plantation: a Study in Ante-Bellum Absentee Ownership," *Journal of Southern History*, IX (February, 1943), 59–74.

13. A case history of a successful cotton planter in the black belt of Alabama who tried to make his plantation produce adequate food for his slaves and failed is recorded by W. T. Jordan, *Hugh Davis and his Alabama Plantation* (University, Ala., 1948), Chap. 6.

14. R. R. Russel, *Economic Aspects of Southern Sectionalism, 1840–1861*. (Urbana, 1924), 203.

CHAPTER XI

Black Labor

THE institution of slavery in the South was not merely a means of human exploitation but a system of race control and relationships. In the land of Dixie, as in other parts of the world, such as South Africa, where black men have dwelt in considerable numbers within white societies, there has arisen the mysterious chasm of race and color. DuBose Heyward in his vivid story, "Porgy," has portrayed the subtle psychological sense of differentness which the Negro feels toward the white man, his ways, and his God. The white man, on the other hand, has often wondered what the Negro was thinking and feeling. On April 13, 1861, Mrs. Chesnut observed in her famous diary that the outward demeanor of the Negro servants seemed to be unchanged by the war, but she could not fathom their real feeling, whether they were genuinely apathetic, "or wiser than we are; silent and strong, biding their time?" [1] Small children do not seem to be aware of the barrier of race. Moreover, the realization of a common humanity between white and blacks becomes keener as the Negro elevates himself by education, cleanliness, the acquisition of wealth, and the white man meets him on intellectual and artistic levels. But in the Old South the barrier of race, lurking fear of insurrection, and the repulsion at the thought of amalgamation immeasurably strengthened the chains of slavery.

At the same time it is apparent that slavery was the Southern method of labor exploitation just as unregulated "wage slavery" was the method employed in England and in the North of exploiting white workers. The expanding Cotton Kingdom needed a large supply of cheap agricultural labor. The original source of supply of black labor for Southern agriculture, the African slave trade, was closed by the legislatures of most of the Southern states during and following the Revolution. At the time of the Federal Constitutional Convention Georgia, alone of the Southern states, permitted the importation of slaves from Africa, and in 1798 Georgia prohibited the maritime slave trade. In 1808 the African slave trade, which had been tolerated for the preceding twenty years as a result of one of the compromises of the Constitutional Convention, was prohibited by Congress. Humanitarian reasons for this closure of the African slave trade were bolstered by economic motives, the fear that further importation would decrease the value of slaves already held and would lead to an overproduction of staple crops. Furthermore, the introduction of wild Africans would increase the danger of servile insurrection. In South Carolina a long-continued debate occurred between the wealthy conservatives, who were opposed to reopening the slave trade, and the radicals, led by a Charleston merchant, Alexander Gillon, who favored the resumption of this cruel traffic. The legislature was finally persuaded in 1803 to legalize the importation of Negroes from Africa and the West Indies. For the next four years there occurred a hectic importation of slaves for speculation and for sale in the state as well as in other parts of the South. During this period South Carolina imported nearly 40,000 Negro bondsmen, absorbing such a large portion of capital that it affected business enterprises.

After 1808 slaves from Africa or the West Indies could be brought into the United States only by smuggling. In 1820 Congress tried to stop smuggling by declaring the maritime slave trade piracy, which exacted a penalty so severe that Southern juries were reluctant to convict offenders. Twenty-two years later the United States entered into a treaty with England for a joint patrol of the west coast of Africa to suppress the nefarious traffic, but anglophobia prevented an agreement to allow British warships to search suspicious American vessels. The Negro historian, W. E. B. Du Bois, who made a study of the problem of suppressing the African slave trade for a Harvard Ph.D. thesis, concluded that approximately 250,000 slaves were smuggled into the United States between 1808 and 1860.[2] However, the census takers of 1870, who cannot be relied upon for strict accuracy, could find only about two thousand Negroes in the United States that admitted African birth. Professor U. B. Phillips in his study, *American Negro Slavery*, has declared that "these importations were never great enough to affect the labor supply in appreciable degree."[3] He has argued that if the African slave trade had been left open it might have resulted in an emancipation movement. In an unrestricted market so many slaves would have been imported in boom times, as to glut the market during depressions. Accordingly, planters would have tried by emancipation to escape from the burden of supporting useless slaves.

The closure of the African slave trade made the upper South the nursery of surplus slaves. When the slave trade was closed, approximately one million slaves were in the United States to produce the future laborers of the South, who in 1860 numbered about four million. The invention of the cotton gin and the westward movement of population into the Gulf region led to the growth of a flourishing internal slave traffic between the upper and the lower South. The oldest tobacco-producing states had a large surplus of servants to sell to the eager cotton planters of the deep South. Every year during the period 1830 to 1860 Virginia exported approximately 9,000 slaves to the lower South, South Carolina about 6,000, and Kentucky about 3,000. Alexandria in the District of Columbia (until 1846), Richmond, Memphis, and Charleston were the most important slave-exporting cities. A considerable number of the slaves taken to the lower South were transported by emigrating masters, but the majority probably were delivered by professional traders.

The slave trade was conducted by a group of men called "Nigger traders," who made considerable fortunes from the traffic. There is disagreement among observers as to whether Southern society looked down upon these merchants of men.[4] The tradition is that Southerners despised the slave traders, and that, although they associated with them freely in business transactions, they did not accept them socially. Nevertheless, successful slave traders occupied respectable positions in Southern society. Nathan Bedford Forrest, the celebrated cavalry leader of the Confederacy, was a slave trader of Memphis whose profits exceeded $50,000 annually. In 1858 he was elected alderman of Memphis. In Charleston, Louis de Saussure and Thomas Norman Gadsden, of aristocratic families, were prominent slave traders though they called themselves by euphemistic titles, such as "auctioneers," "brokers," "commission merchants." De Saussure had a beautiful home on the Battery and derived an income of nearly $11,000 from commissions in the slave trade. The most eminent slave-trading firm in the South was Franklin and Armfield with buying headquarters at Alexandria in the District of Columbia and selling depots at Natchez, Mississippi, and New Orleans. Isaac Franklin married the daughter of a Presbyterian preacher, built a beautiful mansion in the Nashville Basin, and left an estate of three-quarters of a million dollars.

The slaves who were sent to the lower South were usually young men and women in their early twenties, in other words, "prime field hands." They were given new suits of clothes and oiled or "spruced up" for the auction. Buyers examined them carefully, especially their hands, needed for picking cotton, and their backs to see that they were free from the scars of frequent whipping. They were transported to the lower South either in coastal ships or overland by slave coffles in which the men were manacled, while the women and children followed unfettered. Occasionally slaves who were being transported by sea seized control of the ship and steered into a West India port, as was the case of the *Creole* in 1841 which entered Nassau, where the slaves were liberated. The upper South tried to get rid of their vicious and intractable Negroes by selling them to the slave traders doing business with the lower South. Consequently, the states of the lower South passed legislation against the introduction of criminal slaves and required a certificate of good character with each slave imported for sale. Indeed, these states pursued a vacillating course of prohibiting the introduction of slaves for the purpose of sale and then repealing such legislation.

The worst feature of the internal slave trade was the break-up of Negro families. Only Louisiana and later Alabama, by an act of 1852, had laws prohibiting the sale of a child under ten years old from its mother. None of the Southern states prohibited the separation of husband and wife by sale. The numerous sheriff sales of bankrupts and the division of slaves in wills formed constant threats to the forcible separation of Negro families. This separation of slave families was one of the unhappy consequences of the westward movement. White families were also broken up, frequently forever, by the migration of younger sons to the west. On the other side of the balance sheet it must be noted that Southerners made an effort to prevent the separation of Negro families and that many of the wills specifically stipulated that slave families should not be divided or sold out of the state, the county, or even out of the family.

The prices of slaves tended to vary in proportion to the price of cotton. In 1860, however, the cost of slaves was out of all proportion

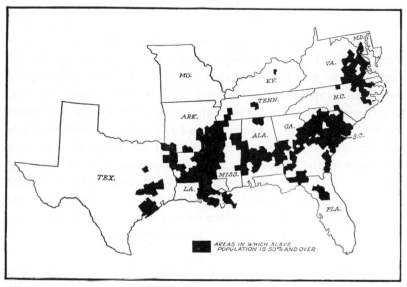

THE BLACK BELT IN 1860

Adapted from C. O. Paullin, *Atlas of the Historical Geography of the United States* (Washington, 1932), Plate 68.

to the profits obtained from cotton, for prime field hands were selling from $1,200 to $1,800, while cotton was selling for 11½ cents. In 1800, when cotton was bringing 36 cents, prime field hands cost only $400. The price of slaves was booming in 1858–59 when Pulliam and Betts, "Auctioneers for Sale of Negroes," at Richmond, Virginia, gave the following quotations: "No. One men bring $1500 to $1550, No. One Girls $1300 to $1350; Boys & Girls from 10 years old to 14 years sell better than we ever saw them sell, 4 feet boys $500 to $550, Girls the same, and so on increasing as they go up in size and likeliness" (MS in possession of the author).

The price of black servants had approximately quadrupled during a period of sixty years, but cotton had declined to one-fourth of its price at the opening of the nineteenth century. Part of this discrepancy in the ratio of cotton and slave values may be accounted for by the fact that slaves could produce much more cotton per hand in 1860 than in 1800. During the last decade of the ante-bellum period, moreover, there was a tremendous speculation in property in slaves, a veritable "Negro fever," which artificially increased their value. Other reasons for this factitious value of slaves were the social distinction involved in owning slaves and the inflationary movement produced by the mining of California gold. During the last decade of the ante-bellum period there was a dearth of hands for the rapidly expanding agricultural region of the Southwest, and new demands for labor were opening in the development of tobacco factories, iron works, construction of railroads, and mining. These facts tended to modify the old rule that the price of slaves was dependent on the price of cotton. The purchase price of slaves began to be based on the hiring wages. At the close of the eighteenth century a prime slave could be hired for $70 a year, plus board and medical expenses, but in 1860 slave factory hands were hired for $200 to $225 annually and agricultural hands for $150 a year.

The high cost of slaves in the last decade of the ante-bellum period had certain unfortunate results. It led to a movement for reopening the African slave trade in order to furnish the small farmer with black labor. It was argued that the reopening of the foreign slave trade would democratize the system of Southern slavery and lead to the solidarity of the South in the defense of its "peculiar institution." In 1856 Leonidas Spratt, an editor of South Carolina, was one of the outstanding propagandists for this move. He had the support of Governor James H. Adams of that state and of certain prominent publicists, such as De Bow of *De Bow's Review* and Edward Pollard, a journalist of Virginia. In 1859 the Southern Commercial Convention at Vicksburg adopted resolutions in favor of reviving the African slave trade. A minority led by Henry S. Foote published a protest, pointing out that the slave states of Virginia, North Carolina, Kentucky, and Missouri were unrepresented at the convention and that the proposal "has been mainly sustained in this body by avowed disunionists . . ." [5] The states of the upper South, which had a surplus of slaves to sell, were opposed to the agitation for the reopening of the African slave trade. They maintained that the revival of the maritime slave trade would increase the danger of servile insurrection and would be accompanied by great cruelty. The large planters in general tended to oppose a movement that would depreciate the value of their slave property.

The treatment of slaves in the ante-bellum South varied according to the disposition and intelligence of the different masters. Undoubtedly there were instances of brutality and of crime in the treatment of slaves by their owners. Drunken masters and sadists at times perpetrated horrible crimes on their black dependents. These cases of abnormality were no more typical of the slave regime than are the lurid accounts of crimes reported in the daily newspapers of the United States of today's society. The Southern laws protected the Negro from wanton cruelty or mayhem, prescribing the death penalty for deliberately murdering a Negro servant. The force of this law was weakened, however, by the fact that slave testimony was not valid against a white man in the courts of law. Furthermore, if a servant was killed by his master or overseer during the administration of moderate correction, the latter was not punishable. Nevertheless, public opinion in the South was a powerful factor in preventing the mistreatment of Negroes. A cruel slavemaster was ostracized by the community. Finally, it was decidedly to the economic interest of the master to treat his slave well, preserve his health, and secure his cooperation.

The history of slavery from the point of view of the Negro remains to be told. Negro accounts of the institution are mostly those of escaped slaves, whose stories were written or edited by the abolitionists. An important body of evidence, far more reliable, is gradually being uncovered in the plantation records and the papers of the planters. In the papers of Ebenezer Pettigrew, a planter of eastern North Carolina, for example, are found some records of remarkable Negroes.[6] They show some slaves who were so intelligent that the master constantly consulted them as advisers on plantation policies, slaves who were foremen, slaves who made real progress in developing skills, slaves who had a passionate attachment to the plantation

—the good earth—and a pride in the crops. They show masters who gave their slaves opportunities to accumulate money by selling rough rice, chickens, eggs, cypress tubs, and shingles, allowing credit at the plantation store. We do not know how many of such slaves were scattered throughout the plantation districts, but their anonymous existence warns us against accepting the abolitionist-Marxist stereotype of an institution which actually was composed of infinitely varied human relationships.

Henry Clay wrote to his overseer in 1833 to rent one of his slaves provided the latter gave his consent. "If Miss Bruce and Gratz," he directed, "will give $120 for Abraham, and he is willing to go, you may hire him to them." [7] This practice of getting the slave's consent for hiring or even for sale was not uncommon in the Old South. John W. Coleman, hemp manufacturer of Woodford County, Kentucky, stipulated in his contracts for hiring slaves: "I am to treat said men well, feed, and clothe them, and pay taxes and physicians' bills, etc., and return them well clothed." [8] In some of his contracts for slave labor he promised to pay the slave $5 a year as a reward for good behavior.

The utilization of the labor of slaves and their treatment as human beings in the Old South have been studied principally from the records of large plantations, which are easily accessible. Our view of Southern slavery, therefore, may be modified when our knowledge of the institution as administered by the farmers and small planters, who seldom kept records or journals, has been enlarged. Nearly half of the slaves in the South did not live on the large plantations laboring under the overseer system but were owned by small masters.[9] In 1860, 47.6 per cent of the Southern slaves were owned by men who had less than twenty slaves. In the upper South the percentage was much higher, 61.7 per cent, but in the lower South, only 38 per cent of the slaves belonged to small slaveholders. The testimony of the Southerners themselves indicates that the conditions of slavery were more humane on the farms and small plantations, where the dark-skinned worker escaped the overseer system and came into frequent contact with the owner, than was the case on the large estates. Nevertheless, the observations of the Northern traveler and agricultural writer, Solon Robinson, disclose that on many of the large plantations of the lower South the slaves were given better medical care, larger quantities of food, and better housing than the slaves of small masters in the upper South.[10]

Was the slave overworked? In determining this question it is necessary to make a distinction between the field slaves and the house servants. The latter, numerically small, fared much better than the field slaves. They worked less, were better fed and clothed, and came more into contact with the refining influences of the master's family than did the field slaves. Frequently on the large plantations there was a superfluity of domestic servants, so that their tasks were light. Often the household servants, especially the Negro "mammy," developed a real affection for their masters, which was warmly reciprocated. Moreover, they acquired a keen sense of pride in belonging to "quality folks," and they looked down upon the common laborers.

The field slaves worked from sunrise to sunset, but the white farmers and the factory hands of New England also worked from "dark to dark." In the rice district slaves were usually assigned tasks, which they often finished before two or three o'clock, and they enjoyed the leisure of the rest of the day. The slaves had a wonderful power of passive resistance which tended to prevent overwork and which the planters recognized. Frederick Law Olmsted estimated that the average white farm hand in the North did twice as much work as the average slave. There was one brutal feature of the work system on large plantations. The slave gang was kept at work frequently by a Negro "driver" who carried a big blacksnake whip which he cracked over the backs of the laborers. He set the pace of work and was responsible for seeing that the slaves did not do a slovenly job.

The abolitionists popularized the idea that slaves on the large plantations of the lower South were deliberately worked to death. Even the eminent historian James Ford Rhodes was under the spell of the abolitionist tradition when he wrote: "Louisiana sugar-planters did not hesitate to avow openly that, on the whole, they found it the best economy to work off their stock of negroes about once in seven years, and then buy an entire set of new hands."[11] Although it may be true that slavery had harsher features on some of the large "factory plantations" of the Southwest than in the upper South, the evidence does not warrant such statements of barbarity. In addition to the caricature of Southern slavery by the abolitionists, the planters of the upper South blackened the reputation of the lower South in order to use the threat of selling a slave "down the river" for disciplinary purposes. Mark Twain in *Puddin'head Wilson* has vividly described the terror of the slaves of being sold "down the river."

Modern research has dispelled some of the false conceptions of the slavery regime propagated by the abolitionists who generalized isolated cases of cruelty as typical of the treatment of the slaves.[12] On the cotton plantations of the lower South the evidence indicates that the slaves did a very moderate amount of work. The records show that during the cotton-picking season, the average quantity of cotton picked per hand was 150 pounds a day, although superior slaves could pick 350 to 500 pounds a day. Today, in the cotton fields of the lower South, the average amount of cotton picked by Negroes remains virtually the same as in ante-bellum days. Furthermore, the average acreage of cotton and corn cultivated by a prime Negro hand, eight acres of cotton and four of corn, was not excessive. On the sugar plantations of Louisiana the slaves worked very hard during the grinding season, but they liked this phase of their work better than their less strenuous occupations, for during this period they were given extra food, abundant coffee, and drams of liquor. The accusation that slaves in the lower South were killed by cruel treatment and inhuman work is refuted by vital statistics of the plantations. The slaves of "Magnolia Plantation" in Louisiana, for example, more than reproduced themselves during the decade 1852–62. In the five years preceding the Civil War there were only eleven runaways from the plantation out of a labor force of 118 slaves, and most of them were back at work within a week. Certainly, if laboring conditions had not been good, the record of runaways would have been greater, although it must be observed that slaves may have tolerated bad conditions because of the relative hopelessness of running away.

An important element in the happiness of the slaves was the food supply. The evidence indicates that in general the slaves were given a nourishing diet, but without much variety. The general rule on slave plantations was to furnish each slave three or four pounds of hog meat weekly. This ration of meat, as far as quantity was concerned, is better than the rationing of two and one-half pounds of meat or less during the recent war period in the United States. The slaves were also given a peck of cornmeal each week, and in some districts they were given a pint of molasses a week. These were standard food supplies issued to slaves by the masters, but the slaves were usually allowed to supplement this diet by cultivating vegetable gardens. Also they obtained fish from the rivers, caught rabbits in home-made traps, and hunted the opossum at night with dogs and an axe to cut down the tree on which this tasty animal took refuge. Food was cheap in the ante-bellum South so that slaves hired to railroad companies in Mississippi were boarded for 15 cents a day. On the plantations at Christmas time the Negroes frequently were given a small supply of whiskey and a feast. Slaves were often allowed to raise hogs and chickens, for the possession of such property was a good insurance policy against their running away.

Olmsted cites a report to Secretary of the Treasury Walker of forty-eight Louisiana planters, who wished to influence the government to maintain the tariff on sugar, that the cost of food and clothing for a working hand was $30 for an entire year, from which this Northern writer inferred that the cost was 5½ cents a day. Yet this calculation does not include the supplies of food grown by the slaves themselves, their little vegetable gardens, the poultry and hogs they raised. The planters needed strong and sturdy slaves for the successful growing and manufacture of sugar, and it was essential that they should be well nourished. The law of Louisiana required that meat should be given daily to the slaves, the only state in the South to have this requirement. The Creole planters were reported to treat their slaves less humanely than the American planters and to evade compliance with the meat law. Not all planters were as intelligent as William J. Minor, whose slaves were allowed to cultivate an acre per family for their personal use. On his several plantations in Louisiana they were permitted to keep chickens and to retain the money they made from selling both chickens and eggs.

The slaves were housed in cabins that were entirely inadequate, according to modern standards, for good health and morality. The slave quarters on the big plantations consisted of a village, usually on a wide street with a row of cabins on each side, with the house of the white overseer at the end of the street. These one-room cabins were almost invariably overflowing with "darkeys." Estimates made of the housing of slaves in Mississippi indicate that, on the average, four or five slaves occupied a cabin; for example, twenty-eight houses were provided for Jefferson Davis's one hundred and thirteen slaves at "Brierfield," seventy-six houses for the three hundred and fifty-five slaves of his brother, Joseph E. Davis, and one hundred and four houses for the four hundred and fifty-two slaves of William N. Mercer. These cabins had large open fireplaces at which the cooking was done. The slave cabins of the ante-bellum period would compare favorably with the houses occupied by most of the Negroes in the modern South. In the ante-bellum period thousands of farmers lived in log cabins no more commodious for their large families than the slave houses.

As to clothing, the house servants often wore the cast-off finery of their masters. The field slaves were issued annually two summer suits, two winter suits, one straw hat, one wool hat, and two pairs of shoes. Most of the slaves went barefoot in summer, as did many of the poor whites. The little Negro pickaninnies wore only one garment, a shift, or an abbreviated nightgown. Sometimes they ran around the plantation clad only in their birthday suits. (The author recalls a little Negro playmate on a farm in North Carolina who wore only one piece of clothing, a cap of many colors.) The Negro women were given linsey-woolsey or calico to make dresses, and they delighted in materials of gaudy colors. On many plantations the Negro women who were unfit for field work wove homespun cloth which was used to clothe the slaves.

The planters tried to protect the health of their human property. They and their overseers often acted in the capacity of amateur doctors, using a family medical book and a medicine chest. Cholera, yellow fever, smallpox, chills, colds, dysentery, whooping cough, and measles were the chief ailments that affected the slaves. To combat these diseases the planters purchased quantities of castor oil, calomel, liniment, quinine, and ipecac. On many of the large plantations there were slave hospitals, and often the white mistress of the plantation cared for sick slaves. On some plantations doctors were employed at a yearly rate to attend sick slaves. Child-bearing slave mothers were allowed a month of absence from field labor, and after they returned to work they were permitted to leave the fields at intervals to nurse their babies. The mortality rates of black babies, as well as white babies, were very high in the Old South. Yet the mortality of mature Negroes in Mississippi, for example, was only slightly more than the deaths of whites. Planters tended to protect their slaves from dangerous and unhealthy work. Irishmen were often employed in unhealthy jobs, such as digging ditches and in handling the bouncing cotton bales which were loaded on the steamboats. If a Negro slave worth $1,500 were killed, that was a grave loss indeed, but it did not make much difference if an Irishman were killed.

Discipline was maintained on the plantation primarily by the overseers. A planter who had as many as thirty slaves usually employed such a supervisor of his black servants. One of the most frequent complaints of the Old South was the difficulty of finding good overseers. The principal causes for this condition were the low social status of the overseer, the insecurity of tenure, and the poor salary he received, which varied from $120 to $600 a year. Stewards or managers of several plantations, however, received salaries of $1,500 or more. The ambitious type of overseer tried to achieve a reputation for himself by striving to make as many bales of cotton for the owner as possible, regardless of the welfare of the slaves. The planters were concerned to prevent the over-driving of the slaves, a factor that led in the ante-bellum period to the substitution of a fixed salary for the overseer instead of compensation by a share of the crop, the practice which prevailed in the colonial period. If an overseer were too harsh, he would be likely to drive the slaves to run away from the plantation, thus causing a considerable financial loss to the owner. On the other hand, if he were too lenient, the slaves would neglect their work, would malinger, and become insubordinate. Other serious faults of overseers which impaired their authority were drunkenness, frequent absences from the plantation, and immorality with the Negro women.

Most large plantations had strict rules to guide the overseer in his management of the slaves. The overseer was sometimes limited by the instructions of the owner never to flog a slave while he was in anger, and to limit his punishment to fifteen lashes. The Negro driver was often the instrument of inflicting corporal punishment, but only in the presence of the overseer. The principal punishment of Negroes was flogging, which was in accordance with the penological practice of the age. They were seldom placed in jail for crimes, and frequently escaped the serious punishment that was given to white criminals. The chief recourse of the slave for protection from cruelty was to appeal to the master, but on absentee or large plantations this safeguard was seldom available. A remarkable set of rules for the management of the plantation of "Beaver Bend" on the Cahaba River in Alabama contains the humane provision "that each and every slave shall communicate to the master all things proper to be known, in the master's judgment, especially such as have reference to his food and its supply, his clothing, or the deficiency thereof, his punishment, the quantity and cause thereof, the existence of any known immorality and the parties engaged in it, etc." [13]

The fact that the slave system rested partly on force is seen in the need of frequent whippings. The diary of a Louisiana cotton planter, Bennet H. Barrow, shows a realistic picture of whipping on a large plantation. Barrow was a successful planter, in good years selling his cotton crop for more than $20,000. He secured excellent cooperation from his slaves and had few runaways. He rewarded the faithful for good work by giving them frequent holidays throughout the year, treating them to a special dinner, giving outstanding workers an extra suit of store-bought clothes, providing them with whiskey for a dance, and donating a money gift before Christmas. He expressed strong disapprobation of a jury clearing a man from the charge of murder who had flogged a slave to death. "Went to town—man tried for Whipping a Negro to Death—deserves death— Cleared!" [14] He also spoke with disgust of a neighbor planter who had the reputation of being a cruel master. Yet Barrow maintained firm discipline over his own slaves by a variety of punishments. Sometimes he devised punishments that would make the slave ridiculous to his fellows, such as exhibiting the culprit on a scaffold with a red flannel cap on his head, making some rascally buck Negroes wear dresses or wash clothes, imprisonment in the plantation jail on week ends and holidays. The most common penalty for misdeeds was whipping. Slaves were flogged for picking trashy cotton, for laziness, for keeping themselves or cottages filthy, or for running away. His diary shows that he engaged in whipping two or three times a week. Certainly the muscles of his right arm must have become habituated to this frequent exercise of punishing his slaves. However, Barrow was not a typical master.

The loss of the services of black labor as the result of slaves fleeing from the plantation was less than one might expect. In all parts of the South slaves occasionally ran away from the plantations because they feared a whipping for some dereliction, or because of a labor strike of a group of slaves against a harsh overseer, or, most frequently, to escape from being sold to the lower South or to revisit their old home places and see their relatives after they had been sold to a distant master. Often these slaves would return of their own accord after they had been absent for a few days hiding in the woods or swamps. The chief loss from flight of slaves out of the land of Dixie fell upon the border states. There were professional "nigger catchers" in the South who at times used bloodhounds to trail the fugitive, but the usual method of recovering absconding slaves was to run advertisements in the newspapers, such as the following:

Ranaway from the subscriber, living at Crab Orchard, Ky., last June, a negro man named *Grandison*, about 24 years of age, very black, wears large whiskers, and is lame in one of his ankles. He is a preacher . . . (offers reward of $400; also advertises for capture of two other Negro men).[15]

After the runaway reached the Ohio River or the Mason and Dixon line he was frequently aided by the Underground Railroad to arrive at Canada. This organization to assist slaves to escape was composed of Quakers and other ardent abolitionists, whose reputed president was the Quaker Levi Coffin of Cincinnati. They established stations or hiding places for the slaves, often the attics of their homes, at distances of a day's journey. They gave the fugitive food and instructions how to reach the next place of refuge. The fleeing slaves traveled at night with the North Star as their guide. Some of the most devoted "nigger stealers" who aided them were Delia Webster, the New England school teacher who purchased a farm in Kentucky along the Ohio River with abolitionist funds, Calvin Fairbank, a Northern preacher in Lexington, Kentucky, who claimed that he had "liberated forty-seven slaves from hell," and the Southern-born Reverend John Rankin, who operated one of the most active stations across the Ohio River at Ripley, Ohio.[16] The Negro historian George Williams declared that the Underground Railroad served as a safety valve for the institution of slavery, for it aided the most dangerous slaves, the natural leaders of insurrection, to escape.

The dangers inherent in the slavery regime in the South were revealed by occasional outbreaks of insurrection and countless rumors of slave plots. Starting back in colonial times when wild Africans were intruded into Southern society, the fear of insurrection occurred at intervals throughout the history of slavery. The stereotype of the Negro as a docile worker, in contrast to the untamable Indian, has been questioned by some modern students. In 1791–95 the South was frightened by the horrible massacres of the whites by the black slaves of Santo Domingo. Five years later there was consternation among the people of Richmond when they discovered a plot to destroy the city by slaves under the lead of "General" Gabriel Prosser. This slave plot led to the formation of a little standing army at the Virginia capital and a movement to colonize free Negroes on the western frontier. In 1822 Denmark Vesey, a free Negro who had purchased his freedom with money obtained by winning a $1,500 lottery, organized a formidable conspiracy among the Negroes of Charleston, South Carolina. Vesey had read the antislavery speeches made in Congress during the Missouri Compromise debates. Among the conspirators was a Negro conjurer, "Gullah Jack," who furnished amulets and charms to the Negroes to make them invulnerable to the white man's weapons. When the plot was revealed by one of the slaves, the people of Charleston fell into a panic of fear, during which many of the Negroes implicated in the plot were hanged.

The complacency of the Southern people was further disturbed in 1829 by the discovery of the circulation within the South of an incendiary pamphlet, *Walker's Appeal to the Colored Citizens of the World*. This violent publication was written by a North Carolina free Negro, David Walker, who had emigrated to Boston. Copies were brought to some of the Southern ports for the purpose of circulating them among the blacks. The alarm created by this insurrectionary document resulted in 1830 in the passage of laws prohibiting the teaching of slaves to read or write in North Carolina, Georgia, and Louisiana.[17]

The most momentous of all the slave revolts occurred in August of the following year, the Nat Turner Insurrection in Southampton County, Virginia. Nat Turner was a slave preacher who cultivated an atmosphere of mystery and prophecy and wielded great influence over the blacks. Although he was well treated by his master, he conceived of a plot to lead the slaves in a revolt to win their freedom. From reading the Bible, especially the Book of Revelation, he had derived fanatical ideas which caused him to see visions of black and white angels fighting. The insurrection was rendered more bloody by the fact that his followers broke into the wine cellars of their masters and fortified themselves with copious draughts of peach and apple brandy. Before the revolt was suppressed over sixty whites as well as many innocent Negroes had been killed.

The Nat Turner Revolt was the last important insurrection in the Old South. Nevertheless, the Southern people continued to be frightened by numerous reported conspiracies. In 1835 a number of Negroes and whites were executed as a result of a wave of hysteria that swept Mississippi caused by an alleged plot of John A. Murrell, "the land pirate," and his confederates to start a slave insurrection. Frances Gaither in the novel *The Red Cock Crows* has drawn a faithful picture of the operation of vigilance committees at this time in condemning whites and Negroes to death, impelled by an incredibly violent fear of servile uprising. In 1856 and 1860 rumors of servile plots spread throughout the South, causing the death of many unfortunate Negroes. These were Presidential election years, filled with political excitement in the South over the rise of the Republican Party. Such dark rumors, when investigated, were usually found to be false, yet they did much to produce at times a pathological state of feeling among the Southern people.

Although the Southern newspapers on occasions tried to suppress rumors of servile insurrection, in political campaigns they tended to magnify them, blaming the Northern abolitionists as responsible for instigating the slaves to rebel. The "jittery" state of public opinion was revealed by the John Brown Raid of 1859. Not a single slave arose to aid this band of Northern fanatics who brought pike heads to distribute among the slaves to kill their masters. Nevertheless, the Southern people were deeply stirred by fear and passion over this incident. The results of actual revolts or of conspiracies, both real and imagined, were to impose more drastic restrictions on slaves and free Negroes as well as to limit the freedom of the press and of speech in the South.

After the discovery of the David Walker pamphlet and the Nat Turner Revolt, the South modified its slave code to secure stricter control over the Negroes. A paramount motive in establishing this new rigor was the fear that the abolitionists would stir the slaves to revolt or run away. After the black code had been perfected in the decade of the 1830's, slaves could not legally be taught to read and write, except in Maryland, Kentucky, and Tennessee; they were prohibited by law from leaving their plantations without a written pass; in the cities as well as on the plantation they were required to be in their houses when the curfew rang, usually at 9 o'clock; Negro preachers were prohibited from exhorting their brethren unless a white person were present; slaves could not own firearms, horses, horns or drums, or give medicine to a white person; they could not legally be employed in printing offices; and they were prohibited from assembling in crowds for dancing or sociable objects without the presence of a white man.

A patrol of white men was established to enforce these laws. The patrols consisted of a captain and three other members, who were appointed at the militia muster or by the county court. They were required to patrol the county once every two weeks, or oftener in times of emergency. Among their duties were the searching of the Negro cabins for firearms and the flogging of slaves found on the roads at night without a pass. Often the patrols were manned by poor whites who got drunk (although it was illegal to drink on patrol) and unmercifully beat Negroes who came across their path. The patrol also captured runaways, for which they received six dollars per capture. The fear of the slaves of the patrol was expressed in the cry "Run, nigger, run! the patter-rollers will ketch you!"

In addition to this legislation for disciplining the slaves, the black codes of the Southern states prescribed a special set of laws for dealing with slave crime and slave relations with the whites. Slave marriages had no legal validity; slave testimony was not valid in the courts against white persons; the wanton murder of a slave by a white man, as previously pointed out, was a capital crime, but the killing of such a person during the administration of moderate punishment was not a legal offense; death was the penalty for rebelling or plotting to rebel; slaves executed by the state for crimes were paid for by state funds; slaves were not tried usually by a jury but by an informal court of justices of the peace.

The draconic laws of the black code were laxly enforced, however, particularly the laws relating to the patrol and to the teaching of slaves to read and write. Joseph Turner, editor of *The Country-man*, published on a plantation near Eatonton, Georgia, declared in 1862 when there was some agitation to repeal the law prohibiting the teaching of Negroes to read: "the law is obsolete, and never has prevented a negro who desired it from learning to read. I have never known a case of punishment for its violation." [18] Southern legislators were in the habit of making extreme laws for emergencies, which were later tempered by the good-natured or the inefficient practice of the Southern people and the liberality of court decisions. Indeed, the laxity of the Southern states in enforcing laws was not confined to the slave code. The Southerner tended to have a cavalier attitude toward laws restraining his personal liberty and to rely upon himself rather than the courts to punish insults and injuries, while at the same time he strenuously insisted upon strict adherence to the Federal Constitution.

The plight of the free Negroes of the Old South was tragic. The majority of them were located in the upper South, particularly in Maryland, where the free colored population of nearly eighty-four thousand balanced the slave population. The Southern state having the smallest number of this class was Mississippi with only seven hundred and seventy-three. The freedmen tended to congregate in the towns and cities, but the considerable free Negro population of North Carolina was mainly rural. Many of this class were the off-spring of illicit relations between whites and blacks. According to Southern laws a person with only a slight admixture of Negro blood in his veins, in North Carolina as much as one-sixteenth, and in Virginia, as much as one-fourth, was classified as a Negro; marriage between a Negro and a white was prohibited; and illegitimate mulatto children followed the status of the mother. The ante-bellum laws in this respect were more liberal than Southern laws of today, for example, the modern Virginia statute which defines a Negro as a person having any quantum of Negro blood, and the North Carolina legislation which permits marriage between whites and persons of Negro descent to the third generation inclusive, but prohibits children with any Negro blood in their veins whatsoever from attending white schools.

In addition to origin by birth from a free mother, the free Negro class was derived from the emancipation of slaves. During and after the American Revolution, Southern masters were influenced by the liberal philosophy of natural rights as well as by the decline of the tobacco trade to free their slaves, particularly by will. In 1782 Virginia passed a liberal manumission law, but in 1805 reversed her policy and made the emancipation process very difficult by requiring the immediate removal of the freedmen from the state. Tennessee also abandoned her generous manumission policy in 1831 by ordering the immediate removal of the freed Negro from the state. Kentucky, by an act of 1851, was one of the last Southern states to require the removal of the slave after emancipation.

Various restrictions stood in the way of the manumission of slaves. In order to prevent masters from liberating old and infirm slaves for the sake of escaping financial responsibility, the Southern states usually required that consent for the emancipation of slaves must be obtained from county courts. In Georgia slaves could not be emanci-pated after 1801 except by the act of legislature, although they could be freed by will outside of the state. Some of the Southern states, Virginia, for example, had laws that if an emancipated slave did not leave the state within twelve months, he was liable to be sold by the state into slavery. In the later ante-bellum period such legislation made it practically impossible for most masters to free their slaves, not only on account of the financial cost, but also because a number of the Northern states prohibited the immigration of free Negroes. Nevertheless, some masters evaded the law by allowing their slaves to live as virtually free persons.

The free Negro in a slave society was an anomaly bitterly resented by the whites. Joel Chandler Harris in his story, "Free Joe and the Rest of the World," has portrayed the pathos and isolation of the free rural Negro in a world of black slaves and whites. In the town he was hated and feared as a competitor by white artisans and mechanics. Southerners regarded free Negroes as the most vicious members of their race, as potential leaders of insurrection. Calhoun in his report to Congress on a bill for preventing the circulation of incendiary publications maintained that free Negroes were found more frequently in jails than any element of the population. Slaveowners believed that the free Negroes tended to corrupt the slaves, sold liquor to them, were thieves and the receivers of stolen property, and set a bad example of idleness.

After the discovery of the David Walker pamphlet and the excitement produced by the Nat Turner Revolt, the legal position of the free Negro in the South deteriorated greatly. In Georgia and Florida he had to have a white guardian, and in other states where there was no such legal requirement he usually secured some white friend to defend him. He had to register with the county officials; his testimony in the courts, save in Louisiana, was invalid against whites; in some states he was prohibited from preaching to Negroes; he was not allowed to buy or sell liquor; and he was subject to curfew laws. His freedom of movement and of assembly was severely limited, and, except in Kentucky, Tennessee, and Maryland, it was illegal to teach free Negroes to read and write. He was constantly in danger of being kidnapped and sold.[19]

Nevertheless, the harsh laws of the free Negro code were only spasmodically enforced, and many free Negroes who legally should have left the state of emancipation remained unmolested. In addition to this laxness of law enforcement, the lot of the free Negroes had other redeeming features. The right of jury trial was not denied to him, and he could sue in the courts. He was permitted to vote in Tennessee until 1834 and was not disfranchised in North Carolina until by the action of the Constitutional Convention of 1835—then by the surprising vote of 66 to 61. Prior to that time it is possible that the free Negroes held the balance of power in some of the eastern counties and towns of the state. In certain of the eastern counties free Negro orphan children were taught to read and write under the apprentice laws, just as were white orphans.

The great majority of free Negroes were employed as domestic servants and agricultural laborers, but there was a considerable proportion of skilled workers among them. In Virginia, for example, there were 4,224 free Negro blacksmiths and 3,728 shoemakers listed in the census of 1860. Free Negroes had almost a monopoly on certain occupations, such as the barber's trade, from which they have been driven since the Civil War by the white man. Free Negroes in the South accumulated money as merchants, hotel keepers, and planters. The year 1830 marks the zenith of the ownership of slaves by free Negroes, most of such slaves being purchased in order to protect relatives but others for exploitation as agricultural labor. An interesting case of the ownership of slaves by free Negroes was the purchase of an eloquent slave preacher by the Pleasant Green Baptist Negro Church of Lexington, Kentucky. When the slave preacher was put up for auction in the settlement of an estate, a friendly white Baptist congregation purchased him for their black brethren, who, in turn paid for him on the installment plan by taking the Sunday collections to the white deacons.[20] The free Negroes of Virginia shared in the revival of prosperity of that state after 1830 so that they owned as much land on the eve of the Civil War as the whole of the race held in the state in 1890. From 1790 to 1850 the proportional growth of the free Negro element in the upper South was greater than either the white or slave population, and despite the deterioration of their legal status during this period, they improved and strengthened their economic position in Southern society.

Although black and white relationships in the South were legally rigid, in actual practice there were some remarkable variations in the status of Negroes. One of the most notable teachers in North Carolina was John Chavis, a free Negro who conducted schools for white children at Raleigh and Hillsborough, teaching the sons of Chief Justice Henderson and such eminent men as Governor Charles Manly and Senator Willie P. Mangum. Also white congregations at times listened to eloquent Negro preachers. Negro women often suckled the children of aristocratic white families. Moreover, among the free Negroes of Louisiana were some wealthy and cultivated persons who had been educated in Paris and who owned large plantations tilled by black slaves. A collection of poetry by Louisiana Negroes, representing a dozen authors, was published in 1845 by Armand Lanusse under the title, *Les Cenelles, Choix de Poésies Indigènes.*

The diary of a free Negro of Natchez, William Tiler Johnson, which has recently been discovered, reveals the large measure of freedom and economic opportunity that a very exceptional Negro could enjoy in a Southern state. Johnson, the son of a white father and a mulatto mother, operated three barber shops, and owned fifteen hundred acres of land and eight slaves. In one year he made sixteen loans totaling two thousand dollars to white men. A Negro sport, he bet on the horse races, bought liquor, spent money on lascivious pleasure, went to the theater, and gambled with cards. He subscribed to four or five Mississippi and Louisiana newspapers as well as to the sporting magazine, *The Spirit of the Times*, the *New York Mirror*, and the *Saturday Evening Post*. In 1851 he was murdered by a white man after he had won a lawsuit against the latter involving the boundaries of his plantation.[21]

Students of Southern history have differed over the question of the vitality of slavery on the eve of the Civil War. The answer to this complex problem requires an evaluation of the profitableness of the institution. It is true that there were important considerations other than economic in perpetuating slavery, such as the need to retain it as a mechanism of social control, the desire for tractable domestic servants, so essential to comfort in a warm climate, and the political value of keeping the Federal three-fifths ratio. Nevertheless, it seems reasonable to conclude that the main consideration in preserving slavery was its economic profitableness, either actual, or presumed.

Slave labor was reluctant labor, because there were few incentives for zealous work in such a system of exploitation. Hostile observers maintained that slaves often went through the motions of labor but accomplished about half the work of a farm hand in the North. Yet white men working in a hot climate also did less work than white laborers in the more stimulating climate of the North. Furthermore, the slaves who worked beside the numerous small slave-owners tended to slow down the labor of the whites and make them less efficient. Since slave labor was based on routine, it was difficult for Southerners to practice scientific or diversified agriculture. This fact contributed to the condition by which the South became wedded to a one money crop, leading to overproduction and low prices.

Despite the fact that slave labor was unpaid, it was in many respects an expensive form of labor. The cost of supervision of the Negro slaves was excessive. A large proportion of the slaves were too old or too young for hard work. Even in a state like Mississippi, which imported from the upper South a large proportion of prime field hands, a planter was fortunate if 60 per cent of his slaves could be classified as "hands." Each plantation carried an overhead expense of virtually old age pensions, and of sickness and unemployment insurance, as well as the cost of rearing Negro children. Too many slaves were withdrawn from productive labor in the fields to act as household servants. In some of the large slaveholding families each member enjoyed the services of a maid or valet. These favored individuals of the master class prided themselves on not lifting their hands to do any menial work. Southerners maintained that black slaves were unsuited to the use of machinery and that they broke or misused high-priced agricultural machines. Consequently, the South could not use its manpower to the best advantage by the introduction of machinery and labor-saving tools.

A large proportion of Southern capital was tied up or "frozen" in slaves. Southerners fell into a vicious practice of investing in slaves to produce more cotton to buy more slaves and land. Indeed, the value of personal property in the Southern states (chiefly slaves) far exceeded the value of real estate; in South Carolina the ratio was nearly three to one. The immobility of Southern capital invested in black chattel property was one of the greatest drawbacks to the use of slave labor. In times of depression the planter could not reduce his labor force nor could he shift his capital easily to other forms of investment.

Since slave labor as managed by the majority of slave-owners was an inefficient system of labor, it could be employed profitably only on rich soils. The natural limits of the expansion of slavery were therefore regulated by the presence of a supply of rich soils which were accessible to markets. It is debatable whether this limit had nearly been reached by 1850. Southern slavery could not advance into the semi-arid lands of New Mexico and Arizona. Slavery survived in the older states of the South, because the surplus of slaves was sold to the lower South. When this area of large cotton and sugar plantations reached the saturation point in buying black labor, slavery would become a financial burden to the slave-owners in the upper South, and they would try to get rid of the incubus of an unprofitable institution by emancipation.

All these economic disadvantages powerfully support a thesis that slavery would have gradually disappeared in the South within the nineteenth century. Professor George Tucker of the University of Virginia argued in a book, *The Laws of Wages, Profits, and Rents* (1837) that slavery was such an inefficient system of labor, that it must expire in the United States when the lower South had used up its best lands, an eventuality which he placed forty or fifty years in the future. The decade of the 1850's happened to be an era of good prices for the cotton planters but they were threatened with all the evils of overproduction. The high capitalization of black labor, $1,500 for a prime field hand, was a dangerous condition for the stability of slavery. The evils of slavery had been intensified by the opening of the fertile lands of the Southwest to cotton culture, leading to the large commercial type of plantation, owned to an undetermined extent by absentee proprietors and operated by overseers. These great estates deprived the relationship between slaves and their master of the paternal character of slavery in the upper South. Furthermore, the Southern grip on the institution of slavery was bound to relax as a result of the frowns of world opinion. Thus slavery would have vanished in the South by a gradual process, like serfdom in Europe. This method of abolishing slavery would have been far more humane and productive of good results than the means adopted by a bloody civil war which has left a bitter and unsolved race problem.

It is extremely difficult, however, to determine the economic vitality of plantation slavery based on its profitableness. To arrive at an accurate answer would require the separation of the question of whether Southern agriculture in the ante-bellum period was a lucrative or a poorly paid form of industry from the problem of the efficiency of slavery. The most eminent student of American Negro slavery, U. B. Phillips, believed that at the close of the ante-bellum period only those slaveholders who lived in the very fertile districts of the South and who had extraordinary managerial ability "were earning anything beyond what would cover their maintenance and carrying charges." [22] Modern studies of slavery in Mississippi, Georgia, and Alabama, based on the papers of some of the large planters, raise grave doubts as to whether the operation of slave plantations in the black belt was lucrative. A student of the cotton kingdom in Alabama concluded that the plantation system hastened the exhaustion of the soil and that in order for planters to make a slender margin of profit a large part of the food supply for the hands had to be raised.[23]

On the other hand, some recent writers have questioned the assumption that slavery was economically unprofitable in the Old South and that slave labor on the plantation was less efficient than white labor. Dr. Lewis C. Gray in his monumental *History of Agriculture in the Southern United States to 1860* has found slave labor efficient, even expert, on the well-managed plantations. Slave labor, under the system of incentives and punishments practiced on these plantations, he maintained, was probably more productive than free Negro labor in the modern South. Competent observers in the ante-bellum South expressed the opinion that slave labor was more efficient than the free Irish labor or the services of the native whites that were available. The relative difference in wages paid to hired white labor and the price of slave labor indicates no marked superiority in value of the free labor available. Slavery had a superior advantage over free labor in that it provided a stable labor supply, free

The Hero of the Common Man, Andrew Jackson

A portrait by Rembrandt Peale, 1778–1860. (Courtesy of the Kirby Hall of Civil Rights, Lafayette College.)

"Shooting for the Beef"

A painting by the Missouri artist, George Caleb Bingham (1811–1879), illustrating a typical frontier sport of competing in marksmanship for the prize of a beef. (Courtesy of the Brooklyn Museum.)

from strikes. Under competent plantation management slave labor had an "irresistible ability to displace free labor" in competition for rich soils accessible to markets.[24] This competitive advantage of slave labor arose primarily from the low subsistence level of the slave —a melancholy evidence of human exploitation.

Accordingly, Dr. Gray has maintained that slavery in the South was economically a strong and vital institution in the years before the Civil War. There was no danger in 1860 of slavery being discarded because of a lack of fresh, fertile lands. Railroads were opening up new sources of fertile land suitable for exploitation by slave labor. Furthermore, slaves were being successfully used in the tobacco factories of Richmond and could be trained to use machinery. Slaves may have been overcapitalized in 1860, he admits, but this was only a temporary phenomenon that would have adjusted itself, just as stocks and bonds that are overvalued today.

Several recent articles, moreover, point to the profitableness of slavery under good managerial ability. A study of the papers of Elisha King, a planter of the black belt of Alabama, shows how a poor man rose to become a wealthy planter owning eight thousand acres of land and one hundred and eighty-six slaves, expanding his possessions through buying on credit and by intelligent management.[25] The career of King could be matched many times in the ante-bellum South. There were also lordly planters like Samuel Hairston of Pittsylvania, who owned nearly two thousand slaves and was reputed to be the largest slaveholder in the South in the last decade of the ante-bellum period, self-made men like Joseph Davis of Mississippi who produced over three thousand bales of cotton annually, and wealthy sugar planters whose incomes were above $100,000. Henry Clay, writing from New Orleans, February 16, 1831, in favor of tariff protection for sugar, maintained that the planters did not receive an average of more than 5 or 6 per cent profit on capital invested in sugar plantations, which is a good profit according to modern standards.[26]

The critics who have attempted to prove the unprofitableness of plantation agriculture based on Negro slavery have almost invariably included interest charges on the investment in slaves and land as an expense. One student has challenged this method of accounting by

arguing that the earning of interest, as well as the wages of management should be regarded, not as an expense, but as a part of the
profit from plantation slavery.[27] Such a method of computing profit,
however, could not apply to the large number of planters who borrowed money to purchase their plantations. Another writer has
observed that erroneous views on the profitableness of slavery have
arisen as a result of reckoning profit on the basis of the assessed or
market value of slaves. Actually the average plantation owner did
not invest much money in slaves but acquired them either by natural
increase or by inheritance. These slaves produced considerably more
than they consumed.[28] The fact that there was an apparent increase
in prosperity among slaveholders as well as non-slaveholders in the
decade of the 1850's may throw some light on the unsolved question
of the profitableness of slavery. Furthermore, the slaveholders obtained a good living out of their farms—hams, fresh eggs, chickens,
fruit, the use of a horse or vehicle for transportation, and other satisfactions which cannot be measured in dollars and cents and therefore are left out in the computing of profits from plantation agriculture.

It must always be remembered in discussing the economics of
Southern agriculture that the Southern slaves and the white farmers
were engaged in producing raw materials. Their labor was deemed
unskilled, although good farming required many skills and much
experience. The Northern industrial worker has been classified as
a skilled laborer producing a finished product. He has always been
more highly rewarded by society, whether justly or not, than the
farmer.[29] Indeed, the Southern agriculturists as a whole were and have
remained poor. In 1850 the average value of land per acre in the
Southern states was $5.34, in the Southwestern states $6.26, and in
the Northwestern states $11.39. Although the Southern farmers did
not wisely use their resources, particularly in failing to preserve the
soil, slavery must be accounted an important factor in the im-
poverishment of the South.

Citations

1. Mary B. Chesnut, *A Diary from Dixie* (New York, 1929), 38.
2. W. E. B. DuBois, "The Enforcement of the Slave Trade Laws," *Annual Report of the American Historical Association for the Year 1891* (Washington, 1892), 173.
3. Phillips, *American Negro Slavery*, 147.
4. Frederic Bancroft, *Slave-Trading in the Old South* (Baltimore, 1931) and Wendell H. Stephenson, *Isaac Franklin, Slave Trader and Planter of the Old South* (Baton Rouge, 1938) have modified the old view of the slave trade.
5. *De Bow's Review*, XXVII (1859), 470.
6. The Pettigrew Papers are in the Southern Collection of the University of North Carolina. Professor B. H. Wall of the University of Kentucky has made some valuable unpublished researches into the lives of individual slaves as revealed in these papers.
7. "Memo. of H. Clay for Mr. Martin made the 20th of Sept., 1833," MS owned by J. Winston Coleman, Jr. of Lexington, Kentucky.
8. Contract of John W. Coleman with John McQuiddie, December 29, 1831, John W. Coleman MSS, 1828–1833, owned by J. Winston Coleman, Jr.
9. R. Hofstadter, "U. B. Phillips and the Plantation Legend," *Journal of Negro History*, XXIX (April, 1944), 109–125.
10. H. A. Kellar (ed.), *Solon Robinson, Pioneer and Agriculturist* (Indianapolis, 1936), I, 454–6; II, 213, 289–302.
11. J. F. Rhodes, *History of the United States from the Compromise of 1850* (New York, 1896–1906), I. 308.
12. Realistic modern studies include C. S. Sydnor, *Slavery in Mississippi* (New York, 1933), R. B. Flanders, *Plantation Slavery in Georgia* (Chapel Hill, 1933), R. H. Taylor, *Slave-Holding in North Carolina* (Chapel Hill, 1926), and A. O. Craven, *The Repressible Conflict, 1830–1861* (University, La., 1939), Chap. II.
13. W. T. Jordan (ed.), "System of Farming at Beaver Bend, Alabama, 1862," *Journal of Southern History*, VII (February, 1941), 80.
14. E. A. Davis, "Bennet H. Barrow, Ante-Bellum Planter of the Felicianas," *Journal of Southern History*, V (November, 1939), 439.
15. Lexington *Observer and Reporter*, May 12, 1849.
16. J. Winston Coleman, Jr., *Slavery Times in Kentucky* (Chapel Hill, 1940), 216; 197–202.
17. Clement Eaton, "A Dangerous Pamphlet in the Old South," *Journal of Southern History*, II (August, 1936), 323–334.

18. *The Countryman,* Turnwold, Putnam Co., Georgia, December 1, November 17, 1862.

19. For admirable studies of the free Negro see, J. M. ENGLAND, "The Free Negro in Ante-Bellum Tennessee," *Journal of Southern History,* IX (February, 1943), 37–58, and J. H. FRANKLIN, *The Free Negro in North Carolina, 1790–1860* (Chapel Hill, 1943).

20. William M. Pratt Diary, Jan. 1, 1856, MS in the University of Kentucky Library.

21. William Tiler Johnson Diary, MS at Louisiana State University.

22. PHILLIPS, *American Negro Slavery,* 392.

23. C. S. DAVIS, *The Cotton Kingdom in Alabama* (Montgomery, 1939); SYDNOR, *op. cit.,* and FLANDERS, *op. cit.*

24. L. C. GRAY, *History of Agriculture in the Southern States to 1860* (Washington, 1933), I, 474.

25. W. T. JORDAN, "The Elisha F. King Family, Planters of Alabama Black Belt," *Agricultural History,* XIX (July, 1945), 152–162.

26. Calvin Colton, *The Life, Correspondence, and Speeches of Henry Clay* (New York, 1864), IV, 294.

27. T. P. GOVAN, "Was Plantation Slavery Profitable?", *Journal of Southern History,* VIII (November, 1942), 513–535.

28. R. W. SMITH, "Was Slavery Unprofitable in the Ante-Bellum South?", *Agricultural History,* XX (January, 1946), 62–64.

29. ALLAN NEVINS, *Ordeal of the Union* (New York, 1947), I, Chap. 14.

CHAPTER XII

The Hero of the Common Man

NO leader of the democratic masses in American history has possessed so masterful and colorful a personality as Andrew Jackson. He became an authentic folk hero—the type of man the common people have always admired, an out-of-doors personality, a man of direct action, a military hero. Arising from plebeian origins, he had the extroverted tastes of the frontier, the prejudices, the religion, and the sense of values of the common people, which enabled him to understand their psychology. Although he was shrewd, he was not an original thinker, expert in the handling of ideas, nor did he have the gift of magnetic speech. Like Washington and Jefferson, he seems also to have lacked a well-developed sense of humor, which has proved so valuable to popular leaders in establishing a bond of union with ordinary men.

Jackson has been accused of being an opportunist, of having no political philosophy, only rich and stubborn prejudices, and of exercising a dangerous military power in government. It is true that he was often autocratic and prejudiced, but his intuitions or sympathies placed him on the right side of the great issues of his day, while the most intellectual statesman of his time, Calhoun, took the wrong course. A combination of a Southerner and a Westerner, he had the notable virtue of being national in outlook in a period when sectionalism was growing. Since he became the leader of the forces known as "Jacksonian democracy," his public career was deeply intertwined with the political development of the Old South.

Born in 1767 in the border region between North and South Carolina, "the garden of the Waxhaws," he was the product of the American frontier. His Scotch-Irish parents were poor, humble people, and his mother was early left a widow. When he was thirteen years old he participated in the Revolutionary battle of Hanging Rock. He acquired an enduring hatred of England as a result of his military experience, which included capture by the British and a sword cut when the indomitable youth refused to clean a British officer's muddy boots. His mother died as a martyr while nursing American soldiers on a prison ship in Charleston harbor, and he was left alone in the world at the age of fourteen years. In the back country he developed into a self-willed and turbulent youth, a "red head," fighting at the least insult, fond of cock fights, and vehement in the use of oaths. From his grandfather in Ireland, a linen weaver and merchant, he inherited a modest sum of money, which he squandered in Charleston betting on the horse races and throwing dice. Here he may have acquired the ceremonious manners of Southern aristocrats that later distinguished him as well as his life-long passion for horse racing. Although he obtained only a smattering of learning, he taught school for a short while and then studied law in the office of Spruce Macay of Salisbury, North Carolina. In this backwoods village he continued his dissipated life, "slicking" his mane of reddish hair down with bear's grease and playing such crude practical jokes as inviting the leading prostitute of the town to a ball of which he was the manager.[1]

In 1788 he emigrated to the growing village of Nashville, Tennessee, where he hung out his shingle as a young lawyer. Possessing precisely the type of personality suited to frontier conditions, he arose rapidly in this community. At the age of twenty-nine he was elected Tennessee's first representative in Congress (1796), and then became successively United States Senator and judge of the Supreme Court of Tennessee. His success arose partly from his connection with the Blount faction in Tennessee politics, but perhaps more from his iron will, his courage, scrupulous regard for honor, and common sense. A crucial step in his career was his election by the officers of the state militia to the position of major-general (1802), which he won over John Sevier by one vote. His whole military career and later election to the Presidency may have depended upon this victory.

One of the best insights into Jackson's personality is afforded by a glance at his dueling activities. On May 30, 1806, he challenged

Charles Dickinson to a duel as a result of bitter words between the two men over a race track dispute. Despite the Tennessee law which forbade dueling, they crossed over the state line into Kentucky and there fought a fatal duel. Dickinson was noted for his consummate skill with a dueling pistol, being regarded as an almost infallible shot. On this occasion the principals stood facing each other at a distance of eight yards, pistols pointing to the ground. At the word "Fire!" Dickinson quickly aimed at his opponent's heart but his bullet only wounded Jackson in the shoulder. Then the relentless Jackson slowly aimed at his opponent, who was standing with folded arms, and pulled the trigger. The hammer stopped at half-cock, but he coolly recocked the pistol and killed his enemy. John Spencer Bassett in his *Life of Andrew Jackson* has branded this unmagnanimous episode as "little less than murder," a deed which lessened Jackson's political influence.[2]

Seven years later, when he was forty-six years old, he engaged in a rough and tumble fight with the Benton brothers. This undignified affair arose out of a duel between Jesse Benton and William Carroll, in which Jackson served as a second for the latter. The duel turned out to be an uproarious farce. After Jesse had fired and missed Carroll, he tried to present as small a target as possible to his opponent's return shot by bending low and pulling his coat tightly around his body. As a result of this stance, an amusing accident occurred. Carroll's bullet traversed Benton's back and wounded his buttocks. Thus Jesse became the laughing-stock of all Tennessee. The humiliated man transferred some of his bitterness of soul arising from this episode to Jackson who had acted as Carroll's second. Gossip aggravated the ill feelings between the Benton brothers and Jackson, so that the latter threatened to horsewhip Thomas Hart Benton on sight. Consequently, when Jackson saw Tom Benton standing in the doorway of a tavern in Nashville, he started after him with his riding whip. In the fracas which followed Jesse, rushing out of the bar room to save his brother, shot Jackson in the shoulder. Later the Bentons and Jackson were reconciled and Thomas Hart, as a Senator from Missouri, became an ardent supporter of Jackson's administration.

Jackson's victory at New Orleans in 1815 made him a national hero and a potential candidate for the Presidency. It is difficult to determine how much personal ambition motivated him to run for this office. Although he professed that he was through with public life after his fiasco as governor of Florida, he subscribed in 1822 to twenty newspapers from all sections of the country—a significant detail. He seems to have been stirred to go after the Presidency by a group of Tennessee politicians, the so-called Nashville Junto, including his neighbor, William B. Lewis, Senator John H. Eaton, and John Overton. These men groomed the Old Hero for the Presidency, arousing his sleeping ambition and subtly enlisting his violent personal animosities. Jackson gained popularity in the North by his Grass Hat letter of May 17, 1823, written to a Pennsylvania protectionist who had sent Mrs. Jackson a grass bonnet. In this letter he expressed approval of a protective tariff. A step in developing his campaign was his election to the Senate in 1823 by the Tennessee legislature. Here he voted for internal improvements and the tariff of 1824, votes that strengthened his candidacy.

During Monroe's last term there was a hectic scramble among ambitious politicians to win the succession to the Presidency. The Federalist party had disappeared and new parties were forming. In the Presidential campaign of 1824 the Southern states produced five of the six candidates, William H. Crawford from Georgia, John C. Calhoun and William Lowndes from South Carolina, Henry Clay of Kentucky, and Andrew Jackson from Tennessee. The only Northern candidate was John Quincy Adams from Massachusetts, the best educated of the political rivals.

Of the chief aspirants to the office of President, Jackson alone depended largely on a reputation of military glory. Moreover, he had shown little fitness to be the executive of a democratic nation. While he was ruling New Orleans following his famous victory he continued martial law after the need for it no longer existed, and when a Creole member of the legislature freely criticized his acts, he had the audacious member arrested and tried by court martial. He also refused to honor a writ of habeas corpus by Judge Hall and even expelled this upholder of law from New Orleans. Later Judge Hall returned to the city, summoned Jackson before the court, and fined him a thousand dollars and costs. His unauthorized invasion of Florida in 1818, his hanging of Arbuthnot and shooting of Ambrister, and his arbitrary conduct as governor of Florida cast serious doubts on his wisdom as an administrator. Indeed, his career had been violent, and Jefferson was right when he observed that Jackson had the autocratic temperament which caused him to disregard constitutions and laws. Jefferson was reported to have declared that although Jackson was an able military chieftain, he was utterly unfit for the Presidency, this man whose passions were terrible.

The campaign of Jackson in 1824 was cleverly managed. Contrary to a common misconception of Jackson, he often heeded the advice of his friends, and he himself was an astute politician. He was very shrewd in not advancing a clear-cut set of proposals, or a constructive platform, but in relying upon his popularity as a military hero. Furthermore, his personality was the kind that the plain people admired, a self-made man with not too much book learning and with the earthy tastes of the common man. In 1822 the legislature of Tennessee nominated Jackson for President. Also a convention at Harrisburg, Pennsylvania, March 4, 1824, declared in his favor, designating Calhoun as candidate for Vice President. After this blow Calhoun decided not to run for the Presidency but to be content, for the time being, with attaining the subordinate office. The legislature of South Carolina nominated William Lowndes as that state's favorite son, but he was eliminated from the race by a fatal sickness. Henry Clay, advocate of "the American System" of protective tariff and internal improvements, divided with Jackson the support of the West.

The candidate who was most feared by all was William H. Crawford, Secretary of the Treasury under Madison and Monroe, and ambassador to France. This dynamic man, of powerful physique and skilled in reading human nature, had been born and educated in Virginia but had removed to Georgia. Here he became the leader of the Radicals or the State Rights school. He was nominated for the Presidency by the Congressional Caucus, a move which probably injured him, since this method of nominating candidates was propagandized as undemocratic by his rivals. In North Carolina a People's Ticket was formed to defeat this candidate made odious as the choice of the caucus. The People's Ticket was a coalition of the enemies of Crawford, pledged to support whichever candidate proved to be the strongest and most likely to defeat the Georgia statesman. The Jackson men were finally able to capture the People's Ticket, carrying the western section of the state and the undeveloped portions of the East bordering on Albemarle and Pamlico sounds.[3]

When the electoral vote was counted, it was found that Jackson had received the largest number of votes, but no candidate had obtained a majority of all the votes cast. Consequently the House of Representatives was forced to make a decision, voting on the three highest candidates, Jackson, Adams, and Crawford. Clay had been last in the electoral vote, and was thus eliminated. However, he was placed in the strategic position of being able to throw his strength to the candidate of his choice and thus virtually determining who should be President. Courted by both sides, Clay decided in favor of Adams and persuaded the Kentucky delegation in Congress to vote for the New Englander. Shortly before the election took place, a Pennsylvania Congressman, George Kremer, who was regarded as somewhat of an eccentric, notorious for wearing a leopard coat, made the charge that a corrupt bargain had been formed between Clay and Adams. He asserted that Clay had agreed to throw his support to Adams in return for a promise by the latter to appoint Clay Secretary of State. Subsequently the Kentuckian was made Secretary of State by President Adams, an appointment which seemed to substantiate the charge that the New Englander and "Harry of the West" had participated in an unscrupulous intrigue to secure the election of Adams. Jackson believed this accusation and, spurred by vindictive feelings, was determined to become a candidate four years later to unseat the beneficiary of a "corrupt bargain."[4]

During this campaign of 1828 "Old Hickory," as he was often called, kept silent on national issues. Indeed, the campaign was one of bitter personalities designed to attract the votes of the unthinking electorate. The old charge of a corrupt bargain between Adams and Clay was used effectively, and Adams was accused of having introduced gambling tables in the Presidential Mansion, because he had installed billiard tables in the White House at his own expense. On the other hand, Jackson's enemies made fun of Rachel, his wife, who smoked a corn cob pipe and was semi-illiterate. Especially, they made malicious remarks about his marriage to Rachel before she had obtained a legal divorce from her former husband, a mistake which had to be rectified by performing a second ceremony two years after the original marriage. His opponents also printed coffin handbills to advertise the fact that during the war against the Creek Indians he had ordered the death of six mutinous militiamen. The real issue in the Presidential campaign was the personality of Jackson, the hero of the common man. He won overwhelmingly over Adams, by an alliance of the South and the West. His candidacy received indispensable aid, however, from James Buchanan in Pennsylvania and Martin Van Buren in New York, decisive states in the election.

The inauguration of Jackson as President on March 4, 1829, was a symbol of the rise of the common man. Jackson treasured the myth of Jefferson riding on horseback to his inauguration and tying his horse with his own hands. He, too, wishing to demonstrate his belief in republican simplicity, walked from his tavern to the inauguration ceremonies, where he read his address. It was a conciliatory document, designed to dispel the fears of many citizens aroused by his previous turbulent and autocratic career. He proclaimed himself an advocate of state rights, strict economy and the extinguishment of the public debt, a judicious protective tariff for the sake of national independence, and a humane Indian policy. Declaring himself opposed to large standing armies, he held that "the bulwark of our defense is the national militia." After the inaugural a reception was held in the White House during which the realistic democracy had little respect for the furniture and rugs of the President's Mansion. "King Mob" trampled with muddy boots on the carpets and stood on the damask seats of the chairs to see the "Old Hero." In fact Jackson was mobbed by ardent democrats who wanted to shake the hand of the victor of the battle of New Orleans. Finally bowls of punch were placed on the White House lawn to lure the democracy out of the house, and the President escaped through a back window. Jackson entered the Presidential Mansion alone, for his wife had died shortly before the inauguration. His close friend, William B. Lewis, lived with him in the White House (much like Harry Hopkins in Roosevelt's administration) and Emily Donelson who had married his wife's nephew presided over his social occasions.

Jackson realized the great power of public opinion in a democracy. Consequently he cultivated newspaper editors, who formed an important group in the so-called Kitchen Cabinet, or his informal coterie of advisers, whom wits represented as meeting in the White House pantry and there deciding the fate of the nation. He made Francis P. Blair, a Kentucky journalist, the editor of the administration organ, the Washington *Globe*. Whenever he wished to influence public opinion, he or his lieutenants would write a communication, and Jackson would order, "Give it to Bla-ar" (Blair)! Amos Kendall, another Kentucky editor, was also an important member of the Kitchen Cabinet, later appointed Postmaster-General. A ghostly figure who seldom appeared in public, he was often a dominating influence in the President's strategy. Jackson's official cabinet was a rather weak body of men, with the exception of the Secretary of State, Martin Van Buren. The cabinet appointments were divided between his own friends and the followers of Vice President Calhoun, with whom there was a silent understanding that the Vice President should succeed the Old Hero after one term.

The source of Van Buren's influence over Jackson remains somewhat a mystery. The tall, angular Tennesseean, with his forthright methods, seems hardly compatible with the suave New York politician called "the Little Magician." Yet Van Buren was an opportunist who studied the character of "Old Hickory" and treated him with unfailing tact. Probably Jackson also admired Van Buren's sagacity as a political manipulator. Observing that the planter-President liked to exercise by horseback riding, Van Buren acquired a horse and often his plump little figure could be seen bobbing up and down on his horse as he rode beside the stern old man. Southerners as a whole never liked Van Buren, regarding him as a designing New York politician. But Jackson declared that he was remarkably frank and guileless and "one of the most pleasant men to do business with I ever saw." [5]

Van Buren strengthened Jackson's attachment to him by his conduct in the amazing Peggy O'Neale affair, in which much of official society in Washington led by Mrs. Calhoun refused to associate with this former barmaid who had married Secretary of War John H.

Eaton, a close friend of the President. Jackson held a cabinet meeting over this social feud and tried to force the members of his official family to receive Mrs. John H. Eaton socially. Van Buren, a widower, unencumbered by female protocol, was attentive to the snubbed lady. At his suggestion Jackson reorganized his cabinet in 1831, purging it of the Calhoun members and appointing Eaton governor of Florida and later minister to Spain, where the lovely Peggy played a brilliant role in Spanish society. Van Buren was at the same time appointed minister to England, but was rejected by the Senate through the deciding vote of Vice President Calhoun. Thereupon Jackson was more determined than ever to make the "Little Magician" Vice President in 1832 and his successor at the following election.

The New York leader had a bond of agreement with the South in a mutual support of the state rights doctrine. Indeed, he had been a zealous supporter of William H. Crawford, the preeminent champion of state rights in the South, and had shifted to the Jackson camp only after the Georgia statesman had been eliminated from the political arena by sickness. But below the Mason and Dixon line, "the Red Fox of Kinderhook" and his cohorts, such as Colonel James A. Hamilton, son of Alexander, Silas Wright, and William L. Marcy, who were sensitive to the labor vote of the North, were distrusted. With the rise to power of Van Buren Southern and Western influences on the administration tended to dwindle.

Although Jackson did not initiate the democratic movement of the 1820's and 1830's, he seized leadership of the movement and rode the groundswell of the democratic revolt. The rise of the common man to political power was accelerated by the War of 1812, which shook American society out of the old grooves, developed a new sense of nationality, and stirred the discontent of the common people. Following the conclusion of the war there was a widespread shift of population from the East to the West. Never before had such a large proportion of the American people lived under frontier conditions; at least half of the population of the United States in 1828 were living under such conditions. Thus the influence of the American frontier on politics, which has contributed to the growth of a democratic spirit, was probably at its height during this period.

Furthermore, the industrial revolution led to a labor movement that encouraged the common man to assert himself politically. The growth of the factory system, nevertheless, did not affect the Southern section of the country very deeply, except in the indirect fashion of enormously stimulating agricultural production for export markets and thus revivifying slavery, which exerted an aristocratic influence. The democratic unheaval of the late 1820's and 1830's followed a decade of political apathy on the part of the American people during the administrations of President Monroe. The passing of the "Virginia dynasty" and the emergence of new leaders, however, resulted in violent political activity.

The rise of Jacksonian democracy within the Southern states cannot be explained in terms of a simple formula. In the Atlantic seaboard states local conditions and sectionalism frequently produced revolts against the control of the conservatives and the Tidewater aristocrats. A brilliant student of the age of Jackson has discounted the influence of the frontier on the rise of the democratic movement in the decades of the 1820's and 1830's and has emphasized the role of the working class in the Northern cities.[6] Below the Mason and Dixon line, however, this influence seems negligible, while the existence of frontier conditions in a large part of the South was undoubtedly an important catalyst of democracy. In the whole country there was a cultural lag between democratic theory and democratic practice. A reaction was due to occur in order to close up the gap between theory and practice.

Jackson became the champion of the interests of the common people partly as a result of circumstances. During his early career, when he was fighting for money and power in Tennessee, he was allied with the upper classes. Eager for capital, he developed many financial interests, such as operating a general store, earning money by his race horses and by his lawyer's fees, conducting a large plantation with slave labor, and speculating in land. Some of his ruthless Indian treaties were made in the interest of land speculators. In 1820 Jackson vehemently opposed Felix Grundy's bill for the establishing of a state loan bank to furnish relief to the debtors suffering from the panic of 1819. The following year he supported Edward Ward, the aristocratic candidate for governor, against William Carroll, champion of the people. Modern research indicates that Jackson was a conservative in Tennessee politics, and that the real champion of democratic reforms in that state was not Jackson but his opponent Governor William Carroll, a former nail merchant with an affable personality, who was governor from 1821 to 1835.[7]

The type of democracy which bears the name of Andrew Jackson was a realistic democracy with all its virtues and defects. Jefferson had attempted to establish a liberal republican form of government, led by gentlemen farmers. Until the Jacksonian movement, the common people were content for the upper class to rule. But by 1828 the psychology of the plain people toward their government had changed, and they wished for direct participation in the government and for the elevation of a man of their choice into the Presidency. In that year the common men came to the polls, demagogic oratory flourished, party slogans, party workers and organizers who had an eye on the plums of office got out the vote. The campaign was personalized. This new type of democracy, composed of the farmers of the West, the yeomen and small planters of the South, and the labor vote of the North was violently partisan and had little interest in the protection of intellectual liberty or the rights of minorities, which had ennobled the brand of democracy that Jefferson had advocated. It was a rough and tumble movement which resulted in the elevation of pushing, mediocre men to office, Jackson's personality was autocratic instead of truly democratic, and he lacked an interest in fundamental *social* reforms.

"Jacksonian democracy" had its roots in Jeffersonian ideas; but it translated democratic theory into practice, extending democratic principles to the national government. It was decidedly more radical than Jeffersonian democracy and less concerned with quality government. Under "Jacksonian democracy" rotation in office was put into practice. This political device was based on the assumption that one citizen was as good as another and that the duties of government should be made so simple that any honest citizen with common sense could administer a public office successfully. The Spoils System was transferred from state politics to the national government. Yet Jackson's removals of Federal officeholders have been grossly exaggerated, for he removed in the first year of his administration only about one-fourth of the incumbent Federal officeholders. A large measure of political democracy was realized by the adoption of the Nominating Convention for President, introduced by the Anti-Masonic Party in 1831, manhood suffrage, adopted first by the frontier states, then extended to the older states, the substitution of popular election of state officials for the old method of selection by the legislature or by appointment, the removal of property qualifications for officeholding, and the election of Presidential electors in all the states, except South Carolina, by the people instead of by the legislature.

Jackson's Indian policy is a good example of his sympathy with the point of view of the frontiersmen and of the common people of the South. He accepted the frontiersman's estimate that the only good Indian was a dead Indian, and he was zealous in robbing Indians of their land by treaties imposed by force or by chicanery. The removal of the Indians from the South was a tragic but inevitable result of westward expansion. In 1825 President Monroe announced as one of his last official acts a policy of the removal of the eastern Indians to an Indian territory beyond the Mississippi River, a policy which his Secretary of War, Calhoun, had advocated. The country selected was the region west of the Arkansas-Missouri state lines, an area which was believed unsuited to agricultural expansion as a result of Major Stephen Long's report of "The Great American Desert." It was believed that the Indians could reside permanently in this area, the present state of Oklahoma, undisturbed by the cupidity of the white man. To Jackson fell the burden of carrying out this policy of removal authorized by Congress in 1830. Treaties were made with the various tribes for exchanging land in the West for their hunting grounds in the eastern states and for their peaceable emigration. Jackson and his successor, Van Buren, had little trouble in removing the northern Indians, but the "Five Civilized Tribes" in the South offered powerful resistance to surrendering their homeland.

The most formidable resistance was made by the Cherokee of Georgia and the Seminole of Florida. The Cherokee had made great advances in the art of civilization. They had become successful farmers and in some cases tilled cotton plantations with slaves. One of their brilliant leaders, the crippled Sequoyah, whose father was a white man, had invented an alphabet for the Cherokee language, and a newspaper, the *Cherokee Phoenix*, had been established at their capitol, New Echota. In 1827 they had organized a government with a written constitution which denied the jurisdiction of the state of Georgia and established a state within a state.

In addition to this repudiation of the sovereignty of Georgia, there was another powerful reason for the removal of the Cherokee, the greed of Georgians for their land. The Cherokee had the double misfortune of owning some fertile cotton land and of having gold discovered in their territory. In 1802 the state of Georgia had given up her claims to western lands on condition that the Federal government should extinguish the Indian title to the lands within her borders. The Federal government, however, was slow in taking the Indians' land away from them by treaty, although President John Quincy Adams did negotiate in 1825 the Treaty of Indian Springs with Chief McIntosh of the Creek tribe for the surrender of a large area of land in Georgia. This treaty was rejected by the Creeks, and McIntosh was killed, but the next year a new treaty resulted in the cession of a considerable portion of the Creek land. The Cherokee, however, announced in 1824 that they would sell no more land to the whites.

During this period of controversy the truculent, red-headed governor of Georgia, George M. Troup, threatened to expel the Indians from the state by force if the Federal government failed to act. In 1828 Georgia extended her laws over the Cherokee nation. Two years later, a Cherokee named Corn Tassel committed a murder and was arrested by Georgia officials and brought to trial before a state court. The Cherokee nation hired the eminent lawyer William Wirt of Baltimore and appealed to the Supreme Court to protect their treaty rights in the famous case of the Cherokee Nation versus the State of Georgia (1831). The Supreme Court ordered the State of Georgia to appear before its tribunal to defend the case, but the governor refused to heed the subpoena, and Corn Tassel was speedily hanged. The majority of the Supreme Court held that the Cherokee were not a foreign nation but a domestic dependent nation in a state of pupilage, and that they were not competent to appear as a party to a suit against a state in the tribunal of the Supreme

Court. Therefore the motion for an injunction restraining Georgia from executing its laws within Cherokee territory was refused.

In 1832 the Supreme Court decided another case, Worcester versus Georgia, which was more favorable to the Cherokee cause. The legislature of Georgia had passed a law making it illegal for white persons to reside in the Cherokee territory without a license from the state and without taking an oath of allegiance to Georgia. Some New England missionaries violated this law and eleven of them were arrested and convicted. Samuel A. Worcester and Elizur Butler, two of the condemned men, appealed to the Supreme Court. Georgia again refused to appear before this tribunal. The Supreme Court then ruled that the Georgia law in question was a violation of the Constitution, which had given to Congress the right to regulate intercourse with the Indians. Worcester was declared entitled to his freedom, but Georgia disdained to obey the mandate of the Supreme Court in favor of the missionaries and the Cherokee. President Jackson, however, refused to use his executive authority to enforce the decision of the court. Thus Georgia was allowed to nullify the decision of the highest Federal court. Jackson's inaction in this case was inconsistent with his policy toward South Carolina when she nullified a Federal law. He is reputed to have said, "John Marshall has made his decision, now let him enforce it."

In December, 1835, the Cherokee, finding that Jackson would not protect them or enforce the decision of the Supreme Court, yielded to their hard fate. They signed a treaty ceding their lands east of the Mississippi for five and one-half million dollars as well as receiving a larger amount of land in the Indian territory than they had held in Georgia. A Southerner, Joel R. Poinsett, who was Secretary of War in Van Buren's administration, supervised their painful removal in 1838. The Cherokee were passionately devoted to their beautiful homeland, containing the graves of their fathers, and the long journey to the setting sun was a "Trail of Tears" to them. Poinsett selected another Southerner, General Winfield Scott, to command the troops that escorted the more than twelve thousand Cherokee to their new home. Instead of giving the contract for furnishing supplies and transportation to white contractors, the War Department awarded the contract to the leading chief, John Ross, who aided greatly in the peaceful removal of the tribe. Nevertheless, at least one-fifth of them died on the way as a result of various hardships and diseases. The Cherokee living in the Great Smoky Mountains of North Carolina were not removed, and some of them remain on reservations in that state to this day.

By the treaties of Dancing Rabbit and Pontotoc (1830–32) the Choctaw and Chickasaw gave up their homeland in the northern part of Mississippi, containing fertile cotton lands. Like the Cherokee, they emigrated to the territory beyond the Arkansas-Missouri line now included in the state of Oklahoma. Here they had to change their habits and modes of life to fit a strange environment. By 1840 the forced emigration of the Southern Indians to the West was largely completed, resulting in the removal of about sixty thousand Indians.

The Seminole Indians of Florida refused to abandon their hunting grounds and fought bitterly against Federal troops from 1836 to 1842. This "nation" was a branch of the Creeks who had emigrated into Florida at the beginning of the eighteenth century, and their name in the Creek language meant "runaways" or "separatists." One of the chief reasons for their fierce struggle to remain in their native haunts was that many fugitive Negroes who had mingled their blood with the tribe were living among them and, in the process of removal, they might be reclaimed by white masters. Furthermore, the Seminole were incensed by the unscrupulous action of United States agents in negotiating a treaty for removal with only a few chiefs. For years these Indians fought the United States regulars and Florida militia in a war characterized by inefficiency and barbarism, costing the United States over twenty million dollars. Protected by the labyrinths of the Everglades and ably led by the gallant mixed-breed, Osceola, they were remarkably successful in frustrating the efforts to remove them. Finally some of their chiefs, including Osceola, were captured while they were approaching under a flag of truce and were imprisoned at Fort Moultrie on Sullivan's Island in Charleston harbor. Here young Osceola died mourning over the fate of his people. Approximately four thousand of the Seminole were finally removed to the Indian territory, but a remnant has survived in Florida to the present day.

One of Jackson's greatest services to the nation was in championing the cause of the common man instead of favoring Big Business. The representative of Big Business in the age of Jackson was the Second National Bank, which had twenty-seven branches scattered through the country controlled by the parent bank at Philadelphia. Nicholas Biddle, the president, was an imperious type of man who had an arrogant disdain of politicians and believed that his business was above the law. His great financial institution had been given valuable special privileges by its charter of 1816, especially the monopoly of keeping the government's deposits, which averaged seven million dollars, without paying interest, and the exclusive privilege of issuing bank-notes which were valid for government dues. The Bank was hated by many in the South and West because of its sound money policy, yet it had also powerful friends in these regions, particularly in South Carolina, where a huge block of its stock, 40,674 shares, was held.

Jackson's hostility to the bank was revealed in his first message to Congress, in which he declared that both the expediency and constitutionality of the institution were doubtful. His cabinet, however, was divided over the wisdom of tackling this powerful financial institution, and Jackson himself wavered at first in his course in regard to the Bank. The charter of the bank would not expire until 1836, but Nicholas Biddle was persuaded by his agent in Washington and by Henry Clay and Daniel Webster, whose retaining fees as attorneys for the Bank were "refreshed" at intervals, to apply for a recharter early in 1832, a Presidential election year. Clay, planning to be a candidate, wished to make the bank question a leading issue of the campaign. The recharter bill passed Congress, but Jackson vetoed it in a fighting message, written largely by Amos Kendall and Roger B. Taney, his Attorney General.

In the bank fight Jackson stood forth as the champion of the common people against predatory business groups. He portrayed this extensive financial institution as possessing a dangerous potential of influencing elections. He denounced the recharter bill as an attempt to "make the rich richer and the potent more powerful," granting to this class exclusive privileges denied to "the humble members of society—the farmers, mechanics, and laborers." [8] He cleverly appealed to the prejudices of the common people by pointing out that a substantial portion of the stockholders were foreigners. Adopting the strict interpretation view of the Constitution, he argued that the Bank was unconstitutional, despite a decision of the Supreme Court to the contrary.

In the ensuing election Jackson, with Van Buren as his running mate, won a smashing victory over Clay. Only South Carolina of the genuinely Southern states refused to vote for him, although the border states of Kentucky, Maryland, and Delaware voted for Clay. Jackson interpreted the election as a mandate from the people to destroy the bank. Despite a report of a Congressional committee that the bank was sound, he determined to remove the deposits of the national government from the bank before the expiration of its charter. The cabinet was divided over the wisdom of this radical move, and Jackson had to remove two Secretaries of the Treasury, one by promotion and another by dismissal, in order to appoint to this office a man who would carry out his will. The new Secretary of the Treasury, Roger B. Taney, executed the policy of weakening the Second National Bank by depositing no more government funds in its vaults and by drawing out gradually the government reserves through means of checks for disbursements. The new depositories for government money were a group of fifteen state banks selected by the Secretary of the Treasury, known as "pet banks." As a punishment for the removal of the deposits from the National Bank, the Senate under Clay's leadership passed an unprecedented resolution of censure against Jackson. However, Senator Thomas Hart Benton after repeated efforts succeeded in January, 1837, in getting the Senate to expunge the famous censure from its journal.

The destruction of the Second National Bank by Jackson has been evaluated by the great American historian, Frederick Jackson Turner, as follows: "The severance of official connection between the national government and the capitalist was one of the most important steps in American history. Thenceforth, the industrial interests were obliged to act by underground methods and by the lobby." [9] Yet the immediate effects of Jackson's war against the bank were pernicious, for he destroyed an institution that was restraining the inflationary trends of the period. Consequently, the government gave the green light to speculation and unsound banking practices which contributed to the panic of 1837.

A policy of the Southern agrarians has been to keep the national government on a course of strict economy. One of the most cherished objectives of Jackson, which had also been a cardinal policy of Jefferson, was to pay off the national debt before he retired from office. In 1835 he succeeded in accomplishing this purpose, and for the first and last time in American history the Federal government was practically free from debt. The Treasury had accumulated a large surplus of money as a result of the huge land sales and receipts from the protective tariff policy. In 1836 Congress ordered the distribution of this surplus among the states in installments, theoretically as loans, but actually as gifts. Some of the Southern states wasted this money in unwise programs of internal improvement, but North Carolina, whose share was $1,433,757.39, devoted most of this gift to establishing free public schools.

Speculation was rife at this time throughout the country and economic conditions were brewing a panic. The tremendous inflation which was occurring was registered in the South by the sharp rise in the price of cotton and slaves. Cotton rose from 7.5 cents in 1830 to 15.2 cents per pound at New Orleans in 1836, the highest price since the boom of 1818. When deflation came as the result of the panic, delayed in the South until 1839, the price dropped to 7.9 cents, reaching the nadir of 4.7 cents in 1844. At the close of 1836 prime slaves were selling for eleven hundred dollars in Virginia, and thirteen hundred dollars in Louisiana, marking an advance of nearly 400 per cent since the end of the eighteenth century. Deflation in the decade of the 1840's reduced their value almost one-half.

This inflation was accompanied by a tremendous speculation in public lands, encouraged by the state banks which issued banknotes without adequate specie basis and lent money recklessly. One of the virtues of the Second National Bank had been that it had maintained a stable uniform currency, partly by forcing state banks to keep a reasonable reserve of specie to pay their bank-notes. The destruction of this institution by Jackson had released a brake on the activity of the state banks in inflating the currency. Contrary to the sentiment of the frontier region from which he had come, Jackson favored a hard money policy. He was sustained in this policy by Senator Thomas Hart Benton of Missouri, who was appropriately nicknamed "Old Bullion." Accordingly, the President, alarmed by the inflationary movement, issued his Specie Circular of July 11, 1836, requiring the payment of hard cash for government land. This measure, designed to strike a blow at speculators and protect the common man against the "non-resident proprietorship" of the public lands, precipitated a disastrous panic which did much to ruin the administration of his successor, Martin Van Buren.[10]

On March 4, 1837, Jackson retired from public life to his plantation near Nashville, "the Hermitage," where he lived until his death in 1845. His career is inseparably connected with the growth of political democracy and the cause of nationalism in the South. It is true that his course as President was not consistently nationalistic. Influenced by Martin Van Buren, he had taken the state rights point of view in vetoing the Maysville (Kentucky) Road Bill in 1830. By adhering to a strict construction of the Constitution in this instance, he delayed the desirable development of a network of national roads uniting the various sections of the country. He also adopted the state rights view in the controversy of Georgia with the national government over the removal of the Cherokee.

Nevertheless, Jackson was one of the greatest of Southern nationalists. By his firmness he contributed powerfully to crushing the nullification movement in South Carolina and asserting the authority of the national government. An ardent expansionist, just before his retirement as President, he signed the proclamation recognizing the independent republic of Texas. Furthermore, he gave the country real leadership, immensely strengthening the powers of the Presidency, especially by his courageous use of the veto power. The veto power had been applied only nine times by all the Presidents who had preceded Jackson, but he vetoed twelve bills of Congress. Other Presidents had vetoed laws because they regarded such laws as unconstitutional or defective technically, but Jackson also vetoed bills which he regarded as unwise or against the interest of the people. In foreign affairs, he raised the prestige of the nation by his "shirt sleeve diplomacy," which, for example, forced France to pay the American spoliation claims dating from the Napoleonic wars. His most deplorable weakness was his encouragement of violent partisanship in American politics.

After his death Jackson's name continued to be a symbol of loyalty to the Union. His staunchest disciples who outlived him, President James Knox Polk, Thomas Hart Benton, Sam Houston, and the Francis Preston Blair family carried forward the torch of nationalism. By a curious reversal of fate, the Whig Party, which had so bitterly fought Jackson in his lifetime, became the strongest force below the Mason and Dixon line to preserve national sentiment. In times of national crisis, such as in 1850 and 1860, the firmness of Jackson in suppressing nullification was an inspiriting example to the upholders of the Union. It was the tragedy of the South that this section failed to hold to the Jackson tradition of nationalism, but followed sectional leaders such as Calhoun, Rhett, and Yancey into secession.

Citations

1. The most colorful biography of Jackson is by MARQUIS JAMES, *Andrew Jackson: The Border Captain*, and *Andrew Jackson, Portrait of a President* (Indianapolis, 1933–1937).
2. J. S. BASSETT, *Life of Andrew Jackson* (Garden City, 1911), I, 64.
3. See A. R. NEWSOME, *The Presidential Election of 1824 in North Carolina* (Chapel Hill, 1939).
4. W. O. LYNCH, *Fifty Years of Party Warfare, 1789–1837* (Indianapolis, 1931), Chap. VI.
5. J. S. BASSETT (ed.), *Correspondence of Andrew Jackson* (Washington, 1926–31), IV, 108–109, and 260.
6. A. M. SCHLESINGER, JR., *The Age of Jackson* (Boston, 1945), Chapters X–XVI; see also JOSEPH DORFMAN, "The Jackson Wage-Earner Thesis," *American Historical Review*, LIV (January, 1949), 296–306.
7. T. P. ABERNETHY, "Andrew Jackson and Southwestern Democracy," *American Historical Review*, XXXIII (Oct., 1927), 64–77.
8. J. D. RICHARDSON, *A Compilation of the Messages and Papers of the Presidents, 1789–1897* (Washington, 1901), II, 590.
9. F. J. TURNER, *The United States, 1830–1850* (New York, 1935), 407–8.
10. See R. C. McGRANE, *The Panic of 1837* (Chicago, 1924), 600–61.

CHAPTER XIII

The Two-Party System
of the Old South

IN contrast to "the solid South" which developed after the Civil War, the ante-bellum South had a vigorous two-party system. Jackson's autocratic measures as President and his violent partisanship produced a strong coalition against him, the Whig party. Formed in 1834, this party took the name "Whig" from the English party label of those opposed to the king. Indeed, cartoonists drew caricatures of Jackson as "King Andrew I" wearing a crown and holding a scepter in his hand. A nucleus of the new party was the group who called themselves National Republicans and who had voted in 1832 for Henry Clay for President. Another element that joined the party was the more extreme Nullifiers, who resented Jackson's stern repression of South Carolina. Other discontented persons who entered the ranks of the opposition were ambitious office-seekers, those who were disgusted with the Spoils System, and the advocates of internal improvements by the Federal government who had been alienated by the Maysville Turnpike veto. Also many Southerners who disliked the influence of Van Buren over the "Old Hero" revolted from administration leadership. The disintegration of the Anti-Masonic Party, which had nominated William Wirt of Baltimore for President in 1831, resulted in some of the members going over to the Whigs. Perhaps the most important factor in the formation of the Whig party in the South was the opposition of conservatives to Jackson's bank policy.

The Jacksonians claimed to be the inheritors of the Jeffersonian tradition with its emphasis on the protection of human rights as opposed to property rights. They elevated the sovereignty of the people and majority rule as their cardinal principles. The Whigs, on the other hand, were identified with the protection of property rights and the advancement of the interests of the business community. Consequently, they were more solicitous for the protection of minority rights. Some of the aristocratic Whigs, in their franker moments, spoke of the common people as "the rabble" and rejected scornfully the doctrine of natural rights and of the equality of man. Indeed, the majority of the party carried on the Federalist tradition of broad construction of the Federal Constitution and an economic program in the interests of the capitalists. In contrast, the Jacksonians, who had the support of the plain people in the South and the laboring vote in the North, wished to restrain by a strict interpretation of the Constitution the powerful industrial groups who sought special favors from the government. Nevertheless, since parties in America are seldom homogeneous but contain both liberal and conservative wings, many humble people belonged to the Whig Party; and vice versa, the Democratic Party in the South eventually became the vehicle of the slave power. Furthermore, a considerable number of Southern Whigs believed in the narrow interpretation of the Constitution and were rightly called State Rights Whigs.[1]

The rise of the Whig Party in Tennessee is especially interesting since this state was the home of Jackson. One of the earliest of the Tennessee Whigs was the frontiersman and wit, David Crockett. This picturesque Indian fighter had been elected in 1827 from western Tennessee to Congress, where he amused his colleagues by his eccentricities and Irish wit. His motives for opposing Jackson, under whom he had fought Indians, were probably a strong sense of independence and jealousy of the fame of Tennessee's favorite son. His opposition to Jackson became pronounced after the latter had removed the government deposits from the National Bank, which incidentally had loaned money to Crockett. The Whigs utilized the opportunity to play up this representative of Tennessee as the opponent of "Old Hickory," and in 1834 invited him to make a tour of the North, arranging enthusiastic receptions and public dinners for him. They intimated that he should run for President, and the immense egotism of Crockett caused him to swallow this flattery. Crockett's name was used as author of a Whig campaign volume satirizing Van Buren, entitled *Life of Martin Van Buren* (1835), but the ghost writer was a Georgia Congressman, Augustin S. Clayton.

Crockett did not develop an important personal following, nor was he as significant in the formation of the Whig party in his native state as were Hugh Lawson White of Knoxville and John Bell of Nashville. White had been an Indian fighter and a judge of the Supreme Court of the state, a man highly respected in Tennessee. He was a strict constructionist, who did not differ greatly in his principles from Jackson. Indeed, he was a friend of the President until 1831, when Jackson tried to persuade him to resign from his position as United States Senator and accept an appointment as Secretary of War in order to permit John H. Eaton to enter the Senate. White refused and became very resentful of the dictatorial manners of the Jackson administration. Moreover, he seems to have resented the growing ascendancy over the President of Van Buren and of the Kitchen Cabinet (whom he called "small men").[2] John Bell represented the conservative business interests and, moreover, he became hostile to Jackson who had opposed his political ambitions. Under the leadership of these men, Tennessee shifted (in the years 1834–36) from an overwhelming support of the Jacksonian party to the Whig camp and remained normally a Whig state as long as that party had a vital existence.[3]

The Whig party in Tennessee seems to have been fostered both by personal animosities and by local needs. East Tennessee desired particularly internal improvements at the expense of the Federal government while middle Tennessee, containing the Bluegrass Basin of Nashville, demanded favorable banking facilities, both of which measures were advocated by the Whig party. Hence a curious coalition of aristocrats and yeomen arose in this state for mutual advantage. The Whigs of East Tennessee had a powerful advocate in "Parson" W. G. Brownlow, editor of the Knoxville *Whig*, who hated abolitionists but loved the Union intensely. Not all of the plain people of this mountainous area, however, voted the Whig ticket, for the Democrats had some plebeian leaders, such as Andrew Johnson of Greeneville, who had been a tailor's apprentice.

A map delineating the location of Whig and Democratic strength in the South shows some very significant correlations. In the lower South the Whigs were strong in the rich delta country and alluvial valley areas of the Mississippi River. The sugar planters of Louisiana supported the Whig party since it stood for a protective tariff. In Alabama the Whigs were clustered in the black counties along the Tennessee River—the Huntsville district—and in the black belt in the middle of the state, of which Montgomery was the center. The Whigs in Alabama normally elected about one-third of the representation in the legislature and in Congress. Only once in Alabama's history were they able to elect the governor. In Georgia the frontier counties, the hill counties of northern Georgia, were pro-Jackson or Democratic, but the cotton area of middle Georgia became Whig under the leadership of the red-headed, belligerent Governor George M. Troup, who formed the State Rights party which joined the national Whig organization.[4]

There was an aphorism concerning the black belt of the lower South, that wherever you found rich soil, there you would find a cotton bale, and sitting on the bale a Negro, and nearby would be a Whig in a silk hat. The great planters joined the Whig party, believing it to be the conservative party, careful of property interests —the broadcloth party. A close correlation existed between Whig strength, concentration of slaves, high land values, and low illiteracy rate of the white population. The Democrats, on the other hand, were strong in the pine barrens and areas of high illiteracy of the white population, of low land values, and of small proportion of slaves.

These generalizations do not apply to South Carolina or the upper South. South Carolina became solidly Democratic. It is true that Calhoun joined the Whigs after the nullification controversy, but only temporarily. The Whig party with its program of a protective tariff, its conservatism in agitating the slavery question, and its broad nationalistic outlook was not a promising vehicle for the Carolinian's views or ambitions. Consequently, he returned to the Democratic party in 1837 by accepting Van Buren's proposal of an Independent Treasury for the Federal government.

In the upper South the Whig party appealed to the business interests as well as to the large conservative planters. Kentucky and

Maryland usually voted for the Whig candidates, partly because of the magnetic influence of Clay, but also because of the hemp interests of Kentucky which demanded tariff protection and the commercial interests of Maryland that needed stable banks. It is a significant fact, however, that Kentucky was pro-Jackson in sentiment as late as 1831, choosing 8 Jacksonian and 4 National Republican Congressmen in that year, although curiously the Clay men won the state legislature.[5] The Bluegrass in the center of Kentucky, the Pennyroyal on the southern border, both rich agricultural areas, and a group of poor counties in the southeast above Cumberland Gap became Whig constituencies. The Democratic strongholds were the mountainous northeast, the tobacco counties in the extreme west, and a block of counties in the hump of the Ohio River where the German and Irish immigrant influence was felt.

In Virginia the constant Whig areas were the Tidewater, the counties along the Great Kanawha River, where the salt, iron, and woolen industries of western Virginia were located. The Whigs were strong in the towns and cities, especially Richmond and the Lynchburg area, where the business interests were powerful. The consistent Democratic districts of Virginia were the upper Shenandoah Valley counties, where the small German farmers were dominant and the southwestern part of the state, also largely occupied by yeoman farmers. The Piedmont area was normally Democratic, but it had a strong Whig element. The Whig leaders, such as Abel P. Upshur and Benjamin W. Leigh, were aristocratic in political thought and were strong believers in state rights.

In North Carolina the distribution of Whig strength has mystified many scholars. The back country and mountainous areas of the state were Whig, while the Tidewater, with the exception of the region of the Albemarle and Pamlico Sounds, was Democratic. The area around Albemarle Sound hoped for Federal aid to construct an ocean inlet into the Sound and obviate the necessity of the long and dangerous trip to Ocracoke Inlet to the south. The western district of North Carolina was also attracted by the Whig program of Federal aid to internal improvements. Moreover, a deep antagonism existed between the West and the planter aristocracy of the East, who had long opposed an equitable representation of the West in the legislature. When the eastern planters supported the Democratic party, partly held in line by the influence of Nathaniel Macon, the yeomen and mountaineers of the West took the opposing side. The leadership of the Whig party, however, was aristocratic, including such men as Governor John Motley Morehead, Senator Willie P. Mangum, William A. Graham, Vice Presidential candidate in 1852, and George E. Badger, Secretary of Navy in the Harrison and Tyler administrations. The Whigs agitated for the calling of the Constitutional Convention of 1835, which gave the people the right to elect the governor and rectified the inequality of representation between the East and West. Consequently, the numerically stronger West was able to elect Whig governors from 1835 to 1850.

The greatest leader of the Whigs was Henry Clay of Kentucky, who stands almost as a symbol of that party. Clay was born in 1777 in Hanover County, Virginia, fifteen miles north of Richmond, the son of a Baptist preacher. He received very little schooling in his youth, and all through his career he suffered from the lack of a sound education. Later in life he liked to picture himself as having suffered as a poor boy, "the mill boy of the slashes," which was a political asset, but actually his family lived in a comfortable frame structure and owned eighteen slaves. One of the important influences on his life was the oratory of Patrick Henry, the great man of Hanover County. His family moved to Richmond, where he became a clerk in a store and later an amanuensis of Chancellor George Wythe, who had a crippled hand. After studying law and being admitted to the Virginia bar, he emigrated in 1797 to Lexington, Kentucky. Here he became the leading criminal lawyer of the state primarily because of his ability as an orator. His marriage to Lucretia Hart, the daughter of a wealthy hemp manufacturer, tended to identify him with the ruling class of planters and hemp manufacturers.[6]

Clay had a personality well suited to success in the youthful state of Kentucky. Tall, six feet, one inch in height, with small gray eyes, and brown hair that became prematurely white, he had the gift of winning friends and influencing people, especially by his wonderful oratorical voice. His warm and genial nature attracted friends to him, and his love of pleasure was another bond of union with the mass of men. He was fond of drinking Kentucky whiskey, playing cards, gambling, dancing, and being the lion at White Sulphur Springs and Olympian Springs in Kentucky. Some of his characteristics are reflected in his many nicknames, "The Cock of Kentucky," "Prince Hal," "Harry of the West," "the Western Star," "the Western Hotspur," and to the Jacksonians, "the Judas of the West."

On his estate of "Ashland" outside of Lexington he raised hemp and fine cattle, horses, and mules. He is credited with introducing Hereford cattle into America in 1817, and he imported merino sheep and jacks of high pedigree into the Bluegrass. That he not only delighted in agriculture but also had a good practical knowledge of farming is shown by an extensive memorandum for his overseer, in which he directs the rotation of crops, corn, wheat, oats, clover, and hemp, and orders the sale of fifty hogs and some fat mules. A list of his taxable property for 1851 which he drafted includes "Ashland," containing 510 acres of land, valued at $40,800, "Mansfield," 125 acres, valued at $6,250, thirty-five horses and mules, one stud horse, "Yorkshire," two jennies, and six head of cattle.[7]

His agricultural interests brought him directly into contact with the institution of slavery, to which he bore a curiously inconsistent relationship. In his early career he had written letters for the *Kentucky Gazette* urging the gradual emancipation of the slaves, but this opposition to the dominant institution did not prevent him from buying, owning, and selling slaves. In 1799 he owned one Negro but the year before he died he had acquired thirty-three taxable slaves, valued at $9,600, and "17 Black tithes under equalization," namely children, valued at $2,000. His will revealed his antislavery feelings, however, for it provided that the issue of his female slaves born after January 1, 1850 should be free, males at twenty-eight years of age, females at twenty-five, that they should be taught to read, write, and cipher, and that they should be sent to Liberia.[8]

In politics, Clay was the advocate of what he called "the American System," which aimed at national self-sufficiency by a tariff policy to encourage American manufacturers and by Federal appropriations for internal improvements. In support of a protective tariff he made a notable argument in Congress in 1824 justifying such a policy by "the home market theory." Unfortunately, Clay's "American System" did not harmonize with the Southerner's concept of the economic interest of his section. Since the South was predominantly an exporting, agricultural region, a high tariff was regarded as an instrument for exploiting the South for the advantage of the North. It was natural, however, that Clay should be an advocate of a protective tariff since the hemp-growing and wool-producing interests of Kentucky demanded tariff protection. Another reason why the "American System" was distasteful to the South as a whole was that it required a liberal construction of the Constitution to sanction Federal appropriations for internal improvements, while the South regarded a strict construction of the Constitution as more suited to its interests.

As the struggle between rival sections began to develop, Clay sought to form an alliance between the West and the North. Not only was he a champion of the National Bank and of a protective tariff, measures desired by the Northern business interests, but also he sided with the North in the opposition to the annexation of Texas, and he was opposed to the extension of slavery. His advocacy of the distribution scheme, which was opposed in the South, was also popular in the North. According to this project the price of western public lands was not to be lowered, but the proceeds from the sale of government lands were to be distributed among the states according to population after 10 per cent had been donated to the state in which the lands lay. This proposal would favor the thickly populated states of the North and deprive the Federal government of a valuable revenue, thus necessitating the maintenance of a high protective tariff. Clay hoped to get the support of the West for this project, which would provide money for internal improvements, but the West preferred a policy of cheap lands, such as Thomas Hart Benton's Graduation Bill, and the preemption of land for squatters, to Clay's panacea.

No man ever desired to be elected President more ardently than did Henry Clay. He was almost a perennial candidate for that office, but he failed to win for a variety of reasons. An eloquent orator and possessing a magnetic personality, he unfortunately had no military record, and twice his party rejected him for a candidate who had the glamor of a military hero. Furthermore, Clay was not on the popular side of many of the great controversies of his day. In a

A SOUTHERNER WITH A NATIONAL OUTLOOK

Portrait of Henry Clay by Oliver Frazier, a Kentucky artist, 1808–1864.

CALHOUN, THE SECTIONAL PATRIOT

A complex personality who loved the Union yet became a sectional leader. A portrait attributed to G. P. A. Healy. (Courtesy of Henry Gourdin Young and the Frick Art Reference Library.)

period of the rising power of the common man, he sought to advance the business interests, the money power of the North. Moreover, he failed to appreciate the ardent desire of his section to expand. His antislavery sympathies, revealed signally at the close of his career by the Pindell letter of 1849 urging the adoption of a plan of gradual emancipation, proved to be an element of weakness in his political career, for he was distrusted by the extremists of both sections.

His solutions of the great problems of his era were compromises, a role that caused him to be called "the Great Pacificator." Compromise was a natural policy for a representative of Kentucky, a border state, and was a sound method of preserving a Union composed of sections with clashing economic interests. It is a significant fact that Clay's successor in the Senate, the Whig leader J. J. Crittenden, was also a compromiser. Clay's constant defeats in the Presidential races caused tears to flow down the cheeks of the respectable and educated classes. The deep affection in which he was held by the Whigs is expressed in the remark of a charming young woman, Ellen McCollam, the wife of a Louisiana planter, who ate gumbo with the old statesman in 1844 and found him a fascinating person, "What a pity such a man should ever die." [9]

The motley elements which composed the Whig party were unable to unite on a Presidential candidate in 1836. Various state legislatures nominated their favorite sons—Webster nominated by Massachusetts, William Henry Harrison by Ohio, and Hugh Lawson White by Tennessee and Alabama. The strongest of these candidates in the South was White. In the election he carried Tennessee and Georgia, Senator Willie P. Mangum of North Carolina received the electoral vote of South Carolina, while Harrison developed surprising strength, winning Maryland, Delaware, and Kentucky. Van Buren, despite his unpopularity below the Mason and Dixon line, was in general supported by the politicians and some influential Southern editors, such as Thomas Ritchie of the Richmond *Enquirer*. Aided by the powerful Federal patronage wielded by Jackson, he won the election. The Democratic candidate for Vice President, Richard Mentor Johnson of Kentucky, did not receive a majority of the electoral vote but was chosen by the Senate, the only time in our history that such a method of election was necessary.

In 1840 the Whigs rejected their most eminent leader, Henry Clay, and nominated William Henry Harrison as their standard bearer. In order to placate Southern Whigs and gain State Rights support, Senator John Tyler was nominated for the Vice Presidency. The Whigs contained so many heterogeneous elements that they were unable to agree on a platform and therefore dispensed with that formality. Harrison was born in the fine old plantation house of "Berkeley" on the James River in Virginia and was educated at William and Mary College. He had been territorial governor of Indiana, in which position he had been aggressive in taking land away from the Indians by treaty. Much of his fame was based on his record as an Indian fighter at the battle of Tippecanoe (1811), in which he won a dubious victory, and on his career as a general in the War of 1812. An aristocrat by birth and rearing, he lived in an imposing mansion at North Bend, Ohio. Nevertheless, he became the beneficiary of an amazing political hoax which represented him as a man of the plain people. A Democratic newspaper of Baltimore sneered at the old gentleman by declaring that he would be content to live in a log cabin on a pension of $2,000 a year, drinking hard cider and studying moral philosophy. The Whig newspapers and orators took up this myth and exploited it.

During the Presidential campaign of 1840 the mass of voters were deluded by slogans and juvenile electioneering devices. Enthusiastic devotees wearing coonskin caps held torchlight processions and, rendered hilarious by hard cider, sang such songs as the "Hard Cider Quick Step." In the villages and towns log cabins were erected at Whig headquarters where barrels of hard cider were always on tap. Whig orators practiced the art of demagogy. In campaigning for Harrison, Webster apologized for not being born in a log cabin but condoned his mistake by declaring that his brother had been born in such a humble dwelling. Clay simplified the issues of the campaign by declaring that it was a contest between palaces and log cabins, between champagne and cider.

Martin Van Buren, the Democratic candidate, was represented as an aristocrat who had no sympathy for the common man. Orators with vivid imaginations pictured him as lavishing great sums of money on luxurious appointments at the White House. He anointed his whiskers with cologne, they said, he wore corsets to reduce his figure, and even his dish rags had lace on them. "Van, Van, is a used-up man!" they shouted, while they emphasized the military glory of their candidate by the slogan, "Tippecanoe and Tyler too!" Such a campaign of hurrah and tomfoolery, reinforced by the effects of the Panic of 1837 on the party in power, resulted in a landslide for the Whigs whose candidates were elected by a majority of 234 to 60 electoral votes.

When Harrison was inaugurated as the first Whig President at the age of sixty-eight, he tried to demonstrate that he was no feeble old man by recklessly exposing himself to inclement weather. Furthermore, he was besieged by a horde of office-seekers who exhausted his strength. Such excessive strain resulted in sickness and death after serving a month as President. He was succeeded by the Vice President, John Tyler, who retained Harrison's cabinet headed by the great Northern Whig, Daniel Webster.

The accession of Tyler to the Presidency brought to the surface the main division among the Southern Whigs—the State Rights wing of the party and the Clay or National Whigs. Tyler was the leader of the State Rights faction, a strong believer in the strict interpretation of the Constitution.[10] A former Jackson adherent, he had joined the Whig Party primarily because of Jackson's action in the nullification controversy. He was a Virginia aristocrat, born on the plantation of "Greenway" in the Tidewater, the son of a former governor of the state. He was graduated at the precocious age of seventeen from William and Mary College. Tall, with a high forehead and unusually long nose, possessing courteous manners, he had a pronounced feeling of family and state pride as well as a stubborn sense of consistency. Among Presidents, he holds a record which will probably never be surpassed, namely, of being a prolific father, with a brood of fourteen children.

After the death of Harrison, Clay assumed that he would be the power behind the throne. Accordingly, he set forth the program of the Whig Party in a series of resolutions which he introduced into the Senate on June 7, 1841. These proposals for legislation to carry out Whig objectives included the repeal of the Sub-Treasury system of Van Buren's administration, the establishment of a National

Bank, the adoption of a higher protective tariff, and the enactment
of his Distribution Bill. The Distribution Bill had passed Congress
in 1833 but did not become a law because of a pocket veto by Jackson. Clay was able to force his Distribution Bill through Congress
in 1841, but it was a fruitless victory. Owing to Southern pressure, an
amendment had been added to the original bill, which prohibited
the distribution scheme from going into effect if the tariff should
be raised beyond the 20 per cent level fixed by the Compromise
Tariff of 1833. Since the tariff was increased above this ceiling in
the next year, Clay's pet bill became inoperative. The important land
act of the Tyler administration was the Preemption Act of 1841, a
victory for the frontier, which allowed any citizen to preempt 160
acres of the public domain at the price of $1.25 an acre.

The dramatic break between Tyler and the majority of his party
occurred over the issue of rechartering a national bank. The President accepted the repeal of the Independent Treasury Act, or the
Sub-Treasury, but balked on the re-establishment of a National
Bank which the Whigs ardently desired. He seemed willing to accept a central bank that could establish branches in the states, but
only with the previous consent of the states involved. Clay's first
bill for the chartering of a National Bank was vetoed. In order to
cater to Tyler's strict construction views, the Whigs drafted a new
plan for a bank which they called a Fiscal Corporation, but he also
vetoed this bill. The Whigs then became thoroughly disgusted with
their recalcitrant President and held a Congressional caucus which
expelled him from the party. In protest of Tyler's recreancy to
party principles, all of his cabinet resigned except Daniel Webster,
who gave as his excuse for remaining that he was negotiating a treaty
with England, the Webster-Ashburton Treaty. Actually, Webster
was hostile to Clay, his rival for leadership in the party, and he had
no desire to increase the ascendancy of the Kentucky Hotspur by
following his lead. Tyler retained the allegiance of a small fraction
of the Whig Party consisting mainly of Southerners. Henry A. Wise
of Virginia became the leader of this "corporal's guard" in Congress who remained loyal to the discredited President. Thus the
Whig Party was split into two warring factions shortly after they
had won a great victory at the polls.

The formation of the Whig Party had the virtue of giving the South a vigorous two-party system. Following the passage of the Kansas-Nebraska Bill of 1854, the Whig Party virtually disappeared, but strong opposition to the Democratic Party in the South did not cease. The Whig Party deserves praise because of its devotion to the preservation of the Union. When the slavery controversy arose, its leaders, such as Henry Clay, John Bell, and the two younger leaders, Alexander H. Stephens and Robert Toombs of Georgia, sought to prevent the agitation of this dangerous question and to preserve national feeling. For this reason, also, the Whigs, in general, opposed the expansionist program of the Democrats and the Mexican War. Finally, the majority of the Whigs held to the doctrine of the liberal interpretation of the Constitution, which is much closer to the view of our own day, and which, if it had prevailed, would have contributed to strengthening the nation and developing its resources.

By 1850 the common man in the South had attained a large measure of *political* democracy, a development which had been aided by the two-party system. In the early years of the republic the Southern states had been ruled by a slaveholding aristocracy. A fundamental step toward realizing political democracy was made in 1792 when Kentucky in its first constitution discarded property qualifications both for voting and for holding office. Georgia also advanced rapidly toward political democracy, in 1798 removing its previous requirement of paying a tax to vote and by 1824 allowing the people to elect all their officers, including the governor and the judges. In 1810 South Carolina yielded to the pressure of her up-country population and granted white manhood suffrage. By 1810 Maryland also had provided for manhood suffrage and had instituted other democratic reforms, such as the adoption of the written ballot instead of the *viva voce* method of voting, the abolition of plural voting, and the elimination of property qualifications for office-holding. Alabama and Missouri, admitted into the Union in 1819 and 1821, placed no property restrictions on voting or holding office, although in order to qualify to become a member of the legislature in Missouri, the payment of state taxes was required. Thus before the emergence of the Jacksonian movement considerable progress had been made toward democracy within the Southern states.[11]

The Jacksonian movement further accelerated the growth of democracy below the Mason and Dixon line. When Mississippians drafted their first constitution, contrary to the dogmas of frontier historians, they made a conservative constitution, which required the governor to own six hundred acres of land or two thousand dollars of wealth and members of the lower house of the legislature to possess one hundred and fifty acres of land or five hundred dollars of wealth. Furthermore, no person who denied the existence of God or of a future state of rewards and punishments could hold office in the commonwealth, and voting was restricted to those who paid a state tax and were enrolled in the militia. Stirred later by Jacksonian democracy, however, the sovereign people held a constitutional convention in 1832 and removed all property qualifications on voting or officeholding and even provided for the election of judges by popular vote. In Tennessee a constitutional convention in 1834 abolished the undemocratic features of the first constitution of the state, which had confined voting to land-owners and had placed property qualifications on officeholding. In Maryland the aristocratic electoral college which had chosen the state senators was abolished by "the revolution of 1837."

The Jacksonian movement failed to make any great headway in Virginia. The western counties demanded the calling of a constitutional convention, for they resented the unjust system of representation in the legislature whereby the smaller Tidewater counties with much less white population were given the same number of representatives as the more populous western counties. The Tidewater aristocrats were unwilling to surrender their minority control over the legislature since they feared that democratic reforms would enable the western counties to impose heavy taxation on the slaveholding East and also vote taxes for internal improvements and schools. Consequently the constitutional convention of 1829–30, which was attended by the most eminent men of the state, including Ex-Presidents Madison and Monroe, Chief Justice Marshall, and John Randolph of Roanoke, was dominated by the conservatives.

Accordingly, the constitution of 1830 did not remove property qualifications from voting, although it extended the suffrage to leaseholders and housekeepers. It was estimated that after the adoption of the new constitution thirty thousand out of a hundred and fifty thousand white men continued to be excluded from voting.[12] The Piedmont counties were given greater representation in the legislature, but the refusal to adopt the white basis for representation caused the western counties to remain discontented. Indeed, there were many threats of the dismemberment of Virginia which came from beyond the Blue Ridge.

The western section of North Carolina, which was under-represented in the legislature, forced the calling of a constitutional convention in 1835. This body adopted some valuable reforms, such as the election of the governor by popular vote, the abolition of borough representation, and the removal of discriminations preventing Catholics from holding office. The new constitution substituted the word "Christian" for "Protestant" in the old constitution, which had declared that "no person who shall deny the being of God, or the truth of the Protestant religion or the divine authority of either the Old or New Testament" should be permitted to hold office in the state.[13] Jews continued to be disqualified from officeholding in North Carolina until 1868. Although the convention of 1835 retained a property qualification on voting for state senators, it placated the western section of the state by abolishing the old system of equal representation of counties, regardless of size and population. The new constitution adopted Federal population, or the three-fifths ratio, as the basis of representation in the House of Commons and the amount of taxes paid as the basis of representation in the Senate.

The power of the aristocracy continued to be strongly entrenched in South Carolina and Louisiana, more so than in any other states of the Union. In 1808 a compromise was made between the Tidewater and the up-country of South Carolina by which half of the lower house of the legislature, which consisted of one hundred and twenty-four members, represented property—slaves and land—as registered by taxation. Thus the lowland aristocracy was able to prevent legislation hostile to their interests from being passed by the white democracy. In 1860 South Carolina was the most aristocratic state in the nation, the only one which continued to choose Presidential electors, the governor, and state officials by the legislature and to require a high property qualification for its chief executive. Thus state-wide elections were not held in South Carolina, only elections in local units, the largest being the congressional district. The constitution of Louisiana of 1812 was also aristocratic in tone, requiring the governor and the members of the legislature to own considerable land and voters to pay a tax. Although the revised constitution of 1845 granted manhood suffrage, Louisiana remained under the rule of gentleman planters, aided by the change in the constitution in 1852 making total population the basis of representation in the legislature.[14]

During the decade of the 1850's another reform movement liberalized the governments of the less democratic Southern states. The Virginia constitutional convention of 1850, called as a result of the pressure of the West, granted complete manhood suffrage, provided for the election of the governor and the county officials by the people, and abolished plural voting. It refused, however, to adopt the white basis for the apportioning of representation in the lower house of the legislature, which was demanded by the West.[15] Missouri, already a relatively democratic state, extended the power of the people in 1850 by providing for the election, instead of the appointment, of judges. In North Carolina, David S. Reid ended the long rule of the state by the aristocratic Whig leaders when he won the election as governor in 1850 on a platform of abolishing the property qualification of fifty acres of land for voting in senatorial elections, a reform adopted seven years later.

The voting records of the Northern and Southern states throw some light on the comparative democracy of the two sections. Recent studies reveal a striking similarity between the North and the South in the exercise of the franchise.[16] In 1820 during the time of President Monroe, when the one-party system prevailed, a national apathy toward voting existed, only seventeen votes being cast for Presidential electors in Richmond, for example, and only fifty-two in Newport, Rhode Island. The real contest in the Jackson-Adams campaign of 1828, however, brought out a greater vote. Nevertheless, in Georgia the percentage of the white population who participated in the election was only 6.3 per cent, the exact percentage which obtained in Connecticut. Although more than

10 per cent of the white population in Alabama voted in this election, slightly over 5 per cent both in Virginia and Massachusetts, and approximately 8 per cent in Tennessee participated in the election. By 1860 these percentages had increased in Virginia to 13.7 per cent, in Massachusetts to 15 per cent, and in Tennessee to 17.4 per cent. Since the Whigs and Democrats were almost evenly matched in the South, the existence of a genuine two-party system was an element of democracy. Furthermore, during the Jacksonian period, it was a habit in the South for the legislature to instruct the United States Senators of the state how to vote. Most Senators obeyed orders, but some Senators, such as John Tyler, resigned rather than sacrifice their political principles.

Despite a large concentration of wealth in the hands of the planters, Southern society was relatively fluid, permitting the rise of men of humble birth to high political position. Indeed, many of the leading statesmen of the Old South came from the yeoman class, such as Andrew Jackson, John C. Calhoun, Alexander H. Stephens, George McDuffie, Albert Gallatin Brown of Mississippi, Joseph E. Brown of Georgia, and Andrew Johnson. The first governor of Virginia elected by the people (1851) was Joseph Johnson, who had been a poor boy without formal schooling, and the governor of the proud Old Dominion in 1861 was John Letcher, the son of a butcher. After the democratic movement of the Jacksonian period, undignified methods of electioneering arose, and the new leadership tended to be less cultured and less independent of public opinion. Thus, it would seem that on the eve of the Civil War remarkable progress had been made in the South since the time of Jefferson in realizing political democracy.

Yet it is unwise to generalize too confidently concerning the democratic status of the Old South. A distinction should be made between the Southwest and the older Atlantic seaboard states, especially in regard to county government and the apportionment of representation in the legislature. In the older part of the South and in Kentucky, the colonial system survived in county government, at least until 1850 and in some instances until the Civil War. The lives of the citizens were affected in many ways by the ruling oligarchies of the counties—the justices of the peace. These local officers met in the courthouse four times a year to try important cases and to transact administrative and legislative duties. There were on an average about thirty-five justices to a county, but only a small minority attended courts except on important occasions. In Virginia the justices of the peace were appointed by the governor upon the recommendation of the county courts until 1851, after which date they were elected by the people. This undemocratic method of appointment of these officials was followed by Kentucky, the child of Virginia. In both of these states also the power of the gentry was strengthened by the *viva voce* method of voting, which remained intact throughout the ante-bellum period. In North Carolina the justices of the peace continued to be appointed by the governor upon the recommendation of the General Assembly, which in practice resulted in the appointment of those candidates recommended by the county representatives. Since the justices of the peace appointed most of the local officials, the effect of this practice was the short ballot for the people of the county. A genuine progress toward democratizing local government, however, took place in the newer states of the South between 1820 and 1850 so that by the latter date eight out of thirteen Southern states had given the voters control over the county officials.[17]

In respect to state government, Alabama, Mississippi, Tennessee, Texas, and Missouri, all lying west of the Appalachian Mountains, had become technically democratic by 1850. In these states the governor was elected by the people, manhood suffrage existed, no property qualifications were imposed on officeholding, the county governments were democratic, and, particularly important, the apportionment of the legislature was on the basis of white population. Yet the creation of democratic machinery does not seem to have been followed by important social reforms for the common people, such as vigorous educational programs, fair taxation, good roads, and control over banks. Too often the sons of the plain people who arose to influential political positions forgot their lowly origins and became zealous agents of the vested interests and the ideology of the slavocracy. The antislavery controversy tended to divert attention from state issues. Furthermore, in many counties courthouse rings or cliques and influential families controlled the local governments and the representatives in the legislature.[18] The political power of a family was demonstrated in Arkansas, where the "Johnson Family" virtually ruled the state from its admission into the Union to 1860.

An important criterion in determining whether the state government was controlled by an aristocracy or by the people was the basis used in apportioning representation in the legislature. The presence of a large slave population in the South, in some states over half of the population, made this question of the principle of apportionment extremely significant. If slaves were counted as freemen or at three-fifths of their number in the allotment of legislators, obviously the planter group and the black belt would have much more power than if the white basis were adopted. In North Carolina, Georgia, and Maryland (until 1852) Federal population, or the three-fifths ratio, was the basis of apportionment. In Louisiana and Maryland (after 1852) total population was the basis of apportionment, the most undemocratic measure of all, since Negro slaves were thus counted at their full number. In South Carolina representation in the legislature was based on a combination of white population and taxes, and in Virginia the white basis was rejected in 1850 in favor of a compromise, or mixed basis, of white population and taxes. In addition to slave representation, some Southern states practiced an undemocratic discrimination against the cities, especially New Orleans, Louisville, and Baltimore, by refusing to give them a fair proportion of representatives in the legislature.

The taxation policies pursued by the Southern states, furthermore, indicated undue power over the government by the planters or the slavocracy. The Southern people during the ante-bellum period conceived of the state as a *laissez-faire* institution and were reluctant to vote money for schools or social services. Consequently, prior to the panic of 1837 taxation was remarkably low. Many of the states, however, acquired large bonded debts when they departed from *laissez-faire* principles in establishing banks and undertaking internal improvements, and as a result taxes were sharply increased during the latter part of the ante-bellum period. In several of the Southern states rudimentary income and inheritance taxes were adopted at this time, but by far the main source of revenue was the general property tax, which in Virginia, for example, constituted 90 per cent of the total amount of tax collected during the decade of the 1850's. All the Southern states, except Arkansas, imposed poll taxes, usually 50 cents or $1, but payment of the tax was not a prerequisite for voting as it became in the post-bellum period.

The planters were able to secure especially light taxation of their slaves. The chief form of taxation of this type of property was a poll tax, such as the Alabama tax in 1852 of $1 on slaves from fifteen to thirty years old, 80 cents on those from thirty to forty years old, and 50 cents on those from forty to fifty years old. In Virginia after 1850 slaves under twelve years of age paid no taxes and those over that age were assessed at no higher than $300 per individual. In North Carolina on the eve of the Civil War land was taxed $1.50 per $1,000 valuation, but slaves, regardless of value, were taxed only by a poll tax of 50 cents. The small amount of taxes paid by the large planters is illustrated by some specific examples recorded in 1849 by Solon Robinson. In Louisiana, Thomas Pugh, one of the largest planters, paid only $200 taxes on his plantation of "Madewood," containing 3,000 arpents of land and 201 slaves, assessed at $206,265. A plantation near Society Hill, South Carolina, containing 4,200 acres, valued at $63,000, was taxed $70 and 254 slaves assessed at $89,900 were taxed $193.04.

The light taxes on slave property caused considerable discontent to arise in the western counties and among the towns and cities. A public-spirited slaveholder of Wake County, North Carolina, Moses Bledsoe, led a movement in 1856 to tax all property, slaves as well as land, *ad valorem*. Three years later the Raleigh Workingmen's Association took up the issue, and a newspaper, the *Ad Valorem Banner*, was founded to agitate the cause. In 1860 the Whig candidate for governor, John Pool, waged his campaign largely on this issue of advocating *ad valorem* taxation. He was defeated, and the question of fair taxation of slaves was pushed into the background by the coming of the Civil War.[19] At the same time the yeomen of western Virginia were becoming more class conscious and entering into politics against the slaveholders. In the Secession Convention of 1860 the western delegates proposed an amendment to the constitution equalizing taxation and abolishing the system of partiality in taxing slave property. Even in South Carolina, the citadel of Southern aristocracy, there arose on the eve of the Civil War an ominous demand from the up-country and the workingmen of Charleston for a democratic reform of the state constitution. But the agitation of the secession issue diverted attention from state politics and social injustice to the absorbing questions of federal relations and Southern nationalism. Thus the privileged position of the wealthy slaveholders was not disturbed by an incipient revolt of the submerged classes, such as came after the Civil War, in the Tillman movement, and in the overthrow of the Bourbons.

Citations

1. For the origins of the Southern Whig Party, see A. C. Cole, *The Whig Party in the South* (Washington, 1913); E. M. Carroll, *Origins of the Whig Party* (Durham, 1925); H. H. Simms, *Rise of the Whigs in Virginia, 1824–1840* (Richmond, 1929); and Paul Murray, *The Whig Party in Georgia, 1825–1853* (Chapel Hill, 1948).
2. L. P. Gresham, "The Public Career of Hugh Lawson White," *Tennessee Historical Quarterly*, III (March–December, 1944), 308.
3. Powell Moore, "The Revolt against Jackson in Tennessee, 1835–1836," *Journal of Southern History*, II (August, 1936), 334–359.
4. Paul Murray, "Economic Sectionalism in Georgia Politics, 1825–1855," *Journal of Southern History*, X (August, 1944), 293–307.
5. John Coffin, "A History of the Whig Party in Kentucky," Unpublished Manuscript, University of Kentucky, Chap. II, 39.
6. The two best biographies of Clay are Bernard Mayo, *Henry Clay, Spokesman of the New West* (Boston, 1937) and G. G. Van Deusen, *Life of Henry Clay* (Boston, 1937).
7. "Henry Clay, List Taxable Property for 1851," MS owned by J. Winston Coleman, Jr., of Lexington, Ky.
8. "Last Will and Testament of Henry Clay, July 10, 1851," MS in Fayette County Court House.
9. J. C. Sitterson, "The McCollams: a Planter Family of the Old and New South," *Journal of Southern History*, VI (August, 1940), 357.
10. See O. P. Chitwood, *John Tyler, Champion of the Old South* (New York, 1939).
11. Fletcher M. Green, *Constitutional Development in the South Atlantic States, 1776–1860* (Chapel Hill, 1930), Chaps. IV and V.

12. C. H. AMBLER, *Sectionalism in Virginia from 1776 to 1861* (Chicago, 1910), 138, and Federal Census of Virginia, 1830.

13. *Proceedings and Debates of the Convention of North Carolina Called to Amend the Constitution of the State* (Raleigh, 1836), Appendix, p. 416.

14. See ROGER W. SHUGG, *Origins of Class Struggle in Louisiana, A Social History of White Farmers and Laborers during Slavery and After, 1840–1875* (University, La., 1939), Chap. V.

15. See CLEMENT EATON, "Henry A. Wise, A Liberal of the Old South," *Journal of Southern History*, VII (November, 1941), 487–490.

16. C. S. SYDNOR, "The One-Party Period of American History," *American Historical Review*, LI (April, 1946), 439–451; F. M. Green, "Democracy in the Old South," *Journal of Southern History*, XII (February, 1946), 3–24.

17. C. S. SYDNOR, *The Development of Southern Sectionalism, 1819–1848* (Baton Rouge, 1948), Chap. II.

18. Professor W. B. Hesseltine has observed "the real central theme of Southern history seems to have been the maintenance of the planter class in control," "Some New Aspects of the Pro-Slavery Argument," *Journal of Negro History*, XXI (January, 1936), 14.

19. C. O. Norton, *The Democratic Party in Ante-Bellum North Carolina, 1835–1861* (Chapel Hill, 1930); C. H. AMBLER, *Francis H. Pierpont, Union War Governor of Virginia and Father of West Virginia* (Chapel Hill, 1937).

CHAPTER XIV

Calhoun and State Rights

T HE growth of sectionalism in the nation from 1820 to 1861 is the dominant political theme of the period. Increasingly the South began to realize the implications of its minority status in the nation and to rely on state rights as a means of protection. The South as "a conscious minority" could follow several paths of development, one which led to Southern nationalism, another, to find allies in the North within the national parties, and a third, to seek defense for its way of life by constitutional amendments. All these methods were advocated by different groups below the Mason and Dixon line. Senator John C. Calhoun sought to defend Southern interests by strengthening the federal character of the central government, by forming an alliance with the West, and finally in desperation, by forming a Southern *bloc* and securing constitutional amendments protecting the South.

Calhoun was a complex personality, not "the cast-iron man" whom Harriet Martineau described, but a flexible person who adjusted himself to the changing economic interests of the South while he thought he was moved only by a devotion to "principle." Indeed, the key to Calhoun's life is to be found in understanding these remarkable changes. The supreme tragedy of his life was not the wreck of his political ambitions through the intrigue of Van Buren, but the fact that despite his genuine love for the Union he was led to advocate measures which tended to destroy it. The factor which prevented Calhoun from being a truly national statesman was the existence of slavery in the South. After the close of the nullification struggle he devoted his life to the preservation of this archaic institution, thus becoming the champion of property rights instead of human rights in the South.

Calhoun was the intellectual leader of the pro-slavery South, formulating the political theories which rationalized its economic interests. He did not originate, however, the doctrines which he so ably advocated, for they were implicit in the political, social, and economic trends of the beleaguered South. Not only was he a one-man "brain trust" for the solution of the problems of his section, but also he became the South's greatest agitator and propagandist for Southern unity against the antislavery forces of the North. Yet a modern reader may wonder whether the oratory and the great forensic battles in the Senate which Calhoun waged against Clay and Webster in behalf of states rights were really significant. When Congressmen voted, they usually voted for their interests regardless of the scintillating sword play of words.

The young Calhoun is an attractive figure in the portrait gallery of the South's heroes. Born in the back country of South Carolina near Abbeville in 1782, he developed into an angular young man, six feet two inches in height, with a superabundant mane of dark hair, deep-set hazel eyes, high cheek bones, strong jutting chin, and a wide mouth. His family belonged to the Scotch-Irish yeomanry who had emigrated from Pennsylvania into the frontier country of the Carolinas. From his Scotch-Irish forbears he had inherited some dominant traits which clearly marked his career as a statesman. He was serious in temperament, lacking in humor, and an aggressive fighter in the political arena, but never descending to fight a duel. Chaste in private life—he never sowed wild oats—he was incorruptible in public life.[1]

Calhoun matured late. Until he was nearly nineteen years old he worked on his father's farm side by side with his slave companion, Sawney. He then decided to get an education, and with all the deep seriousness of his nature he studied two years in the log cabin academy of Moses Waddel at Appling, Georgia, entered the Junior Class at Yale College, was graduated with highest honors from this New England institution in 1804, and prepared for a law career by studying in the famous school of Judge Tapping Reeve at Litchfield, Connecticut. In 1811 he married an heiress of the lowland aristocracy of South Carolina and in that year entered Congress, joining the ranks of the War Hawks.

In the early part of his career Calhoun deserved great praise. "Calhoun," John Quincy Adams wrote on October 15, 1821, "is a man of fair and candid mind, of honorable principles, of clear and quick understanding, of cool self-possession, of enlarged philosophical views, and of ardent patriotism. He is above all sectional and factious prejudices more than any other statesman of this Union with whom I have ever acted." [2] In his speeches before Congress he refused to follow the custom of his period of indulging in florid oratory and artificial gesticulation. He relied upon close reasoning, logical argument, lucid statement, and sincerity to convince his audience. Monroe appointed him Secretary of War, in which position he demonstrated fine ability as an administrator. He reorganized the department to a high degree of efficiency, eliminated corruption, fought earnestly for an adequate system of fortifications and a strong army. One of his most admirable policies was his humanitarian Indian policy by which he sought to civilize the dependent tribes and protect them from exploitation by the powerful fur interests. [3]

The point to be emphasized about the young Calhoun was his ardent nationalism. His career as a War Hawk has already been discussed. During the period following the War of 1812 he voted for the nationalistic program of a protective tariff, the establishment of the Second National Bank, and the Bonus Bill for internal improvements. In speaking on the Bonus Bill, February 4, 1817, he declared that he was "no advocate for refined arguments on the constitution. The instrument was not intended as a thesis for the logician to exercise his ingenuity on. It ought to be construed with plain, good sense. . . ." [4] Later, Calhoun sought to attract the West into an alliance with the South by favoring a land policy that would appeal to the West, even to the extent of granting the public lands to the states to be used for internal improvements.

One of the weaknesses of Calhoun was his intense craving to become President, but he was a man of high principles who would not stoop to unscrupulous means to attain his end. At the height of his career he received a disastrous political blow from which he never recovered. He incurred the bitter enmity of Jackson, an unrelenting hostility that blasted his favorable prospects of attaining his heart's desire. The master architects in defeating Calhoun's ambition were a cabal of Van Buren's friends, intent on making "the Little Magician" the successor of Jackson. The Peggy O'Neale affair had done much to elevate Van Buren in the good graces of the President and to sow distrust of Calhoun in his mind. The breaking point, however, did not occur until May, 1830, when Jackson received proof that the South Carolina statesman had favored a court martial in 1818 to try him for his Florida invasion.

For years Jackson had believed that Calhoun had defended him on that occasion in Monroe's cabinet. Calhoun had allowed the vindictive general to hold this illusion.[5] At a strategic moment in the developing rivalry between Van Buren and Calhoun to succeed to the Presidency a group of Van Buren's friends devised a plot to alienate Jackson completely in his support of the formidable South Carolinian. It was a complicated intrigue, engineered by friends of both Jackson and Van Buren, especially Major William B. Lewis and James A. Hamilton, son of the famous Alexander. The ultimate stage of the plot was reached when Jackson was shown a letter from William H. Crawford, who had been in Monroe's cabinet, revealing the fact that in 1818 Calhoun had advocated a court martial for the obstreperous general. The Old Hero was now thoroughly aroused by this evidence of what he regarded as Calhoun's duplicity. He sent the Crawford letter to Calhoun for his denial or confirmation. The latter replied in a fifty-two page letter, not denying the charge, but observing that this revival of an old and forgotten controversy at this time was an intrigue. The breach between these two leading Southern statesmen became public when the correspondence between them was published early in 1831. The consequences of this quarrel, based on such petty grounds, became far-reaching and tragic, for Calhoun lost his chance to become President, and possibly the course of American history may have thereby been changed.

In the latter part of the 1820's South Carolina, in common with the older Atlantic seaboard states, was suffering an economic decline, a phenomenon which has been called "the rural depression." [6] Cotton sold at the peak of 29.5 cents a pound in June, 1825, thus stimulating heavy planting for the next season, but the price of the staple dropped to 12 cents a pound in 1826 and 9.3 cents during the following year. It was natural that the planters should seek to find some cause for their economic suffering—a scapegoat. Instead of blaming themselves and their forbears for wasteful agriculture that took no thought of the future, and instead of considering the factor of overproduction, they hit upon the protective tariff as the cause of their distress. The tariff was prejudicial to the economic interests of the planters, but the main reasons for their inadequate returns from agriculture were the exhaustion of their soils and their inability to compete in cotton production with the rich virgin soils of the new Southwest.

The policy of a protective tariff, begun in 1816, had led to increases in the customs duties until in 1828 the Tariff of Abominations stirred deep resentment in the South. Even before this unjust law was passed, Robert J. Turnbull had written letters in the Charleston *Mercury,* entitled "The Crisis," protesting violently against the high tariff policy and threatening secession. Dr. Thomas Cooper, president of the University of South Carolina (then called South Carolina College), declared that the time had come for the people of his adopted state to calculate the value of the Union to themselves. In 1828 a committee of the South Carolina legislature had published an ominous document of warning to the North, entitled the *South Carolina Exposition and Protest.* Calhoun was the author, but this fact was kept secret.[7]

The Carolina leader had radically changed his attitude toward the tariff since 1816. At that time he thought that his native state could develop manufactures under the protection of such a law and thus obtain a more balanced economy. But the years had demonstrated the fallacy of his youthful optimism, and he now believed that the agricultural section of the nation was being exploited by the industrial section through the tariff. In 1827 came the turning point in his public attitude to the protection, or subsidizing, of manufactures. The introduction of the Woolens Bill into the Senate brought forward again the issue of tariff protection. The division of yeas and nays on this measure was equal, which forced him as president of the Senate to cast the deciding vote—a negative vote. In New England Webster had also made a remarkable reversal in his stand on the tariff as the economic interest of his section shifted.

During the next year, yielding to the pressure of lesser political leaders in his state, Calhoun drafted an elaborate argument against the constitutionality of the tariff in the *South Carolina Exposition and Protest*. In this document he pointed out that the South exported two-thirds of all domestic products sent to foreign nations by the United States—chiefly cotton, tobacco, rice, sugar, and naval stores. In return for these exports, England and other European countries sent manufactured goods which were taxed at the customs ports for the benefit of New England and the Middle States manufacturers. He observed also that the tariff of 1828, which averaged 45 per cent *ad valorem*, deprived the South of cheap manufactured goods and thus increased the cost of the production of cotton. Furthermore, this bill was imposed by a two-thirds majority on the one-third of the population who produced two-thirds of the exports of the country. He proclaimed that the inhabitants of the South were "the serfs" of the tariff system, which extracted $16,650,000 annually from them in duties, while the national government disbursed to the South less than two million dollars annually. Thus the South was being ruthlessly exploited by the North.

What was the remedy? Not secession, as the radical leaders, Dr. Thomas Cooper, Robert J. Turnbull, and Robert Barnwell Rhett had suggested. Disunion was abhorrent to Calhoun at this time. His remedy was what he liked to call "State Veto," but others called nullification. This legal doctrine was derived primarily from the Virginia and Kentucky Resolutions of 1798, the last of which had declared that the several states had the right to nullify an unconstitutional law. The South Carolina statesman took a more extreme step of declaring that a single state could nullify a Federal law which it regarded as unconstitutional. The Federal government, he maintained, was merely the agent of the states, created by the Constitution, and it could not act legally beyond its written instructions in the compact, or contract, of the Constitution. In the case of grand clashes between the state and the Federal government over a question of the interpretation of the Constitution, there was no common umpire (the Supreme Court could not be considered such, since it was a party of the Federal government). Each state, therefore, had a right to judge whether the Federal government had violated the Constitution. To arrest the operation of an unconstitutional law it was necessary for a specially elected convention to exercise the sovereignty of a state.

Calhoun did not take an active part in the nullification movement until the summer of 1831. The crisis in his career as a national statesman seems to date, not from 1828, but from his quarrel with Jackson which blasted his immediate prospects to become President. His authorship of the *Exposition* was then made public, and on August 28, 1832, he gave a definitive statement of his views on nullification in the "Fort Hill Letter" ("Fort Hill" was the name of Calhoun's home near Pendleton in the up-country of South Carolina). In this document he made important qualifications of the doctrine as expounded by the extremists. He recognized an appeal beyond the sovereign state, namely, a three-fourths majority of the states—the ratifying power of the Constitution. If an amendment conferring upon the Federal government the disputed power should be ratified, the dissatisfied state must submit or leave the Union. Calhoun did not believe that a state could defy the national will and remain within the Union. Even in this modified form the nullification doctrine seems to be an impracticable instrument which would permit a state to refuse to obey a national law that it did not like and thus paralyze the action of the Federal government in carrying out the will of the people.

Calhoun refused to recognize that the Constitution had changed since 1789. Actually a new concept of the nation had arisen which reduced the power of self-determination, or sovereignty, of the individual states. The framers of the Constitution and the Americans of 1789 believed that sovereignty could be divided and that the Constitution gave sovereignty to the national government in some departments of political action and to the state government in other fields. But Calhoun accepted a new definition of sovereignty expounded by the English theorist, John Austin, that sovereignty was indivisible, for the ultimate power of decision cannot be divided. This idea was wittily expressed by John Randolph of Roanoke, who compared sovereignty to a woman's virtue, observing that it was just as absurd to ask a state to surrender part of her sovereignty as to ask a woman to surrender a part of her virginity.

The *South Carolina Exposition* was a statement of South Carolina's grievances and a warning, which was considered and published by the legislature but not formally adopted. The state now waited to see what would be the policy of the new administration in regard to the unjust and oppressive tariff legislation. Since Jackson considered himself a native of South Carolina and was a cotton planter and a slave-owner, the Carolinians expected sympathy and aid from him. In January, 1830, Senator Robert Hayne delivered a magnificent speech in the Senate, seeking to form an alliance between South and West, and defending the South Carolina doctrines, to which Webster replied, asserting national supremacy. In the following April at the Jefferson anniversary dinner, designed to promote the South-West alliance, Jackson gave a toast which was a sharp warning to those hot-headed Carolinians who might attempt the nullification of a Federal law—"Our (Federal) Union—it must be preserved!" Calhoun replied with a nobler toast: "The Union—next to our liberty, most dear. May we always remember that it can only be preserved by distributing equally the benefits and burthens of the Union." [8]

The first effort to call a convention to nullify, in the autumn elections of 1830, was defeated. Two years later, however, a new tariff law was enacted which continued the high level of duties that had exploited the South. The North rejected a compromise, and Jackson refused to veto. South Carolina decided that the time to resist had arrived. By a two-thirds majority the legislature summoned a convention which assembled at Columbia and voted (November 24, 1832) that the Tariff Acts of 1828 and 1832, being unconstitutional, were null and void. The nullification ordinance was to go into effect February 1, 1833, after which date no Federal duties could be collected in South Carolina ports and no appeal from the state courts to the Supreme Court of the United States in regard to the tariff was permissible. The adoption of the nullification ordinance was preceded by a bitter fight between the nullifiers, led by Robert Y. Hayne and James Hamilton, Jr., and the Unionists led by such cool-headed men as James Louis Petigru, Daniel E. Huger, Joel R. Poinsett, and Benjamin F. Perry, editor of the *Greenville Mountaineer*.

South Carolina appealed to her sister states below the Mason and Dixon line to join in this movement of resisting the oppression of the

Federal government. But not a single other Southern state came to her aid by nullifying the obnoxious tariff law. However, Georgia proposed a Southern convention. Disaster then faced South Carolina, especially since Jackson privately announced that he would hang nullifiers on the trees of the state as traitors. Publicly he issued a proclamation written by his Secretary of State, Edward Livingston, declaring nullification to be a destruction of the Union which he would not tolerate. South Carolinians then began to prepare for defending the homeland from the invasion of Federal forces.

In this crisis Calhoun resigned the Vice Presidency and was elected to the Senate by the South Carolina legislature. His journey from his plantation at "Fort Hill" to the national capitol has been compared to Luther's journey to the Diet of Worms. Calhoun did not know whether Jackson would order his arrest for treason when he arrived in Washington or permit him to take his seat in the Senate. In the Senate he spoke earnestly in defense of his native state, but his words had little effect. Henry Clay stepped forward and offered a compromise tariff bill, gradually reducing the tariff duties for a period of nine years until by July 1, 1842, they should stand at a revenue basis of 20 per cent. Privately Clay told his friends that one Congress could not bind later Congresses—a Machiavellian line of argument.

In the meanwhile the South Carolinians had postponed the date of the operation of nullification. On March 1, 1833, the Clay compromise tariff, as well as a "Force Bill," giving the President authority to employ the armed forces of the United States to collect the customs in the disaffected state, were passed. South Carolina then repealed the nullification ordinance, but as a last gesture of defiance, nullified the Force Act. Actually, South Carolina had won in the nullification controversy, for she had accomplished her object of forcing the lowering of the tariff. At the same time the doctrine of nullification received a fatal blow, since South Carolina had been isolated in her struggle against the Federal government. The problem of the state veto has recently been revived on a broader scale in the Council of the United Nations where it remains as difficult a question to solve as in the time of Calhoun.

Calhoun regarded his nullification, or state veto, doctrine as a

Union-saving device that would allay sectional discontent by protecting minority rights. Gradually the former War Hawk lost his enthusiasm for broad national measures and placed the interests of his section above those of the nation. After the subsiding of the nullification movement, he was aroused to a defense of Southern interests by the rise of the Northern abolition movement. The South Carolina statesman was one of the foremost Southern leaders in working for legislation to quarantine his section from the abolition contagion. He appealed to the Northern states to suppress their antislavery societies and the antislavery press. From Congress he demanded that rules be adopted which would prevent the reception of antislavery petitions by Congress—the most thoroughgoing type of gag resolution—and legislation authorizing the Southern states to exclude from the mails publications regarded as incendiary. He believed that slavery was not a national but a local problem which should be exclusively handled by the people of the Southern states, who understood the Negro and who were directly affected by the race problem.

Calhoun had a remarkably prophetic intelligence. Not only did he foresee the War for Southern Independence, but he also predicted that a civil conflict to free the slaves would result in the Negroes becoming, not slaves of individual masters, but slaves of the community. His clairvoyant genius made him gloomy, like Cassandra, for he never quite lost his early nationalism and his love of the Union, which he believed to be in grave danger from the antislavery "fanaticism" of the North. His constant advice to his section was to meet the enemy (the Northern antislavery men) "on the frontier." Making concessions to the abolitionists would not satisfy them, but lead to bolder encroachments on the rights of the South and to more intolerable insults. Therefore the proper course for the South to pursue was not to yield an inch of Southern rights. In order to protect their vital interests, Southerners must give up their party loyalties and unite in an unbreakable phalanx. Realizing that the South's relative strength in the Union was ebbing each day on account of the rapid growth of the North in population and economic resources, he believed that the cause of the South would be lost by pursuing a temporizing course. "If there must be an issue," he said in 1836, "now is our time. We never can be more united or better prepared for the struggle, and I, for one, would much rather meet the danger now, than turn it over to those who come after us." [9] A few years later, he reiterated this advice, "The true policy is to take bold ground and force an issue as soon as possible."

During these years of agitating to arouse the Southern people to realize the dangers of the abolition movement, Calhoun was not unmindful of his frustrated Presidential aspirations. After his return to the Democratic fold during Van Buren's administration, he aspired to win the Presidency by forming an alliance between the South and the West. Such a powerful partnership would curb the menace of the industrial Northern states and might elevate him to the Presidency. In 1843 he launched his candidacy by publishing a campaign biography which he himself wrote, but he induced Representative R. M. T. Hunter of Virginia to assume the paternity of this anonymous panegyric. In April, 1844, his appointment as Secretary of State in Tyler's cabinet gave him a splendid opportunity to win a large political following by championing the annexation of Texas, but he muffed his chance by his foolish Lord Aberdeen letter in which he maintained that annexation of this region was needed to protect Southern slavery.

His claim to be more than a sectional statesman was bolstered by his renewed interest in internal improvements. On this issue primarily he hoped to base an alliance between the South and West. In 1845 he was invited to attend a Southern Convention at Memphis. Here he proposed a great east and west railroad that would connect Memphis and Charleston, a more appealing project to Southerners than Robert Y. Hayne's plan of a line uniting Charleston and Cincinnati. At this convention he returned to his earlier idea of obtaining the aid of the Federal government in undertaking internal improvements. He announced his doctrine that the Mississippi River and its tributaries were so vast that they should be regarded as an inland sea, and therefore they formed a proper object for the expenditure of Federal funds for the improvement of their navigation. Thus Calhoun anticipated some of the aspects of "regional planning" which as a developed program lay far ahead in the next century.

Although he had opposed the Mexican War, he was determined that the South should be treated fairly in the distribution of the spoils.

Consequently he powerfully resisted the adoption by Congress of the Wilmot Proviso (first introduced in 1846) which would have excluded slavery from any territory acquired from Mexico. He elaborated the doctrine that the Constitution protected the establishment of slavery in all Federal territories. Only when a territory had attained the status of a state could it exclude slavery, and Congress had no power to pass legislation prohibiting Southerners from entering the common domain of the nation with their slaves.

When California in the autumn of 1849 drafted a constitution forbidding slavery and applied for admission to the Union, Calhoun was greatly alarmed by this threat to the preservation of the sectional equilibrium in the Senate—a safeguard to slavery. He sought to form a Southern bloc in Congress to protect Southern rights. For this purpose he composed an "Address of the Southern Delegates in Congress to Their Constituents," which presented the dangers that menaced his section from the antislavery crusade and urged Southerners, regardless of party loyalties, to unite to resist encroachment on their rights by the North. As early as 1845–47 Calhoun had attempted to organize a third party based on Southern Rights by which he designed to elevate himself into the Presidency via election by the House of Representatives.[10] When the efforts to form a Southern third party and a Southern *bloc* in Congress failed, he agitated for the calling of a Southern convention, which resulted in the assembly of the Nashville Convention of 1850 (discussed in a later chapter). His last days were spent feverishly trying to alarm and unite the South in order to arrest "the aggression of the North." The only hope for the continuance of the Union, he believed, was for "the South to present with an unbroken front to the North the alternative of dissolving the partnership or of ceasing on their part to violate our rights. . . ." [11]

After Jefferson, Calhoun was the ablest political philosopher produced by the Old South. His ideas of a correct government were formed very much as the political theory of Aristotle was devised, by rationalizing the status quo of the political state in which he lived. Slavery was a social institution which Southerners regarded as of paramount importance, and it must be protected against an aggressive antislavery movement based in the Northern states. The

South was overwhelmingly agricultural, while the industrial interest of the North was becoming increasingly powerful. Politically, the South was a minority group in the nation. How was this section to protect itself within the framework of the Union against a numerical majority that was bent on using its power in Congress to injure the economic interests of the South and its way of life?

Calhoun devoted his magnificent powers of analysis and logic to forge a weapon of defense, a political theory that fitted the needs of the Southern planters. Beginning with a concept of human nature quite different from the romantic idealism of Jefferson or the pessimism of Hamilton, he held that human nature is neither black nor white, but gray—a medium view of human beings. Men are dominated, he thought, by their selfish interests, so that it is essential for a democratic government to provide protection to the minority from the selfishness of the majority. His view of human rights was based on a frank repudiation of the Declaration of Independence with its equalitarian doctrines. He declared that men are unequal and that liberty is the reward of ability and achievement. Therefore liberty must not be thrust upon men, but they must earn it by acquiring the ability to govern themselves. Such ideas he expressed in lucid prose in his essays, *A Disquisition on Government*, and *A Discourse on the Constitution and Government of the United States*, written at the close of his career.

Calhoun's most significant contribution to political theory was made in dealing with the problem of protecting minority rights against a numerical majority. He was only the most prominent of a group of Southern political thinkers who rationalized the status quo of their section into a political theory. Abel P. Upshur, a Tidewater Virginian, in his *A Brief Enquiry into the True Nature and Character of Our Federal Government* (1840) also gave a remarkable analysis of the dangers of majority rule, maintaining that the tyranny of a majority is more destructive of liberty than the tyranny of the few. Calhoun developed an abhorrence for the uncurbed rule of the majority, declaring that the word "democrat" was usually applied to "those who are in favour of the government of the absolute numerical majority to which I am utterly opposed and the prevalence of which would destroy our system and destroy the South." [12] Although this aspect of Calhoun's political thought fits into an anti-democratic tradition, nevertheless, he was a great defender of constitutionalism, an opponent of the totalitarian state, which has a modern validity.

One means of preserving minority rights advocated by Calhoun was the strengthening of the doctrine of state rights, a defense mechanism used by minorities in the North as well as the South. In support of this time-honored device, he proposed the doctrine of the concurrent majority, or of the concurrent voice. The Carolina statesman had observed the working of this formula in the government of his native state. The power of the numerical majority in South Carolina was checked by a compromise in the constitution by which the minority of wealthy slaveholders in the eastern parishes controlled the Senate, which could veto legislation unfavorable to their property interests, while the upland areas of the state, in which the slave interest was weak, was given control of the lower house of the legislature.

Calhoun advocated the application of the doctrine of the concurrent majority to fundamental controversies between the states and the Federal government. He held that in all great clashes between the national government and a state, or group of states, the will of the numerical majority should not be put into force unless the minority consented or concurred. He cited historical examples of this principle such as the working of the jury system, the consuls in the Roman republic, and the Polish diet. He believed that in a nation composed of sections with divergent economic interests the doctrine of the concurrent majority should be exercised in order to preserve liberty. The power to check the numerical majority from adopting an unjust course was needed as a Union-saving device, for it would cause the leaders of a dominant section to be more conciliatory and more cautious in disregarding the rights of weaker sections. In other words, fair compromise would be the basis of an enduring marriage between the sections.

The theory that Calhoun proposed for the protection of minority rights sounds admirable, but it had great practical weaknesses. His agency for the operation of the doctrine of the concurrent majority was the state veto of legislation which was deemed unconstitutional.

Ignoring the function of the Supreme Court of judicial review, he maintained that a state had the right to hold up the execution of an unconstitutional law until three-fourths of the ratifying states—the amending power—could pass on the controversy between the Federal government and the aggrieved state. South Carolina successfully applied this doctrine in the nullification crisis and Northern states practically nullified the Fugitive Slave Act of 1850 by passing Personal Liberty Acts. Nevertheless, Calhoun's doctrine of a state interposition appears impractical as a working instrument of government. At the close of his life he offered another solution of the problem of protecting the South as a conscious minority, namely, the creation of a dual executive for the Federal government, a Southern President and a Northern President, each having a veto power over legislation hostile to the interests of either section.

There is no issue in the modern United States that compares with the slave question of the ante-bellum period in sectionalizing the nation. Today we have minority groups, the Negroes who have multiplied in number from four million in 1860 to fourteen million in 1950, the Jews, the Catholics, and the Communists, whose rights are often threatened or ignored, but we have no powerful geographic section that feels unjustly treated by the nation. Does Calhoun's doctrine of the concurrent majority have any vital application to the modern problem of protecting minority groups? The late Senator William E. Borah of Idaho in arguing against the passage of a Federal anti-lynching law which was violently opposed by Southern Congressmen recurred to the point of view of the dead Carolina statesman. Borah maintained that it was unwise to force a law upon a great minority section like the South by a majority vote of Northern and Western Congressmen. It would be wiser, he said, to let the people of this section handle their own local problems. The progress of education, reason, and persuasive argument constituted a better method of reform. Certainly one of the most efficacious means of protecting minority rights is to guarantee civil rights which will give the minority, through democratic channels, the opportunity to become the majority. Although Calhoun's solutions of the problem of protecting minority rights are untenable, he performed a valuable service to American political theory by warning Americans against a naive faith in majority rule. His contribution was to educate the American people in recognizing the need of protecting minority rights, which has often been forgotten.

Calhoun in his later career became reactionary, rigid in his fixed ideas, absorbed in political abstractions.[13] But his political theorizing was devoted to the practical task of forging intellectual weapons to protect Southern economic interests. Ideas are, in reality, the most powerful of political weapons, which pass by a process of osmosis, or seepage, into the current of political life. The politicians need the slogans, the simplified dogmas, and the imaginative symbols which the intellectuals create. Calhoun furnished these ideas for his section. He was a conservative, however, fearful of the leveling or reforming spirit, and the champion of landed capital against industrial capital. He regarded the rise of Northern capitalism to dominant power in the Federal government as a great menace to the economic interests of the "cotton capitalists" of his section. He believed that the interests of this minority group within the South were also the interests of all Southern people. His argument in behalf of minority rights thus broadened into a defense of the agricultural interest against the exploitation of the industrial interest, which was largely localized in the Northern states. Consequently, there is a definite link between the gaunt, defiant Calhoun of 1850 and the Southern Agrarians of 1930, who in a provocative book, *I'll Take My Stand*, fought a quixotic battle against the industrialization of the South.

The strongest criticism of Calhoun and the Carolina political leaders is that they turned the attention of the people away from progressive reforms within the state to fighting national political issues over slavery. Benjamin F. Perry, the South Carolina Unionist, was sagacious in his comment: "What might not South Carolina now be if her Calhouns, Haynes, McDuffies, Hamiltons and Prestons had devoted their great talents and energies to the commercial and internal improvements of the State, instead of frittering them away in political squabbles, which ended in nothing?" [14] The reforms which South Carolina desperately needed were an enlightened system of public schools, good roads, manufactures, a penitentiary for criminals, railroads, democratic changes in government, such as the abolition of the over-representation of the lowland parishes in the legislature and of the aristocratic method of choosing the governor and Presidential electors. Perry as editor of the *Greenville Mountaineer* and later of the *Southern Patriot* and as a member of the South Carolina legislature fought bravely for these reforms, but Calhoun was the dictator in South Carolina from 1832 to 1850 and he thwarted all the efforts toward progressive reforms within the state, for he did not wish South Carolina to be distracted by bitter internal fights. Rather, he was determined to preserve the unity of the state and devote its harmonious energies to fighting the battles for slavery in Congress and in Presidential elections.

Citations

1. For a critical estimate of Calhoun's personality, see W. H. MEIGS, *Life of John C. Calhoun* (New York, 1917), II, Chap. III.
2. ALLAN NEVINS (ed.), *Diary of John Quincy Adams, 1779–1845* (New York, 1928), 265.
3. Calhoun's early career has been admirably described by C. M. WILTSE, *John C. Calhoun, Nationalist, 1782–1828* (Indianapolis, 1944).
4. R. K. CRALLÉ (ed.), *The Works of John C. Calhoun* (New York, 1853), II, 192.
5. For a defense of Calhoun in this episode, see C. M. WILTSE, *John C. Calhoun, Nullifier, 1829–1839* (Indianapolis, 1949).
6. AVERY O. CRAVEN, *The Coming of the Civil War* (New York, 1942), Chap. III.
7. The two standard studies of the nullification movement are D. F. HOUSTON, *A Critical Study of Nullification in South Carolina* (Cambridge, 1896) and C. S. BOUCHER, *The Nullification Controversy in South Carolina* (Chicago, 1916).
8. R. R. STENBERG, "The Jefferson Birthday Dinner, 1830," *Journal of Southern History*, XIV (August, 1948), 331–356.
9. CRALLÉ, *Works of John C. Calhoun*, II, 486.
10. J. S. RAYBACK, "The Presidential Ambitions of John C. Calhoun, 1844–1848," *Journal of Southern History*, XIV (August, 1948), 331–356.
11. J. F. JAMESON (ed.), *Correspondence of John C. Calhoun, Annual Report of the American Historical Association for 1899* (Washington, 1900), II, 765.
12. *Ibid.*, 399–400.

13. Valuable expositions of Calhoun's political theory are found in W. E. DODD, *Statesmen of the Old South* (New York, 1911); GAILLARD HUNT, *John C. Calhoun* (Philadelphia, 1908); and, J. T. CARPENTER, *The South as a Conscious Minority, 1789–1861* (New York, 1930).

14. L. A. KIBLER, *Benjamin F. Perry, South Carolina Unionist* (Durham, 1946), 302.

CHAPTER XV

Exuberant Imperialism—
A Southerner's War

AS early as 1800 Thomas Jefferson had cast his eye upon Texas
as a natural territory for the expansion of the United States.
In that year he asked Philip Nolan, a wild horse trainer and a protégé
of James Wilkinson, to spy out the land and gather information
about Texas. Nolan set out ostensibly to capture wild horses in this
Spanish domain. Unfortunately, one of Nolan's party deserted and
told the Spaniards what the real purpose of the expedition was.
Nolan was killed in battle with Spanish troops, while the rest of the
party was captured and imprisoned. Spain claimed this vast territory by the right of exploration, but lacking a surplus population
and surplus capital she made little attempt to settle it, except for
founding a few missions, notably Nacogdoches (1716) and San Antonio (1718). Nevertheless, Spain was jealous of interlopers, and
when American filibusters or traders entered Texas they were imprisoned or shot. In 1821 Mexico obtained her independence from
Spain and opened up trade with the American frontier.

The United States had some vague claims to Texas as a result
of the Louisiana Purchase. Napoleon, without justification, had regarded the Rio Grande as the boundary line of Louisiana, and his
foreign minister, Talleyrand, had encouraged the United States to
make extravagant claims of territory under the treaty. But in 1819,
when the United States negotiated a treaty for the purchase of Florida from Spain, our government agreed to surrender any claims we
might have to Texas and accepted the Sabine and Red rivers as our
western boundary. In protest against this surrender, Dr. James Long
led a filibuster expedition (1819) into eastern Texas and captured

the chief Spanish military post of the region, Nacogdoches, but the American filibusters were soon driven out.

The occupation of Texas by Americans began with an elderly Connecticut Yankee, Moses Austin. Possessing a restless, adventurous nature, Austin shifted from place to place until he located in the lead mining district of Missouri, where he became a Spanish subject and made a fortune in lead mining. Later he lost this fortune in a bank failure, a catastrophe which impelled him to seek new adventures in Spanish territories. In 1820 he traveled to San Antonio and received permission from the Spanish authorities to lead an expedition of three hundred American settlers into Texas, provided they were Catholics. Moses Austin died the following year, but his son, Stephen, twenty-seven years old, prevailed upon the new republic of Mexico to confirm the grant made to his father.[1] Thus young Austin became an *empresario,* or contractor, to colonize American settlers in Texas. He himself was given a huge grant of land, and the settlers were granted one labor (177 acres) of farming land and a league (4,428 acres) of grazing land for each head of a family. The *empresario* was also allowed to charge his colonists a fee for his services; Austin charged 12½ cents an acre for cotton lands. In the early years of Texas colonization Austin exercised autocratic powers of government, but he was an able and just administrator. He was only the most prominent of a small group of *empresarios* who were commissioned by the Mexican government to bring population into the vast, vacant expanses of Texas.

By 1835 approximately 25,000 Americans as well as three or four thousand slaves had settled in this border province. The American settlers were supposed to become Catholics, but this requirement was evaded, and in 1834 religious toleration was established by law. The most important lure for immigration was the abundance of cheap cotton lands in the river valleys of eastern Texas. Most of the colonists were respectable citizens, Southern cotton farmers with their slaves, but some were rough characters who moved one jump ahead of the sheriff. "Gone to Texas" frequently had an ominous meaning. Nativity studies of the Census of 1860 indicate that Tennessee contributed more settlers to this south-western frontier than any other state, with Alabama ranking second.

The danger of encouraging a large-scale American immigration into Texas was early revealed to the Mexican government by the Fredonian Revolt. An American *empresario* named Haden Edwards had a quarrel with the Mexican government which led to the annulment of his land grant. Thereupon he led a revolt of American settlers in 1826 and established the Fredonian Republic in the eastern part of Texas near Nacogdoches. The United States refused to recognize or aid the tiny American republic, and Stephen Austin cooperated with Mexican troops in suppressing the rebellion. This uprising, however, alarmed the Mexican government who believed that the United States had incited the leaders. Suspicion was heightened by the fact that before and after the revolt, both President John Quincy Adams and President Andrew Jackson had tried to buy Texas.

After the Fredonian Revolt the Mexican authorities began a policy of restricting settlers from the United States. In 1829 the Mexican government promulgated a decree forbidding slavery. This reform resulted in such a storm of protest by the American colonists that Texas was exempted temporarily from the decree. The next year the Mexican government forbade any further immigration of American colonists into Texas, but this law was never effectively enforced. The old Spanish exclusive policy of trade was revived, so that heavy duties made trade with the United States almost prohibitive. In 1831 military garrisons were established in Texas to control and overawe the Americans. The province of Texas also was joined to the neighboring province of Coahuila, which was dominated by corrupt Mexican officials. Although most of the restrictions were evaded by the Americans, they served to irritate them and to develop a spirit of independence.

In 1832 the first Texan revolution began, not for independence, but for reform. The immediate occasion for hostilities was friction over the enforcement of the Mexican tariff at Brazoria. In the same year Santa Anna led a rebellion against the Mexican government, offering a program of liberalism. He promised the Texan revolutionists that if they would accept his rule, he would grant them the reforms they desired. Urged by Stephen Austin, they accepted the fair promises of the Mexican leader and laid down their arms.

Austin then went to Mexico City to present the three demands of the Americans, tariff reform, repeal of the restriction of American immigration into Texas, and the separation of Coahuila and Texas. After Santa Anna had attained power, however, he threw off the mask of liberalism and became a typical despot. He made facile promises of reform to Austin, but no legislation was passed to carry out these promises. The American leader was arrested on his way back to Texas and thrown into prison on account of an indiscrete letter he had written.

In 1835 relations between Texas and Mexico had become so unbearable that the Texans began a second revolt. The revolt originated at Anahuac at the head of Galveston Bay over a disturbance in connection with the unequal collection of customs and practical jokes on the guards. At first the Americans hoped that the Mexican liberals would join them in an effort to reform the despotic Mexican administration which had recently discarded the federal system of government. Since this cooperation was not secured, the Texans decided to strike for independence. Only by a declaration of independence could they hope for financial support and active sympathy from the United States. In a convention at Washington, Texas, March 2, 1836, they drew up a declaration of independence, based on the doctrine of natural rights and the fact that Santa Anna had overturned the federal system of government.

The Texans suffered two tragic defeats in the early part of the war. In February, 1836, a small band of one hundred and eighty-seven men under Lieutenant-Colonel William B. Travis were defending the church-fortress of the Alamo in San Antonio. Although they had ample warning that Santa Anna was advancing upon them with an army of between six and seven thousand men, they were foolhardy enough to remain in this dangerous position. Among the defenders of the Alamo were James Bowie, brother of the inventor of the bowie knife, and David Crockett, the famous frontiersman. Colonel Travis, a native of South Carolina and a lawyer by profession, issued a high-flown proclamation "To the People of Texas and all Americans in the World," appealing for aid and announcing the determination of the Texans to die rather than surrender. However, only thirty-two men from Gonzales joined the

beleaguered garrison. On March 6, 1836, the Mexican army as-
saulted the Alamo and killed every man of the garrison. The tragedy
of this heroic fight aroused the Texans to avenge their slain com-
rades; "Remember the Alamo!" became their battle cry. The disaster
of the Alamo was soon followed by the massacre of the American garrison at Goliad. Their commander, James W. Fannin, had delayed in
obeying orders to evacuate the town. When he finally began a retreat, his little army was surrounded by the Mexican troops. Faced
by overwhelming numbers, he decided to surrender and trust to the
mercy of the foe. The victorious General José Urrea wished to treat
his prisoners with clemency, but he was overruled by Santa Anna,
who ordered the massacre of the Texans, two hundred thirty-four
in number.

The person who devised the strategy of victory for the rebels was
Sam Houston, who the day after the disaster at the Alamo took
command of the Texan army of three hundred and seventy-four
men. This dynamic leader was born in Virginia, but his family had
emigrated to the wilderness of Tennessee when he was a youth.
Young Houston fought in the War of 1812 under Andrew Jackson, who became his life-long hero. In the frontier state of Tennessee Houston had a rapid rise as a lawyer and politician, being
elected governor at the age of thirty-four (1827). But his promising
career ended disastrously as a result of his marriage to a girl eighteen years old, who accepted Houston, twice her age, because of the
ambitions of her family. Several months after the marriage she left
his home, creating a scandal in which public opinion condemned him.
Dramatically, he resigned his office as governor and went to live
with the Cherokee Indians who gave him the names of "The Raven"
and "The Big Drunk." In 1832 he moved to Texas, where he became an advocate of independence.

For thirty-seven days Sam Houston retreated before the enemy
until he reached the San Jacinto River. Near a ford of this river,
twenty miles from the recently founded village of Houston, he intercepted a portion of the Mexican army under Santa Anna returning from an unsuccessful raid to capture the provisional government
at Harrisburg. The two armies were approximately equal in numbers, about twelve hundred men each.[2] It is interesting to note that

half of the Texan army had recently arrived from the United States. On April 21, 1836, the Texan army surprised completely the Mexican force and won the decisive victory of San Jacinto. The Texans lost sixteen men killed and twenty-five wounded, including Houston, who had his right leg shattered. The Mexicans, according to the fantastic figures of the Texans, lost six hundred and thirty killed, two hundred and eight wounded, and seven hundred and thirty made prisoners, which was three hundred more Mexicans than were present on the battlefield. Among the captured was General Santa Anna, whom the Texans were eager to kill on the spot, but Houston saved him by persuading his men that the Mexican leader would be more valuable to the Texan cause alive than dead. Consequently, the captive Santa Anna sent orders to other Mexican generals to retire and made a secret treaty recognizing the independence of Texas with the Rio Grande boundary. However, this treaty was repudiated by the Mexican government which for the next nine years refused to recognize the independence of Texas. In fact, the Mexican army as late as 1842 twice invaded Texas and captured San Antonio.

Following the victory of San Jacinto the Texans adopted a democratic constitution and elected Sam Houston president of the republic. Not long after they had won their independence, a proposal of annexation to the United States was adopted by a vote of six thousand to one hundred, and a minister, W. H. Wharton, was sent to Washington. The South was eager for the annexation of this region since it offered a field for the expansion of the cotton kingdom and of slavery.[3] Moreover, perhaps as many as five slave states could be carved out of this imperial domain and thus afford a reserve of future slave states to keep the balance of power in the Senate. The Texan government offered two sections of land (1,280 acres) to any American volunteer who served for one year in the Texan army. New Englanders, who since 1803 had opposed westward expansion, were hostile to the annexation of Texas, because they regarded it as "a slaveholder's conspiracy." The year of Texan independence was a Presidential election year in the United States, and President Jackson, although he favored the eventual annexation of Texas, opposed any hasty action because he feared that his advocacy of annexation might jeopardize the chances of Martin Van Buren to be elected President. Consequently, the Texan appeal for annexation was rebuffed. But in 1837 just before Jackson retired from office, he officially received the minister of the "Lone Star Republic," and under authority from Congress recognized its independence.

During the next nine years Texas was a sovereign state with its capital located (after 1839) at Austin on the western edge of settlement. The constitution contained a provision limiting the president's term to two years and making him ineligible to succeed himself. Consequently, during the interim when the veteran Houston was disqualified from serving as executive, Mirabeau Lamar acted as the pinch hitter. This masterful Georgian was a versatile person, being a romantic poet, a soldier, and a statesman. Lamar had grandiose ideas of the future of Texas, which had an area larger than France. Opposing annexation to the United States, he dreamed of extending Texas to the Pacific Ocean. In 1841 he organized an expedition to capture Santa Fé on the east bank of the upper Rio Grande, territory claimed by Texas. The capture of this old Mexican town promised not only an expansion of territory but also money, which was badly needed, and the diversion of the Santa Fé trade to Texas. Furthermore, the people of Santa Fe seemed desirous of joining the new republic. The expedition consisted of two hundred and seventy volunteers as well as some merchants and government officials, including George W. Kendall, editor of the New Orleans *Picayune*, who wrote a vivid account of the adventure. The expedition was poorly planned and the leaders had no knowledge of the best route to Santa Fé. The men suffered terrible privations crossing the plains in a journey of thirteen hundred miles and were reduced to eating their horses. Whenever they came to a prairie dog town they would assault it with impetuous ardor. The governor of New Mexico, Manuel Armijo, easily captured the famished men, who heard the Spanish officers debate whether to kill them on the spot or send them to Mexico City. Finally they decided to send them on foot to the Mexican capital, where the survivors were imprisoned.[4]

About 1840 a famous military unit, the Texas Rangers, was organized to guard the frontier. This picturesque body of men, which included the boyish "Big Foot" Wallace, was under Captain John Coffee Hays and had headquarters at San Antonio. Later they were commanded by the famous Ben McCulloch who became a prominent Confederate general. These mounted troops carried an ideal weapon for fighting on horseback, the Colt revolver, patented in 1836 by Samuel Colt, a Connecticut Yankee. In fact, one of the earliest models of this revolver was called "the Texas" which was used in the "Lone Star Republic" about 1839. It was without a trigger guard, a defect that was remedied by the Walker Colt (1842) named after Captain Samuel Walker of the Texas Rangers. During the Mexican War the Texas Rangers demonstrated the value of the Colt revolver, inducing General Zachary Taylor to order these weapons for his army.[5]

On the whole, Lamar's administration was unsuccessful. His Indian wars, his foreign adventures, and the effect of the Panic of 1837, which reached Texas three years later, ran the Texas debt up close to eight million dollars. As a consequence, Texas bonds depreciated so that they became worth only 15 cents on the dollar. The paper currency of the republic, called "red backs," in 1841 declined in value to 10 cents on the dollar. One of Lamar's extravagances was the Texas navy of seven warships, which was acquired to prevent Mexico from invading Texas by sea. In 1839 he sent this fleet to Vera Cruz bearing James Treat, a diplomatic agent. Treat was authorized to offer Mexico $5,000,000 if that state would recognize the independence of Texas with the Rio Grande as a boundary. When the Mexican Congress indignantly refused to entertain the proposal, the Texas navy was used in aiding a rebellion of Yucatán against the central Mexican government. Furthermore, Lamar pursued a harsh policy toward the Indians, determined to expel most of them from the state and open up additional fertile lands for settlement. When Houston returned to the presidency in 1841, however, he tranquilized the Indian frontier and undertook a policy of financial retrenchment.

The population of Texas expanded rapidly during the period of the Republic and even more rapidly after annexation. In 1847 it had a population of 142,000, exclusive of Indians, but including 39,000 Negroes. After the winning of independence, a considerable portion of the Mexican population, particularly the more prominent citizens, left the principal town of San Antonio. In 1860 the population of the state of Texas had grown to 602,432, of whom 12,443 were Mexicans and 20,553 were Germans.

The Germans were the most valuable of the foreign stocks. The center of German settlement was New Braunfels on the Guadaloupe River between Austin and San Antonio, founded in 1845 by Prince Carl of Solms-Braunfels, agent of the Adelsverein, or Society for the Protection of German Immigrants in Texas. This organization, led by German noblemen, was founded at Mainz on the Rhine in 1844 for the purpose of concentrating German colonization to the United States in Texas. In 1845 four thousand German immigrants came to Texas, but more than a thousand died of disease, especially malaria and dysentery. The Germans in Texas became a thrifty and prosperous group, cultivating their cotton fields without the aid of slaves, teaching their children handicrafts as well as reading and writing, thus setting a good example to their neighbors. Dr. Ferdinand Roemer, who has written the best travel account of early Texas (1849), pointed out the virtues of this new country, particularly the cheap and fertile land, the fluidity of society, and the freedom of trade. He observed that skilled workers were not restricted by guilds as in Europe but that a man might be a jack-of-all-trades, for example, a combination of doctor, baker, apothecary, and horse trader.[6]

In 1839 France, and in the next year, England recognized the independence of Texas. England was very much interested in obtaining a protectorate over Texas, for she saw the great advantage of monopolizing Texas cotton and securing a supply of this raw material, free from the control of the United States. Also the antislavery group in England hoped to abolitionize Texas, an objective that would endanger Southern slavery. In 1843 Great Britain, whose capitalists had considerable investments in Mexico, brought about an armistice between that country and Texas. Sam Houston cleverly played Great Britain against the United States, arousing the fears of the latter that John Bull would dominate Texas, and practicing "coquetry."[7] The Southerners, moreover, were alarmed by the rumor that S. P. Andrews of Houston, Texas, had persuaded the British government to finance a plan to abolish slavery in Texas.

Another factor which made the United States more favorable to annexation was the influence of the Texas bondholders in the United States. Texas was in a chronic state of penury. In order to secure money, the government had made large bond issues which were sold in the United States, especially in the Middle States. Nicholas Biddle, former president of the United States Bank, wrote a forceful letter in favor of annexation, pointing out that if Texas was not annexed by the United States, it would drift into the sphere of British influence. Also the Lone Star Republic had given land scrip to Americans who had fought for independence or had defended the state from Mexico. This scrip was extensively purchased by Northern speculators, who urged the annexation of Texas in order to advance their speculations. Jay Cooke, the great Philadelphia financier, believed that the Texas bondholders in the North exerted enough influence to decide the closely contested question in Congress.

The chief reasons why the United States had rejected the Texan appeals for annexation were the fear that war with Mexico would result and the opposition of the antislavery element in the country. Mexico had given warning that she would declare war against the United States if Texas were annexed. John Quincy Adams, the leader of the antislavery opposition to the acquisition of Texas, pursued a curiously inconsistent policy. While he was President he tried to buy Texas, but in July, 1838, after he had become an antislavery man, he led a filibuster in Congress for three weeks against the resolution of Waddy Thompson of South Carolina for the annexation of Texas. He popularized the idea that the move to acquire Texas was a slaveholder's conspiracy. The same charge was made by the abolitionist Benjamin Lundy in a pamphlet entitled *The War in Texas*. Actually the expansion of slavery had little to do with the settlement of Texas.

President John Tyler was an ardent advocate of the annexation of our southwestern neighbor. Alarmed by reports of British intrigue with regard to Texas, he ordered his Secretary of State, the Virginian Abel P. Upshur, in the autumn of 1843 to begin negotiations for a treaty of annexation with the Lone Star Republic. President Houston, however, assumed an indifferent attitude as a result of his negotiations with England. He was on the point of getting England and France to force Mexico to recognize Texan independence and to guarantee it. He therefore demanded the protection of the United States army during negotiations and pointed out the unfavorable position of the republic in case the United States Senate rejected the proposed treaty. Tyler's representative in Texas, W. S. Murphy, gave Houston the assurance of military protection against Mexico by the United States during the negotiation of a treaty. Upshur was killed, however, February 28, 1844, while he and a Presidential party were inspecting the battleship *Princeton*. He and several cabinet officers were standing near the huge gun "Peacemaker" during an exhibition. The gun blew up and killed the Secretary of State and the Secretary of the Navy, thus interrupting the negotiation of the treaty.

Tyler appointed Calhoun in Upshur's vacant place. Although he disliked the Carolina statesman, he was forced to make this appointment by a maneuver of Henry A. Wise, Congressman from Virginia, who was a dominant force in the Tyler administration. Calhoun made a serious blunder in replying to Lord Aberdeen, the British Secretary of Foreign Affairs, who had declared that the British government was exerting its efforts for the general abolition of slavery throughout the world. The Carolinian's letter to Lord Aberdeen has been called by Professor Channing "the supreme example of Southern provincialism." [8] Calhoun maintained that slavery was a positive good, and cited the miserable examples of free Negroes in the United States as a proof. He declared that the Southern states could not permit Texas to become abolitionized and a refuge of fugitive slaves. Therefore he urged the necessity of annexing Texas as a safeguard to the civilization of the South. Calhoun's Aberdeen letter played an important role in the defeat in June, 1844, of the treaty which he and Upshur had so laboriously negotiated.

The question of the annexation of Texas was then thrown into the arena of politics, to be decided by the Presidential election of 1844. The Southern Whigs as a group were opposed to the annexation of Texas, for the dominant element of the party consisted of men of large property interests who feared that annexation would lead to a war with Mexico and would intensify the controversy over the expansion of slavery. Henry Clay, who expected to be nominated as the candidate of his party, wished to avoid this explosive issue in the campaign. So did Van Buren, the potential candidate of the Democratic Party. In the spring of 1842 Van Buren went on a Southern tour, during which he stopped by the "Hermitage" to see the aged Jackson, but he made a more significant visit to Lexington, where he conferred with his rival, Henry Clay. Although there is no positive evidence to establish the conclusion, it was believed that Clay and Van Buren agreed to eliminate the Texas question from the coming campaign. Later the two politicians published letters on the same day side-tracking the question of the annexation of Texas. Clay wrote his famous "Raleigh (North Carolina) Letter," April 17, 1844, opposing the annexation of Texas "at the present time." He declared that annexation would lead to war with Mexico and that it would not be of advantage to the South since climate and geography would prevent more than two of the possibly five states to be carved from Texas from becoming slave states. Van Buren's letter in the Washington *Globe* opposing annexation lost him the support of Andrew Jackson and the Democratic nomination.

In the Democratic convention of 1844 at Baltimore, Van Buren's enemies succeeded in reviving the two-thirds rule which had first been adopted in 1832. This rule stated that no candidate could be nominated unless he received a majority of two-thirds of the delegates of the convention, a procedure that was continued by the Democratic Party until 1936. Van Buren had a majority of the delegates, but he could not command the necessary two-thirds majority to be nominated. As a consequence of this impasse, the Democrats chose the first "dark horse" candidate in our history, James Knox Polk of Tennessee. He owed his nomination to the advocacy of Andrew Jackson. The old political dictator wrote a letter favoring the selection of Polk, because the latter was an ardent expansionist. Gideon J. Pillow, Polk's law partner, read this letter in the convention at the strategic time. The news of Polk's nomination was flashed to Washington, forty miles away, by the telegraph, the first time this invention had been used in a Presidential campaign. The Whigs tried to belittle the Democratic candidate by the question, "Who is James K. Polk?"

Nevertheless, Polk had had an honorable career in national politics. Although he was born in Mecklenburg County, North Carolina, his early life was spent in the Duck River Valley of Tennessee, to which his father had moved. He was a graduate of the University of North Carolina, where he attained first honors in classics and mathematics. In Tennessee and in Congress he became a devoted follower of Andrew Jackson and one of his chief lieutenants in the bank fight. From 1835 to 1839 he served as Speaker of the House of Representatives, where he refused to be goaded into a duel by his enemies. Later, he redeemed Tennessee from Whiggery by his successful campaign for governor in 1839. He was a very methodical, self-controlled individual, who kept a diary. Serious and conscientious, he drove his frail body unmercifully, working at the job of President until the late hours of night and taking only six weeks' vacation during his four years of office. Perhaps the reason his abilities were unappreciated by his generation was that he was not an orator.

The platform of the Democratic Party expressed the strong mood of imperialism that was rising in the West and the lower South. It cleverly demanded "the reoccupation of Oregon and reannexation of Texas," referring in the latter case to the surrender of our claim to Texas in 1819. The slogan, "Fifty-four forty or fight!" served notice that the Democrats demanded all the western coast of Canada up to the Alaskan boundary of 54°40'. President Tyler was persuaded by some leading Democrats, including Andrew Jackson, to withdraw from the Presidential race so that the forces behind expansion would not be divided in the election. Henry Clay realized too late the strong sentiment in the country for expansion. He tried to straddle the question of the annexation of Texas by his "Alabama Letters," in which he wrote that he approved the acquisition of Texas if annexation could be accomplished without war and without dishonor. New York state decided this fateful election. Here James G. Birney, the candidate of the Liberty Party, withdrew enough votes from antislavery Whigs to defeat Clay. Birney polled 15,812 votes in this pivotal state, while Clay ran only 5,106 votes behind the Democratic candidate in this state. Clay won the upper South with the exception of Virginia, but Polk received the electoral

votes of the rest of the South. Nevertheless, the candidate of westward expansion had only a very slight popular majority over Clay
in the whole South; Polk was actually a minority President, obtaining
merely a plurality of the popular vote.

After the election, Tyler considered that the people had given
the government a mandate to annex Texas. He wished to snatch the

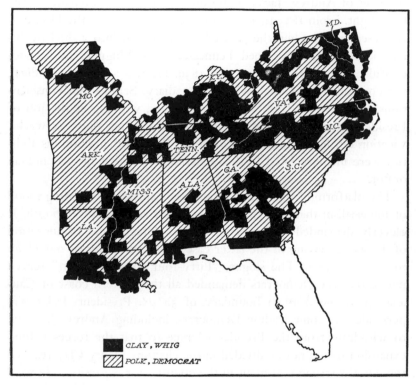

THE PRESIDENTIAL ELECTION OF 1844 IN THE SOUTH

glory of this achievement before he retired from office. Accordingly,
in a message to Congress he suggested quick action on the annexation of the coveted land by a joint resolution of Congress. This procedure required only a majority vote of both houses; the negotiation of a treaty, on the other hand, would have to be ratified by a
two-thirds majority vote of the Senate. His plan was adopted, and
shortly before he left office, Tyler signed the joint resolution offer-

ing annexation to the United States. The vote on annexation in Congress was very close, 27 to 25 in the Senate, and 120 to 98 in the House of Representatives. By the terms of this offer Texas would enter the Union as a state; also she would be allowed to keep her public lands but must pay the debts of the Lone Star Republic; as many as four additional states might be carved out of this huge territory with the consent of Texas, and she must abolish slavery north of the Missouri Compromise line. On July 4, 1845, the people of Texas in a convention accepted annexation under these conditions with only one dissenting vote.

Texas elected Sam Houston to represent the state as the first Senator sent to Washington. Dressed in a picturesque Western fashion, he was famous for whittling sticks during the barrage of eloquence that often disturbed the dozing Senators. He was one of the few Southerners prominent in political life who continued his loyalty to Jacksonian nationalism. Voting against the Kansas-Nebraska Bill, he and John Bell were the only Southern Senators to oppose the wishes of their section in this respect. In 1859 he retired from the Senate once more to become governor of the state. He opposed the agitation of the slavery question, and when the secession crisis came, he courageously "bucked" the sentiment of Texas by refusing to call a convention that might pass a secession ordinance. His career ended in sombre clouds, for on March 18, 1861, he was deposed as governor because he refused to take an oath to support the Confederacy.

The election of Polk brought to the head of the Federal government a Southern imperialist. Polk's appearance and manner were unimpressive, but beneath his quiet reserve there was great tenacity of will and force of character. Since the publication of his frank and manly diary, historians have revised their former low opinion of him and now recognize that he was one of our strongest Presidents. The mantle of old Andrew Jackson who died at the "Hermitage" in the year of Polk's inauguration was conferred upon him, and he carried on the robust nationalism of "Old Hickory" at a period when the trend of the South was away from nationalism to a sectional course. His militant nationalism was expressed in his first message to Congress, December 2, 1845, in which he reasserted the

Monroe Doctrine. This reassertion of the Monroe Doctrine, after a long period of quiescence, has been evaluated by modern students as second only in importance to the original promulgation of the doctrine of President Monroe. But Polk's most enduring claim to fame is that he enormously expanded the boundaries of his country, giving to the United States control of the Pacific Coast. Indeed, he became our greatest expansionist President.

The election of 1844 was one of the most important elections in the history of our country. The victory of Polk strengthened the dominance of the South in the control of the Democratic Party. From 1844 to the election of Lincoln every candidate elected was either a Southerner or a "dough face," a Northern man with Southern sympathies. The ascendancy of the South is revealed by its dictation of the tariff policy of the country. Polk's Secretary of the Treasury, Robert J. Walker, former Senator from Mississippi, wrote the Walker tariff of 1846. It was essentially a tariff for revenue instead of protection, but it placed high ad valorem duties on luxuries such as alcoholic liquors, cigars, and spices. The tariff duties were still further decreased in 1857, when the Southerner, Howell Cobb, Secretary of the Treasury, secured one of the lowest tariffs the nation has ever enjoyed.

The election of Polk had given the green light signal to the expansionist forces of the country. After the annexation of Texas, only the most ardent expansionists in the South were eager to acquire Oregon, which would inevitably be free territory. When Polk's bluff, the threat of war against England, succeeded in acquiring a large part of Oregon for the United States, a sectional fight between North and South arose over the territorial organization of that region. In June, 1847, Calhoun introduced resolutions on the Oregon question which stated the extreme pro-slavery demands. He held that Oregon, being the common territory of the North, the South, and the West, should be open to all citizens with their property, slaves as well as other chattels. He maintained that neither Congress nor a territorial legislature could exclude slavery from this region. The Southerners were quite aware of the fact that Oregon was totally unsuited to the expansion of slavery, but they fought, nevertheless, for sectional prestige, against the legal exclusion of their peculiar institution from this territory. Two Southern Senators, however, Sam Houston and Thomas Hart Benton, voted for the organization of Oregon territory with a restriction against the entrance of slavery. The sectional struggle prevented the organization of a territorial government for this region until August 14, 1848, when President Polk signed a bill establishing the territory with the exclusion of slavery. The people of the Northwest, who had voted with the South for the annexation of Texas, treasured a resentment against the South for its desertion of the Northwest in the move to get all of Oregon.

Polk was determined to take from Mexico the provinces of California and New Mexico, peaceably if he could, forcibly, if he must. He hoped to rob our weak neighbor to the south politely and with the solace of money. He did not want a war, because it might produce a military hero who would be a Presidential candidate, and it would involve heavy taxation. Although he was a Southern slaveholder, he does not seem to have been motivated in the acquisition of territory by the desire of bolstering Southern slavery. Rather, he was the spokesman for the expansionist mood of the country, the agent of manifest destiny.

Relations between the United States and Mexico had been bad ever since our first minister to the Republic of Mexico, Joel R. Poinsett of Charleston, had arrived in 1825 in that miserably governed land. The American ministers had been poorly selected and adapted to establish amicable relations with Mexico. Poinsett intervened in internal politics and got himself mixed up in a struggle between two branches of the Masonic Order, the York rite and the Scottish rite. Finally, Mexico demanded that he be recalled. Then President Jackson sent Anthony Butler, a reprobate, who tried to bribe the Mexican officials to sell Texas. He, too, had to be recalled at Mexico's urgent insistence. Our diplomats were neither able to conclude a favorable commercial treaty with Mexico, nor could they obtain payment for the property damages and injuries done to American citizens during the turmoil of frequent revolutions.

Mexico, too, had her grievances against the United States. Mexicans firmly believed that the United States had given aid to the Texan revolutionists in 1836 and had enabled them to win their independence. As a matter of fact, Americans had furnished both men and money to enable the Texans to free themselves from the corrupt and oppressive rule of the Latin-American republic. Technically, however, the American government had been neutral in that contest. Mexican suspicions were corroborated by a much publicized speech of ex-President John Quincy Adams at South Braintree, Massachusetts, in which he declared that the Southern slaveholders had formed a conspiracy to acquire Texas—a speech that was translated into Spanish and circulated below the Rio Grande. American imperialist ambitions were further revealed when Commodore Thomas Catesby Jones, hearing of a rumor of war between Mexico and the United States, seized the port of Monterey in California in 1842. It was apparent that the United States coveted Mexican border provinces which were weakly defended.

In order to secure payment for our claims, some of which were just and some padded, and to buy California, President Polk sent John Slidell, a prominent Louisiana politician, as Minister Plenipotentiary to Mexico City. Mexico had broken diplomatic relations with the United States immediately after the annexation of Texas. In the fall of 1845, however, the Mexican government had agreed to receive a diplomatic representative, but by the time Slidell arrived, public opinion had become so incensed against the United States that the government did not dare to receive him. The fundamental reason for this insult to the United States was that the Mexicans had learned that Slidell's real mission was to buy California and New Mexico. He was authorized by President Polk to offer as much as $30,000,000 for this vast region. To proud Mexicans, this attempt to mutilate the national domain must be resisted with scorn. Furthermore, the Mexicans were not averse to war with the United States for they had a contemptuous opinion of our military ability and believed that they could defeat the hated *gringos*.

Such was the background of the war with Mexico. The immediate occasion for hostilities, however, was our annexation of Texas and the arrogant claim of Texas to the boundary of the Rio Grande. The Mexican government had never recognized the independence of Texas, and annexation seemed to be the culmination of a plot by the United States to wrest the territory from Mexican hands. The ag-

gressive Texans claimed the Rio Grande to be their southern boundary, and the United States assumed this claim. Actually the province of Texas had not extended beyond the Nueces River, and
Mexico's position was well founded that the southern boundary of
Texas was the Nueces River. The flimsy nature of the American
claim was indicated by the fact that Slidell was authorized to offer
the Mexican government $5,000,000 to recognize the Rio Grande
as the rightful boundary between the United States and Mexico.
When Mexico refused to receive Slidell, on January 13, 1846, Polk
ordered General Zachary Taylor, who was stationed with an army
at the older part of Corpus Christi, located on the north bank of
Nueces River, to move down to the Rio Grande.

In a cabinet meeting on Saturday, May 9, Polk stated that he intended to send a war message to Congress on the following Tues-
day. His Secretary of the Navy George Bancroft the historian advised that the United States should wait until Mexico committed
some definite act of hostility. Polk planned, nevertheless, to ask
Congress for a declaration of war on the basis of Mexico's refusal
to pay American claims and her rejection of our minister, John
Slidell. These claims amounted to only $3,208,314.96 as determined
by a United States commission after the war was over. Fortunately
for Polk's purpose he received that afternoon the news that a skir-
mish had taken place north of the Rio Grande between the army of
Taylor and Mexican troops in which sixteen American soldiers had
been killed. The next day he was busily engaged, with time out to
attend church, in composing his war message. A conscientious
church-goer, he recorded in his diary his regret that he had "to
spend the Sabbath in the manner I have." [9] His message to Congress now had in his eyes a moral justification. Mexican troops he
declared had invaded our territory and had "shed American blood
upon the American soil . . . war exists, and, notwithstanding all our
efforts to avoid it exists by the act of Mexico herself." [10] Congress
responded by declaring war against Mexico on May 13, 1846, by a
vote of 174 to 14 in the House of Representatives and 40 to 2 in the
Senate.

Nevertheless, Polk did not have a unified country behind him in
the prosecution of this war. New England was hostile to a war of

expansion that would decrease her influence in the nation and provide territory for slavery expansion. New England orators branded it a slaveholders' war. James Russell Lowell wrote the Biglow Papers condemning the Mexican War as an imperialistic adventure for the advantage of slaveholders. The President did not wish the Whigs to gain glory or political advantage out of this appeal to arms. It was observed that of the many aspiring politicians who volunteered, the Democrats usually got the good commissions while the Whigs received few plums. Polk had a fear that a Whig military hero would come out of the conflict who would capture the Presidency. He wanted a brief war, partly for patriotic and humanitarian reasons, partly to avoid heavy taxation, but, not least, to prevent the emergence of a military hero. The Mississippi Valley states and Texas supported this war of conquest with enthusiasm. In fact, Tennessee sent so many volunteers that it was called "the volunteer state."

On the other hand, the older Southern states along the Atlantic seaboard were not as ardent for war as were the Southwestern states. Especially the Southern Whigs, who included many large slaveholders and owners of great plantations, were dubious about this war of conquest waged by a Democratic administration. Alexander H. Stephens, later to be Vice President of the Confederacy, joined hands with Abraham Lincoln in opposing the prosecution of an imperialistic war. The great Calhoun also spoke out against this developing imperialism because he foresaw that the territory owned by Mexico for which we were fighting was unsuited to the expansion of slavery. He believed, moreover, that the mongrel population of the region which we hoped to conquer would tend to break down the color line, and that the war would strengthen the central government. He said, "Mexico is forbidden fruit; the penalty of eating it would be to subject our institutions to political death." [11]

Polk had selected General Zachary Taylor, sixty-one years of age, to lead the invading army. Born in Virginia but reared in Kentucky, Taylor had spent a long period of his life on the American frontier. He was a very homely old gentleman, whose dark brown face was deeply lined, and whose sturdy body supported a corpulent stomach. He looked and dressed the part of a plain farmer, and he was fond of talking about crops and his Louisiana cotton plantation tilled by many black slaves. An Illinois volunteer described him as short and very heavy with pronounced face lines and gray hair, and as wearing "an old oil cap, a dusty green coat, a frightful pair of trousers and on horseback looks like a toad." [12] His notorious informality and carelessness in dress led to a funny incident during the Mexican war. He had arranged a conference with Commodore David Conner, commanding the naval blockading squadron, who was known to be fond of ceremony and military pomp. Taylor, therefore, pulled out his wrinkled officer's uniform and donned it for the occasion. Conner, on the other hand, aware of Taylor's distaste for show, put on his oldest and most inconspicuous clothes. When the two met each was amazed at the transformation in the other.

Despite Taylor's unmilitary bearing, he was loved by his soldiers who called him "Old Rough and Ready." In battle he constantly exposed himself on his white horse to the enemy fire and even fought on foot with his soldiers. His bravery and calm demeanor during battle gave his soldiers great confidence in him. He was an unconventional fighter, whose methods were scorned by some West Pointers. They maintained that he failed to get intelligence concerning the enemy, that he neglected sanitation in camp, and that during battle he did not give orders. Yet Taylor was a remarkably humane general who wished to shed as little blood as possible and who would fight to the utter extremity rather than retreat and abandon his wounded soldiers. His humanity extended to the enemy whose civilian population he tried to protect both in their property and persons.

Taylor had little difficulty in defeating the Mexican armies that opposed him. His men found that dysentery, diarrhea, and lack of sanitation in camp were more deadly foes than the Mexican bullets. Taylor's first victories were Palo Alto and Resaca de la Palma on the northeast side of the Rio Grande (in May and September, 1846) in which his army was greatly outnumbered by the Mexicans. Crossing the Rio Grande, he captured Matamoros on the south bank of the river, and, after a courageous fight, the fortified city of Monterrey in northeastern Mexico. After this victory he made the mistakes of permitting the enemy to retire from the city and granting an armistice of eight weeks, instead of trying to crush or capture the

Mexican army. For this failure to follow up his victory he was severely and, perhaps justly, criticized by President Polk and his advisers.

Taylor was now becoming a military hero, and Whig newspapers were mentioning him as a Presidential candidate. Accordingly the Democrats wished to minimize his glory by dividing military honors with another general. The President planned to send an army by sea from New Orleans to Vera Cruz which would march overland to capture Mexico City. He was unable to find a competent Democratic general for the command of this second expeditionary army (he desired to appoint the bombastic Senator Thomas Hart Benton), so that he was forced to appoint General Winfield Scott, a Whig, whom he disliked. By the end of March, 1847, Scott had captured Vera Cruz and was marching overland to the rich and delightful capital of Mexico. In order to strengthen this army, Taylor was ordered to send all his troops, except a force of six thousand, to Scott. Furthermore, he was forbidden to march to Mexico City from the north and was ordered to remain on the defensive at Monterrey. Taylor was bitterly disappointed at this effort to clip his wings, to "break me down," but he resolved to remain at his post and do his duty.

The Mexican War was fought in a loose and undisciplined fashion, largely by volunteers. Lieutenant A. P. Hill of Virginia, fresh from West Point, kept an interesting diary of his participation in the Mexican campaign, seeking martial glory.[18] He found the Mexican soldiers lacking in stubborn resistance, so that most of the time he was pursuing Mexicans as though he were engaged in an old-fashioned fox hunt in Virginia. Nor did he find this war to be glorious, rather it was disgusting to see the lack of discipline of the volunteers. He witnessed them sack a Mexican town, and the next day he saw them on the march wearing beautiful shawls that they had taken and carrying miscellaneous booty with them. Half of the troops were drunk on Mexican *aguardiente*. The bites of the fleas were terrible, and food was scarce and unappetizing, facts which hardly compensated for the smiles of beautiful but unpatriotic senoritas. It was during the Mexican campaign that Ulysses S. Grant developed his habit of solitary drinking.

Before Scott reached Mexico President Polk provided the Latin-American republic with the services of its ablest general and politician, Santa Anna. This adventurer, who had lost a leg in battle, was a dynamic leader despite his corruptness.[14] He regarded himself as the Napoleon of the West, and like his hero, he was immoral, having "five acknowledged bastards." At the beginning of the Mexican War he was in exile in Cuba. Through an intermediary, he offered to negotiate a peace according to Polk's liking, if the President would allow him to go through the blockade and assume charge of the Mexican government. Polk was duped by the fair promises of the Mexican adventurer, despite the latter's record of treachery, and permitted him to pass the blockade. Thus Polk hoped that the war might be brought to a speedy end through the agency of Santa Anna in starting a revolution in Mexico. Then it might be easy for the United States to buy a peace from the prostrate nation. When the Mexican leader returned to his country in August, 1846, his colossal vanity was fed with many enthusiastic *vivas* of the populace. Ignoring his promises, he put himself at the head of the Mexican army and laughed cynically at the American President.

A great stroke of apparent good fortune happened to Santa Anna shortly after he entered his native land. One of the natives intercepted a letter from Scott to Taylor ordering the latter to send all of his soldiers to Scott with the exception of six thousand men. This lucky accident may have given Santa Anna the idea of marching north and destroying the remnant of Taylor's army and then returning to deal with Scott. In February, 1847, he started north with an army far superior to the little American army under Taylor which had occupied Saltillo. Taylor's army had lost most of its best young officers, including Robert E. Lee, Ulysses S. Grant, and George Meade, who had been sent to Scott. His command consisted of approximately seven thousand volunteers and eight hundred regulars. Taylor decided to meet the assault of Santa Anna at the pass of La Angostura, a mile and a half from the ranch of Buena Vista which gave the name to the fierce battle between the Americans and the Mexican army that took place on February 22–23, 1847. Santa Anna's army outnumbered the American army more than four to one, but he was ignominiously defeated and fled in the vanguard of his retreating soldiers. At this battle a Southern officer, Colonel Jefferson Davis of the Mississippi Rifles, arranged his men in a V formation and played a decisive role in the Mexican defeat. He became known as the hero of Buena Vista and ever afterward he thought of himself as a military expert. Following this victory Taylor's army remained inactive, while "Old Rough and Ready" was bitterly ruminating over his treatment by Polk and Secretary of War Marcy.

In the meanwhile General Scott was marching from Vera Cruz to Mexico City, a distance of 250 miles through a difficult terrain and a hostile population. Scott was a Virginian educated at William and Mary College. He was a large and powerful man with a leonine countenance, and, in striking contrast to Taylor, loved pomp and military show. In his naive delight in resplendent uniforms, he bore some resemblance to the German Air Marshal Goering, and he was called "Old Fuss and Feathers." Despite his foibles, he was a student of military science, an able general, and he conducted a skillful campaign against the Mexican armies. He asked for twenty thousand soldiers for this expedition, but received only ten thousand effectives with which to conquer a nation of six million people. Part of the time his army had to live off the country, and in addition to the Mexicans he had to combat "Yellow Jack," the dreaded disease of yellow fever. After winning the battles of Cerro Gordo, Chapultepec, and Churusbusco, Scott entered Mexico City on September 17, 1847. Robert E. Lee and Pierre G. T. Beauregard, later officers of the Confederacy, played an important role in this victorious campaign. Southerners also contributed to the winning of the war in the enthusiastic expedition of Missouri volunteers, "country boys," and a small nucleus of regulars from Fort Leavenworth, led by Stephen Kearny, who seized Sante Fe and California in the summer of 1846 and who, under Colonel Alexander Doniphan, captured the Mexican city of Chihuahua during the following winter.

In Scott's expedition to Mexico City traveled Nicholas P. Trist, Virginian, chief clerk of the State Department, who has been described as "a diplomat with ideals." [15] President Polk had sent him to conclude at the earliest possible moment a peace which would give to the United States the territory that the expansionists coveted. At first General Scott violently resented the presence of this agent of the President. But eventually the two Virginians, both vainglorious, and both mighty warriors, one with the sword, and the other with a copious pen, were reconciled. The administration then became dissatisfied with Trist and ordered him home, partly because he had not followed his instructions and was not sufficiently greedy for Mexican territory. Furthermore, Polk became convinced that a chief reason why Mexico, though defeated, obstinately refused to sue for peace was the presence of a diplomatic agent with the American army. This circumstance gave to the Mexicans the impression that the United States was extremely eager to conclude peace and that therefore, if they waited, the enemy would grant easy terms to them.

Trist decided to disregard his recall and seized the opportunity to make a treaty with the Mexican government. Delay might have led to internal chaos in Mexico so that no responsible government could have been found with whom to negotiate, and the war would have been prolonged. Consequently, he negotiated the Treaty of Guadaloupe Hidalgo, February 2, 1848, when he had no legal authority to do so. The President was furious at Trist for his disobedience, but he accepted the treaty because he feared the development of an irresistible movement to annex all of Mexico. He also feared that the Whig-controlled Congress might refuse to vote appropriations to continue the war. The terms of this treaty gave to the United States the Rio Grande boundary and the vast territory of California and New Mexico. In return, the United States agreed to assume the claims of American citizens against the Mexican government and to pay Mexico fifteen million dollars.

The Mexican War was an adventure in imperialism of the South in partnership with the restless inhabitants of the West. It was provoked by a Southern President and fought largely by Southern generals and by Southern volunteers. It furnished the training school of practical experience for most of the Confederate and Union officers who participated in the Civil War. It gave to the United States a vast territory with a Pacific front that inevitably turned the face of the nation toward Oriental adventure and commerce. One of the most important consequences of the Mexican War was that it precipitated a great sectional struggle between the North and the

South over the status of slavery in this territory, a controversy that eventually led to the Civil War.

An immediate result of the Mexican War was the election in 1848 of Zachary Taylor as President. Taylor had never voted in a Presidential election, but he was Whiggish in sentiment. The vote-getting power of the homely old hero of the war was recognized by the Whig leaders, especially by Thurlow Weed, editor of the *Albany Journal*, John J. Crittenden of Kentucky, and Alexander H. Stephens, who organized a Taylor Club in Congress called "The Young Indians." Accordingly, "Old Rough and Ready" was enthusiastically nominated by the Whigs without a platform, an old custom of that party. Before his nomination Taylor had declared that he would not be the President merely of a party, and he had vacillated in deciding whether to accept the nomination by a Whig convention. The Democrats nominated Lewis Cass of Michigan, the advocate of squatter sovereignty as a method of settling the slavery question in the Federal territories. Taylor won principally because, being a slaveholder, he appealed to some Southern Democrats, and because the Democratic Party in New York lost part of its strength by a revolt of Van Buren, who became the candidate of the Free Soil Party.

According to the view of historians under the influence of the abolition tradition, the Mexican War was a war of conquest, unjustified morally. But such able historians as Professor Edward Channing and especially Justin H. Smith, who has written the classic history of *The War with Mexico,* have held that the war was just. They have maintained that it was practically impossible to obtain satisfaction from Mexico in regard to American claims except by forcible means. The United States was entirely free from blame in annexing Texas, whose independence had been maintained for nine years and recognized by England and France. Both Smith and Channing argued also that Spain and Mexico had held California and New Mexico for years without developing these provinces. It was desirable from the standpoint of civilization that the land should not lie idle but should be seized by a vigorous people who could make use of it. A weak point in the American apology for the Mexican War was the contention that the Rio Grande was the legitimate boundary line of Texas. When Polk ordered Taylor to move from Corpus Christi to the north bank of the Rio Grande, he was invading the territory of a neighbor at peace with us. Although the approximately one hundred and eighteen million dollars which the United States spent in acquiring the coveted territory was a cheap price, many times repaid by the gold of California discovered in the very year of the treaty of Guadaloupe Hidalgo, nevertheless the manner in which we obtained this territory left a heritage of bitterness and distrust of the powerful United States among the weaker Latin-American republics.

The urge for expansion was exceptionally strong in the states of the Southwest. This restless mood may be ascribed in part to the exhaustion of tobacco and cotton lands that made Southerners eager to go west to acquire rich virgin soils. It was motivated also by the high birth rate in the South, for the large families of strapping boys had to make elbow room for themselves. The opening of new cotton lands would give vitality to Southern slavery by increasing the demand for additional slaves, thus enhancing the value of slave property in the South. The South, moreover, needed additional slave states to strengthen its political position in Congress against an aggressive antislavery movement.

Many factors contributed to the growth in the United States of the doctrine of Manifest Destiny, which beckoned to this country to expand over the continent of North America. It was partly inspired by a blatant belief that American democracy was superior to any form of government in the world. Europe was regarded as antiquated and "played out." American institutions, therefore, should be spread to less favored peoples. The Mexican War, resulting in an easy victory, awakened the mood of jingoism and aggressive imperialism in the minds of many Americans, just as the overwhelming victory of Prussia over France in 1870 intensified a militaristic and imperialistic spirit in Germany.

One of the outgrowths of the doctrine of Manifest Destiny was the movement to acquire all of Mexico. In the autumn of 1847 when news arrived of the capture of Mexico City, this movement began to gain momentum. Among the most ardent exponents of the "all-of-Mexico" policy were the colorful Senator Edward A. Hannegan of Indiana and the Senators from New York, who may have voiced the hope of the commercial interests of that state to exploit Mexico. The state of Mississippi also produced some aggressive expansionists in the persons of Robert J. Walker, a member of Polk's cabinet, Jefferson Davis, Senator Henry S. Foote, and John A. Quitman. President Polk was opposed to the absorption of all of Mexico, but he favored obtaining larger territorial gains if Mexico obstinately refused to agree to peace terms. His minimum terms were the acquisition of California, New Mexico, and the Rio Grande boundary, but he had also instructed Trist to ask for lower California and a right of way across the Isthmus of Tehuantepec.[16]

The Southern people were divided in their attitude toward the acquisition of all of Mexico. In general, the Southern Whigs, who represented the large slaveholders of the lower South, were opposed. In this camp also were some leading Democrats of the Atlantic seaboard states, such as the Senators from South Carolina and Virginia. Calhoun made the most powerful speech against the acquisition of all Mexico, for he feared such a conquest would subvert our democratic institutions. On the other hand, *The National Era* of Washington, D. C., an organ of the antislavery forces, advocated the annexation of all of this great Latin-American state. The editor argued that Mexico had already abolished slavery and that this spacious country could be carved into free states, which would send antislavery representatives to Congress. Many Southerners feared that the acquisition of Mexico would not be followed by the opening of that area to slavery. The movement to seize all of Mexico was defeated by the opposition of President Polk, by the circumstance that Congress had been elected a year before the strong drift to secure larger territorial gains had arisen, and finally by the fact that the treaty of Guadaloupe Hidalgo was presented early in 1848 before the expansionist mood had matured. Overshadowing the whole issue was the uncertainty whether the acquisition of Mexico would strengthen the pro-slavery position or the antislavery cause.

Efforts of the United States to acquire additional land and economic rights in Mexico did not cease with the conclusion of the Mexican War. Both President Taylor and President Fillmore sought to negotiate a treaty permitting a New Orleans company to dig a canal across the isthmus of Tehuantepec and granting the United States the right of intervention to protect the canal. But the Mexicans were so bitter against their recent enemy that they refused to consider this proposition made by our minister, the bluff Kentuckian, Robert P. Letcher. In 1853, however, the United States did secure another small slice of Mexico, an area approximately the size of South Carolina below the Gila River in what is now Arizona. This arid region was needed to secure a railroad crossing of the Colorado River and was favored by Southerners who wished to build a transcontinental railroad along the Southern route. James Gadsden, a South Carolina railroad president, was sent to Mexico by President Pierce to negotiate a treaty for this purpose. The Gadsden treaty gave Mexico $10,000,000 for this piece of land, a huge sum in comparison with the amount paid for California and New Mexico. Some critics called it "conscience money."

Another phase of Manifest Destiny was the attacks on Latin-American countries by filibuster expeditions. William Walker, a native of Tennessee, led expeditions into lower California and Sonora in northern Mexico in 1853, and later this small "gray-eyed man of destiny" made himself dictator of Nicaragua. He tried to secure Southern support by proclaiming the legality of slavery in Nicaragua and by triumphal tours of the Southern states. New Orleans became a center of filibuster expeditions in the decade of the 1850's, directed especially against Cuba. Governor John A. Quitman of Mississippi, a Northern man who had settled at Natchez, was an ardent promoter of filibuster expeditions to acquire more slave territory.

In 1852 the election of Franklin Pierce as President brought into power a "dough-face," who smiled upon Southern plans of expansion. He made Jefferson Davis his Secretary of War and principal adviser, and appointed William L. Marcy, another "dough-face," as Secretary of State. Davis hoped to extend Southern influence into the far West by constructing a transcontinental railroad between New Orleans and Southern California. Since it was believed that only one transcontinental railroad would be built for years, there was great rivalry as to the location of its eastern terminus. Davis used army engineers in 1853 to survey the suitable routes across the

Western plains, and he reported in favor of the Southern route because it would be free from snow throughout the year.

The Pierce administration tried to further Southern imperialism by the purchase of Cuba. This rich island was teeming with slaves that could be bought for one-half the price of Southern slaves. Furthermore, if Cuba were admitted into the Union as a state, it would strengthen the pro-slavery cause in Congress. In 1854, Pierce ordered three American diplomats, James Buchanan, Minister to Great Britain, Pierre Soulé, Minister to Spain, and John Y. Mason, Minister to France, to meet and determine the best method of obtaining Cuba. These gentlemen, two Southerners and a Northern pro-slavery man, had a conference at the Belgian seaside resort of Ostend and drew up the notorious Ostend Manifesto. These ministers declared that the United States should offer a large sum to Spain for the purchase of the island but if that nation, "dead to the voice of her own interest, and actuated by a stubborn pride and a false sense of honor," should refuse to sell the island, then the United States must resort to drastic means to obtain it. This country would be justified in wresting it from Spain, "by every law human and divine," particularly the law of self-preservation, to prevent Cuba from becoming "a second Santo Domingo." [17] Such arrogant imperialism was too dangerous politically even for the pro-slavery Pierce, and accordingly his Secretary of State, Marcy, repudiated it. The Ostend Manifesto did the Southern cause serious harm in arousing fear in the North of Southern imperialism to acquire additional foreign territory for slave states.

The activities of filibusters in Mexico, Central America, and Cuba, particularly William Walker, tended to strengthen this fear of Southern aggression. A mysterious organization arose in the South in 1859, the Knights of the Golden Circle, which had for its object the seizure of Mexico and the conversion of this land into slave states. Its founder "General" George W. L. Bickley, a Virginia doctor, traveled through the South seeking recruits for his military order but he had little success except in Texas.[18] Actually, only a small minority of extremists in the South was behind the movement to acquire Cuba and areas of Mexico and Central America.

Later Abraham Lincoln was obsessed with the idea of the danger of the expansion of Southern slavery. In his oft-quoted "House Divided" speech of 1858, he warned Northern voters, "I believe this government cannot endure permanently half slave and half free. Either the opponents of slavery will arrest the further spread of it, and place it where the public mind shall rest in the belief that it is in course of ultimate extinction or its advocates will push it forward till it shall become alike lawful in all the states, old as well as new, North as well as South." This argument ignored economic realism, but it was effective propaganda in portraying the South as an aggressive slavocracy. Lincoln also opposed the Crittenden Compromise in 1860–61 on the ground that the restoration of the Missouri Compromise line of 36°30′ would only lead to a drive of the South to acquire new slave territory to the south of the Rio Grande River and in the Caribbean Sea.

Southern imperialism was handicapped by the fact that the expansion of slavery had certain natural limits.[19] Slavery was such an inefficient and expensive system of labor that it could thrive only on rich soils which were easily accessible to market. Other limiting factors were the question of the security of the slaves, that is, whether they could easily escape, and the existence of a soil and climate suitable for growing routine staple crops such as cotton, sugar, and tobacco. Unfortunately a vast proportion of the soil of the Southwest was arid and unsuited to slaves. Furthermore, Mexican peon labor was cheaper than slave labor. Even today there are few Negroes employed in the Southwest, since their labor is more expensive than the cheap Mexican labor. Economic factors were destined to nullify the political drive to acquire new slave states in the Southwest.

Citations

1. E. C. BARKER, *Life of Stephen F. Austin, Founder of Texas, 1793–1836* (Nashville, 1925).
2. C. E. CASTANEDA (ed.), *The Mexican Side of the Texas Revolution* (Dallas, 1928).
3. J. H. SMITH, *The Annexation of Texas* (New York, 1941), and R. N. RICHARDSON, *Texas, the Lone Star State* (New York, 1943).

4. W. C. BINKLEY, *The Expansionist Movement in Texas, 1836–1850* (Berkeley, 1925).

5. W. P. WEBB, *The Texas Rangers* (New York, 1935); for an excellent discussion of internal conditions in Texas, see W. R. HOGAN, *The Texas Republic a Social and Economic History* (Norman, 1946).

6. FERDINAND ROEMER, *Texas: with Particular Reference to German Immigrations* (San Antonio, 1935).

7. A. W. WILLIAMS and E. C. BARKER (eds.), *The Writings of Sam Houston* (Austin, 1938–1941), IV, 467–468.

8. EDWARD CHANNING, *A History of the United States* (New York, 1921), V, 543.

9. ALLAN NEVINS (ed.), *Polk, the Diary of a President, 1845–1849* (New York, 1929), 86.

10. J. D. RICHARDSON, *A Compilation of the Messages and Papers of the Presidents, 1789–1897* (Washington, 1901), IV, 442.

11. CRALLÉ, *Works of John C. Calhoun*, IV, 308.

12. H. HAMILTON, *Zachary Taylor* (Indianapolis, 1941), 238; see also BRAINERD DYER, *Zachary Taylor* (New York, 1946).

13. Unpublished manuscript in possession of William J. Robertson, Savannah, Georgia.

14. W. H. CALLCOTT, *Santa Anna* (Norman, 1936), 230–243.

15. L. M. SEARS, "Nicholas P. Trist, A Diplomat with Ideals," *Mississippi Valley Historical Review*, XI (June, 1924), 85–98.

16. J. D. P. FULLER, "The Slavery Question and the Movement to Acquire Mexico, 1840–1848," *Mississippi Valley Historical Review*, XXI (June, 1934), 31–48.

17. COMMAGER, *Documents of American History*, I, 334–335.

18. O. CRENSHAW, "The Knights of the Golden Circle," *American Historical Review*, XLVII (October, 1941), 23–51.

19. C. W. RAMSDELL, "The Natural Limits of Slavery Expansion," *Mississippi Valley Historical Review*, XV (September, 1929), 151–171.

CHAPTER XVI

Changing Attitudes Toward Slavery

THE argument which Southerners evolved to justify the institution of slavery is one of the great rationalizations that the human mind has conceived. By 1832 the South had abandoned its former apologetic attitude toward the existence of slavery and had elaborated the pro-slavery argument, a phenomenon of self-persuasion which might be compared to the lotus blossom lulling the conscience of the slaveholders. The pro-slavery argument was, like the philosophy of the Scholastics of the Middle Ages, a product of many minds, a remarkable intellectual achievement, finely articulated, and based on the far-reaching assumption that Negroes are innately inferior to whites. Its cornerstone was conservatism, the rationalization of the *status quo*. The conservative philosophy of the planters pervaded nearly every department of Southern life, creating a political theory, a social ethics, a code of manners, a race theory, a set of economic principles, and a profoundly conservative religion.

The period of apologizing for the existence of slavery in the South extended roughly from the American Revolution to 1832. This liberal attitude toward slavery was explained in part by economic considerations. The exhaustion of tobacco lands and the shift to wheat growing gave to the upper South a surplus of slaves. Slavery was becoming decidedly unprofitable in this region until the invention of the cotton gin in 1793 restored the value of slaves. Washington declared that he had twice as many working Negroes on his estate as could be profitably employed. John Randolph of Roanoke wittily described the economic burden of supporting slavery during this period by remarking that, instead of masters advertising for runaway slaves, the slaves would be advertising for the arrest of fugitive masters.

In addition to economic motives for advocating the emancipation of the slaves, the natural rights philosophy of the Revolutionary period predisposed Southerners to a policy of gradual emancipation. A considerable number of Southerners freed their slaves by will during this period. George Washington set an example by emancipating his slaves by will, so did John Randolph of Roanoke, and Jefferson was prevented from adopting a similar course by his financial bankruptcy. The wills of emancipation indicate that the liberal planters were disturbed by the inconsistency of holding slaves and subscribing to the equalitarian doctrines of the Declaration of Independence. Most of the prominent Virginia leaders, such as Patrick Henry, George Wythe, and James Madison, condemned slavery as an institution that should be eradicated from a free America. George Mason, the proprietor of beautiful "Gunston Hall" on the Potomac, and the master of three hundred slaves, declared slavery to be an infernal school of tyranny for the future leaders of the South, which caused slaveholders to lose sight of "the Dignity of Man which the Hand of Nature had planted in us for great and useful purposes." [1] Furthermore, the most enlightened planters, such as Jefferson, realized that slavery had a pernicious effect on the white population, degrading manual labor, encouraging pride and arrogance, and exposing children to the corrupting influence of licentious slaves.

The grave problem in emancipating slaves was what to do with the freedmen. Practically all Southerners believed that the process of liberation should be gradual and that the freedmen should be colonized. Professor St. George Tucker of William and Mary College proposed in 1796 a plan of gradual emancipation based on liberating all female slaves at birth. Several of the Southern states repealed their colonial laws forbidding the manumission of slaves except for meritorious services, adjudged by the governor and council or the county court, and now permitted emancipation of slaves provided the owner gave guarantees that the freedmen would not become public charges. The experiences of planters who emancipated their slaves, however, were frequently unfortunate. Robert Carter of Nomini Hall emancipated in 1791 more than five hundred slaves by a plan of gradually freeing groups over a period of twenty

years. He tried to rent small patches of land to them, but this practice was not an economic success. The neighbors protested that the
freedmen stole and abused their freedom and corrupted the slaves.
Ironically, two of Carter's sons, whom he had sent to the Baptist
College in Rhode Island (Brown University) in order that they
might escape the immoral influence of slavery, tried to frustrate the
noble experiment of their father. When Carter liberated his slaves
he was influenced by the teachings of the Baptist and Swedenborgian
churches, but also, it is to be noted, the price of slaves had reached
the bottom of a twenty-year decline in this last decade of the eighteenth century.[2]

The Quakers of the upper South were the principal Southern
group that tried to do something practical about removing slavery.
Those planters who apologized for slavery, as a rule, made no positive efforts toward eradicating the institution. Since slavery had not
originated in their generation, they were willing that its removal
should be left to the gradual operation of time. But the Quakers,
who loathed the element of force in human relations, actively sought
to dissolve the institution. One method which they adopted was the
use of antislavery propaganda through the press. In 1819 Elihu
Embree founded *The Emancipator* at Jonesborough, Tennessee, the
first antislavery newspaper in the South. Benjamin Lundy, a saddle-
maker, who worked in Wheeling, Virginia, established in 1821 the
Genius of Universal Emancipation at Baltimore, Maryland. In North
Carolina flourished the Quaker newspaper the *Greensborough
Patriot*, which as late as 1834 championed the cause of freeing the
slaves.

To agitate for the removal of slavery, the Quakers organized abolition societies. Since they were close to slavery, they were practical
enough to urge the gradual rather than the immediate abolition of
the peculiar institution and the amelioration of slavery by repealing
the laws against the education of the slaves. Charles Osborn, a Quaker
preacher born in Guilford County, North Carolina, was the pioneer
organizer of manumission societies in Tennessee (1814–16). After
he had emigrated to Mount Pleasant, Ohio, he published an antislavery newspaper as early as 1817. By the year 1827 fifty antislavery
societies, with a membership of three thousand, were reported in

North Carolina, twenty-five in Tennessee, and eight in Virginia—
a much greater number of antislavery societies than existed in the
North. Besides this method of attacking the institution of slavery,
the Quakers formed free produce societies, pledged not to use products of slave labor, and became operators in the Underground Railroad. The antislavery sentiment in the South was weakened greatly
as many of the Quakers emigrated to free territory beyond the Ohio
River in the first three decades of the nineteenth century. In 1834 the
last meeting of the North Carolina Manumission Society was held
at Marlborough, and in 1860 only about fifteen hundred Quakers
were left in the state.[3]

Most Southerners believed that if the slaves were freed and remained in the South a race conflict would follow and Southern
civilization would be destroyed. Jefferson, Clay, Calhoun, and practically all Southern leaders believed that the removal of the freed
Negro was indispensable to a scheme of emancipation. In 1817 the
American Colonization Society was founded at Washington, D. C.,
to solve this problem by transporting freed Negroes to Africa. Liberals saw in the movement an encouragement to kindly masters to
free their slaves, while conservatives supported the colonization
society as a means of strengthening slavery by removing the objectionable free Negroes already present in the South. The society,
composed largely of Southerners, elected Bushrod Washington, a
nephew of the Revolutionary hero, as the first president. In 1819
agents were sent to the west coast of Africa and acquired from the
native chiefs large areas for a colony which was named Liberia,
"land of freedom," and its capital, Monrovia, in honor of President Monroe. Not until 1847, however, did Liberia become a republic with a Negro as president.

The American Colonization Society failed miserably in its larger
purposes. It was unable to persuade the Federal government to give
financial support to its adventure. Sections of the colony were set
aside for Negro groups from various Southern states, such as Mississippi in Liberia, Maryland in Liberia, and Kentucky in Liberia.
Agents were sent throughout the South to obtain funds and emigrants, and a magazine, the *African Repository*, was published as a
means of propaganda. In Mississippi the society raised approxi-

mately $100,000, and the legislature of Maryland pledged its credit to the amount of $200,000 to aid in the colonization of Maryland Negroes. Some benevolent planters provided in their wills for the emancipation of their slaves and transportation to Liberia. Despite the efforts of the American Colonization Society, a relatively small number of Negroes were sent to Africa, 571 from Mississippi, for example, and 1,363 from North Carolina. The Society transported a total of approximately 12,000 Negroes between 1821, when the first contingent was sent, and 1867. So prodigious was the Negro birth rate that this number was a pitiful fraction of the increase of black babies born in slavery during this period. Thus colonization proved utterly impractical, not only because of the invincible birth rate of the Negro, but also because of the cost and difficulties of transportation to Africa. The American Colonization Society was branded by the abolitionists as a pro-slavery device to get rid of the free Negro, but after 1831 slaveholders gave it slight support.

The Southern Negroes themselves had no enthusiasm to return to their ancient home in the Dark Continent. Having become accustomed to American food, climate, and civilization, they dreaded going to a strange land. Many of those who did emigrate to Liberia died from tropical disease. The interior tribes were hostile and dangerous. Some of the Negroes who emigrated wrote discouraging reports to their masters and brethren in the United States—that the Negroes had farms usually no larger than five acres which they tilled with the hoe without the aid of horses and mules, lived in bamboo houses in a wilderness, and "tell Uncle pleasant that we have snakes here 15 to 20 feet and can Swalow a man, Dear, or a hog with ease." [4] Even to this day Liberia is not an attractive asylum to the American Negro. Sleeping sickness, malaria, hookworm, and dysentery make life precarious. The American Negroes and their descendants have enslaved the interior tribes as late as 1930. Moreover, they developed the idea that manual labor was degrading and a caste system arose—the descendants of slaves were copying the patterns of the white masters.

In January, 1831, William Lloyd Garrison began the publication in Boston, Massachusetts, of *The Liberator*, the first newspaper in the United States devoted to *immediate* abolition of slavery. This

New England printer was a natural agitator who espoused many other reforms besides the abolition of slavery. He had worked for a short time with Benjamin Lundy on the latter's antislavery newspaper in Baltimore, but he knew practically nothing of slavery from observation or experience. Nevertheless, he and his followers indulged in the most bitter attacks against the moral character of the slaveholders in language so extreme that they injured their cause, both in the North and the South. They conceived of the Negro bondsman as a white man enslaved. The platform of *The Liberator* was immediate emancipation of the slaves without any compensation to slaveholders. Since the Federal Constitution sanctioned slavery, Garrison condemned it as a compact with Hell and urged his followers not to vote nor to have anything to do with this iniquitous government. Indeed, he made slavery a great moral issue, upon which he would neither speak with moderation nor accept compromise. In 1857 he and his followers held a Secession Convention at Worcester, Massachusetts, to advocate that the *Northern* states should secede from the union with slaveholders.

The Liberator continued to be published throughout the antebellum period, although it never attained more than three thousand subscribers. During part of its existence it was supported largely by the free Negroes of the North. Southerners claimed that *The Liberator* circulated among the slaves and that it had stirred up the Nat Turner Revolt, but Garrison declared that he did not have a single subscriber in the South at that time. Furthermore, he was a pacifist who discouraged the use of violence in accomplishing reforms. *The Liberator* must be adjudged as an effective gadfly to agitate the question of abolishing slavery and to needle the conscience of the North, but the harm it caused in stirring bitter sectional feelings is incalculable.

The abolition movement in the North was soon organized into very vocal and active societies. The New England Anti-Slavery Society was founded by Garrison in 1832, and during the next year the American Anti-Slavery Society was started in New York City. The Philadelphia group of abolitionists until recently has been neglected by historians, but it contained such effective agitators as the wealthy merchants, Lewis and Arthur Tappan, William Jay, the son of Chief Justice John Jay, and Gerrit Smith, the millionaire of Peterboro. The Northern abolitionists were profoundly influenced by the English antislavery crusade which had led to the abolition of slavery in the British West Indies in 1833. From the reformers across the Atlantic were learned most of the techniques used in advancing the antislavery cause in the United States. The New England and New York societies published tons of lurid and fervid antislavery publications which they sent through the mails to leading men in the South. Although the New York group adopted as their slogan "immediate emancipation," they interpreted this term to mean that "measures looking toward ultimate emancipation be immediately begun"—which was a reasonable program that Jefferson might have approved.

Less spectacular than the eastern abolitionists, but tremendously influential, was the Ohio group led by Theodore D. Weld. The publication of the correspondence of Weld, the Grimké sisters, and of James G. Birney, as well as modern studies of the abolition movement have called attention to this group. Although Garrison remained in Southern eyes the symbol of the antislavery movement, it is probable that the Mid-Western band of abolitionists accomplished more effective work in converting Northerners to the cause than did the Garrisonians.[5] This group arose out of the great religious revivals conducted in the decade of the 1820's by Charles Grandison Finney. These Western abolitionists applied the technique of religious revivals to the abolitionist crusade, emphasizing the point that Southern slavery was a moral sin. Weld compiled a terrible tract called *American Slavery As It Is*, composed of recitals of abnormal and sensational incidents of Southern slavery that he had culled from newspapers and antislavery literature. Oberlin College, Ohio, founded in 1833, became the center of Western abolitionists and also one of the first American colleges to admit Negro students.

In 1839 the Liberty Party was formed to work for the abolition of slavery through political channels. Its first Presidential candidate was James G. Birney, a Kentuckian, who had tried unsuccessfully to establish an antislavery newspaper at Danville, Kentucky. This party, which held the balance of power in the pivotal state of New York in 1844, accidentally aided the election of James K. Polk to the

Presidency by withdrawing votes from Henry Clay. Four years later the Free Soil Party, a fusion of "Conscience Whigs," the old Liberty Party, and the Barnburners of New York, nominated Martin Van Buren as their Presidential candidate. The platform of this third party included the exclusion of slavery from the Federal territories and the granting of free homesteads to settlers. Its slogan was "free soil, free speech, free labor and free men." In the decades of the 1840's and 1850's practical politicians began to realize the advantage of joining the attack against "the Slave Power."

Some of the most effective crusaders of the abolition movement were ministers and writers. At first the conservative churches of the North, such as the Unitarian and Congregationalist, frowned on the radical abolitionists, who tended to injure the valuable Southern trade. The vehement agitator, Parker Pillsbury, was expelled from the Congregational church, and the Garrisonians attacked the churches as the bulwark of slavery. Gradually, however, the churches became powerful centers of antislavery feeling, and prominent ministers such as Theodore Parker, Henry Ward Beecher, and Thomas Wentworth Higginson became ardent abolitionists. A brilliant array of literary talent, including Whittier, Lowell, Emerson, Thoreau, and Horace Greeley, editor of the *New York Tribune*, also waged a relentless literary warfare against Southern slavery.

By far the most influential of the antislavery writers was Harriet Beecher Stowe, the wife of a professor who had taught in Lane Theological Seminary at Cincinnati, where fugitive slaves crossed the Ohio River to freedom. In 1852 Mrs. Stowe published a deeply moving tale of the possibilities of inhumanity in the slavery system entitled *Uncle Tom's Cabin*. This work of propaganda was not based on any real knowledge of slavery (even her later defense of the truth of her novel, *Key to Uncle Tom's Cabin*, was derived from printed sources). By her vivid writing, however, Mrs. Stowe became one of the greatest creators of American stereotypes before Sinclair Lewis portrayed the unforgettable "Babbitt." She created stereotypes of slave traders, idealized portraits of the Negro slave, as well as romanticized versions of aristocrats, which entered deeply into popular thought in the North. Her work was emotional and melodramatic, admirably adapted to the taste of the half-educated audience of readers that had been created by the recently founded public schools. The effectiveness of Mrs. Stowe's novel was tremendously increased by the stage version, which has had one of the longest runs in the history of the theater. *Uncle Tom's Cabin* influenced the rising generation of young voters in the North to vote for the Republican Party. In the South the book was rightly condemned as a distortion of Southern society, and Mrs. Stowe was branded as an immoral and unsexed creature. The Southern states made the mistake of trying to suppress its circulation, but thousands of Southerners read it surreptitiously. Over a dozen proslavery novels by Southern authors arose to counteract the false impression of the Northern novel, but no one has ever heard of them except specialists in Southern literature.

The abolitionists started out by attacking the institution of Southern slavery, but soon they began a violent and indiscriminate denunciation of Southerners and their way of life. They built up a stereotype of slavery and of Southern society that modern historians have found difficult to dispel. Ignoring the handicaps of the Negro as a human being and the rural condition of the South, they blamed all the backwardness of the region, the illiteracy of the people, the exhaustion of the soil, and the lack of industrialization on slavery. The abolitionists painted the South as a land where masters made female slaves their concubines and enslaved their mulatto offspring. The whip never ceased to sear the flesh of their trembling bond servants, for Southerners were cruel and coarse in all the relations of life. The slave trade and the separation of families were a constant staple of their exaggeration. The existence of a substantial middle class of yeoman farmers in the South was ignored, and members of the non-slaveholding class were portrayed as debased creatures. In politics the Slave Power was envisaged as always on the aggressive, striving to pollute free soil and exclude honest laborers from the North from settling on the public domain. In short, the abolitionist propaganda was a black-and-white type of ideology. Their libels of Southern civilization naturally aroused the deepest resentment and intolerance below the Mason and Dixon line. Furthermore, they did not advocate the only fair and practical step toward accomplishing their objective, namely, the use of Federal funds to aid in compensating the owners of slaves for their loss of property as a result of adopting the abolition program.

The abolition movement led to one of the most violent struggles in the history of the nation to suppress civil liberties. Some of the worst offenses against civil liberties occurred in the Northern border states during the decade of the 1830's. Here abolitionists were mobbed countless times and denied their constitutional rights of free speech and freedom of the press. On July 30, 1836, a mob in Cincinnati threw the press of James G. Birney's antislavery newspaper, *The Philanthropist*, into the Ohio River, and in the following year another mob at Alton, Illinois, killed Elijah P. Lovejoy, the brave editor of the abolitionist newspaper, the *Alton Observer*. Colleges such as Marion College in Missouri and Lane Theological Seminary in Cincinnati suppressed academic freedom in regard to the discussion of the emancipation of slaves. In New England Garrison was dragged through the streets by a mob; an academy at Canaan, New Hampshire, which admitted Negro pupils, was transported away by a hundred yoke of oxen; the home of the abolitionist, Lewis Tappan, in New York City was wrecked; and Pennsylvania Hall, a notable forum for the abolitionists, was burned. The tyranny of a mob or of passionate public opinion, indeed, is one of the worst forms of despotism. When public opinion was excited in the South over the appearance of abolitionists in Southern communities or over the rumors of servile insurrections, mobs and vigilance committees usurped the functions of the courts.[6]

In 1835 the abolitionists discovered a shrewd means of advertising their cause, the strategy of presenting petitions to Congress to abolish slavery in the District of Columbia. Southern Congressmen maintained that such petitions should not be received, on the ground that Congress had no jurisdiction over domestic slavery. On the other hand, Northern Representatives, as a group, believed that the antislavery petitions should be received, for the freedom of petition, one of the sacred rights of a democracy, was involved in this issue. The chief presenter of the abolitionist petitions, which came in a flood in 1835–37, was John Quincy Adams, the ex-President, who was now serving as a simple Congressman from Massachusetts. In this new role as the introducer of antislavery petitions, Adams maintained, insincerely, that he was not an abolitionist but was fighting for the freedom of petition. This bald-headed, irascible, and satirical New Englander enjoyed taunting the long-haired orators from the South, and his activities in Congress increased the atmosphere of bitter hatred between the sections. The South was not lacking in violent champions, chief of whom was Henry A. Wise of Virginia, who replied to Adams in kind, and who led a secession of Southern Congressmen from the House of Representatives in 1836 when William Slade of Vermont caustically attacked Southern slavery.

On account of Southern pressure, the lower house of Congress in 1836 adopted the Gag Resolution. Introduced by Henry L. Pinckney of South Carolina, this resolution provided that the House of Representatives should technically receive the abolition petitions, but that they should immediately be laid on the table, without referring them to a committee and without debate. The Gag Rule was continually renewed until it was repealed in December, 1844. The Gag Rule of 1840 read, "That no petition, memorial, resolution or other paper praying the abolition of slavery in the District of Columbia, or any State or Territory, or the slave trade between the States or Territories of the United States in which it now exists, shall be received by the House, or entertained in any way whatever." [7] This rule was finally abandoned when Northern allies withdrew their support and when some Southerners realized that it was doing more harm than good to their cause. Southern chauvinists who insisted on a rigid rejection of abolitionist petitions in Congress did the South a great disservice by alienating the sympathy of many sincere lovers of "democracy" in the North who were indifferent to the reform of abolishing slavery.

Another flaming issue that involved civil liberties was the right of the abolitionists to use the Federal mails to forward their publications into the Southern states. In the summer of 1835 a mob in Charleston, South Carolina, supported by ex-Governor Robert Y. Hayne, entered the post office and destroyed several sacks of mail containing abolition literature. The whole South was aroused to the menace of the circulation of abolition publications below the Mason and Dixon line. It is an established fact that the abolition societies of the North had adopted a concerted plan in 1835 to flood the South with antislavery pamphlets, newspapers, and periodicals. These publications were addressed to white people to persuade them to abandon slavery, but Southerners believed that the abolitionists designed their publications to foment servile insurrections. A small minority of the slaves could read, some of whom were taught illegally by their masters. It was feared in the South that the lurid antislavery literature would fall into the hands of some brooding Nat Turner who would lead a slave revolt.

In a message to Congress, December, 1835, President Jackson recommended that Congress pass a law prohibiting the circulation through the mails in the Southern states of "incendiary publications intended to instigate the slaves to insurrection." [8] Calhoun was opposed to such a law that would enhance the power of the Federal government. Instead, he introduced into the Senate early in 1836 a bill which would accomplish the object of erecting a *cordon sanitaire* against the entry of abolition literature into the South. His bill would have made it illegal for Northern postmasters to receive and forward abolition publications to those states whose laws prohibited the circulation of such publications. This bill failed to pass Congress, but a policy of Federal censorship of the mails, preventing the free circulation of abolition publications in the South, was adopted unofficially by the Postal Department. With impunity, individual postmasters in the South refused to deliver abolition literature. A series of Postmasters-General from the days of Amos Kendall in Jackson's cabinet to Joseph Holt in Buchanan's cabinet permitted this extra-legal censorship of the mails. No attempt was made to discriminate between literature which was a rational discussion of the evils of slavery and that which comprised incendiary appeals to violence. Thus a genuine blockade was set up that protected the minds of Southern whites from the contagion of abolitionist arguments as well as kept the slaves from being inflamed to dissatisfaction or revolt by emotional antislavery literature.[9]

The development of an elaborate argument justifying slavery began in the South before the rise of the abolition movement. South Carolina was the cradle of the pro-slavery argument, which originated as early as 1789. In the Palmetto State the economic and social humus was most suited to the growth of an intellectual defense of slavery. South Carolina had inherited its type of slavery and its attitudes toward the Negro from the rich sugar island of Barbados. Moreover, rice culture was peculiarly adapted to the use of slave labor. The Negroes who worked in the rice fields were blacker and closer to Africa than the slaves of the upper South. Many of the Gullah Negroes, indeed, had been imported during the period when the state reopened the African slave trade, and they needed stricter control than the slaves of the upper South who had been habituated to the white man's society for a considerable period of time. Also the prevalence of malaria in the swampy, coastal region of South Carolina and Georgia caused the wealthy planters to flee from the miasmic lowlands during the spring and summer seasons, leaving the blacks and the overseers to the tender mercies of disease-bearing mosquitoes. It was natural that South Carolina should have discarded the apologetic tone of defending slavery, and that, in such leaders as Senator William Smith, Whitemarsh B. Seabrook, and Doctor Thomas Cooper, president of South Carolina College during the decade of the 1820's, it should have produced some of the early exponents of slavery as a positive good. Later, in 1852, the great classic of slavery defense, *The Pro-Slavery Argument*, containing essays by the South Carolinians, William Gilmore Simms, Chancellor William Harper, James H. Hammond, and others, was published at Charleston.[10] Was this elaborate rationalization of a great social evil motivated by a desire to convince non-slaveholders in order to preserve planter control, or was it evoked to quiet the conscience of Southern slaveholders, or was it a recognition of the moral power of world opinion?

In the upper South a pioneer in producing an able argument in defense of slavery was Thomas Roderick Dew. He was a young professor at William and Mary College who had recently returned from study in Germany. In 1832 he published a pamphlet, *Review of the Debates in the Virginia Legislature of 1831 and 1832*, in which he refuted arguments for the emancipation of the slaves made in the Virginia legislature following the Nat Turner revolt. Dew based his polemic partly upon his study of Aristotle who had justified Greek slavery as a recognition of the natural inequality of man. In addition to deriving a justification of slavery from the order of nature, Dew pointed out that the Bible sanctioned this ancient in-- stitution. These philosophical arguments were buttressed by the economic argument, namely, the lucrative profits obtained from the internal slave trade and the immense property loss that emancipation would entail.

One of the most powerful arguments in the pro-slavery dialectic was the alleged support of the Bible, for the overwhelming majority of Southern people were firmly indoctrinated in a belief in the sacredness of the literal word of the Bible. The apologists of slavery drew their arguments chiefly from the Old Testament which de- scribed a primitive society among the Jews in which the patriarchs held slaves. They also maintained that slavery was ordained by God as a punishment of Canaan, son of Ham, from whom, they affirmed without reliable evidence, the Negroes were descended. In the New Testament the defenders of slavery pointed to the advice that the Apostle Paul had given to a fugitive slave to return to his master as well as Christ's silence in regard to this contemporary institution.

The Baptist, Methodist, and Presbyterian churches in the South, which had condemned slavery in their pioneering period, gradually became pro-slavery as their congregations grew wealthier and more attached to the vested interests of Negro slavery. Leading Southern ministers, such as J. H. Thornwell, B. H. Palmer, Thornton String- fellow, H. B. Bascom, and William A. Smith wrote books and de- livered sermons showing that the institution was approved by God. In 1844 the general conference of the Methodist Episcopal Church requested Bishop James O. Andrew of Georgia to cease his espicopal duties until he had disposed of his slaves acquired by a second marriage. This incident led to the separation of the Southern churches from the national organization and the formation at Louisville in 1845 of the Methodist Episcopal Church, South. During the same year, the Southern Baptists, incensed over the refusal of the national missions board to employ a slaveholder as a missionary, organized the "Southern Baptist Convention."

A myriad of arguments were adduced to show that slavery was needed as a social discipline. If the slaves were emancipated, the pro- slavery argument maintained, they would be uncontrollable, refusing to work, stealing, and committing other crimes. The example of the shiftless free Negro was brought forward as a solemn warning against a wholesale freeing of the blacks. The poor whites and mechanics feared the consequences of competition with hordes of emancipated Negroes. The massacre of the whites in Santo Domingo and the great decline of agriculture in Jamaica after emancipation were cited as proofs of the dangers of emancipation. Religious apologists maintained that the Negro had benefited tremendously from slavery, for he was transported from the barbarism of Africa and was civilized and Christianized in America.

Demagogues raised the bogey of social amalgamation if the slaves were freed and allowed to remain in the country. Deeply rooted in Southern psychology was a fear that the emancipation movement would break down the barriers set up to preserve a pure white race in the South. The census of 1860 clearly indicated that racial antipathy was not enough to prevent considerable miscegenation, for approximately 13 per cent of the Negroes in the United States were mulattoes. The presence of mixed blood among the free Negroes was striking, approximately three-fourths of the free Negroes having an admixture of white blood. New Orleans was notorious for the concubinage system by which Creoles maintained mulatto and quadroon mistresses.

The emphasis in the Old South on the biological inferiority of the Negroes bears some resemblance to the Nazi ideology of race. Most Southerners took it for granted that the Negroes constituted a permanently subordinate race, inferior to the white man in intellect, character, and physiology—a child-like people. Dr. Josiah C. Nott, a physician of Mobile, Alabama, strengthened the ethnological argument justifying slavery by his theory of the plural origin of the races. In 1854, with the collaboration of the archaeologist, George R. Gliddon, he published his work, *Types of Mankind*, in which he maintained that mankind did not have a common progenitor but that the Negro and the white man were separately created species. This theory, which denied the unity of mankind, did not win general acceptance in the South, since it conflicted with the Biblical account of the origin of man. Reverend John Bachman of Charleston, South Carolina, confuted the pluralists in his volume, *The Doctrine of the Unity of the Human Race* (1850), and Dr. John Wesley

Monette of Mississippi wrote a manuscript entitled "The Causes of the Variety of the Complexion and Form of the Human Species," in which he affirmed the primitive unity of the races and explained racial differences as caused by environment and climate. One of the degrading effects of the pro-slavery argument which has continued into our day is the emphasis on the basic inferiority of the Negro to the white man. Although it is impossible at the present time to determine conclusively whether Negroes as a group are equal in innate intelligence and personality to Caucasians, the advances which have been made within recent years in measuring human intelligence tend to throw doubt on the old allegation of the inherent inferiority of the Negro.

In the last decade of the ante-bellum period the pro-slavery argument acquired a militant leadership under Henry Hughes of Port Gibson, Mississippi, William J. Grayson, collector of the port of Charleston, and George Fitzhugh, a Virginia lawyer. Hughes wrote a defense of slavery in 1854 entitled *A Treatise on Sociology*, in which the word "sociology" was first used in the title of an American book. It is interesting to note that the pro-slavery argument led to pioneering efforts, however prejudiced, in developing the science of sociology. Hughes maintained that the advance of civilization in the South had essentially changed Southern slavery, although he produced no valid evidence for his conclusion. He held that slavery had advanced to warranteeism, which gave to the master a trusteeship over the slave and the ownership of the slave's labor only and not of his body. Convinced that slavery was a positive good, he was a strong advocate for reopening the African slave trade under an apprenticeship system. In 1856 Grayson published a vigorous poem, *The Hireling and the Slave*, defending Southern slavery as a paternal institution far more humane than the wage slavery of New England.

Fitzhugh's important contribution was to focus attention on the evils of Northern capitalism, which the abolitionists had ignored in their zeal to reform their Southern brethren. He proclaimed "the failure" of free society, for the condition of the laboring class in the industrial states, he asserted, was worse than that of the Southern slave. Slavery, he maintained, was a wholesome and natural institution for free *white* workers as well as black slaves. He predicted that the North would experience the diseased symptoms of competitive society prevalent in Europe, strikes, the rise of socialism, and the degradation of the laboring class while the South with its harmonious labor system would become the conservative balance wheel of the nation. In the land of plantations the slaves were cared for during sickness, old age, and in times of economic depression, while in the North wages were barely enough to sustain life, child labor of the worst type prevailed, and the workers were ruthlessly exploited by capitalists in a form of wage slavery. These arguments were propagated in *De Bow's Review*, in Southern newspapers, and in two paradoxical books, *Sociology for the South; or, the Failure of Free Society* (1854), and *Cannibals All! or, Slaves Without Masters* (1857). Fitzhugh was not a deep or original thinker, deriving many of his ideas from Carlyle and the English reviews, but he was primarily "a propagandist of the Old South." He did a great deal of harm by exacerbating the relations between the North and the South.

One of the significant phases of the pro-slavery argument was the repudiation of the philosophy of liberalism.[11] Senator James H. Hammond of South Carolina denounced the Declaration of Independence with its doctrine of the equality of men as a fallacious and glittering generalization. On the contrary, he declared that men were naturally unequal and that Negro slavery furnished "a mudsill" for a white democracy. Calhoun supported this argument in behalf of slavery, contending that the Southern slaves freed the master class from drudgery and allowed them the leisure to cultivate the art of politics and refined living. Thus Southern society was idealized as being a Greek democracy, resting on a base of slave labor. The Whig leader, Abel P. Upshur, and later Fitzhugh flatly rejected the romantic liberalism of Thomas Jefferson in favor of a thoroughly conservative and aristocratic caste system. But they misrepresented public opinion in the South, which was devoted to a decentralized white democracy. When Fitzhugh proclaimed an irrepressible conflict between the free form of society and the slave system, which would be resolved by the extension of slavery into the North, he represented only a distinct minority of Southerners. By his extreme editorials in the Richmond press he furnished

Seward and Lincoln with the ammunition for their famous speeches on "the irrepressible conflict" and "the House Divided" doctrine that alarmed Northern workers and small farmers.[12]

Opposing the overwhelming propaganda of the pro-slavery argument was a small group of Southern liberals. No one will ever know the strength of the antislavery sentiment in the South during the period 1831–61, whose finest representatives were persons of tender conscience or critical-minded individuals who were able to free themselves from traditional views. Probably most of the antislavery people were inarticulate because of prudence. The outspoken opponents of slavery, of whom records have been preserved, were chiefly members of the professional class, preachers, college professors, lawyers, and literary men. As regards geographical distribution, they were located principally in the upper South, where Negroes were decidedly less concentrated than in the deep South.

A turning point in the development of the Southern mind was reached in 1831–32 after the shock of the Nat Turner insurrection. The great debate over emancipation that took place in the Virginia legislature following that event brought forward a number of Southern liberals. In the course of the discussion eloquent speeches were made by young men, such as Charles J. Faulkner, James McDowell, and George W. Summers, attacking the evils of slavery and urging the adoption of a plan of gradual emancipation. They based their argument on the danger of servile insurrection, the economic decline of Virginia, which they blamed on slavery, and the pernicious effects of the "peculiar institution" on the whites. Unfortunately, they were unable to agree on a practicable plan of emancipation and of deportation of the freed Negroes. Sectionalism played an important role in the development of antislavery sentiment in Virginia, for the western part of the state felt that the slave-owning planters blocked the progress of the West. Consequently, an antislavery resolution introduced by William B. Preston from the West received the unanimous support of the western delegates. Only nine votes from the combined Tidewater and Piedmont, however, were cast in its favor, including the vote of Jefferson's grandson, Thomas Jefferson Randolph. The measure was lost by 73 negative votes against 58 affirmative votes.[13] After this defeat of the liberals, there was a strong conservative reaction in Virginia which lasted until the surrender at Appomattox.

After 1832 those Southern liberals who protested against the continuance of slavery as a perpetual institution met strong social disapproval. Their position in the South was rendered more difficult by the rising tide of resentment against the Northern abolitionists. Jesse Burton Harrison, educated at Harvard, wrote a reply to Thomas R. Dew's celebrated pro-slavery pamphlet entitled *Review of The Slave Question* (Richmond, 1832) in which he made a noble appeal for freedom of discussion of this grave problem and the adoption of a plan of gradual emancipation. In North Carolina Daniel R. Goodloe, converted to the antislavery cause by reading the Virginia debates of 1831–32, attacked slavery from an economic point of view in a pamphlet entitled, *Inquiry into the Causes Which Have Retarded the Accumulation of Wealth and Increase of Population in the Southern States* (1844). One of the most significant of the antislavery publications by Southerners was *An Address to the People of West Virginia, Shewing that Slavery Is Injurious to the Public Welfare*, published in 1847 by Dr. Henry Ruffner, president of Washington College at Lexington, Virginia. Dr. Ruffner attacked slavery as a wasteful and unsound system of labor which had caused many of the sons of Virginia to emigrate to free soil.

Two concerted efforts were made by liberals in the upper South after the Virginia debate to secure the adoption of a plan of gradual emancipation. In 1834, when a constitutional convention met in Tennessee, memorials for the adoption of a scheme of gradual emancipation were presented which were signed by 1804 persons, chiefly from East Tennessee. A report was finally adopted by the convention, admitting that slavery was an evil: "To prove it to be a great evil is an easy task, but to tell how that evil can be removed is a question that the wisest heads and the most benevolent hearts have not been able to answer in a satisfactory manner." [14] Nothing was done, however, to free the state from the incubus of an admitted evil, primarily because of the race problem, the blind spot of Southerners in visualizing a society of free Negroes and whites living together to the mutual advantage of both races. [15]

The liberals of Kentucky were similarly frustrated in 1849 when a constitutional convention met. An antislavery newspaper, *The Examiner*, was established in Louisville to influence public opinion to send delegates to the convention who would vote for the gradual abolition of slavery in Kentucky.[16] An Emancipation Meeting at Bowling Green, Kentucky, on May 12, 1849, proclaimed that although the group were opposed to "disturbing the right of Masters to their slaves now in being in Kentucky," they desired a clause in the new constitution utterly prohibiting the further introduction of slaves into the commonwealth. This document also declared that all slaves emancipated in the state should be removed to Africa or elsewhere, and finally that a time should be fixed in the new constitution "when the people may vote on prospective emancipation, and declare whether they desire to rid our beloved commonwealth, in a convenient and reasonable time, of the institution of slavery." [17] It was signed by forty-one citizens and ordered to be distributed by means of handbills. Also a state emancipation convention was held at Frankfort, attended by many slaveholders. Despite the fact that ten thousand votes were cast in the state for the election of antislavery delegates, not a single candidate was elected. In this year also the pro-slavery faction succeeded in repealing a law of 1833 prohibiting the bringing of slaves into the state for sale. Furthermore, shortly after the convention met the liberal *Examiner* perished for want of financial support.

No account of Southern liberalism would be complete without recording the crusading efforts of John Hampden Pleasants and Cassius Marcellus Clay. During a brief interim of freedom of discussion enjoyed by the press after the shock of the Nat Turner insurrection, Pleasants wrote brilliant editorials in the Richmond *Whig* urging the emancipation of the slaves. In 1846 he was killed in a duel by a rival editor who had accused him of being an abolitionist. Cassius Marcellus Clay, the son of an aristocratic planter of Kentucky, sacrificed a promising career in politics to advocate the gradual emancipation of the slaves. Clay had been educated at Yale, where he was deeply attracted to the antislavery cause by hearing William Lloyd Garrison speak. Nevertheless, he did not become a militant antislavery man until he had a political quarrel in 1840 with Robert Wickliffe, called "the Old Duke," the largest slaveholder in Kentucky, whose son he defeated for representative in the legislature. In 1845 Clay began the publication of an antislavery newspaper at Lexington which bore the name of *The True American*. Anticipating the attack of a mob, he fortified his printing office with an arsenal of cannon and rifles and by placing a keg of powder with a fuse attached which could be used to blow up the office in case it was invaded by ruffians. He had published his antislavery newspaper only a few months when a huge assembly of citizens resolved that no abolition organ should be tolerated in Kentucky, on the principle that *salus populi suprema lex*. A committee was appointed who, while Clay was sick, entered the amateur fortress of *The True American*, dismantled the presses, and sent them to Cincinnati. A similar fate of suppression by a mob occurred in 1859, when William Bailey, a Northern mechanic, established the *Free South* at Newport, Kentucky, devoted to a policy of organizing the Southern non-slaveholders to use their votes to exterminate slavery.

North Carolina produced three valiant critics of slavery during the last decade of the ante-bellum period. Benjamin Sherwood Hedrick, after study at Harvard, became a professor of chemistry at the University of North Carolina. During the Presidential campaign of 1856 he expressed his free soil views by announcing that he would vote for Fremont. The Raleigh *Standard* launched a campaign to drive him from the state, which succeeded, for he was dismissed from the faculty of the University. Reverend Eli Washington Caruthers was forced to resign his position as pastor of a Presbyterian church at Greensboro, North Carolina, in the summer of 1861 because of his antislavery views. The most significant opponent of slavery that the state produced was the writer Hinton Rowan Helper, a representative of the yeoman class of the Piedmont.

In 1857 Helper published in New York City *The Impending Crisis*, in which he tried to show that the South was far inferior to the North in economic productivity and general civilization as a result of the burden of slavery. Using the statistics of the Census of 1850, he made invidious comparisons. He stated, for example, that the Northern hay crop alone was worth more than all the cotton, rice, tobacco, and hemp produced in the fifteen slave states. (Southerners replied to this spectacular statement by observing that their warm climate permitted their cattle and horses to graze a large part of the year and that the production of hay was really a drain on the economic energies of the Northern people.) He also developed the view that the slaveholding oligarchy had conspired to keep the poor whites in a dependent, illiterate condition. With considerable accuracy he may be called the Karl Marx of the non-slaveholding whites whom he tried to arouse to a sense of class consciousness. Although he was an immediate abolitionist, he hated the Negroes, whom he regarded as the competitors of the poor whites. Like the Georgia pamphleteer, John Jacobus Flournoy, Helper was a Negrophobe, a bitter expulsionist, urging the wholesale shipping of the Negroes to Africa. *The Impending Crisis* was published as a campaign document for the Republican Party, and it became a crime in the South to circulate it.

Southern liberalism had little apparent effect in counteracting the victory of the pro-slavery argument. But the numerous efforts of enlightened planters to ameliorate the harsh features of slavery must be reckoned as a part of Southern liberalism. The aristocratic planter, William H. Fitzhugh of "Ravensworth" in Virginia, adopted a plan of gradually training slaves for the responsibilities of free men, preparatory to liberating them. He settled some of his slaves as tenants on small farms. They paid him a rent for the land and for the stock he furnished, but nothing for the hire of their time. The net profits of this arrangement were set aside for the purchase of their freedom and to send them to Liberia.[18] Jefferson Davis and his millionaire brother, Joseph, adopted on their Mississippi plantations a rudimentary form of self-government for their slaves, with slave courts, and with incentives for working industriously and earning money. John McDonogh, the famous merchant of New Orleans, allowed his slaves to earn their freedom by overtime work on Saturday afternoons. Some benevolent Southerners, like Charles Colcock Jones of Georgia, tried to improve the moral and spiritual side of the Negroes by zealous efforts to give them religious instruction. Also it is an interesting fact that Southerners of the later antebellum period seldom referred to their Negro bondsmen as "slaves" but used such terms as "servants," "hands," and "my people." In the adoption of this nomenclature there seems to be revealed a kinder feeling toward their dark-skinned dependents than the use of the more brutal word "slave" would imply. Or were Southerners ashamed of the stark use of this word?

The endeavors of the Southern liberals and the abolitionist crusade, however, accomplished practically nothing toward revising the black code in the direction of greater humanity. The most progressive step which the Southern states could have taken toward attacking a great social evil was to repeal the laws which virtually prevented individuals from emancipating their slaves. The refusal to make this concession was a great mistake, for by individual emancipations a more liberal spirit might have been generated in Southern society as a whole. At the close of the ante-bellum period nothing had been effected to prevent the sale of husbands from their wives, and only Louisiana and Alabama had laws prohibiting the sale of children under ten years of age from their mothers. All the Southern states, except Maryland, Kentucky, and Tennessee, prohibited the teaching of slaves to read and write. The disability of slaves and of free Negroes, except in Louisiana, to give testimony against white persons in the law courts also remained a practice of the Southern states. Thus the Negro was left poorly protected from cruel or unscrupulous white men, for the force of public opinion was not an adequate substitute for justice in the courts. The failure to revise the slave code, to ameliorate the conditions of Negro bondage, or even to permit the realistic discussion of emancipation, and the refusal of the border states to take any constructive steps toward gradually removing slavery add up to a dark outlook for the cause of Southern liberalism on the eve of the Civil War.

The Southern liberals of the ante-bellum period were lonely individuals, free lances, who were, in general, denied the use of the press or the right of subjecting the Southern social system to sanative criticism. Almost without exception they spurned the epithet of abolitionist, for they advocated a gradual process of emancipating the Negroes. Some of them were belated Jeffersonians who believed in the dignity of man even if he wore a black skin. Perhaps the two most powerful impulses which led them to urge the removal of slavery were moral considerations, as evidenced by the considerable proportion of ministers in their ranks, and by economic realism. Unfortunately, the Southern liberals exaggerated the importance of slavery as a cause of the economic and educational retardation of the South and failed to realize the existence of other powerful contributing factors, such as the dominant ruralism of the South, the westward movement, and the presence of the Negroes in large numbers in the South, irrespective of the institution of slavery.

Citations

1. Quoted in CLEMENT EATON, *Freedom of Thought in the Old South* (Durham, 1940), 19.
2. LOUIS MORTON, *Robert Carter of Nomini Hall* (Princeton, 1941).
3. H. M. WAGSTAFF (ed.), *Minutes of the N. C. Manumission Society, 1816–1834* (Chapel Hill, 1934), and S. B. WEEKS, *Southern Quakers and Slavery* (Baltimore, 1896).
4. MOSES JACKSON, Kentucky in Liberia, to Eliott West, Nicholasville, Ky., March 22, 1846. MS in Wilson Collection, University of Kentucky Library. Another letter in the collection, on the other hand, from Robert Johnson to Thomas Dolan, August 20, 1846 refers to Liberia as "that country where I am known as a man and the only country in which the colored man enjoys undisturbed liberty."
5. G. H. BARNES, *The Antislavery Impulse, 1830–1848* (New York, 1933), argues convincingly on this thesis.
6. CLEMENT EATON, "Mob Violence in the Old South," *Mississippi Valley Historical Review*, XXIX (December, 1942), 351–370.
7. *Congressional Globe*, VII (26th Congress, 1st Session), 150.
8. RICHARDSON, *Messages and Papers of the Presidents*, III, 176.
9. CLEMENT EATON, "Censorship of the Southern Mails," *American Historical Review*, XLVIII (January, 1943), 266–280.
10. Valuable studies of the pro-slavery argument are given by W. S. JENKINS, *Pro-Slavery Thought in the Old South* (Chapel Hill, 1935), and W. B. HESSELTINE, "Some New Aspects of the Pro-Slavery Argument," *op. cit.*
11. W. G. BEAN, "Anti-Jeffersonianism in the Ante-Bellum South," *North Carolina Historical Review*, XII (April, 1935), 102–124.
12. See HARVEY WISH, *George Fitzhugh, Propagandist of the Old South* (Baton Rouge, 1943).

13. J. C. ROBERT, *The Road from Monticello: a Study of the Virginia Slavery Debate of 1832* (Durham, 1941).

14. *Journal of the Constitutional Convention of 1834* (Nashville, 1834), 87–88.

15. C. C. MOONEY, "The Question of Slavery and the Free Negro in the Tennessee Constitutional Convention of 1834," *Journal of Southern History*, XII (November, 1946), 486–509.

16. *The Examiner* was opposed to the Northern abolitionists. It published a plan of emancipation proposed by W. L. Breckinridge, based on freeing all slaves born after 1850 at age of 25 and sending them to Liberia. *The Examiner*, March 3, 1849. A file, February 10, 1847 to March 3, 1849, is owned by the Wisconsin Historical Society.

17. MS in the Thomas Henry Hines Papers, University of Kentucky Library.

18. *The African Repository*, III (August, 1827), 185.

CHAPTER XVII

Commerce in the Old South

THE commerce of the Old South was dominated by the cotton, rice, sugar, and grain factors. These agents of the planters, often Northerners or Englishmen, had counting-houses or warehouses in the leading Southern ports and inland shipping towns. To them the planters sent their staple crops to be sold either to buyers of Northern or English houses or forwarded directly to Liverpool or New York. The factor was a versatile man of business in an agrarian society who performed many different services for the planter besides selling his crops. He purchased or sold slaves for his client, arranged for the hiring of slaves or the placing of the planter's children in distant schools, gave advice concerning the condition of the market or the advisability of selling or withholding his crop, and bought for him a large proportion of the plantation supplies.

The factorage system was a development in the specialization of labor in the South. Thus the planter was relieved of the responsibilities of selling his crop and buying his supplies. He could therefore devote his energies to the problems of slave management and the production of staple crops. But he frequently paid a high price for the services of the factor. The cotton factor received not only 2½ per cent commission for selling the staple crops, but he charged a commission varying from 2½ per cent to 10 per cent for buying supplies for the plantation. Also he deducted from the planter's balance on his books a standard rate for insurance, storage, drayage, weighing, mending, etc., in some instances receiving a rebate from the business firms supplying these services. Some of the rice planters, however, such as Robert F. W. Allston, established such favorable connections with their factors that they rendered many miscellaneous services gratis for the privilege of handling the sale of the rice. Indeed, one of the most recent studies of the rice factor indicates that he realized only a moderate profit from his transactions with the planters and did not unduly exploit his strategic position.[1]

The factor performed a valuable service in furnishing credit to the planter until his crops were harvested. One of the most serious indictments against the factor has been that he exploited the planter by charging exorbitant rates of interest. The ante-bellum period was an era of high interest rates in various sections of the country. Planters paid as much as 12 per cent or more for loans during times of depression. On the other hand, the papers of Elisha F. King, one of the wealthy planters of the black belt of Alabama who usually had a favorable balance in his accounts with the numerous factors he employed, show that he paid only 2½ per cent interest on loans from his factors and that he received a similar rate of interest for his surplus money kept on deposit by them. The planter used the factor as a means of providing a checking account, against which he issued drafts or due bills in settling debts or purchasing Negroes and land.

The most pernicious aspect of the factorage system was the control of the factor in many instances over the cotton planter's production of his crop. When the factor made a loan to a planter, as a rule he attached to the loan a penalty commission clause. He stipulated that all of the cotton crop of the planter should be consigned to him, and that the debtor should cultivate a certain number of acres and send to him a specified number of bales of cotton.[2] If the planter failed to perform his part of the contract, he forfeited a penalty ranging as high as four dollars for every bale below the stipulated number which he omitted to deliver. This harsh condition placed upon loans contributed to the overproduction of cotton and to fastening a one-crop economy on the South. The factorage system, furthermore, hindered the growth of inland towns and concentrated wealth in the seaports. In a few cases, however, an interior town, such as Memphis, overcame this handicap and became itself a center for cotton factors. At the close of the ante-bellum period this city shipped down the Mississippi River nearly four hundred thousand bales of cotton annually.

The prevalent view of the factor as an outrageous exploiter is a one-sided picture, based primarily on the papers of the planters. The much-maligned factor has received more favorable treatment than is usually accorded him in a recent monograph on Ebenezer Pettigrew, an enlightened grain planter of eastern North Carolina.[3] Pettigrew sent his wheat to New York, his corn to Charleston, and his forest products—lumber, shingles and staves—to Norfolk or Baltimore. The firm of New York factors with whom he dealt had branches in the North Carolina ports of Edenton and Plymouth. The factors often saved money for the planter by their advice when to sell and buy, based on an elaborate crop-reporting system, which furnished information about the effects of drought, floods, and disease on growing crops. Some of these commercial agents were vertical factors, who not only did a commission business, but also owned wholesale stores, ships, rope-walks, brick kilns, etc. The factors tried to get the best prices for the staples of their patrons and the fact that many of them went into bankruptcy may throw some light on whether they exploited the planter. The exorbitant freight rates for shipping staples to New York seem to have been a much greater grievance of the planters than factor's commissions. Pettigrew tried to free himself from vassalage to grasping ship-owners by building his own schooner, *Lady of the Lake*, which proved very successful, but this device to eliminate excessive transportation rates was adopted by relatively few planters.

In the colonial period the wealthy merchants often had belonged to the aristocracy, especially in Charleston, South Carolina. With the rise of the cotton kingdom, however, the merchants seem to have declined in social status. Some of the inland merchants started their careers as peddlers, thus acquiring a small amount of capital and then establishing themselves as settled merchants in the villages and towns. The peddlers transported their goods in various ways, by walking through the country-side with packs on their backs, riding horses carrying their merchandise in saddle bags, driving wagons laden with goods, or in the lower South, using pirogues. The packs of the peddlers contained needles, jewelry, handkerchiefs, mirrors, almanacs, ginghams, calicoes, umbrellas, and tinware. Some peddlers specialized in selling fruit trees, seeds, and Bibles. The Connecticut clock-makers distributed their clocks in the

South through peddlers, who sold them on credit to gullible house-wives and farmers. New England peddlers were regarded as guilty of sharp practices, particularly selling adulterated goods, like "wooden nutmegs." Indeed, considerable hostility arose in the South toward peddlers in general, because many of them were feared as dissemi-nators of antislavery propaganda and as agents of insurrection. Some of the Southern states, therefore, passed drastic laws practically tax-ing them out of existence. Alabama, for example, fixed the license fee in 1860 at $300 for vendors on foot, $500 for peddlers on horse-back, and $750 for peddlers using wagons.

The activities of a typical interior merchant of the Old South are delineated in the manuscript diary of Edwin Michael Holt, who kept a store on his farm and later in the village of Graham, North Carolina. Every year in the spring and fall he or his partner made trips to the North to purchase goods. In September, 1841, his brother-in-law who had a store in Caswell County, North Carolina, wrote from Newark, New Jersey, describing a business trip to the North. His first stop had been Philadelphia, where he bought nine hundred dollars' worth of cotton cloth, flannels, hardware, crockery, china, and shoes. From Philadelphia, he had journeyed to Newark, where he purchased hats and saddles and then he completed the purchases of his fall stock in New York City. He found that North Carolina banknotes were receivable in the Northern cities only at a 4 per cent discount, while Virginia and South Carolina paper money was discounted at 3 per cent. On March 24, 1844, Holt recorded that he went to Philadelphia and bought hats, hardware, books, and leather for his store. The goods arrived about two weeks later and were hauled to their destination by wagon, for his store was not located near a railroad. The goods boxes were then opened and a rapid sale followed.

The Holt store in Alamance County was only one of the mani-fold interests of the proprietor. This embryo capitalist established a cotton factory on Great Alamance Creek which furnished cus-tomers for his store. He was also an enterprising farmer, raising about twelve hundred bushels of wheat and killing and salting about ninety hogs annually. He had a saw mill, a grist mill, and made brick with his slaves, whom he also hired to construct a railroad.

One of his most thriving enterprises was distilling whiskey. During a year in which he was particularly active in attending camp meetings and protracted religious gatherings he made twenty-eight hundred gallons of whiskey which he sold for 37 cents a gallon. On December 11, 1846, he jotted down in his diary: "Started wagon to Fayetteville, six barrells of flour, 146 galons Whiskey, 30# butter." [4]

The country merchant in the South operated on a credit basis. In the summer when he traveled to New York or to New Orleans to buy his fall stock of goods he obtained from the wholesale houses a credit of six months without the payment of interest. His ability to obtain credit from the Northern wholesale houses depended on a favorable credit rating, often obtained from local lawyers who collected debts for these Northern firms or from a credit rating agency such as the famous one operated by Lewis Tappan of New York City, which had agents stationed in the South. In turn, the merchant was compelled to sell goods on credit to his farmer customers who rarely had cash until they had sold their crops. A recent student of ante-bellum Southern merchants has found that "at least two-thirds to three-fourths of all merchandise purchased by farmers was obtained on credit." [5] For this service the merchant charged his customers a high mark-up price. He kept a ledger recording the numerous small purchases on credit of each customer. The ledger of William Smith, who owned a store at Smithville, South Carolina, reveals a typical record of few cash purchases; in May 1841, the ledger showed a total of $455.41 sales, of which only $37 were in cash, and in August of that year only $82.10 were paid in cash out of total sales of $604.27. In the autumn after the crops were sold, the store bills were paid. Some of these debts were liquidated also by the acceptance of produce from the farmers, such as whiskey, country linen, feathers, flaxseed, furs, beeswax, corn, cotton and tobacco, and even knitted socks. [6]

The time-stained ledgers of these ante-bellum stores (some of them containing pressed flowers and leaves placed in them perhaps by the storekeeper's daughter) are intensely human documents. They record purchases of a people living a simple rural life, such articles as horse collars, brogans, blue jean cloth, calico and gingham, ½ doz. gunflints, coffee at 20 cents a pound, sugar at 25 cents a pound, plugs of tobacco, and medicine, particularly turpentine, castor oil, as-safoetida, brimstone, and saleratus. The merchant often acted as petty banker, noting in his ledger such sums as 38 cents lent to a customer. He frequently served as postmaster and gave his customers credit on postage. Many of the village stores had a barrel of whiskey or a jug of wine on tap, selling wine for 12 cents a glass, a half pint of whiskey for 7 cents, and a pint of rum or brandy for 25 cents. The ledgers of stores in the upper South indicate that the people were self-sustaining as far as food was concerned, but ledgers of stores in the lower South, such as those of the Hankinson Store at Yokena, Mississippi, on the great river, show large importations of barrels of pork, kegs of lard, sacks of corn, and quantities of flour. The ledger of the store of V. E. Martin at Lafayette, Tennessee (1835), shows that it was a rare customer who did not buy wine, whiskey, rum, or brandy.[7] At these village centers, the farmers gathered on Saturday afternoons, and discussed crops and politics, told yarns, whittled sticks, swapped horses, and practiced the great American art of squirting tobacco juice at some casual target. The heydey of the country store in the South, however, was not attained until after the Civil War. In the ante-bellum period the large planters purchased their supplies in bulk through factors and in turn often sold goods from their commissaries to their numerous poor relations and to the neighboring farmers.

The exporting and importing merchants of the principal Southern seaports made considerable fortunes from commerce. The most famous of these early merchants was John McDonogh of New Orleans, a poor Scotch-Irish boy who came to New Orleans in 1800 and gathered an immense fortune in trade and real estate speculations. Regarded as a miser and eccentric in his life, he left his great fortune when he died in 1850 to found schools for poor boys in New Orleans and Baltimore. Judah Touro, the son of a rabbi of Newport, Rhode Island, who began his career in the Crescent City humbly by the sale of soap, candles, and codfish, through thrift and shrewdness became a millionaire and devoted his wealth to philanthropies so that when he died the city mourned. The career of John Burnside, a Scotch merchant of New Orleans, illustrates the dominance of the agrarian ideal in the South. After he had made a huge fortune, he retired from mercantile pursuits, purchased a baronial estate on the Mississippi River, and became the largest sugar planter in the South.

Southern maritime trade was conducted largely around a triangular voyage. The cotton ports shipped their cotton directly to Europe, but the ships returned to New York, bringing imports of European goods. From New York European and Northern manufactures were sent along the coastal route to Southern ports. Another pattern of trade, a right angle, began with the carrying of cotton to New York, where it was exported to Europe. The returning ships then brought imports to the harbor of the great Northern port, and from here manufactured goods were sent to the South. The phenomenal rise of the port of New York, according to its most able historian, should be attributed to Southern trade more than to the opening in 1825 of the Erie Canal, which gave an outlet to the wheat, pork, and beef of the Northwest.[8] In 1822 Southern products, rice, cotton, tobacco, and naval stores, made up 55 per cent of the exports of New York port, and as late as 1860 cotton ranked "an easy first in New York's exports." This indirect routing of exports and imports through New York was uneconomic, illogical, and a great indictment of Southern business initiative. The commercial passivity of the ante-bellum South contrasts with the bourgeois trading enterprise of the colonial period.

Baltimore was the leading port of the upper South, a far more versatile shipping center than the cotton ports of the lower South. The building of the Baltimore and Ohio Railroad opened up a large wheat-producing country in Virginia and Maryland as tributary to its port. Possessing water power and a deep harbor, the city entered extensively into the manufacture of flour, which was sold to the lower South and to South America. The city had progressive millers and used modern techniques, producing 500,000 barrels of flour annually in the decade preceding the Civil War. From Brazil and Peru, it imported coffee, hides, copper ore, and guano, which it distributed to the upper South. It also had the most important shipbuilding industry of the South, famed for its construction of the fast Baltimore clipper ships. In its shipyards Frederick Douglass worked as a young man, a slave allowed to hire his time, and here he was severely beaten by white mechanics who resented competition with Negroes.

The Virginia towns and ports, Alexandria, Richmond, and Norfolk, were jealous of Baltimore and tried to hinder its trade. Richmond, indeed, was a formidable rival of the Maryland city in the flour-milling industry. Norfolk had many splendid natural advantages to become a prosperous Southern port. In colonial days it had carried on a lucrative West India trade, but this source of commerce received a heavy blow from the Revolution, and later from England's policy of closing the West India trade to American ships. Furthermore, the high protective tariff of the United States on sugar, amounting to 71 per cent in 1844, discouraged trade with the sugar islands of the Caribbean Sea. One of the chief sources of Norfolk exports was the northeastern corner of North Carolina, which became tributary to this Virginia port, largely as a result of the Dismal Swamp Canal, which provided an outlet for the commerce of the Roanoke River Valley and Albemarle Sound. The first canal, completed in 1814, was ineffective since only small boats could navigate it, but by its enlargement in 1828 and again in 1859 it was converted into a valuable artery of transportation. Nevertheless, Norfolk languished as a port partly because of petty jealousies and rivalries in Virginia which prevented the building of railroads and other means of transportation.

The greatest export port of the South was New Orleans, the "Queen of the Mississippi." Each year at least four thousand flatboats and four hundred and fifty steamboats brought their cargoes to this "agricultural focus." The produce of the Missouri and Ohio valleys—grain, flour, furs and hides, bacon, lead, ore, lumber, whiskey—poured as from a cornucopia into this Southern city. To these products of a cooler climate was added the vast freightage of cotton bales and barrels of sugar from the Gulf region. More than three hundred factors advertised in the *Price-Current*, the trade journal of the city.[9] In 1815 Charleston was the leading cotton export port, with New Orleans close behind, but at the close of the ante-bellum period the Creole city surpassed Charleston in exports five to one. For nearly a decade beginning in 1834 New Orleans even outranked New York in the value of its exports.

The second busiest cotton export city was Mobile, which had an extensive river system back of it. Savannah ranked third. This city also enjoyed the distinction of pioneering in the development of steam navigation across the Atlantic. From its harbor there went forth in 1819 the steamship *Savannah* that by a combination of steam and sail crossed to Liverpool, England, in twenty-five days. The remarkable decline of Charleston as a port was caused largely by the southwestward shift of cotton production. On the eve of the Revolution (1772) it had stood third among the American ports and imported more goods than it did during the last two decades of the ante-bellum period. Furthermore, its population of sixteen thousand inhabitants in 1790, just below that of Boston, had increased to only forty thousand by 1860. By comparison, New Orleans had grown from 17,000 people in 1810 to 168,000 fifty years later, and it had become a cosmopolitan city.

Although the bulk of Southern cotton was exported to Europe, a considerable amount went to Boston to be used in New England textile factories. There was also a very interesting shipment of cotton from Memphis and New Orleans up the Mississippi and Ohio rivers to Pittsburgh. Cotton manufacturing was one of the major industries of this city before the Civil War, consuming 13,600 bales in 1857, and shipping its textiles by the Pennsylvania System of canals to Philadelphia.[10] Railroads were seldom used in the transportation of cotton to Northern cities.

The trade of the Southern ports had the disadvantage of being highly seasonal. Cotton was shipped to the great English port of Liverpool or to New York and Boston beginning in the early fall, with exports subsiding sharply in the spring and summer. The most important reason for this phenomenon was that the Southern planter was not in strong enough financial condition so that he could market his crop in a steady year-round distribution. He was frequently in debt to his factor and had to sell his crop as soon as it was gathered. The result was that the Southern farmers and planters disposed of their crops in a mass movement instead of gradually feeding them into the market. Since they lacked the capital to retard the marketing of their crops, they suffered from the glut of staples in the market, cotton especially, which reduced the prices that they received.

Such a seasonal rush to the market also had an adverse effect on the steady development of Southern railroads.

Furthermore, there was a great unbalance between exports and imports of the Southern ports. To take an extreme example, Mobile exported $18,000,000 worth of produce in 1851, but imported only $413,000 worth. The ships which carried the cotton bales to Europe did not bring back European imports to Southern harbors, but rather to Northern ports. In 1850 New York imported more than twice as much as she exported (a considerable proportion of these exports being Southern), while New Orleans exported nearly four times as much as she imported. In Charleston some of the old streets are paved with cobblestones brought back in ballast by empty or semi-empty ships—melancholy reminders that vessels from Southern ports failed to bring back rich cargoes from Europe as in colonial days.

According to the old mercantilistic theory, the Southern ports should have grown rich on this highly favorable balance of trade. Actually, the reverse was true; the Southerners claimed that the North got 40 cents out of every dollar obtained from the sale of cotton. Every summer Southern merchants flocked to New York to buy the year's supply of manufactured goods, paying a high middle-man's profit to the New York merchant or importer. The Northern business men received the profits of insuring cargoes, drayage, broker's fees, freight charges, and high rates of interest. The great Northern city had its agents in all the cotton ports. In 1850 approximately 10 per cent of the white population of Mobile were New York-New Englanders. Indeed, Southerners allowed commercial opportunities to go by default, while they used their capital to buy more slaves and more land to produce more cotton, thus reducing the price of their staple by overexpansion. One of the important reasons why New York absorbed so much of Southern trade and profits was that the merchants of the great metropolis gave Southern customers long terms of credit (at a high rate of interest).

Southerners were constantly in need of credit to finance themselves until the crops were sold or to buy more slaves and land. Consequently they tended to think of banks primarily as institutions to manufacture paper money rather than to serve as depositories of accumulated capital. The first banks in the South were the Bank of Maryland at Baltimore (1790), and the Bank of Alexandria, Virginia (1792), chartered by the state legislatures. The pioneer bank west of the Appalachian Mountains was the Kentucky Insurance Company of Lexington, chartered in 1802, which did a general banking business as well as insuring boats on the Western waters. The Bank of the State of South Carolina, founded in 1812, was exclusively owned by the state, and so successfully was it managed during its long career to 1868 that from its profits a considerable proportion of the state debt was retired. The earliest bank chartered by the Georgia legislature was the Planter's Bank of Savannah, in operation by 1810. Texas was unique among the Southern states in prohibiting, in its constitution of 1845, the creation of banks. Throughout the ante-bellum period, however, this bankless state permitted the circulation of the notes of mercantile firms as substitutes for paper money. In addition to the state banks, branches of the First and of the Second Bank of the United States were established in several of the Southern cities.

Popular pressure for the creation of state banks was stimulated by the hard times in the South and West following the Panic of 1819. In Tennessee, Felix Grundy, the old War Hawk, led the debtor forces in demanding the establishment of a loan bank. The legislature in 1820 chartered the Bank of Tennessee, the capital of which was provided from the sale of state lands, state funds, and the sale of bonds. This institution quickly proceeded to issue copious quantities of bank-notes, which were loaned to hard-pressed debtors apportioned to the counties according to taxes paid. Also a stay law provided that if a creditor refused to accept the bank-notes of the state bank, he had to wait two years before he could force payment of his debt. In 1821 this relief law was declared unconstitutional by the supreme court of the state, and in 1830 the unsound Bank of Tennessee, which had been dubbed the "Saddle-Bags Bank," failed.

When Kentucky yielded to the cries of the debtors for the panacea of cheap money, a dramatic legal battle resulted. In 1820 the legislature chartered the Bank of the Commonwealth of Kentucky which issued a large supply of bank-notes based on public credit without providing an adequate cash reserve for their redemption. These notes, authorized as legal tender for the payment of public dues, were loaned to debtors in amounts not exceeding two thousand dollars to pay "just debts." Within a short while this cheap paper money declined to one-half of its face value. Moreover, the state supreme court in 1823 declared the stay laws passed by the radical legislature unconstitutional, as impairing the obligation of a contract. Thereupon, the debtor group in the legislature abolished the court of appeals and reorganized the judicial system, setting up a "New Court." The "Old Court," however, refused to abdicate, and for two years two supreme courts functioned within the Bluegrass state. Finally, the "Old Court" partly triumphed, and in 1826 the legislature repealed those laws destroying the independence of the judiciary.

The heyday of state banks in the South and the West came during the speculative period prior to the Panic of 1837. In order to provide abundant credit and "rag money," the legislatures created banks without proper safeguards for keeping an adequate specie reserve, established state-owned banks, or subscribed heavily to the capital stock of private banks. The capital for the Bank of the State of Alabama, chartered in 1823, was obtained by selling state bonds in New York and by appropriating for this purpose lands which had been set aside for education and internal improvements. Branches were established in the important towns of the state, and private banking was almost eliminated. The most pernicious feature of the bank's management was that the president and board of electors were elected annually by the legislature. This system resulted in a tremendous inflation of bank-notes and in extensive frauds, especially unwarranted loans to the legislators and politicians. For a brief period, however, the state-operated banks paid all the expenses of the state government from profits. But the Panic of 1837 caused a suspension of specie payments and revealed the unsoundness and dishonesty of the bank administration. After nearly eleven million dollars' worth of state bonds had been squandered to support the bank, Alabama in 1842 abandoned the banking business.[11] Georgia, likewise, had an unfortunate experience with its state system of banks, which had been established largely for the purpose of making easy loans to the citizens. Individual loans were limited to $2,500 and were distributed among the counties according to their population, the rate of interest being fixed at 6 per cent. During the crisis following the Panic of 1837 the bank unwisely expanded its issue of bank-notes and as a result failed.[12]

The Southern and Western states were not only very lax in chartering banks but they exercised slight supervision over them. During the flush times of the early 1830's the number of banks doubled in this area. Some of these ephemeral corporations were known as "wildcat banks" because they recklessly issued vast quantities of paper money and were purposefully located in remote places, frequented by wildcats, where it was difficult to present their bank-notes for redemption in specie. Moreover, the scarcity of coins in the South and West led to the circulation of unsound bank-notes less than one dollar in denomination, called "shin plasters." Much of the paper money issued by the banks of the Southwest was loaned to land speculators. The extent of such speculation is indicated by the enormous expansion of the sales of public land which rose from a total of four million acres in 1834 to twenty million in 1836, an all-time record. The destruction of the Second Bank of the United States by President Jackson and his subsequent policy of depositing government funds in "pet banks" aggravated the evils of speculation.

Jackson's Specie Circular precipitated the severe Panic of 1837, which had been brewing for several years. The South, however, did not feel the full impact of the depression until 1839, when the price of cotton dropped disastrously. Then followed a wave of bank failures; internal improvements were left half-finished; and thousands of farmers and planters abandoned their lands and moved farther west, especially to Texas. The price of cotton continued to decline until it reached bottom in January, 1844, selling for 4.7 cents per pound at New Orleans, the lowest price in ante-bellum history. One of the most lamentable results of this depression was that it led some of the states to refuse to pay their debts. In 1842 Mississippi repudiated five million dollars' worth of bonds which had been invested in the bankrupt state bank, and in the same year the territory of Florida followed Mississippi's example.

The financial debacle had some good results, nevertheless, especially in producing a movement for banking reforms. Also bitter experience caused the retirement of most of the Southern states from the banking business. Louisiana had plunged heavily into financing banks within the state during "the flush times," but later repented of its folly by developing an enlightened regulation of financial institutions. In the Louisiana Specie Reserve system, the state law required banks to keep one-third of their capital as a specie reserve and limited loans of money on deposit to ninety days. The Louisiana banking reforms had considerable influence in the formulation of the National Bank System during the Civil War period.

The leading private banker of the ante-bellum South was James Robb who rose from poverty to great wealth and then lost his fortune. Born in Pennsylvania, he spent his boyhood in Morgantown, Virginia, working as an office boy in a bank. In 1837 he emigrated to New Orleans, where he began to accumulate capital by buying and exchanging uncurrent money. Following the panic he was able to purchase cheaply the stock of the New Orleans Gas Light and Banking Company, which had been granted a thirty-year contract to light the streets of the metropolis. From this enterprise he made a huge profit and then founded the "Bank of James Robb" in New Orleans, with branches in New York, San Francisco, St. Louis, London, and Liverpool. In addition to his banking business, he was a railroad promoter, becoming the first president of the New Orleans, Jackson and Great Northern Railroad. A Whig in politics, he was elected to the upper house of the legislature, where he worked for the property interests. Although he was not opposed to slavery, he frowned upon the agitation of the fire eaters and was a Unionist in his convictions. After he had built a magnificent mansion in New Orleans, adorned with rare paintings, he lost most of his fortune as a result of the Panic of 1857.

The South as a whole, however, suffered from this financial crash less than any section of the country. The world demand for cotton kept its price from declining seriously, thus strengthening the faith of Southerners in King Cotton. Nevertheless, the Panic of 1857 caused the South to realize the danger of relying upon New York City for drafts and bills of exchange, since the tight money situation in that city in 1857 had resulted in considerable loss to cotton exporters. This loss would have been avoided if the marketing of cotton had been conducted directly with European business houses. In 1858–60 Southern banks held more of the country's supply of specie than ever before, a condition resulting from the enlarged production and high prices of Southern staples.

The deposits in Southern banks were not an accurate index of the financial status of the planters and farmers. Checks on banking accounts were rarely used in the Old South. In fact, the economy of this region was based on money to a far less degree than in the Northeast. Slaves did not require money for wages, and the typical farmer handled very little cash in the course of a year, perhaps less than many free Negroes. The financial condition of the rural population can be gauged only by ascertaining the balance of the planter or farmer with his factor or merchant. Debts were settled and money transferred by sight drafts, bills of exchange, or produce. The financial strength or dependence of the factors and merchants, in turn, depended on their balances with the wholesale merchant or commission house in the North and in Europe.

Southern economic life was profoundly affected by the difficulty and slowness of transportation. In 1800 it required about three weeks to travel from Georgia to New York. Although McAdam had invented an improved roadbed of graduated stones which was introduced into this country in the 1790's, this method of building roads was too expensive to be adopted in the thinly populated South. By 1818 Congress had built the National Road between Cumberland, Maryland, and Wheeling, but the prospect of constructing other national roads with Federal funds was blocked by the attitude of the Southern Presidents, Madison, Monroe, and Jackson who vetoed internal improvement bills as being violations of the Constitution.

The Southern states were richly provided with a network of rivers and inland waterways. They participated in the nation-wide enthusiasm for canals which was stimulated by the opening of the Erie Canal in 1825. Their two most ambitious undertakings in the construction of this means of transportation were the Chesapeake and Ohio Canal from Baltimore to Cumberland, Maryland, begun in 1828 and completed in 1850, and the James River and Kanawha Canal which ran from Richmond along the James River with the ambitious goal of connecting with the Kanawha River and thus tapping the trade of the Ohio valley. The state of Virginia chartered a company for this purpose in 1832 and poured millions of dollars into the enterprise, but it never reached its destination, stopping at Buchanan, fifty miles beyond Lynchburg.

A new era of transportation began in the South in January, 1812, when the steamboat *New Orleans*, a side-wheeler, arrived at New Orleans from Pittsburg on a pioneer trip. The prototype of the typical Mississippi steamboat was the *Washington*, constructed by Henry Shreve, a vessel equipped with a high-pressure engine placed on the main deck instead of in the hold, and having a flat, shallow hull and a paddle wheel located at the stern. In 1816 it made a round trip between New Orleans and Louisville in forty-one days. Appointed superintendent of the improvements on the Mississippi River from 1827 to 1841, Shreve invented a steam snagboat to pull up the thousands of snags, planters, and sawyers which obstructed the Mississippi—a boat that was called "Uncle Sam's tooth-puller." One of his most famous achievements was to break up the great log jam in the Red River that had prevented the settlement of northern Louisiana, and on the site of his camp rose the town of Shreveport, incorporated in 1839.

The traffic on the Mississippi became one of the picturesque aspects of Southern life. The steamboat supplemented but did not displace the thousands of flatboats, arks, and broadhorns which floated down the mighty river to New Orleans. The steamboats stopped at intervals at lonely landings for wood, cut by malaria-ridden frontiersmen and free Negroes. Frequently they raced with each other, sometimes with a Negro holding down the valve of the high-pressure engine. The progress of the steamboat in attaining speed was demonstrated by the fact that in 1853 the *Eclipse* made the trip from New Orleans to Louisville in less than four and a half days, while the first boat to go up the Mississippi from New Orleans to Louisville, Shreve's boat, the *Enterprise*, had taken twenty-five days to accomplish this feat. By the latter part of the ante-bellum period some of the steamboats had developed into "floating palaces," often infested with professional gamblers. Gaudy "show boats" also entertained provincial little river towns with theatrical productions. The magic of the great

Mississippi, its romantic atmosphere, has been imperishably preserved in Mark Twain's *Life on the Mississippi* and *Huckleberry Finn*.

Stephen Foster wrote a lively song in 1860 about a magnificent Mississippi boat, the *Glendy Burk*, named after a prominent New Orleans merchant:

> De Glendy Burk is a mighty fast boat,
> Wid a mighty fast captain too;
> He sits up thar on de hurricane roof
> And he keeps his eye on de crew.

> De Glendy Burk has a funny old crew
> And dey sing de boat-man's song,
> Dey burn de pitch and de pine knot too,
> For to shove de boat along.

The tempo of transportation in the South was tremendously increased by the introduction of railroads. The Southern states preceded the North in the development of railroads, following experiments in England. There were two major periods of railroad building below the Mason and Dixon line before the coming of the Civil War. The first one was initiated with the construction of the Baltimore and Ohio Railroad in 1828 and ended during the great depression following the cotton crisis of 1839. This early activity in securing modern means of transportation was promoted by the seaports on the Atlantic coast, especially those which had inferior water communications with the interior, to tap the trade of the hinterland. Another stimulus to railroad building in the older states of the South during this period was the relative decline of their economy on account of the competition of the virgin cotton lands of the Southwest. The second phase of railroad building in the South began in the decade of recovery and prosperity, 1850–60, and was dominated by the desire of *interior* districts to find a market for their crops. During the decade preceding the Civil War, there was a flourishing era of railroad building in which the South surpassed the North in the rate of construction.[13]

The first significant railroad in the South, as well as in the United States, was the Baltimore and Ohio. Charles Carroll, the last living signer of the Declaration of Independence, dug the first spadeful of earth in the construction of the "B & O," July 4, 1828. Two years later the road was in operation between Baltimore and Ellicott's Mills, a distance of thirteen miles, over which ran the primitive locomotive, "Tom Thumb," with huge smokestack belching black smoke from its pine wood fire, and traveling at the terrific speed of twelve miles an hour, or twice as fast as horse travel. By 1853 the "B & O" had reached the Ohio River at Wheeling, realizing its dream of tapping the rich trade of the Northwest. The significance of this railroad is illustrated by the rapid growth of Baltimore, which in 1850 was approximately equal in population to New Orleans, but ten years later had forged far ahead of the "Queen of the Mississippi," attaining a population of 212,418.

The businessmen of Charleston were especially enterprising in promoting pioneer railroads in the South. Alarmed by the declining trade of their city, much of which had been absorbed by a chain of inland towns, they sought to divert the traffic of the Savannah River to their port by constructing a railroad to Hamburg, a village opposite to Augusta. Securing a charter from the legislature in 1828, they obtained capital for their company from the sale of stock to individuals, largely businessmen of Charleston, and to the city corporation. A steam locomotive, built at the foundry at West Point, New York, and named "The Best Friend of Charleston" ran over a few miles of the track in 1830, and three years later the line was completed to Hamburg, a distance of 136 miles, making it the longest railroad in the world at that time. The rails on these early roads were wooden stringers with thin strips of iron nailed on them, the buckling of which became so dangerous that in the decade of the 1850's most of the Southern railroads had changed to the T type of rail, made of wrought iron. Cheaply constructed with slave contract labor, the Charleston and Hamburg Railroad operated at a profit, carrying passengers in cars which looked like stage coaches and cotton bales in primitive freight cars.

An eloquent visionary, ex-Senator Robert Y. Hayne, conceived of the design of connecting Charleston with Cincinnati on the Ohio River by a railroad penetrating the mountains through Cumberland Gap. He was instrumental in 1836 in organizing the Louisville,

Charleston, and Cincinnati Railroad Company and securing charters from the three states through which it would pass. In order to aid the company in financing this tremendous project, the South Carolina legislature chartered the Southwestern Railroad Bank, granting valuable economic privileges to it. In 1837, having obtained a subscribed capital of $8,000,000 for its joint enterprises, the company purchased the Charleston-Hamburg line, from which branches were built to Columbia and Camden. The death of Hayne in 1839 and the tremendous drop in the price of cotton in that year, followed by lean years in the cotton belt, ended this dream of a transmontane road to the Ohio Valley. The failure to build a railroad connecting Charleston with the Northwest was tragic, for the completion of such a project might have prevented South Carolina from precipitating a secession movement.

State, county, and city governments played a dominant role in constructing these highways, cooperating with private individuals and companies. Cities and counties made large subscriptions on condition that the railroad tracks should pass through them. Wheeling, for example, secured for itself the terminus of the Baltimore and Ohio Railroad on the Ohio River by subscribing a million dollars to the stock of the company. The Mobile and Ohio Railroad was prevented for some time from receiving a charter from the Alabama legislature because it proposed to build northward through Mississippi. Richmond and Petersburg were powerful enough in the Virginia legislature to prevent their rival, Norfolk, from building a line westward to Petersburg until the eve of the Civil War because of fear that Norfolk would prosper at their expense. Also efforts to charter a railroad connection between Danville, Virginia, and Greensboro, North Carolina, were frustrated for a number of years because the representatives of eastern North Carolina feared that such a railroad would injure the Wilmington-Weldon line and draw trade from the state to Virginia.

The letter books of John McRae, engineer of the South Carolina Railroad, give intimate glimpses into the problems of building Southern railroads. Slaves were hired from the adjoining planters to grade the roadbed, their masters being paid $10 to $12 a month. Malaria seriously hampered construction in the swampy lowlands during the Spring and Summer. Stockholders were slow in paying installments on their stock and McRae had trouble in securing rights of way. In March, 1847, he wrote that the South Carolina Railroad was doing an immense business in freight so that the Charleston depot had to be closed for seven days and ten new locomotives had been ordered. In the summer of that year he wrote that the people of the state had railroad mania, "the people of the up country and Columbia are in a perfect fever on the Subject of Railroads." But local jealousies interfered with rational planning of railroads, for example, the South Carolina Railroad was not permitted to locate its depot at the Charleston wharves, because of a variety of local interests, including "the fraternity of black barbers," wrote McRae with scorn, because they feared that they would be deprived of the opportunity of shaving the passengers as they passed from the cars to the ocean ships.[14]

The vigorous development of strategic railroads played an important role in making Georgia "the keystone state" of the South. The Georgia Railroad, begun in 1836 at Augusta, reached Atlanta in September, 1845. The company which built it, "The Georgia Railroad and Banking Company," also operated a very successful bank. Its stock, paid for in installments, was purchased largely by Southern businessmen, banks, city councils, and trustees of two Georgia colleges. A financial statement of the company in 1860 showed that it owned 231 miles of track, 56 locomotives, and 634 freight cars, and that it was paying a dividend of 8 per cent. The company boasted of such careful operation that it had never lost a human life on its trains. The Central of Georgia, which traversed the middle of the state from the port of Savannah to Macon, was completed to its terminus in October, 1843, at a cost of approximately $13,000 a mile, which was about half the average cost of constructing railroads in the United States. Financed by Southern capital, this railroad became one of the most powerful corporations below the Mason and Dixon line, with capital stock of $4,000,000, paying 8 per cent interest to its stockholders. In 1858 it adopted a policy of transporting fertilizers to all points on its line for $2 a ton, which tremendously stimulated the use of guano and other fertilizers in Georgia. The Georgia railroads labored under the disadvantage of the prohibition by law of carrying freight on Sunday and especially from the seasonal nature of their traffic, which dwindled greatly in the summer. The freight also was largely eastward bound, the carrying of cotton and food toward the seacoast, with a large proportion of empty cars returning to the West.

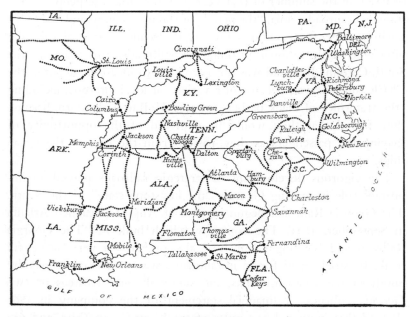

SOUTHERN RAILROADS, 1861

After *Appletons' Railway and Steam Navigation Guide* (New York, March 1861.)

The most unique of Southern railroads was the Western and Atlantic, built, owned, and operated by the state of Georgia. In 1836 the legislature appropriated $1,500,000 in state bonds to construct a railroad between the village of Marthasville (later named Atlanta) on the Chattahoochee River to Rossville on the Tennessee River opposite Chattanooga, thus making connections with railroads going to Memphis and Nashville. The construction of the road, 138 miles in length, was placed in the hands of three commissioners elected by the legislature. After its completion in 1851, a debate was waged at intervals between conservatives and the friends of state operation over the sale or lease of the road and its equipment. Governor Joseph E. Brown was a firm supporter of this business enterprise operated by the state and appointed an able superintendent to manage its affairs. At the close of the ante-bellum period the Western and Atlantic, according to an eminent authority, U. B. Phillips, was "scarcely at all involved in politics." [15] With track and rolling stock in good repair the railroad earned from $800,000 to $900,000 a year, of which more than 50 per cent was profit.

In North Carolina two important railroads were built during the ante-bellum period, the Wilmington and Weldon, traversing the coastal plain, completed in 1840, and the North Carolina Railroad which penetrated the Piedmont. It had been the dream of Joseph Caldwell, president of the University of North Carolina, that a railroad should be constructed from the eastern coast to the western boundary of the state, giving the people of the Piedmont an outlet for their crops. The Whigs, who dominated the western part of the state, demanded such an internal improvement but the Democrats of the eastern Piedmont counties opposed this project. Finally in 1849 after a great sectional fight in which victory was attained by a single vote, the Whigs secured a charter from the legislature for the building of a railroad from Goldsboro (a town on the Wilmington and Weldon line) along the central axis of the state to Raleigh and then to Charlotte, a distance of 232 miles. By 1856 the track was completed, and before the outbreak of the Civil War extensions had been made to Morehead City on the seacoast and westward to Morganton. The state furnished three-fourths of the capital of the company and directed its operation. On the eve of the Civil War the company was in excellent financial shape and its roadbed and rolling stocks were in good condition. Some years after the catastrophe of the war the state leased the railroad to the Southern Railway Company for ninety-nine years.

The development of the Virginia network of railroads was strongly influenced by sectionalism. Since the state had become heavily involved in completing the James River and Kanawha Canal, much of its financial strength was thus diverted from helping private companies in the construction of railroads. Nevertheless, in order to placate the disgruntled western section of the state, the legislature subscribed to three-fifths of the capital stock of the Virginia and East Tennessee Railroad. This railroad, completed in 1858, connected Richmond with Knoxville and Chattanooga by a line across the Blue Ridge Mountains. Also the legislature appropriated several million dollars to build a railroad uniting the James and Ohio rivers via Covington in the extreme western part of the state and Charleston on the Kanawha River. The Civil War, however, prevented the carrying out of this ambitious project which the Virginia orators had predicted would pour a golden harvest into the harbor of Norfolk.

The only important railroad in the state of Kentucky during the ante-bellum period was the Louisville and Nashville. The citizens of Louisville were active in constructing this railroad, since the growth of their city was hampered by the recurrent low level of water in the Ohio River that prevented shipment of coal to the city, and furthermore they feared that Nashville would obtain better rail communications than Louisville and absorb much of the latter's trade. Charters were granted in 1850 by the Kentucky and Tennessee legislatures for the construction of a railroad between Louisville and Nashville, a distance of one hundred and eighty-five miles. Generous subscriptions to the stock of the company were made by the city governments of Louisville and Nashville and by the counties through which the track ran, and bonds were sold in Europe. In 1859 the main line was completed at the cost of over seven million dollars. In the spring of 1861 Louisville obtained rail connections also with Memphis on the Mississippi River by the completion of two small railroads which joined the "L and N" at Bowling Green. The "L and N" became very successful under the management of James Guthrie, a former Secretary of the Treasury in the cabinet of Franklin Pierce. During the Civil War the "L and N" was operated for the benefit of the Federal Army and thus proved a great boon to the North in the invasion of the South through the back door.[16]

The Gulf region was not connected with the upper South by rails until at the close of the ante-bellum period. Furthermore, the states of Louisiana, Arkansas, Texas, and the southern part of Missouri were practically devoid of railroads in 1860 (Arkansas possessing no tracks at all and the other states only a few short lines, such as the one between Houston and the seaport of Galveston). The Mobile and Ohio Railroad, completed in April, 1861, ran northward from Mobile through Meridian, Mississippi, to Columbus, Kentucky, where a ferry transported passengers and goods to Cairo, Illinois. This long railroad was promoted by the citizens of Mobile in order to divert some of the Ohio-Mississippi river trade from New Orleans. Real progress toward its construction occurred after 1850 as a result of a large Federal grant of lands. Senator Stephen A. Douglas cleverly secured Southern votes in Congress for his bill to aid the Illinois Central Railroad by including grants to both the Mobile and Ohio Railroad and the Illinois Central of six alternate sections of land for each mile of track built. Until this threat of losing trade to Mobile had arisen, New Orleans was uninterested in developing railroads, complacently relying on the immense steamboat trade of the Mississippi. But the danger of losing her favored position as Queen of the Mississippi caused the city to push the construction of the New Orleans, Jackson, and Great Northern Railroad, running somewhat parallel to the rival Mobile line through Jackson, Mississippi, until it joined the Mobile and Ohio Railroad at Jackson, Tennessee (January, 1860). A branch line from Grenada, Mississippi, ran into Memphis, thus affording a powerful competing rail line with the Mississippi River traffic.

There were two great transverse lines hooking up the Mississippi River with the Atlantic coast. The Memphis and Charleston railroad, completed in 1857, was composed of several connecting railroads running from Memphis through northern Mississippi at Corinth and northern Alabama to Chattanooga, where connection was made with the Georgia Western and Atlantic to Atlanta. Another west-east railroad artery traversed the heart of the black belt of the lower South beginning at Vicksburg, passing through Jackson, Mississippi, Montgomery, West Point on the Georgia border, to Atlanta. In 1860 there were breaks in this route, however, between Meridian, Mississippi, and Uniontown, Alabama, and between Selma and Montgomery. The first gap was bridged in 1862, when the Confederate government provided funds to construct this vital link of track, but the break between Selma and Montgomery was not completed until 1870. In addition to these main west and east highways, the Florida Railroad connected the Atlantic coast at Fernandina with the Gulf of Mexico at Cedar Keys. Under the vigorous administration of David Levy Yulee, the fire-eating Senator, Northern capital was obtained to complete this line just before the secession of the state. By 1861 over ten thousand miles of track had been laid in the Southern states, largely with local capital, as compared with twenty-two thousand miles built in the states which remained loyal to the Union.

Citations

1. J. H. Easterby, "The South Carolina Rice Factor as Revealed in the Papers of Robert F. W. Allston," *Journal of Southern History*, VII (May, 1941), 160–172.
2. A. H. Stone, "The Cotton Factorage System of the Southern States," *American Historical Review*, XX (April, 1915), 557–665; and Jordan, *Hugh Davis and His Alabama Plantation*, Chaps. 6–7.
3. B. H. Wall, "Ebenezer Pettigrew, an Economic Study of an Ante-Bellum Planter," Unpublished Ph.D. dissertation, University of North Carolina, 1947.
4. L. E. Atherton, *The Pioneer Merchant in Mid-America* (Columbia, Missouri, 1939).
5. The Holt diary is in the Southern Collection of the University of North Carolina.
6. This manuscript ledger is in the University of Kentucky library.
7. MS, University of Kentucky Library.
8. R. G. Albion, *The Rise of the Port of New York, 1815–1860* (New York, 1939), Chap. VI.
9. Wendell H. Stephenson, "Ante-Bellum New Orleans as an Agricultural Focus," *Agricultural History*, XV (October, 1941), 161–174.
10. L. S. Thurman, "The Cotton Industry in Pittsburgh," Unpublished M.A. thesis, University of Pittsburgh, 1947.
11. A. B. Moore, *History of Alabama* (University of Alabama, 1935).
12. See T. P. Govan, "The Banking and Credit System in Georgia, 1810–1860," *Journal of Southern History* (May, 1938), IV, 164–184.
13. R. S. Cotterill, *The Old South* (Glendale, Calif., 1939), 180–185; 215–229.
14. Letter Books of John McRae, Entries of March 25, June 5, 1847, Dec. 1, 1846, MSS, Wisconsin Historical Society Library. There are eighteen books, 1845–1864.
15. U. B. Phillips, *A History of Transportation in the Eastern Cotton Belt to 1860* (New York, 1908), 331.
16. T. D. Clark, *The Beginning of the L & N* (Louisville, 1933).

CHAPTER XVIII

The Progress of Southern Manufactures

M ANUFACTURING in the Southern states did not originate in the post-war "New South," when Henry W. Grady and his fellow editors publicized the expansion of cotton mills. Rather, the South had made an important progress in industry prior to 1860, which was interrupted by the Civil War and resumed in the decade of the 1880's.[1] Southern manufacturing had slowly emerged from the handicraft stage of colonial days. During the eighteenth century and to a lesser extent in the ante-bellum period household industries were carried on by slaves, who were employed on the large plantations to weave cloth, to make bricks, staves, and barrels, to manufacture nails, to boil soap, to do blacksmith work, and even to make artistic furniture. Also in the back country frontier women were engaged in a variety of household industries, particularly the weaving of linsey-woolsey cloth, while their husbands developed into jacks-of-all-trades, making rude furniture, shoes, and agricultural equipment. As late as 1810, according to incomplete census returns, the Southern states were ahead of the rest of the country in the manufacture of homespun cloth and especially in the spinning of flax. In the Piedmont region there were numerous spinning frames in operation, but these rudimentary factories were not equipped with Arkwright machinery, such as had been introduced into New England. The movement of industrialization below the Mason and Dixon line was stimulated to some degree by the War of 1812, but to a much greater extent by the depression of agricultural staples in the period of 1839–1850.[2]

The progress of manufactures below the Mason and Dixon line was impeded by a number of psychological and physical handicaps. The agrarian ideal caused many Southerners of the ante-bellum period to hold prejudices against trade and manufacturing and to regard planting and politics as more honorable occupations. Southern capital was largely monopolized in buying more land and slaves. The accumulation of capital needed to start manufactures was retarded also by the indirect method of selling the Southern agricultural staples, which enabled Northern business men to exploit the South and which contributed largely to perpetuating the colonial status of that region. Lesser reasons for the industrial lag of the South were the necessity of supporting a relatively larger dependent population of children and old people than existed in the North, the avoidance of the South by European immigrant laborers, the aversion of yeomen farmers to give up the independence of the farm and become "mill hands," the belief that Negroes were not suited to the handling of machinery, and the argument that the rise of manufactures would weaken the slave system and the opposition in the South to the protective tariff. Consequently, in 1860 the South produced slightly less than 10 per cent of the manufactures of the United States (measured in terms of value).

The development of cotton mills in the ante-bellum South was socially more significant than the rise of any other industry, for it pointed the way to utilizing the labor of the poor whites in factories. The Southern states enjoyed at least three advantages in the early development of mills. They had excellent water power along the fall line, they could procure cheap white labor, and they could obtain clean, freshly-picked cotton, undamaged by shipping and exposure. The early Southern mills were small establishments engaged in spinning yarn. South Carolina was prominent in pioneering in the development of cotton mills. Here the political leader George McDuffie started the Vaucluse Mill in 1833 as a result of the nullification controversy. This mill and the DeKalb factory (1838) in the same state were exceptions to the usual type of cotton mills below the Mason and Dixon line in that they employed slaves as their chief labor force.

The most influential promoter of the textile industry of the ante-bellum South was William **Gregg** of Charleston, South Carolina. Trained as a watchmaker and silversmith, Gregg became a successful jeweler in Charleston, thus obtaining the capital which he later invested in the cotton mill industry. His interest in this industry had been attracted when as a boy he had been associated with his uncle in an unsuccessful venture in cotton manufacturing in Georgia. As early as 1836 he acquired an interest in the Vaucluse Cotton Mill. His revolutionary role in the development of Southern cotton mills, however, began in 1844 as a result of a tour of New England which he made to observe the operation of the textile industry in that region. Upon his return, he wrote ten articles for the Charleston *Courier,* entitled "Essays on Domestic Industry," which were published in pamphlet form in 1845. In these essays he preached the new gospel of developing manufactures in the South by utilizing the great reservoir of poor white labor that had hitherto been largely neglected. He advocated confining slave labor to agriculture and to the reclamation of swamps. By bringing the poor whites into the factories, he maintained, not only would their labor be profitably employed, but their moral and social condition would be thereby improved. The Southern mills, he thought, should at first confine their efforts to the production of the coarser cotton goods and should import experienced Northern men to aid in starting the factories. He pointed out that by building cotton mills the South could prevent the emigration of its sons to the West. Furthermore, he did not demand tariff protection for these infant industries, primarily because they specialized in making yarn and the cheaper grades of cloth, which needed protection from New England rather than from foreign nations.

Gregg determined to build a model cotton factory to demonstrate the value of his ideas. In 1846 he constructed a remarkable cotton mill at Graniteville, South Carolina, not far from Augusta, Georgia. It was built of granite, "airy and commodious," the grounds landscaped and ornamented with shrubbery and flowers. To house the workers he erected eighty-five cottages in the Gothic style, also of granite, each cottage provided with a large garden. His mill people, he boasted, lived "under parental care," for they were not allowed to solace their arduous labor with alcohol, they were required by their leases to their cottages to send their children to school, and no children "of tender age," that is, under twelve years old, were worked in the factory.[3] Thus Gregg started the first compulsory school system in the South. He was a benevolent despot, who caught truants from his school and punished them personally, but he also gave them picnics and lectures on politeness and thrift. He required that his employees should be moral and sober, and he prohibited such hedonistic practices as dancing in Graniteville. Gregg's paternalistic policy may have been influenced by the Lowell factory in Massachusetts, but it also carried over plantation traditions into industry and the mill village. Graniteville must have been a very thrifty and sober community, but a very dull place in which the sparks of freedom and individuality were smothered.

Graniteville Factory was operated by water power. The superintendent and overseers were Northern men, but the labor force was composed of three hundred "piney woods" folk. The operatives were chiefly women and children over twelve years of age, for the older people who came from the hill districts and pine barrens did not have the flexibility to make good mill hands. The employees worked twelve hours a day, the men receiving four to five dollars a week, the women three to four dollars per week. The mill cottages rented from sixteen to twenty-five dollars a year. These wages were very low, but they compared favorably with wages paid to mill workers in Massachusetts and to agricultural wages in the South. It was an era when respectable, church-going factory owners exploited human labor without recognizing any injustice in making large profits and giving their employees a pitiful share of the returns of their labor.

Although there were failures, the well-managed textile mills in the South during the decade of the 1850's paid good dividends. The Graniteville Mill in its early years paid a 7 per cent dividend and later as much as 18 per cent. Gregg pointed out that the Southern mills had the advantages over their Northern rivals in securing labor 20 per cent cheaper, cotton at one and one-half cents a pound cheaper, and the superiority of bright, freshly picked cotton over shipped cotton. The Southern mills, almost without exception, manufactured the cheaper grades of cloth, osnaburgs, "nigger cloth," sheeting, and yarn. Moreover, their market remained largely below the Mason and Dixon line.[3a]

In North Carolina the Battle family had a pioneer mill at Rocky Mount, but the most important cotton mill leader during the antebellum period was Edwin Michael Holt, whose activities as a merchant have been discussed in the preceding chapter. He gathered the capital for his adventurous enterprise of a cotton mill in his native state from his profits as a farmer, small merchant, distiller, sawmill owner, and miller. In 1837 he erected his mill on Great Alamance Creek in the North Carolina Piedmont, procuring his machinery from the North. With his slaves he made brick for the buildings and cut the timber for his water wheel. His first few years were devoted to spinning yarn, which he transported by wagon to the nearest town, Hillsboro, and to the more distant market of Fayetteville. A considerable amount of his yarn was sold in Philadelphia, Pennsylvania. In 1845 his manuscript diary records the installation of machinery for weaving cloth. He bought fresh, bright cotton for his mill in the near-by towns. Three years later the Holt Mill was paying 7 cents a pound for raw cotton and selling the finished products, yarn, for 15 cents per pound, and sheeting for 7½ cents a yard. In 1849 the mill was running twelve looms which were making sheeting "as good as you ever saw," and selling its goods as fast as they could be made.

But there were ups and downs in the precarious cotton mill business in the South, so that the following year his partner wrote that the factory was paying very poorly, since the cost of cotton was too high for the prices obtained for their cotton yarn and cloth. Furthermore, the water in the creek became at intervals so low that the mill had to stop running. In 1853 a French dyer came to Alamance County and was employed by Holt to teach his mill operatives the art of dyeing cloth. Thus the Holt Mill became the pioneer factory south of the Potomac River in introducing colored cotton cloth made by power looms—"the Alamance plaids." By 1861 the Holt Mill had increased from the original start of over five hundred spindles to twelve hundred spindles and ninety-six looms.

The human side of early textile manufacturing in the South is also illustrated by the records of the Holt Mill. The proprietor arrived at the factory early in the morning and left it after the hands had completed their day's work of twelve hours. He attended strictly to business, eschewing the pursuit of political office, training his sons to be cotton manufacturers with the mottoes: "Stick to business," and "Put your profits into your business." Very religious, he stopped the mill at times in order to permit the hands to attend camp meetings and religious revivals. He built tenement houses for them near the factory and sold them goods from his store. At least on one occasion there was a strike resulting from the overseer "being too tight" with them. Very low wages were paid, and the majority of the workers were women and children. Before his death in 1884 this hard-driving capitalist attained the greatest fortune owned by any individual in the state.

The growth of the cotton mill industry in the South was particularly rapid in the last decade of the ante-bellum period. Although the number of factories in 1860, one hundred fifty-nine in eleven Southern states, was exactly the same as reported by the census ten years before, and although there was an actual decrease of 137 in the number of hands reported, the value of the product of Southern mills had risen 43 per cent. On the eve of the Civil War these mills employed 9,906 hands, of whom approximately two-thirds were female, and the average annual wage was $145.41. The South at that time produced one-third of the national output of yarn. Nevertheless, the expansion of the textile industry in the ante-bellum South should not be exaggerated, for the value of cotton goods manufactured by New England in 1860 exceeded the value of the Southern output almost ten times, and the single town of Lowell, Massachusetts, had more spindles running than the whole South. The largest cotton manufacturing state in the land of Dixie at that time was Georgia, whose thirty-three mills were capitalized at $2,126,103 and employed 2,813 hands. Only three other states listed by the census as "Southern," Virginia, North Carolina, and Alabama, manufactured cotton goods exceeding the value of a million dollars. But Maryland, which was classified by the census officials with the Middle States, had twenty mills that produced nearly three million dollars' worth of cotton textiles.

Another Southern industry was based on the habit of chewing plug tobacco which in the America of the nineteenth century was widespread among all classes of society. President Andrew Jackson injured his frail health by chewing tobacco over a long period of years. The Mormon prophet, Joseph Smith, received a revelation from God against the use of tobacco by his followers after his wife, Emma, had protested vigorously against the practice of the visiting elders who spit on the cleanly swept floors of their house Even the most eminent orators, statesmen, and preachers indulged in this minor vice, and there were Southern tobacco-chewers whose prowess in spitting accurately at the targets of distant spittoons resembled the unerring marksmanship of "Wild Bill" Hickok.[4] Cigarettes were not manufactured in the South until after the Civil War, while cigars were made principally in the North. But the habit of chewing tobacco was responsible for the growth of an industry which ranked third in importance among the manufactures of the Old South. Only flour and lumber exceeded in value the finished product of tobacco within the Southern states. The tobacco factories, concentrated in Virginia and North Carolina, were chiefly plug tobacco establishments, 98 per cent of them being devoted to this manufacture and only 2 per cent to pipe tobacco.

The manufacture of tobacco below the Mason and Dixon line began as a home industry. The tobacco "twists" thus made were peddled in a horse and wagon through the lower South. In the decades of the 1830's small factories were established in Richmond, Petersburg, Lynchburg, Danville, and in Caswell County, North Carolina. Unlike the cotton industry, the tobacco factories employed slaves as their principal labor force. The larger factories in 1860 employed between fifty and one hundred and fifty slaves, principally men, of whom about half were owned by the factories and the others were hired at rates of from $100 to $200 annually, plus food and maintenance.

The processes of manufacturing plug tobacco in the ante-bellum factories were quite simple. The stem was torn from the tobacco leaf by "stemmers," the stripped leaf was then turned over to "twisters," who rolled and twisted it into convenient shape, and finally it was received by "dippers," who dipped the twists into vats of flavoring—licorice, rum, sugar, and spices. The product was then pressed into plugs by a screw and lever press. Appetizing names were given to the different brands, such as "Wedding Cake," "Cherry Ripe," "Nature's Ultimatum," and "Diadem of Virginia." Shortly after the Civil War Washington Duke, a North Carolina Piedmont farmer, peddled a type of smoking tobacco, entitled "Pro Bono Publico," before he founded the great cigarette industry at Durham.

The tobacco manufactured in these Southern towns was sold chiefly to factors in New York and Philadelphia. Although some of this chewing tobacco was peddled in the South by wagons, the Southern merchants as a rule ordered their tobacco through New York and Philadelphia, a roundabout method of purchase which enhanced the profits of Northern business men. After the California gold rush, large quantities of Virginia tobacco were sent to the Pacific coast. The Northern factor received a commission of 5 to 7½ per cent of the sale price, and he granted to his customers a credit of eight months. The Panic of 1857 caused the Virginia and Carolina tobacco manufacturers to combine to remedy their grievances against the Northern factors. In December of that year a Tobacco Manufacturers' Convention, consisting of one hundred delegates, met in Richmond and resolved that all factors should limit their credits upon the sale of tobacco to four months and that the commission should not exceed 6½ per cent.

The leading tobacco manufacturer in Richmond during antebellum days was James Thomas, Jr., whose voluminous papers have been acquired by Duke University. This native Virginian was a poor boy who received only a meager education but who had remarkable business ability and industry. He began his tobacco career in 1829 as the agent of the French government to purchase tobacco in the Virginia markets. Early in the decade of the 1830's he commenced to manufacture chewing tobacco. By 1850 he had become a large manufacturer whose popular brand, "Wedding Cake," was sold in large orders in England, Germany, Australia, and in the distributing centers of New York, Baltimore, and Boston. After the Gold Rush of 1849, he held a virtual monopoly on the trade of chewing tobacco shipped to California. At the close of the ante-bellum period his factory employed one hundred and fifty hands and was manufacturing 1,100,000 pounds of chewing tobacco yearly. He was a devout

Baptist, who on one occasion entertained sixty preachers during a religious convention in the city. His habit of entertaining Baptist preachers caused the wits of Richmond to call his home "Baptist Hotel." Also he liberally supported the Virginia Baptist Seminary (later named Richmond College).

The growth of the tobacco industry in the upper South was phenomenal. By June, 1860, Virginia and North Carolina factories were producing 61 per cent of all plug, smoking, and snuff tobacco manufactured in the United States. Instead of shipping their raw tobacco abroad, as in former times, these states processed two-thirds of the tobacco grown within their boundaries. There had been a steady evolution from small factories to larger units so that in 1860 eighty-five factories, or almost one-fourth in the Virginia-Carolina area, employed fifty or more hands. Richmond, with its fifty-two factories, was by far the largest tobacco manufacturing city in the United States. The eleven Southern states produced a total of $14,612,442 worth of manufactured tobacco and employed 11,321 male and 2,300 female hands.

The Southern iron industry dates back to early colonial days. Lieutenant-Governor Alexander Spotswood in 1716 began mining operations on his huge estate of Germanna on the Virginia frontier in the vicinity of the Rapidan River. His labor force at first consisted of Swiss Germans whom he imported, later of seventy Palatine Germans, and finally of Negro slaves. He exported pig iron to England and developed a profitable business of making iron kettles, pots, and pans, which was continued by his family long after his death in 1740. The largest iron mining company in the colonial period was the Principio Company, founded in 1722, which operated four furnaces and two forges in southern Maryland and northern Virginia. Most of the capital was furnished by English partners, but the Washington family and other Southern planters were also interested in this venture. The company owned a huge amount of land as well as a large number of slaves. During the Revolution the English holdings of the company were confiscated and sold by Maryland. In South Carolina the Aera Furnace, located on a creek of the Catawba River, supplied the cannon balls for the defense of Charleston in 1780. In Kentucky the Bourbon furnace, erected in 1791, made pig iron which was converted by forges into bar iron for the use of blacksmiths and the making of stoves, flat-irons, and cooking utensils for the early settlers of Kentucky. Along the Cumberland River of Tennessee, beginning early in the 1790's, iron furnaces, forges, and bloomeries were developed.

Prior to the founding of Birmingham, Alabama, in 1871, the iron center of the New South, Richmond was the most important iron-manufacturing city below the Mason and Dixon line. Here was located the Belle Isle Iron Works, founded in 1839, which manufactured nails that became famous throughout the land of Dixie. By 1856 this company, its name changed to the Old Dominion Nail Works, was producing over a thousand tons of nails a year. Richmond had the advantage of being located near a coal basin that furnished abundant supplies of cheap bituminous coal. Raw material for the iron-manufacturing industry was obtained from the charcoal-burning furnaces of the Valley of Virginia, which produced a superior grade of iron of great tensile strength. Indeed, the furnaces and forges of the Valley had from the early nineteenth century made bar iron for the numerous blacksmith shops of the South.

The greatest iron company of Richmond, and of the South, was the Tredegar Iron Works which was founded in 1837. The masterful personality behind the success of the Tredegar Works was Joseph Reid Anderson, a graduate of West Point Military Academy, who became sales agent of the company in 1841 and seven years later purchased the business for $125,000. The Tredegar Company secured contracts from the United States government to furnish cannon for the navy. By 1860 the company had sold thirteen hundred cannon to the Federal government. The company also manufactured shells, chain cable, rails and spikes for the expanding railroads, and steam machinery for the Louisiana sugar plantations. The market of this Richmond company was largely in the North, for Southerners were prejudiced against buying home-made iron products. The chief contribution of the company to Southern industrial development was the manufacture of over forty locomotives for Southern railroads. During the Civil War the Tredegar Works played a vital role in Confederate armament, one of the reasons for the stubborn defense of Richmond.

The iron industry of Virginia employed slave labor extensively. Half of the labor force of the Tredegar Company, for example, was slaves. Some of the slave hands were owned by the company, but most of them were hired at rates ranging from $100 a year in 1849 to $175 in 1860. These black laborers were taught the skills needed in the iron industry by trained white mechanics imported from the North. In 1847 this situation led to a strike by the white mechanics, who demanded that slaves should not be used in the skilled processes of puddling and rolling. Anderson replied that he would not relinquish his constitutional right to employ or discharge anyone at his pleasure and notified the strikers that they had discharged themselves.[5] After this event he began more extensively to employ slaves, who made satisfactory employees. White mechanics, however, were reluctant to teach Negroes their acquired skills in the iron industry, for they feared that the Negroes would later usurp their jobs.

Virginia was the leader of the South in 1860 in the development of the iron industry, producing $1,666,885 worth of bar, sheet, and railroad iron. This sum, although small in comparison with the production of Pennsylvania and New York, represented an increase of 194 per cent over the record of 1850. Maryland and Tennessee both made more pig iron than Virginia. Production in these states as well as in Virginia declined during the decade, 1850–60, largely on account of the competition of the Pennsylvania furnaces, which were using anthracite coal instead of charcoal in making pig iron. The iron industry in Kentucky, however, was expanding during this decade, the increase in pig iron manufacture being 27 per cent. At Eddyville, Kentucky, William Kelly discovered as early as 1851 a method of making steel by the "air boiling process" that anticipated the Bessemer process.

The ironmasters and colliers of the South usually supported the Whig Party, primarily because they were ardently in favor of protective tariffs. Until 1846 the iron industry was protected from the cheaper English products by a tariff of $60 a ton on pig iron, $25 a ton on rolled iron, and $17 a ton on bar iron. Although agrarian Southerners succeeded in lowering the tariff in 1846, the iron industry continued to receive considerable protection. The

Southern industrialists also were exponents of state aid to internal improvements and were active in promoting railroads. In general, they remained staunch supporters of the slave regime. Anderson became an ardent secessionist, but he was an exception in this respect to most of the Southern industrialists.

In 1860 the milling of flour and cornmeal still ranked at the top of Southern manufactures. A familiar and picturesque sight on the roads of the upper South was a boy like the young Henry Clay riding to the grist mill with a sack of wheat or corn to be ground into flour or cornmeal for the subsistence of the family. In the lower South much of the flour consumed was brought from the Northwest down the Mississippi River. Thousands of small grist mills all over the South served local needs, but the tendency was to concentrate commercial milling in a few urban centers such as Richmond and Baltimore. At Richmond were located the largest grain mills in the world, a single mill having the capacity of producing a thousand barrels of flour a day. Baltimore was also a great flour-milling city. From these two centers vast quantities of flour were exported to the lower South and to Brazil. According to the report of the Census Bureau of 1860 the value of flour and meal produced in the eleven Southern states which later joined the Confederacy, $37,996,470 yearly, was twice as great as the value of the next most important industry of that region, the sawmill or lumber business.

The processing of the forest resources of the South was a highly dispersed industry. Numerous small sawmills were scattered throughout the land of Dixie, operated by water power or steam engines, producing over nineteen and a half million dollars of wealth per year. Yellow pine lumber, live oak timber for ships, cypress shingles, staves for barrels, were cut from the illimitable virgin forests. Frequently lumbering was a by-product of clearing the land for the purpose of agriculture. The lumber industry in the South employed approximately sixteen thousand persons, the largest labor force engaged in any Southern manufacturing enterprise. There were also over four thousand persons employed in extracting turpentine from the long-leaf pines of the Carolinas and Georgia—a seven and a half million dollar business. In 1860 North Carolina still retained its colonial supremacy in the production of turpentine, furnishing 60 per cent of the turpentine produced in the United States. After the Civil War leadership in this field passed first to Georgia and later to Florida.

The Southern states also supported a variety of minor industries. In 1860 there were within eleven of the Southern states one female and 3,695 male blacksmiths. Three thousand workers were engaged in the leather industry, producing goods to the value of $4,426,870. The carriage and buggy industry employed over four thousand men constructing vehicles worth nearly four million dollars. The making of steam engines absorbed the energies of 4,328 men, whose annual product was worth $5,624,375. Although the South imported huge supplies of shoes from Massachusetts, nearly four million dollars' worth of shoes were manufactured in the Southern states, representing an increase of approximately 90 per cent during the decade. In the Great Kanawha Valley and at Saltville in the Holston Valley of southwestern Virginia much salt was produced by boiling the brine of the salt springs. Of the 12,717,200 bushels of salt produced in the United States in 1859, Virginia's share was 2,076,513 bushels. The eminent Negro leader, Booker T. Washington, born in slavery, worked in the salt works of western Virginia as a boy. Although some cottonseed oil was produced in the South, there were only two small sugar refineries in the land of Dixie, employing a total labor force of thirty-eight persons.

Throughout the ante-bellum period the Southern states depended largely upon the North for the manufacture of agricultural implements. Jefferson had invented a scientific mouldboard for a plow in 1798, a year after Charles Newbold of New Jersey had made the first iron plow in America. The manufacture of plows, however, was carried on chiefly in the industrial center of Pittsburgh and in Illinois, where John Deere was laying the foundations for the largest plow-manufacturing business in the world. A Shenandoah Valley farmer, Cyrus H. McCormick, had patented in 1834 a reaper to harvest the ripe wheat, perhaps the most influential invention made by an ante-bellum Southerner. His invention was not as well suited to the hilly country of the Virginia Valley and the Piedmont as to the level wheat fields of the West, and, being a good business man, he moved to Chicago near the developing Western wheat belt, where in 1848 he began to manufacture his machines. During the Civil War the McCormick reaper was an important factor in the victory of the North. Obed Hussey also received a patent on a successful reaper, December 31, 1833, but unwisely moved from Cincinnati in the West to Baltimore, where he located his factory. In competition with the McCormick reaper, his business declined so greatly that in 1858 he retired from the contest.

In one branch of manufacture, the making of cotton gins, the South had a monopoly in 1860. Alabama was the leading state in the Union in the production of cotton gin machinery while Georgia came second. Daniel Pratt, a native of New Hampshire, was the most successful manufacturer of cotton gins below the Mason and Dixon line. He established a flourishing village at Prattville, Alabama, where in addition to his gin factory he built a cotton mill, a sawmill, and a grist mill. In 1851 he was employing two hundred hands and making annually six hundred gins of a superior quality.

The manufacture of hemp in the South was confined largely to Kentucky and Missouri, where the raw material was grown. In 1800 there were four ropewalks in the Bluegrass state, but by 1810 the number had increased to thirty-eight, giving Kentucky the largest number of rope factories in the Union. These establishments were called ropewalks because in the process of twisting the hemp fibers into ropes the operator, usually a Negro slave, walked to and fro. Instead of manufacturing heavy rope for the navy and for the sailing ships of the merchant marine, which required water-rotted hemp, the Kentucky factories were engaged in making hemp bagging and lighter ropes for the Southern cotton bales, in which the cheaper dew-rotted hemp was used. Kentucky and Missouri had almost a monopoly on this exclusively Southern trade. Three-fourths of the hemp of Kentucky was manufactured into cotton bagging, bale rope, and plow lines. Also some hemp duck cloth for sails was made in Kentucky, and a by-product of the hemp crop was the manufacture of linseed oil from hemp as well as flax seed. The papers of John Coleman, a hemp manufacturer near Versailles, Kentucky, show that he hired a number of slave boys to work in his ropewalk, paying approximately $50 a year for the services of a boy. He sent his coils of rope by steamboat down the Kentucky River to a Louisville commission house (or factor) who charged him 5 per cent for selling his product. Also his factor loaned him money at 6 per cent interest and dispatched by return steamboat such articles as bags of coffee, sugar, glassware, and a cask of oysters.

In 1860 census figures indicate that the production of hemp had remained almost static in Missouri during the preceding ten years but had doubled in Kentucky. In the manufacture of cordage, however, Missouri and Kentucky were of almost equal rank in the nation. After the outbreak of the Civil War the hemp manufacturing industry of Kentucky began rapidly to decline, so that in the decade of the 1880's Lexington ceased to manufacture this fiber. The introduction of iron bands to tie the cotton bales, the substitution of steamships for sailing ships, and the competition of other fibers, such as Manila hemp and jute, rendered the cultivation and manufacture of hemp in the South unprofitable. Recently a perverse use has been found for hemp in the manufacture of the narcotic, marijuana, from the blossom and leaves of the female plant.

Since colonial days when the aristocrats had imported wine from Europe and the poorer people had drunk rum brought by New England ships, taste in the ante-bellum South had changed; the hard liquors had supplanted European wine and West India rum. But the conversion of the South to evangelical religion and the rise of the temperance movement tended to decrease the drinking of alcoholic liquors in this region. In 1860 only one and three-quarters million dollars' worth of whiskey and beer were made in eleven Southern states by 355 establishments. However, Kentucky, incorrectly classified by the Census Bureau with the Western states, had 243 liquor stills and breweries which turned out more liquor than the other eleven Southern states combined. Since these eleven states distilled only 7,244,414 gallons of whiskey in the national total of 88,002,988, it is reasonable to conclude that Southerners imported much of their whiskey from the North, especially from Cincinnati, the greatest market for whiskey in the world at that time.

A now forgotten industry which existed in the Old South was the mining of gold. The Federal government derived its entire gold supply for the coining of money between the years, 1804–27, from the state of North Carolina. Until the discovery of this precious metal in California in 1848 the Southern states were the chief gold-producing region of the United States. In 1830 Mrs. Anne Royall, the sharp-tongued journalist and rampant feminist, visited the North Carolina gold fields, but she had no good words for the long-tailed, cotton-coated Tar Heels whom she saw poking about like snails in the gold mines and using absurd machinery. Over nine million dollars' worth of the glistening metal was extracted from these mines between 1799 and 1860. Gold was discovered also in the foot-hills of north Georgia on Cherokee lands. A mining rush followed in which at least six thousand gold diggers entered the region. John C. Calhoun owned a gold mine at Dahlonega, Georgia, but it did not make him rich. In 1837 the Federal government established a branch mint at Charlotte, North Carolina, and other branches were located at Dahlonega and New Orleans. The gold industry of the South had declined so greatly by 1860 that the mines of that region were producing only about $225,000 worth of bullion annually.[6]

From an economic point of view the South was never liberated from its colonial status. Although its manufactures were develop-ing in a promising fashion during the last decade of the ante-bellum period, still the South remained largely rural. Two-thirds of all exports from the United States to Europe consisted of Southern agricultural products, rice, tobacco, sugar, and cotton. Nevertheless, much of the profit from the sale of these staples went into the pockets of Northern business men, through the cotton factorage system, the indirect trade with Europe via Northern ports, and the purchase of Northern manufactured goods. Thomas Prentice Kettell, editor of *Hunt's Merchants' Magazine*, attempted to show the various ways in which the South was exploited by the North in a book entitled *Southern Wealth and Northern Profits* (1860). He included in his bill of indictment Federal bounties to fisheries, cus-toms duties, profits of Northern manufacturers on goods sold in the South, profits of importers of European goods, profits of factors, brokers, and commission men, interest charges on money loaned to Southerners, profits on the numerous Southern travelers who pa-tronized Northern resorts, and the money sent northward by Yankee teachers and tutors in the South. He pointed out the folly of agitating the slavery question on the part of the North and thus driving out of the Union Southern customers ["suckers"] who were so profitable to the North.

The protective tariff was regarded by the planters and farmers of the South as a means of exploiting their section by the North. This grievance was most irritating in the period 1828–33. The compromise tariff of 1833, gradually lowering duties, was replaced in 1842 by the Whig tariff which raised duties. This revival of high protection led to the Bluffton Movement in South Carolina, a second resistance movement, agitated by Robert Barnwell Rhett, but it did not succeed even in South Carolina. In 1846 the Walker tariff began a long period of moderate duties which lasted until the Civil War. Indeed, Southerners controlled the Federal government, so that the tariff of 1857, largely drawn up by Howell Cobb of Georgia, Secretary of the Treasury, resulted in, as Professor F. W. Taussig observed, "as near an approach to free trade as the country has had since 1816." [7] Furthermore, powerful groups in the South, such as the sugar growers of Louisiana, the hemp growers of Kentucky and Missouri, and the ironmasters of Virginia and Maryland, were in favor of a protective tariff. The chief injury that the tariff did to the South was to raise the price of manufactured goods purchased from the North. The Southern states did not import foreign goods to the degree that the more urbanized North did. In 1860 the amount of customs duty paid in Southern ports was seven million dollars, which was only 14 per cent of the total annual duties collected in the United States. Of course a large proportion of Southern imports from abroad came through the harbor of New York, but the South bought principally Northern goods, and competent estimates indicate that the Southern people consumed less than half of their proper proportion of the foreign goods imported into the United States. [8]

In order to liberate themselves from Northern exploitation, the Southerners considered various proposals: the establishment of direct trade with Europe, the development of Southern manufactures, the boycotting of Northern manufactures, the diversification of Southern agriculture, the building of railroads, and the reopening of the African slave trade. How much the growing sentiment of Southern nationalism contributed to the rise of manufactures below the Mason and Dixon line is impossible to measure. In an address entitled "The Industrial Regeneration of the South" (1852) the Honorable J. H. Lumpkin of Georgia urged his section to free themselves from dependence on the North by developing their own industries. "Will the South, the chivalrous South, remain longer in a condition of colonial servitude?" he asked.[9] William Gregg, eight years later, appealed to provincial patriotism, especially to the devotion of Southern ladies, to patronize Southern manufactures, but he sadly observed the tendency of Southerners to prefer Northern goods. "Graniteville goods," he wrote, "are more popular in New York and Philadelphia than at home." [10]

One of the most influential voices of the South which advocated Southern economic nationalism was *De Bow's Review of the Southern and Western States*. This periodical reflected the interests of the merchants, the planters, and the business men of the South. Its editor, James D. B. De Bow, was a South Carolinian, educated at the College of Charleston, who carried the South Carolina doctrines of Southern nationalism to New Orleans. Here he founded *De Bow's Review* in 1846. In this magazine he encouraged the development of Southern manufactures, direct trade with Europe, the building of railroads, the patronizing of Southern colleges and health resorts, and the organization of Southern commercial conventions. His *Review* also carried articles on the management and care of slaves, the diversification of crops, and improvements in the cultivation of cotton and sugar. In politics he sought to form an alliance between the South and the West, and after 1858 he acted with the Southern fire eaters. His magazine became quite prosperous, rivaling *Hunt's Merchants' Magazine* of the North, and it survived both the Civil War and Reconstruction.

De Bow was quite influential in the deliberations of the Southern Commercial Conventions that were held at intervals between 1837 and 1860 in the leading cities of the South. Such meetings of Southerners from all parts of the land of Dixie were compared by De Bow to the assembly of the Greeks at the ancient Olympic games, since both peoples thus developed a sense of unity and a realization of common aims and grievances. At these meetings many resolutions were passed and much oratory was expended but little was accomplished, except the engendering of ill feeling against the North.

One of the most hopeful proposals made at the Southern Commercial Conventions was to establish a direct trade with Europe.[11] Virginia took the lead in this movement, hoping to restore Norfolk to its pristine glory of colonial days. Governor Henry A. Wise strongly supported this proposal, and in 1856 A. Dudley Mann of Virginia presented a plan of a steam ferry between Norfolk and Milford Haven, England, operated by the construction of four huge steamships of 20,000 tons each, a project estimated to cost seven million dollars. The Virginia legislature granted a charter to the Atlantic Steam Ferry Company in March, 1858, and a number of prominent leaders of the state subscribed to its stock. Also William Ballard Preston was sent to Europe to advance direct trade with the South. He succeeded in interesting some French business men in the project, and the Virginia legislature incorporated in 1858 the Norfolk and St. Nazaire Navigation Company with a board of directors composed equally of Frenchmen and Southerners. A trial ship, the *Lone Star*, was sent out, but the plan failed to mature, partly because the Federal government in 1859 abandoned giving mail subsidies and because of the approach of the Civil War.

Southerners felt keenly their dependence on the North for manufactured goods. It was often asserted that Southerners were rocked in a cradle manufactured in the North, dressed in Northern-made clothes, read Northern books and magazines, used Northern plows and agricultural instruments, sent their children to Northern colleges, and were buried in Northern coffins. Resentment over this economic vassalage to the Yankees was intensified by the rise of the abolition crusade and the attempt to exclude slavery from the territories. After John Brown's Raid in 1859 a strong demand arose to boycott Northern goods. The agitators for Southern nationalism beginning in 1850 proposed commercial non-intercourse with the North. Bills were introduced in state legislatures to levy a tax of 10 per cent on all Northern goods imported into the Southern states. Southern Rights Associations were formed to arouse the people not to patronize Northern resorts like Saratoga Springs or Newport, not to subscribe to Northern magazines or newspapers, nor employ

Yankee teachers in Southern schools, nor send Southern youth to Northern colleges nor use Northern manufactures. Although the state governments failed to pass drastic laws to carry out such a policy, individuals of extreme Southern feelings did boycott Northern manufactures. The fire eater Edmund Ruffin wore a suit of Southern manufacture and Senator Mason of Virginia dramatized Southern nationalism by appearing in a home-spun suit in the national Senate. Lincoln ridiculed such displays by observing that the dignified Senator from Virginia should have come into the Senate barefoot as well as wearing his home-spun suit. "If that's the plan," he remarked, "they should begin at the foundation, and adopt the well-known 'Georgia costume' of a shirt collar and a pair of spurs." [12]

These various efforts to free the South from its colonial status represent an early form of economic planning. Many of the proposals of the ante-bellum "regional planners" and of the Southern Commercial Conventions were sound, but they could not be realized by paper resolutions or the facile dreams of orators. The South was rural, conservative, individualistic, and only by a slow process of education or by drastic economic pressures could Southern ways be radically changed. Furthermore, the South was more prosperous in the decade of 1850–60 than ever before, with cotton selling twice as high as in the preceding decade. If cotton and tobacco had declined disastrously in price at this time, discontent would have aided the reformers and "regional planners." One aspect of the agitation toward economic independence, however, was pernicious—the generation of a bitter anti-Northern feeling in the South. In calling attention to the problems of the South, the Southern Commercial Conventions and the extremists tended to weaken the bonds of the Union.

Citations

1. R. S. COTTERILL, "The Old South to the New," *Journal of Southern History*, XV (February, 1949), 2–8; P. G. DAVIDSON, "Industrialism in the Ante-Bellum South," *South Atlantic Quarterly*, XXVII (October, 1928), 405–425.

2. HERBERT COLLINS, "The Southern Industrial Gospel before 1860," *Journal of Southern History*, XII (August, 1946), 386–402.

3. T. P. MARTIN, "The Advent of William Gregg and the Graniteville Company," *Journal of Southern History*, XI (August, 1945), 389–423. See also BROADUS MITCHELL, *William Gregg, Factory Master of the Old South* (Chapel Hill, 1928).

3a. Nevertheless, some North Carolina cotton mills sent their product to Philadelphia for sale. The Moravian mill at Salem, established in 1837, found its best consignee in Philadelphia. Although the Salem Cotton mill failed in 1854, the woolen mill of Francis Fries, which was in operation by 1840, prospered in manufacturing thirteen varieties of woolen cloth, in carding hatter's wool, and in weaving carpets. Adelaide L. Fries, "One Hundred Years of Textiles in Salem." *North Carolina Historical Review*, XXVII (January, 1950), 1–19.

4. The human side of the tobacco industry is told by J. C. ROBERT, *The Story of Tobacco in America* (New York, 1949).

5. KATHLEEN BRUCE, *Virginia Iron Manufacture in the Slave Era* (New York, 1930).

6. F. M. GREEN, "Gold Mining: A Forgotten Industry of Ante-Bellum North Carolina," *North Carolina Historical Review*, XIV (1937), 1–19; 135–155.

7. F. W. TAUSSIG, *The Tariff History of the United States* (New York, 1888), 115.

8. D. R. DEWEY, *Financial History of the United States* (New York, 1928), 274.

9. *De Bow's Southern and Western Review*, XII (January, 1852), 42.

10. *De Bow's Review*, XXIX (October, 1860), 497.

11. See H. WENDER, *Southern Commercial Conventions, 1837–1859* (Baltimore, 1930).

12. Quoted in A. C. COLE, *The Irrepressible Conflict, 1850–1865* (New York, 1934), 68.

CHAPTER XIX

The Social Pyramid in 1850–60

SERENE white mansions, aristocratic planters, ladies descending graceful staircases in crinoline skirts, slave gangs singing in the cotton fields, and the fragrance of moonlit gardens form a tenacious stereotype of the Old South. Such scenes of glamor and ease for the privileged class actually existed in those areas of the South possessing rich soil and accessibility to markets. This romantic stereotype, however, omits from the landscape the large middle class of farmers, the barefoot women, the log cabins, and the sweaty toil of white men under the hot sun. In actuality, three-fourths of the white population of the ante-bellum South did not belong to slaveholding families, and the typical home was not a "Mount Vernon" or a "Tara Hall" but a log cabin or a modest frame cottage. The stereotype has taken certain real aspects of Southern society, especially the life of the small class of large planters, and has generalized and exaggerated them so that they appear to be typical of the South as a whole.

The romantic image of the Old South is a creation of a number of forces. The abolitionists made a contribution to this distortion by propaganda which represented the land of Dixie as inhabited chiefly by haughty aristocrats, debased "poor whites" and black slaves. The picture of an aristocratic society below the Potomac was also elaborated by the Southerners themselves. Passionately fond of reading Sir Walter Scott's novels, they tended to idealize their anachronistic society in terms of mediaeval chivalry. After the Civil War the psychological need of a compensation for bitter defeat and poverty led to the rise of reminiscences and of romances, such as those of Thomas Nelson Page, James Lane Allen, and John Esten Cooke, idealizing the splendid days "befo' the war." This romantic legend has been perpetuated by modern scenario writers and novelists, notably Stark Young in *So Red the Rose* and Margaret Mitchell in *Gone With the Wind.*

The true profile of the ante-bellum South, however, has been recovered from the exaggerations both of the abolitionists and of the romancers by the researches of recent historians. Especially valuable in this work of restoration have been the unpublished reports of the Census of 1860 which clearly indicate that the South of slavery days was predominantly a region of small independent farmers. Indeed, the social pyramid bulged greatly at the sides, and the social structure was flexible enough to permit the movement of the sons of poor men to a higher economic and social status.

At the apex of the social pyramid were the planters. According to the arbitrary classification of the census bureau, the planter status was based on the ownership of twenty or more slaves engaged in agriculture. The accurate definition of a planter, however, should also include the ownership of a considerable acreage of land, a minimum of between five hundred and a thousand acres, of which at least two hundred were in cultivation. The census of 1860 reported a surprisingly small number of "planters," only 46,274 persons, most of whom were heads of families, owning as many as twenty slaves. Out of this privileged group, only 2,292 persons belonged to the larger planter classification, that is, persons owning as many as one hundred slaves. In the whole land of Dixie, the census officials of 1860 reported finding only one slaveholder, an individual in South Carolina, having an many as a thousand slaves, and only thirteen persons owning between five hundred and one thousand slaves. The large slaveholders, thus, were very few in number and comparable to the millionaires of modern America.

This small privileged class of planters tended to think of themselves as "the South"; they confused their narrow class interests as identical with the welfare of the whole South. Unlike the Northern agriculturists, they cherished the concept of the country gentleman living in the style of an English squire of the eighteenth century—a powerful formative ideal in the Old South. None the less, many of the planters were self-made men, caught up by the restless spirit of America which drove them to buy more land and more slaves on credit in order to grow more cotton and sugar, the profits of which were used, not to pay off their mortgages, but to purchase more black laborers. Frequently, they moved from one exhausted old plantation to a fresh one located in a cruder but more fertile region of the Southwest. Thus these "movers" lost the cultural accumulations and the satisfactions of the more static English squires who quietly lived on inherited estates which they passed on to their sons and grandsons. Some of these large planters belonged to the class of *nouveau riche*, who were described by D. R. Hundley, an amateur sociologist of the Old South, as "cotton snobs." [1]

The landholdings of the larger planters were not as a rule consolidated, but scattered among half a dozen or more plantations. Indeed, it was a more efficient practice to operate units of about one thousand acres in the production of cotton or sugar and of about five hundred acres in the cultivation of rice. Each of these agricultural units utilized approximately fifty slaves under an overseer, but some of the largest planters employed a steward or superintendent to supervise their overseers. The wealthier planters, such as the powerful Wade Hampton family of South Carolina, often invested their surplus profits in the virgin lands of the Southwest. Thus they became absentee owners who administered their distant possessions through overseers guided by an elaborate set of rules for disciplining the slaves. Yet the relative number of absentee planters has been exaggerated. Some planters dispensed with overseers and managed their slaves and plantations themselves, in exceptional cases with the help of Negro foremen.

Instead of generalizing about the lives of the great planters, several case histories will be given. In Virginia the journal of John A. Selden, who had purchased the famous colonial estate of "Westover," on the James River, gives a faithful mirror of the activities of a wheat planter.[2] During the period of agricultural depression from the Revolution to 1830, many of the Virginia and Maryland planters turned from cultivating tobacco to wheat growing and diversified farming. Selden was a practical farmer on a large scale, who personally supervised the various operations of planting wheat, corn, oats, turnips, and clover, the plowing and hoeing of the crops, and the harvesting and sale of them. In 1858 he made twenty-one and a half bushels of wheat per acre, which he described as "the best average I have heard of," and he killed ninety-eight hogs for meat. During the next year he harvested five thousand eight hundred bushels of wheat which he sold in Richmond for $1.50 a bushel. He did not have to worry, however, about being in the high bracket of an income tax; he paid his taxes for the year 1858 in full, amounting to only $244.51. In his abbreviated journal as published by John Spencer Bassett, he does not mention whipping his slaves, of whom he owned sixty-three in 1861, nor does he seem to have been troubled by runaways or excessive sickness among his black laborers. At harvest time he employed extra agricultural labor, paying them 62½ cents and 75 cents a day, a scale of wages which should be evaluated in terms of the price of wheat at $1.50 a bushel and of the price which he paid for chickens at about 15 cents apiece.

With his ample income he purchased such luxuries as a silver tea set for $320, a silver egg cup, and a frock coat, and employed two teachers, an academic teacher and a music teacher, each of whom received $250 a year. He frequently visited by stage the White Sulphur Springs, was a member of the Richmond Whist Club, and on one occasion gave a dinner party for fifty-two persons. He was a public-spirited citizen, active in the Virginia Central Agricultural Society, serving as a justice of the peace without remuneration, and using his slaves to keep his share of the public roads in repair, one of the public services rendered by farmers and planters that partly explains the low taxes paid in money.

The papers of the Allston family of "Chicora Wood" on the Pee Dee River in South Carolina afford an excellent view of the life of the rice planter. "Chicora Wood" lay in the Georgetown District, the heart of the rice country, located north of Charleston. Here the slaves outnumbered the whites six to one. After graduating from West Point Military Academy, Robert F. W. Allston began to combine the career of a large planter with participation in politics, becoming governor of the state in 1856. Like many planters, he expanded his broad acres and his slave force by purchasing on credit, a practice which contributed heavily to his ultimate financial ruin. Eventually he acquired seven plantations, containing over 4,000 acres of land, of which about one-fourth was rice land. "Chicora Wood," his home plantation, contained 922 acres. His slaves increased in number from forty-two Negroes in 1820 to five hundred and ninety in 1864, the year of his death. From his combined plantations he produced a bumper crop in 1859 of 2,581 barrels of rice, each barrel containing six hundred pounds. He estimated that the profits of rice planting under favorable circumstances were 8 per cent, "independent of the privileges and perquisites of the plantation residence." [3] Certainly he was able to live in the style of a gentleman, to own a splendid town house in Charleston, and to escape from the danger of malaria by going to the resort, Pawley's Island, or to his house in the dry pineland region.

Allston had a fine sense of *noblesse oblige* that distinguished the best members of the Southern aristocracy. As a member of the South Carolina legislature, he was an ardent champion of an elementary public school system which would be attended by all classes, the establishment of a normal school "with a model school attached," and increased taxation for schools. He maintained a scholarship at South Carolina College, and was president of the Winyah Indigo Society which operated a school for the poor in Georgetown District. He was a prominent vestryman in the Episcopal Church, and he treated his Gullah slaves with genuine paternalism. Nevertheless, he was strongly in favor of the continuance of slavery, the abolition of which, he declared, would cost him the loss of half of his property.

An insight into the life of the large planters of the deep South is afforded by the diary of Bennet Barrow of West Feliciana Parish in Louisiana. Becoming disgusted with overseers, Barrow supervised his own plantation of five thousand arpents (an arpent was almost equal to an acre) with the aid of a Negro foreman. He worked hard at his vocation of farming, getting excellent performance from his two hundred slaves by a combination of rewards and of rather frequent whippings. He was impatient with slovenly work in the fields and occasionally his temper flared up, as when he broke his sword cane over the skull of a Negro. He carefully supervised the health of his slaves, acting as an amateur doctor. His life as a planter was a rhythm of routine of work, varied by hunting, fishing, attending dances, and going to horse races. He planted about

750 acres of cotton and 300 acres of corn. In 1840 he sold his cotton crop for approximately twenty thousand dollars, but, despite his lucrative returns he was continuously in debt, caused in part by a habit of endorsing the notes of his relatives and friends. In politics he was a Whig, opposed to the "man worship of Andrew Jackson" by the Democrats, but in 1844 because of his ardent wish to see Texas annexed to the United States, he voted for Polk.[4]

The sugar planter of Louisiana was usually a large operator, for the production of sugar required expensive machinery. On the eve of the Civil War the wealthiest sugar planter in Louisiana was John Burnside, an immigrant from North Ireland, who had obtained his capital as a merchant in New Orleans. Burnside had six thousand acres of continuous cane fields, and his sugar plantations and slaves, numbering more than a thousand, were valued at two million dollars. Judah P. Benjamin, the Confederate statesman, was another example of a city man, a lawyer, who purchased an interest in a sugar plantation, "Bellechasse," and introduced the most modern methods of making sugar, such as discarding the old "open kettle" process of boiling the cane juice and using vacuum pans. Benjamin popularized the new scientific techniques in articles in *De Bow's Review*, 1846–48. To "Bellechasse" he would retire from the turmoil of the city on week-ends until he lost the plantation as a result of a flood breaking through the levee and a financial disaster in endorsing the note of a friend.

The more aristocratic type of sugar planter was illustrated by John Hampden Randolph of distinguished Virginia lineage, whose family had emigrated to the deep South when he was a boy. Randolph changed from being a modest cotton planter to a sugar planter about 1846, while the price of cotton was in a slump and the sugar industry was expanding. Although he was forced to borrow much money, he became very prosperous, increasing his number of slaves from 23 in 1842 to 195 twenty years later. His "Forest Home" plantation in Iberville Parish (2,000 arpents), produced a crop of 540 hogsheads which together with his molasses sold for $36,225.26 net. Randolph continued to carry on genteel Virginia traditions in his home in the fertile Southwest. He employed tutors to teach his children the classics and dancing and music masters to give them the accomplishments of polite society. He sent his daughter to a girl's school in Baltimore and one son to the University of Virginia and another to Van Rensselaer Polytechnic in New York. He took frequent trips for pleasure, enjoyed hunting, subscribed to several newspapers, and purchased books, such as Audubon's *Birds of America*, for which he paid $166.67. His taste for magnificence was expressed in building the beautiful home of "Nottaway" in the Virginia style, with fifty rooms and such luxuries as a White Ball Room and an apparatus for gas illumination (1859). He retained his expensive property after the Civil War and continued to live in an aristocratic style until his death.[5]

From travel accounts one gains the impression, however, that many of the planters particularly of the Southwest did not live nearly as well as thrifty farmers of the North although their property was much greater. The major reason for this state was that they were usually "land poor" with their capital frozen in land and slaves. Consequently, they lacked the ready cash to buy some of the comforts of life which the Northerner enjoyed. Frederick Law Olmsted noted the absence in their homes of such things as good reading lamps, good furniture, thermometers, bathtubs, and other equipment. Some of the owners of numerous slaves and large plantations lived in log cabins and ate a monotonous diet of hog, hominy, and execrable coffee.

On the other hand, Frederick A. P. Barnard in 1833 described the gracious manner of living at "Shirley" on the banks of the James, where he enjoyed a rich feast enlivened by champagne and wines of various sorts, held at the fashionable hour of three o'clock in the afternoon. The practice of hospitality was a code of Southerners, both of the aristocrats and of the plain people. It was supported in part by the rural Southerner's keen sense of family, of kinship widely extended, which gave rise to the term "Virginia cousin." Economic conditions also favored the growth of hospitality —the scattered farms and plantations which produced loneliness, bad roads, abundance of food, a superfluity of domestic servants on the plantations, and the lack of decent taverns.

The flavor of the life of the Southwestern planter is contained in the rollicking poem below by General Albert Pike:

Now all good fellows listen, and a story I will tell
Of a mighty clever gentleman who lives extremely well
In the Western part of Arkansas, close to the Indian line;
Where he gets drunk once a week on whiskey and immediately sobers
    himself up completely on the very best of wine,
A fine Arkansas gentleman
Close to the Choctaw line!

This fine Arkansas gentleman has a mighty fine estate,
Of five or six thousand acres or more of land, that will be worth a great
    deal some day or other, if he don't kill himself too soon, and will
    only consent to wait;
And four or five dozen negroes that would rather work than not;
And such quantities of horses, and cattle, and pigs, and poultry, that he
    never pretends to know how many he has got;

This fine Arkansas gentleman makes several hundred bales,
Unless from drought or worm, or a bad stand, or some other damned
    contingency, his crop is short and fails;
And when it's picked and ginned and baled, he puts it on a boat,
And gets aboard himself likewise, and charters the bar, and has a devil
    of a spree, while down to New Orleans he and his cotton float.
This fine Arkansas gentleman
Close to the Choctaw line.

Southerners were hypersensitive about their honor. To accuse a gentleman of an untruth, to insult him, or attack his honor was to provoke a duel. An elaborate etiquette was evolved in regard to sending a challenge and in making preparations for the encounter. One did not fight a duel with a person who did not belong to the category of a "gentleman," but avenged an insult from such a person by caning or horsewhipping him. Challenges were frequently settled by explanations or the good offices of anti-dueling associations, such as the Camden (South Carolina) Anti-Duelling Association, which prevented a duel between James H. Hammond, later a Senator, and an abusive Congressman. Most Southern states passed laws against the practice of dueling, but such legislation was unenforceable against the mores of the people. The Kentucky statute of 1852 punished dueling or carrying a challenge by imprisonment or a heavy fine and by disenfranchisement and disqualification from holding office for a period of seven years. When William L. Yancey,

Representative from Alabama, fought a duel with Congressman T. L. Clingman of North Carolina, the legislature of Alabama passed a special law exempting him from disqualification from officeholding under the Alabama law against dueling. The editor of the Greenville (South Carolina) *Mountaineer*, Benjamin F. Perry, who had killed a rival editor in a duel, condoned this evil practice by saying: "When a man knows that he is to be held accountable for his want of courtesy, he is not so apt to indulge in abuse. In this way duelling produces a greater courtesy in society and a higher refinement." [6] Many a high-minded man recognized the evil of dueling yet accepted a challenge in order to escape the odium of being regarded a coward and thus lose his influence in society.

One of the most attractive virtues nourished by aristocratic plantation society was the practice of chivalry, an ideal which seems virtually extinct in modern industrial America. Chivalry led to the formation of a code of gracious manners, slightly formal and artificial it is true, but recognizing the dignity of human personality. Gentlemen in the Old South were forever getting up from comfortable seats in stage coaches, railroad cars, and public gatherings to give "ladies" a seat. The chivalric or romantic ideal dictated that women should be highly feminine and that they should look up to the male as the protector and the oracle of worldly wisdom. They were shielded from hearing profane or sexy language, and convention required them to blush at the mention of sex. Their functions were to marry early, stay within the sphere of the home, raise numerous children, and uphold the religious tradition. Mrs. Basil Hall, a Scottish traveler, observed at Charleston: "Women are just looked upon as house-keepers in this country." She also protested against the vile custom at social gatherings in the South of women herding together and men segregating themselves. At Darien, Georgia, she commented, "there appears to be no sympathy between the sexes. They have no subjects of conversation in common." [7] She was told by James Couper, a great planter of this region, that the only hope for a man to obtain a rational companion for a wife was to marry a young girl and cultivate her mind. Mrs. Couper was married when she was sixteen.

The Southern "lady" dressed in the romantic vogue, wearing crinoline skirts, reducing her waistline by stays, wearing her hair in curls, or in the Grecian style of head dress, and shading her delicate white complexion from the sun by bonnets and parasols. Southerners strongly condemned the feminist movement in the North, abhorring such vagaries as women speaking in public or wearing the ridiculous costume invented by Miss Amelia Bloomer, editor of *The Lily*. An insight into the attitude of the best Southern men toward women is afforded by Calhoun's letter to his daughter, Anna: "I am not one of those who think your sex ought to have nothing to do with politicks. They have as much interest in the good condition of their country, as the other sex, and though it would be unbecoming them to take an active part in political struggles, their opinion, when enlightened, cannot fail to have a great salutary effect." [7] Two of the most prominent leaders in the feminist and antislavery movements, Sarah and Angelina Grimké, were reared in South Carolina, but they pursued their reforming crusades in the North. Southern women of the upper class were taught in academies or by governesses such subjects as French, music, sewing, Latin, English, art, and polite manners. Among the oldest colleges for women in the nation were the Moravian College at Salem, North Carolina (first a seminary, 1802, and later a college), and Wesleyan Methodist College at Macon, Georgia, founded in 1836.

The diary of Mrs. Isaac H. Hilliard gives a vignette of the blissful life of a sugar planter's wife. In February, 1850, Mrs. Hilliard of Grand Lake, Arkansas, visited the plantation of Bishop Leonidas Polk on Bayou La Fourche in Louisiana, which was a model of paternalism. The Bishop paid a rector $300 to preach to his 370 slaves, and on Sunday afternoons the young Negroes were catechised. The grounds of his estate had an outer hedge of Cherokee roses, and his garden was fragrant with orange trees and with pyramids of Picayune roses. He had an extensive and rare library as well as a collection of prints brought from Italy. Mrs. Hilliard wrote with envy concerning the leisure of the mistress of "Leighton." "She has a faithful nurse (negro) to whose care she abandons her babes entirely. Only when she has a fancy to caress them does she see them. Eight children and cannot lay to their charge the loss of a single night's rest. In another department she is equally fortunate in having

A History of the Old South

a housekeeper who gives out, regulates, and is everything she ought
to be." [9] Also the Polk girls were taught by a white governess. Yet,
four years later this idyllic life came to an end when "Leighton"
was surrendered to creditors.

Despite the romantic tradition, the majority of Southern women
spent laborious lives, cooking, canning, making clothes for the family, milking, gardening, and bearing children. Even the mistresses
of large plantations had many responsibilities in the management of
the inefficient household servants, in attending the sick slaves, and
in supervising the domestic industries, such as weaving cloth and
making soap. Nevertheless, the diaries and reminiscences of ante-
bellum Southern ladies, notably Mrs. James Chesnut, Mrs. Clement
C. Clay, Mrs. Burton H. Harrison, and Mrs. Roger A. Pryor, mirror a very delightful and refined social life enjoyed by the upper
classes.

In this age of awakening interest in the common man, historians
have begun to turn the spotlight of research away from the life of
the gentry to the life of the plain people of the Old South. Contrary to the romantic stereotype, they have discovered that the
typical Southerner was an unostentatious farmer, cultivating a small
acreage of land with his own hands or with the aid of a few slaves.
In Tennessee, for example, two-thirds of the heads of agricultural
families in 1860 tilled farms containing less than two hundred acres.
In North Carolina approximately 70 per cent of the farms at this
time were under one hundred acres. Even in Louisiana, which has
been regarded as the paradise of the large planter, approximately
two-thirds of the agricultural properties were farms of less than a
hundred acres. This large proportion of small farmers is partly explained by the fact that many humble Creole families refused to sell
their farms to neighboring planters and that on the death of the
father the farm was subdivided among the numerous sons. In Mississippi 60 per cent of the agricultural owners had less than one hundred acres of improved land.

Perhaps the most significant fact about the yeoman farmers of the
Old South was that they owned their lands. Investigations of land
ownership in the decade 1850–60 reveal a surprising proportion of
the farmers of the Old South who owned their farms. In Alabama,

which may be taken as representative of the lower South, 74 per cent of the farmers owned their lands in 1850, a high degree of proprietorship which was increased to 80 per cent ten years later. In the Sugar Bowl parishes of Louisiana, 80 per cent of the farming population owned their lands. A similarly independent, land-owning status of the yeoman farmers existed in the upper South where there was about the same proportion of free land-owners as in the lower South. In contrast, the farm tenants of the South in 1930 constituted 57.3 per cent of the farm population, and in states like Georgia and Mississippi, the percentage rose to 65.6 per cent and 66.1 per cent respectively, an unwholesome condition, the reverse of the situation in 1860. The widespread ownership of land in the Old South gave to the farmer a sense of independence and self-respect and provided apparently the economic basis for a democratic policy.

Such statistics make it necessary for us to revise traditional ideas of Southern society during the ante-bellum period. It is apparent from the study of land tenure that there existed a large body of yeoman farmers below the Potomac who constituted a true middle class. A recent school of historians centered at Vanderbilt University have made large claims for this class, maintaining that they enjoyed a remarkable prosperity in the decade 1850–60 during which they increased their holdings both of land and slaves, and that small farms and plantations were frequently side by side, the yeoman ploughing as fertile soil as his rich planter neighbor.[10]

This last conclusion challenges the Phillips-Gray thesis of a large degree of segregation of the planters and yeoman farmers. According to this older view, the small farmers and poor whites were driven by the advance of the plantation from fertile soils into areas of poorer soils.[11] Slave labor was uneconomical on poor land and even on rich land with inadequate communications to market. Certainly the maps of the distribution of slaves and of staple-producing areas show that the slaves and the vast majority of the plantations were concentrated in the rich soil areas and along the river valleys. The yeoman farmers, on the other hand, were most numerous in the uplands—the Piedmont region of the upper South, the hill regions of east Tennessee, northern Georgia, Alabama, and Mississippi—as well as in the poorer soils of the coastal region. This fact does not invalidate a conclusion that frequently planters and farmers lived in juxtaposition, for in contiguous areas the soil is often of unequal fertility. Furthermore, there was considerable fluidity in Southern society so that yeomen did acquire fertile land and become planters.

The dynamics of Southern slavery seems to have been in the direction of greater concentration of slaves into fewer hands rather than the reverse trend of a wider distribution of slave property. In 1850 approximately one-third of the Southern people belonged to slaveholding families, but by 1860 the proportion had declined to slightly over one-fourth of the white population. A case study of Greene County Georgia, for example, shows a remarkable decline of the white populations by 1840 as the plantations and the number of slaves increased. The non-slaveholders, tenants, and unsuccessful farmers tended to move farther west.[12]

This emigration was particularly active in the Atlantic seaboard states in the decade of the 1830's. During this decade South Carolina's population stood almost stationary, registering according to the Federal census a gain of only 0.47 per cent. North Carolina had a rate of increase of only 2.54 per cent and Virginia 6.7 per cent as compared with 8.6 per cent, 12.79 per cent, and 15.12 per cent respectively in the previous decade. The lower South, on the other hand, was increasing in population by huge ratios during these decades, but after 1840 there was constant emigration from the Gulf states to Arkansas and Texas. The nomadic farmers and planters had practiced the same type of soil butchery here as in the older states. Accordingly, after the land had begun to wear out and erosion had carried away much of the top soil, they abandoned their farms. The ever recurring movement of the covered wagons, pulled by oxen and horses, filled with women, children, grandparents, and "household plunder," was a melancholy sight on the dusty roads of the Old South.

The question of how important in the whole economy of the South was the middle class of farmers as compared with the planter group remains an unsolved problem. Professor William E. Dodd in his study of the lower South has pointed out the tremendous and unwholesome concentration of wealth in the hands of a small planter class.[13] The Vanderbilt studies, on the other hand, emphasize the wide distribution of land ownership in the lower as well as in the upper South and the apparent prosperity of the yeoman farmers during the last decade of the ante-bellum period. The quality of land that a farmer tilled was more important than the number of acres which he owned. The fact that the planters tended to monopolize the soils of high fertility and the farmers those of inferior quality meant that the planters in the rich black belts produced the "lion's share" of the money crops, cotton, sugar, and rice.[14] The yeoman farmers, on the other hand, although they owned their little farms, lived a low standard of existence on a hog and corn economy.

With the exceptions of rice and sugar for export, the yeoman farmers raised the same crops as did the planter. Despite the economic advantages of the slave plantation, a considerable part of the Southern cotton crop was grown by small farmers. This group, however, was engaged principally in cultivating subsistence crops, such as wheat, corn, oats, sweet potatoes, and sorghum cane. In the cotton and tobacco districts the typical farmer planted as a rule several acres in cotton or tobacco which furnished him with money to buy goods from the store and pay taxes. To process his cotton for the market he used the planter's gin and press and to grind his corn and wheat, the planter's grist mill, paying a toll of a portion of the grain. The Creole small farmers, in addition to cultivating corn, sweet potatoes, and sorghum cane, raised perique tobacco and a type of rough rice which was different from and sweeter than Carolina rice.

The small farmers also raised a large number of livestock. The landscape of the small farms of the Old South was animated by the grunting of numerous lean hogs, expressively dubbed "razor-backs," which found their own food by rooting in the forests and fields. The small farmer raised a relatively larger proportion of cattle and sheep than did the large planter, often using the public lands for grazing and allowing his cattle largely to feed themselves, even in winter. They were kept tame by placing cakes of salt for them to lick in the neighborhood of the house. Often a substantial yeoman, particularly in the pinelands and mountainous areas, appeared to belong to the "poor whites" because of lack of visible wealth, having only a few acres of corn or cotton, but actually he owned unsuspected wealth in the cattle which were hidden in the woods. The advance of plantation agriculture caused a decline in the production of livestock, for slavery was not especially suited to the raising of cattle.

The overwhelming majority of the yeoman farmers lacked the capital to invest in slaves. A sampling of Mississippi counties in 1860 reveals that 51.56 per cent of the agricultural operators possessed no slaves and that approximately 20 per cent more of the farmers owned less than ten slaves.[15] In Alabama only one-third of the families were slaveholders, and of this minority one-half owned less than five slaves. In North Carolina on the eve of the Civil War nearly three-fourths of the people owned no slaves, and of the small minority who were slaveholders 70.8 per cent owned less than ten slaves. The yeoman farmers who acquired a few slaves usually worked beside their black servants in the fields. Many of the non-slaveholders aspired to acquire slaves, not merely for the purpose of securing laborers or to aid their hard-worked wives, but also for the sake of social prestige. Nevertheless, in the upper South, at least, there was little distinction made in social intercourse between slaveholders and non-slaveholders belonging to the same economic level. Furthermore, in this region there was no dishonor or lessening of respect involved in working in the fields.

A large proportion of the overseers came from the yeoman class. Although the planters have drawn a very unfavorable picture of the overseers as a class, many of them were sons of substantial farmers and even of planters, young men "on the make" who wished to earn money for buying land and Negroes. In the census records of Hancock County, Georgia, for example, of the one hundred and thirty-nine overseers listed, forty-two lived in the homes of the planters and twenty were sons of planters. Jesse Belflowers, the overseer of the rice plantation "Chicora Wood" for twenty-four years, was a respectable yeoman whose salary was increased from three hundred dollars at the beginning of his service to one thousand dollars after he had attained experience. The overseer's position in the Old South was difficult, for very often the sole test of his success was the number of bales of cotton to the acre which he could raise. Consequently, there was little incentive for him to take care of the land or slaves. His tenure was insecure and there was a constant turnover in overseers. The job of managing black slaves required a combination of qualities that was hard to find. He was a rare overseer, indeed, who, like Garland Harmon of Georgia, wrote articles for agricultural magazines and zealously strove to preserve his employer's soil.[16]

It is difficult to find journals and letters of non-slaveholders which give a realistic picture of the life of the yeoman farmer. One of these rare records is a manuscript account of Newton Knight, leader of the Unionists of Jones County, Mississippi, by his son.[17] Jones County is in the pineland belt of southern Mississippi, a region of small slaveless farmers, in which a movement arose during the Civil War to detach the county from the Confederacy and, according to popular legend, establish the "Free State of Jones." Knight, a poor farmer boy, did not receive any schooling in his youth but worked hard on his father's farm. When he was nineteen years old he married, erected a log cabin, and cleared some land for cultivating corn and sweet potatoes. The people of his community marketed their produce, chickens, wool, and grain, at Shubuta, Mississippi, transporting them by oxen, whose slow progress consumed six days going and coming. In such a rural society many articles had to be made by hand. Knight, for example, made shoes for his neighbors and helped them to build log cabins. These yeoman families cooperated with each other in various ways, such as log rollings, corn huskings, and quilting parties. They attended camp meetings, barbecues, and stump speakings. Newton Knight was a primitive Baptist, who seems to have represented the strong streak of Puritanism to be found in the yeoman class of the Old South. Quiet in demeanor, "strictly business," a person who "did not believe in any kind of foolishness," he had a grim and violent side to his nature which led him to kill a Negro. Despite his lack of education (he was finally taught to read and write by his wife) he was a natural leader in his community. Since he resolutely refused to fight against the Union in the Civil War, he was made a hospital orderly by the Confederates. The passage of the "twenty nigger law," exempting owners of twenty slaves from military service, and the plundering of his community by Confederate cavalry caused him to desert and take the leadership

of a guerrilla band of Unionists in the southern part of the state.
The will books in the county courthouses afford a valuable insight into the lives of the plain people of the Old South. The will of Barbary Keistler of Rowan County, North Carolina, May, 1856, shows the personal possessions of an old lady of German extraction who could not read and write but signed her name by making her mark. To her two sons she bequeathed thirty-one dollars in cash, her bed and bedding, a commode, a spinning wheel, a reel, a wash pot, a bucket, a chest, a bake oven, a cupboard, a skillet and a frying pan, and her clothes to be divided among her daughters-in-law.[18] The bill of sale of the personal property of Arnett White of Fayette County, Kentucky, September, 1849, included property valued at $937.03 which included a feather bed, quilts and blankets, a dining table, a bureau, a carpet, churn, crocks, kettles, six silver spoons, one dozen tumblers, a castor stand, a rifle, a saddle and bridle, four hoes, two hay forks, a grain cradle, a hemp brake, stretchers, hackles, a quantity of hemp and corn, two stacks of rye, seven head of cattle, fourteen horses, two sheep, ten hogs, and a large boar. The worldly possessions of a more substantial slave-holding farmer of the Bluegrass region of Kentucky, Daniel B. Kay, as recorded in his will of June, 1854, included: one hundred and sixty acres of land valued at fifty dollars an acre, eight slaves, sixteen horses, twelve silver spoons, eight fine mahogany chairs, one pr. cut glass decanters, one rocking chair, as well as receipts for hemp stored in a warehouse and loans bearing interest.[19]

The monotonous life of these yeoman farmers of the Old South seems very drab to modern eyes. Most of them lived in log houses of the type called "dog-run cabins," consisting of two rooms united under the same roof but with an open space or "breezeway" between them. The boys and girls slept in the loft under the roof. The huge fireplace was equipped with pots, pans, and cranes for cooking. The furniture was largely home-made, the lye soap was home-made, gourds were used for dipping drinking water from the wooden pail; in fact these homes of the yeoman farmers were symbols of a large measure of economic independence. Working from dawn to dark, they accepted the niggardly rewards of their toil and the manifold blows of nature with fortitude, even quiet desperation. Although the generations of farmers which came after the Civil War suffered most keenly from the inheritance of eroded and exhausted soils, the small farmers of the Old South also were often victims of barren land, whose symbol of barrenness was the broomsedge. No historian has portrayed so realistically and poignantly as has Ellen Glasgow in the novel *Barren Ground* the effect of impoverished soil on Southern men and women who unimaginatively accepted their fate, stubbornly opposed to "new-fangled ways," such as experimenting with different crops and new methods of agriculture that might have liberated them.

Nevertheless, the plain people of the Old South had their distinctive amusements which are richly illustrated, with some exaggeration, by the Southern humorists. In such stories as "Polly Peablossom's Wedding" by John Basil Lamar, *Major Jones's Chronicles of Pineville* by William Tappan Thompson, *Fisher's River Scenes and Characters* by Harden E. Taliaferro, "Taking the Census" by Johnson Hooper, and "The Big Bear of Arkansas" by Thomas Bangs Thorpe are delineated the diversions of the common man. Here one may vicariously enjoy with the yeoman his zest in break-down dancing, in singing folk songs, in attending camp meetings, in going to the county court, in getting drunk, in hunting with his hounds, in practical joking, in wrestling and fighting, in shooting at a target for the prize of a beef, and in attending barbecues and corn shuckings.

The yeomen of the South, particularly the mountain whites, have made a valuable contribution to American music and to the literature of ballads and folk songs. Traditional English and Scottish ballads survived in the Appalachians, often modified by the Southern environment. There were lively tunes played by mountain fiddles, such as "Money Musk," "Leather Breeches," "Old Joe Clark," "Sally Good'n," "Weevily Wheat," and "Skip to My Lou." There were melancholy songs about the frustrations of life, like "Barbara Allen." Some of the most creative songs of the Southern uplands were the white spirituals, which expressed the deep religious emotion of a frontier people, dominated by a solemn reverence and an appreciation of the mystery of nature. The favorite theme was the longing for heaven, the "Promised Land," in such songs as "Roll! Jordan, Roll!" In the country churches group singing was directed by a leader with a tuning fork, the group often using songbooks with notes of four shapes. The most popular of these songbooks compiled and in part composed by Southern men were the *Kentucky Harmony* (1815) by Ananias Davisson, *The Southern Harmony* (1835) by William ("Singing Billy") Walker of South Carolina, and *The Sacred Harp* (1844) by Benjamin F. White of Georgia.[20]

An insight into the mentality of the Southern farmers is afforded by the almanacs of the time. These publications, which were sold generally by country stores, ranked next to the Bible as the chief reading matter of the plain people. Not only did they predict weather, but they were also a mine of practical information. Some of them gave the names of members of Congress and of the state legislature, the time of the meeting of the county courts, prices of cotton, temperatures throughout the year, schedule of sunrises and eclipses, jokes, anecdotes, advice in regard to making good butter, getting rid of chinch bugs, mending china, and recipes. Most of the ante-bellum almanacs followed the example of Benjamin Franklin's *Poor Richard's Almanac* in including axioms of conduct, encouraging the middle class virtues. *M'Carter's Country Almanac, Calculated for the Carolinas and Georgia* for the year 1836 published at Augusta, Georgia, gives this advice: "Humble wedlock is better than proud virginity." In the *Christian Almanac for Georgia and South Carolina*, 1830, is an unconsciously amusing article on "Eminent Early Risers," citing examples of great men who arose early in the morning. *Richardson's Virginia and North Carolina Almanac* for 1854 published at Richmond, contains this bit of folklore:

> "When the peacock loudly bawls
> soon we'll have both rain and squalls."

Perhaps the most valuable contribution of the almanacs was their encouragement to scientific agriculture. One of the most famous Southern almanacs was *Affleck's Southern Rural Almanac*, published by Thomas Affleck of Washington, Mississippi, in connection with the advertisement of his Southern Nurseries. Affleck was a significant agricultural reformer in the lower South who used his almanac as a medium for agitating for more scientific agriculture in this region. Especially did he urge farmers to diversify their crops instead of overproducing cotton and to keep business-like records of their agricultural operations. Other almanacs, such as the *Western Farmer's Comprehensive Almanac*, published at Louisville, Kentucky, had brief articles on the management of cattle, rules for overseers, the use of manure, the proper time to sow seeds, crop rotation, and miscellaneous agricultural information.

The number of the "poor whites" in the social structure of the Old South was greatly exaggerated by the abolitionists in order to make a stronger case against the debasing effects of slavery. Travelers also tended to confirm this impression, because they failed to distinguish between "the poor whites" and the yeoman farmers, and because they often carried with them in their mental luggage the stereotype of the South which had been created by antislavery writers. The existence of a class of "poor whites," however, was recognized by the Southerners themselves, who called these unfortunate people, comparable to the slum element of the North, such opprobrious names as "hill billies," "peckerwoods," "dirt eaters," "clay eaters," "poor white trash," "tackies," "piney woods folk," and "crackers." The last epithet was probably derived from the habit of these poor people of reducing their corn to meal by cracking it with a pestle, or possibly the term originated from the long whips which the drivers of ox carts "cracked" over the backs of their plodding animals. The number of the "poor whites" probably did not exceed 10 per cent of the white population of the South.

It was formerly thought that the "poor whites" were descended from the indentured servant class and the transported convicts of colonial days. The modern explanation of their status, however, is that they were "stranded frontiersmen" who became victims of their isolated environment.[21] They were as a rule located in the regions of poor soils, especially "the pine barrens," and the mountains. There were some "poor whites" occupying infertile pieces of land between the plantations who were regarded as nuisances by the planters since they sold liquor to slaves and received stolen property. Consequently the planters tried to get rid of such objectionable neighbors. Environment was not alone the cause of the "poor white" class, but the contempt of the upper classes for these underprivileged people was a factor in their debasement.

Indeed, many complex forces explain the existence of "the poor whites," who incidentally were not confined to the South. Doubtless some of "the poor whites" arrived at their lowly position in life because they desired to escape the law or wished to live a freer life in a semi-frontier region, while others were unfortunate in the struggle for existence, became bankrupts, drunkards, or suffered from poor heredity. Travelers in the South were impressed by the indolence not only of the degraded class but of many villagers, a lethargy which cannot be attributed to climate alone. It is probable also that the abolitionists were partly right in blaming the slavery system for the creation and continuation of this class. Slavery tended to produce a monoply of the richer soils by the planters and the more fortunate yeoman and it retarded the diversification of industry in the South which would have given the landless class larger opportunities for productive work.

Modern students recognize that among the most important causes of the shiftlessness and laziness of the poor whites were disease and lack of a proper diet.[22] The most serious of these diseases were hookworm and malaria, which also affected to a lesser degree the yeomen and the planters. The poor whites lived frequently in regions of sandy soil which was most congenial to the hookworm parasite, and furthermore, the majority of these poor people did not wear shoes. The hookworm enters the body through the feet, passes along the bloodstream to the intestines, where it adheres to the walls by a hook on its body. There it lays numerous eggs and drains the human body of energy. The victim becomes sallow or pale, lustre goes out of the eyes, and sometimes a morbid craving or a calcium deficiency caused the diseased whites of the ante-bellum South to eat the white "hearth clay."

For generations Southern energy was dissipated by this disease that was probably brought to America by African slaves. Although hookworm did affect the Negroes in the South, they seem to have attained some immunity from the disease so that they were not so frequently the victims of its ravages as were the whites. Not until the twentieth century were the Southern people freed from this great incubus. In 1902, Charles W. Stiles, a zoologist in the employ of the Federal government, made a trip through the South, during which he discovered the great havoc wrought by the disease. Accordingly, he began a crusade to free the South from this destroyer of human energy. In 1908, the Rockefeller Sanitation Commission for the eradication of hookworm was created as a result of the efforts of a North Carolina reformer, Walter Hines Page. Rockefeller gave over a million dollars to this cause of rehabilitating the South through eliminating the scourge of disease. Twenty years after the Rockefeller Commission had begun its work, over seven million people had been treated, largely by a simple remedy, a purging of the patient with thymol and epsom salts. Today hookworm has practically disappeared from the South.

The appearance and habits of the "poor whites" bore testimony to their diseases and lack of a balanced diet. Tallow-faced, they were melancholy in aspect, thin and emaciated, frequently with bleary eyes, and faces very wrinkled. The women, who did most of the drudgery, married at extremely early ages, and by the time they were thirty years of age looked like old women. The teeth of the poor whites were almost wholly uncared for, and they relied upon patent medicines or home-made remedies instead of the doctor for the cure of disease. Their poverty-stricken aspect and outlandish clothes caused them to be laughed at as "tackies."

The "poor whites" were not primarily agriculturists but were hunters, fishermen, and stock raisers. Frequently squatters on the public land, they disdained sustained labor in the fields. Usually they had a few "razor-back" hogs and some lean cattle which roamed through the woods subsisting on wiregrass. A small patch of cotton and corn was cultivated, chiefly by the women, to provide a little money for snuff, powder, lead, salt, sugar, and coffee. The diet of the family was monotonous. Besides the game that was killed they lived mostly on corn and hog meat. In some regions sweet potatoes were used for a multitude of needs—as a food in the forms of roasted potatoes, sweet potato pie, sweet potato coffee, as an intoxicant in home brew, and the vines served for mattresses and to feed the stock. From their corn they made corn pone and "big hominy" and distilled it into corn whiskey. The men were frequently drunkards. The piney woods folks were almost invariably illiterate and highly superstitious. The Bible was a sealed book to them, and their religion was of a primitive, fundamentalist type. The most deplorable aspects of the "poor whites" were their lack of ambition and their shiftlessness. Yet they had a type of pride which caused them to disdain begging, and they would not work at any job of domestic or menial service. Furthermore, they regarded themselves as superior to the slaves whom they hated and whom they wished to keep in bondage.

The mountain whites dwelling in the secluded valleys of the Appalachian Mountains have been called "our contemporary ancestors." They preserved the language and even some of the ballads and folklore of the seventeenth century immigrants. They were frontiersmen who remained after the frontier had passed by, hunting bear and deer and raising cattle for subsistence. Occasionally they drove their oxen hitched to covered wagons down to the towns to dispose of their distilled whiskey, apples, chestnuts, and cabbage. It is a mistake to think of all the mountain people as "poor whites." Although there were some individuals among them, especially squatters, who belonged to this category, a considerable proportion of them owned land and cattle and should be classified with the yeomen. Indeed, these mountaineers were a proud and independent people who hated the soft ways of civilization, and outsiders were "furriners" to them. Their primitive ideas of government and justice caused them to carry on vendettas or feuds, in which they held responsible for murder not merely the criminal but his family or clan. After the Civil War they shot revenue officers who attempted to come into their lonely valleys and coves to collect the Federal revenue tax on their distilled whiskey. Olmsted found some of these Southern highlanders antislavery in sentiment, but the majority seldom saw a Negro and had no desire to free the slaves.

Close to the poor whites in the economic scale were the agricultural laborers, who were hired by the farmers and planters particularly during harvest. Their wages were largely determined by the competition of the hiring of slaves. In 1860 the average wage paid for a farm hand with board was $10.37 a month in North Carolina, $21.41 a month in Alabama, $16.66 a month in Mississippi, $13.71 in Indiana, and in the United States the national average was $14.73. Without board the daily wages in North Carolina was 77 cents, the lowest in the nation, in Virginia, 81 cents, in Louisiana, $1.39, in Indiana, 98 cents, in Alabama, 96 cents and in the United States, $1.11.[23] Prime slaves were hired in the tobacco factories of Virginia for approximately $18 a month with board, and on the plantations of Louisiana for as much as $30 a month. The working hours of the white agricultural laborers were from sunrise to sunset. The planters and farmers preferred to hire Negro slaves rather than the poor whites, for they regarded the white laborers as shiftless and inefficient.

In addition to the agricultural laborers there were several other landless groups in the country, the woodchoppers along the Mississippi River who received $50 a month for providing the steamboats with fuel, the Irish ditch-diggers on the sugar plantations, hired to do unhealthy and dangerous work, and the tenants. The last generally tilled the old fields of the planters which had been abandoned as too sterile to waste slave labor on them. Living a marginal existence, they were usually in debt to the planter or the country storekeeper. Indeed, the tenant system did not originate after the Civil War as a result of the freeing of the slaves, but was a pre-war institution for white workers, particularly in the regions of worn-out soil. The emancipation of the slaves and the disruption of the economy of the Old South, however, enormously expanded the use of the tenant system.

The urban class in the South in 1860 was a very small fraction of the population, only 7.8 per cent living in towns of over four thousand inhabitants. At the apex of this urban society was a small group of retired or non-resident planters who had moved to town. Here they built imposing mansions of the Greek Revival style and through overseers supervised their outlying plantations. Closely associated with these "nabobs" were the lawyers, doctors, ministers, teachers, and editors. A large proportion of the income of the professional class was derived from services for the slavocracy. Moreover, the merchants and professional people were dominated by the agrarian ideal, causing them to aspire to own plantations and to acquire slaves. In North Carolina, for example, the professional class on the eve of the Civil War formed about 4 per cent of the total number of persons classified as to occupations by the Census Bureau. A recent study of a Georgia county in the Piedmont has disclosed that over 54 per cent of the professional class owned slaves and that this group enjoyed a greater average wealth than did the merchant class.[24] Except in some of the large seaports, the merchants ranked socially below the professional class.

Skilled laborers were often paid higher wages in the South than in the North. Solon Robinson in 1849 reported that a cotton factory in South Carolina paid its thirty-five hands, some of whom were ten years old, an average wage of $1.90 a week, while a machinist was paid $9 a week. In 1860, a carpenter was paid per day without board, $1.50 in North Carolina, $2.15 in Alabama, $2.47 in Mississippi, $1.65 in Indiana, as compared with the national average of $1.85. In New Orleans skilled labor received as a rule $2 a day while unskilled labor was paid $1 a day, and on the plantations only 50 to 75 cents a day.

In the cities the white mechanics bitterly resented slave competition. On occasions they went on strike when Negro mechanics were employed to work beside them. Sometimes they resorted to mob violence, such as the beating of Frederick Douglass by the ship mechanics of Baltimore. Such prejudices against the Negro mechanic, however, prevailed in the North as well as in the South. The mechanics agitated at various times for legislation excluding Negro mechanics from the cities, and in some cases succeeded, such as in the enactment of a Georgia law in 1845, forbidding colored mechanics or masons, slave or free, from making contracts for the erection or repair of buildings, or the master of slave mechanics from making such contracts. On the plantations, however, much of the skilled labor required for agricultural operations and for the needs of the planter was furnished by slave mechanics, masons, carpenters, coopers, and blacksmiths.

The skilled workmen of the Old South were too individualistic and perhaps too isolated to form effective trade unions and develop a strong sense of class solidarity. In the large cities they organized mechanics associations, which were incorporated by the legislature, but often the purposes of these organizations were to furnish mutual aid to each other or to form lyceums for intellectual improvement rather than for purposes of striking or of regulating the price of labor. The printers seem to have been the most active branch of skilled labor in organizing genuine trade unions, particularly in Augusta, Georgia, and New Orleans. The typographical Society of New Orleans was founded as early as 1835, and after disbanding several times was firmly established in 1852 by Gerard Stith who was later elected Mayor on the American ticket. The strongest of the early unions in the Crescent City was the Screwmen's Benevolent Association, or the union of the stevedores for the cotton ships. Their union paid mutual sick benefits of $3 a week and secured high wages for its members.[25]

The workingmen of the South lived rather insecure lives as was the lot of laborers in other parts of the nation. In the cities open gutters, privies, and unprotected wells were sources of pollution and disease. In this individualistic age there was little control over callous landlords. Also the Irish laborers who worked on the railroads and dug ditches were sadly exploited. Their labor was handled by a contractor who provided them with liquor but paid them very low wages to do the dangerous and unhealthful work from which slaves were protected. The mechanic class and the day laborers bore all the burdens of the risks of their occupation, since the common law doctrine which prevailed in America relieved employers from liability for accidents unless they were directly responsible for the accident. The many hardships of the laboring class are illustrated in a very racy autobiography written by one of them, *The Life and Travels of John Robert Shaw, The Well Digger* (Lexington, Kentucky, 1807). After service in the Revolutionary Army Shaw traveled in Kentucky digging wells, splitting rails, and working with drovers. Despite many vicissitudes, he acquired property and a measure of prosperity, freeing himself from thralldom to liquor and becoming a shouting Methodist.

In the Southern towns and cities the artisans and laboring class were recruited to a considerable extent from foreign immigrants. The large rural districts of the South, on the other hand, were not an inviting region to foreigners; indeed, for every eight immigrants who settled in the North, only one located in the South. The reasons for this avoidance of the land of Dixie were that the principal shipping lines to America terminated in the Northern ports, industrial opportunities also were greater in the North, and the lands of the West were better advertised and more accessible. In the South, on the other hand, competition with slave labor was a deterrent (although this factor has been overemphasized), and the techniques of cultivating Southern staple crops were unfamiliar to European immigrants.

The horde of immigrants who poured into this country in the decade of the 1850's, therefore, sent only a small contingent into the Southern states. Moreover, perhaps 90 per cent of this group settled in the coastal and river towns, New Orleans being the great port of entry for them. The foreign-born in the Southern towns and cities were usually artisans, shopkeepers, cabmen, and specialized laborers, such as workers in the construction of railroads. Despite the overall picture of a relatively small proportion of foreigners in the South, such cities as Baltimore in 1860 had a 24.71 per cent foreign-born population, Richmond 23 per cent, and Mobile 24 per cent. In Charleston 30 per cent of the white population belonged to this category, and in Natchez there were 1,186 foreign-born in a population of 4,680 persons, the Irish numbering 571 and the Germans, 256. The foreign element in Louisville and Memphis was over one-third of the population of those cities, in New Orleans 40 per cent, and in St. Louis 59.76 per cent. Although some of the great Northern cities, like Chicago and New York, had a foreign-born population of approximately 50 per cent, the percentages of many Southern towns were not far behind the ratio of most Northern urban communities.

Citations

1. D. R. Hundley, *Social Relations in Our Southern States* (New York, 1860).
2. J. S. Bassett (ed.), *The Westover Journal of John A. Selden* (Northampton, 1921).
3. J. H. Easterby (ed.), *The South Carolina Rice Plantation as Revealed in the Papers of Robert F. W. Allston* (Chicago, 1945).
4. E. A. Davis, *Plantation Life in the Florida Parishes of Louisiana, 1836–1846, as Reflected in the Diary of Bennet H. Barrow* (New York, 1943).

5. P. S. Postell, "John Hampden Randolph, A Louisiana Planter," *Louisiana Historical Quarterly*, XXV (1942), 149–223.

6. Kibler, *Benjamin F. Perry*, 135.

7. Una Pope-Hennessy (ed.), *An Aristocratic Journey: Being the Outspoken Letters of Mrs. Basil Hall Written during a Fourteen Months' Sojourn in America, 1827–1828* (New York, 1931), 212, 230.

8. Jameson, *Correspondence of John C. Calhoun*, 315–316.

9. Manuscript in Department of Archives, Louisiana State University.

10. F. L. and H. C. Owsley, "The Economic Basis of Society in the Late Ante-Bellum South," *Journal of Southern History*, VI (February, 1940), 24–45; B. H. Clark, *The Tennessee Yeomen, 1840–1860* (Nashville, 1942), H. L. Coles, "Some Notes on Slaveownership and Land Ownership in Louisiana, 1850–1860," *Journal of Southern History*, IX (August, 1943), 380–394.

11. U. B. Phillips, "The Origin and Growth of the Southern Black Belts," *American Historical Review*, XI (July, 1906), 798–816.

12. A. F. Raper, *Tenants of the Almighty* (New York, 1943), 32.

13. W. E. Dodd, *The Cotton Kingdom* (New Haven, 1919), 24.

14. Fabian Linden, "Economic Democracy in the Slave South: An Appraisal of Some Recent Views," *Journal of Negro History*, XXXI (April, 1946), 140–189, a severe criticism of the Owsley school.

15. Herbert Weaver, *Mississippi Farmers*, 1850–1860 (Nashville, 1945).

16. J. C. Bonner, "The Plantation Overseer and Southern Nationalism," *Agricultural History*, XIX (January, 1945), 1–11; and J. S. Bassett (ed.), *The Plantation Overseer as Revealed in His Letters* (Northampton, Mass., 1925).

17. Manuscript in Department of Archives, Louisiana State University.

18. Manuscript in the Courthouse of Rowan County at Salisbury, North Carolina.

19. Manuscript in Courthouse of Fayette County at Lexington, Kentucky.

20. G. P. Jackson, *White Spirituals in the Southern Uplands* (New York, 1913).

21. A. N. J. Den Hollander, "The Tradition of 'Poor Whites,'" in W. T. Couch, *Culture in the South* (Chapel Hill, 1935), 403–431; H. Kephart, *Our Southern Highlanders* (New York, 1913); and S. McIlwaine, *The Southern Poor-White* (Norman, 1939).

22. P. H. Buck, "The Poor Whites of the Ante-Bellum South," *American Historical Review*, XXXI (October, 1925), 44–46.

23. U. S. Bureau of the Census, *Statistics of the United States (Including Mortality, Property, etc.) in 1860* (Washington, 1866), 512.

24. J. C. Bonner, "Profile of a Late Ante-Bellum Community," *American Historical Review*, LXIX (July, 1944), 672.

25. Shugg, *Origins of Class Struggle in Louisiana*, 114–115.

CHAPTER XX

Molding the Southern Mind

ONLY recently have students of the Old South ventured into the realm of the intellectual history of this region. What was the nature of the training which Southern youth received in the schools and colleges of their native section? What influence did the newspapers have on Southern public opinion? What was the type of religion which became dominant below the Mason and Dixon line? Did Southern society respond to the humanitarian movement of the ante-bellum period? The answers to these questions must be tentative, but in this chapter materials are gathered which may illuminate some of the problems raised and provoke fruitful thought on them.

A dark cloud of illiteracy overshadowed the minds of a considerable minority of the Southern people throughout the ante-bellum period. In 1850, according to J. D. B. De Bow, superintendent of the Federal census, the Southern states had an illiteracy ratio among the native white population of 20.30 per cent, the Middle States, 3 per cent, and New England 0.42 per cent. In some parts of the land of Dixie, fully one-third of the white population was illiterate, unable to read the Bible, and signing their names with a cross mark. The large immigrant population of New England, however, was even more ignorant than these unschooled Southerners and the Pennsylvania-Dutch farmers were also woefully illiterate. Since many of the illiterates voted both in the slave and the free states, their ignorance affected the political life of the nation, especially after the rise of Jacksonian democracy. Demagogic politicians appealed to this class of people by affecting the dress and manners of the common man, by treating the sovereign voters to whiskey, and by flattery. Evangelical ministers also aroused suspicions in the minds of common people against men of education and against "ungodly" universities. Furthermore, the florid type of oratory which was the fashion in the ante-bellum South was conditioned at least partly by the limited education of the audiences of farmers and villagers.

The upper class in the South enjoyed reasonably good advantages for giving their children an education. The tutorial system, which had played such an important role among the colonial aristocracy, declined very greatly in the ante-bellum period, and planters seldom sent their sons to England to be educated as they had frequently done before the Revolution. Instead of these methods, the chief educational institutions for the upper class became the "old field schools" and the academies. In 1850 the South led the nation in the support of academies, possessing 2,700 as compared to 2,100 in the Middle States, and 1,000 in New England. Such schools emphasized training in the Greek and Latin classics. Many of the masters of Southern academies were Yankees, but some of the most effective of these nurseries of Southern leaders, such as Zion-Parnassus in Rowan County, North Carolina, David Caldwell's "log cabin college" near Greensboro, North Carolina, and Moses Waddel's academy at Willington in South Carolina were taught by Southern ministers. Since teaching was closely allied with preaching in the Old South, the academies gave their students a strong dose of religion.

The real problem in educating the children of the South was to provide free public schools for the sons and daughters of the yeomen and poor whites. In 1779 Jefferson introduced "A Bill for the More General Diffusion of Knowledge" into the Virginia legislature. He proposed a system of free public school education for all children for three years, supported by taxation. The brighter students should be selected to go to grammar or high schools where they should receive free tuition and board. From the grammar schools the most intelligent children should be chosen to be educated at public expense at the College of William and Mary. Thus "the geniuses" were to be raked from the mass of humanity and educated to become leaders of the republic. The essence of this plan was the selection of the natural aristocracy of intellect from all ranks of society and the education of them for the greatest usefulness. A somewhat similar plan for instructing talented children of the poor at public expense and for a gradation of public schools was presented in 1817 to the legislature of North Carolina by the idealist, Archibald D. Murphey, called "Father of the Common Schools of North Carolina." Neither proposal, however, was adopted, for both were far ahead of the state of public opinion at the time. Indeed, the free school movement in the South, instead of following the Jeffersonian tradition, was an outgrowth of Jacksonian democracy, of the contagious example of the New England reformers, and of shame over the exposure of illiteracy by the census reports of 1840 and 1850.[1]

More than any section of the country, the South was gravely handicapped in the establishment of free public schools. In contrast to Massachusetts which had a density of population of one hundred and twenty-seven inhabitants to the square mile, Southern states like Virginia and North Carolina had respectively only fourteen and twelve white inhabitants to the square mile. The Southern states also had almost impassable roads during seasons of the least need for the agricultural labor of children. From England there was inherited a tradition that only the upper class or the leaders should be educated. Furthermore, the *laissez-faire* conception of the role of government prevailed to an exceptionally strong degree in the South, a belief that the state should not assume a function which was regarded as a private duty. The Southern people paid amazingly light taxes, and the planters did not wish to bear the burden of educating the children of the poor. Moreover, many of the farmers had no appreciation of "book larning" and did not demand free schools for their children, whose labor they needed on the farms except during the three winter months. Indeed, the very poor class of whites displayed an apathy toward education and often neglected to send their children to schools when the opportunity for free education existed. One reason for such indifference was the charity feature of most of the free school systems in the South. Consequently, their pride rebelled at the requirement of making a declaration of poverty before their children could receive free schooling. Another important obstacle was the prevalence among them of such enervating diseases as malaria and hookworm.

During the last three decades of the ante-bellum period, however, the Southern people began to respond to the public school movement which was agitating the nation. In the North, the free school move-

ment had developed in the decade of the 1830's, led by such reformers as Horace Mann and Henry Barnard in Massachusetts and
Governor George Wolf in Pennsylvania. Here not only Jacksonian
democracy, but the pressure of organized labor, which was voiceless
in the South, stimulated the demand for larger educational opportunities for the masses. The work of the Northern reformers was
studied by Southern progressives. Sectionalism also played an important role in the movement for free schools in the South. Those
regions containing few slaves and inhabited predominantly by the
yeomen advocated public education, but the Tidewater and black
belt districts, the location of the slave plantations, opposed such reform since they would have to bear the heaviest burdens of school
taxation. During the decade of the 1840's western Virginia found an
effective spokesman for free schools in President Henry Ruffner of
Washington College, who drafted a memorial to the legislature on
the subject. The Southern educational campaign was led by some
men who had risen from the plain people, such as Andrew Johnson
of Tennessee who had been taught to write by his wife, Christopher
Memminger of South Carolina, and Governor Joseph E. Brown of
Georgia. Other agitators for free schools, however, were enlightened
members of the planter class, such as Governor Henry A. Wise of
Virginia, Robert J. Breckinridge of Kentucky, Governor Robert
F. W. Allston of South Carolina, and William L. Yancey of Alabama.

The fundamental problem in establishing free common schools in
the South was the question of obtaining finances. Virginia in 1810,
followed by other Southern states, established Literary Funds,
usually from sources involving no or little taxation, to provide for
the education of indigent children. Some of the newer states in the
Southwest, such as Alabama, received grants of public land, section
sixteen in each township, for schools. The distribution of the
surplus revenue by the Federal government in 1836–37 resulted in
an increase of the school funds, but after the Panic of 1837 these
funds were in most cases either lost or wasted.

In general, the policy of the Southern states prior to the Reconstruction period was to establish charity schools. In 1811 South
Carolina, for example, passed an act for the establishment of free
schools, but such institutions became in reality charity schools for

orphans and indigent children. The legislature of Virginia in 1846 passed a bill permitting counties to vote to establish free schools by local taxation, but only nine of them took advantage of this opportunity. The first law in Alabama establishing free schools was sponsored by Alexander B. Meek, poet and judge, and passed the legislature in 1854. Nevertheless, the Superintendent of Education in Alabama reported on the eve of the Civil War that nearly one-half of the children of the state were not attending any school and were growing up in ignorance. Georgia did not establish free public schools until 1877, which fact may explain why demagogues have flourished in that state. Although the scattered rural population in the ante-bellum South enjoyed very limited opportunities for education, some of the cities, such as New Orleans, Mobile, Charleston, and Louisville, had excellent public school systems.[2]

The only Southern states that made notable progress in founding free public schools prior to the Civil War were in the upper South —Kentucky and North Carolina. Louisiana had a very progressive system of public schools on paper, but the laws were not carried out. In Kentucky the legislature appropriated over half of the Surplus Revenue received from the Federal government in 1837 as a fund for free schools. At that time approximately one-half of the children of school age in the state had never been to school and one-third of the adults could not read and write. In the agricultural depression of the 1840's an effort was made to repudiate the state debt to the school fund, but the fund was saved as the result of a vigorous fight led by Robert J. Breckinridge. In 1847 Breckinridge was chosen State Superintendent of common schools despite his ardent antislavery views. This member of the Bluegrass aristocracy waged a campaign which led to the adoption by the legislature of a two-cent tax upon all property in the state for the free common schools, the beginning of state taxation for schools in Kentucky. Kentucky was more progressive then than after 1865.

The leadership of North Carolina among the Southern states in popular education was attained partly as a result of the more democratic society of that state and partly as a result of the agitation of two remarkable men, Joseph Caldwell, first president of the University of North Carolina, and Calvin H. Wiley. Caldwell, a graduate of Princeton, published in 1832 eleven letters to the people of the state urging popular education. Wiley, born in the Piedmont region of the state, was a Whig lawyer, editor, and member of the legislature. Before Wiley began his crusade for free public schools, North Carolina had adopted a law in 1839 permitting counties to raise taxes for schools. But there was little centralized control of the public school system by the state, a common defect of the educational systems of other Southern states. Studying the reforms of the New England educational leaders, Wiley began a great educational campaign in his native state. In 1852 the office of State Supertendent of Schools was created and Wiley was appointed to this position, serving from January 1, 1853, to 1866. He accomplished such a revolution that North Carolina had the best system of public instruction in the Southern states prior to the Civil War. In this most advanced educationally of Southern states in 1860, there were 150,000 children enrolled in more than 3,000 schools out of a scholastic population of 221,000. The average school term, however, was only four months, while teachers received an average of twenty-eight dollars a month.

The Civil War shattered the promising beginnings of free schools in the Southern states. In North Carolina the free schools remained open during that conflict, and the Literary Fund, which had been increased to nearly two million dollars, was not diverted to war purposes. After the catastrophe of war the Southern states had to start public school systems anew, with impoverished resources and the great burden of a bi-racial system. Despite its failure to educate the masses, the ante-bellum South was not as backward as the mother country of England in realizing the public obligation to educate all the children, for England did not establish a free school system until after the passage of the Forster Education Act of 1870.

In the schools of the South and of the expanding West the two principal textbooks, which were used for several generations, were Noah Webster's blue-back spelling book and McGuffey's *Eclectic Readers*. Professor William H. McGuffey, the author of the celebrated readers, was teaching at Miami University in Ohio when he published his first reader at Cincinnati in 1836. From 1845 until his death in 1873 he was a professor in the University of Virginia. His readers contained selections of literature, oratory, and poetry which were designed to inculcate morality, patriotism, and devotion to orthodox religion. They also emphasized the cultivation of the virtues which Franklin had extolled, thrift, industry, and obedience. They were written for a generation which placed a high value on oratory, and consequently they inspired young boys to become orators. Furthermore, they were illustrated with sentimental pic tures, particularly those showing affectionate and humane feelings of children toward animals. The McGuffey readers have been re- garded by some authorities as next to the Bible in molding the mind of the plain people of the South and West who had access to few other books.

In the 1840's and 1850's a campaign arose in the South to expurgate the schoolbooks used in that region, which were written mainly by Northerners. An article in *De Bow's Review* (September, 1852) pointed out the sectional bias of these Northern textbooks, such as geographies that "devote two pages to Connecticut onions and broom corn and ten lines to Louisiana and sugar." Regarded as particularly dangerous to the minds of Southern youth were the antislavery senti- ments and innuendoes found in such books as *Peter Parley's* histories, Wayland's *Moral Science* (a college text), Gilbert's *Atlas*, and Whelpley's *Compend of History*. The need for textbooks with a Southern point of view was expressed by a writer in *De Bow's Review* as follows: "We believe that southern life, habits, thought and aims are so essentially different from those of the north that here a different character of books, tuition and training is abso- lutely required." [3] Southern Commercial Conventions urged the necessity of employing Southern men rather than Yankees in the schools, using textbooks written and published in the South, and boy- cotting all Northern colleges and preparatory schools. The largest textbook publishing and distributing house in the South, Morton and Griswold of Louisville, Kentucky, employed a writer to adapt the famous *Peter Parley* readers, written by a Connecticut Yankee, for the Southern trade. [4]

The Southern states concentrated their educational efforts on de- veloping the culture of the upper classes. Consequently the ante- bellum South had a larger proportion of college-trained men than any other section of the country. Since the term "college" was loosely used, some of these college graduates probably received little more than a modern high school education. North Carolina, under the lead of an aristocrat, William R. Davie, was the first state to establish a state university, which opened its doors to students in 1795. Franklin College (the future University of Georgia) was chartered earlier than the University of North Carolina but did not begin instruction until 1801.[5] Although the College of Charleston was incorporated in 1785, it did not develop into a real college until the first quarter of the nineteenth century, and not until 1837 did the city of Charleston assume control over it and make an annual appropriation for its support. Thus it became the first municipal college in the United States. In 1805 South Carolina College was founded at Columbia by the legislature. Thomas Cooper, irreverently called "Old Coot" by the students because of his massive bald head and short, corpulent body which reminded them of a "cooter," or a terrapin, became president in 1821 and introduced into the college a bold spirit of rationalism and free thinking.

The University of Virginia, which began to function in 1825, became the most influential and liberal of Southern institutions of higher learning. It has rightly been called "the lengthened shadow of Thomas Jefferson," for he fought a desperate fight to secure funds from the legislature to start it, he designed its buildings and campus, and he supervised its curriculum. He proposed to divide the university into eight "schools," but this ambitious plan degenerated into one-man departments. He introduced the elective system in the choice of studies, and the students were treated as gentlemen by the adoption of the honor system, which had previously been tried at William and Mary College. They were not compelled to go to chapel or attend religious exercises in this institution founded on the "illimitable freedom of the human mind." Jefferson imported the first faculty largely from England and introduced modern languages and scientific courses into the curriculum. Instead of becoming a democratic institution the school at Charlottesville was patronized chiefly by the aristocratic element of society. Consequently strenuous opposition arose among the people, particularly in western Virginia, toward levying taxes for the support of this state university, which was granted only the paltry sum of $15,000 a year by the legislature.

The oldest institution of higher learning west of the Allegheny Mountains was Transylvania University at Lexington, Kentucky, founded only six years after the admission of the state into the Union. When Horace Holley, a Boston clergyman, became president in 1818, he dreamed of making this university in the wilderness an American Oxford. During the decade of the 1820's its medical and law schools, founded in 1799, were flourishing, and Transylvania attained a larger enrollment than Princeton and had only four less students than Harvard. Holley's liberalism, however, caused the Presbyterians to wage a virulent campaign against him and finally in 1819 to found a rival college, Centre College, in near-by Danville, based on strict Calvinistic doctrine. After Holley was forced to resign the student body declined from an enrollment of 419 in 1826 to 184 in December, 1827. For a while, Transylvania became practically a municipal college and then fell under Methodist influence after Henry Bascom, a prominent Methodist clergyman, was chosen president. In 1837, a faction of its medical school, led by Dr. Charles Caldwell, abandoned Lexington and started the Louisville Medical Institute which later developed into the University of Louisville. The failure of Transylvania University to fulfill its early promise as a result of religious quarrels and its lack of support by taxation is one of the tragedies in the development of Kentucky and the Old South.

Following the rise of the cotton kingdom, colleges and universities were founded in the lower South. In Louisiana, where the population was divided between Catholic Creoles and Protestant Anglo-Americans, the state subsidized the College of Orleans in the metropolis, which was dominated by the Catholic Creoles, and the College of Louisiana at Jackson, which was patronized largely by Anglo-Americans. The University of Alabama was established at Tuscaloosa in 1831, and seventeen years later the University of Mississippi was founded at Oxford. Also over twenty-five religious colleges arose in the South during the last four decades of the ante-bellum period. These colleges originated not only as a result of the luxuriant growth of religious sectarianism, but also because some of the universities, such as those of Virginia and North Carolina, were dominated by the aristocratic Episcopalians or Presbyterians.

The martial spirit of the South nourished some excellent military schools, particularly the Virginia Military Institute, founded at Lexington in 1839, and the South Carolina Military Academy (the Citadel), chartered in 1842 by the legislature. In 1860 Louisiana State Seminary, located in the Red River Valley near Alexandria, was opened for instruction. Supported by state appropriations and by the sale of Federal land grants, the seminary was a military and classical school patterned after "V. M. I." Its first president was William Tecumseh Sherman, later famous as a Union general. When Louisiana seceded, Sherman resigned, and most of the professors and cadets entered the Confederate army. In 1869, after the main building had burned, the Seminary was moved to Baton Rouge, where the following year it was converted into Louisiana State University.

Numerous sons of the planters attended colleges in the North. At Princeton nearly half of the students enrolled in 1850 came from the Southern states. Likewise, at the University of Pennsylvania in 1846 a majority of the students were Southerners, principally medical students. Southern leaders who were educated at Northern colleges included John C. Calhoun, Judah P. Benjamin, and Governor Joseph E. Brown at Yale, William L. Yancey at Williams, Robert Toombs at Union College, Governor Henry A. Wise of Virginia at Washington College, Pennsylvania, Moncure D. Conway, the Virginia liberal, Jabez L. M. Curry, the Alabama statesman, and William Crafts, the litterateur, at Harvard, President Madison and James G. Birney, candidate of the Liberty Party, at Princeton. These Northern institutions do not seem to have had much influence in nationalizing the Southerners who attended them or in producing antislavery critics. During the decade of the 1850's the growth of Southern nationalism led to a campaign to dissuade Southerners from patronizing Northern colleges or preparatory schools where they might absorb pernicious Yankee doctrines. Nevertheless, from 1840 to 1860 Southern students at Harvard and Princeton increased in numbers. Only at Yale was there a striking decrease. In 1859, after the John Brown Raid, over two hundred Southern medical students left the University of Pennsylvania and enrolled at the Richmond

Medical College. In order to provide a Southern university that would teach pure Southern doctrines, especially in regard to slavery, and to train Episcopal ministers, Bishop Leonidas Polk, assisted by Bishop James H. Otey, both of them alumni of the University of North Carolina, founded in 1860 the University of the South at Sewanee, Tennessee.

The outbreak of the Civil War disrupted college life in the Old South. College presidents desperately tried to keep their students in class but many of these spirited young men, alleging that the excited condition of public affairs prevented them from study, and fearing that the war would be over before they could engage in it, left for the battlefield. The University of Mississippi stopped instruction at the outbreak of the war, but the University of Georgia struggled on until the fall of 1863, when it closed its doors, as did the University of South Carolina. The universities of Virginia and North Carolina managed to remain open during the conflict, but ironically, the University of North Carolina was forced to close its doors during Reconstruction from 1870 to 1875. Guilford College, a Quaker institution in North Carolina, suffered perhaps least of the Southern colleges, partly because its endowment, largely invested in Philadelphia, was not impaired to the extent that the funds of other Southern institutions were. William and Mary College suffered such extensive damage to buildings from Northern armies that Congress later recompensed it by an appropriation of $64,000. The buildings of the University of Alabama were also destroyed by Federal troops, an outrage which caused Congress to donate an additional grant of public land for their restoration.

Supplementing the influence of the schools and the colleges upon the Southern mind was the Southern press, which did much to educate the adults and to stimulate a strong interest in politics. In the last decade of the ante-bellum period the circulation of Southern newspapers more than doubled. This phenomenal growth was caused by the relative prosperity of this decade, the expansion of population, and the conversion of weekly into daily papers. The decisive factor in the distribution of newspapers throughout the country was the degree of concentration of population. Predominantly rural states in the North did not make appreciably better records in this

respect than the states below the Mason and Dixon line. Connecticut, for example, had a yearly per capita circulation of newspapers
of 21, Maine, 13, New Hampshire, 3, as compared with Virginia,
25, Alabama, 14, North Carolina, 7, and Louisiana, 47. One of the
strongest of the Southern newspapers, the *New Orleans Picayune*,
had a circulation of 5,600 subscribers of the weekly edition at the
close of the ante-bellum period, while *De Bow's Review* had only
2,500 subscribers.[6] But the influence of newspapers in the Old South
was much more extensive than these statistics indicate, for in country stores, taverns, and courthouse gatherings readers read them to
groups, some of whom were illiterates.

The Southern newspapers devoted little attention to local news.
Instead, they gave elaborate space to debates in Congress, to foreign
news, and to letters on political subjects submitted by anonymous
contributors. Their advertising columns reveal much of the economic and social life of the times, especially the dependence of Southerners on the North for manufactured goods and the dark side of
slavery. Highly partisan politically and remarkably unrestrained in
the abuse of public characters and rival editors, Southern journalism
was spiced with verbal violence and physical conflicts. Indeed, the
cartoon of a Southern editor with a quill in one hand and a dueling
pistol in the other was not entirely out of line with reality.

Despite a restricted circulation, the Southern press of the ante-
bellum period probably exerted a stronger influence on politics than
do the newspapers of today. Indeed, the literary talent of the South
was expressed most potently in the field of journalism rather than
in belles-lettres. The editors of the city papers were a political power
in this era of personal journalism. At the capital of the nation the
most influential Southern journalists were Duff Green of the *United
States Telegraph*, a Calhoun organ, Francis P. Blair who was called
from the editorship of the Frankfort, Kentucky, *Argus of Western
America* to take charge of the *Globe*, spokesman of the Jacksonian
Democracy, and Gales and Seaton, editors of the *National Intelli-
gencer*, the Bible of the Whigs.

The intellectual leader of the upper South, certainly to 1845, was
Virginia. Thomas Ritchie, editor of the Richmond *Enquirer* from
1804 to 1845, wielded a mighty power in behalf of the Democratic

Party and State Rights, while the Whig cause was ably upheld by John Hampden Pleasants of the Richmond *Whig*. An important newspaper of the upper South was the *Baltimore Sun*, a penny paper which had been founded in 1837 by three enterprising Northern printers who had previously established the *Public Ledger* of Philadelphia. During the latter part of the ante-bellum period W. W. Holden of the Raleigh *North Carolina Standard* was the most forceful figure among the Democratic editors of North Carolina. Prior to the Civil War the *Louisville Journal* became the most influential newspaper of Kentucky, edited by the witty Yankee, George D. Prentice, who was the representative voice of the Whigs, advocating moderation on sectional issues and the preservation of the Union. In Tennessee the courageous and colorful "Parson" Brownlow of the Knoxville *Whig* violently defended Southern slavery from the attacks of the Northern abolitionists and just as violently opposed the disunion movement. Other prominent Tennessee newspapers were the Memphis *Daily Avalanche*, the Nashville *Union*, the organ of James K. Polk, and the Nashville *Republican Banner*, edited by Felix Zollicoffer, "the Warwick of Tennessee politics."

In the lower South, Whig and Democratic newspapers were united in upholding the slavery regime, but they divided over such questions as the chartering of a national bank, westward expansion, and the disunion movement. One of the most widely read and quoted of these journals was the *Charleston Mercury*, controlled by the family of Robert Barnwell Rhett, a paper that was *par excellence* the organ of the fire eaters. The Natchez *Free Trader*, the *Woodville Republican* of Mississippi, the Montgomery *Mail*, the *Mobile Register*, edited by the distinguished statesman, John Forsyth, and the *State Gazette* of Austin, Texas, were influential journals that staunchly upheld Southern Rights. There were several well-edited newspapers in New Orleans—the *True Delta*, and the *Bee*, the Creole paper, opposing the fire eaters, and on the other side, the *Delta*, the organ of John Slidell, and the *Crescent*, favoring the secessionist movement. *The Picayune* was one of the most remarkable newspapers in the country, founded in 1837 by a Northerner, George W. Kendall. It was the first penny paper in the lower South and was noted for its alertness in gathering the news. During the Mexican

War Kendall established a pony express which enabled his newspaper to report military news even before the government at Washington was informed. Although *The Picayune* was ardently in favor of western expansion, its general editorial policy was conservative, thus appealing to the New Orleans merchants.

After the abolitionist crusade developed, the discussion of the evils of slavery or of emancipation proposals by the press was deemed dangerous to public safety. Immediately following the Nat Turner insurrection in 1831–32 the Virginia press was unshackled for a brief interim, and the leading Richmond newspapers, the *Enquirer* and the *Whig*, freely discussed the problem of removing slavery from the South. During this period also the *Greensborough Patriot*, published in the Piedmont region of North Carolina, boldly demanded the emancipation of the slaves and the repeal of North Carolina laws prohibiting the education of slaves. From 1832 to the outbreak of the Civil War, however, Southern newspapers did not dare to discuss slavery realistically. Even Northern-born editors, of whom there was a considerable proportion below the Mason and Dixon line, as a rule strongly supported the institution of slavery. This bondage, or uniformity, of the press was in some instances imposed by the powerful vested interests of slave-owners, but was undoubtedly approved by an overwhelming majority both of editors and of the people. In the Southern border region there were a few notable exceptions to the conspiracy of silence. But such manifestations of non-conformity were ruthlessly repressed by mob action. The suppression of *The True American* of Lexington, Kentucky, edited by Cassius Marcellus Clay, of James G. Birney's *The Philanthropist*, of the Parksville, Missouri, *Luminary*, and of the Newport, Kentucky, *Free South* were dramatic warnings.[7]

More influential than the press in molding the Southern mind were the country churches and the preachers. Particularly after "the Great Revival" of 1800 the Southern people were deeply affected by evangelical Protestantism. This phenomenon should be regarded as an American Crusade to convert the masses to emotional Christianity. Thousands of people in the undeveloped areas of the South had been denied the opportunity to join churches because of the rapid expansion of the frontier across the Appalachian Mountains into Kentucky, Tennessee, and the Ohio Valley. A religious apathy also existed among the older settlements of the Atlantic seaboard partly as a result of the disrupting effect of the American Revolution on the churches and the indifference or skepticism of the upper classes who had been affected by deism.

The revival movement began in Logan County, Kentucky, at the close of the eighteenth century. The outstanding personality in this awakening was a Presbyterian preacher, James McGready, a man "superlatively ugly," with an unearthly voice, and possessing the ability of "running people distracted." The revivals were carried on by a peculiarly American gathering—the camp meeting in the woods. The country people from miles around, after the crops were laid by, came with their families, bringing their provisions with them, and camped in tents or in their covered wagons on the camp ground for a week of excitement. Thus the tinder was ready for the revival flame which leapt from community to community throughout the South, not subsiding until 1805.

The camp meetings were often scenes of mass hysteria. Preachers in relays would harangue the huge assemblies from their platforms beneath "brush arbors." At Cane Ridge in Bourbon County, Kentucky, during August, 1801, a crowd estimated at over twenty thousand people attended the greatest of the camp meetings, with eighteen Presbyterian ministers and numerous Methodists and Baptist preachers exhorting. These evangelists concentrated on a technique of frightening people into religion by a description of the horrors of Hell and the torments of damned souls. The more neurotic or sensitive members of the audience became so excited by such preaching and by the deep emotional effect of the camp meeting hymns that they fell into extravagant physical "exercises." Some of them swooned in a trance and their limbs became stiff and fixed, others "shouted" for mercy, then went into the "dancing exercise." Still others laughed hysterically—"the holy laugh," or grimaced, while some had "the jerks," or babbled in unknown tongues, or barked like a dog, going on all fours. Such fantastic manifestations were condemned by the aloof Episcopalians and the more conservative Presbyterians, but they were welcomed by the evangelists as outpourings of God's spirit. Although revivals and camp meetings occurred in cycles throughout the ante-bellum period, the violent physical "exercises" were seldom prevalent in the later revivals. One of the most interesting of these later revival movements occurred in the Northern states after the financial catastrophe of the Panic of 1857.

The Great Revival and subsequent revival movements had profound results, both good and bad, on Southern society. Beneath the tumult and excitement of the camp meetings can be discerned the craving of lonely frontier people for human companionship. These religious orgies performed in a sense the function of the later circus or carnival, bringing excitement and glamor into the lives of isolated farmers and their families, furnishing a much needed social outlet. The camp meetings developed stirring hymns and tunes that affected American music, especially the Negro spirituals. The evangelists influenced Southern oratory in the direction of emotionalism and Biblical illustrations. Some of the camp meetings led to immorality, particularly arising from frequent potations of liquor, and some of the strenuous ministers shattered their nerves by their perfervid exhortations. The Great Revival tended to introduce censorious and ascetic elements into Southern society. The waves of evangelism were an important factor in erasing skepticism from the South and enforcing religious orthodoxy.

On the other hand, the Great Revival led to the rapid expansion of the evangelical churches in the West and South. One admirable result of this religious crusade was a cooperation of Presbyterian, Methodist and Baptist ministers, a harmony later to be dissolved by the rise of denominational warfare. The Great Revival aided the growth of democracy in the Southern region. The central idea of the revival movements was the democratic concept that an individual was not predestined to Hell or Heaven, as Calvinism taught, but could exercise free will and become "saved." This doctrine fitted well into the frontier psychology of optimism and self-reliance and gave dignity to the humblest human being. The evangelists emphasized the equality of the rich man and the poor man, the fine lady and the frontier woman in her linsey-woolsey dress, in the light of eternity. Also in the church government the common man was given training in the practice of self-government.[8]

In the first quarter of the nineteenth century there were many evidences to indicate that the South was passing through a liberal cycle of its history, marked by a rational attitude toward religion. Among the exponents of religious liberalism of this period were Thomas Jefferson after he had retired from the Presidency in 1809, Doctor Thomas Cooper, president of South Carolina College, and Horace Holley, president of Transylvania University. These men, having an optimistic view of human nature, rejected the dogmas of human depravity. They believed that man should use his reasoning faculty fearlessly to investigate the mysteries of religion. Jefferson, for example, advised his grandson to read the Bible with the same detachment and critical faculty that he would adopt in reading Livy or Tacitus. Instead of this attitude resulting in disillusionment and atheism, they believed that the moral law was the natural law of human society. Thus they developed a serenity of mind and a tolerance of variety of opinion that were far different from the complacency of ignorance or a child-like faith in authority. Indeed, the religion of the liberals was ideally suited to form the substratum of a republican type of government.

Religious liberalism in the South received a strong impulse from English exiles who came to America. Of these men, Joseph Priestley, the discoverer of oxygen, was the greatest. Although he did not enter the South but spent the ten years of his life in America within Pennsylvania, he had a remarkable influence on Southern religious liberalism through his writings and his disciples. His book, *An History of the Corruptions of Christianity*, profoundly influenced Thomas Jefferson and may have been the decisive factor in the development of Jefferson's serene religious faith. Two followers of Priestley, Harry Toulmin and Doctor Thomas Cooper, both exiles from England, settled in the South. Toulmin became head of Transylvania Academy and later Secretary of State of Kentucky, in which position he converted Governor James Garrard to Unitarianism. Thomas Paine was another English exile who attained great prominence in America as a religious radical as well as a political pamphleteer. His *Age of Reason* (1796) attacking orthodox ideas of religion was widely read in the South. A friend of Jefferson, Paine had shocked conservative Federalists by a bitter letter criticizing President Washington. Undoubtedly the violent attacks made against his religious ideas in the South as well as in the North were partly motivated by rancorous party politics.

Doctor Thomas Cooper had an amazing career of advocating unorthodox ideas in the South. Jefferson tried to secure his appointment to one of the first professorships in the University of Virginia, but he was prevented by the forces of religious intolerance. However, Doctor Cooper became president of South Carolina College from 1821 to 1834, where he stoutly championed freedom of speech and of thought. When the discoveries of geology began to disturb some of the orthodox leaders of the churches and colleges, Dr. Cooper fearlessly accepted the findings of science and severely condemned Professor Benjamin Silliman of Yale College, the most eminent teacher of geology in America, for warping natural science to harmonize with the Mosaic account of creation in his college textbook. The book of *Genesis*, Dr. Cooper boldly declared, was a collection of "absurd and frivolous tales," and he warned his readers that it was high time to resist the intermeddling of the clergy and their orthodox adherents with the discoveries of natural science.[9]

At Transylvania University President Horace Holley, a graduate of Yale and a Unitarian minister, exerted a liberal influence in Kentucky for nearly a decade (1818–27). Holley opposed the doctrine of the depravity of human nature, upheld the Unitarian faith, and sought to overcome the sectarian spirit by preaching a religion of love and catholic tolerance. Furthermore, his genial manner of living, which included card playing and dancing, was a rebuke to the narrow ascetic spirit of evangelical religion. A similar spirit of tolerance and of rationalism prevailed in the founding of the University of Virginia, which departed from the practices of colleges both in the North and the South in freeing itself from clerical influence.

One of the evidences of the development of religious liberalism in the South was the growth of the Unitarian Church. In 1819 Jared Sparks, the future president of Harvard University and the first editor of Washington's writings, became the pastor of a Unitarian Church at Baltimore. Then Unitarianism spread into the cities of the South during the decade of the 1820's and 1830's. The Unitarian church in Charleston developed vigorously under the Harvard-trained minister, Samuel Gilman, who wrote the nostalgic song, "Fair Harvard." At Raleigh the leading editor of the state, Joseph Gales, and his intellectual wife, Winifred, exiles from England, were propagandizing for the Unitarian faith during the decade of the 1820's and the early 1830's.[10] At Louisville, Kentucky, James Freeman Clarke, another Harvard graduate, while preaching as Unitarian pastor, was chosen superintendent of the public schools of the city. In New Orleans, the Reverend Theodore Clapp, a graduate of Yale, preached to large audiences in an independent church, the building of which was owned by a strange Jewish merchant and philanthropist, Judah Touro, who charged him no rent. With religious ideas quite similar to Unitarian doctrines, Doctor Clapp became an advocate of tolerance toward all classes of people, including Catholics, atheists, and skeptics. He eschewed the brimstone type of sermons and the reliance on supernatural elements common to many of the orthodox preachers.

The liberal phase of Southern religion began to fade in the decade of the 1830's. It had been based on certain rational doctrines, the separation of church and state, and of church and college, the exclusion of the clergy from politics, an emphasis on ethics rather than theology, an unclouded faith in reason as a purifier of superstition, and a belief in the goodness of human nature. The liberal minority, who must fight a never ending battle against the intolerant mores of the people, was defeated. A great resurgence of religious orthodoxy in the South occurred after 1830 as that section began to regiment thought within its borders to protect powerful vested interests that were threatened by the liberal forces of the period.

This change was indicated by the silencing of progressive religious leaders, especially in the colleges. President Holley was driven from Transylvania University primarily because of his liberalism. In the Holley manuscripts preserved at Transylvania College are notes for sermons and letters which indicate that he believed in the validity of religion "independent of a written revelation." A system of espionage was established by his pious enemies who came to his social entertainments, "like serpents into the Garden of Eden," to gather evidence against him in unguarded moments. The fact that nude female statues were exhibited in his home excited horror.

After an attack by the governor before the Kentucky legislature, he was practically forced to resign in 1827, a martyr to the growing intolerance of the churches. He died that year from yellow fever as he was on his way from New Orleans to Boston.[11]

Also the intransigent Dr. Cooper was dislodged from his presidency of South Carolina College in September, 1834. The immediate occasion for his forced resignation was an attack in the legislature because of a pamphlet that he had written against the enactment of laws to stop the carrying of mail on Sundays. In this pamphlet he had declared that avaricious priests had ordained the Sabbath, that Christ had prohibited public prayer, and that payment of the clergy was a pernicious practice. The charges made against him in the legislature bore a curious resemblance to the accusation against Socrates in the fifth century—the promulgation of certain religious opinions "dangerous to the youth and abhorrent to the feelings of the great mass of the community." [12] Perhaps Dr. Cooper would have been guillotined by public opinion long before if he had not been a stout champion of the popular political creed of South Carolina—of state rights, opposition to abolitionists, and the belief that a protective tariff was unconstitutional. Contemporaneously with the victory of orthodoxy in South Carolina, Jefferson's policy of a secular university at Charlottesville, Virginia, was abandoned. Faculty and students by common consent called chaplains to perform services, regularly chosen in rotation from the different sects.

The Southern clergy were disturbed by the dangers of skepticism arising from the new science of geology. Sir Charles Lyell about 1830 had pointed out the vast antiquity of the earth and the implications of fossils in the strata of the earth, which seemed to conflict with the account of the creation given by the Bible. Lamarck's theory of the transmutation of the species was also disturbing to those who believed in the Adam and Eve story. However, Darwin's *The Origin of Species* was not published until 1859 and his *Descent of Man* until 1871. Accordingly, the principal struggle between science and religion in the ante-bellum period was not over the theory of evolution but concerning the findings of geology. The danger of skepticism being produced by the study of science led commencement orators to warn college students against the insidious attacks of science on Christianity. The will of Judge John Perkins of Mississippi endowed a unique chair in the Columbia [S.C.] Theological Seminary, entitled "The Perkins Professorship of Science in Connexion with Revelation" (1861), whose purpose was to teach ministers to defend the faith against the assaults of science. The first Perkins Professor was James Woodrow, the uncle of Woodrow Wilson, who was later dismissed from his position because he believed that evolution was true and did not conflict with the teachings of the Bible.

By 1860 the reaction against religious liberalism had reached the farthest swing of the pendulum. The Unitarian church had not fulfilled its promise of the decades of the 1820's when Jefferson wrote, "I trust that there is not a young man now living in the United States who will not die an Unitarian." [13] Sustained chiefly by New Englanders in the cities, it was moribund on the eve of the Civil War. The prevalent orthodoxy of the South was indicated by the virtual absence of liberal sects below the Mason and Dixon line as registered by the Census of 1860. This enumeration listed in the South only one of the fifty-eight Swedenborgian churches in the United States, only twenty-four of the six hundred and sixty-five Universalist churches, and only three of the two hundred and sixty-four Unitarian churches. Although the South did not support a single one of the seventeen Spiritualist churches, it did have in Kentucky two Shaker communities which were agitated at times by mystical visions. It is a significant index of the religious uniformity of the South in 1860 that the dichotomy which had existed between the religion of the common people and of the aristocrats in the late eighteenth and early nineteenth centuries had been erased. In the latter decades of the Old South the religion of the common people and of the aristocrats had become almost identical in content, a prevailing orthodoxy. The few articulate Southerners who applied a critical spirit to religion, such as the Virginia liberal, Moncure D. Conway, or the agricultural reformer, Edmund Ruffin, or the Louisiana planter, Bennet Barrow, were either ostracized or forced to conceal their unorthodox views.

The growth of a more orthodox spirit in religion within the antebellum South was preceded and accompanied by certain social changes which seem to be related to this religious evolution. In the first place the leaders of a new generation who succeeded the generation of Jefferson, Madison, and Dr. Thomas Cooper, lacked as a whole the culture and emancipation of mind which had distinguished the earlier leaders. The older liberalism had originated across the Atlantic Ocean, but had been closely related to the struggle in America to emancipate men politically and religiously. That impulse, however, was largely spent by 1830. As the Age of Reason declined the Romantic Movement spread from Europe to America, marking a change in taste and elevating emotion and religious feeling. The Jacksonian movement in politics which generated violent partisanship and the following of magnetic leaders with their facile slogans was not conducive to an appeal to reason and a calm investigation of religious dogmas. In so far as the Jacksonian movement led to the rise of the common man, it strengthened the old religious mores of the American people. Furthermore, the South was subjected to the Great Revival and subsequent waves of evangelism which eradicated the skepticism and deism of an earlier epoch. As the Atlantic seaboard lost direct contact with Europe by the cotton and tobacco trade shifting to Northern ports, the South grew more provincial. The intellectual stimulus of European immigration was also greatly diluted by the fact that immigrants now generally avoided the South, except at the ports and the towns along the Mississippi River. Finally, the defense of slavery against the rising tide of abolitionism and of hostile world opinion desperately required the support of a conservative religion that leaned strongly upon a literal interpretation of the Bible.

Nearly three-fourths of the Southern church-goers in 1860 were Methodists and Baptists. The aristocratic churches of the South were the Episcopal and the Presbyterian, the church of the Scotch-Irish. According to a famous saying in the Tidewater South, there were many ways to go to Heaven, but the gentleman would always choose the Episcopalian way. This church of the gentry remained confined largely to the Tidewater areas of the South and was very weak beyond the Appalachian Mountains. Even in the older areas of the South the Episcopalians represented only about 5 per cent of the church membership. In the lower South some of the most prominent men, such as Jefferson Davis and his millionaire brother, Joseph, and Governor Joseph E. Brown of Georgia belonged to the Baptist and Methodist churches. The Baptist and Methodist churches were dominant in the Piedmont, the mountains, and the piney woods districts of the South. The Methodists expanded rapidly partly as a result of the circuit rider who rode on horseback from one little congregation to another in thinly populated regions. The form of church organization of the Baptists, which gave complete autonomy to the separate churches, was suited to the rural communities of the South. Both the Methodist and Baptist churches did not require educated ministers and were closer to the common people because of their high emotional voltage. Frequently the Baptist ministers were farmers for six days of the week and on the seventh were preachers who were prohibited from receiving pay. Some of the more extreme Baptists, called Hard Shells, or Primitive Baptists, practiced foot washings, violently condemned card playing and dancing, sang a primitive music led by a leader without the accompaniment of musical instruments, and opposed missionary societies as unscriptural.

Religion in the South on the eve of the Civil War was still deeply rooted in mediaeval traditions. The conception of a mediaeval Devil being loose in the world constantly tempting men on all occasions was strongly intrenched in the minds of most Southerners. The chief religious problem was to prepare for the life beyond the grave, to secure a passport to Heaven, and to avoid the torments of Hell. Both categories were conceived of as definite physical regions much as the mediaeval man thought of them. Supernaturalism, the belief in miracles, remained an integral part of the religiousness of the South. When severe droughts occurred the ministers prayed for rain as did primitive man. A person who did not go to church was looked upon with profound suspicion, even if he lived an exemplary moral life. Church members attributed great importance to such matters as denominationalism, baptism, and the sacrament of communion. Violent arguments and much ecclesiastical warfare resulted from these differences. The strict observance of the Sabbath was a touchstone of Christian behavior in the South almost as much so as in Puritan New England. Most Southerners believed that God was constantly intervening in human affairs, punishing individuals and societies for their "sins" and rewarding the upright. When the Confederacy was overthrown the devout mycologist, Henry W. Ravenel, wrote in his diary that the defeat should be accepted as the will of providence or of "the great Umpire of nations." [14]

A very significant function of the Protestant churches of the South was the exercise of discipline over the members. This discipline was wielded by church trials and by the penalty of excommunication, which substituted church courts for the temporal courts. The manuscript minutes of the Lulbegrud Baptist Church in Kentucky describe a typical procedure of the exercise of church authority over sinning mortals. Whenever a member transgressed against another, the injured person was required to go alone to the offender and tell him of his fault. If the latter refused to do justice, the offended person should then take one or two members of the church with him and try again to settle the difficulty with the offender. If such efforts failed, the church would hear the case, and if the defendant was found guilty, would either censure him, or accept his explanation, or excommunicate him.

The Baptist and Methodist churches excommunicated persons for a variety of offenses, such as "drinking too much licker," failing to attend church regularly, scolding one's husband, abusing one's wife and child, sexual immorality, particularly "having an heir without a lawful husband," swearing, dancing, gambling, quarreling, fighting, and treating one's father badly. One of the most interesting phases of the disciplinary action of the church was manifested in controlling the slave and free Negro members of the white churches. The manuscript record books of some Baptist churches deposited in the University of Kentucky library show that slaves were excommunicated for stealing, running away from their masters, impudence to their mistresses, and having illegitimate children. In the Providence Baptist Church Record Book, for example, is the sentence of excommunication against Frank, a slave, for the crimes of lying, disobeying his master's commands, and "making too free with women." Also it is recorded, "Mr. Colemans Archabel is Excluded for refusing to hear the Church to answer for his Conduct Shuch as Carnelly Singing biting at a horse nose and report sais that he Swore and Dancest." [15] (Maybe he was full of "corn licker" at the time of such gay conduct.) A record of discipline kept by a Baptist church in North Carolina, 1791–1860, showed five hundred cases tried, of which drunkenness led the list by far, followed in order by quarreling with a member, neglecting the attending of service, and sex immorality.[16]

Closely associated with the religiousness of the South was the growth of the humanitarian spirit. By 1860 real progress had been made in this region in the care of the unfortunate members of society. Although the South prided itself on being free from the "pernicious isms" of the North—feminism, abolitionism, socialism, skepticism, the sparing of the rod in rearing children—it was gradually abolishing cock fighting, gouging, and dueling. A more enlightened attitude toward women was indicated by the passage of a Mississippi law in 1839 giving married women the right to own property separately from their husbands—such property to be free from liability for their husbands' debts.

Moreover, the temperance movement had made considerable headway below the Mason and Dixon line. This reform harmonized with the evangelical religious spirit which had captured large portions of the South. Prominent political leaders, such as Robert Barnwell Rhett of South Carolina, Governor Henry A. Wise of Virginia, and Governor Joseph E. Brown of Georgia, championed the temperance cause. A group of hard drinkers of Baltimore who were converted to the total abstinence cause by an evangelist started the Washington Movement in 1840 to spread the gospel of cold water by the exhortations of reformed drunkards. The Sons of Temperance, organized two years later at Teetotaler's Hall, New York City, enrolled many members in the Southern states. An effective method which they adopted of stopping the drinking of alcoholic liquors was the practice of obtaining pledges of total abstinence. *The Kentucky New Era* of Louisville listed in 1852 two hundred and sixty-five temperance societies in the state as well as eighty post offices where ten or more copies of this temperance newspaper were taken.[17]

In Lexington the contest over outlawing coffee houses which sold liquor swayed back and forth. On January 1, 1853, the prohibition, or no license, party won the city election. Reverend William M. Pratt of Lexington observed the effect: "On Washington's birthday not one in the workhouse, jail, or watchhouse, such an event not known before for years—this is owing to the suppression of the liquor traffic." [18] But the following year the liquor party overwhelmingly defeated the idealists and prohibitionists by electing the city councilmen. The opponents of liquor in Georgia also entered politics and in 1855 cast over six thousand votes for B. H. Overby, a Methodist preacher, the candidate of the Temperance Party for governor.

Furthermore, the Southern states slowly humanized their criminal codes and procedures during the first half of the nineteenth century. Although the mediaeval punishments of flogging, branding, the pillory, dismemberment, and public hangings were retained throughout the ante-bellum period, imprisonment for debt was gradually abolished. The first constitution of Alabama (1819) prohibited imprisonment for debt, and in 1823 Georgia forbade the imprisonment of debtors except in cases of fraud and concealment of property. North Carolina and South Carolina were among the most conservative of the Southern states in abandoning old attitudes toward criminals. In South Carolina 165 offenses were capital crimes in 1813; twenty-two were punishable by death as late as 1850. The *Revised Code* of North Carolina of 1855 abolished the death penalty for housebreaking in the daytime, for the second offense of bigamy, for forgery, horse-stealing, embezzlement by servants, and malicious burning of public bridges, but retained this extreme penalty for seventeen crimes, including arson, sodomy, murder, castration, infanticide, the second offense of circulating incendiary publications, and stealing free Negroes from the state.

Kentucky, by contrast, was one of the most progressive of the Southern states in the treatment of criminals. In 1798 this state adopted a penal code that provided for capital punishment for only one crime committed by free persons, murder, and during the following year established a penitentiary at Frankfort. Kentucky also experimented with the system of separate cells for criminals modeled after the famous Auburn, New York, prison, where the prisoners worked together in the daytime under the rule of silence. Overcrowding of the Frankfort prison led to the abandonment of the solitary confinement system, but under the able administration of the superintendent, Joel Scott, the rule of silence was enforced and a prison textile factory was founded. Unfortunately, Joel Scott in 1825 leased the labor of the convicts of the state for five years, paying the state $1,000 a year. Thus he became the first lessee of convict labor in the South and started a practice which became one of the greatest evils of the New South.

Most of the Southern states tried to make their prison systems economically self-sustaining.[19] In 1817 Georgia established a penitentiary where the prisoners carried on various trades. From 1845 to 1862 Alabama leased the labor of criminals in her penitentiary to private contractors, a pernicious practice followed by Northern as well as Southern states. A successful textile factory was established in the penitentiary at Jackson, Mississippi, which furnished supplies to the Confederate armies. Enlightened reforms were inaugurated by some of the Southern states, such as by the Baltimore prison which had separate quarters for women prisoners and employed a chaplain, by the Richmond prison which was the first in the United States to use honor badges and the grading system as incentives for good behavior, and by Tennessee's precedent in 1836 of rewarding good behavior in prison by lessening the term of service.

On account of its parsimonious policy in regard to taxation, North Carolina did not have a penitentiary until after the Civil War. In 1846 a proposal to establish a state penitentiary at a cost of $100,000 was overwhelmingly voted down. In South Carolina enlightened men such as Governor William Aiken and the Greenville editor, Benjamin F. Perry, advocated establishing a penitentiary, but the people were so conservative that the Senate voted down the proposal in 1849. On the eve of the Civil War Florida and the two Carolinas, however, were the only Southern states which did not have state penitentiaries. In these states the detention of criminals was left to the counties, which operated inadequate jails.

Another humanitarian cause which made considerable progress below the Mason and Dixon line was the enlightened care of the mentally diseased. In colonial days insane people were regarded as possessed by devils and were either chained in jails and poorhouses or allowed to wander at large unsupervised. Urged by the enlightened Governor Francis Fauquier, the legislature of Virginia in 1773 established an insane hospital at Williamsburg. For fifty years it remained the only state hospital for the insane in the United States.

During the first half of the nineteenth century the conception of insanity as a disease which could be cured in many cases by proper care began to spread. The second state institution in the United States exclusively for the insane was established by Kentucky in 1824. Four years later South Carolina was the third state to provide an asylum for the mentally disordered and for epileptics.

The crusade for a more humane treatment of insane people was powerfully aided by the activities of the celebrated Massachusetts reformer, Dorothea L. Dix.[20] This devoted woman traveled throughout the United States speaking before state legislatures and lobbying to get bills passed establishing insane asylums. In 1847–48 she came to Tennessee and North Carolina, where she exposed the wretched conditions in the care of the mentally ill, many of whom were confined in attics, log cabins, poorhouses, and jails while other pauper lunatics were let out to the lowest bidder. As a result of the crusading zeal of this Northern woman these states were aroused to vote appropriations for erecting insane asylums. The institution at Raleigh, North Carolina, which was opened in 1853, was appropriately named "Dix Hill" in honor of the reformer. Before the outbreak of the Civil War all the Southern states, except Florida, had established insane asylums, although the Alabama and Texas institutions did not receive patients until 1861. The census reports indicate that only a small proportion of the insane were cared for in these state institutions. Nevertheless, during the latter part of the ante-bellum period, instead of being confined with chains like animals in jails and poorhouses, the mentally sick were being treated in a more enlightened fashion.

The obligation of the state to care for the deaf, dumb, and blind was tardily performed by most states. In Georgia a remarkable eccentric, John Jacobus Flournoy, who was himself handicapped by deafness and incoherent speech, presented a petition to the legislature in 1833 urging the state to educate its deaf and dumb citizens. The legislature responded by appropriating three thousand dollars for sending some of these dependent persons to the American School for the Deaf at Hartford, Connecticut, founded in 1817 by the great humanitarian, Thomas Gallaudet, but only three of those selected to go were willing to venture to this distant retreat. As early as 1824

Kentucky had founded a school for the deaf and dumb at Danville, which followed the methods used by the American Asylum at Hartford, and in the decades of the 1840's and 1850's other Southern states started similar institutions. Schools were also established for the education of the blind in which the students were taught to read Braille as well as to learn arts and crafts. Yet, according to census reports, only a small fraction of these variously handicapped persons in the South received care and training in state institutions. In the rural society of the Old South there was far less reliance on the government for aid to the unfortunate than has been the practice in recent times.

Citations

1. For a study of illiteracy and the movement for free schools, see Eaton, *Freedom of Thought in the Old South*, Chap. III.
2. C. W. DABNEY, *Universal Education in the South* (Chapel Hill, 1936).
3. *De Bow's Review*, XIII (September, 1852), 260, 262.
4. The records and papers of Morton and Griswold are in the University of Kentucky library. "Peter Parley" was the pen name of Samuel Griswold Goodrich, but this name was not used on the readers published by the firm in the decade of the 1850's, for example, *Goodrich's Sixth School Reader*, edited by Noble Butler (Louisville, 1858).
5. A delightful account of an ante-bellum college is E. M. COULTER, *College Life in the Old South* (New York, 1928).
6. STEPHENSON, "Ante-Bellum New Orleans as an Agricultural Focus," *op. cit.*, 171, 173.
7. CLEMENT EATON, "The Freedom of the Press in the Upper South," *Mississippi Valley Historical Review*, XVIII (March, 1932), 479–499.
8. W. W. SWEET, *Revivalism in America* (New York, 1944), and CLEMENT EATON, "The Ebb of the Great Revival," *North Carolina Historical Review*, XXIII (January, 1946), 1–12.
9. DUMAS MALONE, *The Public Life of Thomas Cooper 1783–1839* (New Haven, 1926).
10. CLEMENT EATON, "Winifred and Joseph Gales, Liberals in the Old South," *Journal of Southern History*, X (November, 1944), 460–474.

11. CHARLES CALDWELL, *A Discourse on the Genius and Character of the Rev. Horace Holley, LL.D.* (Boston, 1828), 218.

12. Columbia *Telescope*, December 20, 1831; quoted in Eaton, *Freedom of Thought*, 286.

13. Quoted in CLARENCE GOHDES, "Some Notes on the Unitarian Church in the Ante-Bellum South," D. K. JACKSON (ed.) *American Studies in Honor of William Kenneth Boyd* (Durham, 1940), 327.

14. A. R. CHILDS (ed.), *The Private Journal of Henry William Ravenel, 1859–1887* (Columbia, S. C., 1947), preface, XVIII.

15. Manuscript in University of Kentucky Library.

16. G. S. JOHNSON, *Ante-Bellum North Carolina: A Social History* (Chapel Hill, 1937).

17. *The Kentucky New Era*, Sept. 4, 1852.

18. Diary of WILLIAM M. PRATT, Jan. 1; Feb. 28, 1853; Jan. 7, 1854.

19. BLAKE MCKELVEY, *American Prisons, A Study in American Social History Prior to 1915* (Chicago, 1936).

20. H. E. MARSHALL, *Dorothea Dix: Forgotten Samaritan* (Chapel Hill, 1937).

CHAPTER XXI

The Chrysalis Stage of
Southern Culture

THE civilization of a regional society, like the physique of a
growing youth, may develop unevenly. In some respects the
culture of the old South was ahead of the general level of the nation,
particularly in the fields of political writing and oratory. Patrick
Henry's speeches, the Declaration of Independence, George Mason's
Declaration of Rights, the Farewell Address of Washington, the
inaugural address of Jefferson and his *Notes on Virginia*, the penetrating political writings of James Madison and John Taylor of
Caroline, John Marshall's opinions, the diary of James K. Polk, and
the profound political essays of Abel P. Upshur and John C. Calhoun
form a body of political thought equal to that of any age. The ante-
bellum South also was perhaps superior to New England and the
Middle States in the development of architecture, landscape gardening, and the fine art of conversation. In the departments of belles-
lettres, of painting, and of science, however, the South in 1860 was
less developed than the more urbanized Northeast, where a remarkable burst of literary productivity took place in the three decades
preceding the Civil War.

In 1860 a very large part of the South was still young and raw. Five
Southern states had no city with a population as large as ten thousand. Alabama, Mississippi, Florida, Arkansas, and Texas had been
states less than fifty years when the Civil War began. These younger,
rural parts of the land of Dixie could hardly be expected to produce
a native literature or engage in creative activity in the fine arts. On
the other hand, there were sections of the South, such as the Atlantic
Tidewater area, where people had dwelt for over two hundred years.

Why did these relatively old regions of the South produce very little literature of a high quality or fail to develop a native art of distinction? The example of Grecian society, based on slavery, which had created a noble art and literature, gave point to this inquiry.

In comparison with New England and the Middle States, the South had many handicaps which retarded the flowering of its intellectual life. Certainly the lack of city life, with its intellectual stimulus and accumulation of wealth, was a very great factor in explaining the greenness of Southern culture. The rural state of Southern society also was accompanied by a large degree of illiteracy and provincialism, with a correspondingly small reading public and an absence of flourishing publishing houses. Furthermore, the South lacked the stimulation of immigration on the large scale that the North enjoyed. In addition to these physical elements, the Southern planters and farmers had a different set of values from the city man in the North. The Southern gentry believed that farming was the most delectable occupation in the world, when the actual physical exertion and sweaty labor were performed by others, and next to planting they placed politics. The cultivation of letters and of the fine arts was regarded as a purely ornamental accomplishment rather than as worthy of a serious profession.

The conservative mood of Southern society in the last three decades before the Civil War had to be broken before a significant intellectual advance could be made.[1] The existence of slavery as an anachronism which required apology adversely affected the growth of a freely conceived literature. Indeed, much of Southern writing in the last three decades of the ante-bellum period was spent in the defense of slavery and Southern life from the undiscriminating attacks of the abolitionists. Also most Southerners had come to believe after 1830 that religion was a type of human experience, a sacred convention, which should not be questioned by the rationalism and bold speculation which had been tolerated in the time of Thomas Jefferson and Doctor Thomas Cooper. The reign of religious orthodoxy was strong in the North as well as in the South, but the ante-bellum South did not nourish an Emerson, or a Theodore Parker, or the organized societies of free thinkers to be found in Northern cities.

Southern culture was in the chrysalis stage of development when it was interrupted by the trauma of the Civil War. In certain respects, such as the lack of intellectual liberty and the failure to produce great men, the period from 1830 to 1860 marks a decline in culture from the golden age of Washington, Jefferson, Madison, and Marshall. Yet during this period a broad basis was being laid for the growth of greater intellectual maturity below the Mason and Dixon line. A new tempo of material progress was evident, and a more democratic concept of culture was emerging. The decade of the 1850's witnessed a significant economic recovery from the doldrums of the 1840's when the price of cotton had reached its lowest point. The rate of railroad building during this decade was greater in the South than in the North, thus increasing the means of communication, which had a direct bearing on mental activity. Since culture usually follows the accumulation of wealth, the increased prosperity of the Southern people was registered in numerous cultural developments, such as the expansion of libraries, the wider circulation of newspapers, and the gradual eradication of illiteracy. Perhaps the most hopeful sign of an intellectual renaissance was the fact that the South possessed a larger number of college-bred men in proportion to its white population than did the North.

Significant indices of the rise of culture in this region were the remarkable growth of public libraries and the increased sale of books. Between 1850 and 1860 the Federal census recorded that the number of volumes in Southern libraries, other than private, had increased fivefold. The three public libraries of Georgia at the beginning of the decade had expanded to two hundred and fifty-eight; the sixteen libraries of South Carolina had multiplied to three hundred and sixty-one; the twenty-one in Virginia to thirteen hundred and fifty. This phenomenal expansion of libraries for the use of the common man must not be interpreted too sanguinely, however, for at the close of the ante-bellum period the number of volumes available to the public in Southern libraries did not average more than a single volume for every two or three white persons. South Carolina was an outstanding exception, possessing one and one-half volumes per white person, which was equivalent to the ratio in Massachusetts. Between 1850 and 1859 the Boston publishing firm of Ticknor and Fields, which dealt in the best current literature of England and

America, expanded its sales in the South from a total of $992 worth of books in 1850 to $10,462 in 1859. At the same time it should be noted that five Northwestern states with almost the same white population as twelve Southern states purchased over twice as many books from the company as did the Southern states.[2]

The South has been described by an eminent scholar as a cultural province of the North, at least until 1830. This region imported its college presidents, its professors, its books, its musical instruments, from the metropolitan centers north of the Mason and Dixon line. But in the decade of the 1830's, influenced by the danger of the abolition movement and by the tariff controversy, the South became more self-conscious and began to take steps in the direction of cultural independence. Signs of such a development were registered in the appearance in 1832 of J. P. Kennedy's *Swallow Barn*, "the South's first novel of importance," the publication of Poe's first story in 1833, of Simms' *Guy Rivers* in 1834, and the founding of the *Southern Literary Messenger* in the same year.[3]

There were two main trends in Southern literature of the antebellum period, a dominant chord of romanticism, expressed in novels and poetry, and a minor tone of realism to be found particularly in Southern humor. The romantic temper of Southern literature was in part an imitation of a larger movement in Europe and the North. Nevertheless, there were special reasons why romanticism flourished in Southern literature. The isolation of the plantations and farms in the land of Dixie created a craving for a dream world of high romance. The aristocratic organization of Southern society bore some resemblance to the serfs and chivalry of mediaeval times, an analogy which undoubtedly contributed to the extravagant admiration by Southerners of the mediaeval romances of Sir Walter Scott. Tournaments were actually held in the Southern states, notably at White Sulphur Springs, Virginia, where Southern youths, clad as knights, tilted with lances at suspended rings, while Southern belles waved their handkerchiefs. The cult of chivalry was nourished by the myth that Southerners were descended from noble Cavaliers.

Furthermore, the attack of the abolitionists on Southern slave society produced a defense reaction, resulting in an effort to idealize the semi-feudal society of the South in novels and poetry. Such romantic writing deflected attention from considering the grave social evils of a slave society. Although Southerners had been trained in the classics, the classical tradition, with its humanism, affected Southern writing very slightly—architecture much more.

Baltimore was the northernmost center of Southern culture. This city was the home of the young cavalier poet, Edward Coote Pinkney, who idealized Southern womanhood in poems of delicate sentiment. Here Francis Scott Key wrote the national anthem, and in this city was born James R. Randall who at the beginning of the Civil War composed that stirring martial song, "Maryland, My Maryland!" The dominant literary figures of Baltimore were William Wirt, the author of *Letters of a British Spy* (1803) and of a biography of Patrick Henry, and John Pendleton Kennedy, the novelist. Both of these men followed the typical pattern of the Southern literary man, namely, an amateur who combined the pursuit of literature with law or politics. Wirt was Attorney General under Monroe and John Quincy Adams and candidate of the Anti-Masonic Party for President, while Kennedy, a Whig who distrusted democracy, served as Secretary of the Navy under Fillmore.

Kennedy was one of the most significant authors in creating the romantic tradition of the Southern plantation. His *Swallow Barn* gives a mellow picture of the aristocratic society of Virginia about the year 1800, a novel reminiscent of Irving's *Bracebridge Hall*. It portrays the virtues of the Southern gentry, their open-hearted hospitality, their devotion to family tradition, their high sense of honor, and their feeling of paternalism. Although he mildly disapproved of slavery, he painted a picture of kindly relations between the masters and their black retainers. He contributed to the growth of the Southern conception of woman as a romantic creature; his heroine, for example, trained a pet hawk in the tradition of mediaeval chivalry. Kennedy's novels are based on authentic episodes and a rich knowledge of the history, the manners, and mores of the older South. His historical romance, *Horse-Shoe Robinson*, written in 1835, resulted from a trip into the up-country of South Carolina where he met a colorful old Revolutionary hero, a scout in the guerrilla warfare between Tories and Patriots. In *Rob of the Bowl* he casts a romantic glamor over the colonial history of Maryland in the days of Charles II. The last important work from his pen, *Quodlibet*, criticizes the crudeness of Jacksonian democracy, but with good humor. Kennedy had tendencies to Jeffersonian liberalism in his early life, but after his marriage to the daughter of a wealthy cotton mill owner of Baltimore, he became a political conservative. If Kennedy was too much an apologist for the privileged classes of Southern society, he atoned for his apostasy from political liberalism by his aid to the struggling young poet, Edgar Allan Poe.[4]

Associated with both Baltimore and Richmond was the South's most famous literary figure, Edgar Allan Poe. Although he was born in Boston in 1809, most of the forty years of his life were spent in the South. His mother, an actress, had died when he was a child, and he was reared in the home of John Allan, a Richmond merchant. He spent a year at the University of Virginia, from which because of his extravagance and gambling debts his foster father withdrew him. He then enlisted in the army and was stationed for a while at Fort Moultrie, Charleston, South Carolina, where he absorbed some of the local color that he portrayed in his short story "The Gold Bug." After a brief term at West Point, from which he was dismissed for neglect of duties, he devoted himself to a literary career. His poetry had little relation to his Southern environment, nor was he concerned with social problems, causes, or politics, but only with sheer beauty. He was obsessed with an interest in the weird, the morbid, and the tragic in life that reflected his melancholy and distraught life, darkened by poverty and an addiction to alcohol. Poe suffered from a complex concerning his dead mother. He believed that the most beautiful thing in the world was a beautiful dead lady, an obsession that colored his highly romantic verse. His poems of love have an ethereal quality such as the unforgettable lines "To Helen" and the sweet melancholy of "Annabel Lee." Not only was Poe the South's greatest artist in verse, but he also became the master technician of the short story in America.

Virginia had the faculty of nourishing local devotion and pride in her writers to an extreme degree. John Randolph of Roanoke was undoubtedly a genuine literary personality whose talent, however, did not come to fruition in the plantation environment. His brilliant, but wasted, literary gift was shown in the satirical phrases which he applied to his enemies and his wonderful improvisations as an orator. Yet he would not discipline himself to become a writer of distinction and he was so intensely a Virginian that he lacked the virtue of detachment. The career of his half-brother, Beverley Tucker, professor of law at William and Mary College, was another example of the blighting effect of intense sectional feeling on literature. Tucker published two novels in 1836, *George Balcombe*, a story of Missouri border life, which Poe pronounced the best American novel, and *The Partisan Leader*, a political novel. In his writings Tucker revealed an aristocratic disdain of the common people and especially of Yankee plebeians. *The Partisan Leader* predicted the secession of the South and a bloody civil war in which the superior race of Southerners would emerge victorious. Virginia also produced a filial poet, Philip Pendleton Cooke, whose best-known poem, "Florence Vane," was in the tradition of excessive romanticism. His brother, John Esten, turned from the study of law to writing historical romances, such as the *Virginia Comedians* and the *Wearing of the Gray*, which idealized the ancient regime in the Old Dominion and the Confederate heroes.

Belles-lettres did not flourish in North Carolina, a land predominantly of small farmers, but in Charleston conditions were more favorable for the cultivation of the muses. In this "capital of the plantations" lived the wit and literary amateur, William Crafts, who had been educated at Harvard. His chief work was a poem describing the gayety of Charleston society during the season of horse racing, entitled *The Raciad*. The most learned inhabitant of Charleston was the crippled lawyer, Hugh Swinton Legaré (pronounced Legree), master of many languages, erudite in the law, a tremendously serious essayist. Minor literary lights in the metropolis and the Carolina Tidewater were William Elliott, educated at Harvard, who wrote *Carolina Sports by Land and Water*, and Caroline Gilman, author of the *Recollections of a Southern Matron*.

Charleston was also the home of the gifted poets Henry Timrod and Paul Hamilton Hayne. Timrod, descended from German stock, lived a poverty-stricken life, supporting himself by serving as a tutor in private families. He wrote some exquisite nature poems, particularly "Spring," which begins:

"Spring with that nameless pathos in the air
Which dwells with all things fair. . . ."

His "Cotton Boll" and "Ethnogenesis" are permeated with a high devotion to the Southern cause. Hayne, a member of the Carolina aristocracy and a graduate of the College of Charleston, abandoned the serious profession of law to cultivate the art of poetry, a calling that doomed him to poverty. He, too, had a sensitive love of nature, expressed in his beautiful "Aspects of the Pines," and a passionate nostalgia for the Old South.

William Gilmore Simms, born in Charleston in 1806, was the most notable novelist of the Old South. He was the only Southerner who made a good living from the profession of belles-lettres in the ante-bellum period, but not because of the encouragement or patronage of the Southern people. A poor boy in an aristocratic city, he won his way upward from the lowly position of a druggist's apprentice by tremendous energy and ability. After a brief career as a lawyer and a newspaper editor, Simms found his true vocation as a story teller. His second marriage to the daughter of a Southern planter enabled him to live the privileged life on the plantation of "Woodlands," with its library of ten thousand volumes. Here and at Charleston he dispensed lavish hospitality and was kind to aspiring young writers. His devotion to the South led him to write apologies for slavery and a history of South Carolina glorifying her past and to take an active part in politics as a champion of secession. Nevertheless, he never succeeded in obtaining from the aristocracy of his native state the social recognition or the appreciation of his works that he craved. His life had a tragic ending, with the destruction of "Woodlands" during the Civil War, the death of nine of his fourteen children, and the loss of the whole of his fortune.[5]

In 1834 he published his first successful novel, *Guy Rivers*, a romance of the Southern border, and in the following year, *The Yemassee*, portraying South Carolina Indians in a style influenced by both Sir Walter Scott and James Fenimore Cooper. These novels had an immense vogue in the North and in England, but not in the South. Simms was a versatile and amazingly prolific author who would not take the time to rewrite and polish his romances. One of the secrets of the extensive sale of his novels was the strong ingredient of melodrama in them. His finest works, *The Partisan, The Forayers,* and *Woodcraft,* portrayed the Revolutionary War in South Carolina as a social conflict, in which the Tories were recruited largely from the poorer classes who resented aristocratic dominance and pride. Simms loved the South passionately and studied deeply its history. He described the Southern frontier and Southern landscape better than any other literary man of his period. He had an excellent talent for realism, which was exhibited in his description of earthy characters such as frontiersmen and yeomen. Lieutenant Porgy, lusty gourmand, fighter, and homely philosopher, was one of the best and most vivid portrayals of character in his novels. On the other hand, his delineation of Southern aristocrats, especially high-bred ladies, whom he did not know from experience, was highly romantic and theatrical.

The reading of a romance by Simms today transports one into a different age of novel writing. *Beauchampe* (1842), for example, is written in the language of a more ceremonious and sentimental period, when the duel flourished and a rather primitive ideal of honor and justice prevailed. It is an almost literal account of a famous crime, in which Beauchampe in 1826 killed the Attorney General of Kentucky, Colonel Sharpe, the seducer of his wife, and was condemned to death.[6] Compared with modern novels, *Beauchampe* is dominated by a spirit of Christian morality, a concept of noble manhood, and despite its sensationalism, it produces the effect of an emotional catharsis characteristic of a Greek tragedy. Simms had a wonderful power of creating suspense which is felt in *Beauchampe* as well as in his other border romances. In *Richard Hurdis, A Tale of Alabama,* and *Border Beagles, a Tale of Mississippi,* he has skillfully reproduced the story of the famous outlaw John A. Murrell, with whose captor, Virgil A. Stewart, he had conversed.

The romantic vogue in the writing of poetry and novels was followed in Georgia by Thomas Holley Chivers and William Alexander Caruthers. Born in the same year as Poe, Chivers was another lugubrious poet who liked to write about death in its physical aspects. He received his medical degree in 1830 from Transylvania University (now College), where is preserved his manuscript dissertation on the treatment of malaria, advocating the use of calomel, and ending with an original verse. His poetry is sensuous—consider his sonnet, "To Isa Sleeping Voluptuous as the Summer South at Noon." A long controversy has existed as to whether Chivers plagiarized Poe's works, or Poe plagiarized the verse of Chivers. Caruthers was a transplanted Virginian who practiced medicine at Savannah. He made an important contribution to romanticizing the history of the South by his novels, *The Cavaliers of Virginia* (1835) and *The Knights of the Horse-Shoe* (1845). He was a Southern liberal, however, who realized the evils of slavery, especially in injuring the yeoman and poor whites. His most significant novel, *The Kentuckian in New-York* (1834), urged the wisdom of sectional understanding and of good will between the North and the South.

One of the most beautiful poems composed by a Southerner was entitled "My Life is Like the Summer Rose," portraying the transitory quality of human life. The author, Richard Henry Wilde, was a Georgia Congressman who later exiled himself from the South and was condemned by Southerners for "wasting" seven years in Italy writing a two-volume life of Tasso. The greatest poet of the South was Sidney Lanier, a native of Macon, Georgia. Lanier was an idealistic young man who probably would have had a distinguished career in music as well as literature if his Georgia environment had not limited his opportunities in that direction. His lovely spiritual poetry, his description of the marshes of Glynn and of the Chattahoochee River, and his role as a reconciler of the North and South lay ahead of him in the Reconstruction period.

West of the Appalachians there were several talented amateurs, who wrote poetry about Southern themes. Theodore O'Hara of Danville, Kentucky, educated in the Catholic St. Joseph's College, fought in the Mexican War and edited the Mobile *Register* and the Frankfort *Yeoman*. His tribute to Southern heroes who were killed in the Mexican War, "The Bivouac of the Dead," is perhaps the most moving and beautiful elegy for soldiers written by an American. Alexander Beaufort Meek, an editor and a politician of Alabama, and Francis Orray Ticknor, a country doctor of Columbus, Georgia, also exalted the South, its flowers and birds, and its knightly breed of men in sonorous verse. The most interesting of the ultra-montane literary men of the South was Albert Pike of Little Rock, Arkansas, a Bostonian by birth, but an ardent Southerner by adoption. He was a giant in stature, a lover of the life of the frontier, a teacher in the schools of Arkansas, prominent in introducing Scottish rite Masonry in the South, an Indian diplomat, and a brigadier-general of the Confederacy, leading Indian troops in the battle of Pea Ridge. Pike wrote glowingly about the mockingbird and the magnolia while his poem, "The Fine Arkansas Gentleman," is a vivid piece of Southern *genre* describing a cotton planter on a spree as a steamboat carries him and his cotton to New Orleans. It is interesting to observe that this largest and most cosmopolitan city of the South did not produce any notable poets or novelists during the ante-bellum period.

The Civil War interrupted or blighted the careers of three of the most admirable of Southern poets. Henry Timrod volunteered as a soldier in the Confederate army (too poor to buy an officer's uniform) and also served as a war correspondent, so seriously injuring his frail body that he died prematurely in 1867. Paul Hamilton Hayne served as a military aide until he was forced to retire because of illness. Sidney Lanier entered Confederate military service shortly after his graduation from Oglethorpe University and was engaged in blockade-running when he was captured. He was confined in a Northern prison from which he emerged in a terrible condition, skin and bones, with the germs of consumption, from which he died an early death. The Civil War, nevertheless, stimulated the writing of martial poetry, such as "The Sword of Robert Lee" by Father Abram Ryan, a Confederate chaplain, "Little Giffen" by Francis O. Ticknor, and "John Pelham" by James R. Randall.

A pleasant relief from the artificial literature of romanticism was furnished by the humorists of the Old South. Unfortunately, they did not act as a solvent of the high-flown romanticism of their section as did Cervantes in Spain, for their work was published chiefly in newspapers and was regarded as trivial and vulgar. The founder of the school of Southern humorists was Augustus Baldwin Longstreet of Augusta, Georgia, descended from New Jersey Dutch stock. He was a versatile man, holding such positions as judge, editor, preacher, college president, and author.[7] Between 1832 and 1835 he wrote humorous sketches describing the mores of the common man of the South, especially on the Georgia frontier, which were first published in his newspaper, the Augusta *State Rights Sentinel,* and later collected in a volume entitled *Georgia Scenes* (1835). A similar vein of humor was exploited by another Georgia editor, William Tappan Thompson (born in Ohio) who wrote *Major Jones's Courtship* and *Major Jones's Chronicles of Pineville,* describing the activities of a naive Georgia bumpkin.

Much of this semi-realistic literature of the Southern frontier was written by newspaper men to entertain their readers or by aristocrats amused by the uncouthness of the cracker. Johnson J. Hooper, a native of North Carolina, who emigrated to Alabama and edited the Montgomery *Journal,* wrote a delightful book entitled, *The Adventures of Captain Simon Suggs,* describing the picaresque adventures on the Alabama frontier of a plausible scamp. The captain of a steam boat on Tennessee rivers, George Washington Harris, created some of the most powerful comic stories of the Old South in *Sut Lovingood's Yarns,* "the humor of discomfiture." The humor of the North Carolina back country was culled by Harden Taliaferro in *Fisher's River Scenes and Characters* and by Hamilton C. Jones in such stories as "Cousin Sally Dilliard" and "McAlpin's Trip to Charleston." In the Southwest flourished the tall tale, notably Thomas B. Thorpe's narration, "The Big Bear of Arkansas," and the incredible stories told about David Crockett, about the mythical character, Mike Fink, and the Texan fighter, "Big Foot" Wallace. Some of the drollest personalities of the Old South, like Governor "Zeb" Vance of North Carolina and Judge Dooley of Georgia, remained oral story tellers and wits whose humor has to a great extent been lost.

The literary productions of the Southern humorists are valuable as sources for the social history of the common people, but they must be used with discrimination.[8] They preserve vivid and authentic accounts of camp meetings, horse racing, country weddings, cracker dances, quilting parties, rude fights in which gouging was practiced, shooting matches, military drills, gander pullings, snatches of old songs like "Bingo," and stories about politicians, preachers, practical jokers, horse traders, confidence men, etc. One of the most valuable works of humor in describing the color and flavor of a vanished period of history is Joseph G. Baldwin's *Flush Times in Alabama and Mississippi* (1853), which portrays the period of speculation in the lower South just before the Panic of 1837. The Negro was seldom used as a subject for comedy by the ante-bellum humorists, a source of literary material which was unexploited until after the Civil War by such innovators as Irwin Russell and Joel Chandler Harris. Mark Twain, who spent his youth in Hannibal, Missouri, was undoubtedly influenced in his development as a humorous writer by his predecessors, the school of Southern humorists of the ante-bellum period.

The growth of an intense sectional feeling seems to have been the strongest force in founding magazines in the ante-bellum South. Nevertheless, the Southern magazines did not as a rule use Southern themes, or local color, or the Negro as sources of literary material. A recent study of Georgia periodicals discloses that at least fifty-seven periodicals were started in this state before the Civil War but that none of them lasted over five years.[9] One of the most attractive of these Georgia periodicals was *The Countryman* published by Joseph A. Turner on his plantation near Eatonton, Georgia. It was a small weekly sheet, designed after Addison's *Spectator*, and contained poetry, romantic stories, wit, and some politicial comment. Joel Chandler Harris worked on this paper as a boy, thus getting his start in journalism and literature.

So many ambitious projects to publish Southern magazines originated in Charleston, the center of Southern pride and nationalism, that this city has been rightly called the graveyard of magazines. The earliest important Charleston periodical was *The Southern Review*, founded in 1828 by Hugh Swinton Legaré, to be the medium for Southern writers. Although handicapped by being a cripple, Legaré belonged to the bluebloods of his state. His literary career was incidental to his pursuit of law and politics, which elevated him to the position of Attorney General in the cabinet of President Tyler. The contents of the *Review* were serious and dull, which probably explains why after four years of struggle against bankruptcy it expired. The most successful of the city's magazines was the *Southern Quarterly Review*, founded in New Orleans in 1842, but transferred the following year to Charleston. Despite the fact that its editor, Daniel K. Whitaker, was a Northerner, the *Southern Quarterly Review* was an ardent defender of slavery against the abolitionists.

In 1857 after the *Southern Quarterly Review* was abandoned, the literary group that met at "Lord John" Russell's bookshop, where Simms held court, founded *Russell's Magazine*, which lasted until the spring of 1860. Charleston also had its woman's magazine, *The Southern Rose* which had blossomed from *The Southern Rosebud*. Edited by Caroline Gilman, the wife of the Unitarian minister of Charleston, it was designed for "ladies" and mirrored the romantic tradition of feminine behavior.

In the upper South the two outstanding periodicals were *Niles' Weekly Register* of Baltimore and the *Southern Literary Messenger* of Richmond. Founded in 1811 by Hezekiah Niles, a Quaker, the *Register* was a forerunner of the modern news magazine, such as *The Literary Digest* or *Time*. It had a national circulation, reporting and digesting news from all over the country and taking a broad national point of view, championing such causes as popular education, democracy, industrialization, and a protective tariff. It remains a valuable mine of the social and political history of the United States, 1811–1849. The *Southern Literary Messenger* enjoyed the longest life of all Southern literary magazines, dating from 1834 and ending in June, 1864. It had a series of able editors, including Edgar Allan Poe, who was paid the salary of fifteen dollars a week, Matthew Fontaine Maury, the scientist, John R. Thompson, and George W. Bagby. Under Poe's editorship it contributed the best literary criticism in America, but after it became ardently pro-Southern in tone, its literary quality suffered from the blight of absorption in sectional defense.

The failures of Southern magazines may be attributed to several factors. Competition with superior English and Northern magazines was undoubtedly an important reason for early bankruptcy of budding Southern periodicals. Southerners preferred to read English magazines such as the *Edinburgh Review, Blackwood's*, and the *Westminster Review*, which were reprinted cheaply for the American market by Leonard, Scott, and Co., of New York. Also *Harper's Magazine, Putnam's, Graham's*, and the *Atlantic Monthly* were sold in the South despite a campaign to boycott them as hostile to Southern institutions. *Godey's Lady's Book*, published at Philadelphia, containing colored plates of the Paris fashions was the delight of Southern ladies. Since Southern periodicals could not pay for contributions, even ardent sectional patriots like Simms sent their best work to paying Northern magazines. Other reasons why Southern magazines perished were the lack of reality and vigor of their articles and verse, the handicap of having few publishing houses located below the Mason and Dixon line, and a much smaller reading public than existed in the Northern states.

In another field of culture, scientific interests, modern research indicates that there was considerable study of the natural sciences below the Mason and Dixon line. Scientific studies occupied an honorable position in the curriculum of Southern colleges. It is true that the study of the Greek and Roman classics was preeminent, but science was quite popular also. The original plan for the curriculum of the University of North Carolina, as drawn up by William R. Davie, the founder, provided for a wide study of the sciences, but this enlightened course was later abandoned to follow the fashion of the period. Nevertheless, President Joseph Caldwell of the University of North Carolina procured impressive electrical equipment for the instruction of the students and in 1827 erected on the campus the first college astronomical observatory in America. In 1856, when the University of Virginia had an enrollment of 558 students, 191 of them were taking courses in chemistry and 143, courses in natural philosophy.[10] South Carolina College required students in 1841 to take courses in physics, astronomy, chemistry, geology, and mineralogy—a larger dose of the natural sciences than is required for graduation in modern colleges. Students gained a love for science and an insight into the scientific method from the contagious example of such able teachers as the LeConte brothers, John and Joseph, who taught at the University of Georgia and South Carolina College, Elisha Mitchell at Chapel Hill, James Woodrow at Oglethorpe University, Dr. Thomas Cooper at Columbia, and the Dutchman, Gerard Troost, who lectured in a hall at the University of Nashville cluttered with stuffed birds, turtles, fossils, minerals, and chemical apparatus.

The methods used in teaching the natural sciences in the colleges of the Old South were amateurish as compared with modern techniques. The professor performed the experiments before the class to illustrate his lectures, but the students seldom had the advantage of working in laboratories and performing experiments themselves. The investigation of the mysteries of nature was severely handicapped by the lack of scientific instruments and laboratories. The best equipped Southern colleges bought apparatus in Europe—telescopes, microscopes, sextants, magnets, quadrants, prisms, thermometers, barometers, and astronomical clocks. The professors were required to teach such a medley of sciences that, by spreading their energies over so many fields, they seldom could become experts and successful experimenters in any one branch of science. Consequently, scientists, both North and South, were engaged chiefly in collecting specimens, classifying flora and fauna, discovering new American species, and making geological surveys—a rather rudimentary stage in the development of science. The fact that scientific courses in colleges were frequently called natural philosophy indicates their large theoretical content. Furthermore, the free pursuit of science was inhibited throughout the country by the dominance of orthodox religion.

In Kentucky, Transylvania University and the University of Louisville were important centers of scientific activity, especially in regard to medicine. From 1819 to 1826 the eccentric professor, Constantine Rafinesque, born in Constantinople of French and German parentage, taught a wide range of sciences at Transylvania University. He claimed to be a universal scholar when he applied to Jefferson for a job at the University of Virginia: "I do not know a single Individual either in the U. St. or in Europe who is *at the same time* equally acquainted with Geology, Mineralogy, Metereology, Zoology, and Botany as I am." This modest scholar did, however, make many expeditions into the wilderness to collect unknown American botanical specimens. He wrote: "I have discovered an immense number of new Plants, Fishes, Shells, fossils, etc. and even some new Quadrupeds!" [11] Dr. Charles Caldwell, professor at Transylvania and later at Louisville Medical Institute, became the foremost advocate in America of the pseudo-science, phrenology. The phrenologists claimed to be able to diagnose the intelligence and character of a person by examination of the shape of the skull, the bumps on the cranium, and the physiognomy. They had a wide-

spread popularity and credence in the decades of the 1830's and
1840's, but were discredited by the "practical phrenologists" who
were intent on reaping a golden harvest.

Charleston was the nucleus of a remarkable group of amateur and
professional scientists. Lewis R. Gibbes taught various branches of
science at the College of Charleston, making contributions to the
knowledge of chemistry, botany, geology, and zoology. John Bachman, a Lutheran minister, cooperated with Audubon to write a
volume, *Quadrupeds of North America* and John Edwards Holbrook wrote a learned work on reptiles, *North American Herpetol-
ogy*, 5 volumes. Stephen Elliott of Beaufort published a volume on
the botany of South Carolina and Georgia in 1821 and was active in
founding the Literary and Philosophical Society of Charleston which
encouraged scientific investigation. One of the greatest American
chemists was J. Lawrence Smith of Charleston, who taught at the
University of Virginia and the University of Louisville. He made
contributions to the knowledge of the chemistry of minerals and
meteorites and to the chemistry of cotton-growing soils. Joel R.
Poinsett, the versatile South Carolina statesman, actively promoted
the investigation of natural science and was one of the founders of
the Smithsonian Institution. Charleston could boast of possessing the
most valuable museum in the South during the last decade of the
ante-bellum period.

Scattered among the planter class and among lawyers, doctors,
and politicians were many amateur scientists. Jefferson was America's first paleontologist, and his example of investigating natural
phenomena was followed by a considerable number of planters, such
as James Hamilton Couper, a wealthy planter of St. Simon's Island,
Georgia, and William Dunbar of Natchez, Mississippi. Henry W.
Ravenel, a planter near Aiken, South Carolina, published a five-
volume study of Carolina fungi shortly before the Civil War. He
corresponded with the Florida botanist, Alvan W. Chapman, author
of *Flora of the Southern States*, Asa Gray at Harvard, and eminent
European botanists. His private journal indicates that his scientific
studies did not disturb his devotion to orthodox religion. He was
an experimentalist who raised superior peaches which he sold profitably in New York, and he encouraged the cultivation of vineyards
for wine making in the South.

Natchez was an attractive rendezvous of cultured planters and pro-fessional men with scientific interests in the rather crude Southwest. Benjamin L. C. Wailes of the near-by village of Washington, a planter with a versatile interest in science, published a volume on the geology and agriculture of Mississippi in 1854 and kept a valuable diary illustrating the social life and intellectual interests of the Natchez region. Another leading investigator of natural science in the Southwest was Dr. John W. Monette of Washington, Mississippi, who made contributions to the study of yellow fever, to the origin of races, and to the physical geography of the Mississippi Valley. Monette, as well as William Charles Wells of Charleston, made contributions to the theory of evolution by natural selection before Darwin published his *The Origin of Species* in 1859. In New Orleans a group of gentlemen interested in the advancement of science organized in 1853 the New Orleans Academy of Sciences, one of a number of Southern societies and lyceums devoted to the cultivation of scientific knowledge.

A significant expansion of the knowledge of science was made by the geological surveys undertaken by all the Southern states ex-cept Florida and Louisiana. The first of these was begun in North Carolina in 1824 by Professor Denison Olmstead of the University at Chapel Hill. Although the legislature appropriated only a pittance, Olmstead devoted his vacations *gratis* to the work. When he returned to Yale, his successor, Professor Elisha Mitchell, a New Englander who taught science for thirty-eight years at the University, carried on the geological survey. Their reports were published by the state, constituting the first geological reports published by state govern-ments in the United States. Mitchell also published in 1842 a pioneer textbook, *Elements of Geology, with an outline of the Geology of North Carolina*. While exploring the mountains in the western part of the state, he lost his life, but his services to the cause of geology were commemorated by naming the highest mountain east of the Mississippi River after him. The ablest geological surveys in the South were undertaken by Oscar Lieber in South Carolina, by David Dale Owen, son of the famous Robert, in Kentucky and Arkansas, by William Barton Rogers in Virginia, and by James M. Safford in Tennessee.[12] William Barton Rogers, professor at the Uni-versity of Virginia, made valuable contributions to the understanding

of the geology of the Appalachian Mountains and later founded the
Massachusetts Institute of Technology. The Southern states were
willing to appropriate money for geological surveys on account of
their practical value in aiding agriculture and the exploitation of
the mineral resources of the South.

Matthew Fontaine Maury, an aristocratic Virginian, pushed back
the frontier of geological knowledge by his exploration of the
oceans. He was placed in charge of the Naval Observatory at
Washington, D. C., which gave him excellent opportunities to carry
on his investigations. By studying deep-sea soundings he discovered
the Atlantic plateau under the Atlantic ocean, which enabled him to
advise Cyrus W. Field as to the best location for laying his cable.
He also charted the routes of winds and currents, discovering the
course of the Gulf Stream. He deserves the honor of being called
the father of the United States Weather Bureau. When the Civil
War came, Maury was given the rank of captain in the Confederate
Navy and sent as an agent to Europe to buy ships for the Confederacy.

A number of alert physicians in the South were not content merely
to practice their profession in a routine manner but made brilliant
advances in medical science. One of the pioneers in developing
modern surgery was Dr. Ephraim McDowell of Danville, Kentucky,
who had studied medicine at the University of Edinburgh. In 1809
he successfully removed a large tumor from the ovary of a patient
whom local physicians believed to be pregnant with twins. This ovari-
otomy has been called "the dawn of abdominal surgery." Another
Southern doctor, Crawford W. Long, experimenting in an obscure
Georgia village in 1842, discovered the use of ether as an anesthetic,
but he neglected to publish his discovery at that time. The state of
Georgia has recognized the epochal value of Dr. Long's achievement by placing a monument to his memory in the Hall of Fame at
the national Capitol. One of the founders of the American Medical
Association in 1846 was Dr. Richard D. Arnold of Savannah who
made scientific studies of yellow fever. Between 1845 and 1849
Dr. Marion Sims, a graduate of South Carolina College and Jefferson Medical College, performed some remarkable experiments in
Montgomery, Alabama, in operating on three slave women afflicted

with fistula. He succeeded in curing them by discovering "the Sims position" and by surgery, an achievement which has caused him to be described as "the father of modern gynecology."

The physician was a highly prized member of Southern society, but the artist received little encouragement from a society that was excessively rural. The chief interest of the planters in painting seems to have been the perpetuation of family pride through portraits. There were a few wealthy planters such as Governor R. F. W. Allston of "Chicora Wood," South Carolina, and Jefferson who showed discriminating taste by adorning their mansions with copies of the great Italian masters. But the gentry disparaged the pursuit by Southern youths of an artistic career as a serious profession. When Matthew H. Jouett (1787–1827) abandoned the honorable profession of law to become an artist, his father lamented that he had educated Matthew at Transylvania University only for him to become "a damned sign painter." This Kentuckian had received instruction in art from Gilbert Stuart in Boston, and he returned home to paint over three hundred and twenty-five portraits, mainly of the Blue-grass aristocracy, for fifty dollars a picture. His notes on conversations with Gilbert Stuart show that he was not an empiric but that he had an intellectual interest in painting.[13] His portraits of Horace Holley, Henry Clay, and Lafayette are marked by sincerity and dignity, and his pictures of children are particularly delightful in capturing the charm of youth.

In the nineteenth century Charleston was the home of several important artists. Thomas Sully, although born in England, spent his youth in this city, and here he began his education as an artist. He moved as a young man to Norfolk and Richmond, where he and his brother painted portraits. Later he went to England to study art under Benjamin West, but he was more influenced by the style of Sir Thomas Lawrence and Gilbert Stuart than by his preceptor. Most of his long artistic career was spent in Philadelphia, where he died in 1872. His portraits of men and women are distinguished for their grace and beautiful color. Other artists who were natives of Charleston or worked there before the Civil War were Henry Benbridge (1744–1812), Edward Malbone (1777–1807), and Charles Fraser (1782–1860). Malbone and Fraser developed an exquisite art of painting miniatures on ivory. Charleston was the home of William H. Brown, the most famous maker of silhouettes in America (see his *Portrait Gallery of Distinguished American Citizens*, 1845). At Waccamaw, South Carolina, was born the artist, Washington Allston, who studied at Harvard College and charmed his contemporaries by his gifted personality. Unfortunately, this scion of South Carolina aristocracy aspired to be a painter in the grand style, but failed to produce great works. When he died in 1843, he left uncompleted his most ambitious attempt, *Belshazzar's Feast*.

Across the Appalachian Mountains traveled Northern or English painters in quest of patrons who would pay money for portraits. In Paris, Kentucky, Chester Harding, a Yankee jack-of-all-trades, painted one hundred portraits at twenty-five dollars each, and with the proceeds went to Europe to study art. His portraits of Daniel Boone and of John Randolph are justly famous. Other wandering painters who have preserved pictorial records of Southern planters and public men were John Wesley Jarvis, the bohemian nephew of John Wesley, William Garl Brown, and Thomas Bangs Thorpe, better known for his humorous stories of the South. Ralph E. W. Earle (1788–1837) married a niece of Mrs. Andrew Jackson and for seventeen years lived in the household of "Old Hickory." His sincere portraits of Jackson and his family have rendered a service to historians comparable to Peale's portraits of Washington. Jackson grew very fond of this artist, who is buried at the "Hermitage."

John James Audubon occupies an honorable position as a Southern painter as well as an eminent naturalist. The mystery of his parentage has never been solved nor has it been definitely determined whether he was a native of New Orleans or Santo Domingo. He was reared in France by a ship captain and received instruction in art from the noted French painter, Jacques Louis David. Audubon came to America as a young man in 1803 and drifted to the frontier where he kept a store at Louisville and at Henderson, Kentucky, and pursued his passion of studying American birds. Audubon had many contacts also with the lower South, painting portraits for a living in New Orleans and Natchez, serving as a tutor on the great plantation of "Oakley" in Feliciana Parish, Louisiana, and exploring the wilds of Florida to obtain paintings of rare birds. In 1838 he published his *magnum opus, Birds of America*, containing exquisite reproductions in color of his paintings of native birds. Approximately five hundred species of American birds, painted in their natural environment, were included in this elephant or life-size edition engraved by Robert Havell of England. He made no money from the sale of this edition, limited to no more than two hundred sets, but the miniature edition brought him means for a comfortable and serene old age.

The most talented native painter of the Southwest was George Caleb Bingham (1811–79). Called "the Missouri artist," Bingham has only recently been recognized as one of the most significant of the ante-bellum artists of Southern origin. Largely self-taught at first, he exploited a rich field of genre painting, describing the life of the Southwest and of the Mississippi River. He had a fine ability to tell a story, as indicated by his picture of a Missouri election, entitled "The Verdict of the People," "Stump Speaking" and his "Raftsmen Playing Cards." In middle life he studied art at Philadelphia and in Dusseldorf, Germany, but his increasing interest in politics, his service in the Union army, and his career as state treasurer of Missouri and as police commissioner of Kansas City caused his art to suffer.[14] The introduction of daguerreotypes in the decade of the 1840's and the development and perfection of photography in the 1850's–60's caused a decline in the business of painting portraits in the United States.

The ante-bellum South produced one sculptor of note, Joel T. Hart of Winchester, Kentucky. Hart had spent his young manhood building stone fences and chimneys and working as a tombstone cutter in a Lexington marble yard. He aspired to become a sculptor, however, and was patronized by Cassius Marcellus Clay, the anti-slavery editor. This self-taught young man had a remarkable talent for carving busts which were excellent likenesses of his subjects. His bust of Cassius Marcellus Clay, now owned by the University of Kentucky, is an arresting work because of the tantalizing and perverse expression on its countenance, which interprets the personality of a fearless non-conformist. Cassius Clay loaned his protegé money to go to Europe, where he studied anatomy and the works of the great masters. His most famous statue was the figure of Henry Clay clad in a frock coat which was ordered by the ladies of Richmond at a cost of $5,000. Hart also made busts of Andrew Jackson, President Millard Fillmore, and Senator J. J. Crittenden. He invented a measuring machine which enabled him to obtain more realistic dimensions and to work three times as rapidly as other sculptors, but he reported that Hiram Powers and other Northern sculptors "hate it like the devil." [15] Much of his later life was spent in Italy carving idealized statues such as "Il Penseroso" and "The Triumph of Chastity." He was a sincere workman with democratic sympathies, revealed in his manuscript letters in the Filson Club, where he wrote with disgust of making "busts of pompous Englishmen" in order to live. Hart's younger contemporary, Edward Virginius Valentine of Richmond, attained celebrity after the Civil War for his statues and busts of Lee and other Confederate heroes.

The artistic taste of the South found its most pervasive expression in architecture and landscape gardening. During the period of the early republic Thomas Jefferson was the dominant influence in architecture. This Virginia aristocrat was a pioneer in introducing into America the Roman revival style of architecture, with its emphasis on the dome, a style admirably suited to the young republic. Jefferson derived his passion for architecture partly from the study of English books on architecture but especially from Palladio, the Italian architect of the Renaissance, whose work on architecture he studied closely. His exquisite taste and skill in architecture were applied in building his home "Monticello," near Charlottesville, Virginia. Unlike most Southern planters, who located their homes near river banks, Jefferson chose as the site for his residence a high eminence with a magnificent view over the Blue Ridge mountains and the Fluvanna River below. In 1769 he began the construction of this noble example of domestic architecture, continued building through the Revolutionary War, and did not complete "Monticello" in its final form until forty years later (1809).

This versatile Southerner was the first great American architect, an amateur in the sense that he refused money for his architectural designs, but a professional in competence and skill. In his *Notes on Virginia*, published in 1784, Jefferson preached the doctrine to his fellow Southerners of constructing their homes in a tradition of beauty as well as of utility. Marquis de Chastellux, who visited

"Monticello" in 1782, wrote that Mr. Jefferson was the first American who consulted the fine arts to discover how to shelter himself from the weather. He designed or remodeled spacious plantation homes with classic facades for his neighbors and friends in Virginia, "Ash Lawn," the home of James Monroe, "Farmington," now the country club of Charlottesville, and "Montpelier," the residence of Madison. In a period in which there were virtually no professional architects in the South each planter had to design his home or select patterns from architectural books. It is a testimony to the taste and refinement of the Southern gentry that so many of them, John H. Cocke, for example, built such beautiful country homes as "Bremo" in Piedmont Virginia.

Jefferson was prominent in the introduction of neo-classicism, especially of the Roman type, into America. While he was minister to France, he saw the celebrated Roman building preserved at Nîmes, called Maison Carrée, which he contemplated for hours as a lover looks on his mistress. When he returned to his native Virginia, he brought a design for the capital at Richmond, copied from the Roman temple at Nîmes, the first use of the classic temple form for an important public building in America (1789). In the planning of the city of Washington and its classic buildings, Jefferson exerted a powerful influence, especially suggesting to Major Pierre L'Enfant the design of placing the Capitol and the President's mansion at opposite ends of a spacious street. He heartily approved of Latrobe's use of tobacco leaves and the ears of Indian corn instead of acanthus leaves for the Corinthian columns in the Capitol's interior.

One of his most distinguished services to Southern architecture was his design of the buildings at the University of Virginia, completed in 1825. He rode almost daily to the site of the University at Charlottesville to superintend the building operations, a round trip of ten miles, and when he was kept at home, he watched the construction with his telescope. The central building was the Rotunda, or Library, with its great Roman dome which dominated a quadrangle of buildings that the eminent authority, Fiske Kimball, has called the most beautiful ensemble of buildings in America.[16] This group contained the pavilions, or homes, of the professors, the recitation rooms, and the dormitories, forming what Jefferson described as "an academical village." Jefferson wished to present to the students exquisite examples of classic architecture that would influence their later lives in erecting homes and public buildings with good taste. Consequently the ten pavilions displayed different styles of classical architecture modeled after Diocletian's baths, the temple of Fortuna Virilis, the theatre of Marcellas, and the designs of Palladio. Most of the columns and capitals of the porticoes, Doric, Ionic, and Corinthian, were imported from Italy. In order to conserve brick Jefferson designed the beautiful serpentine walls of the campus, which the students say Jefferson traced while he was drunk.

The type of architecture that ultimately prevailed in the antebellum South was the style of the Greek Revival. This style was based on the design of a Greek temple—the white temple whose rich colors of classical days had been washed during the transit of the centuries. The vogue of the Greek classical style was not confined to the South but prevailed from New England to Louisiana and as far west as Arkansas. The architect most responsible for the development of the Greek revival style in America was Benjamin Latrobe, an Englishmen who was appointed architect of the Capitol in Washington in 1803. Latrobe was buried in Southern soil at New Orleans, where shortly before his death in 1821 he had designed the Louisiana Bank. The great popularity of the Greek Revival was influenced partly by the heroic struggle of the Greeks to win their independence from Turkey in the decade of the 1820's. Byron had died as a volunteer in the cause of Greek liberty and had popularized the romantic side of this war. So sympathetic were Southerners to the Greek Revolution that the legislature of South Carolina petitioned Congress to recognize the independence of the little country. Furthermore, the education of gentlemen in America was heavily weighted with the learning of the Greek and Latin classics—a fact which facilitated the growth of the Greek Revival style of architecture.

The adoption of the new mode in building occurred rather late in the South, with the exception of Baltimore on the perimeter of the land of Dixie. Yet in the decade of the 1830's and 1840's it developed great momentum as planters gained wealth from cotton, sugar, and wheat. Men who had been born in a log cabin, like Andrew Jackson, followed the new style in building imposing mansions fronted by Greek columns. Jackson's home, "The Hermitage," near Nashville, reconstructed in 1835, was built along classic lines. President James K. Polk was buried in a Greek Doric tomb on the grounds of the state house in Nashville, which was also built in the classic style of architecture. Also the Polk mansion in Tennessee called "Rattle and Snap," built in 1845, was a lofty white residence with a portico supported by ten fluted Corinthian pillars extending two stories high to a pediment.

The houses of the Greek Revival were chiefly constructed of wood, rather than of brick or stone. At times the facade was imposing but the interior was lacking in dignity. The best Southern homes, however, had attractive interiors, with classical marble mantels and beautiful winding staircases. Gay-colored wall paper succeeded the white paneling of Georgian houses. These homes of the Greek Revival style were not slavish imitations of classic models but contained sensible adaptations to the climate and the way of life of the Southern gentry. They were designed for coolness and spacious living, with a central hallway, through which the breeze could blow, with long windows that were shaded with green shutters, and with high ceilings. Few of these houses had bathrooms, but used toilets detached from the house. The weekly bath on Saturday afternoons was usually taken in a small basin or tin tub. The kitchen, presided over by the black cook, was frequently detached from the big house, and food was carried to the dining table by barefooted Negro girls. The wide piazzas beneath the Greek porticoes were a distinct improvement on most of the Georgian houses, for they were admirably adapted for pleasant conversation and for hospitality. The appearance of these serene Greek temple facades gave a quiet dignity and an atmosphere of harmonious leisure to the homes of the Southern aristocrats.

The mansions of the Greek Revival style were found especially in the rich and fertile areas of the South. The newer regions of the South, such as the black belt of Alabama and Mississippi, were the sites of large mansions built in the 1830's and 1840's when this new style had superseded the Georgian houses of the Tidewater. One of

the most beautiful of these homes is "Gaineswood" near Demopolis,
Alabama, which had an oval drawing room and a circular balustrade
on the roof. In the Natchez district of Mississippi are numerous pa-
latial homes, so large that the modern housewife would shrink from
the responsibility of their care. They stand as monuments to the
slave aristocracy, in the days before Federal income taxes were
dreamed of. Every spring they are open for public inspection, at
a fee, during the so-called Natchez Pilgrimage. In the Kentucky
Bluegrass region are found charming one-story classical houses typical of the region, notably "Rose Hill," a Breckinridge home, and
"The Grange" in Bourbon County, built by a slave-trader, Edward
Stone, who was killed in 1826 by slaves whom he was transporting
"down the river."

One of the most original variations of the Greek Revival style in
the South is illustrated by the homes of the Charleston aristocrats.
These houses faced a side lawn or garden hidden from inquisitive
eyes by high walls. The narrow end of the house was placed toward
the street, while the classic portico, facing the garden contained a
double-decker piazza. The house gained height by being placed on
an arched basement. The gateways were made of wrought iron, often
in beautiful designs, such as are found before houses in Savannah,
Mobile, and New Orleans. Frequently, in the lower South and along
rivers of Kentucky influenced by intercourse with New Orleans, the
Greek classic style was combined with iron balconies.

Perhaps the most notable Southern architect after Jefferson was
Robert Mills of Charleston. He has been described as "the first
native-born American regularly trained for the profession of architecture." [17] Educated at the College of Charleston, he studied
under James Hoban, the Irishman, who lived in Charleston for awhile
before he became the architect of the President's Mansion, or the
White House, in Washington. Mills also came under the influence of
Thomas Jefferson, serving as his draughtsman for two years, and
finally he became a pupil of Benjamin Latrobe, an innovator of the
Greek Revival style in America. He was chosen the architect for the
famous Washington Monument in Baltimore, a huge Doric column
completed in 1829, and he also designed the great obelisk, 555 feet
high, in honor of Washington at the nation's capital. Mills did some

notable work in the classic style in his native city. His Records Office in Charleston, built in 1826, is one of the first fireproof buildings erected in America. Mills had been greatly shocked by the fire in Richmond in 1812 that had burned a theater, killing seventy-one people, including the governor of the state. When he was employed to design the Monumental Church erected on the site of the theater which had burned, his attention was drawn to the need of fireproof public buildings. In 1822 he designed the First Baptist Church of Charleston in the form of a Greek temple and later the Jewish Synagogue was built in this style. In 1850 a beautiful Ionic portico was placed in front of the College of Charleston. Mills was not only an architect with high ideals, but he was a humanitarian, whose book, *Statistics of South Carolina* (1826), advocated reforms in the treatment of criminals, the colonization of slaves, etc.

Other talented Southern architects of the Greek Revival were William Jay of Savannah and Gideon Shryock of Lexington, Kentucky. Jay blended artistically the classic style with the use of iron balconies. Shryock, the son of a Kentucky builder, had studied the new style of architecture in Philadelphia. His first important commission was to build the state capitol at Frankfort, which he designed in the Greek temple form (1825). Shryock also was the architect of Morrison Chapel, the principal building of Transylvania University, with its dignified Doric portico, and the Louisville Bank with its elegant Greek facade. One of his most beautiful structures was the state capitol of Arkansas completed in 1836. Although this state was dominated by primitive, frontier conditions, its capitol building was modeled after the temple of Minerva in Ionia. All over the South, the shadow of the ancient civilization of Greece rested. In small villages like Hillsboro, North Carolina, the courthouses were replicas on the exterior of dignified Greek temples; college buildings, such as the group at Washington and Lee University at Lexington, Methodist and Baptist churches, banks, spacious plantation homes, such as "Berry Hill" in Virginia, city homes like Belo House in Winston-Salem, state capitols, such as William Strickland's edifice at Nashville, clubs such as Hibernian Hall in Charleston, all were overcome by the regnant taste for classical architecture. Furthermore, the North and the West shared in this enthusiasm and the victory of the Greek Revival style tended to make the appearance of the sections more alike.

Despite the dominance of the classic vogue, another style of building, the Gothic Revival, attained a minor following in the Old South. Originating in England, this style expressed in architecture the romantic mood which prevailed in the literature of the period. Indeed, the readers of Scott's novels must have found delight in seeing at various places in the South public buildings and private homes constructed in imitation of castles, with stained glass windows, crenellated walls, and pointed arches, and gables. The old capitols at Baton Rouge and Milledgeville, Georgia, have survived into the twentieth century, reminders of this architectural fad of the antebellum South.

The most prominent Southern architect of the Gothic Revival was John McMurtry, born in 1812 near Lexington, Kentucky. This self-educated architect began his career as a practical builder in the Bluegrass region, where the wealthy planters and successful business men of Lexington employed him to construct homes befitting their privileged position in Southern society. McMurtry was taken to England in 1840 by a wealthy resident of Lexington who wished to build a home in the Gothic style. Accordingly, this talented builder had an opportunity to study some of the old castles of England, especially Warwick Castle, and the Tudor manor houses. After his return he constructed during the decades of the 1840's and 1850's some beautiful homes in the Gothic style, especially "Loudoun," "Ingelside," and "Aylesford," located in and near Lexington. In addition to such adaptations of mediaeval designs to the American environment, McMurtry also built dwellings in the Greek revival style, such as the charming "Botherum" in Lexington. In both styles, the spacious veranda, or porch, contributed much to the art of comfortable living in a warm climate.

It is an error to think that the majority of Southerners, or even of the small planter class, in 1860 dwelt in imposing houses of the Greek Revival style. On the contrary, the typical planter lived in a simple frame house, at times unpainted, without any pretense to architecture. The town and city homes of absentee planters in the cotton belt were often white-pillared mansions with Greek facades so familiar to romance, but their country residences were utilitarian structures, even constructed at times of roughly hewn logs.[18] The houses of the overseers were not much better in many cases than the cabins of the slaves. Moreover, the average yeoman farmer dwelt in a frame cottage or a log cabin, often a double log cabin with a breezeway or "dog run" between the two rooms. The chief reason for the failure of the planters to build attractive and durable homes on the cotton plantations was the air of impermanency about these habitations. Many planters regarded their homes as temporary abiding places until the cream of fertility of the soil had been absorbed and then they would sell out and move farther west to virgin land. Ardent Southern nationalists in the decade of the 1850's protested against the reign of the Greek Revival style and also against the minor Gothic Revival fad, but the ante-bellum South was in the chrysalis stage of its culture when the Civil War came and was unable to create a genuinely Southern style of architecture or overcome the inertia of imitation.

Citations

1. CLEMENT EATON, "The Resistance of the South to Northern Radicalism," New England Quarterly, VIII (1935), 215–231.
2. W. S. TRYON, "The Publications of Ticknor and Fields in the South, 1840–1865," Journal of Southern History, XIV (August, 1948), 309, 315.
3. D. R. Fox, Ideas in Motion (New York, 1935), 24–25; see also the splendid chapter, "Cultural Nationalism in the Old South," in MERLE CURTI, The Growth of American Thought (New York, 1943).
4. See provocative interpretations by VERNON L. PARRINGTON, The Romantic Revolution in America 1800–1860 (New York, 1927) and VAN WYCK BROOKS, The World of Washington Irving (New York, 1944).
5. W. P. TRENT, William Gilmore Simms (Boston, 1892).
6. Numerous pamphlets describe this famous murder of the Attorney General of Kentucky, notably The Confession of Jereboam O. Beauchampe, Who was Executed at Frankfort, Ky., on the 7th of July 1826 for the Murder of Solomon P. Sharp (Bloomfield, Ky., 1826).

7. J. D. WADE, *Augustus Baldwin Longstreet* (New York, 1924).
8. CLEMENT EATON, "The Humor of the Southern Yeoman," *Sewanee Review XLIX* (April–June, 1941), 173–183.
9. B. H. FLANDERS, *Early Georgia Magazines: Literary Periodicals to 1865* (Athens, Ga., 1944).
10. See T. C. JOHNSON, *Scientific Interests in the Old South* (New York, 1936).
11. E. M. BETTS, "The Correspondence between Constantine Samuel Rafinesque and Thomas Jefferson," *Proceedings of the American Philosophical Society*, Vol. 87 (1944), 371–373.
12. C. S. SYDNOR, "State Geological Surveys in the Old South," *American Studies in Honor of William Kenneth Boyd*, 86–110.
13. Photostat in University of Kentucky Library; printed in H. MORGAN, *Gilbert Stuart and His Pupils* (New York, 1939), 81–93.
14. See A. CHRIST-JANER, *George Caleb Bingham of Missouri* (New York, 1940).
15. Manuscript in Filson Club Library, Louisville, Kentucky.
16. FISKE KIMBALL, *American Architecture* (Indianapolis, 1928), 83.
17. T. F. HAMLIN, *Greek Revival Architecture in America* (New York, 1944), 53.
18. J. C. BONNER, "Plantation Architecture of the Lower South on the Eve of the Civil War," *Journal of Southern History*, XI (August, 1945), 370–388.

DOUBLE LOG CABIN ON THE CRENSHAW PLANTATION, ALABAMA

Note the "dog run" in the middle of the house. This type of house was occupied by the yeoman farmer and also by the planter in newly opened plantation districts. (Courtesy of the Library of Congress.)

"GAINESWOOD," DEMOPOLIS, ALABAMA, IN THE BLACK BELT

Built in 1842 for General Nathan B. Whitfield, an emigrating planter from North Carolina.

MORRISON HALL, TRANSYLVANIA UNIVERSITY, LEXINGTON, KENTUCKY
Designed by Gideon Shryock and built in 1833, it is a beautiful example
of the classic cult in the South.

"BOTHERUM," LEXINGTON, KENTUCKY
Designed by John McMurtry and completed in 1850 for Madison
Johnson, a lawyer, proclaimed to be the ugliest man in Kentucky;
reputed to be the scene of James Lane Allen's story *Two Gentlemen
of Kentucky*. (Courtesy of J. Winston Coleman, Jr.)

CHAPTER XXII

A Conflict over Morals
and Economics

◆

THE introduction of the Wilmot Proviso in the House of Representatives in 1846 was the signal for a great sectional controversy over slavery. Whatever were the motives of David Wilmot, the
Pennsylvania Congressman who introduced this measure, whether he
was guided by a moral aversion to slavery, or resentment over the
failure of President Polk to recognize his patronage claims, or a
desire to restore his prestige among his constituency which had been
impaired by his vote for the low tariff of 1846, are considerations
of minor importance, for almost certainly some other Northern
Congressman would have introduced a similar measure. On August
8, 1846, he attached a rider to an appropriation bill relating to the
Mexican War, providing that any territory acquired from Mexico
should be forever free from slavery. This bill passed the House of
Representatives repeatedly, but was always defeated in the Senate.
Lincoln declared that while he was a Whig representative in Congress he had voted for the Wilmot Proviso as many as forty times.

  This bill was to ardent Southerners the equivalent of waving a
red cape before a bull. It had tremendous influence in unifying a
South that previously had displayed a considerable variety of political opinions. The Whig party, which had a strong following in the
South, was riven by the Wilmot Proviso into antagonistic Northern and Southern wings. The Southern Whigs voted in a phalanx
against the Proviso, while the Northern Whigs supported it. The
Southern people felt outraged that in a war waged by a Southern
President, "Mr. Polk's War," fought largely by Southern generals
and Southern volunteers, the South was to be denied any of the

fruits of victory. The adoption of the Wilmot Proviso would prevent Southerners with their slaves from treading upon the soil purchased by common blood and treasure. Thus high-spirited Southerners felt that the Wilmot Proviso was an attempt to deny to them equality in the Union. It played into the hands of the fire eaters, or Southern extremists who desired to form a Southern Confederacy.

The outstanding fire eater of the South was William Lowndes Yancey of Alabama. This agitator, born in Georgia, had spent twelve of his most impressionable years in the North. His father was an able lawyer of Abbeville, South Carolina, a friend of John C. Calhoun, who died when Yancey was a child. His mother married a Yankee schoolmaster who took the family to Troy, New York, where he became a prominent minister and abolitionist. Young Yancey attended Williams College for three years and then returned to the South to practice law in the office of the strong Unionist, Benjamin F. Perry of Greenville, South Carolina. At the close of the nullification controversy he edited a strongly Unionist newspaper, the *Greenville Mountaineer*. When he was twenty-two years old he emigrated to the Black Belt of Alabama where he became a planter and editor at Wetumpka. The accidental poisoning of his slaves ended his career as a planter, and he returned to law.

Yancey was a strikingly handsome man, exceedingly proud, and his Northern exile had made him a more pronounced Southerner than his neighbors, even in the matter of dress. His manner was courteous, and the "habitual expression of good humor" on his face hardly comported with the fact that he had killed a man in self-defense and had fought a bloodless duel with the North Carolina Congressman, Thomas L. Clingman. He was the type of individual who scorned compromise. Despite his violent pro-slavery prejudices, he was a liberal in many respects, fighting for free public schools and for the right of married women to control their property, and advocating the white basis instead of the Federal ratio in the apportionment of representatives in the legislature.

The change of Yancey from an ardent Unionist to an equally zealous state rights advocate poses an intriguing question. The transition was made between 1836 and 1840 and seems to have been motivated by his violent resentment to the activities of the Northern abolitionists and to his belief that only by a strict interpretation of the Constitution could the South protect itself from a dangerous antislavery majority.[1] From 1844 to 1846 he was a Representative in Congress, but he resigned out of disgust at the selfishness of party politics and never afterwards did he hold a Federal office.

Yancey has been called "the orator of secession."[2] He spoke with absolute candor, in that blend of fire and musical cadence which never failed to enthrall Southern audiences. He made hundreds of speeches at barbecues and political rallies, not in the interest of his personal ambition, or for party success, but with an almost austere devotion to the cause of the South. In 1848 he drew up a set of resolutions which were adopted by the Alabama Democratic Convention, stating the extreme Southern demand not merely that slavery should be permitted to expand into the common territories of the United States but should be protected by Federal legislation. He sought to arouse the Southern people to realize the dangers to their way of life threatened by the Northern majority. If the Constitution and state rights could not give the South security within the Union, he favored secession and a separate Southern Republic. In the last decade of the ante-bellum period, he had no hope that justice would be granted to the South within the Union or that the Constitution would be faithfully observed by the North. For the purpose of agitation, therefore, he founded the League of United Southerners in 1858 and he was one of the organizers of Southern Rights Associations. To spread the blessings of slavery to poorer men in the South he agitated for the reopening of the African slave trade.

Robert Barnwell Rhett of South Carolina was another significant and masterful figure among the fire eaters. The owner of one hundred and ninety slaves, he belonged to the small privileged class of his native state. His deeply religious nature and his frustrations in his political career gave his life an undertone of sadness. He had no taste for the hedonistic ways of the cavalier; he was vice president of a Young Men's Temperance Society, secretary of the Charleston Port Society for the promotion of the Gospel among seamen; and he refused to fight duels on account of religious scruples. When he failed to attain his political ambitions, he found a haven of solace in his family, who knew that he was a great man. One common characteristic of the fire eaters was very pronounced in Rhett, an exaggerated sense of honor or pride. At the age of thirty-seven, he changed his name from the plebeian nomenclature of Smith to the aristocratic name of Rhett. In that year he began his political career in Congress.[3]

John C. Calhoun was Rhett's master and idol. Yet he differed from the great Carolinian whom he tried to make President, in that he had no love for the Union. One of the most fiery leaders of the nullification movement was this aristocratic South Carolinian, whose slogans were "Liberty" and "the spirit of '76!" Rhett never diluted his language but spoke out in bold and challenging words. The abolition movement enraged him. In 1838 he proposed that the Constitution be amended in order to protect the rights of the South in regard to slavery, or the Union should be peaceably dissolved. The South must act quickly, for by delay Virginia, Kentucky, and Maryland would gradually get rid of their slaves and become lukewarm in the defense of Southern rights. The Southern states should call a Southern Convention and threaten the North with a dissolution of the Union as the best fulcrum by which to obtain Southern rights in the Union.

Rhett treasured a bitter resentment against the North because he believed that the North exploited the South by means of the tariff, the merchant marine which carried Southern cotton, and the internal trade that furnished the South with manufactured articles. In 1844 he began an agitation at Bluffton, South Carolina, called the Bluffton Movement, to summon a state convention in order to resist the raising of the tariff. Calhoun opposed this radical action since it interfered with his ambitions for himself and for the Democratic party. The movement was regarded as a disunion project, but Rhett explained its purpose to be the reform of the Constitution and to prevent the rise of "a consolidated government." Rhett favored all measures to strengthen the South (especially the annexation of Texas.

When the Wilmot Proviso was being considered in Congress, he hoped that it would pass, because it would afford an occasion for the

South to secede. Henceforth, Rhett became an outright disunionist and the agitator for the formation of a Southern republic. He believed that this revolution was to be accomplished by the action of a single state—separate state secession. If South Carolina took the initiative, other Southern states would follow. Like Yancey, Rhett did not believe in compromise, but in forcing the issue between the North and the South. Over his mind hovered the alarming vision of the North growing steadily stronger and the South steadily weaker as the years went by. There was no hope for his native section in following bargaining politicians, nor in waiting until all the Southern states would cooperate to go out of the Union as a body. The South would never secede, he believed, if such a procedure should be followed.

In 1850 Rhett attained one of his ardent ambitions, election to the United States Senate. But the following year South Carolina rejected his leadership by accepting the Compromise of 1850. Then Rhett resigned, "sacrificed his ambition on the altar of liberty." From this time to the eve of the Civil War he was in political retirement. However, his brother, Edmund Rhett, who was in the South Carolina legislature, and his son Robert Barnwell Rhett, Jr., editor of the *Charleston Mercury*, carried on his influence as a Southern fire eater. In 1860 the triumph of the great fire eater came with the secession of South Carolina.

Besides the commanding figures of Rhett and Yancey, there were lesser fire eaters in each Southern state. In Louisiana James D. B. De Bow, a native of South Carolina, the prolific mother of Southern extremists throughout the South, exerted wide influence in developing Southern nationalism through his editorship of *De Bow's Review*, the most important commercial magazine in the South. Another Louisiana fire eater was Pierre Soulé, a native of France who had emigrated to Louisiana, and was elected to the United States Senate, where he became an ardent Southern and pro-slavery advocate. In Mississippi there was Governor John A. Quitman, born in the North, who became a supporter of filibusters in a movement to acquire slave territory. Jefferson Davis was a fire eater until the secession crisis of 1860. In Florida David Levy Yulee, a Senator of part Jewish ancestry, was an extreme champion of Southern interests. The fiery Senator Louis T. Wigfall carried the ultra pro-slavery doctrines of his native South Carolina to Texas. In South Carolina Senator James H. Hammond, the son of a New England school teacher, was a potent agitator for a Southern republic. In Georgia Henry L. Benning was the prophet of the necessity of the South to secede because the North would never let the South alone until her slaves were emancipated.

Virginia produced a brilliant group of extreme pro-slavery publicists, like Professor Beverley Tucker of William and Mary College, George Fitzhugh, author of the book *Cannibals All*, Roger A. Pryor, newspaper editor, and Edmund Ruffin. Ruffin was the most fanatical of the Virginia fire eaters. He had rendered a great service to the whole South in his earlier days by his agricultural reforms. But in the latter part of his life he became a crusader for Southern independence. He spread his doctrines at the Virginia springs, at political rallies, and at agricultural conventions. He developed such a virulent hate of the North that he wore home-spun suits rather than patronize Northern manufacturers. When the South was defeated in 1865 he committed suicide.

The fire eaters were not all of one mind. Some of them like Rhett and Ruffin longed for the independence of the South and hoped that the North would stir the Southern states to secede. Others like Jefferson Davis were secessionists in 1850 but conservative in 1860. They hoped that the North would yield to Southern demands for the protection and expansion of slavery. Some Southern leaders, like Robert Toombs, were opposed to the fire eaters through most of their careers, but became ardent secessionists in 1860, when they became convinced that there was no hope for the protection of Southern rights within the Union. Some of the most extreme fire eaters rejected the doctrines of Jefferson and boldly proclaimed their belief in aristocracy. Professor Beverley Tucker explained Virginia's reluctance to follow the lead of the fire eaters by writing to a fellow extremist in South Carolina, the novelist William Gilmore Simms, that Virginia was "sunk in the slough of democracy, which has no sense of honor." [4] Indeed, all the fire eaters had an exaggerated and unwholesome feeling for "Southern honor."

How shall we estimate the fire eaters in the development of South-

ern history? Were they responsible for the Southern decision to secede from the Union? Every society that is suffering from profound
discontents, from social and economic maladjustments, throws up
individuals who react more intensely to the situation than the majority of the people. Moderate Southerners felt that the fire eaters
were in the same category as the abolitionists in the North—both
groups fanatical and pernicious. It is possible that the fire eaters in
the South and the abolitionists in the North emotionalized sectional
controversies so greatly that they prevented the successful application of compromise and sanity to the issues that led to the Civil
War. One conclusion is certain, that the fire eaters could see only
one side of a question—the Southern point of view.

Various incidents occurred after the conclusion of the war with
Mexico to give the fire eaters splendid opportunities for agitation.
The most dangerous issue threatening the unity of the nation arose
over the status of slavery in the territory acquired from Mexico. The
North was determined to apply the Wilmot Proviso to this vast
new land, or "to monopolize" these common territories as Calhoun
phrased it. At the time Mexico ceded this land to the United States,
the Mexican municipal law forbade slavery in any part of the domain. The Carolina statesman maintained that the moment the United
States took possession of it, the Constitution, which recognized
slavery, applied to it. He deduced from this premise that Southerners had an equal right to immigrate into the common territories
with their slaves, a right which could not be canceled by Congress
or by a territorial legislature. Although Calhoun had vigorously opposed the Mexican War, he was determined that the South should
share equally in the spoils of victory.

This great sectional leader wished to arouse the Southern people
to the dangers of Northern aggression on their rights and to unite the
South to take a firm stand. Accordingly, early in 1849 he called a
meeting of the Southern Senators and Representatives in Washington. To them he presented his draft of an "Address of the Southern
Delegates in Congress to their Constituents," which stated the Southern grievances—violation of the Fugitive Slave Act, constant agitation against the South by abolition societies, the attempt to exclude
Southern slaveholders from the territory acquired by the Mexican

War. The address urged the Southern states to unite, disregarding party success and party ties, anxiety for which had formerly paralyzed their efforts for self-defense. He hoped to impress the North with the gravity of the crisis produced by the attempt to apply the Wilmot Proviso to the Western territory. The resolute stand of a united section, he declared, would cause the North to pause and calculate the consequences of goading the South to disunion. By this maneuver he hoped to save the Union, or if unsuccessful, to unify the South for secession. Unfortunately for his plans, the Southern Whigs refused to cooperate. They entered the Southern caucus to control it and crush any disunion movement. Not only did the Whigs but also some influential Southern Democrats like Howell Cobb of Georgia and President Polk oppose Calhoun's Southern movement as being a dangerous means of increasing sectionalism in the South. Consequently only forty-eight of the eighty-eight members of Congress who attended the Southern caucus signed Calhoun's address. Instead of revealing Southern unity to the North, therefore, it had the opposite effect.

Various solutions were now offered for the settlement of the question of slavery in the territories which threatened to disrupt the Union. President Polk favored extending the Missouri Compromise line of 36° 30′ to the Pacific Ocean. Senator John M. Clayton of Delaware proposed organizing the territories in the Mexican cession without Congressional action on the question of slavery, but leaving the decision to the territorial courts and eventually to the Supreme Court. The Calhoun solution was to allow slavery to exist in all territories of the United States, until the territory became a state, at which time a constitutional convention could decide on slavery or freedom. The Western point of view, represented by Lewis Cass of Michigan, advocated letting the people of the territory decide the question of slavery or freedom. This solution was called "squatter sovereignty," later "popular sovereignty." The adoption of the Wilmot Proviso was the solution of the antislavery Congressmen from the Northern states. But the Virginia legislature, which undoubtedly represented the opinion of the South, declared in a set of resolutions, that if the Wilmot Proviso should be adopted that state would not submit to it, even if it involved the last extremity of disunion.

In this explosive situation, Calhoun turned once more to his favorite idea of an all-Southern Convention. Realizing that if South Carolina issued the call for such a meeting, this fact would prejudice numerous Southerners against the convention, he persuaded some of his political friends in Mississippi to extend the invitation. Accordingly, a convention in Jackson summoned all Southern states to send delegates to Nashville on June 1, 1850, to a Southern Convention. Calhoun's instigation was carefully concealed, and the state of Mississippi was regarded as the originator of the Nashville Convention. The fire eaters hoped to use this convention to bring about a secession movement.

In the autumn of 1849 California, which had suddenly received a large accession of population as a result of the gold rush, applied for admission to the Union with a free state constitution. President Zachary Taylor had sent agents both to California and New Mexico urging the people of these areas to form constitutions and apply for admission as states. His plan was for California and New Mexico to skip the territorial stage of government and enter the Union as states. Thus he hoped to avoid the agitation over whether the land acquired from Mexico should be organized as free or slave *territories.* Although a large slaveholder, President Taylor was in favor of admitting California as a free state without any concessions or compensation to the South. Southern political leaders were alarmed over this prospect. Until 1850 there had been an equal number of slave states (15) and of free states (15) in the Union, thus maintaining a balance of power in the Senate. As long as this equilibrium was preserved, the South could prevent hostile legislation against slavery from being passed, but the admission of California as a free state would deprive this section of its veto. Furthermore, if the Wilmot Proviso should be applied to the rest of the Mexican cession, as the North demanded, there would be no hope for the South of ever improving its political position by the admission of a slave state. The South was deeply incensed over this attempt of the North to exclude Southerners from immigrating with their slaves into a region "purchased by common blood and common treasure," partly because of its declining strength in Congress.

On January 29, 1850, Henry Clay introduced into the Senate a series of resolutions that embodied a comprehensive compromise of the controversies between the North and South over slavery. At this time Clay was seventy-three years of age and for nearly eight years had been in retirement from political office. His return to the Senate in 1849 was motivated by a sincere love for the Union and a desire to prevent its dissolution. He appealed to both hostile sections to assuage their violent partisan feelings and accept a fair compromise. The debate over his compromise proposals brought forward the most distinguished leaders both of the old and of the new generation. Although these full-dress speeches may not have changed a single vote they educated the country on the issues of the day and gained time for compromise. The barrage of oratory on this occasion was really a debate between geographic sections.

John C. Calhoun delivered the ultimatum of the South. He, too, was an old gentleman with one foot in the grave, haggard, and disillusioned. He was too ill to speak on March 4, but Senator James M. Mason of Virginia read his written speech to the Senate while Calhoun sat in his chair with half-closed eyes. His passion to be President had now burned to ashes, and he thought only of the safety of the South, an unchanging South based on slavery. Calhoun warned the North that the bonds of union were snapping one by one, the psychological, emotional, and religious ties. The North was growing stronger every day by the exploitation of the South by tariffs and by a centralized government. He demanded that the North stop its agitation for the abolition of slavery, that the South be admitted to terms of equality in the territories by allowing Southerners to emigrate with their slaves, and that the equilibrium between the North and the South be preserved so that the rights of the South, a minority within the Union, could be protected from the Northern majority. He opposed the admission of California with its free state constitution and advocated constitutional amendments to guarantee Southern rights. Although his speech did not clearly specify the type of constitutional amendments he desired, his last political essay proposed two Presidents, like the consuls of Rome, one chosen from the free states and another from the slave states, each having a veto on Congressional legislation. A few weeks later Calhoun died, despairing of the Union and expressing the sentiment, "The great battle must be fought by you younger men . . . *there* indeed, is my only regret at going—the South—the poor South!" [5]

Senators William H. Seward of New York and Salmon P. Chase of Ohio spoke for the Northern antislavery men. In his speech Seward warned the South against trying to pass a more stringent fugitive slave law, for he said public opinion in the North would not support it. He opposed the expansion of slavery in the Western territories, maintaining that a higher law than the Constitution forbade it, namely, moral conscience. For his higher law doctrine he was condemned bitterly in the South. The advocates of the Wilmot Proviso had in mind not only to exclude slavery from the territory recently acquired from Mexico, but also to serve notice to the South that any further territorial acquisitions, Cuba, for instance, must be free.

Senator Stephen A. Douglas of Illinois represented the feeling of the West. Douglas did not believe that any of the semi-arid territories acquired from Mexico would ever support slavery and therefore abolition on paper would be useless. He was opposed, consequently, to antagonizing the Southern states by the attempt to apply the Wilmot Proviso to the territories. Douglas asserted the doctrine that slavery was a local question, not a national one, and that it depended on local legislation. He favored compromise and granting the South a more effective fugitive slave law. He restated the argument of Lewis Cass for the doctrine of squatter sovereignty.

On March 7, Senator Daniel Webster gave his famous speech advocating compromise. He alone among the prominent speakers did not represent the feeling of his section. Webster maintained that the territories in dispute were not suited to slavery and therefore human bondage would never expand into this region. "I would not take pains," he declared, "uselessly to reaffirm an ordinance of Nature, nor to re-enact the will of God." [6] He urged the North to stop agitating the slavery question, for it would destroy the Union. Thus he alienated the people of New England, especially by his willingness to accept a fugitive slave act. On account of his support of the compromise proposals a storm of abuse and vituperation broke over his head in New England. He was compared by his contemporaries to Benedict Arnold, and Whittier condemned him in his poem "Ichabod" as a statesman who had sacrificed his honor. Actually, he deliberately sacrificed his Presidential ambitions to save the Union.

President Zachary Taylor proved a bitter disappointment to Southerners who had hoped that he would support their sectional interests. His long service in the army had desectionalized him, and he came under the influence of the antislavery Senator Seward. As long as Taylor lived, he blocked the settlement of a compromise along the lines proposed by Clay, against whom he had developed a strong prejudice. When the Southern Whig statesmen, Alexander H. Stephens, Robert Toombs, and Thomas L. Clingman called on Taylor to ascertain his attitude toward the admission of California and the Wilmot Proviso, they found that he favored admission of California as a free state without any compensation to the South and that he would sign the Wilmot Proviso if it passed Congress. They threatened a withdrawal of their section from the Union if this obnoxious measure was forced on the South. Angered by this threat, the old general informed them that if the South resisted the Federal government, he would place himself at the head of an army to suppress rebellion and would hang secession leaders with as little compunction as he had hanged deserters and spies in Mexico.[7] Fortunately for the success of compromise, Taylor died early in July. Vice President Millard Fillmore, who succeeded to the Presidency, was sympathetic to Southern demands and facilitated the adoption of compromise measures.

A sectional truce, the Compromise of 1850, was drawn up, which provided for the admission of California with its free state constitution and the creation of two new territories, New Mexico and Utah, the thirty-seventh parallel being the dividing line between them. No mention of slavery was made in these territorial bills. Thus the principle of non-intervention by Congress in the slavery question within the territories was adopted, permitting the principle of popular sovereignty to operate. The slave trade, but not slavery itself, was abolished in the District of Columbia. A large area of land claimed by Texas was added to the territory of New Mexico, but Texas was compensated by the payment of $10,000,000. Finally, a drastic Fugitive Slave Law was enacted.

The Fugitive Slave Law was drafted by Senator James M. Mason of Virginia. It was the part of the Compromise which led to its undoing, for it offended the moral conscience of many Northern people. The fugitive slave law of 1793 had depended upon state authorities for its enforcement. The Supreme Court in *Prigg versus Pennsylvania* (1842) had decided that the Federal government could not compel a state to enforce Federal laws. The new fugitive slave law, therefore, created Federal commissioners to try fugitive slave cases by a summary process. The slave master, or the slave catcher employed by him, could arrest a Negro and take him before a commissioner and swear an affidavit that the captive belonged to him. If the commissioner decided in favor of the master his fee was $10, but only $5 if his verdict liberated the captive. The marshal, or other Federal officer, was given the authority to call on bystanders to act as a *posse comitatus* to aid in arresting a fugitive or to prevent a rescue by a mob. If a marshal allowed a slave to escape from his custody he was liable to the master for the full value of the slave. This law did not permit the fugitive to testify in his behalf or have a jury trial nor did it safeguard free Negroes from being kidnapped.

In the adoption of the settlement of 1850 the work of Stephen A. Douglas, Senator from the Northern border state of Illinois, was perhaps more decisive than the influence of Henry Clay. Clay insisted upon passing the compromise proposals in one great comprehensive bill, an "omnibus bill," but such a measure could not command a majority vote. Finally, the Compromise was enacted in separate laws during August and September under the leadership of Douglas while Clay was absent from Congress in Newport, Rhode Island. Furthermore, the solution of the slavery question in the territories was based on Douglas's proposals rather than on Clay's plan that the question of slavery be decided by the Mexican law prohibiting slavery.

Before the Compromise measures passed Congress the Southern Convention, summoned to protect the vital interests of the South, had assembled at Nashville, Tennessee. Only nine of the slave states sent delegates, and of the one hundred and seventy-five delegates, a hundred and two came from Tennessee. The Southern Whigs opposed the convention partly because they did not wish to injure the Taylor administration. The meetings were held in the largest church in the city, and the delegates were surrounded by Southern belles and matrons, "like borders of flowers." The delegates were inspired by the occasion and audience to unfurl their most elegant figures of speech, their most graceful gestures, and their richest tones of forensic eloquence; "at one moment, the audience would be startled with the thunders of rock-beating surges; and at another, soothed by the soft zephyrs of a summer sea." One of the most violent of the delegates, Professor Beverley Tucker of Virginia, imitated the vituperative style of John Randolph of Roanoke and was sometimes "forgetful that ladies were present." [8]

Despite the most vehement oratory, the convention had a lame conclusion. Although the delegates passed one resolution demanding that all the Federal territories be open to slavery, they consented, for the sake of preserving the Union, to accept the extension of the Missouri Compromise line of 36°30' to the Pacific, "as an extreme concession." The convention then adjourned until November, but the second session at that time was attended by only fifty-nine delegates, mostly radical secessionists, who passed resolutions urging an economic and social boycott of the North. In the meanwhile, the compromise measures had been adopted, which took the wind out of the sails of the fire eaters. The fiasco of this resistance movement revealed to the Southern nationalists the extreme difficulty of getting the Southern states to cooperate in the defense of Southern Rights, and from now on, fire eaters eschewed "cooperation" as a means of secession and advocated single state secession.

The Southern Movement of 1849–1851, initiated by Calhoun and the bantam-sized Henry S. Foote of Mississippi, was now followed by a reaction. The Whig leaders of the South started a Union movement which soon became non-partisan. The old labels of Whig and Democrat were temporarily laid aside, and campaigns were waged on the question of the acceptance of the Compromise of 1850 by the Union Party and the Southern Rights group. The first Southern state to make a decision on the acceptance of the Compromise measures was Georgia at the close of 1850. The Constitutional Union Party in Georgia was led by Toombs and Stephens, Whigs, and Howell Cobb, who had recently been elected the Democratic Speaker of the National House of Representatives. The Constitutional Union Party won control of the state convention by a large margin, but this body gave warning to the North that Georgia would secede if the Compromise were violated. The "Georgia Platform," adopted by the convention, listed a series of encroachments on Southern Rights which would justify the recourse to secession: abolition of slavery in the District of Columbia, suppression of the internal slave trade by an act of Congress, any law prohibiting the introduction of slaves into the territories of Utah or New Mexico, refusal to admit a slave state into the Union, and serious modification of the Fugitive Slave Law. Georgia's example of the acceptance of the Compromise was followed by the states of the upper South and by Louisiana and Alabama. In Alabama the contest over secession was fought between the Southern Rights group led by William L. Yancey and the Unionists led by the eloquent Whig Congressman, Henry W. Hilliard, who advocated adoption of the Compromise of 1850 as a finality. In the August elections of 1851 the Unionists elected a majority of the legislature and also of the delegation to Congress.

The only Southern states in which the fire eaters remained powerful were Mississippi and South Carolina, yet even in these states they were narrowly defeated by the Unionists in 1851 over the question of the acceptance of the Compromise. In Mississippi Governor Quitman tried to lead a disunion movement, but a state convention called by the legislature voted in favor of accepting the Compromise. In the gubernatorial election of 1851, both of Mississippi's Senators resigned to become candidates for governor, Jefferson Davis for the Southern Rights group, which contemplated secession, and Henry S. Foote for the Union party. Foote had been one of the originators of the Southern Movement, but as soon as the Compromise was adopted he changed his position to advocate its acceptance, thus securing the Whig vote. Jefferson Davis was defeated and retired from political life until recalled by Franklin Pierce to be his Secretary of War. In accepting the Compromise, the Mississippi Convention issued a solemn warning to the North in a resolution, "Resolved, that it is our deliberate opinion, that upon the faithful execution of the Fugitive Slave law, by the proper authorities, depends the preservation of our much-loved Union." [9]

In South Carolina, the Compromise of 1850 was not acceptable to the people, but they were unwilling to follow Robert Barnwell Rhett's leadership in seceding. Instead, the "co-operationists" under the leadership of Senator Andrew P. Butler, Robert W. Barnwell, and James L. Orr, controlled the state convention called to consider immediate secession. The cause of the Union was ably championed by Benjamin F. Perry, editor of *The Southern Patriot* of Greenville, and by the most prominent Whig leader in South Carolina, William C. Preston. The Tidewater parishes were for secession, but the up-country favored cooperation. The convention asserted the right of secession, but favored such a movement only in cooperation with other Southern states.

The Southern Movement and the Compromise of 1850 have been variously interpreted by American historians. Some modern historians have regarded the Southern Movement of 1849–1850 as mainly a bluff, using the threat of secession to secure concessions from the North. It worked, they point out, for the Compromise of 1850 prevented the application of the Wilmot Proviso or the abolition of slavery in the District of Columbia, objectives of the North. On the other hand, the North was the real gainer by the terms of the settlement. The admission of California as a free state destroyed the sectional balance of power in the Senate, depriving the South of its veto over legislation in Congress. The South won the dubious right to take slaves into the territories of New Mexico and Utah, subject to the final approval of the Supreme Court, but this was a hollow victory, for both sides admitted that this territory would never be settled by slaves on account of its climate and soil. The North secured the abolition of the slave trade in the District of Columbia, while the South was placated with the new Fugitive Slave Act, which was quickly scrapped in the Northern states. The greatest advantage derived by the North from the Compromise was that it checked a dangerous secession movement, and thus saved the Union for a decade, during which foreign immigration expanded the population of the North and railroads were built between the Eastern and the Ohio Valley states so that when secession did come in 1860 the Northwest joined the Union cause. The fire eaters were right: the Compromise of 1850 was a bad bargain for the slave interests of the South. It was only "a sectional truce" which permitted the Northern adversary to grow stronger.

The Compromise of 1850 was accepted generally in the North and the South as a great tranquillizing settlement of the differences which had divided the nation. The country was entering upon a cycle of economic prosperity, with cotton selling at 13 cents a pound and the business interests in the North expanding. The conservatives of both sections sighed with relief at the passage of the Compromise measures, which have rightly been called "the Business Man's Peace." The Compromise was regarded as "a final settlement" and it was hoped that slavery agitation would end.

Nevertheless, the Compromise was soon overthrown by the failure of the North to observe its terms, especially in regard to the enforcement of the Fugitive Slave Act. The leaders of the older generation who had a love for the Union had died or disappeared from public life, Calhoun and Zachary Taylor in 1850, Clay and Webster in 1852, and Thomas Hart Benton, who after thirty years of service in the Senate, was defeated for reelection in 1851. The leaders of the new generation were less restrained and more inclined to violent sectional courses. Furthermore, large numbers of Northern people had been converted by 1854 to a belief that the abolition of slavery was a high moral issue which concerned the nation as a whole.

After the passage of the drastic Fugitive Slave Act of 1850 many Northern states where antislavery feeling predominated passed Personal Liberty Acts, which made the recovery of fugitive slaves extremely difficult. These laws stipulated: a heavy penalty against kidnapping; extended the rights of jury trial and the writ of habeas corpus to fugitive slaves and free Negroes; denied the use of state and county jails to confine fugitive slaves; prohibited state officials or citizens from aiding in the arrest or return of fugitive slaves; required state attorneys to defend fugitive slaves at state expense; and in two states, Connecticut and Vermont, granted freedom to all slaves brought within the state. Some of these laws were clear violations of a federal act and constituted a real grievance of the South.

The Fugitive Slave Law proved almost impossible to enforce in the Northern states. Public sentiment in the North was inflamed against the return of fugitive slaves by the publication of *Uncle Tom's Cabin*. The Supreme Court of Wisconsin in the Booth Case (1854) declared the Fugitive Slave Act unconstitutional and re-leased Booth, a member of a mob which had rescued a fugitive slave from jail, from the legal consequences of his act. The Supreme Court of the United States, however, reversed this decision and lectured the Supreme Court of Wisconsin for thus nullifying a Federal law (*Ableman versus Booth*, 1859). Southerners who attempted to reclaim their slaves under the Fugitive Slave Act of 1850 found that it cost more in money and vexatious delays to bring back their fugitives from the North than the slaves were worth. The passage of the Kansas-Nebraska Act of 1854, which annulled the long-standing Missouri Compromise, stirred up so much bitter feeling in the North that the Fugitive Slave Act practically became a dead letter law after this event.

The opposition of public opinion to the enforcement of the act was dramatically revealed in the Anthony Burns Case of 1854. Burns, a slave who had escaped to Boston, was arrested by a United States marshal in order to return him to his master in Virginia. At first he refused to contest the case, for fear that he would be punished more severely when he was sent back to his master. While he was in jail, the city of Boston was inflamed by antislavery agitators and orators, such as Wendell Phillips and Theodore Parker, by posters, and by public meetings. An attempt to rescue him was made by a mob led by Thomas Wentworth Higginson, a prominent New England preacher. Finally, Burns was adjudged to his master by Federal Commissioner Loring. On the day when he was taken to the harbor for the return to Virginia, the street through which he and his escort marched was draped in black. He was placed in a hollow square of soldiers and police. The procession which guarded him included United States cavalry, a battalion of United States artillery, a large number of marines, and the marshal's posse of one hundred and twenty-five men. Twenty-two companies of Massachusetts militia as well as numerous city police formed a cordon to hold back a crowd of fifty thousand people. It cost the government at least $40,000 to send a trembling black slave back to his master.

The Democratic Party won the Presidential election of 1852 with a Northern candidate having Southern principles. Franklin Pierce was victorious over the Whig candidate, General Winfield Scott, a native of Virginia. Nominated by the Democratic Convention because he was known to be a strong opponent of abolitionism in his state of New Hampshire, Pierce was a "dark horse" candidate. When he assumed the executive office in 1853, he tried to carry out the Southern policies of expansion and of protection of slavery. One of his greatest services in this direction was the signing of the Kansas-Nebraska Bill of 1854. According to the distinguished historian, James Ford Rhodes, the Kansas-Nebraska Act was the most momentous bill passed by Congress between the founding of the republic and the outbreak of the Civil War.[10]

Prior to 1854 Southern Congressmen had vigorously opposed the creation of a Nebraska Territory, because it lay north of the Missouri Compromise line and therefore would be a free territory. On the other hand, the settlers in that region were eager to have it organized into a territorial government. The Wyandot Indians and the white immigrants of Nebraska had actually sent two delegates to Washington for that purpose. Moreover, ex-Senator Thomas Hart Benton of the neighboring state of Missouri had begun a campaign for reelection to the Senate on a platform calling for the organization of the Nebraska territory in order that a transcontinental railroad might be built through this region with its eastern terminal at St. Louis. Senator David R. Atchison, leader of the pro-slavery forces in Missouri, determined to defeat Benton by advocating the organization of the territory with the repeal of the Missouri Compromise line. Thus he would kill three birds with one stone, defeat his rival Benton, organize the territory so that a transcontinental railroad could be built to St. Louis, and open up the territory to slavery, thereby protecting Missouri's pro-slavery interests. Atchinson was a friend of Douglas and he put strong pressure on him to report a bill organizing this western territory with a clause repealing the Missouri Compromise restriction.

The question of building a railroad through this relatively unoccupied country was an important factor in promoting legislation relating to the Kansas-Nebraska territory. It was believed that only one railroad connecting the Pacific coast with the East would be built for a long span of time. Consequently, there was great rivalry between the cities of the Mississippi Valley to be chosen the eastern terminal of such a railroad. Government aid in the form of land grants was needed to finance this huge project, but the government survey of land and the establishment of a stable territorial government must precede such grants. The most dynamic railroad states-man in the Senate was Stephen A. Douglas who had secured Federal land grants for the Illinois Central Railroad and the Mobile and Ohio. Born in Vermont, Douglas had emigrated to Illinois as a young man to grow up with the country. Here he came to be known as the "Little Giant," with his big head, powerful shoulders, but unusually short legs. In this western state he had become wealthy, had married a Southern heiress who inherited a slave plantation, and had made large real estate investments in Chicago and Superior City, Minnesota. Consequently, he was an ardent advocate of railroads to the Pacific both along the northern and central routes assisted by government land grants.

Douglas held a strategic position as chairman of the Senate Committee on Territories. To his committee was reported in December, 1853, a bill for organizing the Nebraska Territory which Senator Augustus C. Dodge of Iowa had introduced. In the following January Douglas brought forward a bill for the creation of a single territory of Nebraska. In his report on this measure he said that the Compromise of 1850 had introduced the principle of non-intervention by Congress in determining the status of slavery within the territories, or in other words leaving the question of whether a territory should exclude slavery to the inhabitants. Senator Archibald Dixon of Kentucky proposed an amendment to the bill definitely repealing the slavery restriction clause of the Missouri Compromise. Douglas finally accepted this amendment to gain Southern votes for the passage of his territorial bill. Furthermore, his amended bill also provided for the creation of two territories out of the vast region to the west of Iowa and Missouri, Kansas and Nebraska. The division of the territory was not for the design of permitting a new slave state to be created, but such a division was desired by the people of this region and was expedient in obtaining votes in Congress for the bill. The act as finally passed declared that when the two territories

applied for admission as states they should enter the Union with or
without slavery according to their constitutions. This momentous
bill was passed after Douglas had secured the support of President
Pierce during a visit to the latter in company with Jefferson Davis
on a Sunday when Pierce's scruples against doing worldly work on
the Sabbath had to be overcome. Pierce used his patronage to force
the bill through Congress.

The Southern Congressmen, regardless of party, voted almost
solidly for the Kansas-Nebraska Act. The Whig Senator, Robert
Toombs of Georgia, declared that the repeal of the Missouri Compromise restriction restored to the South "the principle unwisely
surrendered in 1820." [11] Southerners maintained that the Missouri
Compromise had already been violated by admitting California as a
free state when a large portion of its territory lay below the line
of 36° 30′. Only a few Southern members of Congress, Senators Sam
Houston and John Bell, and nine Representatives, all but one from
the Upper South, dared to vote against the bill. Bell believed that
the enactment of this bill would not lead to the advance of slavery
into this region which was unsuited to it, but instead would reopen
a violent agitation of the slavery question. Theodore G. Hunt, a
Whig Congressman from Louisiana, made a noble speech against the
Kansas-Nebraska bill, observing that the South would gain only a
point of honor but no practical advantage from the bill, which
would gravely impair fraternal relations between the North and the
South.[12]

The effects of the Kansas-Nebraska Bill were the opposite from
what Douglas had anticipated. Contrary to the hopes of its sponsors,
the bill did not result in the passage of a Pacific railroad act, because
sectional rivalry prevented it until Southern Congressmen were removed by the secession movement. Instead of settling the irritating
controversy over slavery in the territories by the establishment of the
principle of popular sovereignty, the Kansas-Nebraska Bill revived
more intensely the wrangling over slavery. Although the Missouri
Compromise was simply a law of Congress and could have been
repealed by a subsequent Congress at any time, the North had come
to regard it as a sacred compact. Its annulment aroused the antislavery men in the North to found the Republican Party, whose main

program was to secure the repeal of the Kansas-Nebraska Act. This bill also shattered the Whig Party which had been a great brake against the momentum of sectionalism in politics. Finally the doctrine of popular sovereignty which it embodied proved unworkable and provoked civil war in Kansas.

The Kansas-Nebraska Bill not only led directly to the formation of the Republican Party, but also to the growth of the Know Nothing movement into a national party. The Know Nothings arose out of the Order of the Star Spangled Banner founded in New York City in 1849 to oppose the influence of Catholics and foreign immigrants in politics. The society was pledged to secrecy, and its members invariably replied "I Know Nothing," when questioned concerning their organization, hence the term "Know Nothings." Their platform advocated that an immigrant must have resided twenty-one years in the United States before he could be naturalized, that only native-born Americans and non-Catholics should hold office, and that foreigners should be discriminated against in land legislation. In 1854 the party won Massachusetts, electing a majority of the legislature and the governor, and sending Henry Wilson, an antislavery man, to the United States Senate. Flushed with success in New England and the border states, the party invaded the South during the next year, appealing particularly to the conservative Whigs.

The Know Nothing Party was strongest in the South in the border states. In Maryland the party controlled the city of Baltimore, the center of the Catholic Church in America, from 1855 to 1860. Know Nothing mobs, called "Rip Raps," "Plug Uglies," and "Bloody Tubs," who used awls to mutilate their opponents, terrorized the Democratic voters and drove many of them away from the polls. In 1855 the Maryland legislature was captured by the Know Nothings. The party was also strong in Kentucky where George D. Prentice, editor of the *Louisville Journal*, Garrett Davis, and Robert J. Breckinridge waged a bitter anti-Catholic campaign. In the August, 1855, election mobs in Louisville killed Catholics and foreigners, but the Know Nothings won the state. In Missouri Edward Bates, candidate for the Republican nomination for President in 1860, was a prominent leader. The party was more antiforeign than anti-Catholic in the Southern states, which explains why some Creole Catholics, such as the historian Charles Gayarré, joined it.

The Know Nothings received a severe check in Virginia, however, when their candidate for governor, Thomas A. Flournoy, was defeated by the eloquent Henry A. Wise. Wise condemned the party for its secrecy, its intolerance toward Catholics, and its alliance with the abolition cause. He made a strenuous campaign, concentrating on the western part of the state where he had a large following as a result of his advocacy of the white basis of representation in the Constitutional Convention of 1850. After this reverse, and a defeat in Tennessee by the Democratic candidate for governor, Andrew Johnson, the Know Nothings could make little headway below the Potomac in winning state elections.

The growth of the Know Nothings into a national political organization, the American Party, was accelerated by the break-up of the Whig Party. This great party had followers both north and south of the Mason and Dixon line, and was one of the elastic bands holding the Union together. But the Whigs began to decline after the Compromise of 1850 and the Kansas-Nebraska Act gave their organization a fatal blow. Many of the Whigs in the North entered the Republican ranks, but in the South they either joined the Democratic Party, like Robert Toombs and Alexander H. Stephens, or became Americans, like John Bell. The American Party's ritual contained an oath to preserve the Union. Southerners who wished to find a safer issue than the slavery question turned to this party which sought to divert attention to the nativistic issue. In 1856 the American Party, which by this time had become largely a Southern party, nominated Millard Fillmore for President, but he polled less than half the popular vote given to the Democratic candidate and carried the electoral vote of only one state, Maryland.

The election of 1856 revealed how deeply sectionalism had cut across the political life of the nation. The Democrats in their convention at Cincinnati nominated James Buchanan of Pennsylvania, who had been out of the country as Minister to England during the exciting contest over the Kansas-Nebraska Bill. He was a "dough face," whose record on slavery was without a blemish in Southern eyes. Southern politicians, Senators John Slidell and Judah P. Benjamin of Louisiana, Governor Henry A. Wise of Virginia, Senator James A. Bayard of Delaware, and the Indiana "dough face," Senator Jesse D. Bright, were responsible for his nomination over Pierce and Stephen A. Douglas. Buchanan accepted the Kansas-Nebraska Act and announced his ambition to add Cuba to the territory of the United States. The Democratic platform adopted at Cincinnati was regarded as "a Douglas platform," advocating the doctrine of nonintervention by Congress in the question of slavery within the territories.

The Republicans in convention at Philadelphia passed over the able leaders of the party, Salmon P. Chase, Justice John McLean, and William H. Seward, and selected a candidate of availability, John C. Fremont. Fremont had been born in a Southern state, but he had spent most of his life in the West and he was popularly known as "the Pathfinder" because of his explorations along the Oregon Trail. The chief planks in the Republican platform were the repeal of the Kansas-Nebraska Act and opposition to the extension of slavery into the territories. It had the support of the intelligentsia of the North, the preachers, college professors, and many of the editors, notably Horace Greeley of the *New York Tribune*.

The campaign was one of the bitterest in American history. The Republicans were called "Black Republicans" in the South because of their stand on the slavery question. The Southerners freely threatened that they would secede from the Union if the "Black Republican" candidate was chosen.[13] The crucial state in this contest was Pennsylvania where the slogan "The Union is in danger" plus a liberal use of money probably carried the state for Buchanan. The Republicans appealed to the working men of the North to fight against the aggression of the aristocratic slave power, and they used as propaganda the violent struggle in Kansas between the proslavery and free state groups, "Bleeding Kansas." Although Buchanan won, he did not receive a majority of the popular vote. Moreover, the Republican Party, which drew all of its votes from north of the Mason and Dixon line, polled such a surprising vote that it was an ominous sign for the future of the pro-slavery interests. Buchanan appointed four Southerners and three Northerners to cabinet positions, and his administration continued the ascendancy of the South in the operation of the Federal government.

A weak point in the popular sovereignty formula was the ambiguity of the time at which the decision for slavery or free soil should be made. Should the first territorial legislature make this momentous decision? Senator Douglas thought so, but Southerners dissented from this view. Governor Henry A. Wise rightly declared that the adoption of this view of popular sovereignty meant the virtual exclusion of the South from those territories to which it was applied, for no Southerner would risk the loss of his slaves by taking them into such a dubious situation. The Southerners maintained that the decision of slavery or freedom could be made only by a constitutional convention that applied for the admission of the state to the Union. The outcome of the Kansas-Nebraska bill proved the impracticability of the popular sovereignty doctrine when applied in a violent partisan atmosphere. The normal course of western pioneering and settlement was not permitted to take place. The Kansas question became involved in the fiery furnace of politics. On the one hand the Kansas imbroglio was used to promote the Republican Party and on the other side to save Missouri from the danger of abolition neighbors.

Shortly after the Kansas-Nebraska Act was passed, a movement arose in New England to stimulate the emigration of free-state settlers to make Kansas a free territory. It was recognized that Nebraska, on account of climate and soil, would inevitably be a free state, but there was a question about Kansas. In April, 1854, the New England Emigrant Aid Company was chartered to assist free-state settlers to go to Kansas. Eli Thayer of Worcester, Massachusetts, was the organizer, and some New England capitalists, such as the textile manufacturer, Amos Lawrence, supported this adventure. The organization was to build roads, schools, and churches and to create little New England abolition centers and to make profits. It secured cheap railroad fares and advertised the fertility and salubrity of Kansas, spending $250,000 with no return on its investment. It founded the village of Lawrence, but did not persuade many New Englanders to settle in Kansas. Only 1,240 settlers were assisted the first year, and according to the census of nativity in

1860, the territory had only 4,208 persons of New England birth. The great majority of settlers in Kansas were from the Middle States and the Northwest.

This attempt on the part of New England to decide the question of slavery in the territory by artificially stimulated emigration seemed unfair to the South and explains partly the bloody struggle that followed. Efforts were made by Southern communities to retaliate in kind, especially the expedition of Colonel Jefferson Buford of Alabama into the debatable land. However, the North had decided advantages over the South in any contest over settling Kansas, such as an easy river route down the Ohio and Mississippi, a surplus population, and more capital. Furthermore, the South was handicapped by the great risk of taking slaves into a debatable territory, where they would be enticed to flee by abolitionists. Of the 107,000 people living in Kansas in 1860, only 27,440 had been born in slaveholding states. This region was not suited to the staple crops that made slavery profitable, in other words, it was outside the natural limits of slavery expansion. After all the hullabaloo concerning the spread of slavery, Kansas had only two slaves in 1860.

In the Kansas imbroglio, partisan politics and land speculation played a significant role. The pro-slavery element of Missouri, led by Senator David R. Atchinson and Benjamin F. Stringfellow, regarded Kansas as a natural sphere of influence, the expansion of which the New England element was trying to rob them. Accordingly, in the first election for the territorial legislature, March, 1855, three thousand Missourians, called "Border Ruffians" by Horace Greeley, crossed the boundary line and voted. A pro-slavery legislature was elected, which adopted the slave code of Missouri for Kansas Territory and, in addition, limited officeholding to pro-slavery men and made it a crime to deny that slavery existed legally in the territory. Had there been no illegal voting on either side, the pro-slavery group would none the less have carried this election. The illegal voting of the Missourians was a serious blunder, injuring the Southern cause.

As a result of the struggle between the pro- and antislavery factions two rival governments were set up in Kansas. The capital of the pro-slavery group was located at Lecompton, near the Missouri border. The free-state people held a constitutional convention at Topeka in October, 1855, elected Dr. Charles Robinson as governor, and applied for admission to the Union as a free state. There followed a reign of violence and disorder, partly because of the slavery question, but also on account of the struggle over land claims, the location of town sites, and the salaries and remuneration of office-holding. During this period of violence the free-state town of Lawrence was sacked (May, 1856), its hotel and printing press destroyed, and the home of "Governor" Robinson burned. This outrage was perpetrated by Sheriff S. J. Jones and a posse of seven hundred and fifty men, many of them from Missouri, who were trying to serve warrants on some of the free-state partisans.

Shortly after this event John Brown, who had emigrated to Kansas in a one-horse wagon filled with guns and ammunition, set forth with a little army, consisting chiefly of his four sons, to avenge the death of free-state men. He figured that five antislavery men had been martyred, and that he would exact vengeance in Hebraic fashion, "an eye for an eye, a tooth for a tooth." In the dead of night, May 25, 1856, his band murdered five pro-slavery men on Pottawatomie Creek. Definite proof that Brown committed this crime did not come until after he was hailed as a hero in the North and his body was mouldering in the grave. Nevertheless, he was strongly suspected of the crime, and he and his partisans were attacked by some pro-slavery men in the "battle" of Osawatomie, in which Brown's son, Frederick, was killed. During the Kansas conflict at least two hundred persons were killed and property damage of two million dollars resulted. Prominent antislavery preachers of the North, such as Henry Ward Beecher, pastor of Plymouth Church, Brooklyn, raised money to provide free-soil emigrants to Kansas with Sharp's Rifles, dubbed "Beecher's Bibles."

The Kansas question was making new votes for the youthful Republican Party every day. The Republican Senator, Charles Sumner, used it for his terrible indictment of the South in his speech in the Senate of May 19, 1856, entitled "The Crime against Kansas." Sumner was a Harvard man, who prided himself upon his culture, his classic language, and his New England breeding. Yet this speech, although couched in elegant language, was a disgraceful exhibition.

In it he arraigned Southern civilization and brutally attacked the white-haired Senator from South Carolina, Andrew Pickens Butler. He had the bad taste to refer to an unfortunate habit of the old Carolinian Senator of expectorating while he spoke. Butler's relative, Congressman Preston Brooks, determined to punish this insult. He approached Sumner in the Senate chamber while the latter was working at his desk and beat him over the head with a gutta-percha cane. Sumner was a powerful man, six feet in height, and in struggling to rise from his desk, he tore it from its moorings on the floor. Brooks's attack was undoubtedly a mistake, and probably was not approved by the majority of Southerners. In South Carolina, however, he was a hero, and when he resigned from his seat in Congress he was triumphantly reelected. Many canes were sent to him by his Southern admirers, but in the North he was called "Bully" Brooks. Charles Sumner was so injured that he did not resume his place in the Senate for three years. His seat was kept vacant by Massachusetts during this period, a mute but eloquent reminder of "the barbarity" of slaveholders. Southerners maintained that his wounds were light and that he was only shamming, to which they adduced some suspicious circumstances. To "Bleeding Kansas" the Republicans added the slogan, "Bleeding Sumner."

The Democrats were anxious to settle the Kansas affair as quickly as possible, because the Republicans were making political capital out of it. Senator Robert Toombs of Georgia and Senator Douglas introduced bills to have an impartial vote taken for delegates to a constitutional convention, but these measures were defeated by the Republican-dominated House of Representatives, who wished to use "Bleeding Kansas" for propaganda purposes. Shortly after his inauguration, Buchanan appointed as territorial governor Robert J. Walker of Mississippi, who tried to secure a fair vote on the question of slavery. But both the free-soil men and the pro-slavery group were so bitterly partisan and lawless that he failed in this endeavor. Before he arrived an election had been held to choose delegates to a constitutional convention to meet in September, 1857, at Lecompton. The free-state people had refused to vote so that the delegates chosen were ardently pro-slavery. Under the leadership of John Calhoun, the surveyor general of the territory, they drew up the notorious

Lecompton constitution. This document was submitted to the people for ratification in a very unfair manner. The people of Kansas were given the alternative of voting for the Lecompton constitution with a provision for slavery or for the document without slavery, i.e., no further admission of slaves. In either case they would have to accept the Lecompton constitution, which contained a clause guaranteeing the slave property already in Kansas. This pro-slavery constitution was finally ratified by a vote of 6,143 to 569, the free-soil people abstaining from voting. But in October, as a result of a new election characterized by frauds, a territorial legislature was chosen which was dominated by free-soilers, who ordered the whole constitution submitted to a vote of the people. In this referendum of January 4, 1858, the pro-slavery group refused to vote, with the result that the Lecompton constitution was defeated by a vote of 10,226 to 162.[14]

Nevertheless, President Buchanan was determined to force the pro-slavery Lecompton constitution through Congress. His course was bitterly opposed by two prominent members of his own party, Senator Stephen A. Douglas and Governor Henry A. Wise of Virginia. Douglas had a genuine belief in popular sovereignty, but both he and Wise were resentful over the President's distribution of the patronage. Robert J. Walker and Douglas tried to persuade Buchanan to abandon his unwise Lecompton policy, to no avail, for he had committed himself to extreme pro-Southern politicians who were resolved to make Kansas a slave state. Accordingly, the Democratic party was seriously split into two factions over this issue. A fair compromise was presented to Congress by William H. English of Indiana (largely drafted by Alexander H. Stephens), providing for the submission of the entire Lecompton constitution to the people of the territory. If they accepted this document Kansas would receive a donation of Federal lands within the state identical with the grant made to Minnesota, but if the voters rejected the constitution the territory would have to wait for statehood until its population equaled the number required for a Congressional district (93,560). Republican propaganda unfairly branded this proposal as a bribe to the people of Kansas to accept a pro-slavery constitution, an interpretation which has been followed by older historians. Douglas, motivated apparently by personal political considerations, wavered on the question of voting for the English bill, but finally decided against it. Nevertheless, Buchanan won a dubious victory when he secured the passage of this bill in 1858, but the Democratic Party was disrupted. Kansas remained a territory until January, 1861, when the resignation of Southern Congressmen enabled it to be admitted as a free state.

Two days after Buchanan was inaugurated, on March 6, 1857, the Supreme Court rendered a decision on slavery in the case of *Dred Scott versus Sanford* that was a great technical victory for the South. Dred Scott was the slave of an army surgeon who took him into the free state of Illinois and then into the unorganized territory of Wisconsin and after some years of residence there brought him back to Missouri. Dred brought suit in a Missouri court for his freedom on the contention that he was liberated by residing in free territory. He won a favorable verdict but the case was appealed to the Supreme Court of the state, which in 1852 reversed the decision of the lower court, holding that Dred by returning to Missouri had reverted to his former status of a slave. The widow of the army surgeon transferred the ownership of the slave to her brother John F. A. Sanford of New York, and Dred now appealed to the Federal courts for his freedom, alleging that he was a citizen of Missouri bringing suit against a citizen of New York. The case finally was argued before the Supreme Court of the United States with Montgomery Blair of Maryland as the leading counsel for Dred Scott.

The first question for the court to decide was whether it had jurisdiction over the case. If Dred Scott was not a citizen of Missouri but a slave, he was not entitled to sue in the Supreme Court. The Missouri Supreme Court, which was the proper authority to determine Dred Scott's status, had decided that he was not a citizen of that state. It would have been logical for the Supreme Court to accept this ruling and refuse to grant the plea of Scott with a statement of lack of jurisdiction. Such a course of action would have been in line with a previous ruling in the case of *Strader versus Graham* (1851) involving some Kentucky slaves who crossed into Ohio where they entertained as minstrels and returned to their native state, later suing for freedom. The court had held that the status of slaves who resided temporarily in a free state and returned to their original home was governed by the laws of the state to which they returned.

The majority of the Court had decided to follow the precedent in the *Strader versus Graham* case and rule that Dred Scott was not a citizen of Missouri and therefore the Court had no jurisdiction over the case. Justice Nelson had been assigned the task of writing an opinion to that effect. But the majority learned that two members of the Court, Justice McLean of Ohio and Justice Curtis of Massachusetts, planned to write dissenting opinions in which they would uphold the constitutionality of the Missouri Compromise. Five of the justices came from slave states, and they were much disturbed by this news. McLean was an ambitious man eager to become the Republican candidate for President, while Curtis had been severely criticized in his native state for his vote sustaining the constitutionality of the Fugitive Slave Act, and he may have wished to regain his popularity in the North. Justice James M. Wayne of Georgia was influential in persuading the majority of the Court to reply to McLean and Curtis in an opinion declaring the Missouri Compromise unconstitutional. Justice Grier of Pennsylvania informed President-elect Buchanan of this change of plans by which a majority opinion would declare the Missouri Compromise unconstitutional. Buchanan accordingly in his inaugural address announced that the Supreme Court would shortly render an important decision in the Dred Scott case and that it was the duty of all good citizens cheerfully to accept such a decision.

Chief Justice Taney, nearly eighty years of age, wrote the opinion of the Court, but its force was greatly weakened by the fact that the six concurring judges also wrote opinions reaching the same conclusion by several different processes of reasoning. Taney held that Dred Scott was not a citizen of Missouri and had no right to sue in a Federal Court. It would have been wisdom for Taney to have stopped at this point and to have dismissed the case for lack of jurisdiction. But he proceeded to discuss the broader question of whether Negroes could be citizens of the United States. He declared that Negroes had never been citizens of the United States, that the Constitution was made exclusively for the white people, and that the Negroes had no rights under the Constitution. Furthermore, he declared that slaves were recognized as property by the Constitution and that neither Congress nor a territorial legislature had any right to interfere with a master carrying his slave property into the common territories of the United States. Then came his momentous decision that the Missouri Compromise line of 1820 had always been unconstitutional and therefore null and void.

The announcement of the decision aroused a storm of wrath among the Republicans and antislavery men in the North. The ruling of the Court denied the main plank in the Republican platform which advocated the exclusion of slavery from the territories of the United States by act of Congress. It also made the doctrine of popular sovereignty held by Douglas and the Northern Democrats untenable. The Republicans found in the dissenting opinion of Justice Curtis a statement that Taney's opinions on the unconstitutionality of the Missouri Compromise and the incapacity of Negroes to hold Federal citizenship were *obiter dicta*, or opinions outside of the legitimate limits of the case, and therefore not binding. Accordingly, the Republicans took the position that such unwarranted decisions should not be obeyed and that the personnel of the Court should be changed so as to reverse the Dred Scott decision. Actually, Taney's opinions were not *obiter dicta* any more than many of John Marshall's opinions or the opinions of later judges.

But the Republicans and antislavery men launched a campaign to undermine the authority of the court and bring it into disrepute. Taney's unfortunate statement that at the time the Constitution was drawn up the "Negroes had no rights which the white man was bound to respect" was torn from its context and the venerable judge was misrepresented as expressing this sentiment as his own opinion. The *New York Tribune* declared that the decision was "entitled to just so much moral weight as would be the judgment of a majority of those congregated in any Washington bar-room." [15] Instead of the Dred Scott case settling forever the vexing question of the status of slavery in the territories and removing that sore problem from discussion in Congress it immensely stimulated sectional wrangling and bitterness. The South felt that the North had first nullified the Fugitive Slave Act and now it refused to accept a decision of the Supreme Court which went counter to the antislavery cause.

"HAMPTON" ON THE SANTEE RIVER IN COASTAL SOUTH CAROLINA

Built in 1730; the portico was added in 1791. This rice plantation was owned by the Huguenot Horrys and by the Rutledges.

"WOODLAWN," LOUISIANA

An estate of 1,500 acres and 300 slaves in Louisiana, owned by the mighty Pughs, who had emigrated from North Carolina. Built in 1840, this manor house is an illustration of the legendary South, equipped with such luxuries as a marble bathtub resembling a Roman sarcophagus and a speaking tube to summon servants.

JOHN C. BRECKINRIDGE, PRESIDENTIAL CANDIDATE
OF THE COTTON SOUTH IN 1860

The author's candidate for the most suitable president of the
Confederacy. A portrait in the Filson Club,
Louisville, Kentucky.

To the growing estrangement of the North and South John Brown
gave a mighty impulse by his raid on Harpers Ferry. This Connecticut Yankee had spent most of his life (he was born in 1800)
in a shiftless change from one job to another, such as the trade of a
tanner, farming, and selling wool. He had failed in everything except in producing a bumper crop of twenty children. Deeply religious, although more in the spirit of the Old Testament than in
the gentle spirit of Christ, he was an advocate of the doctrine of
violence—direct action in the antislavery crusade rather than the
use of methods of persuasion and constitutional change. Slavery was
so dark a sin, he believed, that it should be wiped out by the blood
of the masters. By brooding over this crime of Southern slaveholders,
he became a monomaniac on the subject. Indeed, there was a great
mental instability in Brown's family—his grandmother, his mother,
an aunt, and five cousins had been insane. With his long white beard,
stately form, and intensity of gaze, John Brown looked as though
he were a patriarch of Biblical times.

After his escapade in Kansas and his activities in Missouri of
rescuing slaves and taking them to Canada, Brown conceived of a
far more ambitious project of striking a blow at slavery. In 1858 he
drew up a constitution for a Negro republic to be founded in the
mountains of Virginia, which was adopted by a convention of
Negroes and whites at Chatham, Canada. The proposed Negro
state should engage in guerrilla warfare against the white slaveholders
and start a vast slave insurrection over the South. A Negro was
chosen as President of the black Utopia, and Brown was elected
Secretary of War. Oswald Garrison Villard, a distinguished biographer of Brown, says that this project was so fantastic that it is a
serious indictment of his sanity.[16] Yet Brown was so persuasive that
he succeeded in getting the financial support of Gerrit Smith of
Peterboro, New York, a millionaire abolitionist, and of New England
business men and ministers, although he did not reveal to them the
full extent of his plans.

Brown rented a farm on the Maryland side of the Potomac River
near Harpers Ferry, Virginia, where he gathered his little army of
sons, free Negroes, and desperate white abolitionists, twenty-one in
number. On October 16 he marched with his followers against the

Federal Arsenal at Harpers Ferry. This act of attacking an agency
of the Federal government seems crazy, but Brown, who had a keen
sense of the dramatic, planned thus to attract world-wide attention
to his cause as well as gain ammunition and supplies. Brown's invasion was based on the theory that the slaves would rise in insurrection and join his little army. In fact he had a thousand iron pike heads
made by a blacksmith to distribute to the slaves for arms against
their masters—pike heads to be used in an age of guns and cannon.
The arsenal at Harpers Ferry was easily captured, and Brown sent
out a detachment into the countryside to arouse the slaves and to
capture Colonel Lewis Washington, a planter related to George
Washington who owned the sword that Frederick the Great had
presented to Washington. John Brown girded himself with this
historic sword as he stood a siege and an attack in the fire engine
house of the arsenal grounds by United States marines under Colonel
Robert E. Lee. Lee sent Captain "Jeb" Stuart, later to become the
famous cavalry leader of the Confederacy, to demand that Brown
and his followers surrender. When this demand was refused, a small
attacking party led by Lieutenant Israel Green battered down the
door of the arsenal and Green wounded Brown with his sword. This
officer wore only a light dress sword which broke in his hands as he
struck the fanatical leader and consequently Brown survived to become a martyr.

Brown could have been tried for treason by the Federal courts
since he had attacked a United States arsenal. Nevertheless, because
he had also invaded the soil of the sovereign state of Virginia, he was
turned over to the Virginia authorities for trial. Governor Wise
visited him in jail in Charlestown, Virginia, and concluded that he
was sane. It would have been much wiser if the governor had followed his original impulse and had ordered the fanatical leader to be
examined by the superintendent of the State Insane Hospital and
had committed him to this institution. He decided, however, that
Brown was sane and should be tried for his life. The fanatical leader
was assigned counsel and was given a fair trial which resulted in his
condemnation to death. In the meanwhile, the people of Virginia
were deeply excited over this invasion, and Governor Wise, according to his enemies, magnified the danger of a rescue by Northern

abolitionists in order to militarize the state. When Brown was hanged on December 2, more than fifteen hundred troops surrounded the gallows, including cadets of the Virginia Military Institute, among whom was enrolled for the occasion the venerable fire eater, Edmund Ruffin. While he was in prison he wrote noble letters to relatives and friends, and displayed a heroic attitude toward death, making him a martyr in the eyes of the North.

None the less, John Brown's violent act did tremendous damage to a peaceful and rational settlement of the slavery question. The sympathy shown for Brown in the North after his capture led to the belief that Northerners hated the South. It was revealed that money to finance the hare-brained attempt of Brown was furnished by Northern abolitionists and business men. The South blamed the Republican Party for this outrage, but conservative members of that party like Abraham Lincoln condemned John Brown. The great New England literary leader, Ralph Waldo Emerson, however, declared that John Brown had made the gallows as glorious as the Cross. In the South a wave of mob violence against suspected Northerners followed the John Brown invasion. This episode of violence, which should have been interpreted as the misguided act of a fanatic, was an important factor in destroying the fraternal feelings and bonds of sentiment that held the Union together.

The state of bitter feelings which formed a prelude to the Civil War was revealed in the Speakership contest in the House of Representatives, 1859-1860. The voting was held in an atmosphere surcharged with passion, for John Brown had recently been hanged. The Republicans offered as their candidate for Speaker John Sherman of Ohio. Although they were the largest group in the House of Representatives, 119 members, they could not command a majority, for there were 88 administration Democrats, 13 anti-Lecompton Democrats, and 27 Americans or Know Nothings. Sherman could not be elected Speaker largely because he had been one of the fifty leading Republicans who had endorsed Hinton Rowan Helper's *Impending Crisis*, which had been published in 1858 as a campaign document by Horace Greeley. The debates were violent and unworthy of Congress. A pistol dropped to the floor from the pocket of one vehement member, and many representatives were reported to be armed with pistols. For two months the nation's legislative business was suspended while the House of Representatives continued in a deadlock over the selection of a presiding officer. Finally on February 1, 1860, William Pennington of New Jersey, a conservative Republican, was chosen. This struggle over the election of the Speaker foreboded a physical conflict between the two sections of the nation.

The period from 1820 to 1861 was characterized, politically, by the sectionalization of the nation. The lineaments of this sectionalism are traceable in colonial days and in the debates over the adoption of the Federal Constitution. After the Missouri controversy of 1818–1820 and the rise of the abolitionists, the growth of sectionalism, both in the South and North, became virulent. Since well-developed sections are, in reality, incipient nations, the luxuriant development of sectionalism within the United States presents a case history of the forces that make nations. These forces were not merely political, but were based on diverging ways of life, a different set of values, and different views of morals, particularly a conflicting view of slavery.

Citations

1. A. L. VENABLE, "William L. Yancey's Transition from Unionism to States Rights," *Journal of Southern History*, X (August, 1944), 331–342.
2. W. G. BROWN, *The Lower South in American History* (New York, 1903, Chap. II.
3. LAURA WHITE, *Robert Barnwell Rhett: Father of Secession* (New York, 1931), 32, 34, 127.
4. W. P. TRENT, *William Gilmore Simms* (Boston, 1892), 186.
5. "Rhett's Oration before the Legislature of South Carolina, Nov. 28, 1850," J. P. Thomas (ed.), *The Carolina Tribute to Calhoun* (Columbia, 1857), 369.
6. *The Writings and Speeches of Daniel Webster* (Boston, 1903), X, 84.
7. BRAINERD DYER, *Zachary Taylor* (New York, 1946), 381.
8. J. H. INGRAHAM, *The Sunny South or the Southerner at Home* (Philadelphia, 1860).
9. ALLAN NEVINS, *Ordeal of the Union* (New York, 1947), I, 379.

10. J. F. RHODES, *History of the United States from the Compromise of 1850*, I, 490.

11. U. B. PHILLIPS, *The Life of Robert Toombs* (New York, 1913), 119.

12. *Congressional Globe*, 33rd Congress, 1st Session, Appendix, pp. 434–439.

13. CLEMENT EATON, "Henry A. Wise and the Virginia Fire Eaters of 1856," *Mississippi Valley Historical Review*, XXI (March, 1935), 495–512.

14. Excellent modern accounts of the Kansas-Nebraska bill and its consequences are found in CRAVEN, *The Coming of the Civil War*, NEVINS, *Ordeal of the Union*, and ROY L. NICHOLS, *The Disruption of American Democracy* (New York, 1948).

15. CHARLES WARREN, *The Supreme Court in United States History* (Boston, 1924), III, 27.

16. O. G. VILLARD, *John Brown, 1800–1859* (Boston, 1910), 334–336.

CHAPTER XXIII

Secession of the Cotton States

PRIOR to the fateful campaign year of 1860 many of the elastic bands holding the United States together had been broken. As early as 1844–1845 the national Baptist and Methodist churches had divided into hostile Northern and Southern organizations. The Whig party, which had been a powerful cohesive national force in 1850, had been shattered by the Kansas-Nebraska Act. The John Brown Raid had rudely torn the fraternal bonds between the two sections which in the last analysis were the only enduring basis of a union. After this event there was an exodus of Southern students attending Northern colleges, who returned home. As an eminent authority on the Civil War has observed, "the Democratic Party, the Roman Catholic Church, the Episcopal Church, the American Medical Association, and the Constitution were among the few ties that had not snapped." [1]

The Democrats met in convention on April 23 at Charleston, South Carolina, an unfortunate location for moderate decisions. The magnolia gardens and the azaleas in bloom at this season made the city the most wistful and alluring place in America, but it was also the citadel of the fire eaters. The control of the convention was obtained by the followers of Stephen Douglas, partly as a result of the seating of the New York delegation led by Dean Richmond, instead of a contesting group led by Mayor Fernando Wood of New York City who were favorable to Southern Rights. The Douglas men made a mistake in insisting that the platform of the party be adopted before the election of a candidate, hoping by this maneuver to drive out of the convention a few ultra Southerners and insure the election of their candidate. The scheme succeeded too well, leading to the disruption of the party.

The platform which the Northern Democrats advocated left the question of the extension of slavery in the territories to the Federal courts, but, in effect sanctioned the popular sovereignty ideas of Douglas. Such a solution of the slavery issue was unacceptable to the lower South, whose ultimatum was presented by William L. Yancey of Alabama. As this fire eater advanced to the rostrum his compatriots arose to their feet in tribute, and the ladies in the galleries waved their handkerchiefs. In an impassioned speech he tried to persuade the Northern Democracy to accept the Alabama Platform, which stated the minimum demands of the lower South— a Congressional slave code for the protection of slavery in the territories and the nomination of a candidate who accepted the pro-slavery creed. The delegates from the Northern states, however, realizing that such an extreme pro-slavery platform would not carry a single Northern state, rejected Yancey's ultimatum. Accordingly, the Douglas platform was adopted by the convention by a vote of 165 to 138.

When the Douglas platform was adopted, Yancey, following instructions of the Alabama convention, led a bolt of cotton states from the convention hall. The rump convention was unable to nominate a candidate, for after the withdrawal of the Yancey group there did not remain the two-thirds majority of the whole convention requisite for the choice of a nominee. Accordingly the delegates adjourned, to meet at Baltimore on June 18 and the seceders at Richmond. There was still a chance that the Democratic Party might be reunited, but this hope was dashed after the Baltimore convention voted to re-admit some of the old bolting delegations at Charleston, but refused to accept the original Alabama and Louisiana delegations headed by Yancey and Slidell who had applied for admission. Douglas offered to withdraw his candidacy in the interest of party harmony and throw his support to Alexander H. Stephens, but his floor manager, William A. Richardson, and his followers from the Northwest and New York refused to yield.[2] After the decision to seat new delegations from Alabama and Louisiana headed by John Forsyth and Pierre Soulé, a second bolt occurred which took most of the delegates of the upper South from the convention. Then the Douglas adherents nominated their hero for President and Senator Benjamin Fitzpatrick of Alabama for Vice President, who declined and was replaced by Herschel V. Johnson of Georgia. The bolters in Baltimore, joined by some delegates from Richmond, formed the Constitutional Democratic Party, as distinguished from the National Democratic Party, and nominated John C. Breckinridge of Kentucky and Senator Joseph Lane of Oregon as their candidates. Breckinridge, a handsome and eloquent gentleman who had been Vice President in the Buchanan administration, was a staunch supporter of slavery and believed in the theoretical right of secession, but at the same time he was a sincere Union man.

Still another Southern group, who distrusted both Douglas and Breckinridge, formed the Constitutional Union Party. There was only one plank in their platform, the preservation of the Union, the Constitution, and the enforcement of the laws. Meeting also at Baltimore, they chose John Bell of Tennessee as their Presidential candidate, and Edward Everett, a former president of Harvard University, for Vice President. This peace-loving party was composed chiefly of former Whigs, the conservative, older men of the country. Its platform and nominees appealed especially to the border states of the South. Bell would have a good chance of election, if the electoral college failed to return a majority for any one of the candidates and the election were thrown into the House of Representatives.

As a result of the division of the Democrats, a golden opportunity was presented to the Republican party to win the election of 1860. Passing over the outstanding leaders of the party, the Republican convention chose a candidate of availability, the Illinois lawyer and publicized rail-splitter, Abraham Lincoln. The platform which they adopted was a masterpiece of strategy for securing votes. It appealed to the material interests of the East, especially the crucial state of Pennsylvania, by its advocacy of a protective tariff. The Democrats, on the other hand, had alienated the iron interests of Pennsylvania and the wool growers of the Northwest, when, under the leadership of Howell Cobb, Buchanan's Secretary of Treasury, they had lowered the tariff in 1857. The workingmen of the North and the German immigrants were attracted by the homestead plank of the

Republican platform which offered them free farms. The far West was given the bait of a promise of a transcontinental railroad. On the question of slavery the platform steered a middle course, renouncing any purpose of destroying slavery within the states and condemning the John Brown Raid, but placing emphasis on checking the expansion of slavery into the territories. The party printed a large edition of Hinton Rowan Helper's *Impending Crisis* as a campaign document, which was distributed among the working men

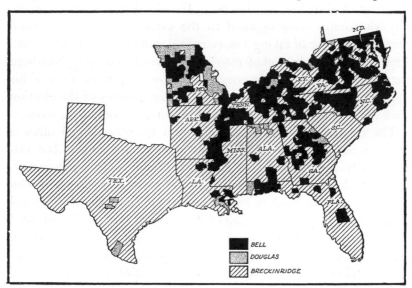

BELL
DOUGLAS
BRECKINRIDGE

THE VOTE FOR PRESIDENT, 1860

and mechanics. Different issues were emphasized in different localities, but the main theme reiterated by the Republican editors during the campaign was not economic interests but the moral issue of checking the expansion of slavery.[3]

Lincoln was elected by a majority of 180 electoral votes to 123 for his opponents, although he received only 39.9 per cent of the popular vote of the country. Douglas carried the electoral vote of only one state, Missouri, and shared the electoral vote of New Jersey with Lincoln. Nevertheless he received 1,376,957 popular votes as compared with 1,866,542 popular votes for Lincoln. John Bell won the electoral vote of a tier of states in the upper South,

Kentucky, Tennessee, and Virginia (by a close vote) and nearly won North Carolina from Breckinridge. In addition to North Carolina and Maryland, Breckinridge carried the states of the lower South. He received, however, only 44.7 per cent of the popular vote of the slave states. Although he himself was opposed to secession, he was the candidate of the Southern extremists, and his lack of support below the Mason and Dixon line presents the strong probability that the Southern people as a whole were not then in favor of disunion. Furthermore, the election revealed that the city electorates were opposed to the extremists, while the rural vote was in favor of taking a more radical stand on the slavery issue.[4] Lincoln won the election of 1860 because he carried every Northern state as well as the Pacific coast by narrow majorities. Even if his opponents had united in these states, modern studies of the election have shown strong probability that Lincoln still would have won.

The election of Lincoln elevated into the Presidential office a leader who was disposed to follow a moderate course, but unfortunately Southerners had a distorted view of his personality. The President-elect was regarded as an uncouth countryman who would be a figurehead in an administration controlled by Seward and the radical antislavery wing of the party. It was widely rumored among the ignorant classes of the South that Hannibal Hamlin, the Republican Vice President, was a mulatto. Southerners believed that Lincoln's real intention was to use his political power to destroy slavery within the Southern states, as indicated by his "House Divided Speech" of 1858 in which he had declared that the nation could not remain half slave and half free. It is true that the Republican platform had denied any such purpose, but political platforms are often forgotten after the campaign, and Southerners feared that slavery within the states would not be safe under Republican rule. It was the fear of future developments rather than present danger that eventually caused the South to secede.

For the moment, however, the South had little to fear from the election of Lincoln. Some of the old Whig leaders pointed out that Lincoln would be powerless to destroy slavery in the Southern states even if he had such a design. The Supreme Court, under the lead of Taney, would shield Southern interests. In the Thirty-seventh

Congress elected in November, 1860, the Republicans would have 29 Senators while the opposition would have 37; in the House of Representatives the opposition could defeat the Republicans by a vote of 120 to 108. Yet there was no guarantee that Northern Democrats would vote for the preservation of slave interests, and the victorious Republican party would necessarily exclude the South from all share in the administration of the national government, for no representative Southerners would accept office from a "Black Republican." Thus the South had come to the end of a long period of control over the Federal government which had been maintained by the mastery of the Democratic party, by the domination of the Supreme Court, and by the election of "dough faces" such as Pierce and Buchanan.

The supreme question of 1860–1861 was whether the country would demonstrate the ability that had previously distinguished Anglo-Saxons of governing by the art of fair compromise. President Buchanan advocated this method of settling the serious controversy before the country in his message of December 3 to Congress. Although he denied the right of secession, nevertheless, following the legal advice of his Attorney General, Jeremiah Black, he declared that the Federal government had no authority to coerce a sovereign state. Upon Congress he placed the responsibility of deciding what was to be done in case South Carolina seceded. At the same time he proposed that Congress should submit to the states certain "explanatory amendments" to the Constitution which would guarantee explicitly the right of holding slaves in the states and protect slave property in the Federal territories during the territorial stage. Moreover, he urged the Northern states to repeal their Personal Liberty Acts. In a noble passage he declared, "Our Union rests upon public opinion, and can never be cemented by the blood of its citizens shed in civil war. If it cannot live in the affections of the people it must one day perish. Congress possesses many means of preserving it by conciliation; but the sword was not placed in their hands to preserve it by force." [5]

Buchanan's policy in this crisis has been severely criticized by the older historians of the nationalist and antislavery school as well as by some recent scholars.[6] They have condemned him for vacillation and weakness during this crisis and have unfavorably contrasted his conduct with the firmness of Andrew Jackson in the nullification movement. Actually, Buchanan tried to create a political atmosphere favorable to compromise and adjustment. He believed that the rights of a minority should be protected and that the decision of the Supreme Court on the question of slavery in the territories should be respected. A strong believer in constitutionalism, he held to the doctrine of divided sovereignty, and therefore did not favor the coercion of a state. The sensible course, he thought, was to refrain from drastic action against a seceding state which would precipitate a civil war. His policy was to gain time for reflection, for he believed that thus the good sense of the people would assert itself.[6a]

The section of the country which most ardently desired to bring about a fair adjustment between the free states and the slave states was the upper South. The upper South was deeply attached to the Union and did not regard the election of the Republican candidate a sufficient justification to secede. Slavery in this region was not so strong a vested interest nor was it needed so much as a means of racial control as in the deep South, for less than one-third of the population consisted of slaves. Furthermore, if war should come as the result of secession, the upper South would be the battle ground. In this crisis, therefore, the upper South was anxious to find a compromise solution, and it was fitting that the leader in this movement was Senator John J. Crittenden, the successor of Henry Clay, "the Great Pacificator."

Crittenden, a venerable gentleman seventy-three years of age, presented his plan of compromise to the Senate on December 18, two days before South Carolina seceded. He proposed the restoration of the Missouri Compromise line of 36° 30′ in the Federal territories, the guarantee of slavery within the states and in the District of Columbia, and the preservation of the interstate slave trade. These provisions were to be adopted as irrepealable constitutional amendments. In regard to the problem of fugitive slaves he advocated the repeal of the Personal Liberty Acts and the compensation by the United States government of slave owners for fugitive slaves lost as a result of the intimidation of Federal officers by mobs, equivalent damages to be assessed on counties in which such outrages occurred. The North was offered concessions in the strict enforcement of the laws suppressing the African slave trade, in a modification of the Fugitive Slave Act freeing Northerners from the duty of serving in posses for the arrest of fugitive slaves, unless there was an attempt to rescue the slave from officers, and in equalizing the fee of the judge in fugitive slave cases regardless of his decision. The most important provision of the Crittenden Compromise was the restoration of the Missouri Compromise line. It was doubtful if any territory would be open to the expansion of slavery under this provision, as both Southerners and Republicans recognized, for New Mexico was unsuited to slavery. Crittenden immediately accepted an amendment, however, which provided that territory hereafter acquired south of that line should be open to slavery. Although the Crittenden Compromise may seem one-sided and primarily an appeasement of the South, it must be remembered that the Southern states threatened to leave the Union and it seemed imperative in order to save the Union to reassure them that Southern rights would not be violated by the Republican victory.

In this crisis the Republicans, with the exception of the business interests in the party, were in no mood for compromise. Too often they had heard the threat of secession made by Southerners to be alarmed for the safety of the Union. The evidence indicates that Lincoln and the Republican party leaders entertained serious misconceptions about the strength and nature of the Union sentiment in the South. They were therefore not disposed to a policy of appeasement of the South.[7] The only practicable compromise would involve a concession in regard to the main plank of the Republican platform, no further extension of slavery in the territories. The prestige and the political interests of the victorious party would be lowered by any compromise on this issue. More important than this consideration, the Republican party had succeeded in making a moral issue of excluding slavery from territory which was naturally and economically unsuited to its expansion. In such an issue many Northern antislavery men had come to believe that a high moral principle was involved, from which there should be no retreat or surrender to expediency.

Faced by the grave prospect of the dissolution of the Union, Congress tried to formulate a plan of compromise. The Republican Speaker of the House appointed a committee of thirty-three members, one from each state, to deal with the problem, but no Douglas Democrats were on this committee. Also Vice President Breckinridge on December 20 appointed a Committee of Thirteen in the Senate which was representative of the various sections. It included Jefferson Davis and Robert Toombs from the lower South, John J. Crittenden from the upper South, Stephen Douglas, leader of the Northern Democrats, and William H. Seward and Ben Wade, two of the most powerful figures in the Republican Party. This committee proved to be the decisive body which determined the fate of the compromise efforts.

When the Senate Committee of Thirteen met, they accepted a motion of Jefferson Davis (December 22) that no report should be adopted unless it received the assent both of a majority of the Republican members and a majority of the other members of the committee. The reason for this procedure was that no measure which was unacceptable to the Republicans would be likely to pass Congress. The key man on the committee, therefore, was William H. Seward, the most prominent Republican leader. This New Yorker was so strongly influenced by the astute politician, Thurlow Weed, editor of the Albany, New York, *Evening Journal* that the connection was recognized in the epigram, "Weed is Seward and Seward is Weed." Before Seward made his decision as to how he would vote on compromise proposals and also whether he should accept a position in Lincoln's cabinet as Secretary of State he consulted Weed. This powerful Republican politician had just returned from Springfield, Illinois, where he had had an interview with Lincoln. Shortly before his pilgrimage to Springfield, Weed, who represented the business interests, had publicly supported compromise on the territorial question in his newspaper. However, in his memorable interview with the President-elect he learned that Lincoln was opposed to the restoration of the Missouri Compromise line. Weed reported this information to Seward, and the latter, accordingly, followed the leader of his party in rejecting compromise on the basis of the Crittenden proposals. The Republican members voted unanimously against this plan of adjustment. The representatives of the lower South on the committee also voted in the negative. This unwise action of the Southerners was taken because the Republicans had voted against the Crittenden compromise, although Toombs, Davis, and other prominent Southern leaders were willing to accept it. Consequently the Senate Committee of Thirteen reported on December 31, eleven days after meeting, that they were unable to agree on any plan of adjustment. Crittenden on January 3, 1861, urged Congress to allow the people of the whole country to vote on his proposals in a solemn referendum, but this plea was rejected by a majority of the Republicans. Delaying tactics by the Republicans prevented a vote in the Senate on the Crittenden Compromise until March 3, when it was rejected by a vote of 20 to 19, after many of the Southern Senators had departed.

The committee appointed by the House of Representatives also made a final report recommending the adoption of some measures that would appease the South. These proposals were the repeal of the Personal Liberty Acts, the enforcement of the Fugitive Slave Act, a Constitutional amendment protecting slavery within the states, and the admission of New Mexico as a state, "with or without slavery" as determined by its constitution. These mild proposals were rejected by the House of Representatives in the last days of February, as well as the Crittenden Compromise, which for over two months had been held back by parliamentary obstruction from a vote. Representative John C. Burch of California and Senators George E. Pugh of Ohio, a Douglas follower, and Joseph Lane of Oregon urged the summoning of a national convention to consider a plan of adjustment, but their plea was brushed aside.

The Virginia legislature called the Washington Peace Conference to meet on February 4 in the national capitol. Twenty-one states sent delegates, but the seven seceded states refused to participate in the conference. Since the number of delegates from each state varied greatly, it was necessary to vote by states. The venerable ex-President John Tyler was chosen presiding officer. The convention adopted a plan of conciliation consisting of six amendments to the Constitution quite similar to the Crittenden proposals. The chief innovation was an amendment that no new territory could be added to the United States (except by discovery and for naval stations), unless a majority of all the Senators from the free states and a majority of all the Senators from the slave states concurred. With the exception of Rhode Island, the New England states voted against every important amendment proposed in the conference. Michigan, Wisconsin, and Minnesota, the children of New England, failed even to send delegates to the conference, and the leaders of the Republican party in those states were opposed to compromise. The final proposals of the Peace Conference were not acceptable to the Southern border states, Virginia, North Carolina, Tennessee, and Arkansas. Nevertheless, the Washington conference, which sat until February 27, probably delayed the secession movement in the upper South.

The efforts of Kentucky to avert war were notable. The legislature of this state urged the calling of a national convention, a proposal which President Buchanan submitted to Congress with his approval. In the latter part of April, Governor Beriah Magoffin appealed to Governor Oliver P. Morton of Indiana and to Governor William Dennison of Ohio to unite with him in a plea for a truce between the hostile sections and the summoning of an extraordinary session of Congress to bring about a peaceful settlement. These partisan Republican governors rejected this constructive proposal, and as a matter of record Congress was not called into extra session by Lincoln until July 4, eighty days after war had started. The Kentucky legislature also on April 3 had issued a call for a border-state conference to meet at Frankfort on May 27, but this convention was attended only by representatives from Kentucky, Missouri, and a single delegate from Tennessee.

The responsibility for the failure of compromise must be shared by Congress, the Southern extremists, and President-elect Lincoln. The real chance for adjustment of the sectional controversy was lost in December, 1860, while the cotton states were in the Union. The blundering and partisanship of Congress during this crisis is one of the great examples of destructive partisanship displayed by Congress comparable to its action in defeating the League of Nations in 1919. Yet the temper of the majority of Northern people also seems to have been uncompromising on the slavery question at this period. One evidence of a conciliatory spirit would have been the repeal of the Personal Liberty Acts, but those of the Northern states which had such laws refused to repeal or significantly modify them after the election of November, 1860, with the exception of New Jersey and Rhode Island.[8]

The Southern extremists also did not wish to facilitate the compromise movement by showing a willingness to make concessions. On December 13 a group of Southern Congressmen met in the room of Reuben Davis of Mississippi and telegraphed a manifesto "To our Constituents" in which they declared that there was no hope of obtaining justice to the South within the Union and advised secession by separate state action and the creation of a Southern Confederacy. Unfavorable to the spirit of compromise was the suspicion entertained by Southerners of Northern politicians, such as Lincoln and Seward, or as "Bull Run" Russell observed: "Disbelief of anything a Northern man—that is, a Republican—can say, is a fixed principle in their minds." [9]

The action of President-elect Lincoln must be counted as a very powerful factor in defeating compromise. As previously described, he exerted his influence to defeat compromise on the territorial question in the Senate Committee of Thirteen. Although it is debatable whether the Republican members of the committee would have voted for compromise regardless of his attitude, Lincoln's influence undoubtedly stiffened the backbone of Republican Senators to vote against the consideration of the Crittenden Compromise by the Senate. Lincoln believed that the restoration of the Missouri Compromise line would lead to an expansionist movement in order to acquire new slave territory. He wrote on December 11 to Congressman William Kellogg of Illinois. "Entertain no proposition for a compromise in regard to the extension of slavery. The instant you do they have us under again; all our labor is lost, and sooner or later must be done over . . . The tug has to come, and better now than later." [10]

Was Lincoln exercising profound statesmanship in rejecting the Crittenden Compromise? There is much reason to question the soundness of his decision, one of the most fateful in the history of the nation. The western territory in dispute was not suited to the natural expansion of slavery and it is doubtful if the restoration of the Missouri Compromise line would have led to anything but a theoretical extension of slavery. In fact when the Republicans obtained control of Congress, they failed to apply the Wilmot Proviso principle in organizing the territories of Colorado, Nevada, and Dakota, an omission which led Stephen Douglas to taunt them with abandoning their principles.[11]

As to Lincoln's fears that the restoration of the Missouri Compromise line would lead to filibustering and a drive to acquire Cuba and Mexico, such apprehension was an unwise basis on which to run the risk of a bloody civil war. There was a practical way of preventing this contingency, namely the proposal of Congressman Emerson Etheridge of Tennessee, spokesman for a caucus of border-state Congressmen, who on January 7 tried to present a plan providing that any annexation of territory to the United States must receive a two-thirds vote of Congress. This provision would have met the main objection of Lincoln to the Crittenden Compromise, but it was opposed both by Republicans and the secessionists. If we criticize Lincoln and the Republicans for taking an uncompromising and unrealistic stand on the expansion of slavery into the Federal territories, we must also condemn those Southerners who were unwilling to surrender the empty right of taking slaves into a region unsuited to the expansion of the "peculiar institution." Both sides were struggling for the advantage in the game of power politics.

During this critical period President-elect Lincoln exercised the silver virtue of being non-committal. The people of the South had genuine fears for the safety of their way of life when the Republicans should assume control of the government, but Lincoln maintained a "perilous silence," probably because he was afraid of the radicals in his own party. In the recently opened Lincoln papers in the Library of Congress is a letter from Professor Schele de Vere of the University of Virginia (March 13, 1861) expressing "the intense anxiety with which the loyal and Union-loving men of Virginia look for some evidence of the conciliatory spirit of the administration." [12] Actually, Lincoln was a decided moderate in regard to the slavery question, being opposed to disturbing slavery in the states, and he tried to appoint a Southerner, Congressman John A.

Gilmer of North Carolina, to his cabinet. But he refused appeals from Alexander H. Stephens, John A. Gilmer, and George D. Prentice to make public statements of his conservative views on the grounds that these sentiments had already been recorded in his speeches. This decision seems to have been a mistake.

When the news of Lincoln's election reached South Carolina, the legislature without a dissenting vote called a convention to consider the question of secession. So strong was the emotionalism of the hour in this state that thousands wore the blue cockade in their hats and formed companies of "minute men." Congressman John D. Ashmore, who had formerly opposed the fire eaters, expressed this emotionalism when he declared that Southerners would never permit Abe Lincoln's banner inscribed with such slogans as "the higher law," "negro equality," "irrepressible conflict," and "final emancipation" to wave over them nor submit to "the logical results" of this victory, "amalgamation." [13] In the election for delegates to the convention the secessionists won an overwhelming victory. Even in the extreme western part of the state, where Unionism had been strongest, the opponents of secession led by Benjamin F. Perry were badly defeated. The old cooperationists or Unionists of 1850–51 now voted for secessionist delegates. Nevertheless, it is interesting to note that a majority of the people of the state did not vote in this critical election for delegates, and it is reasonable to conclude that some of them stayed away from the polls because they were afraid to vote in the negative and thus be branded as "Submissionists." The convention, composed predominantly of elderly men, met first at the capital, Columbia, but adjourned on account of smallpox to Charleston, where on December 20, 1860, they passed an ordinance of secession by a unanimous vote.

Thus the method of precipitating a secession movement by the action of a single state was carried out. By recent experience South Carolina had learned that it was impossible to get the Southern states to cooperate in a resistance movement through an All-Southern Convention. In the previous December, after the John Brown Raid, she had issued a call for a Southern convention to meet at Atlanta and had sent Christopher Memminger, a Charleston lawyer and banker, as a commissioner to persuade Virginia to send delegates, but the leader of the upper South had turned a cold shoulder to this proposal, and it had failed. But now South Carolina received assurances from commissioners sent by Mississippi and Alabama that those states would follow her lead in a secession movement.

After taking the momentous step of dissolving the Union, the Convention appointed Memminger to draw up a Declaration of the Causes of Secession. His statement explained the secession of South Carolina as necessary to assure the safety of slavery and as thoroughly justified by the numerous violations of the Constitution, such as the Personal Liberty Acts, by Northern states. Robert Barnwell Rhett was chosen at the same time by the Convention to compose an address to the people of the slaveholding states. In this document Rhett emphasized the fact that the secession movement was motivated by a desire for self-government and for Southern nationality, comparable to the motives that had produced the American Revolution of 1776. He and his compatriots were irrevocably opposed to any reconstruction of the Union.

South Carolina had taken the initiative in the secession movement, partly because of economic reasons, especially her large stake in the preservation of slavery. Nearly 57 per cent of her population consisted of black slaves, a greater percentage than any other state, and they were held in large blocks. In 1860 eight South Carolinians owned five hundred or more slaves, while in the rest of the slave states only seven individuals held as many. Seventy-two South Carolina planters owned between three hundred and five hundred slaves, as compared to only twenty such slaveholding magnates in Louisiana, the state having the next highest percentage of great planters. Furthermore, South Carolina was the most aristocratic state in the Union, whose boundaries contained a smaller area of land occupied by mountains and unsuited to slavery than most Southern states. Led by Calhoun, Rhett, and Hammond, the Palmetto State had nourished a tradition of independence that had flared forth in the nullification controversy, the Bluffton movement, the Nashville Convention, and finally in 1860. Consequently, South Carolina welcomed an occasion, such as the election of Lincoln, to go out of the Union.

The Gulf states acted hastily in calling conventions and passing ordinances of secession. Mississippi was the second state to leave the Union, on January 9, 1861; Florida seceded the following day, Alabama, January 11, Georgia, January 19, and Louisiana, January 26. The secessionists were in favor of quick measures in precipitating a revolution. They wished to take advantage of the emotional reaction of the people toward the election of Lincoln. Consequently, they were more active and better organized than their opponents whom they branded as "submissionists." They promised that secession would be peaceful and that it would bring prosperity to the South. The secession movement, moreover, was accelerated by interstate commissioners who acted as ambassadors to urge sister states to secede.[14]

In every state there was a group known as cooperationists, who were opposed to immediate secession. They wished to call a Southern convention to discuss the grievances of their section, and, if secession became necessary, they proposed cooperation in seceding and forming a new nation instead of separate state action. Some of the cooperationists hoped by these tactics to produce delay so that compromise and sober second thought would prevent the dissolution of the Union. Most of these moderates admitted the legal right of secession, but questioned its expediency. They were strong in the Piedmont and mountainous sections of the South, where slavery was relatively weak.

In Mississippi the secession feeling was more powerful than in any other state except South Carolina. Like South Carolina, the population of the state was over half Negro, and in certain areas along the Mississippi River, 93 per cent black. The poorer whites followed the leadership of Senator Albert Gallatin Brown, who for a long period had never been defeated at the polls. This politician, who had arisen from the common people, made frequent use of the race issue, portraying the danger and the degradation of the poor whites if the black slaves should be emancipated. In December, 1860, the people of the lower South were alarmed by rumors of Negro insurrection. Furthermore, South Carolina influence had always been strong in the state. Not only had native sons of the Palmetto State emigrated to the rich black lands of Mississippi, but many wealthy Carolinians, including the millionaire, Wade Hampton, drew much of their income from their far-away Mississippi plantations. It was this state that at the instigation of Calhoun had taken the lead in calling the Nashville Convention. To the pride of the planter was joined a frontier spirit of violence and direct action, for the state of Mississippi was less than fifty years old.

In November, 1860, a conference of the political leaders of the state was held in Jackson to determine whether Mississippi should encourage South Carolina to precipitate a secession movement. Jefferson Davis and L. Q. C. Lamar voted for a moderate policy, but they were overruled by the deciding vote of Governor J. J. Pettus, a man with a frontier background. South Carolina was accordingly assured of Mississippi's support in her design of secession, and commissioners to the other Gulf states brought back reports that these states would secede if Mississippi did. The convention which met at the capital, Jackson, was composed of one hundred members, of whom at least sixty were professional men, lawyers chiefly, and small slave owners, or "planters on the make." The vote in the election of delegates to this convention was less than two-thirds of the vote in the Presidential election of 1860.[15] A resolution to submit the ordinance of secession to popular decision was overwhelmingly defeated.

In Florida the secessionists had practically no difficulty in sweeping the state into secession. Senator David Levy Yulee was one of the leading fire eaters of the South, while the governor, Madison S. Perry, a former native of South Carolina, was also an ardent secessionist. Without a dissenting vote the legislature called a convention to meet at Tallahassee, which passed a secession ordinance by a majority of 62 to 7. This vote is surprising in view of the fact that there were only 5,152 slaveholders in the state, with a white population of nearly 78,000. A resolution to submit the ordinance to popular ratification was defeated.

A free debate over the secession issue took place in the Alabama and Georgia conventions, in which those opposed to immediate secession were given a fair hearing. In Alabama the cooperationists, who came principally from the hill country in the northern part of the state, were very strong. Their able leader, Jeremiah Clemens of Huntsville in the Tennessee Valley, made a minority report from a

Committee of Thirteen on Federal Relations which gave a good summary of the point of view of the cooperationists. He proposed a Southern Conference, including the border states, to meet at Nashville, Tennessee, on February 22. He advocated the settlement of the difficulties between the North and the South on the basis of the Crittenden Compromise. Secession should be the last resort of the South, only to be accepted after thorough investigation and discussion, and then, if an ordinance should be adopted, it should be submitted to the vote of the people.

At any time from the beginning of the convention, the secessionists had the power to pass a secession ordinance, but they allowed four days for debate. This tolerance was the policy of wisdom, for a strong intra-state sectional feeling existed between the Union-loving people of north Alabama and the inhabitants of the black belt who were for immediate secession. The strength of the Unionist feeling in the state was registered by the vote for the ordinance of secession of 61 to 39. Thirty-three delegates refused to sign the ordinance and published a broadside giving their reasons for this nonconformity. They maintained that all the Southern states should be consulted before taking such drastic action as separating from the Union, and they demanded that the secession ordinance should be submitted to a popular vote.[16]

In Georgia the most brilliant and the most significant debate of all the Southern states was held on the question of secession. Georgia was a strategic state, for if she voted to remain in the Union, any league of seceded states would be split into two segments. Georgia had always been truculent in defending state rights, and there was hardly a Georgian who would deny the right of secession. It was a question of expediency with them in 1861, an occasion for the exercise of cool judgment instead of passion. Before the members of the legislature passed a bill for the calling of a convention, they invited the two most illustrious men of the state to speak before them. The frank statesman, Alexander H. Stephens, upheld the negative side of the secession debate while the robust, flamboyant Robert Toombs urged his native state to secede. Stephens declared that the election of Lincoln was not sufficient cause for secession. He pointed out that Lincoln was relatively powerless without the control of Congress and of the Supreme Court, which his party did not possess. Also he reminded his audience that the grievance of the tariff had been redressed by the act of 1857, which had been voted for by both South Carolina and Massachusetts. The chief grievance of the South that remained was the existence of the Personal Liberty Acts, but before seceding, an appeal should be made by the South to the Northern states to repeal these unconstitutional laws. He urged delay and the calling of a Southern convention.

Robert Toombs, on the other hand, told the legislature that now was the time to strike for independence. His speech was a tirade against the Northern people who had oppressed and exploited the Southern people. On December 10, however, he wrote to a group in Georgia proposing that an ultimatum be offered to the North in the form of constitutional amendments which would secure the rights of the South. If a majority of the Republicans in Congress should vote for them the South should postpone final action until the legislatures of the Northern states had acted. Ten days later Toombs sent a telegram from Washington to the people of Georgia in which he declared that it was useless to hope that the North would grant to the South her constitutional rights in the Union and that "Secession by the fourth of March next should be thundered from the ballot-box by the unanimous vote of Georgia on the second day of January next" [17] (the date of the election of delegates to the convention).

The secessionist party in Georgia was led by a group of unusually dynamic men. The governor, Joseph E. Brown, who had started life as a poor farmer boy in the mountains of north Georgia, was an ardent secessionist. The two Senators from Georgia, Robert Toombs and Alfred Iverson, were determined to take the state out of the Union. The wealthy Howell Cobb, the leading Democrat of the state, who had recently resigned from Buchanan's cabinet, wrote an address to the people of Georgia declaring that the purpose of the victorious Republican party was the ultimate extinction of slavery, and urging secession before March 4, "each hour that Georgia remains thereafter a member of the Union will be an hour of degradation, to be followed by certain and speedy ruin." [18] His half-brother, T. R. R. Cobb, was an apostle of secession, who was called by

Stephens "the Peter the Hermit of the secession movement in Georgia."

The cooperationists, or "Unionists," in Georgia had abler leaders than in any other state of the lower South. The dominant figure among them in the convention was Herschel V. Johnson, who had been the candidate for Vice President in 1860 on the Douglas ticket. Supporting him were such forceful men as Benjamin H. Hill and Alexander H. Stephens. Outside of the convention the Union cause was advocated by the powerful Methodist divine, Lovick Pierce, and by Judge Garnett Andrews, who remained a Union man through the war. Johnson proposed that a conference of the slaveholding states should be held at Atlanta and that an appeal should be made to the North with a statement of the minimum terms of the South.

The secessionists did most of the campaigning, in which they maintained that secession would not lead to war. For some strange reason Stephens, according to Herschel Johnson, "failed to make a zealous fight against sesession [sic] in the convention." [19] Perhaps the deep melancholy and pessimism of his nature paralyzed his efforts, for he believed resistance to the strong flowing current of secession would be in vain. The Breckinridge men in the convention were arrogant and intolerant toward the moderate delegates and were "rampant for secession." Moreover, fervid appeals for Georgia to secede were made by interstate commissioners from the Gulf states. Nevertheless, the cooperationists made a surprisingly good fight, as shown by the fact that a motion to substitute "cooperation" for immediate secession failed to carry by only sixteen votes in a total vote of 297 members. After this close defeat, the secession ordinance was passed by a vote of 208 to 89.

Louisiana and Texas were the last states in the lower South to secede. In Louisiana there was much Union sentiment, especially among the commercial classes and the sugar planters. The port of New Orleans was enjoying great prosperity, one-half of the total exports of the United States passing through that port. Furthermore, New Orleans had extensive economic connections with the Northwest, which floated its products down to this port of the Mississippi River. The sugar planters of Louisiana, moreover, had no relish to give up the tariff protection which they enjoyed to enter a Confederacy predisposed to free trade. After the election of Lincoln, three of the influential newspapers of the city, the *Picayune*, the *Bee* (the chief Creole paper) and the *True Delta*, were for compromise instead of secession. In December, however, there was a shift of sentiment from opposition to support of secession, caused in part by the failure of the Republicans to reassure the South by guarantees or to accept a reasonable compromise. The most prominent minister of New Orleans, Benjamin M. Palmer, advocated secession in his sermons, which were printed and widely circulated. In the election of January 7 for delegates to a convention, the popular vote for secessionist delegates was 20,448 and for cooperationist delegates 17,296, yet the total vote was 12,766 less than that cast in the Presidential election of the preceding autumn. This decided falling off of the vote may be explained by the failure of Union men to go to the polls. Despite the fact that it was decidedly against the economic interest of Louisiana to withdraw from the Union, the convention, influenced by the contagious example of neighboring states and by a feeling that Southern honor was at stake, passed a secession ordinance on January 26 by a vote of 113 to 17.[20]

In Texas there were complications of geography and race that affected the action of the state in regard to secession. The frontier section was bitterly resentful against the Federal government for its failure to protect the frontier from Indian attacks. Near San Antonio, however, there was settled a group of antislavery Germans who were in favor of the Union. The plantation areas of east Texas and along the Colorado and Red river valleys were secessionist in sentiment. The leader of this group was Senator Louis T. Wigfall, a fire eater who had emigrated from South Carolina. Also the state had recently been thrown into a panic of fear over rumors of servile insurrection, which was believed to be plotted by white abolitionists.

Governor Sam Houston, however, was a strong Unionist, and he refused to summon the legislature into extra session because he feared it would call a secession convention. The powerful opposition of Houston did not prevent the popular will from expressing itself. On December 3, 1860, a group of secessionists at Austin issued an address advocating the election of delegates to a convention at the capital on January 28. The popular pressure on Houston became so insistent that he finally called the legislature in session one week before the meeting of the Austin assembly and it validated the extra-legal convention. Not all the counties sent delegates to this convention, for some counties were so strongly Unionist that they refused to take part in a movement to withdraw the state from the Union. On February 1 the Austin convention by a vote of 166 to 7 passed an ordinance of secession. On account of the irregularity of the elections to the convention, this body provided that the secession ordinance should be submitted to popular vote. Texas was the only state of the lower South to allow the people to vote directly on this issue. The popular vote on the secession ordinance, which was held on February 23, resulted in 46,129 votes for and 14,697 votes against secession.

In surveying the secession movement of the lower South, the evidence points to the conclusion that it was not a conspiracy of a few leaders but a genuinely popular movement.[21] It is true that minorities in Alabama, Georgia, Louisiana, and Texas were opposed to immediate secession. Moreover, the secession movement seems to have been rushed through in its last stages without a thorough canvass. Yet the Southern people had contemplated the probability of dissolving the Union for ten years, and had debated the pros and cons in countless debates. The wave of rejoicing throughout the lower South which followed the passage of the secession ordinances indicated a deep popular approval. The common people of the South, except in the mountain and hilly area which jutted into the South from Pennsylvania, agreed with the aristocrats that the victory of the Republican party was a danger to Southern society which must be met by secession. Rejecting the sagacious advice of the little statesman, Alexander H. Stephens, "Let us not anticipate a threatened evil," [22] six states of the lower South sent delegates to a convention at Montgomery, Alabama, February 4, 1861, which created the Southern Confederacy.

The rise of this new nation was a part of that romantic nationalism of the mid-nineteenth century which was agitating Europe. At last the dream of Southern nationality which the fire eaters had cherished seemed to be realized—the romantic vision expressed by Langdon Cheves ten years earlier at the Nashville Convention: "Unite and you shall form one of the most splendid empires on which the sun ever shone." [23] The decline of the tradition of American nationality below the Mason and Dixon line was one of the great tragedies of our history. Loyalty to the Union, however, survived in the upper South until Fort Sumter was fired upon and the states of this border belt were forced to make a decision whether to fight for or against the Confederacy.

The secession of the lower South marks the end of a long period of sectional adjustment by the fine art of compromise. The exercise of this art is indispensable in a democratic country like the United States containing regions with clashing economic interests and difficult race problems. Traces of old sectional animosity have survived below the Potomac, to be fanned into a flame in 1948 by resentment over President Truman's civil rights program. Today the South remains the most self-conscious of American sections and for years to come is likely to preserve its deep regional feeling. Such a state of feeling may be a powerful force for good, since it resists the standardization of life in America. The true function of this regionalism is to preserve the rich variety of life in the United States, which is so stimulating to the development of literature, art, and intellectual activity.

Citations

1. C. R. Fish, *The American Civil War* (London, 1937), 11.
2. Nichols, *The Disruption of American Democracy*, 317–318.
3. H. C. Perkins (ed.), *Northern Editorials on Secession* (New York, 1942), 2 vols.; see also R. H. Luthin, *The First Lincoln Campaign* (New York, 1944).
4. Ollinger Crenshaw, "Urban and Rural Voting in the Election of 1860," E. F. Goldman (ed.), *Historiography and Urbanization* (Baltimore, 1941), 58–66; and *The Slave States in the Presidential Election of 1860* (Baltimore, 1945).
5. Richardson, *Messages and Papers of the Presidents*, V, 636.
6. See F. W. Klingberg, "James Buchanan and the Crisis of the Nation," *Journal of Southern History*, IX (November, 1943), 455–474.

6a. Actually Buchanan's policy, after the reorganization of his cabinet in January, 1861, was essentially the same as that pursued by Lincoln. He was firm in his resolution not to surrender Fort Sumter. See Kenneth M. Stampp, *And the War Came* (Baton Rouge, 1950).

7. D. M. POTTER, *Lincoln and His Party in the Secession Crisis* (New Haven, 1942).

8. FISH, The American Civil War, 89–97.

9. W. H. RUSSELL, *My Diary, North and South* (Boston, 1863), 64.

10. J. G. NICOLAY and J. HAY, *Complete Works of Abraham Lincoln* (Lincoln Memorial University, 1894), VI, 77–78.

11. J. G. RANDALL, *Lincoln the President* (New York, 1945), I, 240–241.

12. Maximilian Schele De Vere to Frederick Seward, March 13, 1861, Lincoln Papers, Library of Congress.

13. NICHOLS, *Disruption of American Democracy*, 372–373.

14. Basic in the study of the secession movement are DWIGHT L. DUMOND (ed.) *Southern Editorials on Secession* (New York, 1931), and *The Secession Movement, 1860–1861* (New York, 1931).

15. PERCY RAINWATER, *Mississippi, Storm Center of Secession, 1856–1861* (Baton Rouge, 1938), 203–204.

16. W. R. SMITH, *History and Debates of the Convention of the People of Alabama* (*Montgomery*, 1861), 445–447.

17. U. B. PHILLIPS (ed.), "The Correspondence of Robert Toombs, Alexander H. Stephens, and Howell Cobb," *Annual Report of the American Historical Association for the Year 1911* (Washington, 1913), 521, 525.

18. *Ibid.*, 516.

19. "From the Autobiography of Herschel V. Johnson, 1856–1867," *American Historical Review*, XXX (January, 1925), 325–326.

20. See J. D. Bragg, *Louisiana in the Confederacy* (Baton Rouge, 1941), chap I, and Wm. Caskey, *Secession and Restoration of Louisiana* (University, La., 1938).

21. The conflicting interpretation of the forces which led to secession and civil war are admirably presented in HOWARD K. BEALE, "What Historians Have Said About the Causes of the Civil War," *Theory and Practice in Historical Study* (New York, 1946).

22. R. M. JOHNSTON and W. H. BROWNE, *Life of Alexander H. Stephens* (Philadelphia, 1878), 566.

23. R. G. OSTERWEIS, *Romanticism and Nationalism in the Old South* (New Haven, 1949), 7.

Bibliography

(*With emphasis on recent studies*)

———◆———

The Colonial Period

ABERNETHY, T. P., *Three Virginia Frontiers* (University, La., 1940)
———, *Western Lands and the American Revolution* (New York, 1937)
ADAIR, JAMES, *History of the American Indians, particularly those nations adjoining to the Mississippi, East and West Florida, Georgia, South and North Carolina and Virginia* (London, 1775)
ADAMS, J. T., *Provincial Society, 1690–1763* (New York, 1927)
ALDEN, J. R., *John Stuart and the Southern Colonial Frontier* (Ann Arbor, 1944)
AMBLER, C. H., *George Washington and the West* (Chapel Hill, 1936)
ANBUREY, THOMAS, *Travels through the Interior Parts of America* (Boston, 1923), 2 vols.
ANDREWS, C. M., *The Colonial Background of the American Revolution* (New Haven, 1924)
———, *Colonial Folkways* (New Haven, 1921)
———, *The Colonial Period of American History* (New Haven, 1934–1938), 4 vols.
ANDREWS, EVANGELINE W., and CHARLES M. (eds.), *Journal of a Lady of Quality* (New Haven, 1934)
ANDREWS, M. P., *The Founding of Maryland* (New York, 1933)
———, *Virginia, the Old Dominion* (New York, 1937)
BAIRD, C. W., *History of the Huguenot Emigration to America* (New York, 1885), 2 vols.
BALLAGH, J. C., *A History of Slavery in Virginia* (Baltimore, 1902)
———, *White Servitude in the Colony of Virginia* (Baltimore, 1895)
BARKER, C. A., *The Background of the Revolution in Maryland* (New Haven, 1940)
BARTRAM, WILLIAM, *Travels through North and South Carolina, Georgia, East and West Florida . . .* (Philadelphia, 1791)
BEATTY, R. C., *William Byrd of Westover* (Boston, 1932)
BECKER, CARL, *The Declaration of Independence* (New York, 1922)
BEER, G. L., *Origins of the British Colonial System, 1578–1660* (New York, 1908)
———, *The Old Colonial System, 1660–1754* (New York, 1912)

595

BENNETT, H. H., *The Soils and Agriculture of the Southern States* (New York, 1921)

BEVERLEY, ROBERT, *The History and Present State of Virginia*, edited by Louis B. Wright (Chapel Hill, 1944)

BITTINGER, L. F., *The Germans in Colonial Times* (Philadelphia, 1901)

BOLTON, H., *The Spanish Borderlands* (New Haven, 1921)

BOND, B. W., *The Quit-Rent System in the American Colonies* (New Haven, 1919)

BOURNE, E. G., *Spain in America, 1450–1580* (New York, 1904)

BOWES, F. P., *The Culture of Early Charleston* (Chapel Hill, 1942)

BOYD, W. K. (ed.), *William Byrd's Histories of the Dividing Line Betwixt Virginia and North Carolina* (Raleigh, 1929)

——, *Some Eighteenth Century Tracts concerning North Carolina* (Raleigh, 1927)

BREBNER, J. B., *The Explorers of North America 1492–1806* (New York, 1933)

BRIDENBAUGH, CARL, *Cities in the Wilderness: The First Century of Urban Life in America, 1625–1742* (New York, 1938)

BROOKS, CLEANTH, "The English Language in the South," *A Vanderbilt Miscellany, 1919–1944* (Nashville, 1944)

BROWN, ALEXANDER (ed.), *The Genesis of the United States* (Boston, 1891), 2 vols.

BROWNE, W. H. (ed.), *Archives of Maryland* (Baltimore, 1883–1943), 60 vols.

BRUCE, P. A., *Economic History of Virginia in the Seventeenth Century* (New York, 1895), 2 vols.

——, *Institutional History of Virginia in the Seventeenth Century* (New York, 1895), 2 vols.

——, *Social Life of Virginia in the Seventeenth Century* (Richmond, 1927)

——, *The Virginia Plutarch* (Chapel Hill, 1929), 2 vols.

BURNABY, ANDREW, *Burnaby's Travels through North America* (New York, 1904)

BURNETT, E. C., *The Continental Congress* (New York, 1941)

BURNETT, E. C. (ed.), *Letters of Members of the Continental Congress* (Washington, 1921)

CALHOUN, A. W., *A Social History of the American Family from Colonial Times to the Present* (Cleveland, 1917–19)

CHANNING, EDWARD, *A History of the United States* (New York, 1932), 6 vols.

CHASTELLUX, FRANÇOIS JEAN, MARQUIS DE, *Travels in North-America in the Years 1780–1781–1782* (London, 1787), 2 vols.

CHATTERTON, E. K., *Captain John Smith* (London, 1927)

CHILDS, ST. JULIEN R., *Malaria and Colonization in the Carolina Low Country, 1526–1696* (Baltimore, 1940)

CONNOR, R. D. W., *Cornelius Harnett* (Raleigh, 1909)

———, *North Carolina, Rebuilding an Ancient Commonwealth* (Chicago, 1929), 4 vols.

COOK, EBENEZER, *The Sot-Weed Factor; or A Voyage to Maryland* (London, 1708)

CRANE, V. W., *The Southern Frontier, 1670–1732* (Philadelphia, 1929)

CRAVEN, W. F., *Dissolution of the Virginia Company* (New York, 1932)

———, *The Southern Colonies in the Seventeenth Century, 1607–1689* (Baton Rouge, 1949)

CRITTENDEN, C. C., *The Commerce of North Carolina, 1763–1789* (New Haven, 1936)

CROSS, A. L., *The Anglican Episcopate and the American Colonies* (New York, 1902)

CROWL, P. A., *Maryland During and After the Revolution* (Baltimore, 1943)

DAVIDSON, PHILIP, *Propaganda and the American Revolution, 1763–1783* (Chapel Hill, 1941)

DEMOND, R. O., *The Loyalists in North Carolina During the Revolution* (Durham, 1940)

DICKERSON, O. M., *American Colonial Government 1696–1765: A Study of the British Board of Trade in Its Relation to the American Colonies* (Cleveland, 1912)

DODSON, LEONIDAS, *Alexander Spotswood* (Philadelphia, 1932)

DODD, W. E., *The Old South: Struggles for Democracy* (New York, 1937)

DODDRIDGE, JOSEPH, *Notes on the Settlement and Indian Wars of the Western Parts of Virginia and Pennsylvania from 1763–1783 Inclusive* (Albany, 1876)

DONNAN, ELIZABETH (ed.), *Documents Illustrative of the History of the Slave Trade to America* (Washington, 1930–35), 4 vols.

DURAND OF DAUPHINÉ, *A Frenchman in Virginia* (Privately Printed, 1923)

ECKENRODE, H. J., *The Revolution in Virginia* (New York, 1916)

EDDIS, WILLIAM, *Letters from America* (London, 1792)

EGGLESTON, EDWARD, *The Transit of Civilization from England to America in the Seventeenth Century* (New York, 1901)

ETTINGER, A. A., *James Edward Oglethorpe, Imperial Idealist* (Oxford, 1936)

FARISH, H. D. (ed.), *Journal and Letters of Phillip Vickers Fithian, 1733–1774: A Plantation Tutor of the Old Dominion* (Williamsburg, 1943)

FENNEMAN, N. M., *Physiography of Eastern United States* (New York, 1938)

FISKE, JOHN, *Old Virginia and Her Neighbors* (Boston, 1900), 2 vols.

FLETCHER, J. G., *John Smith—Also Pocahontas* (New York, 1928)

FONTAINE, JACQUES, *Memoirs of a Huguenot Family* . . . *1715-1716*, ed. by Ann Maury (New York, 1872)

FORMAN, H. C., *The Architecture of the Old South* (Cambridge, 1948)

FORD, H. J., *The Scotch Irish in America* (Princeton, 1915)

FOSDICK, L. J., *The French Blood in America* (Boston, 1911)

FREEMAN, D. S., *George Washington, a Biography* (New York, 1948), 2 vols.

FRIES, ADELAIDE L., *The Road to Salem* (Chapel Hill, 1944)

———, *Records of the Moravians in North Carolina* (Raleigh, 1922-1947), 7 vols.

GAYARRÉ, CHARLES, *History of Louisiana* (New Orleans, 1885), 4 vols.

GEWEHR, W. M., *The Great Awakening in Virginia, 1740-1790* (Durham, 1930)

GIPSON, LAWRENCE H., *The British Empire Before the American Revolution* (Caldwell, Idaho, and New York, 1936-1946), 6 vols.

GLEN, JAMES, *A Description of South Carolina* (London, 1761)

GLASGOW, MAUDE, *The Scotch-Irish in Northern Ireland and in the American Colonies* (New York, 1936)

GOODWIN, E. L., *The Colonial Church in Virginia* (London, 1927)

GREENE, E. B., and HARRINGTON, V. D., *American Population before the Federal Census of 1790* (New York, 1932)

HAMILTON, P. J., *Colonial Mobile* (Boston, 1897)

HANNA, C. A., *The Scotch-Irish* (New York, 1902), 2 vols.

HANSEN, M. L., *The Atlantic Migration 1607-1860* (Cambridge, 1940)

HARPER, L. A., *The Navigation Laws* (New York, 1939)

HARRELL, J. S., *Loyalism in Virginia* (Philadelphia, 1926)

HART, F. H., *The Valley of Virginia in the American Revolution, 1763-1789* (Chapel Hill, 1942)

HECKSHER, E. F., *Mercantilism* (London, 1935), 2 vols.

HENDERSON, ARCHIBALD, *North Carolina: The Old North State and the New* (Chicago, 1941), 2 vols.

HENDERSON, ARCHIBALD (ed.), *Washington's Southern Tour, 1791* (Boston, 1923)

HENDRICK, B. J., *The Lees of Virginia; Biography of a Family* (Boston, 1935)

HENRY, W. W., *Patrick Henry; Life, Correspondence and Speeches* (New York, 1891), 3 vols.

HEYWARD, D. C., *Seed From Madagascar* (Chapel Hill, 1937)

HILLDRUP, R. L., *The Life and Times of Edmund Pendleton* (Chapel Hill, 1939)

HIRSCH, A. H., *The Huguenots of Colonial South Carolina* (Durham, 1928)

HOLBROOK, H. P. (ed.), *Journal and Letters of Eliza Lucas* (Wormsloe, Georgia, 1850)

HOWE, GEORGE, *The Scotch-Irish and their First Settlement in the Tyger River and other Neighboring Precincts in South Carolina* (Columbia, 1861)

HUGHES, RUPERT, *George Washington* (New York, 1926–30), 3 vols.

HUGHSON, S. C., *The Carolina Pirates and Colonial Commerce, 1670–1740* (Baltimore, 1894)

JAMES, J. A., *The Life of George Rogers Clark* (Chicago, 1928)

JAMESON, J. F., *The American Revolution Considered as a Social Movement* (Princeton, 1926)

JAMESON, J. F. (ed.), *Privateering and Piracy in the Colonial Period* (New York, 1923)

JEFFERSON, THOMAS, *Notes on the State of Virginia* (London, 1787)

JERNEGAN, M. W., *Laboring and Dependent Classes in Colonial America, 1607–1783* (Chicago, 1931)

JOHNSTON, MARY, *Pioneers of the Old South* (New Haven, 1920)

KALM, PER, *Travels into North America* (London, 1772)

KIMBALL, MARIE, *Jefferson, the Road to Glory, 1743–1776* (New York, 1943)

KIMBALL, S. F., *Domestic Architecture of the American Colonies and of the Early Republic* (New York, 1927)

KNIGHT, E. W., *A Documentary History of Education in the South before 1860* (Chapel Hill, 1949), I

KNOLLENBERG, B., *Washington and the Revolution* (New York, 1940)

KOONTZ, L. K., *Robert Dinwiddie: His Career in American Colonial Government and Westward Expansion* (Glendale, Calif., 1941)

———, *The Virginia Frontier, 1754–1763* (Baltimore, 1925)

KRAPP, G. P., *The English Language in America* (New York, 1925), 2 vols.

LABAREE, L. W., *Royal Government in America* (New Haven, 1930)

LANNING, J. T., *The Spanish Missions of Georgia* (Chapel Hill, 1935)

LAWSON, JOHN, *The History of Carolina; Containing the Exact Description and Natural History of That Country* (London, 1714)

LEFLER, H. T. (ed.), *North Carolina History Told by Contemporaries* (Chapel Hill, 1934)

LOWERY, WOODBURY, *The Spanish Settlements within the Present Limits of the United States* (New York, 1901)

McCAIN, J. R., *Georgia as a Proprietary Province* (Boston, 1917)

McCORMAC, E. I., *White Servitude in Maryland, 1634–1820* (Baltimore, 1904)

McCRADY, EDWARD, *The History of South Carolina under the Proprietary Government 1670–1719* (New York, 1897)

McCrady, Edward, *The History of South Carolina under the Royal Government 1719–1776* (New York, 1899)

Mason, Frances N. (ed.), *John Norton and Sons, Merchants of London and Virginia* (Richmond, 1937)

Mereness, N. D., *Maryland as a Proprietary Province* (New York, 1901)

Meriwether, R. L., *The Expansion of South Carolina, 1729–1765* (Kingsport, Tenn., 1940)

Miller, J. C., *Origins of the American Revolution* (Boston, 1943)

Milling, C. J., *Exile Without an End* [*Acadians*] (Columbia, 1943)

Morais, H. M., *Deism in Eighteenth Century America* (New York, 1934)

Morris, R. B., *Government and Labor in Early America* (New York, 1946)

Morris, R. B. (ed.), *The Era of the American Revolution: Studies Inscribed to Evarts Boutell Greene* (New York, 1939)

Morton, Louis, *Robert Carter of Nomini Hall: A Virginia Tobacco Planter of the Eighteenth Century* (Princeton, 1941)

Mowat, C. L., *East Florida as a British Province 1763–1784* (Berkeley, 1943)

Murphy, E. R., *Henry de Tonty, Fur Trader of the Mississippi* (Baltimore, 1941)

Nettels, C. P., *The Roots of American Civilization* (New York, 1946)

——, *The Money Supply of the Colonies before 1720* (Madison, 1934)

Osgood, H. L., *The American Colonies in the Seventeenth Century* (New York, 1904–1907), 3 vols.

——, *The American Colonies in the Eighteenth Century* (New York, 1924), 2 vols.

Parrington, V. L., *The Colonial Mind, 1620–1800:* Vol. I of *Main Currents in American Thought* (New York, 1927)

Phillips, U. B. (ed.), *Plantation and Frontier Documents: 1649–1863* (Cleveland, 1909), 2 vols.

Priestley, H. I., *The Coming of the White Man 1492–1848* (New York, 1930)

Ramsay, David, *History of South Carolina from Its First Settlement to the Year 1808* (Charleston, 1809), 2 vols.

Raper, C. L., *North Carolina: A Study in English Colonial Government* (New York, 1904)

Ravenel, H. H., *Eliza Pinckney* (New York, 1902)

Ravenel, Mrs. St. Julien, *Charleston, The Place and the People* (New York, 1927)

Robert, J. C., *The Story of Tobacco in America* (New York, 1949)

Rowland, K. M., *The Life of Charles Carroll of Carrollton, 1737–1832* (New York, 1918), 2 vols.

Saunders, W. L. (ed.), *Colonial Records of North Carolina, 1662–1776* (Raleigh, 1886–1890), 10 vols.

SAYE, A. B., *New Viewpoints in Georgia History* (Athens, Ga., 1943)

SCHAPER, W. A., "Sectionalism and Representation in South Carolina," *American Historical Association Annual Report, 1900*, Vol. I

SCHLESINGER, A. M., *The Colonial Merchants and the American Revolution, 1763–1776* (New York, 1917)

SCHURICHT, HERMANN, *History of the German Element in Virginia* (Baltimore, 1900)

SCHUYLER, R. L., *The Fall of the Old Colonial System . . .* (Oxford, 1945)

SELLERS, LEILA, *Charleston Business on the Eve of the American Revolution* (Chapel Hill, 1934)

SEMMES, RAPHAEL, *Crime and Punishment in Early Maryland* (Baltimore, 1938)

SKINNER, C. L., *Pioneers of the Old Southwest* (New Haven, 1919)

SPRUILL, J. C., *Women's Life and Work in the Southern Colonies* (Chapel Hill, 1938)

SMITH, A. E., *Colonists in Bondage, White Servitude and Convict Labor in America, 1607–1776* (Chapel Hill, 1947)

SMITH, E. H., *Charles Carroll of Carrollton* (Cambridge, 1942)

SMITH, CAPTAIN JOHN, *The Generall Historie of Virginia, New England and the Summer Isles* (London, 1626)

STEPHENSON, N. W., and DUNN, W. H., *George Washington* (New York, 1940), 2 vols.

SWANK, J. M., *History of the Manufacture of Iron in All Ages* (Philadelphia, 1891)

SWEET, W. W., *The Story of Religion in America* (New York, 1939)

TATHAM, WILLIAM, *An Historical and Practical Essay on the Culture and Commerce of Tobacco* (London, 1800)

TODD, V. H. (ed.), *Christoph Von Graffenried's Account of the Founding of New Bern* (Raleigh, 1920)

TURNER, FREDERICK JACKSON, *The Frontier in American History* (New York, 1921)

U. S. BUREAU OF THE CENSUS, *Heads of Families at the First Census of the United States in the Year 1790* (Washington, 1907–1908), 11 volumes

VAN TYNE, C. H., *The Causes of the War of Independence* (Boston, 1922)

——, *The Loyalists of the American Revolution* (New York, 1929)

VANCE, RUPERT, *Human Geography of the South* (Chapel Hill, 1932)

WALLACE, D. D., *Life of Henry Laurens* (New York, 1915)

WASHINGTON, GEORGE, *The Diaries of George Washington 1748–1799*, edited by J. C. Fitzpatrick (Boston, 1925), 4 vols.

WATERMAN, T. T., and BARROWS, J. A., *Domestic Colonial Architecture of Tidewater Virginia* (Chapel Hill, 1947)

WAYLAND, J. W., *The German Element of the Shenandoah Valley* (Charlottesville, 1907)

WERTENBAKER, T. J., *The Old South: The Founding of American Civilization* (New York, 1942)

——, *The Golden Age of Colonial Culture* (New York, 1942)

——, *Patrician and Plebeian in Virginia* (Charlottesville, 1910)

——, *The First Americans, 1607–1690* (New York, 1929)

——, *Planters of Colonial Virginia* (Princeton, 1922)

——, *Torchbearer of the Revolution: The Story of Bacon's Rebellion and Its Leader* (Princeton, 1940)

WHITAKER, A. P., *Spanish-American Frontier, 1783–1795* (Boston, 1927)

WISSLER, CLARK, *Indians of the United States* (Garden City, 1941)

WOODFIN, M. H. (ed.), *Another Secret Diary of William Byrd of West-over, 1733–1741* (Richmond, 1942)

WRIGHT, L. B., *The Atlantic Frontier, Colonial American Civilization 1607–1763* (New York, 1947)

——, *The First Gentlemen of Virginia: Intellectual Qualities of the Early Colonial Ruling Class* (San Marino, 1940)

——, *Letters of Robert Carter, 1720–1727: The Commercial Interests of a Virginia Gentleman* (San Marino, 1940)

WRIGHT, L. B., and TINLING, M., *The Secret Diary of William Byrd 1709–1712* (Richmond, 1941)

———

Period of the Early Republic
1783–1815

ADAMS, HENRY, *History of the United States* (New York, 1891)

ADAMS, HENRY, *John Randolph* (Boston, 1898)

ANDERSON, D. R., *William Branch Giles* (Menasha, 1914)

BAKELESS, JOHN, *Daniel Boone, Master of the Wilderness* (New York, 1939)

BEARD, C. A., *An Economic Interpretation of the Constitution of the United States* (New York, 1936)

——, *Economic Origins of the Jeffersonian Democracy* (New York, 1915)

BEIRNE, F. F., *The War of 1812* (New York, 1949)

BEVERIDGE, A. J., *Life of John Marshall* (New York, 1916–1919), 4 vols.

BOWERS, C. G., *Jefferson in Power* (Boston, 1936)

——, *Jefferson and Hamilton* (Boston, 1925)

BRANT, IRVING, *James Madison, the Virginia Revolutionist* (Indianapolis, 1941)

——, *James Madison the Nationalist 1780–1787* (Indianapolis, 1948)

Bruce, H. A. B., *Daniel Boone and the Wilderness Road* (New York, 1910)

Bruce, W. C., *John Randolph of Roanoke, 1773-1833* (New York, 1922), 2 vols.

Burt, A. L., *The United States, Great Britain, and British North America* (New Haven, 1940)

Caughey, J. W., *McGillivray of the Creeks* (Norman, 1938)

Channing, Edward, *The Jeffersonian System, 1801-1811* (New York, 1906)

Chinard, Gilbert, *Thomas Jefferson, The Apostle of Americanism* (Boston, 1946)

Clark, T. D., *The Rampaging Frontier* (Indianapolis, 1939)

Cox, I. J., *The West Florida Controversy, 1798-1813* (Baltimore, 1918)

Cresson, W. P., *James Monroe* (Chapel Hill, 1946)

Davis, John, *Travels of John Davis in the United States of America, 1798 to 1802* (Boston, 1910), 2 vols.

Davis, R. B., *Francis Walker Gilmer* (Richmond, 1939)

Dick, Everett, *The Dixie Frontier, A Social History* (New York, 1948)

Dodd, W. E., *Statesmen of the Old South* (New York, 1911)

———, *The Life of Nathaniel Macon* (Raleigh, 1908)

Driver, C. S., *John Sevier* (Chapel Hill, 1932)

Elliott, Jonathan (ed.), *The Debates in the Several State Conventions on the Adoption of the Federal Constitution* (Philadelphia, 1891), 5 vols.

Farrand, Max, *The Framing of the Constitution of the United States* (New Haven, 1913)

———, *Records of the Federal Convention of 1787* (New York, 1911), 3 vols.

Fiske, John, *The Critical Period in American History, 1783-1789* (Boston, 1916)

Greene, E. B., *The Revolutionary Generation 1763-1790* (New York, 1943)

Grigsby, H. B., *The History of the Virginia Federal Convention of 1788* (Richmond, 1890-91), 2 vols.

Hay, T. R., and Werner, M. R., *The Admirable Trumpeter: A Biography of General James Wilkinson* (New York, 1941)

Henderson, Archibald, *The Conquest of the Old Southwest* (New York, 1920)

Hill, Helen, *George Mason, Constitutionalist* (Cambridge, 1938)

Hirst, F. W., *Life and Letters of Thomas Jefferson* (New York, 1926)

Hulbert, A. B., *Boone's Wilderness Road* (Cleveland, 1903)

Hunt, Gaillard, *The Life of James Madison* (New York, 1902)

Jacobs, J. R., *Tarnished Warrior: Major-General James Wilkinson* (New York, 1938)

JENSEN, MERRILL, *The Articles of Confederation* (Madison, 1948)

KIMBALL, MARIE, *Jefferson, War and Peace 1776 to 1784* (New York, 1947)

KINCAID, R. L., *The Wilderness Road* (Indianapolis, 1947)

KOCH, ADRIENNE, *The Philosophy of Thomas Jefferson* (New York, 1943)

KROUT, J. A., and Fox, D. R., *The Completion of Independence, 1790–1830* (New York, 1944)

LATROBE, B. H., *The Journal of Latrobe* (New York, 1905)

LEHMANN, KARL, *Jefferson, American Humanist* (New York, 1947)

LESTER, W. S., *The Transylvania Colony* (Spencer, Ind., 1935)

LYNCH, W. O., *Fifty Years of Party Warfare 1789–1837* (Indianapolis, 1931)

MCCALEB, W. F., *The Aaron Burr Conspiracy* (New York, 1903)

MCLAUGHLIN, A. C., *A Constitutional History of the United States* (New York, 1935)

MCREE, G. J., *James Iredell* (New York, 1857), 2 vols.

MADISON, JAMES, *The Writings of James Madison . . .* edited by Gaillard Hunt (New York, 1900–10), 9 vols.

MALONE, DUMAS, *Jefferson the Virginian* (Boston, 1948)

MAYO, BERNARD (ed.), *Jefferson Himself: The Personal Narrative of a Many-Sided American* (Boston, 1942)

MELLON, M. T., *Early American Views on Negro Slavery* (Boston, 1934)

MOTT, F. L., *Jefferson and the Press* (Baton Rouge, 1943)

MUZZEY, D. S., *Thomas Jefferson* (New York, 1918)

NEVINS, ALLAN, *The American States During and After the Revolution, 1775–1789* (New York, 1924)

NOCK, A. J., *Jefferson* (New York, 1926)

PADOVER, S. K., *Jefferson* (New York, 1942)

PARKS, J. H., *Felix Grundy, Champion of Democracy* (Baton Rouge, 1940)

PRATT, J. W., *Expansionists of 1812* (New York, 1925)

RANDALL, H. S., *Thomas Jefferson* (New York, 1858), 3 vols.

RANDOLPH, SARAH N., *The Domestic Life of Thomas Jefferson* (Cambridge, Mass., 1939)

ROBERTSON, J. A., *Louisiana Under the Rule of Spain, France, and the United States 1785–1807* (Cleveland, 1911), 2 vols.

RODELL, FRED, *Fifty-Five Men* (Harrisburg, 1936)

ROOSEVELT, THEODORE, *The Winning of the West* (New York, 1889–96), 4 vols.

ROWLAND, K. M., *The Life of George Mason, 1725–1792* (New York, 1892)

SCHOEPF, J. D., *Travels in the Confederation* (*1783-1784*) edited by A. J. Morrison (Philadelphia, 1911), 2 vols.

SCHULTZ, CHRISTIAN, *Travels on an Inland Voyage* (New York, 1810), 2 vols.

SELLERS, C. C., *Charles Willson Peale* (Philadelphia, 1947), 2 vols.

SINGER, C. G., *South Carolina in the Confederation* (Philadelphia, 1941)

SWEET, W. W., *Revivalism in America* (New York, 1944)

TRENHOLME, L. I., *Ratification of the Federal Constitution in North Carolina* (New York, 1932)

TOULMIN, HARRY, *The Western Country in 1793* (San Marino, 1948)

THWAITES, R. G., *Early Western Travels* (Cleveland, 1904-1907), 32 vols.

———, *Daniel Boone* (New York, 1902)

VAN DOREN, CARL, *The Great Rehearsal, The Story of the Making and Ratifying of the Constitution of the United States* (New York, 1948)

WARFIELD, E. D., *The Kentucky Resolutions of 1798* (New York, 1887)

WEEMS, M. L., *Mason Locke Weems, His Works and Ways* (New York, 1929)

WILLIAMS, S. C., *History of the Lost State of Franklin* (New York, 1933)

WOLFE, J. H., *Jeffersonian Democracy in South Carolina* (Chapel Hill, 1940)

The Ante-Bellum Period
1815–1860

ABBEY, K. T., *Florida, Land of Change* (Chapel Hill, 1941)

ABERNETHY, T. P., *From Frontier to Plantation in Tennessee* (Chapel Hill, 1932)

———, *The Formative Period in Alabama, 1815-1828* (Montgomery, 1922)

ALBION, R. G., *The Rise of New York Port, 1815-1860* (New York, 1939)

ALDERMAN, E. A., and HARRIS, J. C. (eds.), *Library of Southern Literature* (New Orleans, 1908-13), 16 vols.

ALLEN, J. D., *Philip Pendleton Cooke* (Chapel Hill, 1942)

AMBLER, C. H., *West Virginia, The Mountain State* (New York, 1940)

———, *Sectionalism in Virginia from 1776 to 1861* (Chicago, 1910)

———, *Thomas Ritchie, A Study in Virginia Politics* (Chicago, 1913)

APTHEKER, HERBERT, *American Negro Slave Revolts* (New York, 1943)
ARMSTRONG, MARGARET, *Fanny Kemble; a Passionate Victorian* (New York, 1938)
ATHERTON, L. E., *The Pioneer Merchant in Mid-America* (Columbia, 1943)
AUCHAMPAUGH, P. G., *Robert Tyler; Southern Rights Champion, 1847–1866. A Documentary Study Chiefly of Antebellum Politics* (Duluth, 1934)
BAILEY, T. A., *A Diplomatic History of the American People* (New York, 1946)
BALDWIN, J. G., *The Flush Times of Alabama and Mississippi* (New York, 1853). Recent reprint by Americus Book Company, Americus, Georgia
BALLAGH, J. C., *History of Slavery in Virginia* (Baltimore, 1902)
BANCROFT, FREDERIC, *Slave-Trading in the Old South* (Baltimore, 1931)
BARKER, E. C., *Life of Stephen F. Austin, Founder of Texas, 1793–1836* (Nashville, 1925)
BARNES, G. H., *The Antislavery Impulse, 1830–1844* (New York, 1933)
——, and DUMOND, D. L. (eds.), *Letters of Theodore Dwight Weld, Angelina Grimké Weld, and Sarah Grimké, 1822–1844* (New York, 1934), 2 vols.
BASSETT, J. S., *Anti-Slavery Leaders of North Carolina* (Baltimore, 1898)
——, *Life of Andrew Jackson* (New York, 1911), 2 vols.
——, *Slavery in the State of North Carolina* (Baltimore, 1899)
—— (ed.), *The Southern Plantation Overseer as Revealed in His Letters* (Northampton, Mass., 1925)
BATTLE, KEMP P., *History of the University of North Carolina* (Raleigh, 1907–12), 2 vols.
BEMIS, S. F., *Diplomatic History of the United States* (New York, 1942)
BENTON, T. H., *Thirty Years' View* (New York, 1854–1856), 2 vols.
BERGER, MAX, *The British Traveller in America, 1836–1860* (New York, 1943)
BILLINGTON, R. A., *The Protestant Crusade, 1800–1860; A Study of the Origins of American Nativism* (New York, 1938)
BINKLEY, W. C., *The Expansionist Movement in Texas, 1836–1850* (Berkeley, 1925)
BONNER, J. C., and ROBERTS, L. E., *Studies in Georgia History and Government* (Athens, 1940)
BOWERS, C. G., *Party Battles of the Jackson Period* (Boston, 1922)
BOYD, W. K. (ed.), *Memoirs of W. W. Holden* (Durham, 1911)
BRACKETT, J. R., *The Negro in Maryland* (Baltimore, 1889)
BREMER, FREDRIKA, *Homes of the New World* (New York, 1853), 2 vols.

BROOKS, VAN WYCK, *The World of Washington Irving* (New York, 1944)

BROWN, W. G., *The Lower South in American History* (New York, 1902)

BROWNLOW, W. G., *Sketches of the Rise, Progress, and Decline of Secession* (Philadelphia, 1862)

BRUCE, KATHLEEN, *Virginia Iron Manufacture in the Slave Era* (New York, 1930)

BRUCE, P. A., *History of the University of Virginia, 1819–1919* (New York, 1920–22)

BUCKINGHAM, J. S., *The Slave States in America* (London, 1842), 2 vols.

BUCKMASTER, HENRIETTA, *Let My People Go: The Story of the Underground Railroad and the Growth of the Abolition Movement* (New York, 1941)

BUTLER, PIERCE, *Judah P. Benjamin* (Philadelphia, 1907)

CALHOUN, JOHN C., *The Works of John C. Calhoun*, edited by Richard K. Crallé (New York, 1851–1856), 6 vols.

CALLCOTT, W. H., *Santa Anna* (Norman, 1936)

CAPERS, G. M., JR., *Biography of a River Town: Memphis, Its Heroic Age* (Chapel Hill, 1939)

CARROLL, E. M., *Origins of the Whig Party* (Durham, 1925)

CARROLL, J. C., *Slave Insurrections in the United States, 1800–1865* (Boston, 1938)

CARPENTER, J. T., *The South as a Conscious Minority, 1789–1861* (New York, 1930)

CASH, W. J., *The Mind of the South* (New York, 1941)

CASKEY, W. M., *Secession and Restoration of Louisiana* (University, La., 1938)

CARSON, J. P., *Life, Letters, and Speeches of James Louis Petigru* (Washington, 1920)

CASTANEDA, C. E. (ed.), *The Mexican Side of the Texas Revolution* (Dallas, 1928)

CATE, W. A., *Lucius Q. C. Lamar Statesman of Secession and Reunion* (Chapel Hill, 1938)

CATTERALL, H. T. (ed.), *Judicial Cases Concerning American Slavery and the Negro* (Washington, 1926–1932), 5 vols.

CHANDLER, J. A. C. et al., *The South in the Building of the Nation* (Richmond, 1909), 12 vols.

CHESNUT, MARY BOYKIN, *A Diary from Dixie*, edited by I. D. Martin and M. L. Avary (New York, 1906)

CHILDS, W. T., *John McDonogh, His Life and Work* (Baltimore, 1939)

CHITWOOD, O. P., *John Tyler, Champion of the Old South* (New York, 1939)

CHRIST-JANER, A., *George Caleb Bingham of Missouri* . . . (New York, 1940)

CLAIBORNE, J. F. H., *Mississippi as a Province, Territory, and State* (Jackson, 1880)

CLARK, BLANCHE H., *The Tennessee Yeomen, 1840–1860* (Nashville, 1942)

CLARK, T. D., *The Beginning of the L & N: The Development of the Louisville and Nashville Railroad and Its Memphis Branches from 1836 to 1860* (Louisville, 1933)

——, *A History of Kentucky* (New York, 1937)

——, *The Kentucky* (New York, 1942)

——, *A Pioneer Southern Railroad from New Orleans to Cairo* (Chapel Hill, 1936)

CLARK, V. S., *History of Manufactures in the United States* (New York, 1929), I

CLAY, HENRY, *The Life, Correspondence, and Speeches of Henry Clay*, edited by Calvin Colton (New York, 1864), 6 vols.

CLAY, CASSIUS MARCELLUS, *The Life of Cassius Marcellus Clay. Memoirs, Writings, Speeches* . . . (Cincinnati, 1886)

CLAY-CLOPTON, MRS. VIRGINIA, *A Belle of the Fifties*, edited by Ada Sterling (New York, 1905)

CLEVELAND, C. C., *The Great Revival in the West, 1797–1805* (Chicago, 1916)

COHEN, S. J., "Three Notable Ante-bellum Magazines of South Carolina," *Bulletin of University of South Carolina*, no. 42, pt. II (Columbia, S. C., 1915)

COLE, A. C., *The Whig Party in the South* (Washington, 1913)

——, *The Irrepressible Conflict, 1850–1865* (New York, 1934)

COLEMAN, J. W., JR., *Slavery Times in Kentucky* (Chapel Hill, 1940)

CONWAY, M. D., *Autobiography, Memories and Experiences* (London, 1904), 2 vols.

COPELAND, FAYETTE, *Kendall of the Picayune* (Norman, 1943)

COTTERILL, R. S., *The Old South* (Glendale, Calif., 1939)

COUCH, W. T. (ed.), *Culture in the South* (Chapel Hill, 1934)

COULTER, E. M., *College Life in the Old South* (New York, 1928)

——, *Georgia, A Short History* (Chapel Hill, 1947)

——, *Thomas Spalding of Sapelo* (University, La., 1940)

——, *William G. Brownlow, Fighting Parson of the Southern Highlands* (Chapel Hill, 1937)

CRAVEN, AVERY O., *The Coming of the Civil War* (New York, 1942)

——, *Edmund Ruffin, Southerner, A Study in Secession* (New York, 1932)

——, *The Repressible Conflict, 1830–1861* (University, La., 1939)

Bibliography 609

CRAVEN, AVERY O., *Soil Exhaustion as a Factor in the Agricultural History of Virginia and Maryland, 1606–1860* (University of Illinois Studies in the Social Sciences, XIII, no. I, Urbana, 1926)

CRAVEN, AVERY O. (ed.), *Essays in Honor of William E. Dodd* (Chicago, 1935)

CRENSHAW, O., *The Slave States in the Presidential Election of 1860* (Baltimore, 1945)

CRUM, M., *Gullah: Negro Life in the Carolina Sea Islands* (Durham, 1940)

CURTI, MERLE, *The Growth of American Thought* (New York, 1943)

CURTIS, G. T., *Life of James Buchanan* (New York, 1883), 2 vols.

DABNEY, C. W., *Universal Education in the South* (Chapel Hill, 1936), I

DABNEY, T. W., *One Hundred Great Years: The Story of the Times-Picayune from Its Founding to 1940* (Baton Rouge, 1944)

DABNEY, VIRGINIUS, *Liberalism in the South* (Chapel Hill, 1932)

DAVENPORT, F. G., *Ante-Bellum Kentucky, A Social History, 1800–1860* (Oxford, Ohio, 1943)

———, *Cultural Life in Nashville on the Eve of the Civil War* (Chapel Hill, 1941)

DAVIDSON, DONALD, *The Tennessee* (New York, 1946), 2 vols.

DAVIS, C. S., *The Cotton Kingdom in Alabama* (Montgomery, 1939)

DAVIS, E. A., *Plantation Life in the Florida Parishes of Louisiana 1836–1846, as Reflected in the Diary of Bennet H. Barrow* (New York, 1943)

DE BOW, J. D. B., *The Industrial Resources, etc., of the Southern and Western States* (New Orleans, 1853), 3 vols.

———, *The Interest in Slavery of the Southern Non-Slaveholder* (New York, 1860), A Pamphlet

DEMAREE, A. L., *The American Agricultural Press, 1819–1860* (New York, 1941)

DENMAN, C. P., *The Secession Movement in Alabama* (Montgomery, 1933)

DEVOTO, BERNARD, *The Year of Decision: 1846* (Boston, 1943)

DEW, THOMAS, *Review of the Debates in the Virginia Legislature of 1831 and 1832* (Richmond, 1832)

DICKEY, D. C., *Seargent S. Prentiss, Whig Orator of the Old South* (Baton Rouge, 1945)

DODD, DOROTHY (ed.), *Florida Becomes a State* (Tallahassee, 1945)

DODD, W. E., *The Cotton Kingdom* (New Haven, 1919)

———, *Jefferson Davis* (Philadelphia, 1907)

DOUGLASS, FREDERICK, *Life and Times of Frederick Douglass, Written by Himself* (Hartford, Conn., 1889)

DREWRY, W. S., *The Southampton Insurrection* (Washington, 1900)

DuBois, W. E. B., *The Suppression of the African Slave-Trade to the United States of America, 1638–1870* (New York, 1896)

DuBose, J. W., *The Life and Times of William Lowndes Yancey* (Birmingham, 1892)

Dumond, D. L., *Antislavery Origins of the Civil War in the United States* (Ann Arbor, 1939)

Dumond, D. L. (ed.), *Letters of James Gillespie Birney, 1831–1857* (New York, 1938), 2 vols.

——, *Southern Editorials on Secession* (New York, 1931)

——, *The Secession Movement, 1860–1861* (New York, 1931)

Dunbar, Seymour, *A History of Travel in America* (New York, 1937), 4 vols.

Dupre, Huntley, *Rafinesque in Lexington, 1819–1826* (Lexington, 1945)

Dyer, Brainerd, *Zachary Taylor* (New York, 1946)

Easterby, J. H., *History of the College of Charleston* (Charleston, 1935)

Easterby, J. H. (ed.), *The South Carolina Rice Plantation as Revealed in the Papers of Robert F. W. Allston* (Chicago, 1945)

Eaton, Clement, *Freedom of Thought in the Old South* (Durham, 1940)

Elliott, E. N. (ed.), *Cotton is King, and Pro-Slavery Arguments . . .* (Augusta, 1860)

Featherstonhaugh, G. W., *Excursion through the Slave States* (New York, 1844)

Felton, Rebecca L., *Country Life in Georgia in the Days of My Youth* (Atlanta, 1919)

Fielder, H., *Sketch of the Life and Times and Speeches of Joseph E. Brown* (Springfield, 1883)

Fish, C. R., *The Rise of the Common Man, 1830–1850* (New York, 1941)

——, *The American Civil War, an Interpretation* (New York, 1937)

Fitzhugh, George, *Cannibals All! or, Slaves without Masters* (Richmond, 1857)

——, *Sociology for the South, or the Failure of Free Society* (Richmond, 1854)

Flanders, B. H., *Early Georgia Magazines: Literary Periodicals to 1865* (Athens, Ga., 1944)

Flanders, R. B., *Plantation Slavery in Georgia* (Chapel Hill, 1933)

Flippin, P. S., *Herschel V. Johnson of Georgia* (Richmond, 1931)

Folmsbee, S. J., *Sectionalism and Internal Improvements in Tennessee 1796–1845* (Knoxville, 1939)

Foner, P. S., *Business and Slavery; The New York Merchants and the Irrepressible Conflict* (Chapel Hill, 1941)

Foreman, Grant, *Indian Removal* (Norman, Oklahoma, 1932)

Fox, E. L., *The American Colonization Society, 1817–1840* (Baltimore, 1919)

Franklin, J. H., *The Free Negro in North Carolina 1790–1860* (Chapel Hill, 1943)

——, *From Slavery to Freedom, a History of American Negroes* (New York, 1947)

Frazier, E. F., *The Negro in the United States* (New York, 1949)

Freidel, Frank, *Francis Lieber, Nineteenth Century Liberal* (Baton Rouge, 1948)

Fuller, J. D. P., *The Movement for the Acquisition of All Mexico 1846–1848* (Baltimore, 1936)

Gabriel, R. H., *The Course of American Democratic Thought: An Intellectual History Since 1815* (New York, 1940)

Gaines, F. P., *The Southern Plantation* (New York, 1924)

Ganaway, L. M., *New Mexico and the Sectional Controversy, 1846–1861* (Albuquerque, 1944)

Gambrell, H. P., *Anson Jones: The Last President of Texas* (Garden City, 1948)

Garrison, W. P., and F. J., *William Lloyd Garrison* (New York, 1885–1889), 4 vols.

Godbold, Albea, *The Church College of the Old South* (Durham, 1944)

Goldman, E. F. (ed.), *Historiography and Urbanization: Essays in American History in Honor of W. Stull Holt* (Baltimore, 1941)

Gray, L. C., *History of Agriculture in the Southern United States to 1860* (Washington, 1933), 2 vols.

Green, E. L., *George McDuffie* (Columbia, 1936)

——, *History of the University of South Carolina* (Columbia, 1916)

Green, Fletcher M., *Constitutional Development in the South Atlantic States, 1776–1860* (Chapel Hill, 1930)

Hall, Captain Basil, *Travels in North America in the Years 1827–1828* (Edinburgh, 1830)

——, *Forty Etchings, from Sketches made with the Camera Lucida, in North America in 1827 and 1828* (Edinburgh, 1829)

Hamer, P. M., *History of Tennessee* (New York, 1933), 4 vols.

Hamilton, Holman, *Zachary Taylor: Soldier of the Republic* (Indianapolis, 1941)

Hamilton, J. G. deR. (ed.), *The Papers of Thomas Ruffin* (Raleigh, 1918–1920), 4 vols.

——, *The Correspondence of Jonathan Worth* (Raleigh, 1909), 2 vols.

Hamlin, T. F., *Greek Revival Architecture in America* (New York, 1944)

Harden, E. J., *Life of George M. Troup* (Savannah, 1859)

HATCHER, W. B., *Edward Livingston, Jeffersonian Republican and Jacksonian Democrat* (University, La., 1940)

HAWK, E. Q., *Economic History of the South* (New York, 1934)

HELPER, H. R., *The Impending Crisis of the South* (New York, 1857)

HESSELTINE, W. B., *The South in American History* (New York, 1943)

HILL, J. D., *The Texas Navy* (Chicago, 1937)

HOGAN, W. R., *The Texas Republic, A Social and Economic History* (Norman, 1946)

HOFSTADTER, R., *The American Political Tradition and the Men Who Made It* (New York, 1948)

HOOLE, W. S., *The Ante-Bellum Charleston Theatre* (Tuscaloosa, 1946)

HOPKINS, J. F., *A History of the Hemp Industry in Kentucky* (Lexington, 1951).

HOUSTON, D. F., *A Critical Study of Nullification in South Carolina* (Cambridge, 1896)

HOWARD, J. T., *Stephen Foster, America's Troubadour* (New York, 1935)

HUDSON, A. P. (ed.), *Humor of the Old Deep South* (New York, 1936)

HUNDLEY, D. R., *Social Relations in Our Southern States* (New York, 1860)

HUNT, GAILLARD, *John C. Calhoun* (Philadelphia, 1908)

HUNTER, R. M. T., "Correspondence of Robert M. T. Hunter, 1826–1876," edited by C. H. Ambler, *American Historical Association Annual Report*, 1906, Vol. II (Washington, 1918)

INGLE, EDWARD, *Southern Sidelights: A Picture of Social and Economic Life in the South a Generation before the War* (New York, 1896)

JACK, T. H., *Sectionalism and Party Politics in Alabama, 1819–1842* (Menasha, Wisconsin, 1919)

JACKSON, D. K. (ed.), *American Studies in Honor of William Kenneth Boyd* (Durham, 1940)

JACKSON, G. P., *White Spirituals in the Southern Uplands* (Chapel Hill, 1933)

JACKSON, L. P., *Free Negro Labor and Property Holding in Virginia, 1830–1860* (New York, 1942)

JAMES, MARQUIS, *Andrew Jackson: The Border Captain* (Indianapolis, 1933)

———, *Andrew Jackson: Portrait of a President* (Indianapolis, 1937)

———, *The Raven; A Biography of Sam Houston* (Indianapolis, 1929)

JENKINS, W. S., *Pro-Slavery Thought in the Old South* (Chapel Hill, 1935)

JERVEY, T. D., *Robert Y. Hayne and His Times* (New York, 1909)

JOHNSON, G. G., *Ante-Bellum North Carolina: A Social History* (Chapel Hill, 1937)

JOHNSON, Z. T., *The Political Policies of Howell Cobb* (Nashville, 1929)
JOHNSON, T. C., *Scientific Interests in the Old South* (New York, 1936)
JOHNSTON, R. M., and BROWNE, H. H., *Life of Alexander H. Stephens* (Philadelphia, 1878)
KANE, HARNETT T., *Deep Delta Country* (New York, 1944)
KELLAR, H. A. (ed.), *Solon Robinson, Pioneer and Agriculturist, 1825–1845* (Indianapolis, 1936), 2 vols.
KENNEDY, J. P., *Swallow Barn; or, A Sojourn in the Old Dominion* (Philadelphia, 1832)
KEPHART, HORACE, *Our Southern Highlanders* (New York, 1913)
KETTELL, T. P., *Southern Wealth and Northern Profits* (New York, 1860)
KIBLER, L. A., *Benjamin F. Perry, South Carolina Unionist* (Durham, 1946)
KING, GRACE E., *Creole Families of New Orleans* (New York, 1921)
KNIGHT, E. W., *Public Education in the South* (Boston, 1922)
KONKLE, B. A., *John Motley Morehead and the Development of North Carolina, 1796–1866* (Philadelphia, 1922)
LOMAX, J. A., and ALAN, *American Ballads and Folk Songs* (New York, 1934)
LONGSTREET, A. B., *Georgia Scenes* (Augusta, 1840)
LYELL, SIR CHARLES, *A Second Visit to the United States of North America* (London, 1849)
MACKAY, CHARLES, *Sketches of a Tour in the United States and Canada* (London, 1859), 2 vols.
MACY, JESSE, *The Anti-Slavery Crusade* (New Haven, 1919)
MALONE, DUMAS, *The Public Life of Thomas Cooper, 1783–1839* (New Haven, 1926)
McCORMAC, E. I., *James K. Polk* (Berkeley, 1922)
McILWAINE, SHIELDS, *The Southern Poor-White from Lubberland to Tobacco Road* (Norman, 1939)
McKELVEY, BLAKE, *American Prisons* (Chicago, 1936)
MARTIN, S. W., *Florida During the Territorial Days* (Athens, Ga., 1944)
MAYO, BERNARD, *Henry Clay, Spokesman of the New West* (Boston, 1937)
MEADE, R. D., *Judah P. Benjamin, Confederate Statesman* (New York, 1943)
MEIGS, W. H., *Life of John C. Calhoun* (New York, 1917), 2 vols.
MEINE, F. J. (ed.), *Tall Tales of the Southwest, an Anthology of Southern and Southwestern Humor, 1830–1860* (New York, 1937)
MERRITT, ELIZABETH, *James Henry Hammond, 1807–1864* (Baltimore, 1923)

MEYER, L. W., *The Life and Times of Colonel Richard M. Johnson of Kentucky* (New York, 1932)

MILTON, G. F., *The Eve of Conflict: Stephen A. Douglas and the Needless War* (Boston, 1934)

MIMS, EDWIN, *Sidney Lanier* (Boston, 1905)

MINOR, B. B., *The Southern Literary Messenger, 1834–1864* (New York, 1905)

MITCHELL, BROADUS, *Frederick Law Olmsted, A Critic of the Old South* (Baltimore, 1924)

——, *William Gregg, Factory Master of the Old South* (Chapel Hill, 1928)

MOORE, A. B., *History of Alabama* (University of Alabama, 1935)

MORISON, S. E., and COMMAGER, H. S., *The Growth of the American Republic* (New York, 1942), 2 vols.

MOTT, F. L., *American Journalism: A History of Newspapers in the United States through 250 Years* (New York, 1941)

——, *A History of American Magazines* (Cambridge, 1930), I and II

MUMFORD, LEWIS, *The South in Architecture* (New York, 1941)

MYRDAL, GUNNAR, *An American Dilemma: the Negro Problem and Modern Democracy* (New York, 1944), 2 vols.

NEVINS, ALLAN, *Ordeal of the Union* (New York, 1947), 2 vols.

NEWSOME, A. R., *The Presidential Election of 1824 in North Carolina* (Chapel Hill, 1939)

NICHOLS, R. F., *The Disruption of the American Democracy* (New York, 1948)

NORTON, C. C., *The Democratic Party in Ante-Bellum North Carolina, 1835–1861* (Chapel Hill, 1930)

ODUM, H. W., *Southern Regions of the United States* (New York, 1921)

OLMSTED, F. L., *A Journey in the Seaboard Slave States with Remarks on Their Economy* (New York, 1856)

——, *A Journey in the Back Country in the Winter of 1853-4* (New York, 1907), 2 vols.

——, *A Journey through Texas* (New York, 1860)

OSTERWEIS, R. G., *Romanticism and Nationalism in the Old South* (New Haven, 1949)

OWEN, MARIE B., *Alabama: A Social and Economic History of the State* (Montgomery, 1938)

OWEN, THOMAS M., *History of Alabama and Dictionary of Alabama Biography* (Chicago, 1921), 4 vols.

PARKINS, A. E., *The South: Its Economic-Geographic Development* (New York, 1938)

PARKS, J. H., *Felix Grundy, Champion of Democracy* (University, La., 1940)

PARRINGTON, V. L., *The Romantic Revolution in America 1800–1860:* Vol. II of *Main Currents in American Thought* (New York, 1927)

PATRICK, R. W., *Jefferson Davis and His Cabinet* (Baton Rouge, 1944)

PERKINS, H. D. (ed.), *Northern Editorials on Secession* (New York, 1942), 2 vols.

PETER, ROBERT, and JOHANNA, *Transylvania University: Its Origin, Rise, Decline and Fall* (Louisville, 1896)

PHILLIPS, U. B., *American Negro Slavery* (New York, 1918)

——, *The Course of the South to Secession: an Interpretation by Ulrich Bonnell Phillips,* edited by E. M. Coulter (New York, 1939)

——, *Georgia and State Rights* (Washington, 1902)

——, *A History of Transportation in the Eastern Cotton Belt to 1860* (New York, 1908)

——, *The Life of Robert Toombs* (New York, 1913)

——, *Life and Labor in the Old South* (Boston, 1929)

PHILLIPS, U. B. (ed.), "Correspondence of Robert Toombs, Alexander H. Stephens, and Howell Cobb," *American Historical Association Annual Report,* 1901, Vol. II (Washington, 1912)

POAGE, G. R., *Henry Clay and the Whig Party* (Chapel Hill, 1936)

POLK, JAMES K., *Diary of James K. Polk During His Presidency, 1845–1849,* edited by M. M. Quaife (Chicago, 1910), 4 vols.

POSEY, W. B., *The Development of Methodism in the Old Southwest, 1783–1824* (Tuscaloosa, 1933)

POTTER, D. M., *Lincoln and His Party in the Secession Crisis* (New Haven, 1942)

POWER, TYRONE, *Impressions of America During the Years 1833, 1834, and 1835* (Phila., 1836)

Pro-Slavery Argument, The; as Maintained by the Most Distinguished Writers of the Southern States, Containing the Several Essays on the Subject of Chancellor Harper, Governor Hammond, Dr. Simms and Professor Dew. (Charleston, 1852)

PULSZKY, FRANCIS, and THERESA, *White, Red, Black, Sketches of Society in the United States* (London, 1853), 2 vols.

RAINWATER, P. L., *Mississippi, Storm Center of Secession, 1856–1861* (Baton Rouge, 1938)

RANCK, J. B., *Albert Gallatin Brown, Radical Southern Nationalist* (New York, 1937)

RANDALL, J. G., *The Civil War and Reconstruction* (Boston, 1937)

RAVENEL, H. H., *Life and Times of William Lowndes of South Carolina, 1782–1822* (Boston, 1901)

RAVENEL, H. W., *The Private Journal of Henry William Ravenel* edited by A. R. Childs (Columbia, S. C., 1947)

RAY, P. O., *Repeal of the Missouri Compromise* (Cleveland, 1909)

RENIERS, PERCEVAL, *The Springs of Virginia* (Chapel Hill, 1941)

RHEA, LINDA, *Hugh Swinton Legaré, A Charleston Intellectual* (Chapel Hill, 1934)

RHODES, J. F., *History of the United States from the Compromise of 1850* (New York, 1893–1906), 7 vols.

RICHARDSON, R. N., *Texas, the Lone Star State* (New York, 1943)

RIPPY, J. F., *Joel R. Poinsett* (Durham, 1935)

ROBERT, J. C., *The Road from Monticello: A Study of the Virginia Slavery Debate of 1832* (Durham, 1941)

———, *The Tobacco Kingdom: Plantation, Market, and Factory in Virginia and North Carolina, 1800–1860* (Durham, 1938)

ROBBINS, R. M., *Our Landed Heritage: The Public Domain, 1776–1936* (Princeton, 1942)

ROEMER, FERDINAND, *Texas; with Particular Reference to German Immigrations* (San Antonio, 1935)

ROGERS, E. R., *Four Southern Magazines* (Charlottesville, 1902)

ROOSEVELT, THEODORE, *Thomas H. Benton* (Boston, 1899)

ROWLAND, DUNBAR, *History of Mississippi: The Heart of the South* (Chicago, 1925), 2 vols.

———, *Jefferson Davis, Constitutionalist, His Letters, Papers, and Speeches* (New York, 1923), 10 vols.

RUSSEL, R. R., *Economic Aspects of Southern Sectionalism, 1840–1861* (Urbana, Ill., 1924)

SAXON, LYLE, *Fabulous New Orleans* (New York, 1928)

———, *Old Louisiana* (New York, 1929)

SEARS, L. M., *John Slidell* (Durham, 1925)

SCHLESINGER, A. M., *New Viewpoints in American History* (New York, 1922)

SCHLESINGER, A. M., JR., *The Age of Jackson* (Boston, 1945)

SCHURZ, CARL, *Henry Clay* (Boston, 1899), 2 vols.

SHANKS, H. T., *The Secession Movement in Virginia, 1847–1861* (Richmond, 1934)

SHIPPEE, L. B. (ed.), *Bishop Whipple's Southern Diary, 1843–1844* (Minneapolis, 1937)

SHRYOCK, R. H., *The Development of Modern Medicine* (Philadelphia, 1936)

———, *Georgia and the Union in 1850* (Durham, 1926)

SHUGG, R. W., *Origins of Class Struggle in Louisiana: A Social History of White Farmers and Laborers during Slavery and After, 1840–1875* (University, La., 1939)

SIEBERT, W. H., *The Underground Railroad from Slavery to Freedom* (New York, 1898)

SIMKINS, F. B., *The South, Old and New, a History 1820–1947* (New York, 1947)

SIMMS, H. H., *Life of John Taylor* (Richmond, 1932)

——, *A Decade of Sectional Controversy, 1851–1861* (Chapel Hill, 1942)

——, *Rise of the Whigs in Virginia, 1824–1840* (Richmond, 1929)

SIMMS, W. G., *The Partisan; a Tale of the Revolution by the Author of "The Yemassee"* (New York, 1835)

——, *Beauchampe or the Kentucky Tragedy* (Phila., 1842)

SITTERSON, J. C., *The Secession Movement in North Carolina* (Chapel Hill, 1939)

SMEDES, SUSAN D., *A Southern Planter* (New York, 1860)

SMITH, J. F., *White Pillars; Early Life and Architecture of the Lower Mississippi Valley Country* (New York, 1941)

SMITH, J. H., *The Annexation of Texas* (New York, 1941)

——, *The War with Mexico* (New York, 1919), 2 vols.

SMITH, W. E., *The Francis Preston Blair Family in Politics* (New York, 1933)

SONNE, N. H., *Liberal Kentucky, 1780–1828* (New York, 1939)

SPILLER, R. E. *et al.*, *Literary History of the United States* (New York, 1948), 3 vols.

STARKEY, MARION L., *The Cherokee Nation* (New York, 1946)

STEPHENSON, W. H., *Alexander Porter, Whig Planter of Old Louisiana* (Baton Rouge, 1934)

——, *Isaac Franklin, Slave Trader and Planter of the Old South* (Baton Rouge, 1938)

STILLWELL, L., *John Cabell Breckinridge* (Caldwell, Idaho, 1936)

STRINGFELLOW, THORNTON, *A Brief Examination of Scripture Testimony on the Institution of Slavery* (Richmond, 1841)

SYDNOR, C. S., *The Development of Southern Sectionalism, 1819–1848* (Baton Rouge, 1948)

——, *Slavery in Mississippi* (New York, 1933)

——, *A Gentleman of the Old Natchez Region: Benjamin L. C. Wailes* (Durham, 1938)

SWEARINGEN, MACK, *The Early Life of George Poindexter, a Story of the First Southwest* (New Orleans, 1934)

SWISHER, C. B., *Roger B. Taney* (New York, 1935)

TASISTRO, LOUIS F., *Random Shots and Southern Breezes* (New York, 1842), 2 vols.

TAYLOR, R. H., *Ante-Bellum South Carolina* (Chapel Hill, 1942)

——, *Slave-Holding in North Carolina* (Chapel Hill, 1926)

THOMAS, D. Y., *Arkansas and Its People, A History 1841–1930* (New York, 1930), 4 vols.

THURMAN, L. S., "The Cotton Industry in Pittsburgh." M.A. Thesis, University of Pittsburgh, 1947

TRENT, W. P., *William Gilmore Simms* (Boston, 1892)

——, *Southern Writers* (New York, 1895)

TREXLER, H. A., *Slavery in Missouri, 1804-1865* (Baltimore, 1914)

TURNER, F. J., *The Significance of Sections in American History* (New York, 1932)

———, *The Rise of the New West, 1819-1829* (New York, 1906)

———, *The United States, 1830-1850; The Nation and Its Sections* (New York, 1935)

TYLER, L. G., *Letters and Times of the Tylers* (Richmond, 1884-1896), 3 vols.

VAN BUREN, A. D., *Jottings of a Year's Sojourn in the South* (Battle Creek, Mich., 1859)

VAN DEUSEN, G. G., *Life of Henry Clay* (Boston, 1937)

VAN DEUSEN, J. G., *Economic Bases for Disunion in South Carolina* (New York, 1928)

VILLARD, O. G., *John Brown, 1800-1859* (Boston, 1910)

VON ABELE, R., *Alexander H. Stephens: A Biography* (New York, 1946)

WADE, J. D., *Augustus Baldwin Longstreet* (New York, 1924)

WALL, B. H., *Ebenezer Pettigrew, an Economic Study of an Ante-Bellum Planter* (Ph.D. Thesis, University of North Carolina)

WALLACE, D. D., *The History of South Carolina* (New York, 1934), 4 vols.

WAGSTAFF, H. M., *State Rights and Political Parties in North Carolina, 1776-1861* (Baltimore, 1906)

WARDELL, M. L., *A Political History of the Cherokee Nation, 1838-1907* (Norman, 1938)

WEAVER, C. C., *Internal Improvements in North Carolina Previous to 1860* (Baltimore, 1903)

WEAVER, HERBERT, *Mississippi Farmers, 1850-1860* (Nashville, 1945)

WEEKS, S. B., *Southern Quakers and Slavery* (Baltimore, 1896)

WEINBERG, A. K., *Manifest Destiny: A Study of Nationalist Expansion in American History* (Baltimore, 1935)

WENDER, H., *Southern Commercial Conventions, 1837-1859* (Baltimore, 1930)

WERTENBAKER, T. J., *Norfolk, Historic Southern Port* (Durham, 1931)

WHITE, LAURA, *Robert Barnwell Rhett; Father of Secession* (New York, 1931)

WHITFIELD, T. M., *Slavery Agitation in Virginia, 1829-1932* (Baltimore, 1930)

WILTSE, C. M., *John C. Calhoun, Nationalist, 1782-1828* (Indianapolis, 1944)

———, *John C. Calhoun, Nullifier, 1829-1839* (Indianapolis, 1949)

WISE, B. H., *Life of Henry A. Wise of Virginia, 1806-1876* (New York, 1899)

WISE, JOHN S., *The End of an Era* (Boston, 1902)

WISH, HARVEY, *George Fitzhugh, Propagandist of the Old South* (Baton Rouge, 1943)

WOODSON, C. G., *The Education of the Negro Prior to 1861* (Washington, 1919)

——, *The Negro in Our History* (Washington, 1941)

——, *The Mind of the Negro as Reflected in Letters Written during the Crisis, 1800–1860* (Washington, 1926)

WRIGHT, J. M., *The Free Negro in Maryland, 1634–1860* (Baltimore, 1921)

YOAKUM, H., *History of Texas from its First Settlement in 1685 to its Annexation to the United States* (Austin, 1935), 2 vols.

Index